TEXAS
LEGAL RESEARCH

TEXAS
LEGAL RESEARCH

SECOND EDITION

Pamela R. Tepper
Peggy N. Kerley

DELMAR
CENGAGE Learning™

Australia • Brazil • Japan • Korea • Mexico • Singapore • Spain • United Kingdom • United States

DELMAR
CENGAGE Learning™

Texas Legal Research, Second Edition
Pamela R. Tepper, Peggy N. Kerley

Acquisitions Editor: Christopher Anzalone

Editorial Assistant: Judy A. Roberts

Developmental Editor: Jeffrey D. Litton

Project Editor: Eugenia L. Orlandi

Production Coordinator: Linda J. Helfrich

Art & Design Coordinator: Douglas J. Hyldelund

Cover Design: Douglas J. Hyldelund

For product information and technology assistance, contact us at
Cengage Learning Customer & Sales Support, 1-800-354-9706

For permission to use material from this text or product, submit all requests online at **cengage.com/permissions**
Further permissions questions can be emailed to
permissionrequest@cengage.com

Library of Congress Control Number: 96-26537

ISBN-13: 978-0-8273-7682-3

ISBN-10: 0-8273-7682-0

Delmar
Executive Woods
5 Maxwell Drive
Clifton Park, NY 12065
USA

Cengage Learning is a leading provider of customized learning solutions with office locations around the globe, including Singapore, the United Kingdom, Australia, Mexico, Brazil, and Japan. Locate your local office at:
international.cengage.com/region

Cengage Learning products are represented in Canada by
Nelson Education, Ltd.

For your lifelong learning solutions, visit **delmar.cengage.com**

Visit our corporate website at **www.cengage.com**

Printed in the United States of America
15 16 17 18 19 20 11 10 09 08

CONTENTS

≡ CHAPTER 6:   Administrative Law   162

≡ CHAPTER 7:   The Digest System   213

≡ CHAPTER 8:   Legal Encyclopedias and American Law Reports   237

≡ CHAPTER 11:   Shepard's Citators   322

≡ CHAPTER 12:   Additional Legal Research Materials   351

☰ CHAPTER 13:   Legal Research by Computer   387

PREFACE

Legal research is probably the most important subject to master, as it is the tool used to find the law. Often legal research is taught at the beginning of a paralegal's training program. This means that the law, its terms and precepts, are a complete mystery. Knowing this, we wanted to develop a text that would be both informative and practical. What we have developed, through years of teaching, is a text that meets those needs. Checklists are included for many subjects discussed in the chapters, a feature that is somewhat unique to legal research textbooks. The checklists can be used in the library to assist the paralegal in finding the required law to complete an assignment or as refreshers in recalling how to use the legal research tools. In teaching legal research, we realized that our students wanted a guide that would take them from the searching stage to the finding stage and then to the analysis stage. The checklists ensure success with all assigned projects, and best of all, a thorough knowledge of the law is unnecessary.

Moreover, this textbook is unique because it focuses on Texas legal research as well as general research tools. Such uniquely Texas sources as writ histories are featured. A significant portion of each chapter is devoted to the Texas aspects of the subject of the chapter. Both the national and Texas sources for legal research, therefore, will be at the paralegal's fingertips.

The textbook is divided into chapters with the first three chapters focusing on general information about the American and Texas legal systems, including an overview of the court systems and the sources of American law. These chapters are important, as they form the basis for understanding the law and how it works—**the mechanics**. Learning the mechanics is the prerequisite to understanding the process of finding the law.

Once the mechanics are mastered, the student is ready for the next three chapters, which focus on the sources of the law—judicial opinions, statutes, constitutions, and administrative law. Understanding where to locate the general sources of the law is essential to legal research. Some new sections have been added to the text in this edition, for example, the section on how to brief a case. This is an important function to master for any legal professional. Knowing where to find the primary sources of the law and knowing how to dissect them are critical skills a paralegal needs for achieving success in legal research.

Success in legal research comes only when the paralegal knows where to find the law. Chapters 7 and 8 focus on the "finding tools" used in legal research: the digest system, legal encyclopedias, and the *American Law Reports*. These chapters are essential to master, as they form the basis of legal research. By mastering these chapters, the paralegal's task of mastering the computerized legal research found in Chapters 13 and 14 will be easier. Computerized legal research has become the research method of choice for most legal research, but mastering the manual method of research is important for two reasons: (1) a paralegal must have a visual understanding of how the books work and their contents, and (2) many paralegals simply will not have access to computerized research, thus making manual research the only alternative. To complement these methods of finding the law, Chapter 12 introduces the paralegal to sources such as looseleaf series, hornbooks, and restatements that combine finding the law with other general legal research sources.

The chapters on Texas writ histories and proper citation form (Chapters 9 and 10) have been expanded. The chapter on Texas writ histories has been expanded to include criminal petition histories—an area unique to Texas. The chapter traces the history of writs of review and petitions and gives some practical points on the subject. The chapter also shows the paralegal how to properly cite the writ and petition histories. The chapter on proper citation form also has been expanded. More forms of citations have been added to assist the paralegal in understanding how to properly cite legal sources. And more importantly, the chapter will help the paralegal conquer *The Bluebook* and the *Greenbook*.

The final touches are added to legal research in helping the student master *Shepard's* citators, or Shepardizing. Checking whether a case is still "good law" or whether it has been "overruled" is critical to completing any research project. The chapter on *Shepard's* citators (Chapter 11) reminds the paralegal of the wide range of citators available and that use of supplements is critical to the process. The paralegal will learn not only to check for writ histories but also to Shepardize all cases used in legal research. Citing an overruled case not only can be an embarrassment, but it may cost a paralegal professionally.

The second edition has some new features that enhance the book, promote student understanding, and make the book easier to use. There are two glossaries for important legal terms—a running glossary, which is in close proximity to the boldfaced term in text, and a more traditional end-of-the-text glossary that is alphabetized for quick reference. Glossary terms that correspond to *Ballentine's Legal Dictionary and Thesaurus* (Delmar/LCP, 1995) are indicated by a dagger (†) following the terms. In addition, a summary section and review questions have been added to each chapter, and all the exercises have been expanded and updated to challenge the paralegal's knowledge and understanding of the subject.

The intent of the first edition has not changed in the second edition. It has always been our hope that this text will be the one to which the paralegal will refer in completing assignments even after the legal research class has finished. The checklists can always be used as quick reference guides when a refresher regarding legal research is needed. With this in mind, this legal research book has been written for paralegals—to focus on their needs.

CHAPTER 1

INTRODUCTION TO LEGAL RESEARCH

§ 1.1 Overview of Legal Research

Generally

Legal research is a big jigsaw puzzle. Each piece has a place, just as each fact in a case has a place. **Legal research** can be visualized as the process of locating authorities that define and explain the legal strengths and weaknesses of a client's position—the puzzle is pieced together to create a picture. Depending on the attorney's needs, the legal assistant's role is (1) to assist in locating the law and specific factual information to permit a thorough and accurate assessment of the client's legal position, and (2) to ensure that all authorities supporting the client's position have been located and brought to the attorney's attention.

Before beginning the complex process of legal research, you must be familiar with the litigation procedures that are the basis for legal research and the courts through which the litigation process moves systematically. A brief review of litigation procedures follows in this chapter. An overview of the court system is presented in Chapter 2. Subsequent chapters discuss the tools used in legal research, including reporters, encyclopedias, digests, citators, looseleaf services, and electronic databases.

The Legal Assistant's Perspective

This set of course materials presents legal research from the legal assistant's perspective. Legal research involves not magic, but skills that will improve through frequent and proper use. This book presents a clear step-by-step approach to the basic tools and most often consulted sources that are used in legal research. You will find that these tools and sources, once understood (and hopefully mastered), will work effectively for virtually any research project you may encounter in your remaining student days and in your future career as a practicing legal assistant.

Not all research in a law firm focuses exclusively on legal issues and litigation. There may often be occasions where a research assignment involves a quest for factual information that may be important to a particular client or to an attorney who advises a particular client. The nature of a "find the facts" assignment usually is apparent or spelled out by the attorney making it. Typical of the "nonlegal" factual assignments that might be directed to a legal assistant are the following:

TERMS

legal research†   A study of precedents and other authority for the purpose of developing or supporting a legal theory or position.

1. Determine the stockholders who own more than 5% of a company.
2. Locate title information in a major real estate transaction.
3. Secure an address for an important witness who has left the state to avoid testifying in a major securities fraud case.

Answers to factual data research problems are often available in computer-accessed databases. How to conduct such research is discussed in detail in Chapter 14.

Although factual research is important, most research assignments in a law firm call for research of legal issues (the "law"), such as **liability** (deciding who is legally responsible). The distinction between "law" and "fact" is one that you should always keep in mind. Simply stated, a **fact** is something that can be objectively verified (in the words of *Ballentine's Legal Dictionary and Thesaurus,* "[a]n actual occurrence, as distinguished from the legal consequences of the occurrence; something that took place, not something that might or might not have occurred; an act or deed; that which exists; that which is real; that which is true"), whereas **law** refers to legal conclusions that can be drawn from collections of facts. For example, suppose that a person injured (fact) in an automobile accident (fact) where the other car was driven by a drunken driver (two facts: identity of driver and drunkenness) wants to sue the nightclub where the drunken driver became intoxicated (fact). Assuming the facts are all agreed to, the legal issues that need to be researched may include:

1. Can the nightclub be held liable (responsible) under any circumstances for the acts of a patron to whom it served drinks, after the patron leaves the club?
2. If the club can be held legally liable at all, what must be proved by the injured person in order to convince a court or jury to hold the club liable in a specific case?

The answers to the above questions would enable the attorney to evaluate the facts as presented by the client to determine whether there is a solid basis for recommending that the client sue the nightclub or its employees. Because of the importance of legal issue research (much of which is

---

TERMS

liability†   A legal responsibility such as a debt one is required to pay, an obligation one must discharge, the circumstance one is in when he or she has breached a contract, or a person's responsibility after he or she has committed a tort that causes injury.

fact†   An actual occurrence, as distinguished from the legal consequences of the occurrence.

law†   The entire body of rules of conduct created by government and enforced by the authority of government.

litigation-oriented), the materials that follow devote more attention to this research than to factual research.

Legal research can be an enigma. Piecing together facts and finding cases to support legal conclusions you would like to draw from a fact situation is both frustrating and challenging. Legal research can be handled more easily if you remember that in most instances there is not the perfect case, or even *the* case that will ensure that your position will be upheld in litigation. Generally, you will find authorities that either support or contradict a legal position. Some authorities are stronger than others; but remember, you can only locate authorities that are there. Do not expect the impossible.

The only way to become a skilled legal researcher is to learn to use a myriad of legal research sources, including primary authorities such as cases, statutes, constitutions, and administrative rules and regulations; finding tools such as digests, encyclopedias, and citators; and secondary sources, such as treatises and legal periodicals. All of these legal sources will help you piece the puzzle together.

Introduction to the Research Process

Beginning Legal Research

Legal research must begin with a basic understanding of the methodology, or process, involved. Legal research seeks answers to questions. Each question must be clearly formulated, otherwise the answer will probably not be precise. The process of setting up a legal research assignment should begin with formulating the search, based on the "who, what, when, where, how, and why" questions. Developing the legal research question is much simpler when basic fact information has been secured. Elements common to virtually all cases include the parties, nature and location of events, the basis of an action, possible defenses, and relief sought. For example, some questions that may be asked:

1. *People.* Who are the parties or potential parties in the case being researched?
2. *Documents.* What provisions does the commercial lease contain that would allow for its early termination?
3. *Remedy sought.* Does the client's case revolve around dollar damages, or will an injunction, a request that another party cease doing some action, be necessary?

Once the facts have been assembled, the next area of concern in legal research is locating a source for the answers to the fact and legal issue questions. How does the researcher know which books from among thousands in the law library should be consulted? If there are several sources, how does a researcher determine which is more reliable? After a source has been located, how can the answer be quickly and accurately pinpointed? How can the researcher be certain the answer is the *right* answer?

Conducting a Research Project

By following the steps outlined in this book of (1) analyzing the research question so that it becomes quite focused, (2) determining the court jurisdiction in which case research should be concentrated, and (3) locating possible sources within the jurisdiction, the research process should be both accurate and complete. If you skip one step, overlook one source, or select the wrong jurisdiction, the research results will be flawed. Herein lies the problem, particularly for a new legal assistant. How can I keep so much information straight? How do I know if I followed through on every cross-reference discovered in my research? The answer is, write it down. Keep a dated log of your research assignment, including the question(s) researched, sources checked, results within each source, and, unless too cumbersome, copies of any successful results in the search quest. Figure 1–1 is a guide to preparing a log of your search results.

FIGURE 1–1
Log of search results

1. Make complete, legible notes. If you are unable to identify the source of a quotation that is pertinent to your research issue because you failed to write down the complete source information, that quotation will be of no benefit.

2. Use a looseleaf notebook or index cards to record the information from each search. The looseleaf notebook can be divided into separate tabs to correspond to the major issues of your research assignment. Copy all cases or statutes that you feel may be useful in your legal research memorandum to the attorney. Alphabetize the cases, either at the end of the notebook or within the section to which they apply. If one case will be used with more than one issue, make a copy for each section of the notebook. You might also consider using only one copy of the case, but marking the section for one case with a particular color of ink and the section for another case with a different color of ink. If you utilize the index card method for recording search results, use one card for each case or statute. Divide the issues with colored index tabs.

3. Prepare a log with the following information:

   Name of case for which the research is being conducted
   Issue researched
   Words or phrases used in search
   Sources researched
   Results of research
   Date of research

Check and assess your log periodically. Compare what you have done with what you think you should have done. Look for any gaps. Did you trace each cross-reference lead? Did you check pocket parts, if available, for every primary source utilized? This is one of the most important, but often overlooked, aspects of legal research for the beginning legal assistant. A second critical aspect of legal research is Shepardizing each primary source to determine if the case or statute is still good law. (Refer to Chapter 11 for Shepardizing guidelines.) Do *you* have any unanswered questions about the research assignment or its results? If so, the chances are that your supervising attorney will too. Are you comfortable with the results? Remember, the results may not be favorable. That does not necessarily mean that your research has been incomplete; it may mean simply that the law is not on your side in the particular case.

Concluding Legal Research

One of the most difficult tasks in legal research is answering the question, "How do I know when my research assignment is completed?" A new legal assistant may answer, "It is never done." The point at which a research project should be concluded is nebulous. There is no warning that one is almost finished or that one "finished" several research steps ago.

Speed and accuracy in research may not be synonymous. Once you think you *might* be finished, check one new source. If the answers continue to lead you to the same case or the same statute, chances are good that the assignment is complete. However, when in serious doubt, do not stop without trying one new source.

Once you are confident that you have exhausted all possible legal research sources, organize the research and prepare a comprehensive written report for your attorney, documented with your search results. Be prepared to defend your report and to answer questions. Preparation in the beginning of the research assignment should translate into preparation for bringing the assignment to a conclusion with confidence.

All of these questions and issues will be explored and answered to the extent possible in the chapters that follow. A strong word of caution here: Always supplement the knowledge you gain from these materials by consulting any specific "how to use this publication or source" guidelines provided by the publisher of the print or on-line service you are using.

Effective research of legal issues depends in part on understanding the purpose of the research in terms of the litigation process that is always at the forefront of an attorney's thought process. The results of research have real meaning only when translated into an impact on the client's case. Such impact may vary depending on the stage of litigation. The overview that follows briefly summarizes the litigation process.

§ 1.2 The Litigation Process

Litigation procedures differ from state to state. The underlying concepts, however, are the same. Only the terminology varies. **Litigation** is the process of bringing a case to court to enforce a legal right one is claiming.

Initiation of the Litigation Process

The parties to a civil lawsuit are the plaintiff and the defendant. The **plaintiff** is the person who brings the lawsuit by filing a **complaint** (in Texas, a **petition**), which is the original pleading that sets forth a claim for relief or recovery. The **defendant** is the person against whom relief or recovery is sought. The complaint or petition, terms that are often used interchangeably, sets forth the names of the parties, the facts of the case, and a request for relief or recovery. **Relief** sought is often in the form of a request for money from the defendant. It may also be in the form of a request to the court to order the defendant to stop doing something or to fulfill some obligation to the plaintiff. Relief can also take the form of a divorce or the grant of the right to a landlord to evict a tenant. Figure 1–2 is an example of a petition that might be filed in a Texas court in a personal injury case arising from an automobile accident.

The petition is presented to the clerk of court or other appropriate court officer. A **summons** (in Texas, a **citation**) is then issued by the appropriate court officer. This is the process by which a party is given notice that he or she has been sued. The citation names the court and the

---

TERMS

litigation† A legal action; the area of the law concerning trial work.

plaintiff† A person who brings a lawsuit.

complaint† The initial pleading in a civil action, in which the plaintiff alleges a cause of action and asks that the wrong done him or her be remedied by the court.

petition† The name given in some jurisdictions to a complaint or other pleading that alleges a cause of action.

defendant† The person against whom an action is brought.

relief† A person's object in bringing a lawsuit; the function or purpose of a remedy.

summons† The process by which an action is commenced and the defendant is brought within the jurisdiction of the court.

citation† A writ issued by a judge, ordering a person to appear in court for a specified purpose.

FIGURE 1–2
Example of a
Petition

NO. 96-245-A

_____[*plaintiff*]   IN THE _____ COURT

v.   DALLAS COUNTY, TEXAS

_____[*defendant*]   [92ND JUDICIAL DISTRICT]

PLAINTIFF'S ORIGINAL PETITION

TO THE HONORABLE JUDGE OF SAID COURT:

_____ [*Name*], plaintiff, complains of _____ [*name*], defendant, and for cause of actions shows:

I.

_____ [*Plead parties, e.g.,* Plaintiff is an individual residing in _____ County, Texas. Defendant is an individual residing in _____ County, Texas, who may be served with process at _____ (*address*), _____ County, Texas.]

II.

_____ [*Set forth facts giving rise to cause of action, e.g.,* on or about _____ ,19___, plaintiff was operating her 19___ _____ on _____ Avenue, in _____ (*city*), Texas, driving in a westerly direction. As plaintiff drove through the intersection of _____ Avenue and _____ Way, plaintiff's car was violently and unexpectedly struck by a 19___ _____ being driven by defendant in a southerly direction on _____ Way.]

III.

The occurrence made the basis of this suit, referred to in Paragraph II, and the resulting injuries and damages were proximately caused by the negligent conduct of defendant in one or more of the following respects: _____ [*Itemize negligent conduct, e.g.,*

a. In failing to keep such lookout as a person of ordinary prudence would have kept under the same or similar circumstances.
b. In failing to timely apply the brakes to the vehicle in order to avoid the collision in question.
c. In failing to apply the brakes to the vehicle in order to avoid the collision in question.
d. In driving the vehicle at a rate of speed that was greater than that which an ordinarily prudent person would have driven under the same or similar circumstances.
e. In failing to turn the vehicle to the right in an effort to avoid the collision in question.
f. In failing to stop, yield, and grant the privilege of immediate use of the intersection in obedience to a stop sign erected by public authority.

FIGURE 1–2
(continued)

g. In failing to proceed into the intersection only when it might safely be entered without interference or collision with traffic using _____ Avenue.]

Each of these acts and omissions, singularly or in combination with others, constituted negligence that proximately caused the occurrence that made the basis of this action and plaintiff's injuries and damages.

IV.

_____ [*Describe injuries and unliquidated damages incurred by plaintiff, e.g.,* As a result of the negligent conduct of defendant, plaintiff suffered severe bodily injuries to the head, neck, back, and spine. She sustained a compound fracture of the right tibia, and a ligamentous tear in the right knee. Her entire body was bruised, battered, and contused, and she suffered great shock to her entire nervous system. The injuries are permanent in nature. The injuries have had a serious effect on plaintiff's health and well-being. She suffers from limitation of motion of the right knee, nervousness, dizziness, nausea, and fatigue. Some of these ill effects are permanent and will abide with plaintiff for a long time in the future, if not for her entire life. The specific injuries and their ill effects have, in turn, caused plaintiff's physical and mental condition to deteriorate generally, so that specific injuries and ill effects alleged have caused and will, in all reasonable probability, cause plaintiff to suffer the consequences and ill effects of this deterioration throughout her body for a long time in the future, if not for the balance of her natural life. As a further result of the nature and the consequences of her injuries, plaintiff has suffered great physical and mental pain, suffering, and anguish, and in all reasonable probability she will continue to suffer in this manner for a long time into the future, if not for the balance of her natural life. Prior to the incident, made the basis of this action, plaintiff was _____ years of age and had a life expectancy of _____ years according to the Standard Ordinary Tables of Mortality.

By reason of all of the above, plaintiff has suffered losses and damages in a sum that exceeds the minimum jurisdictional limits of the Court and for which she sues.]

V.

_____ [*Set out claim for liquidated and special damages for medical care and treatments, e.g.,* As a further result of all of the above, plaintiff has incurred the following expenses for medical care and attention; physicians' fees, $_____; for medical supplies, appliances, and medicine, $_____ hospitalization, $_____; nursing services, $_____. These expenses were incurred for necessary care and treatment of the injuries resulting from the incident complained of. The charges are reasonable and were the usual and customary charges made for such service in _____ County, Texas.

_____ [*Allege probable need for reasonable and necessary future special damages for care and treatment, e.g.,* As a further result of the injuries sustained by plaintiff, there is a reasonable probability that she will require further

FIGURE 1–2
(continued)

medical care and attention and will incur future reasonable and necessary expenses for her medical care and attention.]

VI.

_____ [*Allege special damages based on lost wages, e.g.,* At the time of the incident complained of, plaintiff was gainfully employed as a _____ (*describe occupation, e.g.,* copy editor) and was earning $_____ per _____ (*indicate time period, e.g.,* day). As a further result of the injuries sustained by plaintiff, she has suffered physical impairment and has been unable to attend to her occupation for _____ (*time period*) and has been damaged as a result in the sum of $_____ for which she now sues.]

_____ [*If appropriate, allege probable future special damages for loss of earning capacity, e.g.,* It is reasonably probable that plaintiff's physical impairment results from the foregoing injuries is of a lasting nature and that her earning capacity will be diminished for the balance of her life.]

VII.

_____ [*Include property damage allegations, e.g.,* As a proximate result of the negligence of defendant, plaintiff's 19___ _____ was damaged in the following respects: _____ (*describe in general terms*). Immediately prior to the collision, plaintiff's automobile had a reasonable cash market value of $_____; immediately thereafter its value was $_____, to plaintiff's damage in a sum in excess of the minimum jurisdictional limits of the Court. (Continue with loss of use allegations, if appropriate; *see* Chapter 20, *Damages in Tort Actions* [Matthew Bender, 1982–1991].)]

WHEREFORE, plaintiff requests that defendant be cited to appear and answer, and that on final trial plaintiff have:

1. Judgment against defendant for a sum in excess of the minimum jurisdictional limits of the Court, with interest at the legal rate from _____, 19___, until judgment.

2. Interest after judgment at the rate of _____% per annum until paid.

_____
(Attorney)

[Certificate of Service]

nature of the action and demands that the defendant answer the petition within a specified period of time.

A copy of the petition and citation must be given to the defendant so that the defendant has knowledge of the lawsuit and can exercise the right to respond to the allegations in the petition. The procedure of handing (or delivering) these documents to the defendant is referred to as **service of process.**

Texas statutes and court rules provide for service of the citation by any sheriff or constable, any person authorized by law to make service of process, and any person authorized by written court order who is not less than eighteen years of age.

Service by mail may be effected by mailing to the defendant, by certified or registered mail, return receipt requested, a true copy of the citation, with a copy of the petition attached.

Service on a corporation or partnership is normally accomplished by the delivery of the citation to one of its authorized agents, such as an officer or attorney.

The Answer

After the citation is properly served, the defendant has an opportunity to file an answer. An **answer** is the defendant's official response to the allegations contained in the petition. The answer must be filed within a period of time specified by state statute or court rules. Figure 1–3 shows an answer that might be filed in a Texas state case where the defendant was sued for damages allegedly resulting from the plaintiff's failure to repair a garage involved in a real estate transaction.

Figure 1–3 only illustrates generally the format and a possible approach of an answer in a specific factual setting. The specifics of each answer vary from case to case. Multiple forms of answers are available, including cross-claims, third-party complaints, and counterclaims. A **cross-claim** is a claim filed by one defendant against another defendant

---

TERMS

service of process†   Delivery of a summons, writ, complaint, or other process to the opposite party, or other person entitled to receive it, in such manner as the law prescribes, whether by leaving a copy at the party's residence, by mailing a copy to the party or the party's attorney, or by publication.

answer†   A pleading in response to a complaint. An answer may deny the allegations of the complaint, demur to them, agree with them, or introduce affirmative defenses intended to defeat the plaintiff's lawsuit or delay it.

cross-claim†   A counterclaim against a coplaintiff or a codefendant.

FIGURE 1–3
Defendant's
original answer

NO. 96-245-A

_____[*plaintiff*]   IN THE _____ COURT

v.   DALLAS COUNTY, TEXAS

_____[*defendant*]   [92ND JUDICIAL DISTRICT]

DEFENDANT'S ORIGINAL ANSWER

TO THE HONORABLE JUDGE OF SAID COURT:

Now comes the defendant, _____ [*name*], and in answer to Plaintiff's Original Petition would respectfully show the court as follows:

I.

Defendant specially excepts to said petition in its entirety because nowhere in said petition, is it alleged that defendant made any misrepresentations as to presently existing facts, and that in the absence of such allegations said petition fails to state a ground of recovery upon which relief may be granted. And of this special exception, defendant prays judgment of the court.

II.

Defendant specially excepts to Paragraph _____ [*specify*] of said petition wherein it is alleged that _____ [*specify allegation to which exception is being made, e.g.,* that certain personal property of the plaintiff became damaged in the sum of Fifty Dollars ($50.00) from being mildewed], for the reason that said allegation is _____ [*specify objection, e.g.,* that it is too vague, general, and indefinite in that it does not specify the particular items of property that allegedly became damaged, and that therefore defendant is not given fair notice of what plaintiff expects to prove under said allegation and is not enabled properly to prepare any defense thereto.] And of this special exception, defendant prays judgment of the court.

III.

Defendant specially excepts to Paragraph _____ [*specify*] of said petition, wherein it is alleged that _____ [*specify the allegation to which exception is being taken, e.g.,* that Plaintiff has undergone physical and mental suffering,] for the following reasons [*specify, e.g.,*

(1) Any promises or representations (if any were made) that defendant would repair or alter the construction of the floor of plaintiff's garage were made after the property had been sold and possession thereof had been delivered to plaintiff. Since said promises or representations, if any, were made after the consummation of the sale of the property, plaintiff could not have relied upon the representations or promises as an inducement to enter into the contract and, therefore, any damages arising from the failure to

perform said representations and promises cannot be recovered in a suit for breach of warranty.

(2) The only cause of action alleged by plaintiff in his petition is one of breach of warranty in the sale of real estate, and damages for physical and mental suffering are not recoverable in an action for breach of warranty, the proper measure of damages being the difference between the value of the property as warranted and its value as actually conveyed].

Therefore, said allegations as to physical and mental sufferings are immaterial and would be prejudicial to defendant if read to the jury trying this cause, and said allegation should, therefore, be stricken from the plaintiff's petition.

And of this special exception, defendant prays judgment of the court.

IV.

Defendant specially denies _____ [*specify denial of allegations in plaintiff's petition, e.g.,* that he made any representations to the plaintiff in connection with the sale of the property involved in this case].

V.

Defendant enters a general denial and demands a trial by jury.

VI.

Answering further herein, if the same be necessary, defendant further alleges _____ [*specify affirmative defenses such as waiver, satisfaction of obligation, e.g.,* that plaintiff has waived the right to damages, if any he ever had, by remaining in possession, making payments on his note owed defendant of Nineteen Hundred Dollars ($1900.00) within ninety (90) days from the date of contract of sale of the property, and further making payments on the balance of said note monthly and up to and including the month of July 1995].

_____

(Attorney)

[Certificate of Service]

FIGURE 1–3
(continued)

in the same lawsuit. A **third-party complaint** brings in a party who was not within the original group of parties. A **counterclaim** is a claim that the defendant has against the plaintiff. There are specific pleading requirements for raising each of these claims in an answer. The sample pleading in Figure 1–4 is an example of how an answer with a counterclaim might be framed.

The Pretrial Phase of Litigation

Once the answer has been filed, there is a period of time before the case is ready for trial. During this pretrial period, several important activities normally take place, including a pretrial conference, discovery, and the filing of various pretrial motions, which are often provided for, and governed by, rules of court and state statutes. Although pretrial conferences are discussed first, Texas permits discovery to go forward as the first step in the pretrial stage, to be followed by a pretrial conference.

Pretrial Conference

Many courts require that a case go to a **pretrial conference** after the petition and answer have been filed. During this conference, the judge and attorneys attempt either to settle the dispute without the necessity of a lengthy and expensive trial or, at a minimum, to narrow the issues for trial. For example, frivolous claims or defenses may be eliminated. If a settlement does not evolve from the pretrial conference, a trial date is then set on the court's **docket**, a calendar of lawsuits with their dates of trial that is prepared and maintained by the clerk of the court.

TERMS

third-party complaint† A complaint filed by the defendant in a lawsuit against a third person whom he or she seeks to bring into the action because of that person's alleged liability to the defendant.

counterclaim† A cause of action on which a defendant in a lawsuit might have sued the plaintiff in a separate action, which is stated in a separate division of a defendant's answer.

pretrial conference† A conference held between the judge and counsel for all parties prior to trial, for the purpose of facilitating disposition of the case by, among other actions, simplifying the pleadings, narrowing the issues, obtaining stipulations to avoid unnecessary proof and limiting the number of witnesses.

docket† A list of cases for trial or other disposition; a court calendar.

NO. 96-245-A

_____[*plaintiff*]   IN THE _____ COURT

v.   DALLAS COUNTY, TEXAS

_____[*defendant*]   [92ND JUDICIAL DISTRICT]

DEFENDANT'S ORIGINAL ANSWER AND COUNTERCLAIM

TO THE HONORABLE JUDGE AND JURY OF SAID COURT:

Comes now, _____ [*name of defendant*], and files this answer and counterclaim, and would show as follows:

I.

As authorized by Rule 92 of the Texas Rules of Civil Procedure, defendant asserts a general denial herein.

II.

For further answer, if such be necessary, defendant would show _____ [*specify in this and other numbered paragraphs specific reasons for denying liability to the plaintiff, e.g., that there has been a failure of consideration and a lack of consideration in that plaintiff failed to perform services in accordance with the agreement asserted by him*].

III.

Defendant would further answer and defend, if such be necessary, by showing that the agreement alleged by plaintiff is not expressed in a writing complying with the Texas Real Estate Licensing Act or the Statute of Frauds.

IV.

Defendant would further answer and defend, if such be necessary, by showing that plaintiff's claim has been the subject of an accord and satisfaction or release.

V.

Defendant would further answer and defend by showing that plaintiff was in a position of trust and confidential relationship with defendant, and that he breached his fiduciary obligation by creating and causing defendant to sign documents that he has now chosen to interpret to provide him with monies far in excess of any services.

VI.

Defendant would further answer and defend, if such be necessary, by showing that the amounts claimed by plaintiff and paid to him are grossly disproportional

FIGURE 1–4
Defendant's original answer and counterclaim

FIGURE 1–4
(continued)

to the consideration and to the value of the services performed by plaintiff, are unconscionable and are in violation of Tex. Bus. & Com. Code §§ 17.45, 17.46, and 17.50 (the Texas Deceptive Trade Practices Act)].

COUNTERCLAIM

VII.

Defendant realleges Paragraphs _____ [*specify, e.g.,* II through VI as though fully set out herein].

VIII.

_____ [*Specify basis for asserting a claim against the plaintiff, e.g.,* defendant has in connection with the transaction herein paid plaintiff amounts in excess of Twenty-one Thousand Dollars ($21,000) to which, owing to the facts and law hereinbefore set forth, plaintiff was not entitled. Defendant prays for the relief accorded by Tex. Bus. & Com Code § 17.50(b), including three times actual damages and attorneys' fees].

WHEREFORE, defendant prays that plaintiff take nothing by his suit, that defendant have judgment on this counterclaim, and that the court grant such other and further relief as to which defendant may show itself justly entitled.

_____
(Attorney)

[Certificate of Service]

Discovery

Discovery is the process through which the parties search for information relevant to the issues of a case. Discovery is intended to simplify the issues for trial by identifying those about which the parties genuinely disagree and to enable the parties to avoid any surprises at the time of trial

TERMS

discovery† A means for providing a party, in advance of trial, with access to facts that are within the knowledge of the other side, to enable the party to better try his or her case.

in furtherance of the general goal of using court proceedings to find the "truth." There are four major categories of discovery:

1. **Depositions** are oral statements made outside the courtroom, under oath, by witnesses or parties to the action in response to questions from the opposing attorneys. A court reporter records the questions and answers verbatim. The deposition may be used at the time of trial with the same force and effect as if the person giving the deposition, the **deponent**, were testifying in person at trial. Federal and parallel state procedural rules permit the introduction of a witness's prior deposition testimony to **impeach** (discredit) a witness on the basis of prior inconsistent statements, contradiction of facts, bias, or character (as to propensity for truth and veracity).

2. **Interrogatories** are written questions that must be answered in writing, under oath, by the opposing party. Nonparty witnesses may not be required to answer interrogatories.

3. **Request for production of documents** is a request to a party to produce documents and other tangible evidence that is relevant to the case. A similar request to a nonparty witness is called a **subpoena duces tecum**.

4. **Request for admission** is a written statement of facts concerning the case which is directed to a party and which that party is required to admit or deny. Statements that have been admitted do not have to be proven at trial. Failure to timely respond to a request for admission may result in the proffered statements being deemed admitted.

TERMS

depositions†   Transcripts of witnesses' testimonies given under oath outside of the courtroom, usually in advance of the trial or hearing, upon oral examination or in response to written interrogatories.

deponent†   A person who gives a deposition.

impeach†   To charge a public officer with defective performance in office.

interrogatories†   Written questions put by one party to another, or, in limited situations, to a witness in advance of trial.

request for production of documents   A request to a party to produce documents and other tangible evidence that is relevant to the case.

subpoena duces tecum†   A written command requiring a witness to come to court to testify and at that time to produce for use as evidence the papers, documents, books, or records listed in the subpoena.

request for admission†   Written statements concerning a case, directed to an adverse party, that he or she is required to admit or deny. Such admissions or denials will be treated by the court as having been established, and need not be proven at trial.

Pretrial Motions

During the pretrial stage, several motions may be filed. A **motion** is a request for the court to rule on a particular issue in the case. One of the most widely used pretrial motions is a **motion for summary judgment**, a motion that asks the court for an immediate judgment for the party filing the motion because both parties are in agreement on the facts and the party who introduces the motion claims that he or she is entitled to a favorable judgment as a matter of law. Another often used pretrial motion is the **motion in limine**, which seeks to limit the admission of certain evidence at trial because of prejudice, confusion of issues, or irrelevancy.

The Trial

Following the completion of discovery, pretrial conference, and any hearings on pretrial motions, the case is ready for **trial**, a judicial examination and determination of issues between the parties to an action.

The trial may be a **bench trial**, a trial before a judge alone, or a **jury trial**, a trial before a panel of citizens from the community in which the trial is taking place, which has been selected to hear a certain case and determine the truth of the evidence presented by the parties. Potential jurors normally included citizens who have registered to vote in a particular jurisdiction and who have not served on another jury for a designated period of time. A list of potential jurors may be obtained from the clerk of court prior to the trial date.

The selection of the jury involves **voir dire**, a process by which the lawyers for both parties question prospective jurors to determine whether they should be allowed to sit on the jury.

TERMS
---

motion†   An application made to a court for the purpose of obtaining an order or rule directing something to be done in favor of the applicant.

motion for summary judgment   An application made to the court requesting that the action be disposed of without further proceedings.

motion in limine†   A motion made before the commencement of a trial that requests the court to prohibit the adverse party from introducing prejudicial evidence at trial.

trial†   A hearing or determination by a court of the issues existing between the parties to an action.

bench trial†   A trial before a judge without a jury.

jury trial†   A trial in which the jurors are the judges of the facts and the court is the judge of the law.

voir dire   A process by which the lawyers for both parties examine potential jurors to determine whether they are qualified and acceptable to act as jurors in the case.

Prospective jurors may be rejected by a **challenge for cause,** a party's challenge of a particular juror's ability to serve for a specific reason. For example, if the juror is partial to one of the parties or has a financial interest in the outcome of the trial, the juror may be challenged for cause. Once challenged, the juror is dismissed. There are no limits to the number of challenges for cause that can be made by either party.

In addition, a prospective juror may be excluded through a **peremptory challenge,** a request by a party to a judge that a prospective juror not be permitted to serve on the jury. No reason or cause is required for this type of jury challenge, but the number of peremptory challenges each party is permitted to make may be limited by statute or court rule.

The trial process includes:

- **opening statement**—a statement by the counsel for each party setting forth the basis for the party's case,

- **direct examination**—examination of witnesses by the lawyers who called them to testify,

- **cross-examination**—the period during which opposing lawyers have the right to challenge the truthfulness of the evidence and testimony,

- **closing statement**—statements made by each side to emphasize issues and evidence that it believes the judge or jury should consider in its deliberation, and

- **jury instructions**—written instructions that may be suggested by both parties but are ultimately edited and issued by the judge to assist the

---

TERMS

challenge for cause†   An objection, for a stated reason, to a juror being allowed to hear a case.

peremptory challenge†   A challenge to a juror that a party may exercise without having to give a reason.

opening statement†   A statement made by the attorney for each party at the beginning of a trial, outlining to the judge and jury the issues in the case and the facts that each side intends to prove.

direct examination†   The first or initial questioning of a witness by the party who called the witness to the stand.

cross-examination†   The interrogation of a witness for the opposing party by questions designed to test the accuracy and truthfulness of the testimony the witness gave on direct examination.

closing statement†   Making the closing argument (also referred to as a final argument) in a case; summing up.

jury instructions†   Directions given to the jury by the judge, just before the jurors are sent out to deliberate and return a verdict, explaining the law that applies in the case and spelling out what must be proven and by whom.

jurors in applying the facts and law to the case in order to reach a decision.

Verdict or Judgment

The jury retires to a private room with the judge's instructions to apply the rules to the evidence presented by the witnesses and exhibits. After deliberations, the jury reaches a **verdict**, or finding of fact, as to which side wins, based on the specific answer(s) to question(s) submitted to the jury. The verdict may include not only a decision as to the "winner" of the lawsuit, but in the case of a verdict in favor of the plaintiff the award of monetary damages or of other relief. The verdict is entered by the judge in the court record and becomes a **judgment**, or final decision, in a case.

Appeals

Either party in a lawsuit has the right to appeal a final judgment if the party believes a judicial error was made during trial that unfavorably influenced the verdict. An **appeal** is the referral of a case to a higher court for review. A **final judgment** is one that disposes of all parties' interests and all issues, leaving nothing in the suit for further decision except as necessary for carrying the decree into effect. By contrast, an **interlocutory order** is an order that is not final and does not dispose of every issue, every requested ground for relief, and every party's interest in the cause. An interlocutory order is not reviewable by an appellate court unless expressly allowed by statute. (*See, e.g.,* Tex. Civ. Prac. & Rem. Code Ann. § 51.014 [Vernon 1986].)

Legal error must be shown before an appeal is granted by the Supreme Court. Appeals to the Texas Court of Appeals are granted as a right. An error of fact alone is insufficient for an appeal. For example, a party may

---

TERMS

verdict† The final decision of a jury concerning questions of fact submitted to it by the court for determination in the trial of a case.

judgment† In a civil action, the final determination by a court of the rights of the parties, based upon the pleadings and the evidence; in a criminal prosecution, a determination of guilt.

appeal† The process by which a higher court is requested by a party to a lawsuit to review the decision of a lower court.

final judgment† A judgment that determines the merits of the case by declaring that the plaintiff is or is not entitled to recovery.

interlocutory order† An order that is not final, but only intermediate, and does not determine or complete the action.

claim that the verdict was either excessive or inadequate or that it was not supported by any evidence. A party might also argue that the judge refused to properly instruct the jury.

All presentations to the appellate court are on the basis of the record of the lower court. No new evidence and no new testimony from witnesses may be presented. Depending on the rules of the court system involved, lawyers for both parties may appear before the higher court in oral argument, arguing the merits of the appeal and answering any questions of the appellate court judges. Texas permits such appearances before the Court of Appeals by any party filing briefs in accordance with court rules, but the time allotted is limited to thirty minutes for each party's principal presentation. (*See* Tex. R. App. Proc. 75 (a), (f).) Similar rules prevail for oral argument before the Texas Supreme Court. (*See* Tex. R. Civ. P. 498.)

Appellate judges listen to the oral argument, review the trial records and briefs, conduct independent legal research, and reach a decision, which is supported with their reasons for the ruling. If a party is dissatisfied with the decision of the appellate court, that party can then file an appeal with the next court level that has appellate jurisdiction of the matter.

Appeals, however, cannot go on forever. At some point a dissatisfied party will find the door closed to further appeal. For example, a question of state law not involving an issue of either federal constitutional or statutory law, once resolved by the Texas Supreme Court, will not be taken up on appeal by the United States Supreme Court, which is the only court that could possibly review a decision of the Texas Supreme Court.

Summary

1.1 Overview of Legal Research

Legal research is the process of locating authorities that define and explain the legal strengths and weaknesses of a client's position—the puzzle being pieced together to create a picture. The legal assistant's role is to assist in locating the legal and specific factual information to permit a thorough and accurate assessment of the client's legal position and to ensure that all authorities supporting the client's position have been located and brought to the attorney's attention. The process of setting up a legal research assignment should begin with formulating the search based on the "who, what, when, where, how, and why" questions. The legal assistant should maintain a log of all sources checked in the research process, including the result of each search.

1.2 The Litigation Process

Litigation procedures differ from state to state. Litigation is the process of bringing a case to court to enforce a legal right one is claiming. This process begins when the plaintiff files a complaint (or petition in Texas), which is the original pleading that sets forth a claim for relief or recovery against the defendant. After the petition is filed, a summons (or citation in Texas) is issued to give notice to a defendant that he or she has been sued. After proper service of process, delivering of the petition and citation to the defendant, the defendant has an opportunity to file an answer, an official response to the allegations of the petition. Once the answer has been filed, before the case is ready for trial, there is a pretrial conference, discovery, and the filing of various pretrial motions. Discovery, the process through which the parties search for information relevant to the issues of a case, consists of four major categories: deposition, interrogatories, request for production of documents, and request for admission. Following the completion of pretrial activities, the case is ready for either a bench or jury trial. The trial process includes an opening statement, direct examination, cross-examination, closing statement, and jury instructions. After deliberations, a jury reaches a verdict, or finding of fact, as to which side wins. The verdict is entered by the judge in the court record and becomes a judgment of final decision. Each party in a lawsuit has the right to appeal a final judgment if the party believes that a judicial error was made during trial that unfavorably influenced the verdict. An appeal is the referral of a case to a higher court for review.

Review Questions

1.   Define legal research.

2.   Explain the difference between fact research and legal issues research.

3.   Define litigation.

4.   Identify the two major parties in litigation.

5.   Name three types of relief that might be sought in litigation.

6.   How does a person who has been sued learn of the lawsuit?

7.   In Texas, who may serve a citation?

8.   How is service on a corporation or partnership accomplished?

9.   What is the purpose of a pretrial conference?

10.   List the four major types of discovery.

Exercises

1. Prepare a list of all law libraries in your area. Include the telephone number, address, and hours of operation.

2. Visit your county law library or any other local library that offers a legal collection and become familiar with the location of the various types of legal publications mentioned in this text.

3. Prepare a diagram of the library visited to reflect the location of Texas legal publications.

4. Compare a petition filed in state court and a complaint filed in federal court. What are the differences?

5. Obtain a copy of an answer filed in your federal district court.

6. Locate a copy of an answer filed in your state district court.

7. Locate and review a copy of a subpoena for state and federal courts.

8. Contact the central jury room in your courthouse for a list of requirements for jury service in your county.

9. Obtain a copy of a directory listing for the county, district, and federal courts in your area.

10. Contact your district and federal courts to obtain a copy of a citation.

CHAPTER 2

OVERVIEW OF COURT SYSTEMS

§ 2.1 Court Systems Generally

When disputes arise between parties, a common place to seek a resolution is a court. A **court** is a forum where disputes between members of a society are decided using procedures that are generally accepted as fair. There must be a *real* "controversy," however, or, as the United States Constitution states, "cases and controversies." Unless there is a *real* dispute that the courts can adjudicate, a court can reject hearing the case. There are three instances when a court will reject a case because there really is not a dispute between the parties. They are rooted in the doctrines of **standing, mootness,** and **advisory opinions.**

Standing

A litigant must have an injury to bring a lawsuit. An illusory injury or some tangential interest in a dispute is not sufficient. The plaintiff, the party filing the lawsuit, must have a legally protected right such that the party will be affected by the outcome. For example, assume that a group of citizens file a lawsuit against the United States government alleging that they will be injured or affected by legislation that restricts Medicare rights for the elderly. All of the citizens are in their thirties, so none of them are eligible for Medicare. This citizens' group would not have standing to challenge the legislation, as none of them would be affected.

Advisory Opinions

Another area where courts will not hear cases is when a controversy does not exist, but the litigants are seeking the advice of the court in the event a controversy develops. The litigants are a creating a "hypothetical" situation and asking the court to render a decision in a "what if" situation.

TERMS
---

court† A part of government, consisting of a judge or judges and, usually, administrative support personnel, whose duty it is to administer justice; the judicial branch of government.

standing† The position of a person with respect to his or her capacity to act in particular circumstances.

mootness† Of no actual significance; a case is moot when it involves only abstract questions, without any actual controversy between the parties.

advisory opinions† Judicial interpretations of legal questions requested by the legislative or executive branch of government.

The court will not do this. Parties cannot seek the advice of a court. There must be a real dispute between real parties.

Mootness

When a dispute has resolved itself prior to the court making a final decision, the case is said to be *moot*. Thus, when a court's decision cannot have any affect on the controversy or the reason the parties filed the lawsuit no longer exists, the court will not render a decision, as the matter is moot. For example, a lawsuit is filed by an unsuccessful bidder to a construction contract against the United States government. The successful bidder proceeds with the contract while the lawsuit is pending. All monies under the contract have been paid to the successful bidder, and by the time the case reaches the court, the project is complete. There are no real issues to resolve and, therefore, the case may be deemed moot. There are exceptions to this rule, such as the issue is recurring and likely to be raised again by the parties or the issue is one that the court deems will have wide public policy effects, such as the abortion issue and AIDS cases. But the exceptions are limited, and the court must have a case to adjudicate.

As outlined in Chapter 1, a lawsuit begins when a party claiming to have been injured or in need of a remedy files a complaint or petition with the clerk of an appropriate court. Courts in which cases are filed and initially tried are called **courts of original jurisdiction,** or **trial courts.** This chapter discusses the trial courts and the importance of choosing the proper court to begin a lawsuit.

Trial courts do not have the power to review their own decisions. A higher court, known as an **appeals court,** has the power to review decisions of trial courts. At the appellate level, in most cases, the court only reviews the trial court record and the law. Neither witnesses nor testimony are presented to the appeals court. In certain cases, however, particularly in state court systems, including Texas, an appellate court may sit as a trial court, with the case on appeal being relitigated before it. This is called a **trial de novo,** which means "anew."

TERMS

---

courts of original jurisdiction   Trial courts, where cases are filed and initially tried, as distinguished from appellate courts.

trial courts†   Courts that hear and determine cases initially, as opposed to appellate courts; courts of general jurisdiction.

appeals court†   A court in which appeals from a lower court are heard and decided.

trial de novo†   A new trial, a retrial, or a trial on appeal from a justice's court or a magistrate's court to a court of general jurisdiction.

A working understanding of court systems is important to effective legal research, particularly in ensuring that the research project has been thorough. It would be a mistake, for example, to decide to conclude a research project upon finding an intermediate appellate court decision that solidly supports the position your firm wants to take on behalf of a client. It is possible that a higher court in the same jurisdiction may have, in the same or another case, rejected the position of the case you have found. In such a case, the higher court's ruling would be the prevailing law of the jurisdiction you are researching.

There are two general court systems in the United States: the federal and the state. Federal courts hear certain types of cases, normally involving issues of federal concern, whereas state courts hear cases that involve state disputes, such as a suit based upon a violation of a state stature or a suit on a debt. A general outline of these systems appears in Figure 2–1.

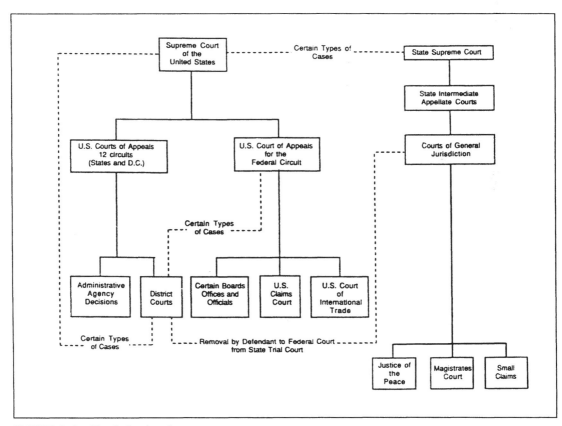

FIGURE 2–1 The federal and state court systems

§ 2.2 Overview of the Federal Court System

The American judicial system is founded in the United States Constitution. Article III creates one Supreme Court and empowers Congress to create other courts that it deem necessary. From this grant of power, Congress has created two levels of courts that are inferior to the Supreme Court: the United States District Courts and the United States Circuit Courts of Appeals. This three-tiered court system makes up our federal judicial system.

Federal District Courts

The trial courts in the federal court system are the United States District Courts. Along with the District of Columbia, each state has at least one district court. The number of district courts created within a state depends on various factors: population, size of the state, and case load of the courts. When Congress determines that more than one district court is necessary, a geographical label—such as northern, central, middle, southern, eastern, or western—will differentiate the districts. Texas is divided into four districts, each with several "divisions" for administrative convenience, as set out in the following text. (*See* 28 U.S.C. § 124.)

NORTHERN DISTRICT OF TEXAS
Room 15C22, U.S. Courthouse
1100 Commerce Street
Dallas, TX 75242

Dallas Division (Dallas, Ellis, Hunt, Johnson, Kaufman, Navarro, and Rockwall Counties)

Fort Worth Division (Comanche, Erath, Hood, Jack, Palo Pinto, Parker, Tarrant, and Wise Counties)

Amarillo Division (Armstrong, Briscoe, Carson, Castro, Childress, Collingsworth, Dallam, Deaf Smith, Donley, Gray, Hall, Hansford, Hartley, Hemphill, Hutchinson, Lipscomb, Moore, Ochiltree, Oldham, Parmer, Potter, Randall, Roberts, Sherman, Swisher, and Wheeler counties)

Abilene Division (Callahan, Eastland, Fisher, Haskell, Howard, Jones, Mitchell, Nolan, Shackleford, Stephens, Stonewall, Taylor, and Throckmorton counties)

San Angelo Division (Brown, Coke, Coleman, Concho, Crockett, Glasscock, Irion, Menard, Mills, Reagan, Runnels, Schleicher, Sterling, Sutton, and Tom Green counties)

Wichita Falls Division (Archer, Baylor, Clay, Cottle, Foard, Hardeman, King, Knox, Montague, Wichita, Wilbarger, and Young counties)

Lubbock Division (Bailey, Borden, Cochran, Crosby, Dawson, Dickens, Floyd, Gaines, Garza, Hale, Hockley, Kent, Lamb, Lubbock, Lynn, Motley, Scurry, Terry, and Yoakum counties)

EASTERN DISTRICT OF TEXAS
Room 212, U.S. Courthouse
Beaumont, TX 77701

Tyler Division (Anderson, Cherokee, Gregg, Henderson, Panola, Rains, Rusk, Smith, Van Zandt, and Wood counties)

Sherman Division (Collin, Cooke, Denton, and Grayson counties)

Texarkana Division (Bowie, Franklin, and Titus counties)

Paris Division (Delta, Fannin, Hopkins, Lamar, and Red River counties)

Lufkin Division (Angelina, Houston, Nacogdoches, Polk, Sabine, San Augustine, Shelby, Trinity, and Tyler counties)

Beaumont Division (Hardin, Jasper, Jefferson, Liberty, Newton, and Orange counties)

Marshall Division (Camp, Cass, Harrison, Marion, Morris, and Upshur counties)

SOUTHERN DISTRICT OF TEXAS
P.O. Box 61010
Houston, TX 77208

Houston Division (Austin, Brazos, Colorado, Fayette, Fort Bend, Grimes, Harris, Madison, Montgomery, San Jacinto, Walker, Waller, and Wharton counties)

Brownsville Division (Cameron and Willacy counties)

Corpus Christi Division (Aransas, Bee, Brooks, Duval, Jim Wells, Kenedy, Kleberg, Live Oak, Nueces, and San Patricio counties)

Galveston Division (Brazoria, Chambers, Galveston, and Matagorda counties)

Laredo Division (Jim Hogg, La Salle, McMullen, Webb, and Zapata counties)

Victoria Division (Calhoun, DeWitt, Goliad, Jackson, Lavaca, Refugio, and Victoria counties)

McAllen Division (Hidalgo and Starr counties)

WESTERN DISTRICT OF TEXAS
Hemisfair Plaza
655 E. Durango Boulevard
San Antonio, TX 78206

San Antonio Division (Atascosa, Bandera, Bexar, Comal, Dimmit, Frio, Gonzales, Guadalupe, Karnes, Kendall, Kerr, Medina, Real, and Wilson counties)

Austin Division (Bastrop, Blanco, Burleson, Burnet, Caldwell, Gillespie, Hays, Kimble, Lampasas, Lee, Llano, Mason, McCulloch, San Saba, Travis, Washington, and Williamson counties)

El Paso Division (El Paso County)

Waco Division (Bell, Bosque, Coryell, Falls, Freestone, Hamilton, Hill, Leon, Limestone, McLennan, Milam, Robertson, and Somervell counties)

Del Rio Division (Edwards, Kinney, Maverick, Terrel, Uvalde, Val Verde, and Zavalla counties)

Midland-Odessa Division (Andrews, Crane, Ector, Martin, Midland, and Upton counties)

Pecos Division (Brewster, Culberson, Jeff Davis, Hudspeth, Loving, Pecos, Presidio, Reeves, Ward, and Winkler counties)

Each federal district court system also includes a court known as the United States Bankruptcy Court. Bankruptcy courts are adjuncts to the district courts and have exclusive jurisdiction of bankruptcy proceedings, which are governed by the federal Bankruptcy Act (11 U.S.C.). The judges who preside over these courts are appointed for a term of fourteen years, subject to reappointment.

Jurisdiction of the Federal District Courts

A court's power and authority to hear and decide a case is known as its **jurisdiction**. In general, this means that the court has the power or "competence" to decide a particular kind of controversy. A federal district court, for example, has jurisdiction to hear cases involving federal questions and diversity cases.

─────────────────── TERMS ───────────────────

jurisdiction† In a general sense, the right of a court to adjudicate lawsuits of a certain kind; in a specific sense, the right of a court to determine a particular case.

Federal question jurisdiction usually arises in cases involving a federal statute or the United States Constitution. When a federal statute requires that a case be brought in federal court, the court is said to have **exclusive jurisdiction**, and it must hear the case.

Often, however, a case can be heard by either a federal court or a state court. When a litigant has a choice of courts in which to file a lawsuit, the courts are said to have **concurrent jurisdiction**. For example, a dispute involving a claim of a wrongful firing of an employee and a violation of the equal protection clause raises both state and federal issues and can be filed in either a state court of general jurisdiction or a federal district court. A claim of wrongful discharge is a state law cause of action, whereas a claim of a violation of the equal protection clause of the United States Constitution is a federal question involving federal constitutional law.

The second category of jurisdiction that can be exercised by a federal district court is **diversity jurisdiction**. Diversity cases involve disputes between citizens of different states where at least $50,000 is in controversy. The diversity must be complete. If there are multiple parties in a lawsuit and one of the defendants is from the home state of the plaintiff, diversity is destroyed. The case is no longer appropriately filed in the United States District Court. The traditional justification for diversity jurisdiction is that it protects out-of-state litigants from local biases, reflecting a view that state courts tend to favor their own residents over nonresidents. For example, if a controversy arises in Texas, between a citizen of Texas and a citizen of Oklahoma, a Texas state court may favor its own citizen over a noncitizen. This "fairness" justification, however, has been heavily criticized in recent years, and some scholars argue that today the only justification for diversity jurisdiction is that it allows litigants a tactical choice between trying a case in a federal or a state court.

As in other trial courts, the federal district courts have the authority to resolve disputes among litigants and ultimately can render a final decision. The decisions by United States District Court judges can be appealed in the United States Court of Appeals.

TERMS

federal question jurisdiction† The power of federal courts to adjudicate a question created by any case arising under the Constitution or any treaty or statute of the United States; it also exists in any case based upon diversity of citizenship.

exclusive jurisdiction† Jurisdiction when only one court has the power to adjudicate the same class of cases or the same matter.

concurrent jurisdiction† Two or more courts having the power to adjudicate the same class of cases or the same matter.

diversity jurisdiction† The jurisdiction of a federal court arising from diversity of citizenship, i.e., the existence of a controversy between citizens of different states, when the jurisdictional amount has been met.

United States Courts of Appeals

A party who is dissatisfied with the decision of a federal district court may appeal to the appropriate United States Court of Appeals. These courts, of which there are thirteen, are the intermediate appellate courts in the federal judicial system. Twelve of the courts serve designated geographic areas that are referred to as circuits. A circuit is a regional grouping of states with one state acting as the central location for that circuit. All states, the District of Columbia, and all United States protectorates are covered by this system.

In addition, the District of Columbia Circuit hears appeals from decisions of federal administrative agencies. A Federal Circuit Court of Appeals was created by Congress in 1982 to hear cases on appeal from United States District Courts in patent, copyright, and trademark cases, and cases where the United States is a defendant. It also hears appeals from the United States Claims Court and the United States Court of International Trade, as well as reviews administrative rulings of the United States Patent and Trademark office.

Except for the District of Columbia and federal circuits, each circuit covers a minimum of three states. Texas is part of the Fifth Circuit, along with Louisiana, Mississippi, and the District of the Canal Zone. The central headquarters for the Fifth Circuit is New Orleans, Louisiana. The list that follows shows the jurisdictions of United States Circuit Courts.

District of Columbia: District of Columbia

First: Maine, Massachusetts, New Hampshire, Puerto Rico, Rhode Island

Second: Connecticut, New York, Vermont

Third: Delaware, New Jersey, Pennsylvania, United States Virgin Islands

Fourth: Maryland, North Carolina, South Carolina, Virginia, West Virginia

Fifth: District of the Canal Zone, Louisiana, Mississippi, Texas

Sixth: Kentucky, Michigan, Ohio, Tennessee

Seventh: Illinois, Indiana, Wisconsin

Eighth: Arkansas, Iowa, Minnesota, Missouri, Nebraska, North Dakota, South Dakota

Ninth: Alaska, Arizona, California, Idaho, Montana, Nevada, Oregon, Washington, Guam, Hawaii, Northern Mariana Islands

Tenth: Colorado, Kansas, New Mexico, Oklahoma, Utah, Wyoming

Eleventh: Alabama, Florida, Georgia

Federal: All federal judicial districts

The basic function of the federal appeals courts is to review decisions of the district courts within their circuits. This is usually done through three-judge panels (some circuits have as many as twenty judges sitting at one time) that are empowered to act on behalf of the court. In some cases, however, upon petition of a party, the circuit court may grant a rehearing *en banc,* that is, before all the judges of the circuit.

United States Supreme Court

A litigant who is dissatisfied with the decision of a circuit court of appeals may appeal to the United States Supreme Court. Created by Article III of the United States Constitution, the Supreme Court is the highest court in the United States and the court of last resort for matters of federal law and federal constitutional issues.

The Supreme Court has the power to hear cases from both the federal and state courts and is the final authority for all cases over which it asserts jurisdiction. It is one court, currently consisting of nine justices, one of whom serves as chief justice. These justices, appointed for life by the president with Senate confirmation, preside in person over all proceedings before the Court.

Most of the Supreme Court's work is appellate, reviewing decisions of lower federal courts and state high courts. The Court has **original jurisdiction** (meaning that it functions as a trial court) in only a narrow class of cases defined by the Constitution, particularly those "in which a state shall be a party." (U.S. Const. art. III, § 2.) Typical examples would include suits by one state against another concerning boundaries, water rights, or the right to tax.

Most cases heard by the Supreme Court come on appeal from decisions of United States Courts of Appeals or state supreme courts. In a few instances, federal statutes grant a right to appeal a federal district court decision directly to the Supreme Court. One of the most imporant statutes of this type is one allowing a direct appeal from a district court decision that holds a federal law unconstitutional in a civil action to which the United States or one of its agencies, officers, or employees is a party. (*See* 28 U.S.C. § 1252.)

Only in an extremely limited number of situations is a dissatisfied party entitled to Supreme Court review as a matter of law. For example, such a right exists by virtue of 28 United States Code section 1252 when

---

TERMS

---

original jurisdiction† The jurisdiction of a trial court, as distinguished from the jurisdiction of an appellate court.

the decision being appealed has invalidated an act of Congress on constitutional grounds.

The usual method of requesting an appeal to the United States Supreme Court is through a petition for a writ of certiorari. A **writ of certiorari** is an order to the lower court to produce a certified record of the proceedings before the lower court to enable the court issuing the writ to inspect those proceedings to determine whether any errors of law have occurred that would require reversal of the lower court's decision.

The granting of a writ is discretionary with the Court. In most cases (over ninety-five percent) the Court denies the writ. When the Court grants a writ, it usually limits review to issues involving constitutional rights, major conflicts among the federal courts of appeals or between a federal court of appeals and a state court of last resort, or cases in which substantial issues of federal law have not been, but should be, decided by the Supreme Court.

All United States Supreme Court terms begin on the first Monday in October, and terms usually end sometime in early July. During this time period, the Court reviews the requests to hear cases and determines which cases will be heard. Often when cases are accepted by the Court for review, the parties, usually the attorneys, will present their cases before the Court in **oral argument**, which means the full Court has an opportunity to hear the parties' arguments and question their constitutional soundness. Each side is normally given thirty minutes to present their argument. After the argument is concluded, the justices gather to discuss the case, determine its result, and assign responsibility for writing the opinions of the Court.

§ 2.3 The State Court System

In General

Each state has its own independent court system created by its respective state constitution. The type of court system established in each state

---

TERMS

writ of certiorari† A writ issued by a higher court to a lower court requiring the certification of the record in a particular case so that the higher court can review the record and correct any actions taken in the case which are not in accordance with the law; the Supreme Court of the United States uses the writ of certiorari to select the state court cases it is willing to review.

oral argument† A party, through his or her attorney, usually presents the party's case to an appellate court on appeal by arguing the case verbally to the court, in addition to submitting a brief.

varies. Some states have a three-tiered system that includes a trial court, an intermediate appeals court, and a state supreme court. There are approximately twenty-three states, however, that have only a trial court and one level of appeals court.

It is important when you are researching the law of an unfamiliar state that you begin by finding out the structure of the state's court system. Keep in mind that the names of the courts vary among the states. For example, in New York, one of the lowest trial courts is the New York Supreme Court, and the highest appellate court is the New York Court of Appeals. The intermediate appeals courts are the Appellate Divisions of the Supreme Court. Yet in Massachusetts, the trial level court is the Superior Court, the intermediate court is the Appeals Court, and the highest court of review is the Supreme Judicial Court. Consequently, do not assume that a state's highest court is always the supreme court. Be cautious then researching unfamiliar states.

The Texas Court System

The Texas Constitution created the Texas court system. This is a three-tiered system consisting of trial courts, appeals courts, and *two* highest courts. Texas is unique in that it is the only state that has two high courts of last resort. The structure of the Texas court system and the interrelationships of the courts are diagramed in Figure 2–2.

Trial Level Courts

Overview The structure of the state trial court system and the jurisdictions of its various units seem complex at first glance. The rules regarding trial court jurisdiction, however, are set out clearly by the Texas Constitution and statutes enacted by the Texas Legislature. A solid working knowledge of court jurisdiction, both civil and criminal, is essential to effective legal research. It is particularly important to distinguish between **courts of general jurisdiction** (those that are able to hear any cases not exclu-

───────────────────◀ TERMS ▶───────────────────

court of general jurisdiction†   Generally, another term for trial court; that is, a court having jurisdiction to try all classes of civil and criminal cases except those which can be heard only by a court of limited jurisdiction.

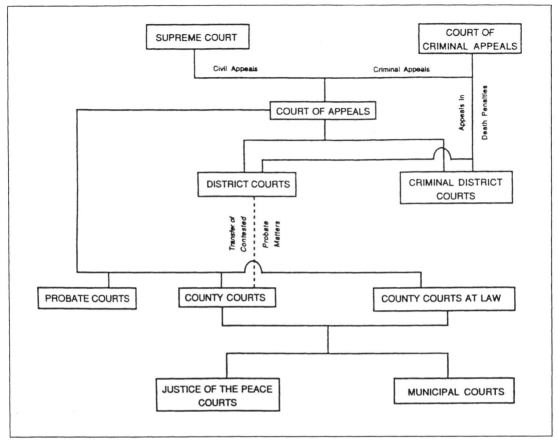

FIGURE 2–2   The Texas court system

sively assigned by law to some other court) and **courts of limited jurisdiction** (those that are able to hear only cases that fall within specific
constitutional or statutory guidelines).

The materials that follow outline the various trial courts and their
scopes of jurisdiction. The intent here is to *introduce* this subject, not to
provide a research tool for answering all jurisdictional issues that arise.
These materials offer sufficient information to allow you to identify most

<hr>

TERMS

court of limited jurisdiction†   A court whose jurisdiction is limited to civil
cases of a certain type or which involve a limited amount of money, or whose
jurisdiction in criminal cases is confined to petty offenses and preliminary
hearings.

situations in which a jurisdictional issue may need to be addressed as part of a research project. If you need to conduct in-depth research, you should also consult good secondary sources, for example, an encyclopedia such as *Texas Jurisprudence* (*see* Chapter 8, *infra*) or a specialized treatise such as W. Dorsaneo's *Texas Civil Litigation,* particularly Chapter 2, "Jurisdiction of Texas Courts."

There are four major trial courts in Texas: municipal courts, justice of the peace courts (called justice courts), county courts, and district courts, as illustrated in Figure 2–3. In addition, there are small claims courts that are, in effect, adjuncts of the justice courts. The types of cases these courts can hear vary and will be discussed in the sections that follow.

Municipal Courts Municipal courts are courts that have limited jurisdiction in criminal cases. They are established within a community or city, and they have jurisdiction of criminal cases arising under municipal ordinances and state law when class C tickets are issued by city police officers. They have concurrent jurisdiction with the justice courts of state criminal charges in which the maximum penalty to be imposed is a fine of $200 or less, usually class C misdemeanors.

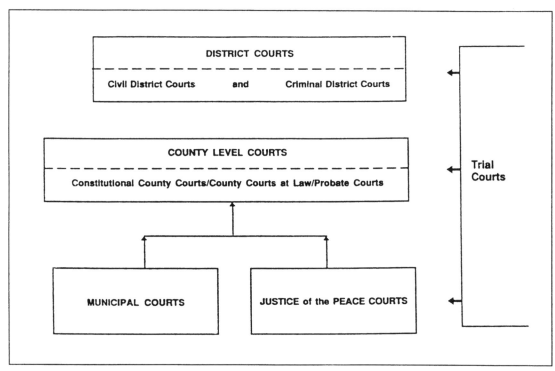

FIGURE 2–3 Diagram of Texas trial courts

Cases filed in municipal court may be heard before a judge or a jury. Normally, either party has the right to have a case heard before a jury, which consists of six persons. After a verdict is rendered, a party who is dissatisfied with the result in a municipal court has the right to appeal to a county court, which, if appeals procedures have been properly followed, must try the case "de novo" (anew) as though the proceedings before the municipal court had never occurred.

Justice of the Peace Courts The justice of the peace courts are created under the Texas Constitution, article 5, section 19, and the Government Code sections 27.031 and 27.032 of *Vernon's Statutes*. Each Texas county is divided into several precincts, and in each precinct, there is a justice of the peace who holds court.

Justice courts have jurisdiction of both criminal and civil matters. On the criminal side, this jurisdiction extends to cases in which the fine to be imposed does not exceed $200. On the civil side, unless another court has been granted jurisdiction over the subject matter of an action, a justice court has original exclusive jurisdiction over cases in which there is an amount in controversy of $200 or less. This is considered to be the court's **small claims jurisdiction**. In addition, the justice court shares concurrent original jurisdiction with the district and county courts in civil cases in which the matter in controversy exceeds $200 but does not exceed $5,000.

Justice courts have exclusive jurisdiction over forcible entry and detainer actions. **Forcible entry and detainer actions** are typically eviction actions that involve the right of possession to a piece of real estate but do not involve title. The amount in controversy in a forcible entry and detainer action is irrelevant. The action deals solely with the right of possession without regard to the amount in controversy.

Another area of specialty for the justice courts is the issuance of peace bonds. **Peace bonds** are orders by the court that prevent individuals from contacting each other because of prior hostilities or disturbances between the parties. Once the peace bond is issued, the individual against whom the bond is issued has the responsibility of making a bond to refrain from

---

TERMS

small claims jurisdiction† The power of a court of limited jurisdiction to adjudicate the litigation of small claims, that is, claims not exceeding a specified limited amount, which varies according to state statute.

forcible entry and detainer action† An action to obtain a summary remedy for obtaining possession of real property by a person who has been wrongfully put out or kept out of possession.

peace bonds† Bonds that a court requires be posted by a person who has threatened to commit a breach of the peace.

harming or destroying another person's property for a period of one year from the date of the issuance of the bond. The justice of the peace courts set the amount of the bond.

As courts of limited jurisdiction, justice courts are exclusively denied jurisdiction to hear cases involving suits for divorce, suits to recover damages for slander, suits involving defamation of character, suits for the title of land, and suits for the enforcement of liens on land.

Justice of the peace courts are not **courts of record**. The proceedings are not transcribed by a court reporter, so no written record reflecting the findings of the court is kept. Consequently, if a justice of the peace case is appealed to the county court, the case is tried de novo ("anew"), as though the proceedings before the justice court never occurred.

Small Claims Courts   The justices of the peace in each county jointly preside over a small claims court, which exercises concurrent jurisdiction with the justice courts in actions for the recovery of money when the amount claimed does not exceed $1,000. For small claims courts in counties with a population of 400,000 or more, the jurisdictional limit is $5,000.

County Courts   County courts make up a second major category of trial courts in Texas. The are two types of county courts: constitutional and legislative. The Texas Constitution establishes one county court in each county (called constitutional county courts). (Tex. Const. art. 5, § 16.) It also authorizes the legislature to create other courts and to prescribe their jurisdiction. (Tex. Const. art. 5, § 1.) The legislature has taken this authority seriously and has created several other courts, including county courts-at-law (called legislative or statutory county courts), probate courts, criminal district courts, and family district courts. These courts have jurisdiction over cases that otherwise would be within the jurisdiction of justice courts and district courts (which also were created by the state constitution).

Constitution County Courts   Constitutional county courts are courts mandated by the state constitution. (Tex. Const. art. 5, §16.) Constitutional county courts usually have original jurisdiction of civil cases where the amount in controversy exceeds $200 but is less than $5,000.

A constitutional county court has criminal jurisdiction only if there is no statutorily created criminal district court in the county. In that case, the county court has original jurisdiction over all misdemeanors except

---

TERMS

courts of record†   Generally, another term for trial courts.

those involving official misconduct and those in which the fine to be imposed does not exceed $200.

Not only are the constitutional county courts trial courts, but they also act as courts of appeal for the justice of the peace and municipal courts. The amount in controversy for an appeal must exceed $20 exclusive of costs. Because of the lack of written record, review by the constitutional county court on appeal from a justice of the peace court is by trial de novo. The justice court decision is virtually erased, and the litigants begin the same case again. A decision rendered in the constitutional county court may be appealed to the Texas Court of Appeals.

Finally, constitutional county courts in Texas have original jurisdiction to hear probate matters only in counties in which there is no statutory probate court, county court-at-law, or other statutory court exercising the jurisdiction of a probate court. A probate court is a court that hears matters involving estates, wills, trusts, and guardianships. Some more populated counties have individual probate courts that handle only probate matters. Many of the less populated counties do not. For example, Dallas County has three probate courts, whereas Denton County has none.

It is important to remember that the authority of the constitutional county courts is granted by the Texas Constitution and Texas statutes. These courts do not have the ability to hear all cases in controversy. In fact, there are specific limitations on their authority set out in the Government Code section 26.043, including suits involving damages for slander or defamation of character, suits for divorce, suits for the forfeiture of a corporate charter, suits involving rights to property over $500, suits seeking to invoke eminent domain, and suits for the recovery of land.

Legislative County Courts Legislative county courts (also called county courts-at-law or statutory courts) are statutory courts created by the Texas Legislature pursuant to constitutional authorization. Approximately 118 legislative county courts have been created in 48 counties in Texas.

The type of case these courts can hear varies. Some of these courts have been authorized to handle civil cases where the amount in controversy exceeds $500 but is less than $5,000, whereas others may hear cases involving amounts up to $100,000. County courts-at-law have concurrent jurisdiction with district courts over civil cases where the amount in controversy exceeds the amount over which constitutional county courts have jurisdiction. To determine a particular county court's jurisdiction, it is important to review the statute that created the court.

District Courts District courts are constitutional trial courts of general jurisdiction. (Tex. Const. art. 5, § 8.) They serve as the primary trial courts in Texas. Over two hundred separate district courts have been created by the state legislature pursuant to constitutional mandate. In addition, pursuant to authority granted by the Texas Constitution permitting the legislature to create other courts (Tex. Const. art. 5, § 1), the legislature has created statutory district courts. These are specialized district courts that deal with criminal, family, and juvenile matters.

District courts have traditionally had jurisdiction of civil cases in which the amount in controversy exceeds $500. There is no specified upper dollar limit to district court jurisdiction. More important, district courts have "original jurisdiction of all actions, proceedings, and remedies, except in cases where exclusive, appellate or original jurisdiction" has been conferred by the constitution or by statute "on some other court, tribunal, or administrative body." (Tex. Const. art. 5, § 8.) In practical terms this means that district courts can hear all cases that the justice courts and county courts do not or cannot hear and that have not been assigned to the statutorily created, specialized district courts. Consequently, the subject matter jurisdiction of the district courts is generally defined by exclusion.

In criminal matters, the district courts and criminal district courts have original jurisdiction over felonies as well as misdemeanors involving official misconduct. The types of cases heard in criminal district courts are murders, rape, kidnapping, and arson to name a few.

Family District Court   One of the specialized district courts is the family district court. This court deals exclusively with family law matters such as divorce, child custody, and support issues. Because of the abundance of family matters filed in the district courts, some counties have judges, called **masters**, who assist the district court judge in moving their dockets. The masters are appointed by the family court district judge and approved by the county commissioners' court. These masters can hear virtually all family court matters and are subject to appeal to the district court judge.

Juvenile Courts   Due to the substantial increase of juvenile crime, a number of district courts are designated as juvenile courts. Not all counties have juvenile district courts, but large counties, such as Dallas County, have two. These district courts handle matters such as neglect cases, termination of parental rights, adoptions, paternity, and criminal offenses involving minors (persons under eighteen years old). Crimes such as murder, burglary, and rape can be heard by juvenile district court judges. Oddly enough, juvenile cases are considered civil and are treated as such, so the civil rules of procedure and civil rules of evidence apply. The laws

TERMS

masters†   Persons appointed by the court to assist with certain judicial functions in specific cases.

have changed somewhat regarding juveniles, however. When a juvenile commits an adult-like crime such as murder, he or she can be certified as an adult and tried under adult rules. This means that the protections afforded juvenile offenders, such as the sealing of their records and the prohibition against using the offense against the juvenile as an adult, are eliminated.

Choice of Court As pointed out in the preceding discussion, more than one court may have jurisdiction over a certain matter. When this situation occurs, the courts are said to have concurrent jurisdiction, and the party filing the lawsuit makes the decision about the court in which to file.

Choice of court decisions are usually based on practical or tactical considerations. For example, an attorney who desires a speedy handling of the case may choose to file in a county court, since the docket is usually less crowded than the dockets in district courts. An attorney desiring more formal proceedings may choose a county or district court over a justice court where the proceedings are relatively informal.

A situation can arise where two suits involving the same parties and issues are filed in courts having concurrent jurisdiction. When this occurs, the issue is which court has **dominant jurisdiction**. The general rule is that "the court in which suit is first filed acquires dominant jurisdiction to the exclusion of other coordinate courts." (*Curtis v. Gibbs,* 511 S.W.2d 263, 267 [Tex. 1974].) Jurisdictional conflicts, however, can become complicated and may have to be researched in-depth. (*See, e.g.,* W. Dorsaneo, *Texas Civil Litigation* § 2.01[6].)

A Checklist In choosing a court, consider the following:

1. Determine if the dispute is a federal or state issue.
2. If federal, determine in which district court to file the case.
3. If Texas state court, determine the subject matter of the case and the amount in controversy.
4. If more than one court has proper jurisdiction, consider which court is the best strategically in which to file the case.
5. Know your court rules of procedure.
6. When a final decision is rendered, determine where the appeal should be filed.
7. If in Texas, determine whether the case is a criminal or civil matter.

TERMS

dominant jurisdiction The power of one court over another to adjudicate the issues where two suits involving the same parties and issues are filed in courts of concurrent jurisdiction.

Appellate Courts

When a final decision is rendered by a trial court, the dissatisfied party may, in its discretion, seek review in the appropriate Texas court of appeals. There are presently fourteen courts of appeals in Texas.

Texas Courts of Appeals The intermediate court of appeals in Texas is known as the Texas Court of Appeals. The courts of appeals in Texas are divided into fourteen districts, each numbered and called a Supreme Judicial District. Houston is presently the only locality with more than one court of appeals. The Supreme Judicial Districts are as follows:

First District: Houston [1st Dist.] (formerly Galveston)

Second District: Fort Worth

Third District: Austin

Fourth District: San Antonio

Fifth District: Dallas

Sixth District: Texarkana

Seventh District: Amarillo

Eighth District: El Paso

Ninth District: Beaumont

Tenth District: Waco

Eleventh District: Eastland

Twelfth District: Tyler

Thirteenth District: Corpus Christi

Fourteenth District: Houston [14th Dist.]

When a case is appealed, it is heard by a panel of three justices. After all the appropriate preliminary procedures are completed, the court of appeals acquires jurisdiction to hear the case and render a decision. Usually, an appeals court issues a written opinion announcing and explaining its decision.

Since 1981, the Texas Court of Appeals has had appellate jurisdiction over both civil and criminal cases. This change occurred through a 1980 amendment to the Texas Constitution, effective in 1981. Prior to 1981, criminal appeals were handled by the Court of Criminal Appeals, but because of case backlogs causing excessive time lags, the appeals system in Texas was changed. Now all cases, civil and criminal, are appealed to the Court of Appeals with one exception, death penalty cases, which are appealed directly to the Texas Court of Criminal Appeals, discussed later in this chapter.

Texas Supreme Court   The court of last resort in civil cases is the Texas Supreme Court, which is composed of nine justices with one justice acting as the chief justice. In 1981, the Texas Supreme Court was relieved of its criminal jurisdiction and, therefore, is limited to hearing civil cases only.

The method for appealing a case to the Texas Supreme Court is through an application for a **writ of error**. The application for the writ of error points out what the applicant claims are errors of law in the lower court's decision.

Although an application for review may be filed, it may not be granted. Only a limited number of cases are granted review. The Supreme Court may act only if the court of appeals has exercised its appellate jurisdiction. (Tex. Const. art. 5, § 3.) By virtue of this authority, the Texas Supreme Court can hear cases from the court of appeals only where:

1. material questions of law exist, and the courts of appeals disagree about the proper application of the law;
2. conflicts among the different judicial districts exist on a point of law;
3. a state statute is determined unconstitutional;
4. a case involves the Texas Railroad Commission;
5. a case involves state revenues;
6. a substantive error of law is made by a court of appeals; or
7. disputes involve divorce, custody, or visitation.

Once a decision has been rendered by the Texas Supreme Court, a dissatisfied litigant may appeal to the United States Supreme Court by a petition for a writ of certiorari.

Texas Court of Criminal Appeals   The Texas Court of Criminal Appeals is the court of last resort for cases involving criminal matters. Prior to 1981, the Texas Court of Criminal Appeals heard all appeals on criminal cases. As previously mentioned, since 1981 the Texas Court of Appeals has been authorized to hear both civil and criminal matters. A case on further appeal

---

TERMS

writ of error† A formal order issued by an appellate court, directed to the lower court, ordering it to transfer the record for review and for the correction of errors of law that the appellant alleges were committed by the lower court.

is then directed to either the Texas Supreme Court or the Texas Court of Criminal Appeals.

Most appeals to this court are requested by filing with the court a **petition for discretionary review**, which points out errors in the lower court's decision. The Court of Criminal Appeals may accept or reject the case for review. Only in a case that involves imposition of the death penalty does a defendant have an automatic right of appeal to the Texas Court of Criminal Appeals.

Since the jurisdictions of the Court of Criminal Appeals and the Texas Supreme Court are not concurrent, neither court can review the other's decision. The only court that may review an appeal from the highest courts in Texas is the United States Supreme Court.

Summary

2.1 Court Systems Generally

Cases are filed in a court when a dispute arises between parties. There must be a case and controversy for a court to hear a case. Cases where the parties do not have standing and cases that are advisory opinions or are moot will not be heard by a court. Trial courts hear the original dispute between the parties, and after a final decision, they are subject to review by a higher court of appeals. The two types of court systems in the United States are the federal and state systems.

2.2 Overview of the Federal Court System

The federal trial courts are known as United States District Courts, each state having more than one. Texas has four district courts: northern, southern, eastern, and western. The United States District Courts can hear two kinds of cases—those involving diversity of citizenship where more than $50,000 is in controversy, and federal question cases involving a federal statute or the United States Constitution. A party can appeal a United States District Court decision to one of thirteen United States Courts of Appeals. Parties who are dissatisfied with a decision of the United States Court of Appeals can appeal to the United States Supreme Court.

--- TERMS ---

petition for discretionary review† A request that the appellate court review a case even though review is not required by law but takes place solely at the discretion of the court.

The United States Supreme Court does not have to hear all appeals and has the discretion to accept or reject an appeal.

2.3 The State Court System

Many state courts have a three-tiered court system while others have a two-tiered system. Texas has a three-tiered system with trial courts, courts of appeals, and two high courts. The trial courts consist of municipal courts, justice of the peace courts, legislative and constitutional county courts, and district courts. Some of the trial courts are specialized courts, such as probate, family, and juvenile courts. Cases from trial courts can be appealed to one of the fourteen Texas Courts of Appeals. Cases decided by a Texas Court of Appeals can be appealed to the Texas Supreme Court or the Texas Court of Criminal Appeals.

Review Questions

1. Define a *court*.

2. Under what circumstances can a court refuse to hear a case?

3. What types of cases can a federal district court hear?

4. How many federal districts does Texas have and what are their designations?

5. How many United States Courts of Appeals exist and in which circuit is Texas?

6. What is the usual method of requesting an appeal to the United States Supreme Court?

7. What is the jurisdiction requirement of cases filed in a Texas district court?

8. What Texas court would hear an eviction action?

9. How many Texas intermediate courts of appeals exist and what judicial district has two courts of appeals?

10. Identify the two highest courts in Texas.

Exercises

1. Using Figure 2–1, which illustrates the federal and state court systems, which courts can hear cases involving controversies of $50,000 or more?

2. Which courts in Texas can hear cases involving $100,000 or more?

3. An injured party has a claim under the federal law named Americans with Disabilities Act. Which court has jurisdiction to hear the case?

4. A Texas resident wants to file a federal civil rights action against her employer for sexual harassment. The parties are in Grayson County. In which district and division would the case be filed? If the plaintiff lived in Grayson County and the defendant-employer resided in Henderson County, in which district and division would this case be filed?

5. A decision has been rendered by a Missouri United States District Court. Where would the appeal be filed?

6. Which court can hear cases from the Texas Supreme Court and the Texas Court of Criminal Appeals?

7. A person has violated a Houston city ordinance regarding recycling. Which court has jurisdiction to hear this case?

8. Recently your wealthy uncle died and left you a sizable inheritance. Which Texas court could entertain your case? If your uncle died in Dallas County, which court would hear the case? In Denton County?

9. Your sixteen-year-old sister has just been arrested for murdering your step-father. Which courts could hear the case?

10. You have just lost a personal injury lawsuit in El Paso County. In which Texas Court of Appeals would you file your action?

CHAPTER 3

LEARNING THE LAW

§ 3.1 Primary Sources of the Law

As discussed in Chapter 1, legal research is the process of finding the law and determining how it applies to a legal problem. Knowing the proper legal authority to apply in a case is critical. The four primary sources of the law are constitutions, judicial opinions, statutes and treaties, and administrative rules and regulations. Before mastering the process of legal research, you must understand each of these sources and the role they play in our legal system.

Constitutions

A **constitution** is a political document created by a government. It sets the foundation for the allocation of power between the divisions in a government referred to as the **branches of government**. Inherent in a constitution are the fundamental rules by which people must live. It defines the basic rights of citizens and how citizens are to be governed.

The United States Constitution

The United States Constitution, which shaped the American system of government, is the "supreme law of the land." With its origins dating back to 1781 in the Articles of Confederation, the United States Constitution is the oldest surviving written constitution. It consists of eight articles and twenty-six amendments.

Articles As approved by the requisite number of states in 1787 and 1788, and taking effect on March 4, 1789, the original seven articles of the United States Constitution created the form of government under which the United States has operated to the current time. Essential to the constitutional framework, carefully worked out in the Constitutional Convention in 1787, was the division of governmental authority among three branches

---

TERMS

constitution† The system of fundamental principles by which a nation, state, or corporation is governed.

branches of government† Three divisions into which the Constitution separates the government of the United States, specifically, the executive branch, the legislative branch, and the judicial branch.

of government. Article I creates a **legislative branch** (Congress) that enacts laws to regulate the conduct of American citizens. Article II creates an **executive branch**, with the president as the commander in chief, that coexists with the legislative branch. Article III creates a **judicial branch**, with the one United States Supreme Court as the highest court in the land and other inferior courts.

Amendments   Article V of the Constitution established a mechanism for proposing and ratifying amendments, ensuring that the Constitution would become a "living document" that could be responsive to changing needs of the peoples whose lives it governs. The first ten amendments, known as the **Bill of Rights**, were ratified in 1791. These amendments grant us many of our fundamental rights, such as the freedoms of speech, press, religion, and assembly (First Amendment); the right of the people to keep and bear arms (Second Amendment); the freedom against unreasonable searches and seizures (Fourth Amendment); the privilege against self-incrimination, the right to due process, the right not to be subjected to double jeopardy, and protection against uncompensated takings of property (Fifth Amendment); and the right to trial by jury, with specific procedural protections (Sixth Amendment).

Throughout the years, many amendments have been proposed, but only twenty-six have been approved. As an internal protection to haphazard change, Article V requires that a proposed amendment must have approval of three-fourths of the total number of state legislatures to become final. Consequently, it is not an easy task to have a new amendment passed. The equal rights amendment was one of the more recent

---

TERMS

legislative branch†   With the judicial branch and the executive branch, one of the three divisions into which the Constitution separates the government of the United States; the legislative branch is primarily responsible for enacting the laws.

executive branch†   With the legislative branch and the judicial branch, one of the three divisions into which the Constitution separates the government of the United States; the executive branch is primarily responsible for enforcing the laws.

judicial branch†   With the legislative branch and the executive branch, one of the three divisions into which the constitution separates the government of the United States; the judicial branch is primarily responsible for interpreting the laws.

Bill of Rights†   The first ten amendments to the United States Constitution; the portion of the Constitution that sets forth the rights that are the fundamental principles of the United States and the foundation of American citizenship.

amendments that was unable to receive the requisite state approvals. It never became part of the Constitution.

The Texas Constitution

Overview   Each of the fifty states has a constitution that governs its citizens. The document that created the Texas system of government is the Texas Constitution. In contrast to the United States Constitution, which is relatively short, the Texas Constitution is a lengthy document, consisting of seventeen articles with hundreds of subsections, covering a wide range of specific governmental activities. The Texas Constitution establishes on the state level the three basic branches of government: the legislative (Article III), the executive (Article IV), and the judicial (Article V). See Chapter 5 for a listing of the titles of each article.

The Texas Constitution has undergone many changes since the days of independence from Mexico in 1836. Following bitter battles over its contents after the Civil War, a constitutional convention was convened in 1875 to draw up the basic document by which we live today. The Constitution of Texas was formally ratified in 1876. Under Article 1, section 1, of the Texas Constitution, Texas is a free and independent state, subject only to the United States Constitution.

Amendments   The power to amend the Texas Constitution is delegated to the people of Texas from the constitution itself. Article 17, section 1, of the Texas Constitution states that the voters shall have the right to amend the constitution. Normally, proposed amendments begin with the state legislature in Austin. If an amendment proposed by a state representative is approved by the legislature, it is submitted to the voters for approval. A majority vote is necessary for a proposed amendment to become effective. Although the governor issues a proclamation after an amendment is approved by the voters, if the governor fails or neglects to proclaim the amendment, the amendment is still effective. It is the will of the people that governs the amendment process in Texas.

Judicial Opinions

Another source of law, known as judicial opinions, or **case law**, is created by both federal and state courts. Case law is the written decisions

---

TERMS

---

case law†   The law as laid down in the decisions of the courts in similar cases that have previously been decided.

rendered by courts. Judicial opinions may be referred to by a number of names such as judicial decisions, case decisions, or opinions.

Judicial opinions have their origins in the common law of England. **Common law** is based upon principles of custom, fairness, and justice. In the beginning, courts did not create a written record of most decisions. To assist judges in making future decisions, the principle of **stare decisis** evolved. Stare decisis suggests that future decisions involving similar facts should have the same result. The basis of the stare decisis principle is precedent. A **precedent** is a rule of law announced by a court that is followed by other courts. Resorting to precedent results in greater consistency and fairness in judicial opinions, which in turn enables people to enter legal relationships more knowledgeably and allows them to weigh the consequences of their behavior with better predictability.

A precedent, however, may not always be followed. The distinction must be made between *binding* and *nonbinding* precedents. A **binding precedent** is a decision of a higher court that must be followed by a lower court. For example, a decision by the Texas Supreme Court must be followed by a Texas Court of Appeals.

By contrast, a **nonbinding precedent** does not have to be followed. Using the Texas Supreme Court as the example again, assume that a Florida court decides a case on the legality of a spouse assisting a terminally ill spouse to commit suicide. A Texas court has the same issue before it. Does the Texas court have to follow the Florida case? The answer is "no." The Florida case is nonbinding precedent for a Texas court. The Texas court is free to reach its own decision in the matter. Similarly, Texas has several "divisions" of an intermediate appellate court, and a decision in one does not become a binding decision for other courts at the same level. This rule

---

TERMS

common law† Law found in the decisions of the courts rather than in statutes; judge-made law; English law adopted by the early American colonists, which is part of the United States' judicial heritage and forms the basis of much of its law today.

stare decisis† The doctrine that judicial decisions stand as precedents for cases arising in the future.

precedent† Prior decisions of the same court or a higher court that a judge must follow in deciding a subsequent case presenting similar facts and the same legal problem, even though different parties are involved and many years have elapsed.

binding precedent† Previous decisions of a higher court that a judge must follow in reaching a decision in a case.

nonbinding precedent Previous decisions of a higher court that a judge may, but does not have to, follow in reaching a decision in a case.

holds generally for all situations in which there are multiple courts at the same level of responsibility.

There are occasions when courts can sidestep a binding precedent by recasting the facts so that they do not seem to fall within the framework of the precedent. This is referred to as **distinguishing a case**. Court decisions, however, generally follow the precedents.

Because of the growth of our judicial system, the need to have a written compilation of court decisions developed. Most decisions can be found in a **case reporter** or other commercial publications such as **looseleaf reporter services**. Both publish the full texts of court decisions, often including separate concurring and dissenting opinions (if any were issued) in addition to the official "opinion of the court" that governs the specific case. The case reporters are treated in-depth in Chapter 4, and the looseleaf services in Chapter 12.

Statutory Law and Treaties

Statutes

The law passed by the United States Congress or the Texas state legislature and signed into law is referred to as **statutory law**. Once passed, statutory law is released in three forms of interest to a legal researcher: slip laws, session laws, and statutory codes.

A **slip law** is the unbound and unedited but final version of a recently passed law. The slip law is published usually in a pamphlet or single-sheet form. The chronological compilations of the slip laws enacted by a legislative session are referred to as the **session laws**. Session laws are published at the close of a legislative session. Both the federal and Texas

---

TERMS

distinguishing a case† To explain why a particular case is not precedent or authority with respect to the matter in controversy; to point out significant differences.

case reporter† Official, published reports of cases decided by courts, giving the opinions rendered in the cases, with headnotes prepared by the publisher.

looseleaf reporter services Official reports of cases decided by courts that are published in a notebook-style format that can be easily updated by substituting more recent pages for the original ones.

statutory law† Law that is promulgated by statute, as opposed to law that is promulgated by the judiciary.

slip law† A single judicial decision published shortly after it has been issued by the court and well before it is incorporated into a reporter.

session laws† The collected statutes enacted during a session of a legislature.

legislatures publish session laws. Eventually, slip laws and session laws are bound into **statutory codes**, which contain the current statutory law. The federal statutes are known as the *United States Code*, and the Texas state statutes are known as *Vernon's Annotated Texas Statutes*, or "Blacks" (the books are black). Often the new statutory law changes are found in the pocket supplements or pocket parts at the end of each volume. These supplements should always be consulted when evaluating the current status of the law. Statutory codes are discussed further in Chapter 5.

Treaties

Treaties are a primary source of law. Entered into by the president of the United States, treaties form the basis of international agreements between the United States and foreign nations. They govern rights, especially in the trade area. Treaties can dictate anything from the cost of a foreign car to copyright rights in videos and CDs (compact discs). Therefore, they can be an important source of law.

Administrative Law

Although considered a source of law, administrative law is a segment of statutory law. Derived from a legislative grant of authority from either the United States Congress or a state legislature, **administrative law** is the law created by, and governing, administrative agencies. An **administrative agency** is a governmental body that regulates the conduct of individuals, business entities, and governmental bodies. From the legislative grant of authority, these agencies have been delegated powers to (1) establish an expertise in their areas of authority, (2) promulgate rules and regulations in furtherance of their statutory authority, and (3) administer and enforce those rules and regulations through enforcement and other proceedings.

The United States Congress established the basic guidelines for administrative agencies in the Administrative Procedure Act (APA). The act provides for agency regulation of policy making, public access to agency

---

TERMS

statutory codes† The published statutes of a jurisdiction, arranged in systematic form.

administrative law† The body of law that controls the way in which administrative agencies operate; regulations issued by administrative agencies.

administrative agency† A board, commission, bureau, office, or department, of the executive branch of government, that implements the law that originates with the legislative branch.

information, and public participation in promulgating rules. Most states have similar administrative procedure acts that govern their state agencies. The Texas Administrative Code, for example, sets the basic parameters governing Texas administrative agencies. Administrative law is discussed further in Chapter 6.

§ 3.2   Classifications of the Law

Laws that govern the actions of individuals in a community and the enforcement of those laws are varied in nature. There are two major classifications of law: civil and criminal. Laws in each classification can be further subdivided into two general categories that reflect how they function: procedural and substantive.

Civil

Civil law involves disputes between two or more persons. The "person" may be an individual, a corporation, or a local, state, or federal government. A court action, referred to as a **lawsuit**, is brought by a party to seek monetary or nonmonetary relief for some type of injury suffered because of the actions of another party.

The relief sought by a party, referred to as a **remedy**, may take the form of **monetary damages** or **equitable relief.** For example, life lost in an automobile accident cannot be replaced, nor can serious injuries be undone. Monetary compensation, known as **compensatory damages**, is the only relief that can be bestowed upon the injured party for its loss.

TERMS

civil law†   Law based upon a published code of statutes, as opposed to law found in the decisions of courts.

lawsuit†   An informal term for an action or proceeding in a civil court, but not for a criminal prosecution.

remedy†   The means by which a right is enforced, an injury is redressed, and relief is obtained.

monetary damages†   The sum of money that may be recovered in the courts as financial reparation for an injury or wrong suffered as a result of breach of contract or a tortious act.

equitable relief†   A remedy available in equity rather than at law; generally relief other than money damages.

compensatory damages†   Damages recoverable in a lawsuit for loss or injury suffered by the plaintiff as a result of the defendant's conduct.

However, there is a difficulty inherent in this type of remedy. How much money compensates the victim? What are the standards for establishing the amount and length of the compensation? The goal is to make the one who caused the injury bear the costs and make the injured party whole again.

Some types of injuries are easily measured in dollar terms. For example, where personal property is destroyed, a monetary award will enable the injured party to obtain a comparable substitute. In personal injury cases, the major types of measurable economic losses are medical expenses, lost wages, and expenses to provide replacements or substitutes for activities prevented by the injuries. Such losses are usually referred to as **special damages**.

Other type of losses, however, are not so easily measured. These include such injuries as physical pain, mental suffering, and injuries to dignity and honor such as libel and slander, loss of enjoyment of life, and loss of consortium. These injuries are not translatable into dollars and cents in any objective way, yet monetary damages, known as **general damages**, are allowed, since no other remedy could any more effectively return to the injured party something for his or her loss. Anything less would have the effect of allowing the party that inflicted these types of injuries to escape responsibility.

A second type of money damages is **nominal or token damages**. This award is made by the court in cases where a party is unable to prove measurable substantial damages. The wrongful act is acknowledged with minimal compensation.

The court also has the authority to award **punitive damages**, also called **exemplary damages**. Punitive damages, if awarded, are not in-

---

TERMS

special damages† Damages that may be added to the general damages in a case, and arise from the particular or special circumstances of the case; the natural but not necessary result of a tort; damages arising naturally but not necessarily from a breach of contract.

general damages† Damages that are the natural and probable result of the wrongful acts complained of.

nominal or token damages† Damages awarded to a plaintiff in a very small or merely symbolic amount where no actual damages have been incurred, but the law recognizes the need to vindicate the plaintiff, or some compensable injury has been shown, but the amount of that injury has not been proven.

punitive damages† Damages that are awarded over and above compensatory damages or actual damages because of the wanton, reckless, or malicious nature of the wrong done by the plaintiff.

exemplary damages† Damages that are awarded over and above compensatory or actual damages for the purpose of making an example of the plaintiff to discourage others from engaging in the same kind of conduct in the future.

tended to compensate an injured party for the types of losses covered by compensatory damages. Rather, the goal of punitive damages is to punish the wrongdoer and hopefully control the wrongdoer's future behavior and send a message to others that there may be serious economic consequences to intentionally injuring someone.

Punitive damages are awarded only in cases where the defendant's conduct is considered to have been done with such a high degree of intention and deliberation as to be characterized as having been done with malice, a fraudulent or evil motive, or such a conscious and deliberate disregard for the well-being of others that the conduct may be called willful or wanton.

An equitable remedy is a remedy based upon principles of fairness and justice. In cases when monetary damages are insufficient or inappropriate or the court is unable to determine the proper amount of damages, an equitable remedy may be awarded. The **injunction**, an order by the court directing an individual or company to refrain from performing, or directing one to perform, a particular act, is an equitable remedy. An example of a case where an injunction might be in order is in a labor strike against an employer. The company asks the court to order the striking employees to refrain from harassing and committing acts of violence against company personnel or premises.

A second form of equitable remedy, **specific performance**, is a court order directing a party to perform a contractual obligation. For example, a home owner has contracted for remodeling and additions to an existing property. The contractor, without reason, is wavering and refuses to complete the contract. The court could order the contractor to specifically perform the terms of the contract. This court-ordered performance results in equity or fairness to the complaining party.

Criminal

Criminal law, unlike civil law, involves a wrongful act committed by an individual against society, even though the brunt of the injury caused by the wrongdoer may have fallen on a single person. What behavior is

---

TERMS

injunction† A court order that commands or prohibits some act or course of conduct.

specific performance† The equitable remedy of compelling performance of a contract, as distinguished from an action at law for damages for breach of contract due to nonperformance.

criminal law† Branch of the law that specifies what conduct constitutes crime and establishes appropriate punishments for such conduct.

considered criminal is set out in state and federal statutes that both define the nature of the behavior being criminalized and provide for penalties to be imposed on those persons convicted of violating the statutes. Thus, a **crime** is an offense committed by an individual that breaks a state or federal law, for which punishment in the form of imprisonment, fines, or, in some instances, death, may be imposed.

The type of crime is measured by degrees of the severity of a particular offense. The lowest level of criminal offense, the **misdemeanor**, is punishable by a fine and/or imprisonment for a maximum of one year. Typical misdemeanors are public intoxication, shoplifting, and assault and battery. A **felony** is the highest level of criminal offense. Punishment for this crime ranges from one year to the death penalty. Murder, rape, arson, and armed robbery are examples of felonies.

State legislatures have enacted criminal codes or guidelines for the conduct of their citizens. The range of requisite punishment that a court or jury can impose for violation of the criminal code is established within the code. However, criminal codes and the severity of punishment for an offense vary from state to state.

Texas has passed the Texas Penal Code to regulate the conduct of its citizens. This code defines the penalties and punishments for those who violate Texas criminal laws.

Procedural and Substantive

The rights and duties of individuals in a society encompass the substance of the law, commonly referred to as **substantive law**. Substantive law is the source of obligations incurred by people toward each other, and it imposes liability, civil and/or criminal, for violations of those obligations. Substantive law is what gives rise to a cause of action, and it

---

TERMS

crime† An offense against the authority of the state; a public wrong, as distinguished from a private wrong; an act in violation of the penal code; a felony or a misdemeanor.

misdemeanor† A crime not amounting to a felony; in many jurisdictions, misdemeanors are offenses for which the punishment is incarceration for less than a year or the payment of a fine.

felony† A general term for more serious crimes, as distinguished from lesser offenses, which are known as misdemeanors; in many jurisdictions, felonies are crimes for which the punishment is death or more than one year of imprisonment.

substantive law† Area of the law that defines right conduct, as opposed to procedural law, which governs the process by which rights are adjudicated.

determines how a dispute will be decided. For example, if a person crosses the street when a signal light is red and gets hit by a car, the substantive law would decide which party is liable.

Procedural law, sometimes referred to as remedial or adjective law, establishes how rights and duties are enforced or how redress for violations can be obtained. It determines such matters as the court in which a lawsuit must be filed and court deadlines within the lawsuit.

Separate rules of procedure have been established for both civil and criminal law. The Federal Rules of Civil Procedure and the Federal Rules of Criminal Procedure must be followed in all cases within the federal court system. States have adopted civil and criminal procedures for litigation within the framework of the state court system.

In Texas, the procedural rules are the Texas Rules of Civil Procedure and Texas Rules of Criminal Procedure. These rules are followed for cases filed in Texas state courts. The federal and Texas rules of procedure are substantially different. Always use the proper rules and be aware of the differences between the federal and Texas state court rules.

§ 3.3 Distinguishing Between Primary and Secondary Authority

Collectively, constitutions, judicial opinions, statutes and treaties, and administrative law are the **primary sources** of the law. Primary authority may be either mandatory or persuasive.

Mandatory authority is binding legal authority—that is, authority that must be followed by a court. You must identify this type of authority in your legal research. For example, if the Texas Supreme Court were to decide that women could contractually agree to serve as surrogate mothers for other couples and in so doing agree to sever their parent-child relationships with the children born of such arrangements, future decisions on that issue by trial and intermediate appellate courts in Texas would have to be followed. The supreme court case would be mandatory authority.

TERMS

procedural law† The law governing the manner in which rights are enforced; the law prescribing the procedure to be followed in a case.

primary sources The collective term for the main sources of the law: constitutions, judicial opinions, statutes and treaties, and administrative law.

mandatory authority Binding legal authority that a court must follow in making a decision in a case.

Persuasive authority is legal authority that sets a standard but does not have to be followed by a court. Persuasive authority is generally used to convince a court why a precedent should be followed. Whether a court follows a persuasive authority is purely discretionary. Returning to the "surrogate mother" example from the preceding paragraph, if no Texas court had yet decided this issue but a high court in another state had, the authority from the other state would be only persuasive authority in Texas. It would not be binding in any way on any Texas state court.

Secondary authority is the term applied primarily to legal sources that offer interpretations of the law by (mainly) law professors, practicing attorneys, law students, or other legal scholars. Secondary authority is found in a range of publications: law reviews, legal encyclopedias and treatises, books, and hearings before legislative committees, to name a few—all of which are covered later in this volume.

Although often based on careful research in primary sources, secondary sources are not the law. Secondary authority is not binding on a court, although it has on occasion been the case that courts, including the United States Supreme Court, have been greatly influenced by a particularly well-reasoned point of view appearing in a secondary source.

§ 3.4 Getting Ready to Research

Are you begin your legal research, there are certain preliminary factors that must be considered. Always determine the court in which a case will be filed. Will the court be a United States district court or a Texas state court? The court where a case is filed will have a direct bearing on the laws that apply and the procedures that will need to be followed. Often you will begin your research by locating an applicable statute, then you will find judicial opinions that have interpreted the statute. Legal research is not complete until all applicable sources of law have been exhausted and evaluated.

Although the next chapter deals with judicial opinions, research may well be more appropriately begun with other sources, for example, with a legal encyclopedia or digest, discussed in Chapters 7 and 8, respectively.

TERMS

persuasive authority†   Authority that is neither binding authority nor precedent, but which a court may use to support its decision if it chooses.

secondary authority†   Nonbinding or persuasive authority that is not the law itself but simply commentary upon or a summary of the law.

Both sources lead you to cases that will assist you in finding the law. Where you begin depends upon your assignment. Often the best source for one type of research may not be particularly useful for another. To be successful in legal research, you need to be flexible and responsive to the needs of each specific assignment.

A Checklist

1. Determine whether your case is civil or criminal.
2. Locate statutes that apply.
3. Locate cases that apply.
4. Determine whether a constitutional provision may apply.
5. Determine whether an administrative rule or regulation applies.
6. Determine if the authority found is mandatory or persuasive.
7. If possible, use authority that is binding and mandatory.
8. Review secondary authority to find primary sources of the law.

Summary

3.1   Primary Sources of the Law

There are four primary sources of the law. They are constitutions, judicial opinions, statutes and treaties, and administrative rules and regulations. Constitutions set the foundation for government at the federal and state levels. The United States Constitution sets forth the structure of government for the United States federal government, while the Texas Constitution sets the basis of government in Texas. Judicial opinions are the written decisions handed down by courts. Both state and federal courts create judicial opinions. Statutes are the laws created by legislatures, whereas treaties are agreements created by the United States government with foreign nations. Administrative rules and regulations are the laws created by the federal and state administrative agencies.

3.2   Classifications of the Law

The law can be classified into different categories. The main classifications are civil and criminal law. Civil law involves disputes between two or more persons who are seeking a remedy for the wrongdoing. The remedy can be monetary or equitable. Criminal law involves a wrongful act committed by an individual against society and usually has penalties for the wrongdoing, such as monetary restitution, fines, or imprisonment. The distinction between substantive and procedural law is another classification. Substantive law imposes liability and determines the rights and obligations of the parties, whereas procedural law identifies the procedures that are followed in the court system.

3.3 Distinguishing Between Primary and Secondary Authority

The primary sources of the law may be mandatory or persuasive authority. Mandatory authority must be followed by a court and is legally binding on that court. Persuasive authority may be followed by a court and is not legally binding on that court. Other sources of law are the secondary authorities that interpret the primary sources of law.

Review Questions

1. What are the primary sources of the law?

2. How many articles and amendments does the United States Constitution presently contain?

3. Define the principles of *stare decisis* and *precedent*.

4. Distinguish between a binding and nonbinding precedent.

5. What is statutory law and in what three forms is it released?

6. Who creates administrative law? What act provides the basic guidelines for federal administrative law?

7. Distinguish between monetary and equitable remedies.

8. Distinguish between civil and criminal law.

9. What is mandatory authority? Persuasive authority?

10. What is the difference between primary authority and secondary authority?

Exercises

1. Find a copy of the United States Constitution. What was the last amendment passed, and what right was granted?

2. What constitutional amendment deals with the right to a speedy trial?

3. Find a copy of the Texas Constitution. What article establishes who can amend the constitution?

4. A Texas court has to determine whether surrogacy contracts are legal. The two leading case decisions are in New Jersey and California. New Jersey held

the contracts void as against public policy, and California held the contracts legal and binding. What would the result be in Texas, and which court would Texas follow, if any?

5. Choose a law that has recently been passed by your state legislature and determine:

    a. legislative session

    b. the author or sponsor of the law

    c. the date it was passed

    d. the date it was signed into law

6. Plan a trip to your local courthouse and find the following:

    a. a lawsuit that has a claim for damage

    b. a lawsuit that has a claim for an equitable remedy

    c. a lawsuit that has punitive damages

7. Plan a trip to a criminal court and locate the following:

    a. a case involving a misdemeanor

    b. a case involving a felony

For each case, determine the parties to the case and the crime involved.

8. Locate a copy of the Texas Rules of Civil Procedure. Review the table of contents and determine which rules deal with the following:

    a. motion for summary judgment

    b. motion for continuance

    c. request for production of documents

9. Identify the types of Texas mandatory authority.

10. Visit a local library and identify the following secondary sources:

    a. the Texas encyclopedia

    b. a general legal encyclopedia

    c. a Texas law review article

CHAPTER 4

JUDICIAL OPINIONS AND CASE REPORTERS

§ 4.1   Judicial Opinions

Introduction

To thoroughly evaluate the law, a legal researcher must understand how to read a judicial opinion and understand its components. Judicial opinions are a primary source of law in legal research. Unless you can understand the components of case opinions, you will be at an impasse.

Most judicial opinions are found in a **reporter**. A reporter is a book that contains "case law," the written reports of judicial decisions of controversies litigated before various courts. The National Reporter System, published by West Publishing Company, is comprised of a number of reporters that publish cases from all federal courts and all state appellate courts. Very few of the West reporters include any trial court opinions. At the intermediate appellate court level, most decisions are not published. Those appearing in the reporters have been selectively chosen for publication.

Citations

All judicial opinions are identified by a citation. A *citation* is the formal notation that identifies the case. It normally includes the name of the case, the reporter series and the specific reporter volume in which the case is found, the page where the case begins, and the date (year) of the opinion. The citation for the landmark United States Supreme Court case of *Brown v. Board of Education* is as follows:

347 U.S. 483 (1954)

This citation conveys very precise information that is crucial to legal research. It names the court, the date of the decision, and exactly where the case can be found in a specific reporter:

Reporter: U.S. (stands for *United States Reports*)

Court: U.S. Supreme Court (only cases from this court are found in the *United States Reports*)

Date of decision: 1954

TERMS

reporter†   Court reports, as well as official, published reports of cases decided by administrative agencies.

Volume of *U.S. Reports*:   347

Page on which *Brown* begins: 483

§ 4.2 The Components of a Judicial Opinion

Judicial opinions in West reporters have standard components. These are the caption, the docket number, the name of the court, the syllabus, the case headnotes, the attorneys, the majority opinion, and the concurring and dissenting opinions, if any. For an illustration of the components of a judicial opinion, see Figure 4–1.

Caption

Technically, the **caption** of the case identifies the parties involved in the case and the court issuing the decision. Often the caption is characterized as the *name* of the case. It is also referred to as the *style* or *heading* of the case. The terms are used interchangeably. When a case begins in the trial court, the parties are normally referred to as the plaintiff and the defendant. The *plaintiff* is the party filing the lawsuit and the *defendant* is the party responding to the lawsuit. Most trial court cases are not published. Texas does not publish any state trial level decisions.

When a case is appealed, the name designations may change. The name of the party bringing the appeal, the **appellant**, may appear first, and the name of the party responding to the appeal, the **appellee**, may appear second. If a case is on appeal with the Texas Supreme Court, the parties are referred to as **petitioner** and **respondent**, the party bringing the appeal being the petitioner, and the party responding to the appeal being the respondent.

TERMS

caption† A heading; in legal practice, it generally refers to the heading of a court paper.

appellant† A party who appeals from a lower court to a higher court.

appellee† A party against whom a case is appealed from a lower court to a higher court.

petitioner† A person seeking relief by a petition.

respondent† The party against whom an appeal is taken to a higher court, *i.e.*, the successful party in the lower court; the appellee.

FORECA, S.A., Petitioner,

v.

GRD DEVELOPMENT COMPANY,
INC. et al., Respondents.

No. C–7370.

Supreme Court of Texas.

July 13, 1988.

Rehearing Denied Nov. 16, 1988.

Manufacturer of amusement rides sued to recover for defendants' alleged breach of purchase agreement. The 171st District Court, El Paso County, Peter S. Peca, Jr., J., entered judgment in favor of manufacturer for lost profits, and defendants appealed. The El Paso Court of Appeals, Eighth Supreme Judicial District, Fuller, J., 747 S.W.2d 9, reversed, and manufacturer appealed. The Supreme Court, Kilgarlin, J., held that "subject to legal documentation" provision in handwritten document executed by parties after they had agreed on material terms of sale did not establish, as matter of law, that no sales agreement had been reached.

Judgment of Court of Appeals reversed; judgment of trial court affirmed.

Robertson, J., dissented and filed opinion in which Wallace, Mauzy and Culver, JJ., joined.

Sales ⚖=53(1)

"Subject to legal documentation" provision in handwritten document executed by parties after they had agreed on material terms of sale of six amusement park rides did not establish, as matter of law, that no sales agreement had been reached; rather, existence of enforceable contract was question for jury.

Russell H. McMains, McMains & Constant, Corpus Christi, David K. Anderson, Caddell & Conwell, Houston, for petitioner.

Gerald B. Shifrin, El Paso, for respondents.

KILGARLIN, Justice.

At issue in this case is whether negotiations between the parties to this suit produced a valid, enforceable contract. Based on a jury verdict finding a breach of contract, the trial court rendered judgment for Foreca, S.A. (Foreca) for $389,940. The court of appeals reversed the judgment of the trial court, holding that the written instruments contained a condition precedent to the formation of a contract that had not been met. 747 S.W.2d 9 (Tex.App.). The court of appeals rendered a take nothing judgment in favor of GRD Development Company, Inc. (GRD) and George R. Dipp. We reverse the judgment of the court of appeals and affirm the judgment of the trial court.

The negotiations underlying this lawsuit involved the purchase of six amusement park rides. Foreca is a Belgium corporation. GRD is a Texas corporation with its principal place of business in El Paso, Texas. GRD and its owner and president, George R. Dipp, planned to open the Magic Landing Amusement Park in El Paso. In this endeavor, they sought to purchase six amusement park rides. On September 2, 1983, Foreca's president, Wim Poulussen, wrote Dipp and offered to sell and deliver six amusement park rides for approximately $2,000,000. The September 2 letter discussed financing and expressed Foreca's awareness that GRD wanted delivery of the rides before the end of January 1984. The letter concluded, as follows:

As a general rule of the house all offers are subject to:

—satisfactory legal and financial documentation,

—legal restrictions or prior sale of one or more machines.

On September 12, 1983, GRD responded to the Foreca proposal, agreeing to the terms in general but proposing a different financing structure. Soon thereafter, the parties arranged to meet in El Paso.

After negotiating in person in El Paso with George Dipp, Poulussen prepared a handwritten document dated October 19, 1983. The document contained several pro-

FIGURE 4–1

FORECA, S.A. v. GRD DEVELOPMENT CO., INC.   Tex. **745**
Cite as 758 S.W.2d 744 (Tex. 1988)

visions: (1) the cost of six amusement park rides ($1,950,000); (2) the terms of payment; and (3) delivery information, including warranties. Provision 4, the genesis of much of the current controversy, read:

> 4. SUBJECT TO LEGAL DOCUMENTATION CONTRACT TO BE DRAFTED BY MR. DUNLAP.

Mr. Dunlop (not *Dunlap*) was Foreca's attorney in Houston. The document also provided that George Dipp and Paul Dipp would guarantee certain promissory notes and GRD would bear legal and out-of-pocket costs. Both Poulussen and George Dipp initialed the document. Foreca presented evidence that Poulussen advised George Dipp, during this meeting, that Foreca could not deliver the rides in February 1984 unless an immediate commitment to purchase was made. Poulussen testified that Dipp replied that such a commitment had been made.

On November 22, 1983, GRD wrote to Poulussen and informed him of GRD's decision "not to pursue any further negotiations" with Foreca. Foreca brought suit alleging breach of contract. The jury found: that the September 2 and October 19, 1983 documents constituted a buy and sell agreement; that GRD, by the November 23, 1983 letter, repudiated the agreement; that Foreca was ready, willing and able to perform under the agreement; and that Foreca would have made $389,940 profit on the deal.[1]

Foreca contends that the September 2 and October 19, 1983 writings constitute an agreement breached by GRD. GRD responds that no enforceable agreement existed because the "subject to legal documentation" provision in the October 19, 1983 instrument constitutes an uncomplied with condition precedent. GRD concludes

that the court of appeals properly construed the meaning of an unambiguous contract provision.

This case involves a situation increasingly common in business negotiations. GRD and Foreca negotiated over the sale of amusement park rides. Agreement was reached as to certain material terms, yet another formal document was contemplated by the parties. Was the contemplated formal document a condition precedent to the formation of a contract or merely a memorial of an already enforceable contract?

Professor Corbin's writing is instructive on this question:

> One of the most common illustrations of preliminary negotiation that is totally inoperative is one where the parties consider the details of a proposed agreement, perhaps settling them one by one, with the understanding during this process that the agreement is to be embodied in a formal written document and that neither party is to be bound until he executes this document. *Often it is a difficult question of fact whether the parties have this understanding*; and there are very many decisions holding both ways. These decisions should not be regarded as conflicting, even though it may be hard to reconcile some of them on the facts that are reported to us in the appellate reports. *It is a question of fact that the courts are deciding, not a question of law; and the facts of each case are numerous and not identical with those of any other case. In very many cases the question may properly be left to a jury.*

A. Corbin, *Corbin on Contracts* § 30 at 97 (1963) (emphasis added). Professor Corbin is not alone among commentators in espousing this view. *See, e.g.,* J. Calamari &

---

1. The jury issues, in pertinent part, read as follows. Issue No. 1:
    Do you find that the writings of September 2, 1983 ... and October 19, 1983 ... constituted an agreement whereby Foreca would sell and GRD ... would buy the six amusement park rides ...?
    Issue No. 2:
    Do you find that GRD ..., by its letter of November 22, 1983, repudiated the agreement, if any, with Foreca?

Issue No. 3:
    Do you find that Foreca would have been ready, willing, and able to perform its agreement, if any, with GRD?
Issue No. 4:
    What profit, if any, would Foreca have made if GRD ... had purchased the six amusement park rides from Foreca, pursuant to the agreement, if any?

FIGURE 4–1   *(continued)*

746 Tex.   **758 SOUTH WESTERN REPORTER, 2d SERIES**

J. Perillo, *Contracts* § 2–7 (3d ed. 1987). Restatement (Second) of Contracts § 27 (1979);[2] Note, *Contemplated Written Agreements—Contract or Memorial*, 26 Baylor L.Rev. 132 (1974); 17 Am.Jur.2d *Contracts* § 28 (1964).

This court quoted with approval, more than a decade ago, this excerpt from Professor Corbin's treatise. In *Scott v. Ingle Bros. Pacific, Inc.*, 489 S.W.2d 554 (Tex. 1972), we encountered a similar contract formation dispute. Scott sold a mop manufacturing plant to Ingle. The purchase agreement provided that an employment agreement "[had] been prepared" whereby Scott would manage the business for five years at a stated salary. No such employment agreement had actually been reduced to writing. A dispute arose, and Ingle discharged Scott. Scott brought suit for breach of an employment contract. In a unanimous opinion, Chief Justice Greenhill posed the question before the court:

> [W]as that portion of the "purchase agreement" dealing with the employment of the seller, Scott, an enforceable contract? This depends upon the intention of the parties. An agreement simply to enter into negotiations for a contract later does not create an enforceable contract. But parties may agree upon some of the terms of a contract, and understand them to be an agreement, and yet leave other portions of an agreement to be made later.

Scott, 489 S.W.2d at 555. Thus, the intention of the parties would be determinative: "Whether the execution of a separate employment agreement was, and is, essential to a mutuality of assent is a question of the intention of the parties." *Id.* Upon restating the principle that intention is usually an inference to be drawn by the fact finder, the court held that whether the clause in the purchase agreement was meant to be a contract was for the trier of fact to determine. *Id.* at 557. *See* Note, *Contem-*

plated Written Agreements—Contract or Memorial, 26 Baylor L.Rev. 132 (1974). *See also Preload Technology, Inc. v. A.B. & J. Construction Co., Inc.*, 696 F.2d 1080, 1090 (5th Cir.1983); *Kanow v. Brownshadel*, 691 S.W.2d 804, 806 (Tex.App.—Houston [1st Dist.] 1985, no writ); *Frank B. Hall & Co., Inc. v. Buck*, 678 S.W.2d 612, 629 (Tex.App.—Houston [14th Dist.] 1984, writ ref'd n.r.e.), *cert. denied*, 472 U.S. 1009, 105 S.Ct. 2704, 86 L.Ed.2d 720 (1985); *John E. Mitchell Co. v. Anderson*, 520 S.W.2d 927, 934 (Tex.Civ.App.—Waco 1975, writ ref'd n.r.e.); *Houston Chronicle Publishing Co. v. McNair Trucklease, Inc.*, 519 S.W.2d 924, 928 (Tex.Civ.App.—Houston [1st Dist.] 1975, writ ref'd n.r.e.).

Scott guides our analysis today. Accordingly, we hold that it is a question of fact in this case whether the terms agreed to and embodied in the September 2 and October 19, 1983 writings were intended to be the final expressions of the contract or were only preliminary negotiations which the parties did not intend to have legal significance until execution of the contemplated legal documentation. This question was properly submitted to and answered by the jury in fulfillment of its fact finding responsibilities. In some cases, of course, the court may decide, as a matter of law, that there existed no immediate intent to be bound. This case, however, is not such a case. The evidence as to the intent of the parties is disputed. More important, the "subject to legal documentation" language is not conclusive on intent to contract. *See Scott*, 489 S.W.2d at 556. The jury's resolution of this issue should be allowed to stand.

The judgment of the court of appeals is reversed, and the judgment of the trial court is affirmed.

ROBERTSON, J., dissented and filed an opinion in which WALLACE, MAUZY and CULVER, JJ., joined.

---

2. Comment c to section 27 of the Restatement (Second) of Contracts sets forth the following circumstances which may be helpful in determining whether a contract has been concluded: the extent to which express agreement has been reached on all the terms to be included; whether the contract is of a type usually put in writing; whether it needs a formal writing for its

full expression; whether it has few or many details; whether the amount involved is large or small; whether it is a common or unusual contract; whether a standard form of contract is widely used in similar transactions; and whether either party takes any action in preparation for performance during the negotiations.

FIGURE 4–1   *(continued)*

RIO GRANDE LAND & CATTLE CO. v. LIGHT   Tex. 747
Cite as 758 S.W.2d 747 (Tex. 1988)

ROBERTSON, Justice, dissenting.

I respectfully dissent. The majority has constructed a somewhat persuasive argument; however, in the process, it has divorced itself from a basic tenet of contract construction.

The sole issue presented in this case is simple: Is the phrase "subject to legal documentation" an ambiguous term? Under settled rules of contract construction, ambiguity is a question of law for the court to decide by examining the contract as a whole in the context of the circumstances present when the contract was drafted. *Coker v. Coker*, 650 S.W.2d 391, 394 (Tex. 1983); *R & P Enterprises v. LaGuarta, Gavrel & Kirk, Inc.*, 596 S.W.2d 517, 518 (Tex.1980). And if a contract is written so that a provision can be given a definite legal meaning, then it is not ambiguous and the court will therefore construe the contract as a matter of law. *Universal C.I.T. Credit Corp. v. Daniel*, 150 Tex. 513, 518, 243 S.W.2d 154, 157 (1951). This is the exact situation presented in this case.

During trial, *neither* party contended that the term "subject to legal documentation" was ambiguous. Absent any dispute as to ambiguity, it thus became the trial court's duty to construe the contract as a matter of law.

It is well settled that terms such as "subject to" create a condition precedent. *Hohenberg Brothers Co. v. George E. Gibbons & Co.*, 537 S.W.2d 1, 3 (Tex.1976). And, in this case, the term established a condition precedent to the formation of the contract. Inasmuch as the required "legal documentation" never took place, no contract was established between Foreca and GRD.

I would therefore affirm the judgment of the court of appeals.

WALLACE, MAUZY and CULVER, JJ., join in this dissenting opinion.

RIO GRANDE LAND & CATTLE COMPANY et al., Petitioners,

v.

George E. LIGHT, III et al., Respondents.

No. C-7582.

Supreme Court of Texas.

Sept. 21, 1988.

Rehearing Denied Nov. 16, 1988.

Cattle producers brought action against owners and operators of feed lot for wrongful conduct in housing and feeding of cattle. The 224th District Court, Bexar County, Carolyn Spears, J., entered jury verdict in favor of producers, and appeal was taken. The San Antonio Court of Appeals, Fourth Supreme Judicial District, 749 S.W.2d 206, affirmed as modified in part and reversed in part, and feed lot operators petitioned for review. The Supreme Court held that: (1) interest provisions applicable to contracts ascertaining sum payable was inapplicable to determine prejudgment interest; (2) equity was appropriate basis for award of prejudgment interest in case in which damages could not be measured from face of contract; and (3) limitation of prejudgment interest to 6% per annum, rather than statutory interest rate applicable to judgments, was improper.

Reversed in part and remanded.

1. Interest ⟶39(2.30)

Interest provisions applicable only to "contracts ascertaining the sum payable" did not apply to determination of prejudgment interest in case in which contract provided no guidance in ascertaining measure of damages suffered by party to contract. Vernon's Ann.Texas Civ.St. arts. 5069-1.03, 5069-1.05.

2. Interest ⟶39(2.30)

Equity was appropriate basis for award of prejudgment interest in case for

FIGURE 4–1   *(continued)*

By contrast, some states do not change the party designation from *plaintiff* and *defendant* on appeal. If case law is needed from other jurisdictions, pay attention to the party designations, as they may differ from those used in Texas.

Caption styles vary. A divorce case uses the caption "In the Matter of the Marriage of" followed by the names of the parties. A criminal case may list "State" or "People" or a similar term as the party bringing the action. Criminal cases also may use the caption *Ex parte* followed by the name of the person to the court action. In a probate action or dispute over property, the caption *In re* may be used. The caption *In re* is also used in juvenile proceedings.

A caption may list multiple parties. When referring to the case, the first name listed on each side is the name used to identify the case. Figure 4–2 provides examples of different captions.

Docket Number

The **docket number** is the file number for a case. Knowing a docket number will assist you in finding information on a case from research sources that are filed by docket number. For example, local courts often maintain files by docket number, and you may want to review the complete file of a particular case. Giving the clerk of a court or other court personnel the docket number will give you access to the file.

You need to check the docket number assigned at each level of litigation. Docket numbers change at each court level. All documents filed with a court can be reviewed simply by knowing the docket number. See Figure 4–1 for an example of a docket number (No. C-7370).

Date of the Case

All cases identify the month, date, and year the case was decided. Many cases, however, identify more than one date. For example, the caption in Figure 4–3 identifies the date the case was submitted and the date the case was decided. For research purposes, the date the case was decided by the court is the important date. Sometimes the parties to a case will request that the court reconsider the decision. In such cases, these dates may be noted as well. Do not be confused by all the date references. Focus only on the date the case was decided.

TERMS

docket number†   The number given to a case when it is on a list of cases for trial or other disposition.

!

John J. COSTELLO, Jr., M.D., P.A. and All
Saints Episcopal Hospital, A Non–Profit
Corporation d/b/a All Saints Episcopal
Hospital

v.

William J. SMITH and Debra Smith.

2

The STATE of Texas, ex rel., John
F. HEALEY, Jr., District
Attorney, Relator,

v.

Honorable Walter S. McMEANS,
Judge, County Court at Law
No. 2, Respondent.

In the Matter of R.W., a Minor.

No. 13–93–418–CV.

Court of Appeals of Texas,
Corpus Christi.

Don HAGLER, Petitioner,

v.

The PROCTOR & GAMBLE MANUFAC-
TURING COMPANY, Respondent.

WILLIAMS DISTRIBUTING COMPANY
a/k/a B.C. Williams Bakery Service,
Inc., Appellant,

v.

Roy FRANKLIN and Etta B.
Franklin, Appellees.

No. 05–93–00960–CV.

Court of Appeals of Texas,
Dallas.

FIGURE 4–2   Examples of different captions

FIGURE 4–3

Cathy Lynn WARDEN, Appellant,

v.

The STATE of Texas, Appellee.

No. 06–93–00048–CR.

Court of Appeals of Texas,
Texarkana.

Submitted Nov. 16, 1994.

Decided Dec. 12, 1994.

Rehearing Overruled March 14, 1995.

Syllabus

The **syllabus**, or summary, of the case is a paragraph that references a court's decision and gives an overview of the facts and the prior proceedings of the case. The syllabus is normally prepared by the publisher (in some instances, by the court reporter) and is *not* the law of the case. You must never rely on or quote the court syllabus in legal research. The syllabus should be used solely as a quick reference guide for determining the general issues addressed in a case and providing a framework for reading the opinion, should that seem appropriate. If a case is one that should be used, always read the full opinion of the court. (See Figure 4–1.)

Attorneys

Included in all court opinions are the names of the attorneys who represented the parties in the action. This information is not critical to understanding a court decision, but it may be extremely useful should it become necessary to consult with attorneys who have handled similar cases. (See Figure 4–1.)

TERMS

syllabus†   The headnote of a reported case.

Case Headnotes

Many case reporters print case headnotes at the beginning of the case. A case **headnote** is a paragraph summary of a point of law contained within the case. Cases may have only one headnote or many headnotes. The publisher who prepares the headnotes decides on the number of headnotes needed to digest each case. As with the syllabus, the headnotes should be used as a quick reference, and not as legal authority.

Included in the reporter headnotes published by West Publishing Company is an additional feature, the West topic and key number, which is part of the West Digest Key Number System. This system was developed by West and is used in all their reporters and encyclopedias. The indexing of each point of law under a unique topic and key number provides an excellent means of locating additional cases on the same topic. This system is discussed in greater detail in Chapter 7.

West Publishing Company also publishes Texas court opinions in the *Southwestern Reporter*. The Texas opinions have headnotes with a West topic and key number assigned to each paragraph. The topic and key numbers found in the headnotes can assist in finding Texas cases. In West compilations such as General Digests, cases are arranged alphabetically and clearly by state under each topic and key number.

Not all case reporters employ West's key number system. At least one other legal publisher, Lawyers Cooperative Publishing Company (LCP), has produced its own unique headnote system that is of value primarily in finding related cases and materials in other LCP publications.

See Figure 4–4 for a comparison of the different headnote styles. Figure 4–4(a) is the *Supreme Court Reporter* version of *City of Dallas v. Stanglin,* and Figure 4–4(b) is the *Lawyer's Edition* version of the same case.

Opinion of the Case

At the beginning of most opinions, the name of the judge assigned to write the opinion appears. An **opinion** in a case consists of the holding,

---

TERMS

headnote† A summary statement that appears at the beginning of a reported case to indicate the points decided by the case.

opinion† A written statement by a court that accompanies its decision in a case and gives the court's reasons for its decision. Although "decision" and "opinion" are often used interchangeably, the terms are not synonymous: a decision is the judgment in the case; an opinion gives the reasoning on which judgment is based.

490 U.S. 19   CITY OF DALLAS v. STANGLIN   1591
Cite as 109 S.Ct. 1591 (1989)

Florida v. Royer, 460 U.S. 491, 502, 103 S.Ct. 1319, 1326–27, 75 L.Ed.2d 229 (1983), the casing of a store, *Terry, supra,* 392 U.S., at 6, 88 S.Ct., at 1872, or the provision of a reliable report from an informant that wrongdoing is imminent, *Illinois v. Gates,* 462 U.S., at 225–227, 103 S.Ct., at 2325–2326, nothing about the characteristics shown by airport traveler Sokolow reasonably suggests that criminal activity is afoot. The majority's hasty conclusion to the contrary serves only to indicate its willingness, when drug crimes or antidrug policies are at issue, to give short shrift to constitutional rights. See, *e.g., Skinner v. Railway Labor Executives Assn.,* 489 U.S. 602, 636, 109 S.Ct. 1402, 1423, 103 L.Ed.2d 639 (1989) (MARSHALL, J., dissenting).[4] In requiring that seizures be based on at least some evidence of criminal conduct, 831 F.2d, at 1419, the Court of Appeals was faithful to the Fourth Amendment principle that law enforcement officers[18] must reasonably suspect a person of criminal activity before they can detain him. Because today's decision, though limited to its facts, *ante,* at 1587, disobeys this important constitutional command, I dissent.

490 U.S. 19, 104 L.Ed.2d 18

 |₁₉CITY OF DALLAS, et al., Petitioners

v.

Charles M. STANGLIN, Individually, and d/b/a Twilight Skating Rink.

No. 87–1848.

Argued March 1, 1989.

Decided April 3, 1989.

City filed petition for writ of certiorari after the Texas Court of Appeals, Fifth

District, 744 S.W.2d 165 declared city's ordinance limiting use of dance halls to persons between ages of 14 and 18 violative of those persons' associational rights. After granting certiorari, the Supreme Court, Chief Justice Rehnquist, held that: (1) ordinance did not infringe on First Amendment right of association, and (2) ordinance was rationally related to legitimate purpose and did not violate equal protection clause.

Reversed and remanded.

Justice Stevens, with whom Justice Blackmun joined, concurred in judgment.

1. Constitutional Law ⬦91
   Theaters and Shows ⬦3.50

City ordinance restricting admission to certain dance halls to persons between ages of 14 and 18 did not infringe on First Amendment right of association; dance hall patrons were not engaged in any form of intimate or expressive association, and there was no generalized right of "social association" that included chance encounters in dance halls. U.S.C.A. Const.Amend. 1.

2. Constitutional Law ⬦242.1(4)
   Infants ⬦13
   Theaters and Shows ⬦3.50

City ordinance restricting admission to certain dance halls to persons between ages of 14 and 18 did not violate equal protection clause because it was rationally related to city's legitimate effort to protect teenagers within that age group from what could be corrupting influences of older teenagers and young adults. U.S.C.A. Const.Amend. 14.

---

4. The majority also contends that it is not relevant that the DEA agents, in forcibly stopping Sokolow rather than simply speaking with him, did not "use the least intrusive means available." *Ante,* at 1587. On the contrary, the manner in which a search is carried out—and particularly

whether law enforcement officers have taken needlessly intrusive steps—is a highly important index of reasonableness under Fourth Amendment doctrine. See, *e.g., Winston v. Lee,* 470 U.S. 753, 760–761, 105 S.Ct. 1611, 1616–1617, 84 L.Ed.2d 662 (1985).

FIGURE 4–4(a)   Headnote style: *Supreme Court Reporter*

U.S. SUPREME COURT REPORTS   104 L Ed 2d

HEADNOTES

Classified to U.S. Supreme Court Digest, Lawyers' Edition

Constitutional Law § 960 — freedom of association — teenage dance hall patrons

1a-1f. A city ordinance restricting admission to certain dance halls to persons between the ages of 14 and 18 does not interfere with the associational rights, guaranteed by the Federal Constitution's First Amendment, of patrons of a dance hall that is subject to the ordinance, where (1) such patrons are not members of any organized association, (2) hundreds of such patrons congregate at the dance hall each night, and most of them are strangers to one another, (3) the dance hall admits all who are willing to pay the admission fee, and (4) there is no suggestion that such patrons take positions on public questions or perform other similar activities; the First Amendment secures no right of such patrons to associate in the dance hall with persons outside their age group, because (1) coming together to engage in recreational dancing (a) is not a form of intimate association protected by the First Amendment, and (b) does not involve the sort of

TOTAL CLIENT-SERVICE LIBRARY® REFERENCES

4 Am Jur 2d, Amusements and Exhibitions § 23; 16A Am Jur 2d, Constitutional Law §§ 533, 534, 536, 750; 42 Am Jur 2d, Infants § 18

12 Am Jur Legal Forms 2d, Licenses and Permits §§ 164:73, 164:74

USCS, Constitution, Amendments 1, 14

US L Ed Digest, Constitutional Law §§ 404, 929, 960

Index to Annotations, Children; Dancehalls; Equal Protection of Law; Freedom of Association

Auto-Cite®: Cases and annotations referred to herein can be further researched through the Auto-Cite® computer-assisted research service. Use Auto-Cite to check citations for form, parallel references, prior and later history, and annotation references.

ANNOTATION REFERENCES

The Supreme Court and the First Amendment right of association. 33 L Ed 2d 865.

Public dances or dancehalls as nuisances. 44 ALR2d 1381.

Exclusion from place of public entertainment or amusement, for reason other than race or color, as violation of equal protection clause. 1 ALR2d 1165.

FIGURE 4–4(b)   Headnote style: *Lawyers' Edition*

DALLAS v STANGLIN
(1989) 490 US 19, 104 L Ed 2d 18, 109 S Ct 1591

expressive association that is so protected; and (2) the Federal Constitution does not recognize a generalized right of "social association" that includes chance encounters in dance halls.

Constitutional Law § 319 — equal protection — rational relationship

2. In order for laws to be valid under the equal protection clause of the Federal Constitution's Fourteenth Amendment, it need only be shown that they bear some rational relationship to a legitimate state purpose, unless such laws create suspect classifications or impinge upon rights protected under the Federal Constitution.

Constitutional Law § 932 — expression associated with conduct

3. Although it is possible to find some kernel of expression in almost every activity a person undertakes, such a kernel is not sufficient by itself to bring the activity within the protection of the Federal Constitution's First Amendment.

Constitutional Law §§ 319, 404 — equal protection — dance halls — age restrictions on admission

4a-4d. A city ordinance restricting admission to certain dance halls to persons between the ages of 14 and 18 is valid under the equal protection clause of the Federal Constitution's Fourteenth Amendment, because (1) dance hall patrons are not a suspect classification, (2) the ordinance does not infringe on any right protected by the Federal Constitu-

tion, and (3) a rational relationship exists between the age restriction and the city's interest in promoting the welfare of teenagers, since the city could reasonably conclude that (a) teenagers might be susceptible to corrupting influences if permitted, unaccompanied by their parents, to frequent a dance hall with older persons, and (b) limiting dance hall contacts between juveniles and adults would make less likely illicit or undesirable juvenile involvement with alcohol, illegal drugs, and promiscuous sex; the fact that the city might otherwise be able to achieve its objectives through increased supervision, education, and prosecution of those who corrupt minors does not mean that the ordinance does not survive rational-basis scrutiny, which is the most relaxed and tolerant form of judicial scrutiny under the equal protection clause; the fact that the city allows teenagers and adults to roller-skate together does not mean that the ordinance violates the equal protection clause, because (1) skating involves less physical contact than dancing, and (2) although the differences between the two activities may not be striking, the differentiation need not be striking in order to survive rational-basis scrutiny.

[See annotation p 1078, infra]

Constitutional Law §§ 316, 400, 401 — equal protection

5. In the sphere of local economic regulation, it is only the invidious discrimination, the wholly arbitrary act, which cannot stand consistently with the equal protection clause of the Federal Constitution's Fourteenth Amendment.

SYLLABUS BY REPORTER OF DECISIONS

For the express purpose of providing a place where teenagers can socialize with each other but not be

subject to the potentially detrimental influences of older teenagers and adults, a Dallas ordinance authorizes

---

FIGURE 4–4(b) *(continued)*

the reasoning, and the dicta of the court. The **holding** is the result the court has reached. It is the principle for which the case stands, although it often may be expressed in terms of simply announcing which party has "won." The **reasoning** of the case is the legal basis upon which the court relies to reach its result. The reasoning may include any source of legal material that a court determines is relevant. The sources can be both primary and secondary. **Dicta**, or **obiter dicta**, are additional comments or remarks made by the court that are immaterial to the court's resolution of the dispute before it. Dicta is not the law of the case and has no precedential authority.

Additional Opinions of the Court

When unanimity is impossible, additional opinions from the other judges who sat on the case may be issued. The **majority opinion**, which is the main opinion in most cases, is the decision of the court and is the law decided by the court. The majority opinion always comes first in the published case.

A judge who agrees with the result but does not agree completely with the reasoning may issue a concurring opinion. A judge who completely disagrees with the result may issue a dissenting opinion. There are also other types of opinions such as per curiam and plurality opinions. These various types of opinions are discussed in the following text.

Concurring Opinion

A judge who agrees with the result in a case but is not satisfied or not in agreement with the court's reasoning may write a **concurring opinion**. A concurring opinion often offers additional analysis of the issues pre-

---

TERMS

holding†   The proposition of law for which a case stands; the "bottom line" of a judicial decision.

reasoning   The legal basis upon which the court relies to reach its result in a case.

dicta (obiter dictum)†   Expressions or comments in a court opinion that are not necessary to support the decision made by the court; they are not binding authority and have no value as precedent.

majority opinion†   An opinion issued by an appellate court that represents the view of a majority of the members of the court.

concurring opinion†   An opinion issued by one or more judges that agrees with the result reached by the majority opinion rendered by the court, but reaches that result for different reasons.

sented in the majority opinion or adds a different perspective of the issues. A concurring opinion is not written for all cases. Any concurring opinions are usually found immediately after the majority opinion.

Dissenting Opinion

A judge or justice who disagrees with the majority opinion is referred to as a dissenter and may issue a dissenting opinion. The **dissenting opinion** disagrees with the majority opinion entirely or in part as to the result. Although a dissent is rarely as widely cited as the majority opinion, it can be a useful tool when analyzing many legal problems.

Sometimes the dissent will add insight into an opposing position or suggest a trend in the law. Indeed, a particularly well-argued dissent in a case involving an unsettled area of law can become widely used should later courts adopt that dissenter's position as the majority position. Dissenting opinions are always placed in the reporters after the majority and concurring opinions.

Concurring in Part and Dissenting in Part Opinion

Judges may agree with part of a decision and disagree with another part of a decision. An opinion reflecting the views of a judge in this position is referred to as a **concurring in part and dissenting in part opinion**. This is a hybrid of a concurring and a dissenting opinion that is often seen in United States Supreme Court decisions.

Per Curiam Opinion

A **per curiam opinion** is a judicial opinion given by the entire court as one body. No particular judge is given responsibility to write the opinion. Generally, a per curiam opinion is written when a court determines that the issues of law either are so firmly established as not to need

---

TERMS

---

dissenting opinion†   A written opinion filed by a judge of an appellate court who disagrees with the decision of the majority of judges in a case, giving the reasons for his or her differing view.

concurring in part and dissenting in part opinion   An opinion of the court in which the judges agree with a part of a decision and disagree with another part of the decision.

per curiam opinion†   An opinion, usually of an appellate court, in which the judges are all of one view and the legal question is sufficiently clear that a full written opinion is not required and a one- or two-paragraph opinion suffices.

further explanation or are in areas of the law that the court does not want to treat specially in the case at hand. Per curiam opinions are legal precedents.

Plurality Opinion

In some cases, even though a majority of the judges sitting on a case have agreed to the decision, they may not have agreed on their reasons for the decision. The result can be the issuing of two or more opinions on behalf of the decision. In all likelihood, in such cases there will be one opinion joined by more judges than any other opinion.

A **plurality opinion** is the name applied to an opinion joined by the most members of the court in a case where there is no majority opinion. A good example of a plurality opinion can be found in *Regents of the University of California v. Bakke,* 438 U.S. 265 (1978), an affirmative action case. Because the reasoning in a plurality opinion does not reflect the analysis of a majority of the court, it may have limited precedential value.

Memorandum Opinions

A decision where the court merely states its ruling or gives an order but not an explanation for its decision is a **memorandum opinion**. Usually, these opinions are short, not more than a few lines. These decisions are not appealable, since they are simply an announcement of the court's intended decision. The most common place to find memorandum opinions is in United States Supreme Court decisions. (See Figure 4–5 for an illustration of a memorandum opinion.)

Disposition

The **disposition** of the case identifies whether a higher court has agreed or disagreed with the lower court's decision. Words such as *affirmed* or *reversed* signal the higher court's view of the lower court's decisions.

TERMS

plurality opinion† An appellate court opinion joined in by less than a majority of the justices, but by more justices than the number joining any other concurring opinion.

memorandum opinion† A court decision, usually consisting of a brief paragraph announcing the court's judgment, without an in-depth opinion.

disposition† A court's ruling, decision, or judgment in a case.

Affirmed   When a higher court agrees with a lower court's decisions, the case is **affirmed**. By affirming a judgment, decree, or order, the appellate court is giving its "stamp of approval" and telling the world the decisions is valid. The lower court's decision, therefore, must stand as it was rendered.

Reversed   A higher court can completely change the result or decision of a lower court. This is known as the court reversing the judgment of the lower court. When a case is **reversed**, the lower court's decision is thrown out, and any previous decision is void.

Vacated   Another term that is often seen as part of the disposition of a case is **vacated**. All this means is that the lower court's decision has been canceled or voided.

Remanded   Many cases that are reversed are also **remanded**. Usually the court states that the case has been *reversed and remanded*. When a case is remanded, it is sent back to the lower court for further action. The higher court may instruct the lower court to change its original decision, reform it, change the irregularities as specified by the appellate court, or have a new hearing.

Source of the Opinion

Whether a case comes from an official or unofficial reporter is irrelevant to the accuracy of the case. The terms *official* and *unofficial* relate only to which reporter is recognized by a jurisdiction. The content of the case decision is the same, but in unofficial reporters, the legal publishers create commentary such as summaries and headnotes. This distinction is discussed further in the following text.

TERMS

affirmed†   The upholding of a lower court's decision or judgment by an appellate court.

reversed†   The overthrow or annulment of a prior decision.

vacated†   A judgment, decree, or other order of a court that is annulled, set aside, made void, or canceled.

remanded†   A case that is returned by an appellate court to the trial court for further proceedings, for a new trial, or for entry of judgment in accordance with an order of the appellate court.

§ 4.3 The Reporters

In the American judicial system, a vast number of court decisions are written for and published in case reporters. Reporters are generally organized by court, state, and geographic region. The most comprehensive reporter system with numerous interrelated units is known as the National Reporter System, published by West Publishing Company.

Two terms you will encounter with some frequency are *official reporter* and *unofficial reporter*. An **official reporter** has been designated by or on behalf of a court as one accepted as a matter of law as containing the final valid versions of the opinions issued by the court. An **unofficial reporter** exists side-by-side with an official reporter and is not endorsed by the court as containing the official versions of cases. In many instances, this may seem to be a distinction without clear meaning, particularly since West reporters function for some states as official reporters and for others as unofficial reporters. You should ascertain in all instances which case law compilation serves as the official reporter for the jurisdiction you are researching.

Reporters, including those in the National Reporter System, can be broken down into five general categories: United States Supreme Court reporters, federal reporters, specialized reporters, state reporters, and regional reporters, all of which are discussed in detail in the following text.

Slip Opinions and Advance Sheets

When a written opinion is issued by a court, it is not initially printed in book form. It is first printed in single-sheet or pamphlet form known as a **slip opinion**, or slip decision. Slip opinions are printed without headnotes or any other publisher additions and are individually paginated. Many courts now transmit slip opinions by facsimile (FAX) machine when time is of the essence.

TERMS

---

official reporter   The publication containing reports of cases that has been designated by or on behalf of a court as the one that is to be accepted as a matter of law as containing the final valid versions of the opinions issued by that court.

unofficial reporter   A publication containing reports of cases that has not been endorsed by the court as containing the official versions of the cases heard by the court.

slip opinion†   A single judicial decision published shortly after it has been issued by the court and well before it is incorporated into a reporter.

Cases next appear in an **advance sheet**, a softcover pamphlet that is published prior to the issuance of a hardcover bound volume in a reporter set. The advance sheets are edited, normally have headnotes, and usually identify the exact volume and page where the case will appear in the hardcover volume. Remember, the advance sheets may not contain the precise final form of a court opinion. The bound volume, if available, should be used to ensure accuracy.

United States Supreme Court Reporters

Decisions issued by the United States Supreme Court can be found in three reporters: *United States Reports, Supreme Court Reporter,* and *United States Supreme Court Reports, Lawyers' Edition.* All three Supreme Court reporters contain the full texts of the Court's opinions. Two of them, the *Supreme Court Reporter* and the *Lawyer's Edition,* contain some potentially valuable research-assisting features. In addition to these reporters, there are various weekly printed publications and on-line services that allow faster access, if needed, to Supreme Court opinions. Foremost among the printed publications are *United States Law Week* and *Supreme Court Bulletin.*

Some courts' opinions appear in both official and unofficial reporters. When a case from such a court is cited into more than one reporter, the citations are known as **parallel citations**. An assignment to "find the parallel cites" is an assignment to locate the citations of a case in all the reporters in which it appears. Always use the official citation, if available, when citing a United States Supreme Court case.

Official citation alone: *City of Dallas v. Stanglin,* 490 U.S. 19 (1989)

Official citation with parallel citations: *City of Dallas v. Stanglin,* 490 U.S. 19, 109 S. Ct. 1591, 104 L. Ed. 18 (1989)

United States Reports

The official reporter for United States Supreme Court cases is *United States Reports,* which is abbreviated as U.S. in case citations. *United States Reports* is published by the United States Government Printing Office. This reporter contains the entire judicial opinion rendered by the high court

---

TERMS

advance sheet†   A printed copy of a judicial opinion published in looseleaf form shortly after the opinion is issued.

parallel citation†   A citation to a court opinion or decision that is printed in two or more reporters.

in an unedited form. Early Supreme Court publications were compiled by individuals and identified by the individuals' names. The early Supreme Court reporters are referred to as **nominative reporters**.

Although published officially by the United States Government, the first ninety volumes of *United States Reports* still include references to the early nominative reporters. The early *United States Reports* and the nominative reporters are as follows:

Reporter	Nominative Citation	*U.S. Reports* Citation	Dates
Dallas	1–4 Dallas	1–4 U.S.	1790–1800
Cranch	1–9 Cranch	5–13 U.S.	1801–1815
Wheaton	1–12 Wheaton	14–25 U.S.	1816–1827
Peters	1–16 Peters	26–41 U.S.	1828–1842
Howard	1–24 Howard	42–65 U.S.	1843–1860
Black	1–2 Black	66–67 U.S.	1861–1862
Wallace	1–23 Wallace	68–90 U.S.	1863–1874

The following is a sample citation from a nominative reporter:

Marbury v. Madison, 5 U.S. (1 Cranch) 137 (1803).

Although *United States Reports* is the official Supreme Court reporter, a given case is not available in it until long after it is issued. Often a year passes before a case appears in the bound *United States Reports* volume. Consequently, *United States Law Week*, the *Supreme Court Bulletin,* or the *Supreme Court Reporter* may have to be cited.

Supreme Court Reporter

One of the unofficial reporters for United States Supreme Court cases is the *Supreme Court Reporter,* which is abbreviated as S. Ct. in case citations. *Supreme Court Reporter* is published by West Publishing Company. This unofficial reporter has a research-assisting feature that *United States Reports* does not have, which is case headnotes with the key number system. Editors at West review the cases and determine important points of law in each. Editors then abstract these points from the case, summarizing each in a short paragraph, and assigning to each paragraph a topic and key

---

TERMS

nominative reporters Early reports of United States Supreme Court cases that were compiled by individuals and identified by the individuals' names.

number in the West numbering system, which is used in all West reporters and digests.

The first *Supreme Court Reporter* volume was published in 1882. The first *United States Reports* volume to correspond with the *Supreme Court Reporter* is volume 106. The *Supreme Court Reporter* has published all Supreme Court cases since 1882. The *Supreme Court Reporter* publishes advance sheets approximately every two weeks when the United States Supreme Court is in session, beginning the first Monday of each October.

In addition to the texts of decisions that make up most of each volume, **front matter**, the materials at the beginning of the volume, can provide valuable research guidance. Included in the front matter of the *Supreme Court Reporter* are a table of contents, a list of Supreme Court justices throughout history, special orders, a cross-reference table to *United States Reports* citations, a table of cases reported in the volume, and a listing of statutes and rules cited.

Lawyers' Edition

The other unofficial reporter is the *United States Supreme Court Reports, Lawyers' Edition,* commonly referred to as *Lawyers' Edition*, published by Lawyers Cooperative Publishing Company (LCP), a division of Thomson Legal Publishing Inc. The *Lawyer's Edition* has headnotes that identify the points of law in the case, similar to those in the *Supreme Court Reporter*. However, the *Lawyer's Edition* does not use the West Topic and Key Number System, but, instead, uses a series of annotation commentaries for case identification and research.

The *Lawyers' Edition* is now in its second series. The cases are reported in roughly chronological order. The first series has completely separate cases from its later edition. The series is always identified in the citation: *L. Ed.* or *L. Ed. 2d.* Pay close attention to the different series notations or you may pull the wrong case accidentally. The *Lawyers' Edition* has different features than *United States Reports* and the *Supreme Court Reporter*. In addition to its own headnotes and case summaries, the *Lawyers' Edition* includes summaries of the briefs of counsel as well as commentaries known as annotations for some cases. (See Chapter 8.)

Similar to West's efforts to link its publications through its key number system, LCP has created a link among its various publications that is

---

TERMS

front matter Materials at the beginning of a book that can provide valuable research guidance, *e.g.,* tables of contents, cases, statutes, rules, and cross-references.

referred to as the Total Client-Service Library (TCSL). Only LCP publications are referenced in this system.

As with the *Supreme Court Reporter*, the *Lawyers' Edition* has an extensive table of contents. Parallel citations are given to *United States Reports* as well as statements of cases, points and authorities of counsel, and annotations.

Star Paging

The paging systems differ in each United States Supreme Court reporter. Since most law libraries do not have all three Supreme Court reporters, a system had to be developed to coordinate the official and unofficial Supreme Court reporters. The system is star-paging. **Star paging** is a pagination system used in the unofficial reporters to reference the official reporter pages that correspond to the pages in the unofficial reporter. The reason for star paging is that when referencing a case, its official reporter citation, if available, must be used.

The system is easy to use. In the *Supreme Court Reporter*, a symbol is used in the unofficial reporter to reference the official pages. The symbol is an upside-down T: $\bot$. The beginning and ending of each page in the official reporter is noted in the unofficial reporter. Not much is left to chance, as the official citation is given above the caption, and you can follow the official pages accordingly. Think of star paging as placing an overlay of the official reporter case and having the same text presented twice.

For an illustration of star paging, see *City of Dallas v. Stanglin* in Figure 4–5(a), which is taken from the *Supreme Court Reporter*. Note the official citation above the caption: 490 U.S. 19. Find the first star-paging entry, which is page 20 on page 1592 of the *Supreme Court Reporter*. Page 20 is the official page in *United States Reports*. Notice that you are on a completely different page in the *Supreme Court Reporter*. Say you were interested in quoting the passage on page 1594, second column, of the *Supreme Court Reporter* that begins, "While the First Amendment does not in terms protect a 'right of association,' our cases have recognized that it embraces . . . ," and you know you must reference the official page. The official page is 23, found on page 1594 of the *Supreme Court Reporter*. But also notice that the word *embrace* has the star-paging symbol right in the middle of it. The original text was hyphenated. The quotation, therefore, is on pages 23 and 24 of *United States Reports*. Now check the same section

---

TERMS

star paging   A pagination system used in unofficial reporters to reference the official reporter pages that correspond to the pages in the unofficial reporters.

in *United States Reports* (Figure 4–5[c]) and observe the hyphenated word in the original. By following the star-paging system, you are able to identify the official reporter and official pages without using *United States Reports.*

The star-paging system is important to master because it is used in other reporters besides the *Supreme Court Reporter.* The *Lawyers' Edition* uses star paging, but with a different identification. Rather than using the upside-down T, the *Lawyers' Edition* uses paragraph breaks to denote the *United States Reports* coordinating pages. The passage identified on page 1594 of the *Supreme Court Reporter* is found on page 25 of the *Lawyers' Edition* (see Figure 4–5[b]), which indicates the passage is found on page 23 of *United States Reports.*

Weekly Reporters

United States Law Week Although not technically a reporter, *United States Law Week* (cited as *U.S.L.W.*) essentially functions as one for the period before an advance sheet to a reporter is issued. *United States Law Week* is a weekly publication issued by the Bureau of National Affairs (BNA).

United States Law Week is published in two volumes, the *Supreme Court* volume and the *General Law* volume. The *Supreme Court* volume contains the complete texts of the latest United States Supreme Court decisions, summaries of cases being appealed to the court, requests for petitions for writs of certiorari, summaries of oral arguments, and discussions of future cases to be heard before the Court. Cases are published in *U.S.L.W.* usually within days of being issued. *United States Law Week* does not offer publisher-prepared headnotes or research aids. The *General Law* volume contains summaries of a highly selective number of cases from lower federal and state courts and discusses current legal developments not specifically related to Supreme Court decisions.

Supreme Court Bulletin Commerce Clearing House (CCH) publishes the *Supreme Court Bulletin,* a weekly volume similar to *United States Law Week*'s Supreme Court volume. The *Supreme Court Bulletin* contains the complete texts of Supreme Court decisions, as well as the Court's calendars, proceedings, and orders.

Federal Reporters

Cases from the United States Circuit Courts of Appeals and the United States District Courts are published in a series of federal reporters. These are *Federal Cases, Federal Reporter, Federal Supplement,* and *Federal Rules Decisions.* All the federal case reporters are published by West Publishing

Florida v. Royer, 460 U.S. 491, 502, 103 S.Ct. 1319, 1326–27, 75 L.Ed.2d 229 (1983), the casing of a store, *Terry, supra,* 392 U.S., at 6, 88 S.Ct., at 1872, or the provision of a reliable report from an informant that wrongdoing is imminent, *Illinois v. Gates,* 462 U.S., at 225–227, 103 S.Ct., at 2325–2326, nothing about the characteristics shown by airport traveler Sokolow reasonably suggests that criminal activity is afoot. The majority's hasty conclusion to the contrary serves only to indicate its willingness, when drug crimes or antidrug policies are at issue, to give short shrift to constitutional rights. See, *e.g., Skinner v. Railway Labor Executives Assn.,* 489 U.S. 602, 636, 109 S.Ct. 1402, 1423, 103 L.Ed.2d 639 (1989) (MARSHALL, J., dissenting).[4] In requiring that seizures be based on at least some evidence of criminal conduct, 831 F.2d, at 1419, the Court of Appeals was faithful to the Fourth Amendment principle that law enforcement officers[18] must reasonably suspect a person of criminal activity before they can detain him. Because today's decision, though limited to its facts, *ante,* at 1587, disobeys this important constitutional command, I dissent.

490 U.S. 19, 104 L.Ed.2d 18

⌊19CITY OF DALLAS, et al., Petitioners

v.

Charles M. STANGLIN, Individually, and d/b/a Twilight Skating Rink.

No. 87–1848.

Argued March 1, 1989.

Decided April 3, 1989.

City filed petition for writ of certiorari after the Texas Court of Appeals, Fifth

District, 744 S.W.2d 165 declared city's ordinance limiting use of dance halls to persons between ages of 14 and 18 violative of those persons' associational rights. After granting certiorari, the Supreme Court, Chief Justice Rehnquist, held that: (1) ordinance did not infringe on First Amendment right of association, and (2) ordinance was rationally related to legitimate purpose and did not violate equal protection clause.

Reversed and remanded.

Justice Stevens, with whom Justice Blackmun joined, concurred in judgment.

1. **Constitutional Law** ⇐91
  Theaters and Shows ⇐3.50

City ordinance restricting admission to certain dance halls to persons between ages of 14 and 18 did not infringe on First Amendment right of association; dance hall patrons were not engaged in any form of intimate or expressive association, and there was no generalized right of "social association" that included chance encounters in dance halls. U.S.C.A. Const.Amend. 1.

2. **Constitutional Law** ⇐242.1(4)
  Infants ⇐13
  Theaters and Shows ⇐3.50

City ordinance restricting admission to certain dance halls to persons between ages of 14 and 18 did not violate equal protection clause because it was rationally related to city's legitimate effort to protect teenagers within that age group from what could be corrupting influences of older teenagers and young adults. U.S.C.A. Const.Amend. 14.

---

4. The majority also contends that it is not relevant that the DEA agents, in forcibly stopping Sokolow rather than simply speaking with him, did not "use the least intrusive means available." *Ante,* at 1587. On the contrary, the manner in which a search is carried out—and particularly

whether law enforcement officers have taken needlessly intrusive steps—is a highly important index of reasonableness under Fourth Amendment doctrine. See, *e.g., Winston v. Lee,* 470 U.S. 753, 760–761, 105 S.Ct. 1611, 1616–1617, 84 L.Ed.2d 662 (1985).

FIGURE 4–5(a)   An example of star paging: *Supreme Court Reporter*

1592   109 SUPREME COURT REPORTER   490 U.S. 19

Syllabus

For the express purpose of providing a place where teenagers can socialize with each other but not be subject to the potentially detrimental influences of older teenagers and adults, a Dallas ordinance authorizes the licensing of "Class E" dance halls, restricting admission thereto to persons between the ages of 14 and 18 and limiting their hours of operation. Respondent, whose roller-skating rink and Class E dance hall share a divided floorspace, filed suit in state court to enjoin the ordinance's age and hour restrictions, contending, *inter alia*, that they violated the First Amendment and the Equal Protection Clause of the Fourteenth Amendment. The trial court upheld the ordinance, but the Texas Court of Appeals struck down the ordinance's age restriction, holding that it violated the First Amendment associational rights of minors.

Held:

1. The ordinance does not infringe on the First Amendment right of association. Respondent's patrons, who may number as many as 1,000 per night, are not engaged in a form of "intimate association." Nor do the opportunities of adults and minors to dance with one another, which might be described as "associational" in common parlance, involve the sort of "expressive association" that the First Amendment has been held to protect. The teenagers who congregate are not members of any organized association, and most are strangers to one another. The dance hall admits all who pay the admission fee, and there is no suggestion that the patrons take positions on public questions or perform other similar activities. Moreover, the Constitution does not recognize a generalized right of "social association" that includes chance encounters in dance halls. *Griswold v. Connecticut*, 381 U.S. 479, 483, 85 S.Ct. 1678, 1681, 14 L.Ed.2d 510, distinguished. Pp. 1594–1595.

* The syllabus constitutes no part of the opinion of the Court but has been prepared by the Reporter of Decisions for the convenience of the

2. The ordinance does not violate the Equal Protection Clause because there is a rational relationship between the age restriction for Class E dance halls and the city's interest in promoting the welfare of teenagers. Respondent's claims—that the ordinance does not meet the city's objectives because adults and teenagers can still associate with one another in places such as his skating rink and that there are other, less intrusive, alternatives to achieve the objectives—misapprehend the nature of ⌐₂₀rational-basis scrutiny, the most relaxed and tolerant form of judicial scrutiny under the Equal Protection Clause. Under this standard, a classification that has some reasonable basis does not offend the Constitution because it is imperfect. Here, the city could reasonably conclude that teenagers might be more susceptible to corrupting influences if permitted to frequent dance halls with older persons or that limiting dance-hall contacts between adults and teenagers would make less likely illicit or undesirable juvenile involvement with alcohol, illegal drugs, or promiscuous sex. While the city permits teenagers and adults to rollerskate together, skating involves less physical contact than dancing, a differentiation that need not be striking to survive rational-basis scrutiny. Pp. 1595–1597.

744 S.W.2d 165 (Tex.App.1987), reversed and remanded.

REHNQUIST, C.J., delivered the opinion of the Court, in which BRENNAN, WHITE, MARSHALL, O'CONNOR, SCALIA, and KENNEDY, JJ., joined. STEVENS, J., filed an opinion concurring in the judgment, in which BLACKMUN, J., joined, *post*, p. 1597.

————

Craig Lee Hopkins, Dallas, Tex., for petitioners.

Daniel J. Sheehan, Jr., Dallas, Tex., for respondent.

reader. See *United States v. Detroit Lumber Co.*, 200 U.S. 321, 337, 26 S.Ct. 282, 287, 50 L.Ed. 499.

FIGURE 4–5(a)   *(continued)*

Chief Justice REHNQUIST delivered the opinion of the Court.

Petitioner city of Dallas adopted an ordinance restricting admission to certain dance halls to persons between the ages of 14 and 18. Respondent, the owner of one of these "teenage" dance halls, sued to contest the constitutional validity of the ordinance. The Texas Court of Appeals held that the ordinance violated the First Amendment right of persons between the ages of 14 and 18 to associate with persons outside[21] that age group. We now reverse, holding that the First Amendment secures no such right.

In 1985, in response to requests for dance halls open only to teenagers, the city of Dallas authorized the licensing of "Class E" dance halls.[1] The purpose of the ordinance was to provide a place where teenagers could socialize with each other, but not be subject to the potentially detrimental influences of older teenagers and young adults. The provision of the ordinance at issue here, Dallas City Code § 14–8.1 (1985), restricts the ages of admission to Class E dance halls to persons between the ages of 14 and 18.[2] This provision, as [22]enacted, restricted admission to those between 14 and 17, but it was subsequently amended to include 18–year olds. Parents,

guardians, law enforcement, and dance-hall personnel are excepted from the ordinance's age restriction. The ordinance also limits the hours of operation of Class E dance halls to between 1 p.m. and midnight daily when school is not in session. § 14–5(d)(2).

Respondent operates the Twilight Skating Rink in Dallas and obtained a license for a Class E dance hall. He divided the floor of his roller-skating rink into two sections with moveable plastic cones or pylons. On one side of the pylons, persons between the ages of 14 and 18 dance, while on the other side, persons of all ages skate to the same music—usually soul and "funk" music played by a disc jockey. No age or hour restrictions are applicable to the skating rink. Respondent does not serve alcohol on the premises, and security personnel are present. The Twilight does not have a selective admissions policy. It charges between $3.50 and $5 per person for admission to the dance hall and between $2.50 and $5 per person for admission to the skating rink. Most of the patrons are strangers to each other, and the establishment serves as many as 1,000 customers per night.

Respondent sued in the District Court of Dallas County to enjoin enforcement of the

---

1. Dallas also licenses Class A, B, and C dance halls, which differ in the number of days per week dancing is permitted; Class D is for dance instruction. Persons under 17 must be accompanied by a parent for admission to Class A, B, and C dance halls. Dallas City Code §§ 14–1, 14–8 (1985–1986). A dance-hall license is not needed if the dance is at any of the following locations: a private residence from which the general public is excluded; a place owned by the federal, state, or local government; a public or private elementary school, secondary school, college, or university; a place owned by a religious organization; or a private club. *Ibid.*

2. Section 14–8.1 of the Dallas City Code provides:

"(a) No person under the age of 14 years or over the age of 18 years may enter a Class E dance hall.

"(b) A person commits an offense if he is over the age of 18 years and:

"(1) enters a Class E dance hall; or

"(2) for the purposes of gaining admittance into a Class E dance hall, he falsely represents himself to be:

"(A) of an age from 14 years through 18 years;

"(B) a licensee or an employee of the dance hall;

"(C) a parent or guardian of a person inside the dance hall;

"(D) a governmental employee in the performance of his duties.

"(c) A licensee or an employee of a Class E dance hall commits an offense if he knowingly allows a person to enter or remain on the premises of a dance hall who is:

"(1) under the age of 14 years; or

"(2) over the age of 18 years.

"(d) It is a defense to prosecution under Subsections (b)(1) and (c)(2) that the person is:

"(1) a licensee or employee of a dance hall;

"(2) a parent or guardian of a person inside the dance hall; or

"(3) a governmental employee in the performance of his duties."

FIGURE 4–5(a)   *(continued)*

age and hour restrictions of the ordinance. He contended that the ordinance violated substantive due process and equal protection under the United States and Texas Constitutions, and that it unconstitutionally infringed the rights of persons between the ages of 14 and 17 (now 18) to associate with persons outside that age bracket.[3] The trial court upheld the ordinance, finding that it was rationally$_{23}$ related to the city's legitimate interest in ensuring the safety and welfare of children.

The Texas Court of Appeals upheld the ordinance's time restriction, but it struck down the age restriction. 744 S.W.2d 165 (1987). The Court of Appeals held that the age restriction violated the First Amendment associational rights of minors. To support a restriction on the fundamental right of "social association," the court said that "the legislative body must show a compelling interest," and the regulation "must be accomplished by the least restrictive means." *Id.*, at 168. The court recognized the city's interest in "protect[ing] minors from detrimental, corrupting influences," *ibid.*, but held that the "City's stated purposes ... may be achieved in ways that are less intrusive on minors' freedom to associate," *id.*, at 169. The Court of Appeals stated that "[a] child's right of association may not be abridged simply on the premise that he 'might' associate with those who would persuade him into bad habits," and that "neither the activity of dancing *per se*, nor association of children aged fourteen through eighteen with persons of other ages in the context of dancing renders such children peculiarly vulnerable to the evils that defendant City seeks to prevent." *Ibid.* We granted certiorari, 488 U.S. 815, 109 S.Ct. 51, 102 L.Ed.2d 30 (1988), and now reverse.

[1] The dispositive question in this case is the level of judicial "scrutiny" to be applied to the city's ordinance. Unless laws "create suspect classifications or im-

pinge upon constitutionally protected rights," *San Antonio Independent School Dist. v. Rodriguez*, 411 U.S. 1, 40, 93 S.Ct. 1278, 1300, 36 L.Ed.2d 16 (1973), it need only be shown that they bear "some rational relationship to a legitimate state purpose" *id.*, at 44, 93 S.Ct., at 1302. Respondent does not contend that dance-hall patrons are a "suspect classification," but he does urge that the ordinance in question interferes with associational rights of such patrons guaranteed by the First Amendment.

While the First Amendment does not in terms protect a "right of association," our cases have recognized that it embraces$_{24}$ such a right in certain circumstances. In *Roberts v. United States Jaycees*, 468 U.S. 609, 104 S.Ct. 3244, 82 L.Ed.2d 462 (1984), we noted two different sorts of "freedom of association" that are protected by the United States Constitution:

"Our decisions have referred to constitutionally protected 'freedom of association' in two distinct senses. In one line of decisions, the Court has concluded that choices to enter into and maintain certain intimate human relationships must be secured against undue intrusion by the State because of the role of such relationships in safeguarding the individual freedom that is central to our constitutional scheme. In this respect, freedom of association receives protection as a fundamental element of personal liberty. In another set of decisions, the Court has recognized a right to associate for the purpose of engaging in those activities protected by the First Amendment—speech, assembly, petition for the redress of grievances, and the exercise of religion." *Id.*, at 617–618, 104 S.Ct., at 3249.

It is clear beyond cavil that dance-hall patrons, who may number 1,000 on any given night, are not engaged in the sort of

---

3. The Court of Appeals held that respondent had standing to assert the associational rights of the teenage patrons of his establishment. 744 S.W.2d 165, 168 (1987). That issue has not been raised before us.

FIGURE 4–5(a)   *(continued)*

DALLAS v STANGLIN
(1989) 490 US 19, 104 L Ed 2d 18, 109 S Ct 1591
APPEARANCES OF COUNSEL

Craig Lee Hopkins argued the cause for petitioners.
Daniel J. Sheehan, Jr. argued the cause for respondent.
Briefs of Counsel, p 1077, infra.

OPINION OF THE COURT

[490 US 20]
Chief Justice **Rehnquist** delivered the opinion of the Court.

[1a] Petitioner city of Dallas adopted an ordinance restricting admission to certain dance halls to persons between the ages of 14 and 18. Respondent, the owner of one of these "teenage" dance halls, sued to contest the constitutional validity of the ordinance. The Texas Court of Appeals held that the ordinance violated the First Amendment right of persons between the ages of 14 and 18 to associate with persons outside
[490 US 21]
that age group. We now reverse, holding that the First Amendment secures no such right.

In 1985, in response to requests for dance halls open only to teenagers, the city of Dallas authorized the licensing of "Class E" dance halls.[1]

The purpose of the ordinance was to provide a place where teenagers could socialize with each other, but not be subject to the potentially detrimental influences of older teenagers and young adults. The provision of the ordinance at issue here, Dallas City Code § 14-8.1 (1985), restricts the ages of admission to Class E dance halls to persons between the ages of 14 and 18.[2] This provision, as
[490 US 22]
enacted, restricted admission to those between 14 and 17, but it was subsequently amended to include 18-year-olds. Parents, guardians, law enforcement, and dance-hall personnel are excepted from the ordinance's age restriction. The ordinance also limits the hours of operation of Class E dance halls to between 1 p.m. and midnight daily when school is not in session. § 14-5(d)(2).

---

1. Dallas also licenses Class A, B, and C dance halls, which differ in the number of days per week dancing is permitted; Class D is for dance instruction. Persons under 17 must be accompanied by a parent for admission to Class A, B, and C dance halls. Dallas City Code §§ 14-1, 14-8 (1985-1986). A dance hall license is not needed if the dance is at any of the following locations: a private residence from which the general public is excluded; a place owned by the federal, state, or local government; a public or private elementary school, secondary school, college, or university; a place owned by a religious organization; or a private club. §§ 14-1, 14-8.

2. Section 14-8.1 of the Dallas City Code provides:
"(a) No person under the age of 14 years or over the age of 18 years may enter a Class E dance hall.
"(b) A person commits an offense if he is over the age of 18 years and:
"(1) enters a Class E dance hall; or

"(2) for the purposes of gaining admittance into a Class E dance hall, he falsely represents himself to be:
"(A) of an age from 14 years through 18 years;
"(B) a licensee or an employee of the dance hall;
"(C) a parent or guardian of a person inside the dance hall;
"(D) a governmental employee in the performance of his duties.
"(c) A licensee or an employee of a Class E dance hall commits an offense if he knowingly allows a person to enter or remain on the premises of a dance hall who is:
"(1) under the age of 14 years; or
"(2) over the age of 18 years.
"(d) It is a defense to prosecution under Subsections (b)(1) and (c)(2) that the person is:
"(1) a licensee or employee of a dance hall;
"(2) a parent or guardian of a person inside the dance hall; or
"(3) a governmental employee in the performance of his duties."

FIGURE 4–5(b)   An example of star paging: *Lawyers' Edition*

U.S. SUPREME COURT REPORTS   104 L Ed 2d

Respondent operates the Twilight Skating Rink in Dallas and obtained a license for a Class E dance hall. He divided the floor of his roller-skating rink into two sections with moveable plastic cones or pylons. On one side of the pylons, persons between the ages of 14 and 18 dance, while on the other side, persons of all ages skate to the same music—usually soul and "funk" music played by a disc jockey. No age or hour restrictions are applicable to the skating rink. Respondent does not serve alcohol on the premises, and security personnel are present. The Twilight does not have a selective admissions policy. It charges between $3.50 and $5.00 per person for admission to the dance hall and between $2.50 and $5.00 per person for admission to the skating rink. Most of the patrons are strangers to each other, and the establishment serves as many as 1,000 customers per night.

Respondent sued in the District Court of Dallas County to enjoin enforcement of the age and hour restrictions of the ordinance. He contended that the ordinance violated substantive due process and equal protection under the United States and Texas Constitutions, and that it unconstitutionally infringed the rights of persons between the ages of 14 and 17 (now 18) to associate with persons outside that age bracket.[3] The trial court upheld the ordinance, finding that it was rationally
[490 US 23]
related to the city's legitimate interest in ensuring the safety and welfare of children.

The Texas Court of Appeals up-held the ordinance's time restriction, but it struck down the age restriction. 744 SW2d 165 (1987). The Court of Appeals held that the age restriction violated the First Amendment associational rights of minors. To support a restriction on the fundamental right of "social association," the court said that "the legislative body must show a compelling interest," and the regulation "must be accomplished by the least restrictive means." Id., at 168. The court recognized the city's interest in "protect[ing] minors from detrimental, corrupting influences," ibid., but held that the "City's stated purposes . . . may be achieved in ways that are less intrusive on minors' freedom to associate," id., at 169. The Court of Appeals stated that "[a] child's right of association may not be abridged simply on the premise that he 'might' associate with those who would persuade him into bad habits," and that "neither the activity of dancing per se, nor association of children aged fourteen through eighteen with persons of other ages in the context of dancing renders such children peculiarly vulnerable to the evils that defendant City seeks to prevent." Ibid. We granted certiorari, 488 US 815, 102 L Ed 2d 30, 109 S Ct 51 (1988), and now reverse.

[2] The dispositive question in this case is the level of judicial "scrutiny" to be applied to the city's ordinance. Unless laws "create suspect classifications or impinge upon constitutionally protected rights," San Antonio Independent School Dist. v Rodriguez, 411 US 1, 40, 36 L Ed 2d 16, 93 S Ct 1278 (1973), it need only

---

3. The Court of Appeals held that respondent had standing to assert the associational rights of the teenage patrons of his establishment. 744 SW2d 165, 168 (Tex App 1987). That issue has not been raised before us.

FIGURE 4–5(b)   *(continued)*

DALLAS v STANGLIN
(1989) 490 US 19, 104 L Ed 2d 18, 109 S Ct 1591

be shown that they bear "some rational relationship to a legitimate state purpose" id., at 44, 36 L Ed 2d 16, 93 S Ct 1278. Respondent does not contend that dance-hall patrons are a "suspect classification," but he does urge that the ordinance in question interferes with associational rights of such patrons guaranteed by the First Amendment.

While the First Amendment does not in terms protect a "right of association," our cases have recognized that it embraces
[490 US 24]
such a right in certain circumstances. In Roberts v United States Jaycees, 468 US 609, 82 L Ed 2d 462, 104 S Ct 3244 (1984), we noted two different sorts of "freedom of association" that are protected by the United States Constitution:

"Our decisions have referred to constitutionally protected 'freedom of association' in two distinct senses. In one line of decisions, the Court has concluded that choices to enter into and maintain certain intimate human relationships must be secured against undue intrusion by the State because of the role of such relationships in safeguarding the individual freedom that is central to our constitutional scheme. In this respect, freedom of association receives protection as a fundamental element of personal liberty. In another set of decisions, the Court has recognized a right to associate for the purpose of engaging in those activities protected by the First Amendment—speech, assembly, petition for the redress of grievances, and the exercise of religion." Id., at 617-618, 82 L Ed 2d 462, 104 S Ct 3244.

[1b] It is clear beyond cavil that dance-hall patrons, who may number 1,000 on any given night, are not engaged in the sort of "intimate human relationships" referred to in Roberts. The Texas Court of Appeals, however, thought that such patrons were engaged in a form of expressive activity that was protected by the First Amendment. We disagree.

The Dallas ordinance restricts attendance at Class E dance halls to minors between the ages of 14 and 18 and certain excepted adults. It thus limits the minors' ability to dance with adults who may not attend, and it limits the opportunity of such adults to dance with minors. These opportunities might be described as "associational" in common parlance, but they simply do not involve the sort of expressive association that the First Amendment has been held to protect. The hundreds of teenagers who congregate each night at this particular dance hall are not members of any organized association; they are patrons of the same business establishment.
[490 US 25]
Most are strangers to one another, and the dance hall admits all who are willing to pay the admission fee. There is no suggestion that these patrons "take positions on public questions" or perform any of the other similar activities described in Board of Directors of Rotary International v Rotary Club of Duarte, 481 US 537, 548, 95 L Ed 2d 474, 107 S Ct 1940 (1987).

[1c, 3] The cases cited in Roberts recognize that "freedom of speech" means more than simply the right to talk and to write. It is possible to find some kernel of expression in almost every activity a person undertakes—for example, walking down the street or meeting one's

FIGURE 4–5(b)   *(continued)*

DALLAS *v.* STANGLIN   19

Syllabus

CITY OF DALLAS ET AL. *v.* STANGLIN, INDIVIDUALLY AND DBA TWILIGHT SKATING RINK

CERTIORARI TO THE COURT OF APPEALS OF TEXAS, FIFTH DISTRICT

No. 87–1848. Argued March 1, 1989—Decided April 3, 1989

For the express purpose of providing a place where teenagers can socialize with each other but not be subject to the potentially detrimental influences of older teenagers and adults, a Dallas ordinance authorizes the licensing of "Class E" dance halls, restricting admission thereto to persons between the ages of 14 and 18 and limiting their hours of operation. Respondent, whose roller-skating rink and Class E dance hall share a divided floorspace, filed suit in state court to enjoin the ordinance's age and hour restrictions, contending, *inter alia*, that they violated the First Amendment and the Equal Protection Clause of the Fourteenth Amendment. The trial court upheld the ordinance, but the Texas Court of Appeals struck down the ordinance's age restriction, holding that it violated the First Amendment associational rights of minors.

Held:

1. The ordinance does not infringe on the First Amendment right of association. Respondent's patrons, who may number as many as 1,000 per night, are not engaged in a form of "intimate association." Nor do the opportunities of adults and minors to dance with one another, which might be described as "associational" in common parlance, involve the sort of "expressive association" that the First Amendment has been held to protect. The teenagers who congregate are not members of any organized association, and most are strangers to one another. The dance hall admits all who pay the admission fee, and there is no suggestion that the patrons take positions on public questions or perform other similar activities. Moreover, the Constitution does not recognize a generalized right of "social association" that includes chance encounters in dance halls. *Griswold v. Connecticut,* 381 U. S. 479, 483, distinguished. Pp. 23–25.

2. The ordinance does not violate the Equal Protection Clause because there is a rational relationship between the age restriction for Class E dance halls and the city's interest in promoting the welfare of teenagers. Respondent's claims—that the ordinance does not meet the city's objectives because adults and teenagers can still associate with one another in places such as his skating rink and that there are other, less intrusive, alternatives to achieve the objectives—misapprehend the nature of

FIGURE 4–5(c)   An example of star paging: *United States Reports*

rational-basis scrutiny, the most relaxed and tolerant form of judicial scrutiny under the Equal Protection Clause. Under this standard, a classification that has some reasonable basis does not offend the Constitution because it is imperfect. Here, the city could reasonably conclude that teenagers might be more susceptible to corrupting influences if permitted to frequent dance halls with older persons or that limiting dance-hall contacts between adults and teenagers would make less likely illicit or undesirable juvenile involvement with alcohol, illegal drugs, or promiscuous sex. While the city permits teenagers and adults to roller-skate together, skating involves less physical contact than dancing, a differentiation that need not be striking to survive rational-basis scrutiny. Pp. 25–28.

744 S. W. 2d 165, reversed and remanded.

REHNQUIST, C. J., delivered the opinion of the Court, in which BRENNAN, WHITE, MARSHALL, O'CONNOR, SCALIA, and KENNEDY, JJ., joined. STEVENS, J., filed an opinion concurring in the judgment, in which BLACKMUN, J., joined, *post*, p. 28.

Craig Hopkins argued the cause for petitioners. With him on the briefs were *Analeslie Muncy* and *Kenneth C. Dippel.*

Daniel J. Sheehan, Jr., argued the cause and filed a brief for respondent.*

CHIEF JUSTICE REHNQUIST delivered the opinion of the Court.

Petitioner city of Dallas adopted an ordinance restricting admission to certain dance halls to persons between the ages of 14 and 18. Respondent, the owner of one of these "teenage" dance halls, sued to contest the constitutional validity of the ordinance. The Texas Court of Appeals held that the ordinance violated the First Amendment right of persons between the ages of 14 and 18 to associate with persons out-

---

*Briefs of *amici curiae* urging reversal were filed for the National Institute of Municipal Officers by *William I. Thornton, Jr., Frank B. Gummey III, William H. Taube, Roy D. Bates, Robert J. Alfton, James K. Baker, Robert J. Mangler, Neal E. McNeill, Dante R. Pellegrini, Clifford D. Pierce, Jr., Benjamin L. Brown,* and *Charles S. Rhyne;* and for the United States Conference of Mayors et al. by *Benna Ruth Solomon.*

FIGURE 4–5(c)   *(continued)*

DALLAS *v.* STANGLIN   21

19   Opinion of the Court

side that age group.   We now reverse, holding that the First Amendment secures no such right.

In 1985, in response to requests for dance halls open only to teenagers, the city of Dallas authorized the licensing of "Class E" dance halls.[1] The purpose of the ordinance was to provide a place where teenagers could socialize with each other, but not be subject to the potentially detrimental influences of older teenagers and young adults.   The provision of the ordinance at issue here, Dallas City Code § 14–8.1 (1985), restricts the ages of admission to Class E dance halls to persons between the ages of 14 and 18.[2]   This provision, as

---

[1] Dallas also licenses Class A, B, and C dance halls, which differ in the number of days per week dancing is permitted; Class D is for dance instruction.   Persons under 17 must be accompanied by a parent for admission to Class A, B, and C dance halls.   Dallas City Code §§ 14–1, 14–8 (1985–1986).   A dance-hall license is not needed if the dance is at any of the following locations: a private residence from which the general public is excluded; a place owned by the federal, state, or local government; a public or private elementary school, secondary school, college, or university; a place owned by a religious organization; or a private club.   *Ibid.*

[2] Section 14–8.1 of the Dallas City Code provides:

"(a) No person under the age of 14 years or over the age of 18 years may enter a Class E dance hall.

"(b) A person commits an offense if he is over the age of 18 years and:

"(1) enters a Class E dance hall; or

"(2) for the purposes of gaining admittance into a Class E dance hall, he falsely represents himself to be:

"(A) of an age from 14 years through 18 years;

"(B) a licensee or an employee of the dance hall;

"(C) a parent or guardian of a person inside the dance hall;

"(D) a governmental employee in the performance of his duties.

"(c) A licensee or an employee of a Class E dance hall commits an offense if he knowingly allows a person to enter or remain on the premises of a dance hall who is:

"(1) under the age of 14 years; or

"(2) over the age of 18 years.

"(d) It is a defense to prosecution under Subsections (b)(1) and (c)(2) that the person is:

FIGURE 4–5(c) *(continued)*

enacted, restricted admission to those between 14 and 17, but it was subsequently amended to include 18-year-olds. Parents, guardians, law enforcement, and dance-hall personnel are excepted from the ordinance's age restriction. The ordinance also limits the hours of operation of Class E dance halls to between 1 p.m. and midnight daily when school is not in session. § 14–5(d)(2).

Respondent operates the Twilight Skating Rink in Dallas and obtained a license for a Class E dance hall. He divided the floor of his roller-skating rink into two sections with moveable plastic cones or pylons. On one side of the pylons, persons between the ages of 14 and 18 dance, while on the other side, persons of all ages skate to the same music—usually soul and "funk" music played by a disc jockey. No age or hour restrictions are applicable to the skating rink. Respondent does not serve alcohol on the premises, and security personnel are present. The Twilight does not have a selective admissions policy. It charges between $3.50 and $5 per person for admission to the dance hall and between $2.50 and $5 per person for admission to the skating rink. Most of the patrons are strangers to each other, and the establishment serves as many as 1,000 customers per night.

Respondent sued in the District Court of Dallas County to enjoin enforcement of the age and hour restrictions of the ordinance. He contended that the ordinance violated substantive due process and equal protection under the United States and Texas Constitutions, and that it unconstitutionally infringed the rights of persons between the ages of 14 and 17 (now 18) to associate with persons outside that age bracket.[3] The trial court upheld the ordinance, finding that it was ra-

---

"(1) a licensee or employee of a dance hall;

"(2) a parent or guardian of a person inside the dance hall; or

"(3) a governmental employee in the performance of his duties."

[3] The Court of Appeals held that respondent had standing to assert the associational rights of the teenage patrons of his establishment. 744 S. W. 2d 165, 168 (1987). That issue has not been raised before us.

FIGURE 4–5(c)   *(continued)*

DALLAS *v.* STANGLIN   23

19   Opinion of the Court

tionally related to the city's legitimate interest in ensuring the safety and welfare of children.

The Texas Court of Appeals upheld the ordinance's time restriction, but it struck down the age restriction. 744 S. W. 2d 165 (1987). The Court of Appeals held that the age restriction violated the First Amendment associational rights of minors. To support a restriction on the fundamental right of "social association," the court said that "the legislative body must show a compelling interest," and the regulation "must be accomplished by the least restrictive means." *Id.,* at 168. The court recognized the city's interest in "protect-[ing] minors from detrimental, corrupting influences," *ibid.,* but held that the "City's stated purposes . . . may be achieved in ways that are less intrusive on minors' freedom to associ-ate," *id.,* at 169. The Court of Appeals stated that "[a] child's right of association may not be abridged simply on the premise that he 'might' associate with those who would per-suade him into bad habits," and that "neither the activity of dancing *per se,* nor association of children aged fourteen through eighteen with persons of other ages in the context of dancing renders such children peculiarly vulnerable to the evils that defendant City seeks to prevent." *Ibid.* We granted certiorari, 488 U. S. 815 (1988), and now reverse.

The dispositive question in this case is the level of judicial "scrutiny" to be applied to the city's ordinance. Unless laws "create suspect classifications or impinge upon constitution-ally protected rights," *San Antonio Independent School Dist. v. Rodriguez,* 411 U. S. 1, 40 (1973), it need only be shown that they bear "some rational relationship to a legitimate state purpose," *id.,* at 44. Respondent does not contend that dance-hall patrons are a "suspect classification," but he does urge that the ordinance in question interferes with asso-ciational rights of such patrons guaranteed by the First Amendment.

While the First Amendment does not in terms protect a "right of association," our cases have recognized that it em-

FIGURE 4–5(c)   *(continued)*

24   OCTOBER TERM, 1988

                  Opinion of the Court   490 U. S.

braces such a right in certain circumstances.   In *Roberts* v.
United States Jaycees, 468 U. S. 609 (1984), we noted two
different sorts of "freedom of association" that are protected
by the United States Constitution:

> "Our decisions have referred to constitutionally pro-
> tected 'freedom of association' in two distinct senses.
> In one line of decisions, the Court has concluded that
> choices to enter into and maintain certain intimate
> human relationships must be secured against undue in-
> trusion by the State because of the role of such rela-
> tionships in safeguarding the individual freedom that is
> central to our constitutional scheme.   In this respect,
> freedom of association receives protection as a funda-
> mental element of personal liberty.   In another set of
> decisions, the Court has recognized a right to associate
> for the purpose of engaging in those activities protected
> by the First Amendment—speech, assembly, petition
> for the redress of grievances, and the exercise of reli-
> gion." *Id.*, at 617–618.

It is clear beyond cavil that dance-hall patrons, who may
number 1,000 on any given night, are not engaged in the sort
of "intimate human relationships" referred to in *Roberts*.
The Texas Court of Appeals, however, thought that such patrons were engaged in a form of expressive activity that was
protected by the First Amendment.   We disagree.

The Dallas ordinance restricts attendance at Class E dance
halls to minors between the ages of 14 and 18 and certain excepted adults.   It thus limits the minors' ability to dance
with adults who may not attend, and it limits the opportunity
of such adults to dance with minors.   These opportunities
might be described as "associational" in common parlance,
but they simply do not involve the sort of expressive association that the First Amendment has been held to protect.
The hundreds of teenagers who congregate each night at this
particular dance hall are not members of any organized association; they are patrons of the same business establishment.

FIGURE 4–5(c)   *(continued)*

Company and are the only systematically compiled published sources of federal case law.

Federal Cases

The earliest reporter to publish federal opinions was *Federal Cases* (cited as *F. Cas.*). *Federal Cases* published the early federal cases from both the appellate and trial levels and has over 20,000 cases cited in alphabetical order. Although this reporter was published from 1894 to 1897, it contains decisions issued only up to 1882. This reporter is not as widely used as the other reporters and has limited value.

Federal Reporter

When first published in 1880, the *Federal Reporter* contained both appellate and trial court decisions. Today, it consists primarily of cases from the United States Circuit Courts of Appeals. It also contains decisions of the Temporary Emergency Court of Appeals.

The *Federal Reporter* has three series, identified and cited as *F., F. 2d* or *F. 3d*. The first series of the *Federal Reporter* covers the years 1880 to 1924 and consists of 300 volumes. The second series began in 1924 and continues to 1993. In 1993, the *Federal Reporter* began publishing its third series. Since the *Federal Reporter* is a West publication, it has headnotes, topic and key numbers, and publisher summaries.

Federal Supplement

As the federal judiciary grew and published decisions became more voluminous, West in 1932 created the *Federal Supplement*, cited as *F. Supp.* There is presently only one *F. Supp.* series, consisting of over 800 numbered volumes.

The *Federal Supplement* contains primarily cases from the United States District Courts. It also reports cases decided by the United States Court of International Trade and the Special Court under the Regional Rail Reorganization Act, as well as rulings of the Judicial Panel on Multi-District Litigation. As a West publication, *Federal Supplement* has all the West research aids.

Federal Rules Decisions

Challenges to procedural matters and evidentiary issues grew at the federal level. As a response to the volume of cases dealing with these issues, another federal reporter was created in 1940, called *Federal Rules Decisions,* cited as *F.R.D.* The *Federal Rules Decisions* publishes only cases dealing with civil and criminal procedural challenges and evidentiary questions. The cases contained in *F.R.D.* are from both the appellate and trial level courts.

Miscellaneous Specialty Reporters

Since the late 1970s, West has initiated publication of several specialized case reporters in its National Reporter System, complete with the standard West reporter research aids (syllabi, headnotes, and key numbers).

The *Military Justice Reporter,* cited as *M.J.,* began publication in 1977. Since that time, it has been the official reporter of decisions from the United States Court of Military Appeals and the various Courts of Military Review for the Army, Navy-Marine, Coast Guard, and Air Force. The *Military Justice Reporter* will be used almost exclusively for judicial research of a military legal issue. Care should be taken when reviewing a military justice issue, as the laws and rules of the military are comparatively unique to our civil law system.

The *Bankruptcy Reporter,* cited as *Bankr.,* was developed in 1979 to cover the increased litigation in the bankruptcy field. Because of the economic reversals in several important segments of the economy over the past fifteen years, the number of bankruptcy filings has soared. This reporter includes decisions from the United States Bankruptcy Courts in addition to federal appellate cases, reprinted from other reporters, that concern bankruptcy matters.

The *United States Claims Court Reporter,* cited as *Cl. Ct.* was begun in 1982 after Congress established the United States Claims Court. This reporter includes the decisions of that court, which is a trial court, as well as relevant appellate decisions, reprinted from other reporters, from the Court of Appeals for the Federal Circuit and the United States Supreme Court.

The *Education Law Reporter,* cited as *Educ. L. Rep.* began in 1982. This reporter contains selected decisions from both state and federal courts dealing with education law.

The *Social Security Reporter,* cited as *Soc. Sec. Rep.,* was first published in 1983 and is subject-specific.

State Reporters

All fifty states have case reporters, with some states having both an official and unofficial reporter. The current trend for many states is to discontinue the publication of the official state reporter and adopt the unofficial West regional reporter as authoritative. The unofficial state reporters are generally published by West. When a state has both an official and unofficial reporter, however, the official reporter should always be cited, as it is the authoritative source.

Regional Reporters

The regional reporters are state reporters that publish decisions from the state courts. There are seven regional reporters, all published by West: *Northeastern, Northwestern, Southeastern, Southwestern, Atlantic, Pacific,* and *Southern.* All are presently in their second series. Texas cases are in the *Southwestern Reporter.* Listed below are the states in each regional reporter.

Atlantic Reporter	First series:	Volume 1–200 from October 1885 to 1938
	Second series:	Volume 1–600(+) from 1938 to present
	States covered:	Maine, Connecticut, New Hampshire, New Jersey, Vermont, Pennsylvania, Rhode Island, Delaware, Maryland, Washington, D.C.
Northeastern Reporter	First series:	Volume 1–200 from July 1885 to 1936
	Second series:	Volume 1–580(+) from 1936 to present
	States covered:	Illinois, Indiana, Massachusetts, New York, Ohio
Northwestern Reporter	First series:	Volume 1–300 from April 1879 to 1942
	Second series:	Volume 1–480(+) from April 1942 to present
	States covered:	Michigan, Iowa, Nebraska, North Dakota, South Dakota, Wisconsin, Minnesota
Pacific Reporter	First series:	Volume 1–300 from December 1883 to 1931
	Second series:	Volume 1–825(+) from 1931 to present
	States covered:	Arizona, Kansas, Oklahoma, California (copyright in 1884), Montana, Oregon, Colorado, Nevada, Utah, Idaho, New Mexico, Washington, Wyoming, Hawaii, Alaska
Southeastern Reporter	First series:	Volume 1–200 from February 1887 to 1939
	Second series:	Volume 1–415(+) from 1939 to present
	States covered:	Virginia, West Virginia, North Carolina, South Carolina, Georgia
Southern Reporter	First series:	Volume 1–200 from February 1887 to 1941
	Second series:	Volume 1–585(+) from 1941 to present
	States covered:	Alabama, Louisiana, Florida, Mississippi
Southwestern Reporter	First series:	Volume 1–300 from December 1886 to 1928
	Second series:	Volume 1–820(+) from February 1928 to present
	States covered:	Arkansas, Kentucky, Missouri, Tennessee, Texas

Each series grows on a daily basis and, consequently, the expansion of the volume of reporters continues.

Some states use the regional reporters as official state reporters, and others do not. Listed below are the states that have the regional reporter as their only reporter.

State	Regional Reporter
Alabama	Southern
Alaska	Pacific
Colorado	Pacific
Delaware	Atlantic
District of Columbia	Atlantic
Florida	Southern
Indiana	Northeastern
Iowa	Northwestern
Kentucky	Southwestern
Louisiana	Southern
Maine	Atlantic
Minnesota	Northwestern
Mississippi	Southern
Missouri	Southwestern
North Dakota	Northwestern
Oklahoma	Pacific
Rhode Island	Atlantic
South Dakota	Northwestern
Tennessee	Southwestern
Texas	Southwestern
Utah	Pacific
Wyoming	Pacific

All the remaining states have both an official reporter and a West regional reporter publishing their cases.

Texas is a special case. Texas has not published an official reporter since 1962. Although its reported decisions appear in *Southwestern 2d,* Texas has not designated *Southwestern 2d* as an official reporter.

Many states publish a state official reporter and have a West unofficial reporter. Whether a regional reporter is adopted by a state is discretionary with each state. Some states such as California and New York have a number of case reporters. For example, recent California Supreme Court decisions can be found in *California Reporter 3d (Cal. 3d),* the official reporter, and in two West reporters, *Pacific Reporter 2d (P.2d)* and *California Reporter 2d (Cal. Rptr. 2d).* Consequently, the two unofficial reporters use a star-paging system similar to the one found in the *Supreme Court Reporter* for page consistency in the unofficial volumes. New York also has a number of case reporters: *New York Supplement 2d (N.Y.S.2d)*, an unofficial reporter, and three official reporters—*New York Reports 2d (N.Y.2d)*, for the New York Court of Appeals, its highest court; *Appellate Division Reports 2d (A.D.2d)* for the appellate division of its Supreme Court, its lowest appellate court; and *Miscellaneous Reports 2d (Misc. 2d)*, which contains a limited selection of trial court cases.

Other states use the West regional reporter for the publication of cases from their appellate courts. Regional reporters contain decisions from the courts of several states. To respond to the demands from lawyers for state-specific reporters, and for reasons of economy and convenience, West has created individual state case reporters as offprints from their regional reporters. They are essentially the regional reporter with only one state contained in the series. Listed below are the states that have state-specific reporters.

Regional Reporter	State	Reporter Name
Pacific	California	*California Reporter*
Northeastern	Illinois	*Illinois Decisions*
Southwestern	Texas	*Texas Cases*
Southeastern	North Carolina	*North Carolina Reporter*
Southern	Louisiana	*Louisiana Cases*
Southern	Florida	*Florida Cases*
Southwestern	Missouri	*Missouri Cases*
Pacific	Colorado	*Colorado Cases*
Northeastern	Indiana	*Indiana Cases*
Northeastern	Ohio	*Ohio Cases*
Northeastern	Massachusetts	*Massachusetts Decisions*
Southeastern	Georgia	*Georgia Cases*
Northwestern	Wisconsin	*Wisconsin Reporter*
Northeastern	New York	*New York Supplement*

Texas Reporters

Throughout the state's history, Texas cases were published in a variety of sources and in a variety of forms. The following text reviews the Texas reporters.

Texas Supreme Court

Prior to 1962, the state of Texas had a number of case reporters. Early Texas Supreme Court cases for the period 1840 to 1844 were decided by the Supreme Court of the Republic of Texas and are reported in the second part of *Dallam's Digest,* beginning at page 357 of the volume. This digest may be seen on library shelves with the title *Dallam's Texas Decisions* or *Dallam's Opinions.* The first part of the volume consists of digests of statutes.

Cases from the year 1845 were historically lost until 1986 when the *University of Texas Law Review* published a special sesquicentennial issue. Included in the issue were the lost cases of the 1845 term of the Texas Supreme Court in an article entitled *The Missing Cases of the Republic* (65 Tex. L. Rev. 372 [1986]).

Beginning in 1846, Texas Supreme Court cases were published in *Texas Reports* (cited as *Tex.*), which was the official reporter for Texas Supreme Court cases until 1962 when the Texas Legislature stopped appropriating funds for the publication of an official reporter, even though Texas still has a statute mandating the publication of an offical reporter. Consequently, the only reporter for Texas Supreme Court cases since 1962 has been *Southwestern 2d* and its state-specific offprint, *Texas Cases* (cited as S.W.2d.), but it is not an official reporter because it has not been designated as such. Texas Supreme Court cases decided between 1886 and 1962 can be found in both *Texas Reports* and the *Southwestern Reporter.*

The advance sheet that publishes the most recent Texas Supreme Court cases is the *Texas Supreme Court Journal.* Texas Supreme Court decisions are also published in advance sheets for West's *Southwestern Reporter,* but these advance sheets are not as current as the *Texas Supreme Court Journal.*

Texas Court of Criminal Appeals

Prior to 1962, the Texas Court of Criminal Appeals cases were published in *Texas Criminal Reports* (cited as *Tex. Crim.*) and the *Southwestern Reporter.* Since 1962, all Court of Criminal Appeals cases have been published in the *Southwestern Reporter.* Careful attention should be paid to the dates of cases in Texas, as they will determine the authoritative nature of the reporters.

Texas Court of Appeals

From 1892 to 1911, decisions of the Texas Courts of Civil Appeals were published in *Texas Civil Appeals Reports* (cited as *Tex. Civ. App.*), the official reporter. After 1911, *Texas Civil Appeals Reports* was eliminated and Texas

Courts of Civil Appeals cases were found solely in the *Southwestern Reporter*, which became its official reporter.

Since 1962, all cases from the Texas appellate courts have been published in *Southwestern Reporter 2d* or the Texas-specific version, *Texas Cases*. These are not, however, official reporters.

Miscellaneous Texas Case Reporters

Between 1876 and 1892, many criminal cases from the early Texas Court of Appeals were printed in the first thirty volumes of *Texas Appeals Reports* (cited as *Tex. App.*). The civil cases published during that time were privately edited and compiled by two judges, White and Willson. The cases are found in a four-volume reporter identified by the judges' names. The first volume is identified as *1 White & W.*, with the subsequent volumes cited as *Willson* only.

A Checklist

When using case reporters, keep the following in mind:

1. Determine the citation of the case.
2. Identify the appropriate reporter and series of the reporter.
3. Find the correct volume of the reporter.
4. Open to the designated page of the citation, which is the beginning of the case.
5. Determine whether the reporter is the official or unofficial source for the jurisdiction you are researching.
   a. If official, the citation and text of the decision is authorative.
   b. If unofficial, determine the official reporter and whether the unofficial volume utilizes star paging. Always cite to the official reporter citation.
6. Pay attention to the cases covered in the reporter.
7. Be sure you are in the correct jurisdiction, especially when working with regional reporters.
8. Always search for cases from a jurisdiction's highest court. If one is not found, use a lower court decision. Know the court system of the jurisdiction you are researching.

§ 4.4 Evaluating Cases: The Case Brief

Once the paralegal finds relevant cases, the tedious task of reading, reviewing, and digesting the cases begins. All paralegals will want to develop a synopsis of each relevant case to present to the attorney or use for themselves as a reminder of the general propositions presented in the case. Your synopsis of the case is called a **case brief**. It evaluates pertinent legal points in the case and, as the words suggest, is brief.

Everyone has their own version of what information should be contained in a brief. Consequently, if the attorney you are working with wants certain information in a case brief, then put in that information. Otherwise, identify the name of the case, state the relevant facts, identify the issue and holding, and evaluate the court's reasoning.

Name of the Case

The case brief should state who is suing whom, for example, *ABC Corporation v. Smith*. The citation should contain the year the case was decided, as this will assist you in quickly locating the case later.

Relevant Facts

The relevant facts of the case should be set forth in the brief. Chronological order is best. It aids in understanding the case and promotes continuity. *Do not* copy the facts verbatim from the case. The details of the actual case may be unnecessary for briefing purposes. Think about what facts are needed to illustrate the points you are trying to convey, and think about whether you or your attorney could read your fact statement in your brief and know exactly what the case is about. A long description of a scenic highway may be irrelevant if your case focuses on a contract issue. Think of yourself as a reporter with a limited amount of print space. You want only the facts, just the facts.

TERMS

case brief† An outline of the published opinion in a case, made by an attorney or a paralegal for the purpose of understanding the case.

Issue and Holding

The *issue* is the question the court is being asked to decide. The *holding* is the decision by the court—essentially it is the answer to the **issue**. Both need to be included in the case brief.

Often the court will state the issue literally in a case. For example, "The issue before us is . . ." That makes your job easier. But when the issue is not easily identified, try to find the holding. The holding usually is easier to find. The court does not hide its holding because that is the heart of the case, it is that for which the case stands. Consequently, the court is usually blatant in its pronouncement of the holding and makes statements such as "We hold that . . .," "Our decision is . . .," or "Our result in this case is . . ." Once you have stated the holding, you can formulate the issue by simply turning the holding into a question with words such as *whether, did,* or *does.* The holding and issue virtually mirror each other.

We will use *City of Dallas v. Stanglin* to illustrate this point. The holding in the case is that the Dallas ordinance does not infringe on any constitutionally protected right of association and that a national relationship exists between the age restriction for class E dance halls and the city's interest in promoting the welfare of teenagers. Now you can simply record the holding as a question to formulate the issue.

Court's Reasoning

The basis of the court's decision is known as the *reasoning* or *rationale.* This section of the brief tells what legal principles the court relied upon to reach its holding, or result. Discuss the general legal points the court addresses, but *do not* start citing the cases the court used in your reasoning section. This could turn your brief into a dissertation. Ignore the temptation to be too detailed. An exception to this rule, however, may be made where a case has overruled or is overruled by the case you are briefing or one particular case is relied upon by the court to support the court's reasoning. For example, if the case you are briefing overrules established law, your first sentence in the reasoning section of your brief should read, "This case overrules *Smith v. Smith* and establishes that . . ."

issue†   A material point or question arising out of the pleadings in a case, which is disputed by the parties and which they wish the court to decide.

A Sample Brief

City of Dallas v. Stanglin

490 U.S. 19, 109 S.Ct. 1591, 104 L.Ed.2d 18 (1989)

Facts: The City of Dallas enacted an ordinance in 1985 that restricted the use of certain dance halls by teenagers between the ages of fourteen and eighteen. Stanglin, the respondent, operates the Twilight Skating Rink in Dallas, Texas, and obtained a class E dance hall license in accordance with the Dallas City Code § 14.-81 (1985). Stanglin sued the City of Dallas to enjoin the enforcement of the statute as it violated substantive due process and equal protection under the United States and Texas constitutions. Stanglin claimed that it unconstitutionally infringed on the rights of persons between fourteen and eighteen to freely associate with persons outside their age bracket. The Texas Court of Appeals upheld the ordinance's time restriction but struck down the age restriction. The case was appealed to the United States Supreme Court.

Issue: Does the Dallas ordinance infringe on any constitutionally protected right of association, and does a rational relationship exist between the age restriction for class E dance halls and the city's interest in promoting the welfare of teenagers?

Holding: The Court held that the Dallas ordinance does not infringe on any constitutionally protected right of association and that a rational relationship exists between the age restriction for class E dance halls and the city's interest in promoting the welfare of teenagers.

Reasoning: The Court focused on the First Amendment right of association. The Dallas city ordinance restricts attendance of minors between the ages of fourteen and eighteen at class E dance halls. The dance hall patrons were not engaged in any form of intimate or expressive association. As such, there was no generalized right of social association that included chance encounters in dance halls. Therefore, the ordinance did not infringe on the First Amendment right of association. Further, the city ordinance did not violate the equal protection clause as it was rationally related to the city's legitimate effort to protect its teenagers from older teenagers and young adults and their corrupting influences. The ordinance promotes the welfare of teenagers. The judgment of the Texas Court of Appeals was reversed.

Summary

4.1 Judicial Opinions

Most judicial opinions are found in reporters, which is a book that contains judicial decisions. There are a number of reporters for appellate decisions. Most trial court decisions are not published. All court opinions are identified by a citation, which is the formal notation that identifies the location of the case.

4.2 Components of a Judicial Opinion

Judicial opinions usually have a caption and docket number that identify the case. Some opinions have a syllabus or case summary. The case also may have headnotes, which identify points of law in the case. All judicial opinions contain a holding, reasoning, and dicta, which are found in the majority opinion. Opinions that offer other or different reasoning are concurring or dissenting opinions that can be found in the case.

4.3 The Reporters

Reporters are either official or unofficial. Whether a reporter is official or unofficial is determined by the jurisdiction publishing the case. Some jurisdiction have both official and unofficial reporters. Others simply rely on West Publishing's regional reporters, which are designated as Atlantic, Pacific, Southern, Northeastern, Southeastern, Southwestern, and Northwestern. The United States Supreme Court has three reporters—*United States Reports, Supreme Court Reporter,* and *Lawyers' Edition.* The federal appellate court decisions are generally found in the *Federal Reporter, Federal Supplement,* and *Federal Rules Decisions.* Texas cases are found in the *Southwestern Reporter* or *Texas Cases,* the Texas-specific version of the *Southwestern Reporter.*

4.4 Evaluating Cases: The Case Brief

After researching the cases, those chosen must be evaluated and briefed. The case brief should identify the name of the case, the citation, and the year the case was decided. It should also state the facts, the issue, the holding, and the court's reasoning. The case brief should be concise and generally should not cite cases.

Review Questions

1. Define a reporter.

2. What are the components of a judicial opinion?

3. What is the difference between a petitioner and respondent and a plaintiff and dependant?

4. Define a court's holding, reasoning, and dicta.

5. Distinguish between a majority opinion and dissenting opinion.

6. Distinguish between an official and unofficial reporter.

7. State the names of all the regional reporters. Which reporter has Texas cases?

8. What is star paging and in which United States Supreme Court reporters can this system be found?

9. Identify the reporters that contain federal cases.

10. What are the general components of a case brief?

Exercises

1. Locate 109 S. Ct. 1591 and answer the following:
    a. What is the name of the case?
    b. Who wrote the majority opinion?
    c. Who was the petitioner?
    d. What was the court of appeals's holding?
    e. Did the United States Supreme Court reverse of affirm the Texas Court of Appeals?
    f. How many headnotes are in the case?
    g. When was the case argued?
    h. What are the parallel cites?

2. Locate 650 F.2d 1065 (1981) and answer the following:
    a. Identify the name of the case.
    b. What federal circuit decided the case?
    c. What did the case involve? What was the case about?
    d. Did the court reverse or affirm the lower court?
    e. From what federal district was the case appealed?

3. Determine who wrote the majority opinion in *Time, Inc. v. Hill*, 87 S.Ct. 534 (1967). Who wrote the dissenting opinion? The concurring opinion?

4. Identify the case names and state of origin for each of the following citations:
    a. 423 S.E.2d 491
    b. 494 N.W.2d 608
    c. 246 So. 2d 648
    d. 62 N.E.2d 772
    e. 575 P.2d 540
    f. 395 A.2d 169
    g. 610 N.E.2d 779
    h. 273 P.2d 585
    i. 521 S.W.2d 461

5. Find the parallel cite for *Hodson v. Minnesota*, 110 S. Ct. 2926 (1990).

6. The only volume your library has is the *Lawyers' Edition*. You want to use a quote in *Burger v. Kemp*, 97 L. Ed. 2d 638 at 651 (1987), which states "we generally presume that the lawyer is fully conscious of the overarching duty of complete loyalty to his or her client." You realize, however, that you must cite to *United States Reports*. Using star paging in the *Lawyers' Edition*, determine where the quote would be located in *United States Reports*.

7. Locate 314 S.W.2d 763 (1958) and determine:

   a. Court of origin
   b. County of origin
   c. Final court of decision

8. Locate 891 S.W.2d 640 (Tex. 1995) and answer the following:

   a. What is the name of the case?
   b. How many headnotes are in the case?
   c. Who wrote the court's opinion?
   d. What is the court of origin?
   e. Who was the plaintiff?

9. (A) Identify the names of the following cases and the years they were decided:

   a. 890 S.W.2d 42
   b. 853 S.W.2d 193
   c. 401 S.W.2d 316
   d. 683 S.W.2d 885
   e. 550 S.W.2d 18
   f. 641 S.W.2d 321
   g. 275 S.W.2d 869
   h. 109 S.W.2d 288
   i. 98 S.W. 233
   j. 596 S.W.2d 561

   (B) Identify the Texas Intermediate Appellate Division (city) where the following cases were decided:

   a. 463 S.W.2d 757
   b. 866 S.W.2d 665
   c. 82 S.W.2d 753
   d. 173 S.W. 262
   e. 628 S.W.2d 101
   f. 866 S.W.2d 243
   g. 197 S.W. 364
   h. 516 S.W.2d 452
   i. 369 S.W.2d 917
   j. 749 S.W.2d 202

10. Brief *Helms v. Gonzalez*, 885 S.W.2d 535 (Tex. App.—Eastland 1994).

CHAPTER 5

STATUTES, CONSTITUTIONS, AND RULES

§ 5.1 Statutes, Constitutions, and Rules: An Introduction

Legal research often should begin with *statutes,* laws enacted by the legislative body of a government. The legislature, whether federal or state, was created by a *constitution*, the fundamental law of a nation or state.

Statutes are a logical starting point for research because of their pivotal role in the legal system. Court decisions often involve statutory analysis, and a judicial decision may be modified or overturned by a legislature through enactment of a statute. (A legislature, however, cannot overturn a Supreme Court decision holding a particular statute unconstitutional.) Moreover, administrative regulations exist by virtue of authority vested in agencies by legislatures through statutes.

Clearly, an understanding of statutory law and the sources to consult in order to conduct statutory research is essential for effective research. That understanding must include the origin of the statute in both the federal and state legislative systems. The two systems have many similarities.

§ 5.2 Researching Federal Statutes

The Federal Legislative Process

All federal statutory research must begin with a basic understanding of the federal legislative system. The researcher should be aware of the process involved in converting an idea for a change in a federal law or the enactment of a new piece of legislature into law. For example, what was the beginning of the concept of drug testing for federal employees? Who introduced the idea and when? Was the original concept altered before the passage of the law? The steps listed below trace the passage of federal legislation and contain the answers to these questions.

Statutory Process—Federal System

1. Preliminary inquiry on bill proposed by legislator, executive branch, committee, or special interest group.

2. Introduction of bill in original text, referred to as the introduced print. With the exception of a revenue bill, which must originate in the House, a bill may originate in either the House or the Senate. A bill in the House begins with the prefix "H.R.," followed by a sequentially assigned number, beginning with the first bill introduced in the House during the two-year Congress. A bill introduced in the Senate

begins with the prefix "S," followed by a sequential number. This number remains with the bill only during the Congress in which it is introduced. A new number is assigned if the bill is introduced in the next Congress even if the bill is identical.

3. Bill referred to committee or committees having jurisdiction over the subject matter of the bill.

4. Hearings on bill. Hearings include testimony from experts or other interested individuals. This testimony is recorded and transcribed, but not always published.

5. Bill reported out of committee. A committee report including committee's version or reported print of bill is produced. For purposes of determining legislative intent, the courts often view committee reports as an insight into the legislature's reasons for enacting a bill. Committee reports normally include the text of the bill as reported out of the committee, including a detailed analysis of each section, anticipated accomplishments and changes to existing laws, full texts of laws to be repealed, and the committee's reason for its recommendations on the bill. Committee reports are assigned identifying numbers and are printed. Each chamber numbers its committee reports sequentially in a single series during the two-year congressional term. Since 1969, the numbers also reflect the number of the Congress during which the report was issued. For example, "House Report No. 97-1254."

6. Consideration by the full chamber. The bill is placed on a calendar, a listing of all bills that various committees have indicated are ready for the full chamber's consideration. The majority of legislation is passed without legislative debate. If floor debate occurs, however, the floor debate is recorded, transcribed, and printed in the *Congressional Record*.

7. Passage or defeat. Final House or Senate version of bill.

8. Other house—same procedure as above.

9. Referred to conference committee if texts passed by each House differ. A conference committee version of the bill may result. The published conference committee report includes text of any compromise amendments and conference committee recommendations for action. This report is another source that offers important information on legislative intent.

10. Passage by second House. The *enrolled* (passed) bill is signed by the speaker of the House or the president of the Senate and then sent to the president. The enrolled bill is not available to the public.

11. If the bill is vetoed, there is a presidential veto message. Congress may override a veto by a two-thirds majority vote in both houses.

12. If approved by the president, slip law is then printed in the *United States Code Congressional and Administrative News* (commonly cited as *U.S.C.C.A.N.*) and in the *United States Code Service (U.S.C.S.)* advance sheets, subsequently bound into *United States Statutes at Large* and annual volumes of *U.S.C.C.A.N.*, and then classified into appropriate titles of the *United States Code*.

Sources for Federal Statutes

Federal Slip Laws

The *slip law* published immediately after the enactment of a statute contains the first authoritative and official text of the new statute. At the end of each congressional session, the slip laws for that session are placed in chronological order in a hardback collection called the *United States Statutes at Large*, the official compilation of the acts and resolutions of each session of Congress published by the United States Printing Office.

The only identification number in the slip laws is the **public law number**, the number that was assigned once the statute completed the legislative process, for example, P.L. 101-433. The first part of this number represents the congressional session that enacted the law, and the second part reflects the order of its chronological enactment.

United States Statutes at Large—Federal Session Laws

Session laws is the name given to the body of laws enacted by a federal or state legislature during one of its sessions. The session laws are first compiled in pamphlet form during the session. At the end of a legislative session, the session laws are arranged in bound volumes in the chronological order in which they were passed.

The official session law publication for all federal law is *United States Statutes at Large* (cited as *Stat.*). **Public laws** are acts that relate to the public as a whole. **Private laws** are acts that are directed at individuals or specific

---

TERMS

public law number The number of a statute in the slip laws that is assigned once the statute has completed the legislative process.

public laws† Laws dealing with the relationships between the people and their government, between agencies and branches of government, and between governments themselves.

private laws† The rules of conduct that govern activities occurring among or between persons, as opposed to the rules of conduct governing the relationship between persons and their government.

matters. Both public and private laws that are enacted in a session of Congress and all concurrent resolutions, presidential proclamations, and reorganization plans are cumulated and published by the United States Government Printing Office two or three years after the end of a legislative session.

If you need to do up-to-date research, this slow publication process makes it necessary for you to rely on commercial publications, such as the *United States Code Congressional & Administrative News* (cited as *U.S.C.C.A.N.*), a legislative history source published by West, or the *C.I.S. Microfiche Library,* prepared by a private publisher, for the texts of recently enacted statutes. The *U.S.C.C.A.N.* is the earliest and most convenient source for the full text of public laws. It is found in most libraries. (See the discussion later in this chapter.)

A correct statute citation includes the title number, code abbreviation, section number, and year.

The *United States Statutes at Large* contains the following important types of information to assist in research:

1. The house or senate bill number
2. The date of enactment
3. The purpose of the act
4. Title or short title of the act
5. Definitions
6. Operative provisions
7. Remedy or enforcement provisions

The large volume of legislation enacted each session requires a streamlined method for locating a particular statute. If you are asked, for example, to research the subject of handling potential drug abuse in the federal workplace, searching every volume of session laws and determining those laws that were amended or repealed would be a formidable task. There is an easier means of conducting session law research by subject or topic order in the *United States Code.* (See the discussion later in this chapter.)

Compilations of Federal Statutes

Overview Case law can be found, depending on the jurisdiction, in both official and unofficial reporters. The same is true for federal statutes. Official compilations of statutes are published either by the government or private parties it authorizes to publish the statutes on its behalf. Unofficial compilations are published by private publishing companies on their own initiative.

There are three sources of the federal code: one official code, *United States Code* (cited as *U.S.C.*), and two unofficial codes, *United States Code Annotated* (cited as *U.S.C.A.*) and *United States Code Service* (cited as *U.S.C.S.*).

Although these three codes contain many similar features, including organization and research aids, one major difference is that *United States Code* reports only the actual text of the code, while others include annotations and research aids to assist with interpretation and analysis. Consequently, the unofficial codes may prove to be more helpful in research. Code compilations provide access to statutory law, by subject, that cannot be achieved through session laws.

Official Compilation of Federal Statutes: *United States Code* (*U.S.C.*)
The *United States Code* (*U.S.C.*) is the official code or collection of public laws categorized by topics and sections. The process of collecting and organizing public statutes by topic, adding amendments, and deleting repealed, superseded, or expired statutes is referred to as **codification**. *United States Code* does not include private laws or temporary provisions, such as a budget allocation, and it excludes laws that have been repealed. It does include amendments to the statutes. A new edition of the *U.S.C.* is published by the United States Government Printing Office approximately every six years. Current changes are incorporated through the issuing of interim cumulative bound supplements. In using the *U.S.C.*, you should keep in mind that it is not highly regarded by legal research specialists as a research tool because of its infrequent supplementation.

Research tools found in the *U.S.C.* include a title outline, an index, a conversion table, and a popular name table.

Title Outline   There are fifty general titles of the code that are listed in the front of each *U.S.C.* volume, as shown in Figure 5–1. The titles are divided into chapters and subchapters.

The title outline may enable the researcher to locate quickly one or more titles that contain statutes that relate to the research topic. Because of the generality of titles, researching only the title outline may not be sufficient. In the illustration of the history of the law that provides for drug testing of federal employees, the title outline reveals only that federal employees are discussed in Title 5. Additional searching is necessary to locate the subtopic of drug testing.

TERMS

codification†   The process of arranging laws in a systematic form covering the entire law of a jurisdiction or a particular area of the law; the process of creating a code.

TITLES OF UNITED STATES CODE

*1. General Provisions.

2. The Congress.

*3. The President.

*4. Flag and Seal, Seat of Government, and the States.

*5. Government Organization and Employees; and Appendix.

†6. [Surety Bonds.]

7. Agriculture.

8. Aliens and Nationality.

*9. Arbitration.

*10. Armed Forces; and Appendix.

*11. Bankruptcy; and Appendix.

12. Banks and Banking.

*13. Census.

*14. Coast Guard.

15. Commerce and Trade.

16. Conservation.

*17. Copyrights.

*18. Crimes and Criminal Procedure; and Appendix.

19. Customs Duties.

20. Education.

21. Food and Drugs.

22. Foreign Relations and Intercourse.

*23. Highways.

24. Hospitals and Asylums.

25. Indians.

26. Internal Revenue Code.

27. Intoxicating Liquors.

*28. Judiciary and Judicial Procedure; and Appendix.

29. Labor.

30. Mineral Lands and Mining.

*31. Money and Finance.

*32. National Guard.

33. Navigation and Navigable Waters.

‡34. [Navy.]

*35. Patents.

36. Patriotic Societies and Observances.

*37. Pay and Allowances of the Uniformed Services.

*38. Veterans' Benefits.

*39. Postal Service.

40. Public Buildings, Property, and Works.

41. Public Contracts.

42. The Public Health and Welfare.

43. Public Lands.

*44. Public Printing and Documents.

45. Railroads.

*46. Shipping; and Appendix.

47. Telegraphs, Telephones, and Radiotelegraphs.

48. Territories and Insular Possessions.

*49. Transportation; and Appendix.

50. War and National Defense; and Appendix.

---

*This title has been enacted as law. However, any Appendix to this title has not been enacted as law.
†This title was enacted as law and has been repealed by the enactment of Title 31.
‡This title has been eliminated by the enactment of Title 10.

Page III

FIGURE 5–1   Titles of *U.S.C.*

Index   The *U.S.C.* General Index is an alphabetical subject matter index of federal statutes that includes code sections, as shown in Figure 5–2. The page in Figure 5–2 includes the topic of "Drug Abuse Prevention, Control and Treatment" and the subtopic of "Testing programs," which then lists "Drug-free Federal workplace. Federal employees, criteria, requirements, etc."

For the index to be helpful, the researcher must first select descriptive words or phrases that can be used to locate pertinent statutes. Once words or phrases descriptive of the facts of the case being researched have been identified (and written down in a list), they can be checked through the General Index. The index will direct the researcher to the specific title(s) and section(s) where the full statutory text can be found. For example, to locate the index entries shown in Figure 5–2, the researcher might have started a search with such words as *drug abuse, drug testing,* and *workplace.*

Remember to review not only the index for the main volumes but also the index in the most recent cumulative annual bound supplement. The latter index will reference all statutes enacted after the publication of the main volume index and before the cutoff date for including revisions in the most recent cumulative supplement.

Popular Name Table   If the popular name of an act is known, it is possible to locate the statute in *U.S.C.* by using the table entitled Acts Cited by Popular Name in the tables volume (1988 edition). This table lists each act's public law number, date of enactment, a *Stat.* citation, and, where applicable, *U.S.C.* title and section numbers. See Figure 5–3 for a sample page containing the entry for the "Federal Employee Substance Abuse Education and Treatment Act of 1986."

For statutes enacted after the publication of the main volume, consult the popular name table in the most recent cumulative supplement.

Conversion Tables   The popular names and tables volume of *U.S.C.* contains a Table of Revised Titles to show where statutes that have been revised or renumbered appear in the *U.S.C.* current edition. See Figure 5–4.

A Table of Internal References, also found in the tables volume (1988 edition), provides a valuable finding aid. This table cross-references what one federal statute has to say about another. In the words of the publisher, this table "lists those sections of the United States Codes that are referred to in other sections of the Code together with citations to the referring sections." This table should be reviewed prior to "finalizing" a research project. Another Code section can affect the application or operation of the section under review.

The *Statutes at Large* Conversion Table reflects the acts of Congress in chronological order and their location in the *U.S.C.* Assume that you know the date of enactment of a statute but do not know where to find the

DRUG ABUSE PREVENTION, CONTROL AND TREATMENT—Continued

Technical assistance to State and local governments, Director of National Institute on Drug Abuse, 42 § 290ee

Temporary restraining order, court may enter to preserve, requirements, 21 § 853

Temporary scheduling of substance in schedule I, authority of Attorney General, 21 § 811

Territories,
   Courts, injunctions, jurisdiction, 21 § 882
   Inclusion in term "State", 21 § 802

Testing programs,
   Criminal investigations in military departments, forensic examinations, procedures, etc., 10 § 912a note
   Drug-free Federal workplace, Federal employees, criteria, requirements, etc., 5 § 7301 note, Ex. Ord. No. 12564
   Implementation, preconditions, availability of results, etc., 5 § 7301 note

Tetrahydrocannabinols, schedule I drug, designation, 21 § 812

Thebacon, schedule I drug, designation, 21 § 812

Third party transfers, property subject to criminal forfeiture, effect, 21 § 853

3,4-Methylenedioxyphenyl-2-propanone, "listed precursor chemical" as meaning, 21 § 802

Time, administrative inspection warrant, execution and return, 21 § 880

Toluene, "listed essential chemical" as meaning, 21 § 802

Tort claims arising in foreign countries in connection with operations of DEA abroad, payment by Attorney General, 21 § 904

Trade secrets, inspection, information acquired, use or revelation prohibited, 21 § 842

Traffic. Drug traffic prevention functions, generally, ante, this heading

Training programs on controlled substance law, local, State and Federal personnel, 21 § 873

Training programs or activities, "drug abuse prevention function" as meaning, 21 § 1103

Transfer,
   Forfeited property to Federal, State, or local agency, Attorney General authorized, 21 § 881
   Funds, for veterans with alcohol or drug abuse dependence, 42 § 300y-1
   Regulated person, listed chemical or tableting or encapsulating machines, requirements, 21 § 830

Transferee of property subject to forfeiture, hearing to determine interests, 21 § 853

Traveling expenses, advisory committee members, 21 § 874

Treasury Department,
   Attorney General to direct advance of funds from, 21 § 886
   Drug transactions, proceeds of illegal drug transactions forwarded by Attorney General to Treasurer, 21 § 881
   Officers, etc., of transfer, investigative, law enforcement, etc., functions relating to illicit traffic to Attorney General, 5 App., Reorg. Plan No. 2 of 1973

Treaties, conventions, protocols or international agreements,
   Convention for Limiting the Manufacture and Regulating the Distribution of Narcotic Drugs, export prohibitions, exceptions, etc., 21 § 953
   Effect on classification of controlled substances in schedules, 21 §§ 811, 812
   Import and export, registration consistent with obligations under, 21 § 958
   International Opium Convention of 1912 for the Suppression of the Abuses of Opium, Morphine, Cocaine and Derivative Drugs, export prohibitions, exceptions, etc., 21 § 953
   Psychotropic substances, ante, this heading
   Registration requirements to be consistent with, 21 § 823
   Single Convention on Narcotic Drugs of 1961, generally, ante, this heading

Treatment,
   Demonstration projects of national significance, etc., 42 § 290aa-14
   "Drug abuse prevention function" as meaning treatment programs, etc., 21 § 1103
   Programs, etc., data collection by Secretary, 42 § 290aa-11
   Utilization of military facilities for programs, etc., 42 § 290ff

Treatment evaluation programs, establishment, purposes, etc., 42 § 300y-2

Treatment grants and contracts, reduction, treatment waiting period, requirements, limitation, etc., 42 § 290aa-12

Trial,
   Burden of proof, 21 § 885
   Injunctions, violation, jury, 21 § 882

Trial or appeal of criminal case involving forfeiture of property, intervention, bar on, 21 § 853

Trimeperidine, schedule I drug, designation, 21 § 812

Trust Territory of Pacific Islands, inclusion in term "State", 21 § 802

Trustees, appointment by court upon entry of order of forfeiture, criminal forfeitures, 21 § 853

2-Butanome, "listed essential chemical" as meaning, 21 § 802

Ultimate user,
   Applicability of registration requirement, 21 § 822
   Defined, 21 §§ 802, 951
   Exemption from import and export registration requirement, 21 § 957

Underserved populations, consideration to applications for programs and projects aimed at, 21 § 1177

Uniform forms for, procedures for submission, etc., applications of State, etc., governments for grants and contracts, 42 § 290ee

Uniform methodology and technology for determining extent and kind of drug abuse and effects, investigation and publication of information, 42 § 290aa-2

United Nations, generally, this index

United States, defined, 21 §§ 802, 951

FIGURE 5–2   *U.S.C. General Index*

ACTS CITED BY POPULAR NAME   Page 958

Federal Deposit Insurance Act—Continued
  Mar. 31, 1980, Pub. L. 96–221, title III,
    §§ 302(b), 308(a), (d), title V, § 521, 94
    Stat. 146, 147
  Dec. 26, 1981, Pub. L. 97–110, title I, §§ 102,
    103, 95 Stat. 1513
  Oct. 15, 1982, Pub. L. 97–320, title I, §§ 111,
    113, 116, 117, 141(a)(1), title II, § 203, title
    IV, §§ 404(c), 410(d), (g), 423, 424(d)(6),
    (10), (e), 425(b), (c), 427(d), 429, 433(a),
    title VII, § 703(a)–(c), 96 Stat. 1469, 1473,
    1476, 1479, 1488, 1492, 1512, 1520,
    1522–1525, 1527, 1538
  Jan. 12, 1983, Pub. L. 97–457, §§ 1, 3, 4, 10,
    96 Stat. 2507, 2508
  May 16, 1983, Pub. L. 98–29, § 1(a), 97 Stat.
    189
  Nov. 30, 1983, Pub. L. 98–181, title VII,
    § 702(a), 97 Stat. 1267
  Oct. 27, 1986, Pub. L. 99–570, title I,
    §§ 1359(a), 1360, 100 Stat. 3207-27,
    3207-29
  Aug. 10, 1987, Pub. L. 100–86, title I,
    §§ 101(g), 102(b), 103, title V, §§ 502(a)–(g),
    (l), 503, 504(b), 505(a), 507, 509(a), (b),
    title VIII, § 801, 101 Stat. 563, 566,
    623-627, 629-635, 656
  Nov. 18, 1988, Pub. L. 100–690, title VI,
    § 6185(d)(1), 102 Stat. 4356

Federal Deposit Insurance Corporation Act
  June 16, 1933, ch. 89, § 8 ("Sec. 12B"), 48
    Stat. 168 (See Title 12, § 1811 et seq.)
  See Federal Deposit Insurance Act

Federal District Court Organization Act of 1978
  Pub. L. 95–408, Oct. 2, 1978, 92 Stat. 883
  Pub. L. 96–4, § 1, Mar. 30, 1979, 93 Stat. 6

Federal District Court Organization Act of 1980
  Pub. L. 96–462, Oct. 15, 1980, 94 Stat. 2053

Federal District Court Organization Act of 1984
  Pub. L. 98–620, title IV, subtitle B,
    §§ 404-411, Nov. 8, 1984, 98 Stat. 3361,
    3362

Federal Drivers Act
  Pub. L. 87–258, Sept. 21, 1961, 75 Stat. 539
    (Title 28, § 2679)
  Pub. L. 89–506, § 5(a), July 18, 1966, 80 Stat.
    307

Federal Drug Law Enforcement Agent Protection Act of 1986
  Pub. L. 99–570, title I, subtitle U, §§ 1991,
    1992, Oct. 27, 1986, 100 Stat. 3207-59
    (Title 21, §§ 801 note, 881)

Federal Election Campaign Act of 1971
  Pub. L. 92–225, Feb. 7, 1972, 86 Stat. 3 (Title
    2, § 431 et seq.; Title 18, §§ 591, 600, 608,
    610, 611; Title 47, §§ 312, 315, 801 et seq.)
  Pub. L. 93–443, title II, title III, Oct. 15,
    1974, 88 Stat. 1272-1289
  Pub. L. 94–283, title I, §§ 101-115 (f), (h), (i),
    May 11, 1976, 90 Stat. 475-496
  Pub. L. 95–127, Oct. 12, 1977, 91 Stat. 1110
  Pub. L. 95–216, title V, § 502(a), Dec. 20,
    1977, 91 Stat. 1565
  Pub. L. 96–187, title I, §§ 101-113, Jan. 8,
    1980, 93 Stat. 1339-1366
  Pub. L. 96–253, May 29, 1980, 94 Stat. 398

  Pub. L. 97–51, § 130(a), Oct. 1, 1981, 95 Stat.
    966
  Pub. L. 98–63, title I, § 908(g), July 30, 1983,
    97 Stat. 338
  Pub. L. 98–620, title IV, § 402(1), Nov. 8,
    1984, 98 Stat. 3357
  Pub. L. 100–352, § 6(a), June 27, 1988, 102
    Stat. 663

Federal Election Campaign Act Amendments of 1974
  Pub. L. 93–443, Oct. 15, 1974, 88 Stat. 1263

Federal Election Campaign Act Amendments of 1976
  Pub. L. 94–283, May 11, 1976, 90 Stat. 475

Federal Election Campaign Act Amendments of 1979
  Pub. L. 96–187, Jan. 8, 1980, 93 Stat. 1339

Federal Emergency Relief Act of 1933
  May 12, 1933, ch. 30, 48 Stat. 55

Federal Employee Substance Abuse Education and Treatment Act of 1986
  Pub. L. 99–570, title VI, Oct. 27, 1986, 100
    Stat. 3207-157

Federal Employees Benefits Improvement Act of 1986
  Pub. L. 99–251, Feb. 27, 1986, 100 Stat. 14

Federal Employees' Compensation Act (1908)
  May 30, 1908, ch. 236, 35 Stat. 556
  Sept. 7, 1916, ch. 458, § 41, 39 Stat. 750

Federal Employees' Compensation Act (1916)
  Sept. 7, 1916, ch. 458, 39 Stat. 742 (See Title
    5, § 8101 et seq.)
  Apr. 11, 1940, ch. 79, 54 Stat. 105
  July 18, 1940, ch. 633, 54 Stat. 762
  Oct. 14, 1949, ch. 691, title I, §§ 101-108,
    title II, §§ 201-209, 63 Stat. 854-865
  Sept. 26, 1950, ch. 1049, § 2(a)(2), 64 Stat.
    1038
  Aug. 1, 1956, ch. 837, title V, § 501(e), 70
    Stat. 883
  June 29, 1957, Pub. L. 85–71, 71 Stat. 242
  Aug. 8, 1958, Pub. L. 85–608, title III, §§ 301,
    302, 72 Stat. 538
  Sept. 13, 1960, Pub. L. 86–767, title I,
    §§ 101-103, 105, title II, §§ 201-210, 74
    Stat. 906
  Aug. 30, 1964, Pub. L. 88–508, 78 Stat. 666
  July 4, 1966, Pub. L. 89–488, §§ 2-12, 14, 80
    Stat. 252-256
  Sept. 6, 1966, Pub. L. 89–554, § 8(a), 80 Stat.
    632, 643

Federal Employees' Compensation Act Amendments of 1949
  Oct. 14, 1949, ch. 691, 63 Stat. 854

Federal Employees' Compensation Act Amendments of 1960
  Pub. L. 86–767, Sept. 13, 1960, 74 Stat. 906
  Pub. L. 87–339, Oct. 3, 1961, 75 Stat. 751

Federal Employees' Compensation Act Amendments of 1966
  Pub. L. 89–488, July 4, 1966, 80 Stat. 252

Federal Employees Flexible and Compressed Work Schedules Act of 1978
  Pub. L. 95–390, Sept. 29, 1978, 92 Stat. 755
    (Title 5, §§ 5550a, 6101 note)
  Pub. L. 97–160, Mar. 26, 1982, 96 Stat. 21

FIGURE 5–3 *U.S.C. Acts Cited by Popular Name*

TABLE I—REVISED TITLES   Page 50

TITLE 31—MONEY AND FINANCE

[This title was enacted into law by Pub. L. 97-258, § 1, Sept. 13, 1982, 96 Stat. 877. This table shows where sections of former Title 31 were incorporated in revised Title 31.]

Title 31 Former Sections	Title 31 New Sections	Title 31 Former Sections	Title 31 New Sections
1	Rep.	52-3(h)	753
2	701, 1101	52-3(i)	754
11(a)	1105	52-3(j), (k)	753
11(b), (c)	1106	52-3(l)	755
11(d)-(f)	1105	52-3(m)	753
11(g)(1st-3d sentences)	1106	52-4(a)	733
11(g)(last sentence)-(1)(1st sentence)	1105	52-4(b)	731
11(i)(last sentence),(j)	1108	52-5	732
11(k)(1)	1105	52-6	735
11(k)(2)	1113	52-7	736
11 note	1105	52a	Rep.
11a	1109	52b, 52c	731
11b	T. 2 § 661	53(a)(1st sentence words before 5th comma)	712
11c	1110	53(a)(1st sentence words after 5th comma, last sentence)	719
11d	1104	53(b)	712
12	Rep.	53(c)-(e)	719
13	1105	53(f)	718
14	1107	54	716
15	1108	55	Rep.
16(1st sentence)	501	56	731
16(2d, 3d sentences)	502	57, 58	Rep.
16(last sentence related to preparation of budgets and appropriations)	1104	59, 60(1st sentence)	712
16(last sentence related to appropriations request)	1108	60(last sentence)	715
16a	502	61	719
16b	Rep.	65(a)-(e)	Rep.
16c	502	65(f)	3511
17(a)(related to employees)	521	65a	3501
17(a)(related to expenses)	522	65b	3521
17(b), (c)	Rep.	66(a)	3511
18, 18a	1111	66(b)(less Treasury Department)	3512
18b	1104	66(b)(related to Treasury Department)	3513
18c	1112	66(c)	3512
19	1105	66a	3512
20	1113	66b	3513
21	1104	66c	3326
22-24	1108	66d	3514
25	1105	67(a)-(c)	3523
26	Rep.	67(d)(1)-(3)	713
27	1103	67(d)(4)	719
28	1114	67(e)(1)-(5), (7)	714
41	702	67(e)(6)(A)	719
42(a)(1st sentence words before comma)	702	67(e)(6)(B)	718
42(a)(1st sentence words after comma, last sentence), (b)	703	67(f)	3524
42a	703	68	9601
43(1st par.)	703	68a	9603
43(2d par. 1st, 2d, 4th, last sentences)	772	68b	9604
43(2d par. 3d sentence)	779	68c, 68d	9602
43(3d par.)	772	71(related to accounts)	3526
43(last par.)	775	71(related to claims)	3702
43a	703	71a	Rep.
43b(a)-(c)	773	72, 73	Rep.
43b(d), (e)	774	74(1st, 2d paras. last par. words after 4th comma)	3526
43b(f)	776	74(last par. words before 4th comma)	3529
43b(g)	771	75	3521
43b(h)	778	76(1st, last sentences)	3324
43b(i), (j)(less last 13 words before colon)	775	76(2d, 3d sentences)	3323
43b(j)(last 13 words before colon)	776	77	3323
43b(k)	775	78	3522
43b(l), (m)	776	79	Rep.
43b(n), (o)	774	80-80c	3522
43b(p)	771	81	3522
43b(q)	773	82	3521
43b(r)	779	82a	3325
43c	777	82a-1, 82a-2	3557
44(1st sentence)	711, 731, 3301, 3323, 3324, 3521, 3522, 3526, 3529, 3531, 3541, 3702, (See § 2(b) of Pub. L. 97-258)	82b	3325
		82b-1	3521
		82c	3528
		82d(words before semicolon)	3541
		82d(words after semicolon)	3529
		82e(related to 31:82b)	3325
		82e(related to 31:82c)	3528
		82e(related to 31:82d)	3529
44(2d, last sentences)	3526	82f(related to disbursing officers)	3325
45	Rep.	82f(related to certifying officers)	3528
46	704	82g(related to disbursing officers)	3322
46a to 48	Rep.	82g(related to certifying officers)	3528
49	3511		
49a	5120		
50, 51	Rep.		
51-1	702	82h	T. 7 § 1032a
51a, 52(a), (b)	731	82i	3526
52(c), (d)	711	82j to 82p	Rep.
52-1(related to appointment, pay and assignment)	731	83, 84	Rep.
52-1(related to direct)	711	85	T. 48 § 1469-1
52-2	732	86	3702
52-3(a)-(d)	751	87, 88	Rep.
52-3(e)-(g)	752		

FIGURE 5–4 *U.S.C.* Table of Revised Titles

statute in the *U.S.C.* Using the Conversion Table, you can locate the pertinent *U.S.C.* title and section numbers.

One inherent danger in embracing a statute as it appears in *U.S.C.* is that any provisions that may have been declared unconstitutional by the Supreme Court remain in the code until they are either repealed or amended by Congress in response to the Court's actions. Research, therefore, should include a search of the annotated versions of the code, as discussed below, and *Shepard's* (see Chapter 11) to determine subsequent judicial treatment of a section of the code, such as "Has a case disagreed with or held unconstitutional that particular section of the code?" In addition, always check the pocket parts of these resources.

Unofficial Federal Codes   Two publications of the annotated code, the *United States Code Annotated (U.S.C.A.)* and *United States Code Service (U.S.C.S.)*, are referred to as "unofficial publications" because they are published by private companies in a situation where the United States government publishes the *U.S.C.* as the "official" version of federal statutes. The unofficial publications are divided into the same fifty general titles as the *U.S.C.* and contain the same wording as the *U.S.C.*

For timely and comprehensive research, the unofficial publications are more practical research tools. They are published faster and contain excellent references to other sources in addition to the text of the statute.

The unofficial publications of the federal statutes differ from the official *United States Code* in two areas. First, the unofficial codes are annotated, that is, they include summaries of cases that have either applied or interpreted sections of the code and references to other sources that interpret or analyze particular sections of the code. These annotations are the essence of *U.S.C.A.* and *U.S.C.S.* and are what make these sources such valuable research tools. Second, *U.S.C.A.* and *U.S.C.S.* both offer internal cross-references to other sections of the code, a potentially valuable feature in statutory research that is not provided in *U.S.C.*

United States Code Annotated (U.S.C.A.)   West Publishing Company published the first annotated edition of federal statutes, *United States Code Annotated*, or *U.S.C.A.* In addition to the text of the statutes, *U.S.C.A.* also includes the complete text of the United States Constitution, the Federal Rules of Civil and Criminal Procedure, the Federal Rules of Evidence, the Internal Revenue Code, the Federal Rules of Appellate Procedure, and cross-references to administrative rules and regulations.

Annotations.   Refer to Figure 5–5, which shows the annotation aids contained in *U.S.C.A.* for § 7301 of Title 5, relating to conduct of federal employees. These aids, which are representative of such aids throughout *U.S.C.A.*, include:

1. source of the section, including public law number, date of the enactment of the law, and citation to the *United States Statutes at Large*;

2. historical notes explaining references in the statute, amendments and effective dates of amendments, and cross-references to other *U.S.C.A.* sections;

3. cross-reference to *U.S.C.C.A.N.* legislative history;

4. "Notes of Decisions" annotation, which lists and describes cases dealing with a particular statutory section;

5. West digest topic and key number reference;

6. *Code of Federal Regulations* reference; and

7. *Corpus Juris Secundum* citations.

Supplements. The frequent updating of *U.S.C.A.* makes it more current than the *U.S.C.* Noncumulative quarterly pamphlets issued three times a year are replaced by annual cumulative pocket parts in the back of each *U.S.C.A.* volume. To do thorough research in *U.S.C.A.*, it is necessary to check the bound volume, pocket parts to the bound volume, any supplementary pamphlets to the bound volume, and the most recent softbound set of *U.S.C.A. Statutory Supplement* pamphlets.

Tables and Indexes. The *U.S.C.A.* offers three research aids that are similar to ones found in *U.S.C.*, namely, a detailed index, a conversion table for *United States Statutes at Large*, and a popular name table at the end of the last volume of the General Index. See Figure 5–6 for an example of the *U.S.C.A.* popular name table. The index, in particular, is an excellent finding aid. It is far more detailed than the *U.S.C.* index and is one of the key advantages to using *U.S.C.A.*

In addition to the soft-cover multivolume general index, each *U.S.C.A.* title has an individual index. This index is usually located in the last volume of a multivolume title.

The *U.S.C.A.* tables volume includes separate tables that enable the user to reference different statutory citations into their current *U.S.C.* or *U.S.C.A.* citations, including tables of revised titles (titles of the code that have revised and renumbered since adoption of the code in 1926); revised statutes 1878 (showing where sections of these statutes will be found in *U.S.C.A.*); *United States Statutes at Large* (showing where the acts of Congress will be found in *U.S.C.A.*—by far the largest table); and proclamations, executive orders, and reorganization plans.

The beginning of each volume of statute texts includes a popular name table. In addition, the General Index lists the popular name acts for all titles.

The tables and indexes in the *U.S.C.A.* supplement volumes and pamphlets are the same as those contained in *U.S.C.*

5 § 7301 EMPLOYEES Part 3

Historical and Revision Notes

Derivation: **United States Code** **Revised Statutes and Statutes at Large**

5 U.S.C. 631 (last 16 words) R.S. § 1753 (last 16 words).

Explanatory Notes

The words "employees in the executive branch" are substituted for "persons who may receive appointments in the civil service".

Standard changes are made to conform with the definitions applicable and the style of this title as outlined in the preface to the report.

Delegation of Functions. For the delegation to the Office of Personnel Management of authority of the President to establish regulations for the conduct of persons in the civil service under former section 631 of this title, see section 601 of Ex.Ord.No.11222, May 8, 1965, 30 F.R. 6469, set out as a note under section 201 of Title 18, Crimes and Criminal Procedure.

For the delegation to the Office of Personnel Management of various functions vested in the President, see Ex.Ord.No. 11228, June 14, 1965, 30 F.R. 7739, set out as a note under section 301 of Title 3, The President.

Emergency Preparedness Functions. For assignment of certain emergency preparedness functions to the Office of Personnel Management, see Parts 1, 28, and 30 of Ex.Ord.No.11490, Oct. 28, 1969, 34 F. R. 17567, set out as a note under section 2292 of Title 50, Appendix, War and National Defense.

Code of Ethics for Government Service. House Concurrent Resolution No. 175, July 11, 1958, 72 Stat. B12 provided that:

"Resolved by the House of Representatives (the Senate concurring), That it is the sense of the Congress that the following Code of Ethics should be adhered to by all Government employees, including officeholders:

"CODE OF ETHICS FOR GOVERNMENT SERVICE

"Any person in Government service should:

"1. Put loyalty to the highest moral principles and to country above loyalty to persons, party, or Government Department.

"2. Uphold the Constitution, laws, and legal regulations of the United States and of all governments therein and never be a party to their evasion.

"3. Give a full day's labor for a full day's pay; giving to the performance of his duties his earnest effort and best thought.

"4. Seek to find and employ more efficient and economical ways of getting tasks accomplished.

"5. Never discriminate unfairly by the dispensing of special favors or privileges to anyone, whether for remuneration or not; and never accept, for himself or his family, favors or benefits under circumstances which might be construed by reasonable persons as influencing the performance of his governmental duties.

"6. Make no private promises of any kind binding upon the duties of office, since a Government employee has no private word which can be binding on public duty.

"7. Engage in no business with the Government, either directly or indirectly, which is inconsistent with the conscientious performance of his governmental duties.

"8. Never use any information coming to him confidentially in the performance of governmental duties as a means for making private profit.

"9. Expose corruption wherever discovered.

"10. Uphold these principles, ever conscious that public office is a public trust."

EXECUTIVE ORDER NO. 9845

Ex.Ord.No.9845, Apr. 28, 1947, 12 F.R. 2799, formerly set out as a note under this section, which permitted Bureau of Reclamation employees to accept appointments as constables or deputy sheriffs under state or territorial laws, was revoked by Ex.Ord.No.11408, Apr. 25, 1968, 33 F.R. 6459.

FIGURE 5–5 An example of annotation aids from *U.S.C.A.*

Ch. 73   EMPLOYMENT LIMITATIONS   5 § 7311

EXECUTIVE ORDER NO. 11491

Ex.Ord.No.11491, Oct. 29, 1969, 34 F.R. 17605, as amended, is now set out as a note under section 7101 of this title.

Library References

United States ⬤41.   C.J.S. United States § 41.

Code of Federal Regulations

Determinations, etc., of suitability, see 5 CFR 731.201 et seq.
Employment of relatives, see 5 CFR 310.101 et seq.
Federal labor relations organization, programs, etc., see 5 CFR chap. XIV.
Nondisciplinary separations, etc., see 5 CFR 715.201 et seq.
Political activities, see 5 CFR 733.101 et seq.

Notes of Decisions

Power of federal government 1
State regulation or control 2

---

1. Power of federal government

The federal government has power to control objectionable official conduct by its employees and officers. State of Ohio v. U. S. Civil Service Commission, D.C. Ohio 1946, 65 F.Supp. 776.

2. State regulation or control

Congress must clearly manifest an intention to regulate for itself activities of its employees, which are apart from their governmental duties, before the police power of the state is powerless. Railway Mail Ass'n v. Corsi, N.Y.1945, 65 S.Ct. 1483, 326 U.S. 88, 89 L.Ed. 2072.

FIGURE 5–5   *(continued)*

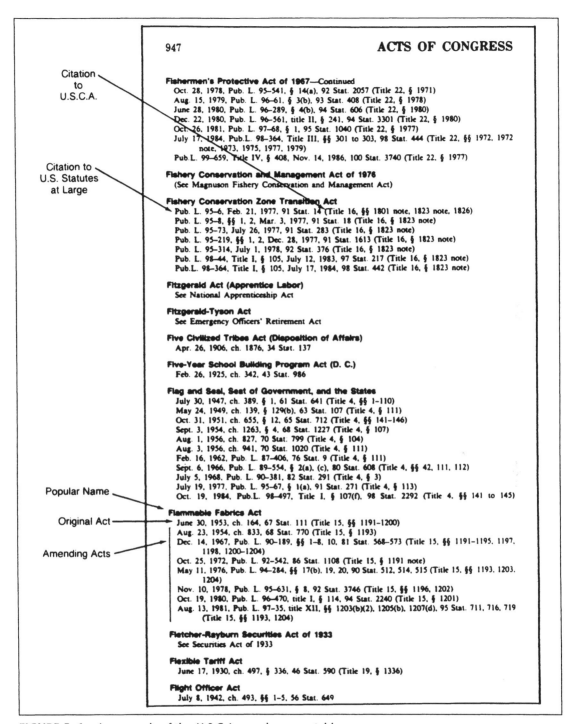

947   **ACTS OF CONGRESS**

Fishermen's Protective Act of 1967—Continued
  Oct. 28, 1978, Pub. L. 95–541, § 14(a), 92 Stat. 2057 (Title 22, § 1971)
  Aug. 15, 1979, Pub. L. 96–61, § 3(b), 93 Stat. 408 (Title 22, § 1978)
  June 28, 1980, Pub. L. 96–289, § 4(b), 94 Stat. 606 (Title 22, § 1980)
  Dec. 22, 1980, Pub. L. 96–561, title II, § 241, 94 Stat. 3301 (Title 22, § 1980)
  Oct. 26, 1981, Pub. L. 97–68, § 1, 95 Stat. 1040 (Title 22, § 1977)
  July 17, 1984, Pub.L. 98–364, Title III, §§ 301 to 303, 98 Stat. 444 (Title 22, §§ 1972, 1972
      note, 1973, 1975, 1977, 1979)
  Pub.L. 99–659, Title IV, § 408, Nov. 14, 1986, 100 Stat. 3740 (Title 22, § 1977)

Fishery Conservation and Management Act of 1976
  (See Magnuson Fishery Conservation and Management Act)

Fishery Conservation Zone Transition Act
  Pub. L. 95–6, Feb. 21, 1977, 91 Stat. 14 (Title 16, §§ 1801 note, 1823 note, 1826)
  Pub. L. 95–8, §§ 1, 2, Mar. 3, 1977, 91 Stat. 18 (Title 16, § 1823 note)
  Pub. L. 95–73, July 26, 1977, 91 Stat. 283 (Title 16, § 1823 note)
  Pub. L. 95–219, §§ 1, 2, Dec. 28, 1977, 91 Stat. 1613 (Title 16, § 1823 note)
  Pub. L. 95–314, July 1, 1978, 92 Stat. 376 (Title 16, § 1823 note)
  Pub. L. 98–44, Title I, § 105, July 12, 1983, 97 Stat. 217 (Title 16, § 1823 note)
  Pub.L. 98–364, Title I, § 105, July 17, 1984, 98 Stat. 442 (Title 16, § 1823 note)

Fitzgerald Act (Apprentice Labor)
  See National Apprenticeship Act

Fitzgerald-Tyson Act
  See Emergency Officers' Retirement Act

Five Civilized Tribes Act (Disposition of Affairs)
  Apr. 26, 1906, ch. 1876, 34 Stat. 137

Five-Year School Building Program Act (D. C.)
  Feb. 26, 1925, ch. 342, 43 Stat. 986

Flag and Seal, Seat of Government, and the States
  July 30, 1947, ch. 389, § 1, 61 Stat. 641 (Title 4, §§ 1–110)
  May 24, 1949, ch. 139, § 129(b), 63 Stat. 107 (Title 4, § 111)
  Oct. 31, 1951, ch. 655, § 12, 65 Stat. 712 (Title 4, §§ 141–146)
  Sept. 3, 1954, ch. 1263, § 4, 68 Stat. 1227 (Title 4, § 107)
  Aug. 1, 1956, ch. 827, 70 Stat. 799 (Title 4, § 104)
  Aug. 3, 1956, ch. 941, 70 Stat. 1020 (Title 4, § 111)
  Feb. 16, 1962, Pub. L. 87–406, 76 Stat. 9 (Title 4, § 111)
  Sept. 6, 1966, Pub. L. 89–554, § 2(a), (c), 80 Stat. 608 (Title 4, §§ 42, 111, 112)
  July 5, 1968, Pub. L. 90–381, 82 Stat. 291 (Title 4, § 3)
  July 19, 1977, Pub. L. 95–67, § 1(a), 91 Stat. 271 (Title 4, § 113)
  Oct. 19, 1984, Pub.L. 98–497, Title I, § 107(f), 98 Stat. 2292 (Title 4, §§ 141 to 145)

Flammable Fabrics Act
  June 30, 1953, ch. 164, 67 Stat. 111 (Title 15, §§ 1191–1200)
  Aug. 23, 1954, ch. 833, 68 Stat. 770 (Title 15, § 1193)
  Dec. 14, 1967, Pub. L. 90–189, §§ 1–8, 10, 81 Stat. 568–573 (Title 15, §§ 1191–1195, 1197,
      1198, 1200–1204)
  Oct. 25, 1972, Pub. L. 92–542, 86 Stat. 1108 (Title 15, § 1191 note)
  May 11, 1976, Pub. L. 94–284, §§ 17(b), 19, 20, 90 Stat. 512, 514, 515 (Title 15, §§ 1193, 1203,
      1204)
  Nov. 10, 1978, Pub. L. 95–631, § 8, 92 Stat. 3746 (Title 15, §§ 1196, 1202)
  Oct. 19, 1980, Pub. L. 96–470, title I, § 114, 94 Stat. 2240 (Title 15, § 1201)
  Aug. 13, 1981, Pub. L. 97–35, title XII, §§ 1203(b)(2), 1205(b), 1207(d), 95 Stat. 711, 716, 719
      (Title 15, §§ 1193, 1204)

Fletcher-Rayburn Securities Act of 1933
  See Securities Act of 1933

Flexible Tariff Act
  June 17, 1930, ch. 497, § 336, 46 Stat. 590 (Title 19, § 1336)

Flight Officer Act
  July 8, 1942, ch. 493, §§ 1–5, 56 Stat. 649

Citation
to
U.S.C.A.

Citation to
U.S. Statutes
at Large

Popular Name

Original Act

Amending Acts

FIGURE 5–6   An example of the *U.S.C.A.* popular name table

United States Code Service (U.S.C.S.)   A second unofficial, commercial edition of the entire federal code is the *United States Code Service,* which is published by Lawyers Cooperative Publishing Company (LCP) and referred to as *U.S.C.S.* This edition also retains the title and section numbers of the *U.S.C.* and incorporates research aids similar to those found in *U.S.C.A.,* including tables and index.

Annotations.   Compared to *U.S.C.A.,* the *U.S.C.S.* normally contains fewer annotations but typically provides longer abstracts of relevant cases. The *U.S.C.S.* contains numerous cross-references to selected law review articles. It also annotates both administrative agency decisions and court opinions that have discussed a particular section.

One difference between the *U.S.C.A.* and the *U.S.C.S.* annotations is in the organization and indexing of annotations. For example, *U.S.C.A.* uses alphabetical topic indexes, while *U.S.C.S.* uses quite detailed topic outlines.

A major strength of the *U.S.C.S.* is the section entitled Research Guide, which includes non-West research sources such as *A.L.R., Am. Jur.,* and law reviews.

Supplements.   Replacement volumes and pocket parts update *U.S.C.S.* in addition to softcover *U.S.C.S.* volumes called *Cumulative Later Case and Statutory Service (C.L.C.S.S.),* published three times each year, that contain statutory amendments and annotations of cases arising after the publication of the last pocket supplement. The *C.L.C.S.S.* volumes are organized by title and section numbers and include a comprehensive index.

The *U.S.C.S. Advance Service* compiles, in monthly pamphlets, the text of newly enacted public laws, presidential proclamations, and executive orders. This service does not contain cases or annotations. However, it does include a list of amendments after the publication of the last *C.L.C.S.S.* The noncumulative pamphlet features a supplemental *United States Statutes at Large* table and a Table of Code Sections Added, Amended, Repealed or Otherwise Affected, in addition to a cumulative index.

Another feature is the public law section, a monthly compilation of slip laws. This feature, shown in Figure 5–7, illustrates the monthly compilation of slip laws in the *U.S.C.S.*

Tables and Indexes.   At the end of each title is an individual index. In addition, the *U.S.C.S.* includes tables of revised titles, revised statutes 1878, *United States Statutes at Large,* executive orders, proclamations, reorganization plans, and acts by popular names. The use of these tables is similar to the use of the tables found in *U.S.C.* and *U.S.C.A.,* discussed in earlier sections of this chapter.

Selection Criteria—*U.S.C.A.* and *U.S.C.S.*   The unique requirements of a research assignment control which unofficial publication should be used. For example, if there is a need to correlate the statutory research with other West key number system publications or West's encyclopedia *Corpus*

```
                        STATUTES AT LARGE


                   Stat.      USCS
    Pub. L.  Section  Page  Title  Section      Effect


                    1990 March 6 (cont'd)


    101-250   2(1)          20    3244(a)      Amd.
    (cont'd)  2(2)          20    3244(a)(1)-(4) Amd.
              3             20    3244(b)(1)   Amd.
              4       97    20    3271(d)      Amd.


                        1990 March 13


    101-251          98           Spec.        Unclass.
    101-252          99           Spec.        Unclass.


                        1990 March 14


    101-253          100          Spec.        Unclass.


                        1990 March 15


    101-254   1(a)    101   20     351 nt.     New
              1(b)                Spec.        Unclass.
              2(1)          20    351a(2)      Amd.
              2(2)          20    351a(17), (18) Added
              3(a)          20    351b(a)      Amd.
              3(b)    102   20    351b(b)      Amd.
              4(a)          20    351c(c)      Amd.
              4(b)          20    351d(g)(2)   Amd.
              5(1)    103   20    351d(b)(3)   Amd.
              5(2)          20    351d(b)(5)
                                 [(b)(4)]      Redes.
              5(3)          20    351d(b)(4)   Added
              6(1)          20    351d(d)(1)   Amd.
```

FIGURE 5–7   Public law section from the *U.S.C.S. Advance Service*

Juris Secundum (C.J.S.), the choice should be *U.S.C.A.* If the goal is to locate either *American Law Reports (A.L.R.)* annotations or law review articles that are not included in the West reporting system, *U.S.C.S.* is the preferable choice. If the most up-to-date research is needed, *U.S.C.S.* offers an additional advantage with its monthly updates.

Statutory Research Aids

The official and unofficial codes offer excellent research potential. As is true with case research, however, other nonofficial research aids are also available. These research tools are often simpler to use than the lengthy, complicated code volumes. Some of the statutory research aids that should be consulted in legislative research include the following publications.

United States Code Congressional & Administrative News (U.S.C.C.A.N.)

As an update to *U.S.C.A.*, West publishes the *United States Code Congressional & Administrative News* (commonly cited as *U.S.C.C.A.N.*) during each session of Congress.

The *U.S.C.C.A.N.* contains a reprint of the *United States Statutes at Large* version of statutes and legislative histories. Valuable legislative historical information contained in this reprint includes:

1. the number of the final House or Senate bill enacted,
2. the number of the prior version of the bill that did not become law,
3. the committee assigned to the bill,
4. committee report numbers,
5. dates of floor debates,
6. dates of passage of the bill in the House and Senate,
7. volume of the *Congressional Record* containing the floor debate and passage in the House and Senate, and
8. references to any presidential message.

This monthly "advance sheet" pamphlet contains the full text of bills that became public law during that time period, executive orders, proclamations, legislative histories, and congressional and administrative highlights. At the end of each congressional session, this publication is reissued in bound volumes.

Both the monthly and annual volumes contain a Table of Legislative Histories listing all public laws passed during the year, with citations to each law's committee reports and relevant *Congressional Record* citations.

One of the most important features of *U.S.C.C.A.N.* is its inclusion of the full texts of House and Senate reports, conference reports, and any statements the president may have made at the time the law was signed. This is the most readily available source of these materials.

United States Law Week (U.S.L.W.) The Bureau of National Affairs (BNA) publishes weekly this complete text of what the publisher considers to be significant public laws enacted during the previous week and summaries of recent court decisions.

Congressional Information Service, Inc. (CIS) Congressional Information Service, Inc. (CIS) offers a monthly pamphlet that simplifies the task of compiling legislative histories for recently enacted statutes. In its *Annual Legislative Histories of U.S. Public Laws* volume, each public law is listed and briefly abstracted and is accompanied by citations to the bill number, committee reports, hearings, and the *Congressional Record*. Monthly pamphlets are then cumulated at the end of the year into two bound volumes. Volume 1 contains summaries of bills as introduced, testimony provided at committee hearings, committee reports, and information regarding dates of debates (which are contained in the *Congressional Record*). Volume 2 is a comprehensive index pamphlet published monthly, then cumulated quarterly and annually. Ultimately the annual volumes are cumulated into multiyear volumes. These index volumes enabled a researcher to locate a public law by its name or title, subject matter, or bill number. The index also contains information about witnesses who testified at committee hearings and the names of committee chairpersons.

In addition, CIS publishes an extremely valuable guide entitled *C.I.S. Index and Abstracts,* which provides full indexing of every document issued by Congress, not just legislative history materials. The companion *C.I.S. Microfiche Library,* available in most academic law libraries, gives ready access to the full text of every congressional document.

Congressional Record The *Congressional Record,* published by the United States Government Printing Office, is an excellent source of legislative history. It is the official record of activity on the floor of the House and Senate. As such, it contains nearly verbatim transcripts of both floor debates and speeches. It also publishes the texts of presidential messages to Congress, votes on proposed amendments, conference committee reports, and selected bills.

The *Congressional Record* is easy to use because of the separate hardcover index entitled *Congressional Record Index* that is published at the end of each congressional session. This index includes two excellent status tables entitled History of Bills Enacted into Public Law and History of Bills and Resolutions that list, by bill and resolution numbers, each bill and resolution passed by either the House or Senate and a summary of the legislative history of that bill or resolution, as well as citations to, but not a full record of, committee hearings.

The *Congressional Record* is published in a daily paperback edition whenever at least one chamber of Congress is in session. A cumulative hardbound volume is published at the end of each congressional session.

CCH *Congressional Index* The *Congressional Index*, a weekly pamphlet published by Commerce Clearing House (CCH), quickly makes available basic information about congressional activity while Congress is in session. There is a cumulative volume published at the end of each Congress. This publication contains a list of publish laws passed by bill number, the date the bill was introduced, a history of the bill, the sponsor of the bill, and a very detailed subject index. This publication also contains membership rosters for Senate and House committees and subcommittees, presidential vetoes, and voting records for each bill.

Other helpful features of the *Congressional Index* include a summary of all bills introduced, a membership list for House and Senate committees and subcommittees, and records of votes. This publication, however, does not contain references to the *Congressional Record*.

Analyzing Federal Statutes

Statutory analysis differs from case law analysis. An analysis of a case is based on an event that has occurred (a decision has been rendered by a court of appropriate jurisdiction), but a statute is enacted by a legislature to cover an event that will (or will possibly) occur in the future. Statutes are generally broadly drafted. Cases are more limited and generally impact narrower issues.

Some statutes replace, clarify, or enlarge particular areas of common law. Other statutes establish a new area of law, based on the impact of such factors as social changes, technology, geography, employment, and economics.

If there is a difference in a statute and a common law precedent, the statute generally is considered to be a higher and more persuasive authority. The meaning of a statute must be challenged in a legal setting before a statute will be interpreted by the judicial branch. The court's interpretation is based on a determination of the intent of the legislature when it enacted the statute and whether the legislature acted within its constitutional authority in the enactment. Determining what a body of several hundred individuals, or even a congressional committee of ten members, intended ten years ago when it initially drafted a piece of legislation is difficult.

To analyze a federal statute, complete the steps outlined in the following text in connection with the preparation of a legislative history.

Researching Federal Legislative Histories

A **legislative history** encompasses all the documents that contain the information the legislature considered, and the debates in which it engaged, prior to its decision to approve or reject a particular bill. Statutes often are subject to varying interpretations after the fact. They may not be crystal clear "on their face." Legislative histories can become crucial when courts are called upon in a case subsequent to the passage of a statute (or the refusal to pass a proposed statute) to discern what the legislature intended to accomplish by passing (or not passing) the statute. If the application of a statute to a particular type of issue is in dispute, for example, a court would normally look for external aids beyond the text of the statute to determine the intent of the legislative body when it passed the bill.

The court's authority is limited to determining what the legislative intent was and, if a constitutional challenge has been raised, whether the legislature acted within its constitutional authority when it enacted the legislation. It is not within the court's authority to rewrite a statute.

A legislative history should include both the statute as originally enacted and its amendment. Remember that an amendment signals the need for a change in the original statute. That change might be necessary because of a flaw in the construction of the bill, changes in public policy, or problems that occurred as a result of the enactment of the statute.

Practical Tips for Tracing Federal Legislative History   If you are asked to produce a legislative history, the first thing you must do is clarify exactly what the attorney is asking you to do. Lawyers often use the term *legislative history* in two senses. If they say "get me the legislative history of a particular act," they usually want you to obtain and organize the documents—bills, hearings, reports, debates—produced by Congress in considering the legislation. If, on the other hand, they ask for the legislative history of a particular phrase or section of the act, they want you to locate the particular passages within the documentation that refer to that phrase or section.

The process of analyzing a statute must begin with its actual wording. Each word should be given its most literal meaning. Often the introductory paragraphs of a statute contain a statement of purpose or other information helpful in determining the meaning of the statute. Defini-

---

TERMS

legislative history†   Recorded events that provide a basis for determining the legislative intent underlying a statute enacted by a legislature.

tions set forth within a statute also can be extremely valuable aids to statutory analysis. In addition, you should carefully read the remedy or penalty provisions found in the body of the statute.

Evidence of intent for legislation may be found in the bill as it was initially introduced in the legislature, amendments to the bill, congressional debate, and reports from legislative committees to which the bill was assigned.

The following steps should be used when you are asked to secure or prepare a legislative history:

1. Determine if the legislative history of the statute has already been compiled. The only practical approach is to ask a *law* librarian whether such a history is available. Possible sources of existing legislative histories include:

   a. *U.S.C.C.A.N.* or CCH's monthly pamphlets;

   b. CCH's *Public Laws—Legislative Histories on Microfiche,* available beginning with the 96th Congress. This service contains necessary elements of a legislative history, with the exception of hearing transcripts;

   c. LEGI-SLATE, an on-line service that permits subscribers to trace legislation from beginning to end. For information about becoming a subscriber, contact LEGI-SLATE, 777 North Capitol Street, Washington, D.C., 20002, (202) 898-2300 or (800) 877-6999;

   d. *Sources of Compiled Legislative Histories,* compiled by Nancy Johnson and published by the American Association of Law Librarians; and

   e. Congressional Information Service (CIS) which began publishing a separate volume of legislative histories in 1984.

2. Locate congressional committee reports and hearings transcripts through the *C.I.S. Microfiche Library,* which should be available in an academic law library. If you do not have access to this collection, identify the congressional committees that considered the legislation and contact them to obtain the documents you need. Committee reports are published in bound volumes entitled the *Serial Sets.* The *U.S.C.C.A.N.* also includes some committee reports.

3. Review the historical data at the end of the statute in the official and unofficial codes.

4. Check the notes of decisions after the statute in *U.S.C.A.* and *U.S.C.S.* to locate cases interpreting the statute. Opinions in those cases may contain detailed legislative histories, albeit from the perspectives of the judges writing the opinions.

5. Use the *American Law Review (ALR)* to locate annotations that have interpreted the statute.

6. Search for any looseleaf publications, treatises, or law reviews citing the statute. Some major treatises, for example, Matthew Bender's multivolume sets *Weinstein's Evidence* and *Moore's Federal Practice*, are built around the organization of federal statutes and rules dealing with specific topics, for example, the Matthew Bender books deal with evidence and civil procedure, respectively. These publications contain both valuable analyses and helpful legislative history materials.

7. Review the Table of Statutes and Rules Cited in *Am. Jur. 2d* to determine if the statute has been discussed.

8. Consult unofficial research texts, including *U.S.C.C.A.N.*, CCH's *Congressional Index,* the *Texas House Journal* and the *Texas Senate Journal*, and CIS publications.

9. Shepardize the official source of the statute in all citator volumes and supplements from the date the statute was enacted into law.

10. Update research by checking supplements to the particular statutory code, including annual pocket parts and pamphlets.

11. If you encounter problems while preparing a legislative history, contact your Congress representative or senator's office for assistance. Congressional assistants can often provide you with copies of the bill or committee report.

12. For information on the status of legislation and availability of Senate legislative documents, call the Senate Document Room at the number listed below between 9:00 A.M. and 5:30 P.M., Monday through Friday. A written request is required to obtain a single copy of Senate bills, public laws, and conference reports. Only six items may be included on one request, and only one request per individual per day will be filled.

    Senate Document Room B-04
    Hart Office Building
    Washington, D.C. 20510
    (202) 224-7860

13. To obtain information relating to House legislative documents, call the House Document Room at the number listed below between 9:00 A.M. and 6:00 P.M., Monday through Friday. Telephone and fax orders are accepted by the House Document Room (but not the Senate Document Room). You may request two copies of no more than twelve items. However, only one request per individual per day will be filled.

    House Document Room, B-18
    House Annex No. 2
    Washington, D.C. 20515
    (202) 225-3456
    Fax: (202) 226-4362

14. A copy of congressional hearings may be obtained, for a charge, by telephone, fax, or mail request from 8:00 A.M. to 4:00 P.M., Monday through Friday, at the address listed below. Checks, money orders, and VISA and MasterCards are accepted.

    Superintendent of Documents
    GPO Congressional Sales Office
    Washington, D.C. 20402-9315
    (202) 512-2470
    Fax: (202) 512-2250

15. If you do not know the bill number, call the Congressional Legislative Office at (202) 225-1772. When you call, have information available to assist in locating the bill, including the date the bill was introduced, the sponsor of the bill, or the subject matter of the bill.

§ 5.3   Researching State Statutes

The State Legislative Process

Federal and state statute organization and publication processes are similar. With a few exceptions, the legislative process entailed in passing state laws mirrors that involved in the passage of federal laws. The majority of the states, including Texas, have a dual house (bicameral) legislative system similar to the United States Congress.

As with federal statutes, research of state statutes, to be done thoroughly, requires knowledge of the legislative process. In Texas, the process is that which is described below.

Statutory Process—Texas

1. A bill is introduced in either house and assigned a number to indicate the house and sequence of its introduction. The introduced bill is stamped with a filed date. A "blue back," which is a blue legal-sized sheet stapled to the back of the filed version, contains a short history of the bill throughout the legislative process.

2. The bill is assigned to a committee having jurisdiction over the subject matter of the bill.

3. The committee reports the bill out and issues a committee "report." This report is merely another version of the bill, not a report in the sense of a discussion or analysis. The *House Committee Report* includes a section-by-section analysis of the bill and valuable background information. Another attachment is a Fiscal Note, which reflects the fiscal implications and projected costs of the bill's enactment. A

House Committee Report Form is also attached to the bill to indicate the committee's vote. The Senate Committee Report includes all changes made in that House's committee. However, the Senate Committee Report does not include a bill analysis. The Senate version of the bill is the only version that is single-spaced.

4. When a bill is reported from committee, it goes to the floor for a second reading and any subsequent floor amendments, and then for a third reading during which it may also receive floor amendments.

5. When the bill has been read for a third time, it is printed in engrossed (final) form and sent to the other house for the same process listed above. If the bill is amended in the second house, it must be returned to the original house for approval. In the event the originating house does not approve the changes, the bill is then assigned to a conference committee that produces a Conference Committee Report. A bill that does not have to go to conference committee is voted on for a third time and becomes enrolled if passed.

6. A bill bearing the stamp "enrolled" is sent to the governor for signature. The signed copy of the bill is available only in the Texas Secretary of State's office.

Texas Statutory Research

Texas statutes are compiled in *Vernon's Texas Statutes and Codes Annotated*. *Vernon's* is often referred to as the "Black Statutes," since the volumes in the set have black covers. Do not assume that the entire text of all bills that are passed will appear in *Vernon's*. Local and special interest bills such as those establishing special districts for water, hospital, soil conservation, utility, and road maintenance, and those setting hunting laws for a particular area of the state, are not included.

Vernon's is a starting point for compiling a legislative history. Each article or section of the code contains a complete record of the original legislation and subsequent amendments. An examination of all session laws listed at the end of the statute may reveal how the law evolved and whether a particular section or language was added or appeared in the original law.

Annotations at the end of the statutes include:

■ **Historical references:** cites to original legislation and subsequent amendments

■ **Cross references:** cities to related or qualifying articles in the state code

■ **Law review commentaries:** cites to articles in law journals that have interpreted the statute

■ **Library references:** refers to West digests and *Corpus Juris Secundum*

History of Texas Statutes

Texas session laws have been published regularly since the days when Texas was a republic. The early session laws appeared in *Gammel's Laws,* published between 1822 and 1897, which has become the most important nineteenth century source of Texas legislation.

In 1854, the legislature authorized a revision and recodification of the laws, with the first releases appearing in 1856. *George Paschal's Digest,* which had first appeared in 1806 and had served until 1856 as an unofficial code, then became the authoritative source for Texas laws.

A second unofficial compilation of early statutes was *Sayles' Early Laws of Texas.* The major value of *Sayles,* however, was in researching land titles.

The Codes of 1856, or the "Old Code," consisting of the Penal Code and the Code of Criminal Procedure, were the first codes authorized and adopted by the legislature. The Old Code, referred to in *Vernon's* by the abbreviation "O.C.," was the only official compilation of Texas's laws for a number of years.

In 1879, the first complete and official revision of the statutes was adopted, based on the final edition of *Paschal's Digest.* Subsequent revisions were issued in 1895, 1911, and 1925 by Sayles, who first published annotated statutes in 1888 and followed up with supplementary volumes. The name of the volumes was changed in 1914 to *Vernon's Sayles* because of a copyright buyout. The 1925 revision, *Vernon's Texas Statutes and Codes Annotated,* is generally referred to as the "Black Statutes."

Vernon published an unannotated centennial edition in 1936 and 1948. Supplements to the 1948 edition published through 1974 were referred to as the "Red Statutes" because of their red bindings. These statutes were inconvenient to use because of their size and lack of indexing. West Publishing Company began the publication of *Vernon's* in 1969. The Secretary of State subsequently certified *Vernon's* as the official statutes.

Session Laws

The session laws, consisting of all bills, concurrent resolutions, and joint resolutions that pass into law, are published in *General and Special Laws of Texas* (generally referred to as "the session laws") following each legislative session.

Throughout the legislative session and immediately following the session, recent session laws are published in paperback by West in *Vernon's Texas Session Law Service.* Only the final version of the bill, authenticated by the Secretary of State's office, appears in the session laws. Underlining in the session law represents new language in a preexisting statute. A "cross-through" in a statute indicates language that has been removed from the statute.

The contents of the session law include:

1. chapter, which is used for citing the bill;
2. bill number;
3. caption and text of the bill;
4. *Vernon's* statute number to which the bill was assigned;
5. date of the bill's passage;
6. vote total;
7. date of governor's signature; and
8. effective date of the bill.

A typical house bill passed by the legislature is shown in Figure 5–8. The bill includes the votes it received in both houses, the date the act was signed into law by the governor, and its effective date.

Sample contents pages from *Vernon's Texas Session Law Service* are shown in Figure 5–9.

The compilation of early session laws, entitled *Laws of Texas, 1822–1897,* is generally referred to by the name of the compiler, Gammel. This set originally consisted of ten volumes dating back to the time of the Mexican Republic.

To facilitate research in the early session laws, Cadwell Walton Raines published an index in 1906, entitled *Analytical Index to the Laws of Texas 1823–1905,* with material arranged by subject and referencing the volume and page number in the *Gammel* volumes.

Codification of State Laws

All laws passed by the state legislature during regular and special sessions are arranged in the session law compilations in the chronological order in which they were enacted. If you attempt to locate a law on a specific subject in the session laws, for example, a law on jury trials, the law may be elusive. However, all state laws are organized by title or subject in *Vernon's,* as is true of the arrangement of federal statutes in the *United States Code.* Only nineteen of an eventual twenty-seven titles or subjects have been codified to date (through the 1995 Texas legislative session).

Texas state laws compiled in annotated form by West Publishing are known as *Vernon's Texas Statutes and Codes Annotated.* The annotated statutes and codes furnish references to valuable research tools, such as legislative reports and law reviews. To determine whether there have been changes to a particular article or section, all supplements must be checked. Annotated codes, like *U.S.C.A.* or *U.S.C.S.,* contain references to cases or other sources that have interpreted or referred to a particular statute,

Ch. 980, § 3.02   74th LEGISLATURE—REGULAR SESSION

and the Texas Workers' Compensation Commission shall enter into an interagency contract under Chapter 771 to pay the costs incurred by the office in implementing this subsection.

ARTICLE 4. MISCELLANEOUS PROVISIONS

SECTION 4.01. The changes in law made by this Act to Chapter 2003, Government Code, and Sections 407.046, 411.049(b), 413.031(d), and 415.034, Labor Code, apply only to a hearing that begins on or after January 1, 1996. A hearing held before or pending on January 1, 1996, is governed by the law in effect immediately before September 1, 1995, and that law is continued in effect for that purpose.

SECTION 4.02. This Act takes effect September 1, 1995.

SECTION 4.03. The importance of this legislation and the crowded condition of the calendars in both houses create an emergency and an imperative public necessity that the constitutional rule requiring bills to be read on three several days in each house be suspended, and this rule is hereby suspended.

Passed by the House on March 9, 1995, by a non-record vote; the House concurred in Senate amendments on May 26, 1995, by a non-record vote; passed by the Senate, with amendments, on May 3, 1995, by a viva-voce vote.

Approved June 16, 1995.

Effective September 1, 1995.

CHAPTER 981

H.B. No. 1125

AN ACT

relating to the forced sale of a co-owner's interest in certain real property.

Be it enacted by the Legislature of the State of Texas:

SECTION 1. Title 4, Property Code, is amended by adding Chapter 29 to read as follows:

*CHAPTER 29. FORCED SALE OF OWNER'S INTEREST IN CERTAIN
REAL PROPERTY AS REIMBURSEMENT FOR PROPERTY
TAXES PAID BY CO-OWNER ON OWNER'S BEHALF*

Sec. 29.001. APPLICATION OF CHAPTER. This chapter applies only to real property that is:

(1) received by a person as a result of the death of another person:

(A) by inheritance:

(B) under a will;

(C) by a joint tenancy with a right of survivorship: or

(D) by any other survivorship agreement in which the interest of the decedent passes to a surviving beneficiary other than an agreement between spouses for community property with a right of survivorship: and

(2) not exempt from forced sale under the constitution or law of this state.

Sec. 29.002. PETITION FOR FORCED SALE. (a) A person who owns an undivided interest in real property to which this chapter applies may file in the district court in a county in which the property is located a petition for a court order to require another owner of an undivided interest in that property to sell the other owner's interest in the property to the person if:

(1) the person has paid the other owner's share of ad valorem taxes imposed on the property for any three years in a five-year period; and

FIGURE 5–8   A typical house bill

74th LEGISLATURE—REGULAR SESSION Ch. 982, § 1

(2) the other owner has not reimbursed the person for more than half of the total amount paid by the person for the taxes on the owner's behalf.

(b) The petition must contain:

(1) a description of the property;

(2) the name of each owner of the property;

(3) the interest held by each owner of the property;

(4) the total amount paid by the petitioner for the defendant's share of ad valorem taxes imposed on the property; and

(5) if applicable, the amount paid by the defendant to the petitioner to reimburse the petitioner for paying the defendant's share of ad valorem taxes imposed on the property.

Sec. 29.003. HEARING ON PETITION FOR FORCED SALE. At a hearing on a petition filed under Section 29.002, the petitioner must prove by clear and convincing evidence that:

(1) the petitioner has paid the defendant's share of ad valorem taxes imposed on the property that is the subject of the petition for any three years in a five-year period;

(2) before the date on which the petition was filed the petitioner made a demand that the defendant reimburse the petitioner for the amount of the defendant's share of ad valorem taxes imposed on the property paid by the petitioner; and

(3) the defendant has not reimbursed the petitioner more than half of the amount of money the petitioner paid on the defendant's behalf for the defendant's share of ad valorem taxes imposed on the property.

Sec. 29.004. COURT-ORDERED SALE. On completion of the hearing on a petition filed under Section 29.002, if the court is satisfied that the petitioner has made the requisite proof under Section 29.003, the court shall enter an order that divests the defendant's interest in the real property that is the subject of the petition and that orders the petitioner to pay to the defendant an amount computed by subtracting the outstanding amount of money the defendant owes to the petitioner for payment of the defendant's share of ad valorem taxes imposed on the property from the fair market value of the defendant's interest in the property as determined by an independent appraiser appointed by the court. The court's order may also direct the defendant to execute and deliver to the petitioner a deed that conveys to the petitioner the defendant's interest in the property.

SECTION 2. The importance of this legislation and the crowded condition of the calendars in both houses create an emergency and an imperative public necessity that the constitutional rule requiring bills to be read on three several days in each house be suspended, and this rule is hereby suspended, and that this Act take effect and be in force from and after its passage, and it is so enacted.

Passed by the House on May 12, 1995, by a non-record vote; passed by the Senate on May 27, 1995: Yeas 31, Nays 0.

Approved June 16, 1995.

Effective August 28, 1995, 90 days after date of adjournment.

CHAPTER 982

H.B. No. 1765

AN ACT

relating to the regulation of the fitting and dispensing of hearing instruments.

Be it enacted by the Legislature of the State of Texas:

SECTION 1. Section 1, Chapter 366, Acts of the 61st Legislature, Regular Session, 1969 (Article 4566–1.01, Vernon's Texas Civil Statutes), is amended by amending Subdivisions (3) and (13) and adding Subdivisions (14) and (15) to read as follows:

FIGURE 5–8 *(continued)*

TABLE OF CONTENTS

―――――

1990 Fourth, Fifth and Sixth Called Sessions

1990 Fourth Called Session

1990 Fifth Called Session

FIGURE 5–9   Sample contents from *Vernon's Texas Session Law Service*

TABLE OF CONTENTS

1990 Sixth Called Session

FIGURE 5–9   *(continued)*

legislative history of the statute, and other research sources. *Vernon's* contains a subject matter index and topic outline, in addition to conversion tables similar to those found in *U.S.C.* See Figure 5–10 for an example from the Table of Civil Statutes, Codes and Acts, Amended, New or Repealed.

State Legislative Histories

Researching state legislative histories is complicated by the absence of published committee reports, debates, and hearing transcripts. The *Texas Senate Journal* and *Texas House Journal* each contain *summary* reports of proceedings and final debates. Another source of information for state legislative history is the note section of the annotated code. References to legal encyclopedias and law review articles and detailed tables that cross-reference session law and statutes are also included.

Guidelines for Preparing Texas Legislative Histories

Materials for researching state legislation are not assembled in one place or one source. The process through which a bill becomes law in the Texas legislature is outlined earlier in this chapter. Research sources for legislative histories are outlined in the following text.

Research Sources for Texas Legislative Histories

1. A bill file is maintained on a bill from its initial introduction and contains all pertinent changes and documents that have an impact on the bill. This file is an excellent research tool. Original bill files for the 1st to the 62nd Legislatures, 1846–1971, are located in the Texas State Archives in the Lorenzo de Zavala State Archives & Library Building in Austin, Texas. The files for 1973 to the present are in the Legislative Reference Library, Room 207B, State Capitol Building, Austin, Texas.

2. The original bill files from the 63rd through the current legislature have been microfilmed and may be obtained from the Dallas Public Library, Houston Public Library, and the Legislative Reference Library.

3. If the governor vetoes a bill during the legislative session, the veto message will be printed in the *House* or *Senate Journal*. However, if the veto follows the legislature's adjournment, the message may be found in either the original bill file or the Legislative Reference Library. Any official message of the governor when the bill becomes law without signature is also filed in the Legislative Reference Library.

4. Any attorney general opinions requested by legislative committees may be obtained only through the Attorney General's Opinion Committee. (Note: All Texas Attorney General opinions are available in

TABLE 2—CUMULATIVE

CIVIL STATUTES, CODES AND ACTS
AMENDED, NEW, OR REPEALED

74th LEGISLATURE, REGULAR SESSION, 1995

CIVIL STATUTES

Art.	Effect	Acts 1995 Regular Session Ch.	Sec.
46c–1 to 46c–3	Repealed	165	24(a)
46c–6, subd. 1	Repealed	165	24
46c–6, subd. 2	Repealed	165	24
46c–6, subd. 3(b)	Amended	165	20
46c–6, subd. 3(e)	Amended	165	20
46c–6, subd. 3(f)	Repealed	165	24
46c–6, subd. 10(d)	Amended	636	1
46c–6, subds. 4 to 10	Repealed	165	24
46c–8 to 46d–15	Repealed	165	24(a)
46d–16A to 46d–22	Repealed	165	24(a)
46f–1	Repealed	165	24(a)
46f–2	Repealed	165	24(a)
46f–4 to 46h	Repealed	165	24(a)
46i–1 to 46i–9	Repealed	165	24(a)
179d, sec. 41	Amended	76	14.57
179g, sec. 1.02(2)	Repealed	76	6.55
179g, sec. 1.02(9)	Repealed	76	6.55
179g, sec. 1.02(10)	Repealed	76	6.55
179g, sec. 2.01(*l*)	Repealed	76	6.55
179g, sec. 2.02	Repealed	76	6.55
179g, sec. 2.021	Repealed	76	6.55
179g, sec. 2.03(a)	Repealed	76	6.55
179g, secs. 2.04(a) to (f)	Repealed	76	6.55
179g, sec. 2.04(h)	Repealed	76	6.55
179g, sec. 2.04(k)	Repealed	76	6.55
179g, sec. 2.05(a)	Repealed	76	6.55
179g, sec. 2.06(a)	Repealed	76	6.55
179g, sec. 2.06(c)	Repealed	76	6.55
179g, secs. 2.07 to 2.11	Repealed	76	6.55
179g, sec. 2.111	Repealed	76	6.55
179g, secs. 2.12(a) to (f)	Repealed	76	6.55
179g, sec. 2.13	Repealed	76	6.55
179g, sec. 2.14	Repealed	76	6.55

T2–1

FIGURE 5–10 Sample from the Table of Civil Statutes, Codes and Acts, Amended, New, Repealed

academic law libraries and other large libraries in Texas.) Recent Attorney General Opinions are generally available on WESTLAW and LEXIS.

5. Both the *Senate* and *House Journals* contain indexes in the final volume for each session. *Both* journals should be searched for a particular subject, since each journal contains only bills introduced in that house. Indexes available include subject matter, author, or bill number.

6. The Legislature Council, a state agency that assists the House and Senate with bill drafting and research and computer services, produces several outstanding research tools. The council publishes a Summary of Enactments after each legislative session that includes the author and sponsor of the bill, the effective date, and a synopsis of the bill's effect on present law. The current edition of this summary may be purchased from "House Bill Distribution," Texas Legislative Council, P.O. Box 12128, Austin, Texas 78711. Earlier editions are located at the Legislative Reference Library or State Depository Libraries. This council also publishes a Veto Proclamations at the end of every session that lists the reasons for the governor's veto.

7. The Legislative Information System (LIS) Bill History is a computer printout on each bill. Computer records are on-line during the legislative session, then they are printed and taken off-line. Public computer terminals are available in the capitol in the Legislative Reference Library for free computer searches on bills from the current legislative session. Bound volumes of these printouts, Bill History, list all bills by bill number, and contain the complete bill history. The page numbers from the computer listing of bills will not match the bound volume. For correct page numbers for a bill history, consult the appendix in the back of both the *House* and *Senate Journals*. Additional indexes available from LIS include a Subject Index to Bills, which provides only a general subject category, Bills by Committee, Bills by Author, and Bills Passed by Author, Subject, which lists only those bills that passed both houses.

8. In addition to written transcripts, audio tapes from the 63rd Legislative session (1973) to the present are available for House and Senate floor proceedings and committee hearings. The House tapes are available from the Committee Coordinator's office on the first floor of the Reagan Building in Austin, Texas. Senate tapes may be purchased from the Senate Staff Services, Room G-27, Capitol Building, Austin, Texas.

9. During each legislative session, a legislative "hotline" is maintained to provide information on newly enacted legislation. That number is available through the Legislative Reference Library, (512) 463-1252.

During the even-numbered years when the legislature is not in session, contact the Legislative Reference Library for assistance in compiling legislative histories.

§ 5.4 Researching Constitutions

The federal government and each state has its own constitution. Amendments to the original constitution make research more difficult. Both the present version of the federal or state constitution and any prior versions, along with amendments, should be researched in compiling a thorough history of a constitutional provision.

Federal Constitution

The United States Constitution is the "Supreme law of the land." This document organizes the government into different departments with designated responsibilities, prescribes the extent and manner of the exercise of the government's sovereign powers, and enumerates the fundamental rights of the people.

History of the Federal Constitution

The Constitution of the United States was drafted at the Constitutional Convention in Philadelphia in 1787 and ratified by all the states between 1787 and 1790. The first ten amendments to the Constitution, referred to as the Bill of Rights, were proposed in 1789 and ratified in 1791. Two hundred years later, the United States Constitution contains only twenty-six amendments.

There was no official record of the Constitutional Convention. One important reference for the history and intent of the Constitution, however, is *The Federalist* papers, essays of James Madison, John Jay, and Alexander Hamilton in favor of the convention's adoption of the Constitution.

Researching the Federal Constitution

The logical starting point for constitutional research is the Constitution itself. The text of the federal Constitution and amendments is found in the official and unofficial compilations of federal statutes, *U.S.C.*, *U.S.C.A.*, and *U.S.C.S.*

One benefit to using an annotated code in constitutional research is the wealth of research aids, including brief abstracts of cases, that have considered a particular section of the Constitution. In addition, *U.S.C.A.* contains cross-references to other West publications. The *U.S.C.S.* includes cross-references to *A.L.R.* and other LCP publications, as well as law reviews.

Library of Congress Edition

The Congressional Research Library publishes a smaller, less cumbersome annotated text of the Constitution. This one-volume publication, *The Constitution of the USA, Analysis and Interpretation,* includes the actual text of the Constitution, historical background of the Constitution, and legal decisions on pertinent sections of the Constitution.

Digests

Volume 17 of the *United States Supreme Court Reports Digest, Lawyers' Edition* published by LCP contains the text of the Constitution. West also publishes the entire text in its *United States Supreme Court Digest.* In addition, other federal and state digests discussed in Chapter 7 contain abstracts of cases in which constitutional issues have arisen.

Legal Encyclopedias, Treatises, and Legal Periodicals

Constitutional research should include legal encyclopedias, treatises, and legal periodicals. In addition to their own discussions, legal encyclopedias often contain citations to cases that focus on constitutional issues. Treatises and legal periodicals offer extensive treatment of particular constitutional issues by legal scholars. See Chapters 8 and 12 for detailed discussions of these secondary sources.

State Constitution

The Texas Constitution is the supreme authority for the operation of the Texas government. It parallels the organization of the federal Constitution, although it is much longer. The Texas Constitution was adopted February 15, 1876. The seventeen articles of the Texas Constitution, through amendments of 1984, are as follows:

I. Bill of Rights	X. Railroads
II. The Powers of Government	XI. Municipal Corporations
III. Legislative Department	XII. Private Corporations
IV. Executive Department	XIII. Spanish and Mexican Land Titles
V. Judicial Department	XIV. Public Lands and Land Office
VI. Suffrage	XV. Impeachment
VII. Education	XVI. General Provisions
VIII. Taxation and Revenue	XVII. Mode of Amending the
IX. Counties	Constitution of This State

Vernon's Constitution of the State of Texas Annotated contains brief summaries of cases in which courts have interpreted the Texas Constitution.

Researching the Texas Constitution

The procedure for conducting state constitutional research mirrors that for federal constitutional research, both in procedure and in types and locations of documents.

Text of the Constitution

Researching a section of the Texas Constitution requires familiarity with the organization and contents of the base document. The index furnishes a quick overview of both the organization and contents.

Historical Records

In order to determine the intent of those who drafted the Texas Constitution, it may be necessary to review the historical documents surrounding the first Constitutional Convention that are available from the Legislative Reference Library in Austin, Texas, or State Depository Libraries.

Legal Encyclopedias, Treatises, and Legal Publications

Texas Jurisprudence III, the state legal encyclopedia, includes information on cases that have interpreted sections of the Texas Constitution and all relevant citations. Treatises such as Dorsaneo's *Texas Civil Litigation* and other legal publications often include scholarly treatments of the Texas Constitution or state constitutional law topics.

Other State Constitutions

Assume that the section of the Texas Constitution you are researching has not been interpreted by the courts in Texas. What is the next step in your research process? Other states may have similar constitutional provisions that have been judicially interpreted. Printed sources and computer research databases such as WESTLAW and LEXIS, discussed in Chapter 13, should be searched for interpretations of similar provisions in other states.

§ 5.5   Researching Rules of Court

An unprecedented growth in litigation within the past few years has reinforced the need for a tighter regulation of the litigation process by the courts. The substance of these regulations ranges from administrative (color and size of paper to be used for court documents) to procedural (length of time for various litigation actions) to court dress and demeanor (requirement for a coat and tie in the courtroom).

Federal Rules

Chapter 1 discussed the power of the United States Supreme Court to enact rules for all federal courts. This chapter has introduced you to *U.S.C.A.* and *U.S.C.S.* Both publications contain the rules of civil and criminal procedure for federal courts. In *U.S.C.A.*, the civil rules follow Title 28 and the Federal Rules of Criminal Procedure follow Title 18. The *U.S.C.S.* publishes these two sets of procedural rules in separate volumes.

West publishes *Federal Rules Decisions*, which contains only cases that have interpreted either federal statutes or rules. Figure 5–11 is the table of statutes and rules from volume 160 of *Federal Rules Decisions*. Lawyers Cooperative Publishing Company also publishes *Federal Rules Service*.

Rules for the lower federal courts have been issued by the United States Supreme Court and are found in *U.S.C.A.* and *U.S.C.S.* In addition, the lower federal courts have the authority to enact their own rules. Many of the lower court rules are administrative in nature, but the majority are substantive.

Locating a rule on a particular subject in a specific federal court can be difficult and time-consuming. Refer to the *Federal Rules Service*, which publishes all rules alphabetically by state.

West publishes an annual "Texas Rules of Court—Federal." This volume contains the following rules:

STATUTES AND RULES

For full-text of statutes and rules see WESTLAW.

STATUTES

UNITED STATES CODE CONGRESSIONAL AND ADMINISTRATIVE NEWS

1990. p. 267—160 F.R.D. 142
1990. p. 6802—160 F.R.D. 532
1990. p. 6875—160 F.R.D. 532
1982. p. 4434—160 F.R.D. 75
1982. p. 4446—160 F.R.D. 75

UNITED STATES CODE ANNOTATED

15 U.S.C.A.—Commerce and Trade

Sec.
78j(b)—160 F.R.D. 561
78j(b)—160 F.R.D. 631

18 U.S.C.A.—Crimes and Criminal Procedure

Sec.
2510 et seq.—160 F.R.D. 691
3626—160 F.R.D. 114

20 U.S.C.A.—Education

Sec.
1681–1683—160 F.R.D. 474

28 U.S.C.A.—Judiciary and Judicial Procedure

Sec.
473(a)(2)(B)—160 F.R.D. 30
1332(a)(1)—160 F.R.D. 532
1367(c)—160 F.R.D. 660
1821(b)—160 F.R.D. 166
1920(2)—160 F.R.D. 166
2255—160 F.R.D. 436

29 U.S.C.A.—Labor

Sec.
201 et seq.—160 F.R.D. 540
216(b)—160 F.R.D. 146
401 et seq.—160 F.R.D. 691
626(b)—160 F.R.D. 22
706(8)(D)—160 F.R.D. 142
1001 et seq.—160 F.R.D. 70
1001 et seq.—160 F.R.D. 527

35 U.S.C.A.—Patents

Sec.
271—160 F.R.D. 134
271(g)—160 F.R.D. 1

42 U.S.C.A.—The Public Health and Welfare

Sec.
1983—160 F.R.D. 8
1983—160 F.R.D. 61
1983—160 F.R.D. 565
2000e et seq.—160 F.R.D. 22
2000e–3—160 F.R.D. 8
9607(a)(3)—160 F.R.D. 655
9622(a)—160 F.R.D. 123
12102(2)—160 F.R.D. 142

Constitution

Amend.
1—160 F.R.D. 478
5—160 F.R.D. 478

UNITED STATES

United States District Court Rules

D.Kan., Rule 206—160 F.R.D. 616
D.Kan., Rule 206—160 F.R.D. 620
D.Kan., Civil Rule 206(f)—160 F.R.D. 605
D.Mass., Rule 116.1—160 F.R.D. 6
D.Neb., Rule 15.1—160 F.R.D. 118
D.N.J., Rule 40, subd. A—160 F.R.D. 37
E.D.Va., Rule 20(A)—160 F.R.D. 78
N.D.Ill., General Rule 5, subd. A—160 F.R.D. 100
S.D.N.Y., Civil Rule 3(d)—160 F.R.D. 452
S.D.N.Y., Civil Rule 3(g)—160 F.R.D. 452
W.D.Wash., Rule 2(e)(1)—160 F.R.D. 134

AMERICAN BAR ASSOCIATION

Rules of Professional Conduct

Rule
1.1—160 F.R.D. 51
1.9—160 F.R.D. 134
1.9 comment—160 F.R.D. 134
1.10—160 F.R.D. 134
3.2—160 F.R.D. 524

KANSAS

Kansas Statutes Annotated

60–427—160 F.R.D. 161
60–437—160 F.R.D. 161
65–5602—160 F.R.D. 161
65–5603(a)(3)—160 F.R.D. 161

XLV

FIGURE 5–11 Table of Statutes and Rules from *F.R.D.*

Federal Rules of Civil Procedure

Federal Rules of Evidence

Federal Rules of Appellate Procedure with Fifth Circuit Rules and IPOs

Local Federal District Court Rules

Bankruptcy Court Rules

Multidistrict Litigation Rules

Local federal rules are also available in *U.S.C.A.* and *U.S.C.S.* Another West publication discussing federal court rules is *Federal Rules Handbook.*

For assistance in obtaining current local court rules, check with your firm's law library or the local or county law library. Copies of local rules normally can be obtained from the court clerk's office at a nominal cost.

State Rules

The state courts' civil, criminal, and appellate rules of procedure generally track the federal rules. In Texas, *Vernon's Texas Rules Annotated—Civil Procedure* compiles and annotates the Texas Rules of Civil Procedure. In addition to the rules, Vernon's includes historical notes, annotations, and library references.

West also publishes an annual pamphlet containing state court rules for most states. For example, *Texas Rules of Court—State—1995* compiles the following types of rules:

Texas Rules of Civil Procedure

Texas Rules of Civil Evidence

Texas Rules of Criminal Evidence

Texas Rules of Appellate Procedure

Rules Governing Procedure for Making a Record of Court Proceedings by Electronic Recording

Local Rules of Courts of Appeals

Local District Court Rules

State Bar Rules

Texas Rules of Disciplinary Procedure

Texas Lawyer's Creed

Rules Governing Admission to the Bar

Rules Governing Participation of Law Students and Unlicensed Graduates

Code of Judicial Conduct

Rules for Removal or Retirement of Judges

Rules of Judicial Administration

Mandatory Reports of Judicial Appointments and Fees

Standards and Rules for Certification of Shorthand Reporters

Rules Governing Texas Equal Access to Justice Program

State Court rules often provide practical information, including the clerk's office hours, type of paper to be used for court pleadings, and the acceptability of facsimile transmissions.

Municipal Law

Many legal issues arise that do not involve federal or state issues. For example, a homeowner is annoyed by the sudden appearance of a large billboard at the corner of his residential street and wants to know whether the billboard meets the city's codes. The answer to the homeowner's question can usually be obtained by checking the municipal codes at the local library, law library, or city secretary or attorney's office.

Cities often operate under a charter. Acting under the authority of the charter, a city, through its governing body (city council, mayor, or county board of supervisors) passes "ordinances" or "resolutions." Proposed ordinances may be published in full text in the local newspaper.

Once you have located the appropriate code for a research issue, such as the placement of a billboard in a residential neighborhood, the research techniques are quite similar to those used to locate state or federal statutes. Most municipal codes include an index and the city charter.

Within its jurisdiction, a municipal ordinance has the same effect as a law. If a municipal ordinance conflicts with a state statute, the state statute is controlling. For example, if there were a Texas statute prohibiting billboards within three hundred feet of a state highway and a municipality passed an ordinance permitting the placement of such a billboard within two hundred feet of the state highway, the statute would be the effective legal standard.

The validity of an ordinance is based upon a lack of conflict with all other statutes, the state constitution, and the charter under which a city operates. Ordinances are presumed to be valid, but are subject to the establishment of unconstitutionality by any party challenging the ordinance.

Ordinances are subject to the same standards of interpretation as are statutes. Intention of the body enacting the ordinance is given heavy weight in any instance of interpretation.

A municipal resolution normally relates to temporary or administrative municipal matters. It cannot be enforced as a statute.

§ 5.6 Computer-Assisted Legal Research

Many of the manual research techniques outlined in this chapter can be duplicated with the computer databases discussed in Chapter 13. For example, *U.S.C.A.* is included in the WESTLAW database, and *U.S.C.S.* is in the LEXIS database. Both of these services are updated regularly.

Successful statutory research by computer requires a basic knowledge of the legislative process in addition to the ability to quickly and accurately search by computers. Search queries or questions directed to the computer should be carefully planned and executed to obtain the maximum results from the particular computer database searched.

In addition to *U.S.C.A.* and *U.S.C.S.*, numerous state statutes are available in both annotated and unannotated form. Four databases containing federal statutes are available through WESTLAW: (1) *United States Code* (USC), (2) *United States Code Annotated* (USCA), (3) *United States Code Annotated Index* (USCA-IDX), and (4) *United States Public Laws* (US-PL). Federal statute research should begin with the first three of these databases. LEXIS' CODES library contains federal statutes. Statutes may also be found in such libraries as GENFED, STATES, and the subject libraries. The USCODE file is a file containing the federal code (*U.S.C.S.* version), the Constitution, and public laws. Codes for all fifty states are maintained on LEXIS. Session laws of several states are also included on the two computer databases.

Legislative history research is simplified through computer-assisted legal research. Information on public laws introduced in the current congressional session is available through WESTLAW's BILLCAST (BC). BILLCAST archives (BC-Old) contain information on public bills introduced in prior sessions. WESTLAW also offers the *Congressional Record* (CR) for sessions after 1984. Certain provisions of the United States Code are available on WESTLAW's Legislative History (LH) database. The State Net (Statenet) database on WESTLAW includes both federal and state legislation and administrative matters, in addition to proposed legislation for all states. You can access information relating to state legislation on WESTLAW's From the State Capitols (FTSC) database.

Both WESTLAW and LEXIS have the full text of the United States Constitution in their databases. Some state constitutions may also be accessed by computer.

Before making the decision to perform statutory research manually, you should investigate the computer research options available. For a researcher very experienced in using electronic databases, use of the computer may be faster, less expensive, and more complete than a manual search. Manual searches using annotated codes, however, will usually yield excellent results and do so efficiently.

§ 5.7   Checklist for State and Federal Statutory Research

Many of the steps required to research a case can be adapted to statutory research, as outlined below:

1. Make a list of search words and terms that might be used to locate the pertinent act. For example, in the illustration of drug testing for federal employees, the paralegal searched for terms such as *drug abuse*, *drug testing*, and *workplace*.
2. Select the code to be used: *U.S.C, U.S.C.A, U.S.C.S., Vernon's Texas Codes Annotated*, or *Vernon's Annotated Revised Civil Statutes of the State of Texas*.
3. Read the preface pages of the first volume of the code to become familiar with the organization and abbreviations in the volume.
4. Check the index to the code for the search words or terms.
5. Review any cross-references to other statutes within the code.
6. Check annotations, legal periodicals, legal treatises, legal encyclopedias, and looseleaf services on the research topic.
7. Shepardize the pertinent statutes.
8. Read cases located by Shepardizing that relate to the legal issue being researched.
9. Check the legislative history of pertinent statutes.

Summary

5.1   Statutes, Constitutions, and Rules: An Introduction

Legal research often should begin with statutes, the laws enacted by the legislative body of a government. The legislature, whether federal or state, was created by a constitution, the fundamental law of a nation or state.

5.2 Researching Federal Statutes

All federal statutory research must begin with a basic understanding of the federal legislative system. The slip law published immediately after enactment of a statute contains the first authoritative and official text of the new statute. At the end of each congressional session, the slips for that session are placed in chronological order in a hardback collection called the *United States Statutes at Large*, the official compilation of the acts and resolutions of each session of Congress published by the United States Government Printing Office. A statute is given a public or private law number, representing the congressional session that enacted the law and the order of the statute's chronological enactment. *Session laws* is the name given to the body of laws enacted by a federal or state legislature during one of its sessions. There are three sources of the federal code, one official code, the *United States Code*, and two unofficial codes, *United States Code Annotated* and *United States Code Service*. A legislative history encompasses all documents that contain the information the legislature considered, and the debates in which it engaged, prior to its decision to approve or to reject a particular bill. A legislative history should include both the statute as originally enacted and any amendments.

5.3 Researching State Statutes

Federal and state statute organization and publication processes are similar. Texas Statutes are compiled in the official *Vernon's Texas Statutes and Codes Annotated* (the "Black Statutes"), published by Vernon's (for West Publishing Company). *Vernon's* is a starting point for compiling a legislative history. Throughout the legislative session and immediately following the session, recent session laws are published in paperback by West in *Vernon's Texas Session Law Service*. Several laws passed by the state legislature during regular and special sessions are arranged in *Vernon's* by title or subject. Research sources for Texas legislative histories include a bill file maintained in Austin, the Legislative Council, the *Senate Journal* and *House Journal*, Legislature Information System Bill History, and audio tapes for House and Senate floor proceedings and committee hearings.

5.4 Researching Constitutions

The present and prior versions of a federal or state constitution and any amendments should be researched in compiling a thorough history of a constitutional provision. The logical starting point for constitutional research is the Constitution itself. Legal encyclopedias, treatises, and legal periodicals often contain citations to cases that focus on constitutional issues. The Texas Constitution is the supreme authority for the operation of the Texas government. It parallels the organization of the federal

Constitution, although it is much longer. There are seventeen articles to the Texas Constitution, and over three hundred amendments. The procedure for researching the Texas Constitution mirrors that for federal constitutional research.

5.5 Researching Rules of Court

The rules governing appearances before the federal courts include the Federal Rules of Civil Procedure, Federal Rules of Evidence, Federal Rules of Appellate Procedure, Local Federal District Court Rules, Bankruptcy Court Rules, and Multidistrict Litigation Rules. The state courts' civil, criminal, and appellate rules of procedure generally track the federal rules. In Texas, *Vernon's Texas Rules Annotated—Civil Procedure* compiles and annotates the Texas Rules of Civil Procedure. West publishes annual pamphlets containing state court rules for most states and rules for each federal district in the state.

5.6 Computer-Assisted Legal Research

Much of the manual research relating to statutes, constitutions, and rules can be duplicated easier, faster, and sometimes less expensively with the computer databases of WESTLAW and LEXIS. Both WESTLAW and LEXIS have the full text of the United States Constitution in their databases. Before making the decision to perform statutory research manually, you should investigate the computer research options available.

5.7 Checklist for State and Federal Statutory Research

Many of the steps required to research a case can be adapted to statutory research. Make a list of search words and terms that might be used to locate the pertinent act. Select the official or unofficial code to be used. Check the index to the code for your search words or terms. Check annotations, legal periodicals, legal treatises, legal encyclopedias, and looseleaf services on the research topic. Finally, Shepardize the pertinent statutes.

Review Questions

1. Define statute.

2. What is the official session law publication for all federal law?

3. What is a public law number?

4. Identify the official and unofficial codes for federal statutes.

5. What is one source for significant public laws enacted within the previous week?

6. Explain the meaning of a legislative history.

7. What is another name for *Vernon's Texas Statutes and Codes Annotated*?

8. How many articles does the Texas Constitution contain?

9. Identify two sources for locating attorney general opinions.

10. Name two sources for the Texas Rules of Civil Procedure.

Exercises

1. Locate the Senate Bill enacted in the 74th session of the Texas legislature relating to a magistrate's orders for emergency protection for victims of family violence or the offense of stalking and violation of a protective order. List the following information:

   a. Senate bill number
   b. date approved
   c. effective date of the bill

2. In *U.S.C.S. Cumulative Supplement* for 1996, locate changes to the local rule 11 of the United States Court of Appeals for the Fifth Circuit, enacted on January 9, 1996. List the following information relating to that change:

   a. subject matter of the rule
   b. change

3. Locate Senate Bill 667 passed in the 1995 legislative session and furnish the following information:

   a. code amended
   b. chapter number of code amended
   c. requirements of amendment

4. In the 1996 Supplement to *Vernon's Annotated Revised Civil Statutes,* locate the statute relating to the regulation of auctioneers and furnish the following information:

   a. chapter number
   b. article number

5. Using the *U.S.C.C.A.N. Supplements* for 1996, locate the recently enacted public law governing the telecommunications industry and provide the following information:

   a. the public law number
   b. short title of the act
   c. The *United States Statutes at Large* citation

6. Use *C.F.R.* to locate the 1995 changes to the opening of the fishing trawling seasons off the Texas coast of the Gulf of Mexico, and provide the following information:

    a. the *C.F.R.* number.
    b. the section number relating to the Texas closure period
    c. the closure period

7. Locate the Senate bill enacted during the 74th Texas Legislature relating to notification of a victim of stalking about the defendant's release on bail.

    a. What is the Senate bill number?
    b. What article of the Code of Criminal Procedure is amended by this act?
    c. What date was the act approved?
    d. What was the effective date of the act?

8. The Texas Civil Practices and Remedies code was amended to allow extra time for financial institutions to respond to depositions on written questions.

    a. Name the section of the code that was amended.
    b. How many additional days does a financial institution have to respond to depositions on written questions?

9. Refer to the 1996 amendment to the Federal Rules of Appellate Procedure and furnish the following information relating to the filing of an appellate brief in the Fifth Circuit:

    a. How many levels of extensions of time for filing a brief are available?
    b. What constitutes "timely filing" for all papers except briefs and appendices?
    c. What constitutes "timely filing" for briefs and appendices?

CHAPTER 6

ADMINISTRATIVE LAW

§ 6.1 An Introduction to Administrative Law

Overview of Administrative Law

In the broadest sense, *administrative law* involves the study of how those parts of our system of government that are neither legislatures nor courts make decisions. These entities, referred to as *administrative agencies,* are typically located in the executive branch of government and are usually charged with the day-to-day details of governing. Agencies are assigned specific tasks by the legislature and perform these tasks by making decisions and supervising the procedures by which these decisions are carried out. For example, Congress has charged the Federal Department of Health and Human Services (HHS) with the administration of the nation's social security program. Under that mandate, HHS does two things: (1) it makes general social security policy (within the terms of the statute), and (2) it processes individual applications for, and terminations of, social security benefits. Affected persons who disagree with the agency's decisions on either the substance of the social security program or the procedures under which that program is implemented, and whose grievances are not resolved within the agency, may normally take their dispute into federal court for resolution.

The purpose of the chapter is twofold: (1) to present an overview of administrative law, emphasizing how agencies operate, which provides the larger context in which agency research projects take place, and (2) to give you the information you need to find agency regulations and administrative decisions, which is what you most likely will be asked to do in your role as a legal assistant.

Nature and Function of Agencies

By the 1930s the growth of government made it imperative that the system of agencies, which had long been a part of government activity, be greatly expanded. The New Deal era marks the beginning of modern administrative law. Since that time, agencies have become a pervasive influence in daily life.

There is hardly any function of modern government that does not in some way involve an administrative agency. The reason for this is really very simple: agencies are the only entities in government equipped to deal with the day-to-day minutiae of governing. It may be one thing, for example, for Congress to decide to regulate trucking companies, but the last thing that Congress wants to decide is how much Company *X* may charge to carry a package from New York to Chicago. Environmental protection is now a matter of national concern, but a court is unlikely to have the expertise necessary to decide precisely what specific air pollution control equipment is best suited for coal-fired power plants. Two themes constantly sound in administrative law: agencies are established (1) to take care of the details of regulation (promulgating and enforcing rules and regulations) and (2) to develop expertise in a particular area of regulation.

Administrative agencies are established by legislatures and are empowered by them to carry out specific tasks. Most administrative agencies are designated as executive branch agencies. Others are established as independent regulatory commissions.

No matter how a legislature chooses to deal with an agency, your first task in learning about an agency is simple: read the agency's enabling and administrative procedure acts. An **enabling act** is the primary source of an agency's authority—what the agency does must be within the framework of its legislative authorization. An **administrative procedure act**, discussed in detail in the following text, outlines the processes an agency must use in conducting its activities.

Administrative agencies are often referred to as the fourth branch of the government. They have extensive power and authority subject to review and checks by the three principal branches of government.

Administrative agencies regulate conduct their rule making and adjudication processes, the latter allowing for resolution of disputes. For example, there may be various applicants for a limited number of operating licenses, and the agency must decide which applicant should receive the license. It must also provide for enforcement of agency rules and regulations once a license is granted. Virtually all federal agencies, and most state agencies, follow the general procedures outlined below in conducting their rule making and adjudication proceedings.

Agencies' rule-making procedures are similar to the legislative process. A proposed law, or in administrative law terms, a **rule** or **regulation**, drafted by the agency is normally published and open to public scrutiny

---

TERMS

enabling act† A statute that grants new powers or authority to persons or corporations.

administrative procedure act† A statute enacted by Congress and statutes enacted by state legislatures that regulate the way in which administrative agencies conduct their affairs and that establish procedures for judicial review of the actions of agencies.

rule† An order of a court or an administrative agency made in a particular proceeding with respect to the disposition of the case or some aspect of the case; a regulation issued by an administrative agency.

regulation† A rule having the force of law, promulgated by an administrative agency.

and response through one of two types of rule-making procedures: informal or formal. Both are important to agency functioning. Although informal rule making may seem at first glance to be very "formal," it is different from formal rule making. The type of proceeding your client is facing may affect the type of research that needs to be conducted.

In **informal rule making**, also referred to as **notice and comment rule making**, a proposed rule is published in a manner provided by law. For example, federal agencies publish them in the *Federal Register*, discussed later in this chapter. The public is given the opportunity to submit comments about the proposed rule to the agency sponsoring the rule. After the period of time, the agency reviews all information and makes a final determination whether to pass the proposed rule. If the rule is passed, notice of its passage is published in the *Federal Register* if it is a federal agency, or in some other official publication.

Procedures for **formal rule making** are more complicated. In formal rule making, a trial-type proceeding occurs. Once notice of a proposed rule is published, all interested parties are invited to formally appear before the agency and present testimony, documentation, or any information a participant believes relevant to final agency action on the proposed rule. Formal adjudication procedures can be time-consuming and often continue for months at a time. For example, with the issue of what percentage of peanut butter should be peanuts, the agency conducted a full trial-type proceeding. The issue was whether peanut butter should consist of either 87% or 90% peanuts. The proceeding went on for over a year, with many citizens and organizations participating. If a rule is passed by the agency, notice of its passage will be published.

Agencies also can regulate conduct through their adjudication procedures, which, as with rule making, appear in both informal and formal forms. **Adjudication procedures** resemble court proceedings. Normally

---

TERMS

informal rule making   The procedure by which a proposed rule is published in a manner provided by law, the public is given an opportunity to submit comments about it to the agency sponsoring the rule, and the agency reviews all information and makes a final determination whether to pass the proposed rule.

notice and comment rule making   Another term for informal rule making.

formal rule making   The procedure by which a proposed rule is published in a manner provided by law and a trial-type proceeding is held to which all interested parties are invited to appear before the agency and present testimony, documentation, or any information relevant to final agency action on the proposed rule.

adjudication procedures   Proceedings similar to those of a court that take place before, and under the guidance of, an agency administrative law judge who makes a final decision on the issue in question.

these proceedings take place before, and under the guidance of, an agency administrative law judge who makes the final decision. In informal adjudication, the proceeding often results in a settlement or the payment of a negotiated fine or penalty. Formal adjudication, however, is conducted as a trial-type proceeding with witnesses, examination, the rules of procedure, and evidence. The result is a written opinion, similar to a court opinion.

Guidelines for Agency Operations: Administrative Procedure Acts

The early history of administrative agencies is cloudy. A written catalog of rules and regulations was not maintained in a central system in the beginning. Since there were no specific rules or laws in force to govern the agencies, many actions of federal agencies were held unconstitutional by the United States Supreme Court. In 1946, Congress remedied this problem by enacting a regulatory statute, the Administrative Procedure Act (APA) (5 U.S.C. § 1 *et seq.*).

The federal APA provides the most important set of standards governing administrative agencies and their rule-making and adjudication procedures. It governs federal agencies and has served as the model for many state administrative procedure statutes. State acts differ considerably, so in researching a specific state's system, you *must* refer to that state's administrative procedure act.

The APA establishes procedures agencies must follow in issuing rules and regulations. The act suggests ways to conduct agency proceedings without offending the due process clause of the fifth amendment to the United States Constitution.

Through the years, the Administrative Procedure Act has been amended by the Freedom of Information Act, the Privacy Act, the Government in the Sunshine Act, and the Regulatory Flexibility Act. All these acts are found in Title 5 of the *U.S.C.* under the Administrative Procedure Act. They give additional rights to public notice and access to administrative procedures.

§ 6.2 Federal Agency Research

Finding Federal Agencies

To obtain general information about administrative agencies, consult the *United States Government Manual* published by the Office of the Federal

Register. This manual provides information about each agency's structure, authority, and personnel. The manual also discusses in detail the functions of all agencies from the executive branch down to the smallest office or bureau.

From a very practical standpoint, what you may need most in a particular situation is the name, address, and telephone number of a federal agency. These are provided in the *United States Government Manual.* You can also find them in the *Federal Yellow Book,* an extensive telephone directory for federal agencies. If you need to contact agencies and their officials with any frequency, the latter publication is indispensable.

Focusing exclusively on the larger agencies, the *Federal Regulatory Directory* also provides information on administrative agencies. Published by Congressional Quarterly, Inc., this annual publication offers topical discussions on current agency issues and activities.

Most federal agencies publish general information in pamphlets and periodicals. These publications are helpful for understanding the basic structure and function of a particular agency.

Agency Rules and Regulations

Introduction

To locate proposed and effective administrative rules and regulations, two main sources should be consulted: the *Federal Register* and the *Code of Federal Regulations* (C.F.R.). The *Federal Register* is to the *C.F.R.* what the *United States Statutes at Large* is to the *U.S.C.,* namely, the *Federal Register* and *United States Statutes at Large* are the sources where new rules and statutes, respectively, are first published, whereas the *C.F.R.* and *U.S.C.* are the final compiled versions of codified rules and statutes, respectively.

Agencies also publish and distribute texts of their own rules and regulations. Agency publications often are easier to use than the *Federal Register* and *Code of Federal Regulations.* However, never use an agency publication, which is a secondary source, to the exclusion of the primary source material.

Federal Register

Introduction   Publication of administrative rules and regulations did not begin until 1936. Prior to that time, there was no accessible source in which to find or review administrative decisions or proposed rules or regulations. In response, Congress passed a law that provided for the publication of all federal administrative rules and regulations in a publication known as the *Federal Register* (cited as *Fed. Reg.*). The *Federal Register* began publication in 1936. Unless exempted by a statute, all proposed rules and regulations must be published in the *Federal Register*. Generally, if publication of an administrative rule or regulation does not occur, the rule or regulation is not legally effective.

The *Federal Register* is a softbound, newspaper-like publication that is published on weekdays and circulated by the United States Government Printing Office. The *Federal Register* reports all proposed rules and regulations, making them available to the public. The proposed rules and regulations in the *Federal Register* contain helpful information. Not only are summaries and background information provided, but a contact person is also given for those interested in further information about the rule or regulation and its ultimate effective date.

In total, the *Federal Register* consists of hundreds of volumes because of its frequency of publication. In addition to administrative rules and regulations, the *Federal Register* also includes presidential proclamations and executive orders. See Figure 6–1 for sample pages from a typical issue of the *Federal Register*.

Indexes to the *Federal Register* The *Federal Register* is a beginning point for researching federal administrative rules and regulations. To begin legal research in the *Federal Register*, start with its indexes. The indexes list agency and subject entries for access to proposed administrative rules and regulations. Two indexes assist in accessing the *Federal Register*. General Indexes and the *CIS Federal Register Index*.

The General Indexes General indexes provide access to the proposed rules and regulations and other published material in the *Federal Register*. The indexes of rules, regulations, and amendments are published weekly, quarterly, and annually. To effectively and efficiently locate agency regulations or information, it is important to know which agency issued the regulation. See Figure 6–2 for a sample page from the *Federal Register* index.

If the name of the agency is not known, it may be difficult to locate your information. An agency name may be located by using the *United States Government Manual*, discussed earlier in this chapter.

CIS Federal Register Index A more effective, comprehensive, and easier-to-use index is the *CIS Federal Register Index,* first published in 1984. This index is issued weekly and has cumulative issues. The *CIS Federal Register Index* cites its entries by the subject of the regulation, the specific name of the regulation with the agency, the agency docket number, a calendar of effective dates, and the anticipated *C.F.R.* number to be assigned to the regulation once it is codified.

Daily Table of Contents Each daily issue of the *Federal Register* includes a table of contents that alphabetically lists the agency's regulations

Proposed Rules

Federal Register

Vol. 55, No. 136

Monday, July 16, 1990

This section of the FEDERAL REGISTER contains notices to the public of the proposed issuance of rules and regulations. The purpose of these notices is to give interested persons an opportunity to participate in the rule making prior to the adoption of the final rules.

DEPARTMENT OF AGRICULTURE

Agricultural Marketing Service

7 CFR Part 927

[Docket No. FV-90-151 PR]

Proposed Expenses and Assessment Rate for Marketing Order Covering Winter Pears Grown in Oregon, Washington, and California

AGENCY: Agricultural Marketing Service, USDA.

ACTION: Proposed rule.

SUMMARY: This proposed rule would authorize expenditures and establish an assessment rate under Marketing Order 927 for the 1990–91 fiscal year established for that order. The proposal is needed for the Winter Pear Control Committee (committee) to incur operating expenses during the 1990–91 fiscal year and to collect funds during that year to pay those expenses. This would facilitate program operations. Funds to administer this program are derived from assessments on handlers.

DATES: Comments must be received by July 26, 1990.

ADDRESSES: Interested persons are invited to submit written comments concerning this proposal. Comments must be sent in triplicate to the Docket Clerk, Fruit and Vegetable Division, AMS, USDA, P.O. Box 96456, room 2525–S, Washington, DC 20090–6456. Comments should reference the docket number and the date and page number of this issue of the Federal Register and will be available for public inspection in the Office of the Docket Clerk during regular business hours.

FOR FURTHER INFORMATION CONTACT: Patrick Packnett, Marketing Order Administration Branch, Fruit and Vegetable Division, AMS, USDA, P.O. Box 96456, room 2525–S, Washington, DC 20090–6456, telephone 202–475–3862.

SUPPLEMENTARY INFORMATION: This rule is proposed under Marketing

Agreement and Marketing Order No. 927 (7 CFR part 927) regulating the handling of winter pears grown in Oregon, Washington, and California. The order is effective under the Agricultural Marketing Agreement Act of 1937, as amended (7 U.S.C. 601–674), hereinafter referred to as the Act.

This proposed rule has been reviewed by the Department of Agriculture (Department) in accordance with Departmental Regulation 1512–1 and the criteria contained in Executive Order 12291 and has been determined to be a "non-major" rule under criteria contained therein.

Pursuant to the requirements set forth in the Regulatory Flexibility Act (RFA), the Administrator of the Agricultural Marketing Service (AMS) has considered the economic impact of this proposed rule on small entities.

The purpose of the RFA is to fit regulatory actions to the scale of business subject to such actions in order that small businesses will not be unduly or disproportionately burdened. Marketing orders issued pursuant to the Act, and rules issued thereunder, are unique in that they are brought about through group action of essentially small entities acting on their own behalf. Thus, both statutes have small entity orientation and compatibility.

Approximately 90 handlers of winter pears are subject to regulation under this marketing order each season. There are approximately 1,800 winter pear producers in Washington, Oregon, and California. Small agricultural producers have been defined by the Small Business Administration (13 CFR 121.2) as those having annual receipts of less than $500,000, and small agricultural service firms are defined as those whose annual receipts are less than $3,500,000. The majority of the handlers and producers of winter pears may be classified as small entities.

The winter pear marketing order, administered by the Department, requires that the assessment rate for a particular fiscal year shall apply to all assessable pears handled from the beginning of such year. An annual budget of expenses is prepared by the committee and submitted to the Department for approval. The members of the committee are handlers and producers of winter pears. They are familiar with the committee's needs and

with the costs for goods, services, and personnel in their local area and are thus in a position to formulate appropriate budgets. The budgets are formulated and discussed in public meetings. Thus, all directly affected persons have an opportunity to participate and provide input.

The assessment rate recommended by the committee is derived by dividing anticipated expenses by expected shipments of pears (in standard boxes or equivalents). Because that rate is applied to actual shipments, it must be established at a rate which will produce sufficient income to pay the committee's expected expenses. Recommended budgets and rates of assessment are usually acted upon by the committee shortly before a season starts, and expenses are incurred on a continuous basis. Therefore, budget and assessment rate approvals must be expedited so that the committee will have funds to pay its expenses.

The committee met on June 1, 1990, and unanimously recommended 1990–91 fiscal year expenditures of $4,943,738 and an assessment rate of $0.315 per standard box, or equivalent, of assessable pears shipped under M.O. 927. In comparison, 1989–90 fiscal year budgeted expenditures were $4,501,022 and the assessment rate was $0.335.

Major expenditure items this year in comparison to 1989–90 budgeted expenditures (in parentheses) are $3,859,775 ($3,737,038) for paid advertising, $317,767 ($187,693) for contingencies to cover unanticipated expenses, and $350,661 ($211,870) for research designed to improve winter pear yields and quality. The committee has budgeted $145,000 for industry development, of which $100,000 would be held in reserve for use in the event of a consumer-related industry crisis. The balance of $45,000 would cover marketing and promotional services and other services to be provided by the Northwest Horticultural Council under a consultant agreement. The remaining expenses are primarily for program administration and are budgeted at about last year's amounts.

Assessment income for the 1990–91 fiscal year is expected to total $4,266,068 based on shipments of 13,543,072 packed boxes of pears. Other available funds, including $20,000 in prior year assessments, $36,000 in miscellaneous

FIGURE 6–1 Title page from the *Federal Register*

Federal Register / Vol. 55, No. 136 / Monday, July 16, 1990 / Proposed Rules

income, $94,500 in voluntary intrastate assessments, and a reserve of $527,170 carried into this fiscal year, would also be utilized to cover proposed 1990–91 fiscal year expenditures. The committee's reserves are within authorized limits.

While this proposed action would impose some additional costs on handlers, the costs are in the form of uniform assessments on all handlers. Some of the additional costs may be passed on to producers. However, these costs would be significantly offset by the benefits derived from the operation of the marketing order. Therefore, the Administrator of the AMS has determined that this action would not have a significant economic impact on a substantial number of small entities.

Based on the foregoing, it is found and determined that a comment period of 10 days is appropriate because the budget and assessment rate approval for the pear program needs to be expedited and the committee needs to have sufficient funds to pay its expenses, which are incurred on a continuous basis.

List of Subjects in 7 CFR Part 927

Marketing agreements, Reporting and recordkeeping requirements, Winter pears.

For the reasons set forth in the preamble, it is proposed that 7 CFR Part 927 be amended as follows:

PART 927—WINTER PEARS GROWN IN OREGON, WASHINGTON, AND CALIFORNIA

1. The authority citation for 7 CFR part 927 continues to read as follows:

Authority: Secs. 1–19, 48 Stat. 31, as amended; 7 U.S.C. 601–674.

2. New § 927.230 is added to read as follows:

§ 927.230   Expenses and assessment rate.

Expenses of $4,943,738 by the Winter Pear Control Committee are authorized, and an assessment rate of $0.315 per standard box, or equivalent, of pears is established for the fiscal year ending June 30, 1991. Unexpended funds from the 1990–91 fiscal year may be carried over as a reserve.

Dated: July 10, 1990.

William J. Doyle,

Associate Deputy Director, Fruit and Vegetable Division.

[FR Doc. 90–16476 Filed 7–13–90; 8:45 am]

BILLING CODE 3410-02-M

7 CFR Parts 1001, 1002 and 1004

[Docket Nos. AO–14–A62 and AO–14–A62–RO1, AO–71–A77 and AO–71–A77–RO1, and AO–160–A65 and AO–160–A65–RO–1; AMS–88–105 and DA–89–028]

Milk in the New England, New York-New Jersey and Middle Atlantic Marketing Areas; Extension of Time for Filing Exceptions to the Recommended Decision on Proposed Amendments to Tentative Marketing Agreements and to Orders

AGENCY: Agricultural Marketing Service, USDA.

ACTION: Extension of time for filing exceptions to proposed rule.

SUMMARY: This notice extends until August 1, 1990, the deadline for filing exceptions to a recommended decision issued May 18, 1990, concerning proposed amendments to the New England, New York-New Jersey and Middle Atlantic milk marketing orders. Additional time to prepare exceptions was requested on behalf of a number of cooperative associations and proprietary handlers. Those requesting the extension state that more time is needed because of the voluminous nature of the record and exhibits on which the decision is based.

DATES: Exceptions now are due on or before August 1, 1990.

ADDRESSES: Exceptions (seven copies) should be filed with the Hearing Clerk, room 1083, South Building, United States Department of Agriculture, Washington, DC 20250.

FOR FURTHER INFORMATION CONTACT: Constance M. Brenner, Marketing Specialist, USDA/AMS/Dairy Division, Order Formulation Branch, room 2968, South Building, P.O. Box 96456, Washington, DC 20090–6456 (202) 447–7183.

SUPPLEMENTARY INFORMATION: Prior documents in the proceeding:

Notice of Hearing: Issued June 7, 1988; published June 20, 1988 (53 FR 21825).

Supplemental Notice of Hearing: Issued September 29, 1988; published October 4, 1988 (53 FR 38963).

Notice of re-opened Hearing: Issued August 10, 1989; published August 16, 1989 (54 FR 33709). (To consider changes in Class II pricing for 40 orders)

Partial Recommended Decision: Issued September 20, 1989; published September 26, 1989 (54 FR 39377).

Partial Final Decision: Issued December 12, 1989; published December 18, 1989 (54 FR 51749).

Order Amending the New York-New Jersey Order: Issued January 25, 1990; published January 31, 1990 (55 FR 3198).

Recommended Decision: Issued May 18, 1990; published May 25, 1990 (55 FR 21558).

Notice is hereby given that the time for filing exceptions to the recommended decision with respect to the proposed amendments to the tentative marketing agreements and to the orders regulating the handling of milk in the New England, New York-New Jersey and Middle Atlantic marketing areas which was issued May 18, 1990, is hereby extended to August 1, 1990.

This notice is issued pursuant to the provisions of the Agricultural Marketing Agreement Act of 1937, as amended (7 U.S.C. 601–674), and the applicable rules of practice and procedure governing the formulation of marketing agreements and marketing orders (7 CFR part 900).

List of Subjects in 7 CFR Parts 1001, 1002 and 1004

Milk marketing orders.

The authority citation for 7 CFR parts 1001, 1002 and 1004 continues to read as follows:

Authority: Secs. 1–19, 48 Stat. 31, as amended; 7 U.S.C. 601–674.

Signed at Washington, DC, on July 10, 1990.

Kenneth C. Clayton,

Acting Administrator.

[FR Doc. 90–16474 Filed 7–13–90; 8:45 am]

BILLING CODE 3410-02-M

FEDERAL COMMUNICATIONS COMMISSION

47 CFR Part 73

[MM Docket No. 90–263; FCC 90–193]

Broadcast Service; Settlement Agreements Among Applicants for Construction Permits

AGENCY: Federal Communications Commission.

ACTION: Proposed rule.

SUMMARY: The Commission adopts a Notice of Proposed Rule Making (Notice) initiating this proceeding as part of a comprehensive effort to eliminate the potential for abuse of its processes. In particular, the Notice considers imposing limitations on payments that can be made to settle cases involving competing applications for construction permits for new broadcast stations or modifications to facilities of existing stations.

DATES: Comments are due by August 23, 1990, and reply comments are due by September 7, 1990.

FIGURE 6–1   *(continued)*

FEDERAL REGISTER INDEX, January—December 1990
ANNUAL

Acquired Immune Deficiency Syndrome, National Commission

See National Commission on Acquired Immune Deficiency Syndrome

ACTION

RULES

Drug-free workplace requirements; contracts or grants, 21681
Freedom of Information Act; implementation, 50330
Uniform fee schedule and administrative guidelines, 20152
Lobbying restrictions, 6736
Nondiscrimination on basis of handicap:
Federally-assisted programs and activities, 52136
Federally-conducted programs and activities, 47755

PROPOSED RULES

Locally generated contributions in older American volunteer programs, 42218
Regulatory agenda, 16800, 45118

NOTICES

Agency information collection activities under OMB review, 27275, 27664, 27847, 29643, 35441, 39311, 40407, 40412, 48875
Foster grandparent and senior companion programs; income eligibility levels, 10268, 51136
Grants and cooperative agreements; availability, etc.:
MiniGrant program, 3243
Special volunteer programs—
After school, weekend, and summer time youth illicit drug use prevention demonstration project, 23116
VISTA projects—
Regions 2, 3, 4, 8, and 9, 8968
Student community service projects, 52198
Senior Executive Service:
Performance Review Board; membership, 41119
VISTA program guidelines, 9343

Actuaries, Joint Board for Enrollment

See Joint Board for Enrollment of Actuaries

Administration Office, Executive Office of the President

RULES

Freedom of Information Act; implementation, 46037

PROPOSED RULES

Freedom of Information Act; implementation:
Fee schedule and administrative guidelines, 29219

Administration on Aging

See Aging Administration

Administrative Conference of the United States

RULES

Recommendations:
Administrative practice and procedure, 34209, 53269
Biotechnology, Federal regulation; agency adjudicatory decisions, indexing and public availability; visa denials processing and review; and social security disability determinations, use of medical personnel; correction, 1665

PROPOSED RULES

Recommendations:
Ombudsmen; uses by Federal agencies, 13279
Risk communication as regulatory alternative for protecting health, safety, and environment, 13538

NOTICES

Meetings:
Adjudication Committee, 3428, 9476
Administration Committee, 9151, 42590, 46849
Financial Services Regulation Special Committee, 37913, 46536
Financial Services Special Committee, 6409
Government Ethics Regulation Special Committee, 24134, 29077
Governmental Processes Committee, 37913, 41363, 43392
Judicial Review Committee, 41363, 43392
Model Rules Working Group, 5865, 18923, 25855, 41363
Plenary Session, 20485, 49926
Regulation Committee, 2119, 5865, 9476, 14988, 21764
Rulemaking Committee, 14330, 25855, 40211, 43013

Administrative Office of United States Courts

NOTICES

Registry fee; assessment method change, 42867

Advisory Committee on Federal Pay

See Federal Pay, Advisory Committee

Advisory Council on Historic Preservation

See Historic Preservation, Advisory Council

African Development Foundation

RULES

Drug-free workplace requirements; contracts or grants, 21681

NOTICES

Meetings; Sunshine Act, 958, 28133, 29292, 49751

Agency for Health Care Policy and Research

NOTICES

Clinical practice guidelines development, 35185
Committees; establishment, renewal, termination, etc.:
AIDS and HIV infection; clinical practice guidelines development panel, 50776
Grants and cooperative agreements; availability, etc.:
Medical treatment effectiveness research program, 33170
Medical technology assessments:
Heart-lung transplantation, 42776
Single and double lung transplantation, 42776
Meetings:
Cesarean Section Patient Outcomes Research Advisory Committee, 36702
Clinical practice guidelines, 35186
Acute post-operative pain management, 42898
Pressure sores management; risk assessment, prevention, and early intervention, 48904
Urinary incontinence in adults, 40240
Gastroenteritis Patient Outcomes Research Advisory Committee, 36703
General Research Support Services Advisory Committee, 33169
Health Care Policy, Research, and Evaluation National Advisory Council, 46577
Medical Treatment Effectiveness Guideline Development Support Advisory Committee, 33169
Meetings; advisory committees:
February, 1876
June, 23808, 25373
September, 36316
October, 38855

Agency for International Development

See International Development Cooperation Agency

RULES

Acquisition regulations:
Disadvantaged enterprises; contracting and subcontracting requirements, 8469, 39153
Major systems acquisition procedures and advisory and assistance services, 39975
Miscellaneous amendments, 6801
Commodity transactions financed by A.I.D.; practice and procedure rules, 34231
Disaster relief, economic development, and other assistance; food commodities transfer for food use, 23638
Drug-free workplace requirements; contracts or grants, 21681
Freedom of Information Act; implementation, 43328
Lobbying restrictions, 6736

FIGURE 6–2 Index page from the *Federal Register*

that appear in the issue, along with page references. See Figure 6–3 for a sample table of contents page.

Code of Federal Regulations (C.F.R.)

Introduction The subject arrangement and codification of agency rules, regulations, and amendments created by the agencies are found in the *Code of Federal Regulations* (cited as *C.F.R.*). The *C.F.R.* is updated yearly with new bound volumes, and updates are also issued at quarterly intervals throughout the year.

The *C.F.R.* is presently published under fifty titles in pamphlet form. Each title is divided into chapters, parts, and sections. Although similar to *U.S.C.*, citing *C.F.R.* is different. The title is the general subject area, with section and parts related to specific areas under the title. Therefore, if you have identified section 7.1 of Title 1, your citation would read: 1 C.F.R. § 7.1.

Unlike many legal materials, new volumes are printed each year with the current text of the effective regulations, including amendments and deletions of the previous twelve months. Consequently, the latest issue of *C.F.R.* should be consulted for current regulations. For a sample of *C.F.R.* materials, see Figure 6–4.

Since all regulations are first published in the *Federal Register,* both the *Federal Register* and *C.F.R.* must be consulted for the current status of an administrative rule or regulation. Check the cover of the *C.F.R.* you are consulting to determine the cut-off date for inclusion of revisions (for example, "Revised as of April 1, 1995"). In general, titles are revised according to the following schedule:

Title 1 through Title 16: January 1

Title 17 through Title 27: April 1

Title 28 through Title 41: July 1

Title 42 through Title 50: October 1

Due to the staggered publication of *C.F.R.*, all subsequent indexes of the *Federal Register* must be consulted for completeness.

Another important point is that all material appearing in the *Federal Register* does not necessarily appear in *C.F.R.* Preambles to rules and regulations in the *Federal Register*, which may be very helpful in understanding and interpreting regulations, are not included when the regulation is codified in *C.F.R.*

Indexes and Finding Aids A general index to *C.F.R.* is issued annually as a separate softbound pamphlet entitled *C.F.R. Index and Finding Aids*. It has an alphabetical listing of administrative agencies (such as the Bureau

Contents

Federal Register

Vol. 55, No. 133

Wednesday, July 11, 1990

Agricultural Marketing Service
PROPOSED RULES
Milk marketing orders:
   Middle Atlantic et al., 28403

Agriculture Department
See also Agricultural Marketing Service; Farmers Home
   Administration; Forest Service; Soil Conservation
   Service
RULES
Organization, functions, and authority delegations:
   Science and Education, Assistant Secretary, et al.;
      Resource Conservation and Recovery Act, 28369

Air Force Department
NOTICES
Privacy Act:
   Systems of records, 28427

Army Department
NOTICES
Environmental statements; availability, etc.:
   Base realignments and closures—
      Fort Douglas, UT, 28433

Arts and Humanities, National Foundation
See National Foundation on the Arts and the Humanities

Bonneville Power Administration
NOTICES
Environmental statements; availability, etc.:
   Riverside and Anaheim, CA; surplus power sale and
      exchange agreement, 28436

Census Bureau
PROPOSED RULES
Foreign trade statistics; Shipper's Export Declarations
   eliminated, 28404
NOTICES
Surveys, determinations, etc.:
   Service industries; annual, 28425

Centers for Disease Control
NOTICES
Meetings:
   Childhood Lead Poisoning Prevention Advisory
      Committee, 28456

Civil Rights Commission
NOTICES
Meetings; State advisory committees:
   Arizona, 28425
   North Carolina, 28425

Commerce Department
See Census Bureau; Export Administration Bureau;
   International Trade Administration; National Oceanic
   and Atmospheric Administration

Committee for the Implementation of Textile Agreements
NOTICES
Cotton, wool, and man-made textiles:
   Singapore, 28426

Commodity Futures Trading Commission
RULES
Foreign futures and options transactions:
   London Futures and Options Exchange, 28372

Community Services Office
NOTICES
Grants and cooperative agreements; availability, etc.:
   Discretionary grants programs, 28550

Defense Department
See also Air Force Department; Army Department
PROPOSED RULES
Acquisition regulations:
   Commercial products acquisition and distribution, 28514
NOTICES
Federal Acquisition Regulation (FAR):
   Agency information collection activities under OMB
      review, 28433
Meetings:
   DIA Advisory Board, 28427
   Women in Services Advisory Committee, 28427

Education Department
NOTICES
Special education and rehabilitative services:
   Blind vending facilities; arbitration panel decision under
      Randolph-Sheppard Act, 28434

Energy Department
See also Bonneville Power Administration; Federal Energy
   Regulatory Commission
NOTICES
Agency information collection activities under OMB review,
   28441
Grant and cooperative agreement awards:
   Tecogen, Inc., 28435
Meetings:
   Nuclear Facility Safety Advisory Committee, 28435
Methanol from unutilized domestic natural gas; assessment
   of production costs, 28436
Natural gas exportation and importation:
   Nortech Energy Corp., 28451

Environmental Protection Agency
RULES
Air programs; State authority delegations:
   California, 28393
Hazardous waste program authorizations:
   New Mexico, 28397
PROPOSED RULES
Water pollution control:
   State underground injection control program—
      Hazardous waste, disposal injection restrictions; acidic
         wastewater, 28415
NOTICES
Agency information collection activities under OMB review,
   28453

FIGURE 6–3   Table of contents page from the *Federal Register*

Telecommunication

47

PART 80 TO END

Revised as of October 1, 1990

CONTAINING
A CODIFICATION OF DOCUMENTS
OF GENERAL APPLICABILITY
AND FUTURE EFFECT

AS OF OCTOBER 1, 1990

With Ancillaries

Published by
the Office of the Federal Register
National Archives and Records
Administration

as a Special Edition of
the Federal Register

FIGURE 6–4   Sample pages from the *C.F.R.*

Table of Contents

iii

FIGURE 6–4 *(continued)*

FIGURE 6–4   *(continued)*

Federal Communications Commission § **80.1**

80.969 Illumination of operating controls.
80.971 Test of radiotelephone installation.

Subpart U—Radiotelephone Installations Required by the Bridge-to-Bridge Act

80.1001 Applicability.
80.1003 Station required.
80.1005 Inspection of station.
80.1007 Bridge-to-bridge radiotelephone installation.
80.1009 Principal operator and operating position.
80.1011 Transmitter.
80.1013 Receiver.
80.1015 Power supply.
80.1017 Antenna system.
80.1019 Antenna radio frequency indicator.
80.1021 Nameplate.
80.1023 Test of radiotelephone installation.

Subpart V—Emergency Position Indicating Radiobeacons (EPIRB's)

80.1051 Scope.
80.1053 Special requirements for Class A EPIRB stations.
80.1055 Special requirements for Class B EPIRB stations.
80.1057 Special requirements for Class C EPIRB stations.
80.1059 Special requirements for Class S EPIRB stations.
80.1061 Special requirements for 406.025 MHz EPIRBs.

Subpart W—Global Maritime Distress and Safety System (GMDSS)—[Reserved]

Subpart X—Voluntary Radio Installations

GENERAL

80.1151 Voluntary radio operations.
80.1153 Station log and radio watches.

VOLUNTARY TELEGRAPHY

80.1155 Radioprinter.
80.1157 Facsimile.
80.1159 Narrow-band direct-printing (NB-DP).
80.1161 Emergency position indicating radiobeacon (EPIRB).

VOLUNTARY TELEPHONY

80.1165 Assignment and use of frequencies.

AUTOMATED SYSTEMS

80.1169 Automated Maritime Telecommunications System (AMTS).
80.1171 Assignment and use of frequencies.

ON-BOARD COMMUNICATIONS

80.1175 Scope of communications of on-board stations.
80.1177 Assignment and use of frequencies.
80.1179 On-board repeater limitations.
80.1181 Station identification.
80.1183 Remote control for maneuvering or navigation.

MOBILE-SATELLITE STATIONS

80.1185 Supplemental eligibility for mobile-satellite stations.
80.1187 Scope of communication.
80.1189 Portable ship earth stations.

RADIODETERMINATION

80.1201 Special provisions for cable-repair ship stations.

AUTHORITY: Secs. 4, 303, 48 Stat. 1066, 1082, as amended; 47 U.S.C. 154, 303, unless otherwise noted. Interpret or apply 48 Stat. 1064-1068, 1081-1105, as amended; 47 U.S.C. 151-155, 301-609; 3 UST 3450, 3 UST 4726, 12 UST 2377.

SOURCE: 51 FR 31213, Sept. 2, 1986, unless otherwise noted.

GENERAL

Subpart A—General Information

§ **80.1 Basis and purpose.**

This section contains the statutory basis for this part of the rules and provides the purpose for which this part is issued.

(a) *Basis.* The rules for the maritime services in this part are promulgated under the provisions of the Communications Act of 1934, as amended, which vests authority in the Federal Communications Commission to regulate radio transmission and to issue licenses for radio stations. The rules in this part are in accordance wtih applicable statutes, international treaties, agreements and recommendations to which the United States is a party. The most significant of these documents are listed below with the short title appearing in parenthesis:

Communications Act of 1934, as amended—(Communications Act).
Communications Satellite Act of 1962, as amended—(Communications Satellite Act).
International Telecommunication Union Radio Regulations, in force for the United States—(Radio Regulations).

FIGURE 6–4 *(continued)*

Agreement Between the United States of America and Canada for the Promotion of Safety on the Great Lakes by Means of Radio, as amended, and the Technical Regulations annexed thereto—(Great Lakes Radio Agreement).

International Convention for Safety of Life at Sea, 1974, as amended, and the Annex thereto—(Safety Convention).

Vessel Bridge-to-Bridge Radiotelephone Act—(Bridge-to-Bridge Act).

(b) *Purpose.* This part states the conditions under which radio may be licensed and used in the maritime services. These rules do not govern radio stations operated by agencies of the U.S. Government.

§ 80.2 Other regulations that apply.

The Commandant, U.S. Coast Guard has promulgated regulations which affect radiotelecommunication equipment carriage and power source installation requirements for certain ships. Inquiries concerning applicable U.S. Coast Guard regulations are to addressed to the Commandant, U.S. Coast Guard, Washington, DC 20593, or to the nearest District Headquarters Office of the U.S. Coast Guard.

§ 80.3 Other applicable rule parts of this chapter.

Other FCC rule parts applicable to licensees in the maritime services include the following:

(a) *Part 0.* This part describes the Commission's organization and delegations of authority. Part 0 also lists available Commission publications, standards and procedures for access to Commission records and location on Commission monitoring stations.

(b) *Part 1.* This part includes rules of practice and procedure for license applications, adjudicatory proceedings, procedures for reconsideration and review of the Commission actions; provisions concerning violation notices and forfeiture proceedings; and the environmental processing requirements that, if applicable, must be complied with prior to the initiation of construction.

(c) *Part 2.* This part contains the Table of Frequency Allocations and special requirements in international regulations, recommendations, agreements, and treaties. This part also contain standards and procedures concerning marketing of radio frequency devices, and for obtaining equipment authorization.

(d) *Part 13.* This part contains information and rules for the licensing of commercial radio operators.

(e) *Part 17.* This part contains requirements for construction, marking and lighting of antenna towers.

(f) *Part 21.* This part contains rules concerning point-to-point microwave service authority relating to communication common carriers.

(g) *Part 42.* This part contains rules concerning the preservation of records of communication common carriers.

(h) *Part 43.* This part contains rules concerning reports of communication common carriers.

(i) *Part 61.* This part contains tariff rules applicable to communication common carriers.

(j) *Part 62.* This part contains rules concerning interlocking directorates relating to communication common carriers.

(k) *Part 63.* This part contains rules concerning the extension of lines and discontinuance of service by communication common carriers.

(l) *Part 64.* This part contains miscellaneous rules relating to communication common carriers.

(m) *Part 68.* This part contains technical standards for connection of terminal equipment to the telephone network.

(n) *Part 87.* This part contains rules for the aviation services. Some maritime frequencies are authorized for use by aircraft stations for safety and distress, public correpondence and for operational communications.

(o) *Part 94.* This part contains rules concerning the private microwave service relating to point-to-point communication requirements.

[51 FR 31213, Sept. 2, 1986, as amended at 55 FR 20398, May 16, 1990]

§ 80.5 Definitions.

Alaska—public fixed station. A fixed station in Alaska which is open to public correspondence and is licensed by the Commission for radio communication with Alaska-Private fixed stations on paired channels.

FIGURE 6–4   *(continued)*

of Alcohol, Tobacco and Firearms) and subject entries (such as wine labeling or alcohol percentages allowed for beer). It is heavily cross-referenced, which facilitates faster and more accurate research. The index will cite the title and specific section of the title that is being referenced. However, the updates for *C.F.R.* must also be consulted for completeness. See Figure 6–5 for sample pages from the *C.F.R.* index.

The *C.F.R. Index and Finding Aids* also has a Parallel Table of Authorities and Rules. This table can be used only if the citation to a statute, presidential document, or regulation is known. By locating the citation to the authority in the table, you can find the coordinate *C.F.R.* reference.

As an alternative to the *C.F.R. Index and Finding Aids,* you could consult, if available, two commercial indexes to the *C.F.R.* Both are far more detailed and potentially more helpful than the *C.F.R.* volume. Martindale-Hubbell publishes a large four-volume set entitled *Code of Federal Regulations Index*, which is revised annually. It is updated with three quarterly softcover volumes, and the fourth release each year consists of the new annual set, which incorporates all supplement material for the year. The *Code of Federal Regulations Index* published annually since 1981 by Congressional Information Service is also a good alternative.

***C.F.R.* Updating Procedures**   The *C.F.R.* updating procedures are fairly complicated. You need to be very careful in researching in this set to ensure that you have the most current information available. The *C.F.R.* volumes are updated only once a year on a staggered basis. Consequently, any changes after publication of the latest *C.F.R.* update volume will be found in the *Federal Register* (see discussion earlier in this chapter) and noted in two *C.F.R.* coordinate publications: *LSA: List of CFR Sections Affected* and *CFR Parts Affected*.

LSA: List of CFR Sections Affected   All changes occurring after publication of the *C.F.R.* volume are noted in *LSA: List of CFR Sections Affected*. See Figure 6–6 for a sample of materials from this publication. This is a monthly publication that is cumulated once a year. There is, however, no single annual issue of *LSA*. The titles are cumulated in four separate "annuals" according to the following schedule:

Issue	*Cumulates Changes for Specific Titles*
December	Titles 1–16
March	Titles 17–27
June	Titles 28–41
September	Titles 42–50

For historical research, there are three sets of *LSA: List of CFR Sections Affected* volumes that compile the *C.F.R.* sections affected for their respective time periods. The period 1949–1963 is covered by one volume, and the periods 1964–1972 and 1973–1985 are each covered by two volumes.

CFR Index

Revised as of January 1, 1990

Published by
the Office of the Federal Register
National Archives and Records Administration

as a Special Edition of
the Federal Register

FIGURE 6–5   Sample pages from the *C.F.R.* index

Table of Contents

FIGURE 6–5 *(continued)*

LIST OF CFR TITLES, CHAPTERS, SUBCHAPTERS, AND PARTS

(Revised as of January 1, 1990)

TITLE 1—GENERAL PROVISIONS

Chapter I—Administrative Committee of the Federal Register (Parts 1—49)

SUBCHAPTER A—GENERAL

Part
1   Definitions.
2   General information.
3   Services to the public.

SUBCHAPTER B—THE FEDERAL REGISTER

5   General.
6   Indexes and ancillaries.

SUBCHAPTER C—SPECIAL EDITIONS OF THE FEDERAL REGISTER

8   Code of Federal Regulations.
9   United States Government Manual.
10   Presidential Papers.

SUBCHAPTER D—AVAILABILITY OF OFFICE OF THE FEDERAL REGISTER PUBLICATIONS

11   Subscriptions.
12   Official distribution within Federal government.

SUBCHAPTER E—PREPARATION, TRANSMITTAL, AND PROCESSING OF DOCUMENTS

15   Services to Federal agencies.
16   Agency representatives.
17   Filing for public inspection and publication schedules.
18   Preparation and transmittal of documents generally.
19   Executive orders and Presidential proclamations.
20   Handling of the United States Government Manual statements.
21   Preparation of documents subject to codification.
22   Preparation of notices and proposed rules.

Chapter II—Office of the Federal Register (Parts 50—299)

51   Incorporation by reference.
219   Flexible subsidy program for troubled projects.

Chapter III—Administrative Conference of the United States (Parts 300—399)

301   Organization and purpose.
302   Bylaws of the Administrative Conference of the United States.
303   Employee responsibilities and conduct.
304   Public availability of documents and records.
305   Recommendations of the Administrative Conference of the United States.
310   Miscellaneous statements.
315   Model rules for implementation of the Equal Access to Justice Act in agency proceedings.
316   Roster of dispute resolution neutrals.
326   Enforcement of nondiscrimination on the basis of handicap in programs or activities conducted by Administrative Conference of the United States.

FIGURE 6–5 *(continued)*

CFR INDEX

A

Accidents

See Safety

Accountants

Commodity Futures Trading Commission, rules relating to suspension or disbarment from appearance and practice, 17 CFR 14

Form and content of and requirements for financial statements, Securities Act of 1933, Securities Exchange Act of 1934, Public Utility Holding Company Act of 1935, Investment Company Act of 1940, and Energy Policy and Conservation Act of 1975, 17 CFR 210

Practice before Alcohol, Tobacco and Firearms Bureau, 31 CFR 8

Practice before Farm Credit Administration, 12 CFR 623

Practice before Internal Revenue Service, 31 CFR 10

Practice before Thrift Supervision Office, 12 CFR 513

Accounting

See also Uniform System of Accounts

Acquisition regulations, contract administration

Agriculture Department, 48 CFR 442

Commerce Department, 48 CFR 1342

Defense Department, 48 CFR 242

Energy Department, 48 CFR 942

Environmental Protection Agency, 48 CFR 1542

Justice Department, 48 CFR 2832

Labor Department, 48 CFR 2942

National Aeronautics and Space Administration, 48 CFR 1842

Transportation Department, 48 CFR 1242

Veterans Affairs Department, 48 CFR 842

Acquisition regulations, contract cost principles and procedures

Agency for International Development, 48 CFR 731

Commerce Department, 48 CFR 1331

Defense Department, 48 CFR 231

Energy Department, 48 CFR 931

Environmental Protection Agency, 48 CFR 1531

General Services Administration, 48 CFR 531

Justice Department, 48 CFR 2831

Labor Department, 48 CFR 2931

National Aeronautics and Space Administration, 48 CFR 1831

Transportation Department, 48 CFR 1231

Veterans Affairs Department, 48 CFR 831

Acquisition regulations, cost accounting standards

Agriculture Department, 48 CFR 430

Defense Department, 48 CFR 230

Environmental Protection Agency, 48 CFR 1530

General Services Administration, 48 CFR 530

Health and Human Services Department, 48 CFR 330

Justice Department, 48 CFR 2830

Labor Department, 48 CFR 2930

National Aeronautics and Space Administration, 48 CFR 1830

FIGURE 6–5 *(continued)*

1 U.S.C.	CFR
112	1 Part 2
112b	22 Part 181
113	1 Part 2
133	32 Part 151

2 U.S.C.	
136	36 Parts 701–703
431—432	11 Parts 100, 101, 104, 110, 114
431	11 Part 109
432—433	11 Part 102
432	11 Parts 103, 105, 110, 113
434	11 Parts 104, 108, 109
437	11 Part 107
437d	11 Parts 100, 101, 110, 111, 114, 115
437f—437g	11 Part 5
437g	11 Part 111
438	11 Parts 5, 100–105, 108–115
439	11 Part 108
439a	11 Part 113
441a—441b	11 Part 110
441a	11 Parts 106, 113
441b	11 Part 114
441d—441i	11 Part 110
441d	11 Parts 102, 109
441i	34 Part 73
451	14 Part 374a
	47 Part 64
453	11 Part 108

3 U.S.C.	
202	22 Part 2a
	31 Parts 13, 409
208	22 Part 2a
	31 Part 13
301	32 Parts 40, 719
	35 Part 3

5 U.S.C.	
App	10 Part 7
4a	17 Part 145
10	17 Part 10
22	32 Parts 157, 238, 718
73	34 Part 73
132 note	36 Parts 401, 402
133	32 Part 257
201 et seq	29 Part 100
301	7 Parts 2003, 3017
	37 Parts 15, 15a
302—305	18 Part 388
483a	22 Part 22
500 et seq	18 Part 1
500	29 Parts 103, 580
	31 Parts 8, 10
	37 Parts 1, 2, 10
501	28 Part 9
	41 Part 114-52
503	29 Part 580
504	1 Part 315
	5 Part 2430
	7 Part 1
	12 Parts 308, 509b, 747
	13 Part 132
	14 Parts 14, 373, 1262
	15 Part 18

5 U.S.C.—Continued	CFR
	16 Parts 3, 1025
	17 Parts 148, 201
	19 Part 212
	21 Parts 5, 12
	22 Part 134
	24 Part 14
	28 Part 24
	29 Parts 16, 102, 2204, 2704
	31 Part 6
	32 Part 155
	34 Part 21
	39 Part 960
	40 Part 17
	43 Part 4
	45 Part 13
	46 Part 502
	47 Part 1
	49 Parts 826, 1016
504 note	13 Part 132
	21 Part 12
522	1 Part 456
	7 Parts 600, 2810, 3011
	8 Part 103
	39 Part 601
	49 Part 1244
551 et seq	14 Parts 201, 211, 302
	16 Part 1025
	18 Parts 281, 286
	29 Part 1910
	40 Part 124
	43 Parts 4, 2650
551—559	31 Parts 8, 10
551—558	21 Parts 10, 12, 13
551—557	18 Parts 3, 6, 8, 154, 375, 382, 385, 388
551	17 Part 10
	28 Part 540
	29 Part 580
	44 Part 1
	46 Part 502
	49 Part 1003
552—556	29 Part 98
552—552a	48 Part 2424
552	1 Parts 51, 301, 302, 304
	4 Part 303
	5 Parts 293, 294, 300, 511, 532, 536, 736, 1204, 1260, 1303, 1631, 1703, 1820, 2411, 2502
	7 Parts 1, 295, 370, 412, 510, 600, 661, 798, 900, 1520, 1701, 2003, 2018, 2101, 2200, 2507, 2610, 2620, 2700, 2710, 2902, 2903, 3010, 3305, 3403, 3600, 3601, 3700, 3701, 3800, 3801, 3900, 3901, 4000, 4001, 4100
	8 Parts 103, 343c
	9 Parts 165, 110, 204, 390
	10 Parts 0-2, 9, 110, 202, 861, 1004, 1500, 1502, 1504, 1534
	11 Part 4
	12 Parts 4,

FIGURE 6–5   *(continued)*

LSA

List of CFR Sections Affected

June 1995

Save this issue for Titles 28–41 (Annual)

Title 1–16
Changes January 3, 1995
through June 30, 1995

Title 17–27
Changes April 3, 1995
through June 30, 1995

Title 28–41
Changes July 1, 1994
through June 30, 1995

Title 42–50
Changes October 3, 1994
through June 30, 1995

FIGURE 6–6 Sample pages from *LSA: List of CFR Sections Affected*

LSA—LIST OF CFR SECTIONS AFFECTED

The LSA (List of CFR Sections Affected) is a monthly publication designed to lead users of the Code of Federal Regulations (CFR) to amendatory actions published in the Federal Register (FR). It should be shelved with current CFR volumes. Entries are by CFR title, chapter, part, and section. Proposed rules are listed at the end of appropriate titles.

HOW TO USE THIS FINDING AID

The CFR is revised annually according to the following schedule:

Titles 1–16—as of Jan. 1
17–27—as of April 1
28–41—as of July 1
42–50—as of Oct. 1

To bring these regulations up to date, consult the most recent LSA for any changes, additions, or removals published after the revision date of the volume you are using. Then check the CUMULATIVE LIST OF PARTS AFFECTED appearing in the Reader Aids of the latest Federal Register for less detailed but timely changes published after the final date included in this publication.

The page numbers listed to the right of each LSA entry indicate where the specific amendments begin in the Federal Register. **Boldface** page numbers under a particular title indicate that the page numbers span 2 years. **Boldface** is used to distinguish the previous year from the current year.

Cite a page reference from this publication using the volume number (i.e. 60 FR for 1995) and the page number. Example: 24727 cite as 60 FR 24727. For your convenience, the volume number has been included in the Table of Federal Register Issue Pages and Dates.

ISSUES TO BE SAVED

There is no single annual issue of the LSA. Four ANNUAL ISSUES must be saved: the DECEMBER issue is the ANNUAL for Titles 1–16; the MARCH issue is the ANNUAL for Titles 17–27; the JUNE issue is the ANNUAL for Titles 28–41; the SEPTEMBER issue is the ANNUAL for Titles 42–50. ANNUAL ISSUES to be saved are clearly designated on the cover.

PARALLEL TABLE OF AUTHORITIES AND RULES

Following Title 50 is an update to Parallel Table of Authorities and Rules found in the CFR Index and Finding Aids. This table contains authority citations added to or removed from the Parallel Table of Authority and Rules as a result of documents published in the Federal Register since January 1, 1995.

TABLE OF FEDERAL REGISTER ISSUE PAGES AND DATES

A table is included at the end of this publication which identifies the volume number, the inclusive page numbers, and the corresponding Federal Register issue dates for the period covered.

INDEXES

An INDEX to the daily Federal Register is published monthly and is cumulated for 12 months. A separate volume, the CFR Index and Finding Aids to the entire Code of Federal Regulations, is revised as of January 1 each year.

INQUIRIES AND SUGGESTIONS

Rob Sheehan was Chief Editor of the LSA. The LSA was prepared under the direction of Richard L. Claypoole, assisted by Maxine L. Hill. INQUIRIES, telephone 202–523–5227.

FIGURE 6–6 *(continued)*

100 LSA—LIST OF CFR SECTIONS AFFECTED

CHANGES JULY 1, 1994 THROUGH JUNE 30, 1995

TITLE 36 Chapter II—Con.

292.40—292.48 (Subpart F) Revised 36882
296 Authority citation revised 5260
296.1 (a) amended 5260
296.3 (a)(6) added; (i) revised............5260
296.4 Heading and (a) revised; (c) added 5260
296.7 (b)(4) added 5260, 5261
296.13 (e) added 5260, 5261
296.19 Revised 5260, 5261
296.20 Added 5260, 5261
296.21 Added 5260, 5261

Chapter VII—Library of Congress (Parts 700—799)

701 Authority citation revised **55811**
701.35 Revised **55812**
704 Authority citation revised **35034**
704.23 Added **35034**
704.24 Added **35035**
704.30 (Subpart B) Removed **35035**
705 Added......................................**38367**

Chapter XII—National Archives and Records Administration (Parts 1200—1299)

1207.36 (d), (g), (h) and (i) revised 19639, 19643
1209.100 Revised; eff. 8–25–95...........33040, 33058
1209.105 Amended; eff. 8–25–95 ....33041, 33058
1209.110 (c) revised; eff. 8–25–95.......33041, 33058
1209.200 Revised; eff. 8–25–95...........33041, 33058
1209.215 Revised; eff. 8–25–95...........33041, 33058
1209.220 Revised; eff. 8–25–95...........33041, 33058
1209.225 Revised; eff. 8–25–95...........33041, 33058
1209 Appendixes A and B revised; eff. 8–25–95 ....33042, 33058
1230 Heading revised 13908
1230.12 (d)(1)(i) amended 13908
1236 Revised 29990
1258.2 (c)(1) through (5) revised; interim 5580
Regulation at 60 FR 5580 confirmed..................................26828
1258.12 (b) removed; interim............5580
Regulation at 60 FR 5580 confirmed..................................26828

Chapter XIV—Assassination Records Review Board (Parts 1400—1499)

Chapter XIV Established................33349

Proposed Rules:

1—199 (Ch. I) 36108
7 37734
 ....4394, 13662, 26857
13 58804
 ....19013, 20374, 29523, 29532
14 39228
36 38149
68 3599
215 18886
217 18886
219 18886
242 45924
 ....6466, 24601
292 32633
701 48580
26392
702 48193
800 ....50396, 61859
86
1191 48542
1207 53706
1209 65607
1400—1499 (Ch. XIV) 32930
1400 7506
1410 34193

TITLE 37—PATENTS, TRADEMARKS, AND COPYRIGHTS

Chapter I—Patent and Trademark Office, Department of Commerce (Parts 1—199)

1 Technical correction **45757**
  Authority citation revised 14518
  Technical correction 16920, 27598
1.1 (i) added 20220
1.9 (a) revised...............................20220
1.11 (e) revised 14518
1.12 (c) revised 20221
1.14 (e) revised 20221
1.16 (a), (b), (d) and (f) through (i) revised 43740
  (a) through (g) revised; (k) and (l) added 20221
1.17 (b) through (g), (j) and (m) through (p) revised....................43740
  (h) and (i) revised; (q), (r) and (s) added 20221

NOTE: **Boldface page numbers indicate 1994 changes.**

FIGURE 6–6 *(continued)*

JUNE 1995 101

CHANGES JULY 1, 1994 THROUGH JUNE 30, 1995

1.18 Revised...**43741**
1.20 (c), (e), (f), (g), (i)(1) and (j)
   revised **43741**
   (j) revised; eff. 7–11–95.................25618
1.21 (p) removed.................................**43741**
   (l) revised 20222
1.28 (a) revised 20222
1.45 (c) revised 20222
1.48 Revised 20222
1.51 (a) and (b) revised 20222
1.53 Heading and (a) through (e)
   revised...20223
1.55 Revised 20224
1.59 Revised 20224
1.60 Heading and (b) revised............20224
1.62 (a) and (e) revised 20225
1.63 (a) revised 20225
1.67 (b) revised 20225
1.78 (a)(1) and (2) revised; (a)(3)
   and (4) added 20225
1.83 (a) and (c) revised 20226
1.97 (d) revised 20226
1.101 (a) revised 20226
1.102 (d) revised...............................20226
1.103 (a) revised...............................20226
1.129 Undesignated center head-
   ing and section added...............20226
1.131 (a) revised...............................21044
1.137 (c) revised...............................20227
1.139 Added.....................................20227
1.177 Revised....................................20227
1.192 (c)(1) through (7) redesig-
   nated as (c)(3) through (9);
   (a), (c) introductory text,
   new (7), new (8) introductory
   text, new (v) and (d) revised;
   new (c)(1) and new (2) added
  14518
1.312 (b) revised...............................20227
1.313 (a) revised...............................20227
1.314 Revised....................................20227
1.316 (d) revised...............................20228
1.317 (d) removed 20228
1.412 (c)(6) added 21439
1.421 (a) revised...............................21440
1.445 (a) revised...............................**43741**
   (a)(5) added 21440
1.482 (a)(1) and (2)(ii) revised...........**43741**
1.492 (a)(1) through (5), (b) and
   (d) revised...................................**43742**
   (a)(5) correctly revised **47082**
1.601 (f), (g), (j) through (n) and
   (q) revised; (r) and (s) added
  14519
1.602 (c) revised...............................14519
1.603 Revised....................................14519

1.604 (a)(1) revised...........................14519
1.605 (a) revised...............................14519
1.606 Revised....................................14520
1.607 (a)(4) revised; (a)(6) added
  14520
1.608 Revised....................................14520
1.609 (b)(1), (2) and (3) revised 14520
1.610 Revised....................................14520
1.611 (b), (c)(6), (7) and (d) re-
   vised; (c)(8) redesignated as
   (c)(9); new (c)(8) added...............14521
1.612 (a) revised...............................14521
1.613 (c) and (d) revised...................14521
1.614 (a) and (c) revised....................14521
1.615 Revised....................................14521
1.616 Revised....................................14521
1.617 (a), (b), (d), (e), (g) and (h)
   revised...14522
1.618 (a) revised...............................14522
1.621 (b) revised...............................14522
1.622 (b) revised...............................14522
1.623 Heading and (a) introduc-
   tory text revised 14522
1.624 Heading, (a) and (c) revised
  14523
1.625 (a) introductory text re-
   vised...14523
1.626 Revised....................................14523
1.627 (b) revised...............................14523
1.628 Revised....................................14523
1.629 (a), (c)(1) and (d) revised.........14523
1.630 Revised....................................14524
1.631 (a) revised...............................14524
1.632 Revised....................................14524
1.633 (a), (b), (f), (g) and (i) re-
   vised 14524
1.636 Revised....................................14524
1.637 (a), (b), (c)(1)(v), (vi), (2)(ii),
   (iii), (3)(ii), (4)(ii), (d) introductory text, (e)(1)(viii),
   (2)(vii), (f)(2) and (h)(4) revised; (c)(1)(vii), (e)(1)(ix)
   and (2)(viii) added; (c)(2)(iv),
   (3)(iii) and (d)(4) removed.........14524
1.638 Revised....................................14525
1.639 (a), (b), (c) and (d)(1) revised
  14525
1.640 (a), (b), (c), (d) introductory
   text, (1), (3) and (e) revised
  14525
1.641 Revised....................................14526
1.642 Revised....................................14526
1.643 (b) revised...............................14527
1.644 (a) introductory text, (1),
   (2), (b), (c), (d), (f) and (g) re-
   vised 14527

NOTE: **Boldface page numbers indicate 1994 changes.**

FIGURE 6–6 *(continued)*

102   LSA—LIST OF CFR SECTIONS AFFECTED

CHANGES JULY 1, 1994 THROUGH JUNE 30, 1995

TITLE 37 Chapter I—Con.

1.645 (a), (b) and (d) revised 14527
1.646 (c)(5) redesignated as (c)(6); (a)(1), (2), (b), (c) introductory text, (1), (4), new (6), (d) and (e) revised; new (c)(5) added 14527
1.647 Revised 14528
1.651 (a), (c)(1), (2), (3) and (d) revised 14528
1.652 Revised 14528
1.653 (a), (b), (c) introductory text, (1), (4), (d), (g) and (i) revised; (c)(5), (f) and (h) removed 14528
1.654 (a) and (d) revised 14529
1.655 Revised 14529
1.656 (b)(1) through (6) redesignated as (b)(3) through (8); (a), new (b)(5), new (6), (d), (e), (g), (h) and (i) revised; new (b)(1) and (2) added 14529
1.657 Revised 14530
1.658 (a) and (b) revised 14530
1.660 (e) added 14530
1.662 (a) and (b) revised 14530
1.664 Revised 14530
1.666 (b) revised 20228
1.671 (h) redesignated as (i); (a) introductory text, (c)(1), (2), (6), (7), (e), (f), (g) and new (i) revised; new (h) and (j) added 14530
1.672 Revised 14531
1.673 (a), (b) introductory text, (c), (d), (e) and (g) revised........14532
1.674 (a) revised 14533
1.675 (d) revised 14533
1.676 (a)(4) revised 14533
1.677 Revised 14533
1.678 Revised 14533
1.679 Revised 14533
1.682 Revised 14533
1.683 Revised 14534
1.684 Removed 14534
1.685 (d) and (e) revised 14534
1.687 (c) revised 14535
1.688 Revised 14535
1.690 (a), (b) and (c) revised............14535
1.701 Added 20228
1.750 Revised; eff. 7-11-95 25618
1.760 Heading revised; eff. 7-11-95 25618
1.765 (a) revised; eff. 7-11-95 25618
1.780 Revised; eff. 7-11-95 25618
1.785 Revised; eff. 7-11-95 25618
1.790 Added; eff. 7-11-95 25619

1.791 Added; eff. 7-11-95....................25619
3.21 Revised 20228
3.81 (b) revised 20229
10.9 (c) revised 21440

Chapter II—Copyright Office, Library of Congress (Parts 200—299)

201 Authority citation revised 38371, 67635
    Authority citation revised 25998, 34168
    Technical correction 28019
201.1 (b) amended 34168
201.5 (b)(2)(iv) and (c)(1)(iii) amended 34168
201.6 (c) amended; interim...............38371
201.7 (c)(4)(ii) amended 34168
201.10 (d)(1) and (3) amended 34168
201.11 Amended 67635
    (f), (g)(3)(iii)(B), (v) and (vi) amended 34168
201.15 (c) amended........................34168
201.16 Removed 34168
201.17 (a), (b)(2), (5), (h)(1)(i), (iii), (2)(i), (3)(iii)(A) and (9) amended 67635
    (k) revised 67636
    (b)(2)(A) and (B) redesignated as (b)(2)(i) and (ii); (c)(1), (g) introductory text, (h)(4)(iii) and (8) amended................34168
201.26 (b)(2) amended......................34168
201.29 Added................................25998
201.31 (d)(2) revised; (d)(3) and (4) redesignated as (d)(6) and (7); new (d)(3), new (4) and (5) added..58789
201.32 Added; interim 38371
202 Policy decision 21983
    Authority citation revised 34168
202.2 (b)(1) amended 34168
202.3 (b)(3)(ii) amended; (b)(8) redesignated as (b)(9); new (b)(8) added; (c)(2) Footnote 6 revised..................................15875
    (b)(5)(i)(D) amended..................34168
202.18 Removed 34168
202.19 (b)(1)(ii), (iii)(B) and (e)(3) amended 34168
202.20 (b)(2)(iii) amended.................34168
202.22 (d)(6)(iii) amended.................34168
202.23 (e)(1) and (2) amended 34168
202 Appendix A amended 34168
203 Authority citation revised........34168
203.3 Revised 34168

NOTE: Boldface page numbers indicate 1994 changes.

FIGURE 6–6   *(continued)*

Also published in *LSA* are tables that cite the *U.S.C.* sections relied upon to promulgate a rule or regulation. The *U.S.C.* references are cited opposite the *C.F.R.* section. These tables are published monthly. (See Figure 6–7.)

CFR Parts Affected *LSA*, as previously discussed, is the monthly publication of changes in the *Code of Federal Regulations*. On a daily basis, a section entitled CFR Parts Affected in This Issue appears toward the front of the *Federal Register*. Also on a daily basis, the CFR Parts Affected is cumulated into a monthly table (for example, CFR Parts Affected During March) that appears in the Reader Aids section at the back of each issue of the *Federal Register*.

Accordingly, the most recent issue of the *Federal Register* in the month subsequent to the last month for which the *LSA* pamphlet has been issued must be consulted to ensure thorough research through this method. If the "lag time" since the last *LSA* volume is more than one month, you need to consult the end-of-the-month compilation in the *Federal Register* for the missing months.

Agency Adjudications

Finding Agency Decisions

From the authority delegated to them by Congress, federal administrative agencies have the power not only to promulgate rules and regulations but also to enforce them through adjudicatory proceedings that are similar to court proceedings. For example, the Environmental Protection Agency, which is authorized to regulate chemical waste disposal, is empowered to hear charges that its regulations have been violated and to issue decisions on those charges.

Agency adjudicatory decisions are released to the public in several ways. Over thirty federal agencies release slip opinions or advance sheets of decisions. Information offices of the agencies normally distribute these materials to interested attorneys, news organizations, and publishers and make them available to the public by request. A list of the agencies that are official publishers of administrative decisions appears in Figure 6–8.

Agency decisions can be difficult to monitor as they are normally issued in a random manner. They may, however, be located in the *Official Publications of Federal Administrative Agencies* published by the Government Printing Office. Unfortunately, although indexed by subject, this publication is not well organized, nor is it produced systematically.

Better sources for finding agency decisions are the unofficial publications of commercial publishers such as the Bureau of National Affairs (BNA), Commerce Clearing House (CCH), and Prentice-Hall. These publications are usually in looseleaf form. See Chapter 12 for a full discussion

PARALLEL TABLE OF AUTHORITIES AND RULES   175
Additions to Table I, January through March 1989

This table lists the sections of the U.S. Code, U.S. Statutes at Large, Public Laws, and Presidential documents which are being added to Table I as a result of authority citations carried in the **Federal Register** during January through March 1989. Recent legislation is carried by public law number.

Table I is in the CFR Index and Finding Aids revised as of January 1, 1988. Additions during 1988 are in the December 1988 LSA (List of CFR Sections Affected).

In order to determine the **Federal Register** page number of a parallel CFR citation, consult this LSA and the appropriate Annual Issue of the LSA for that CFR title.

U.S. Code:	CFR	5 U.S.C.—Con.	CFR
2 U.S.C.:		3395	5 Part 317
441i	34 Part 73	3397	5 Part 317
5 U.S.C.:		3701	29 Part 100
73	34 Part 73	4111	34 Part 73
201 et seq	29 Part 100	5112	5 Part 339
301	7 Parts 2003, 3017	5333—5334	5 Part 531
	37 Parts 15, 15a	5336	5 Part 531
302—305	18 Part 388	5383	5 Part 534
551—557	18 Parts 375, 388	5511—5512	32 Part 527
552—556	29 Part 98	5512	40 Part 13
552—552a	48 Part 2424	5514	20 Part 361
552	7 Parts 2902,		40 Part 13
	2903, 3403, 3700, 3701, 3800,		41 Part 105–56
	3801, 4000, 4001, 4100		47 Part 1
	10 Part 2		49 Part 92
	16 Part 456	5569—5570	22 Part 19
	28 Part 701	5734	41 Part 101–7
	32 Parts 285, 298b	6332	5 Part 630
	38 Part 1	7201	5 Part 300
	39 Part 946	7204	5 Part 300
552a	5 Part 1001	7301	31 Part 0
	22 Part 1507	7342	34 Part 73
	40 Part 13	7351	34 Part 73
552b	5 Part 1632	7701 et seq	5 Parts 300, 330
	12 Part 791	8151	5 Part 330
553	16 Part 305	8439	5 Part 1645
	21 Parts 338, 340, 349, 640	8461	5 Part 844
	46 Parts 571, 588	8474	5 Parts 1620,
	49 Parts 1004, 1035, 1071, 1185,		1632, 1633, 1645
	1314	8477	29 Parts 2584, 2585
608c	7 Part 1	App. 2	34 Part 33
702—704	21 Part 640	App. 4	5 Part 1633
1101 note	5 Part 950	App. 207	10 Part 1010
1103	5 Part 300	5 U.S.C. App.:	
1201 et seq	5 Part 1200	4—5	34 Part 73
1302	5 Part 300	7 U.S.C.:	
2301—2302	5 Part 300	4a	17 Part 12
2621	7 Part 1	61	7 Part 1
2714	7 Part 1	87e	7 Part 1
3101	28 Part 0	136 et seq	40 Part 31
3103	28 Part 0	136—136y	40 Parts 16, 153, 156, 158,
3302	5 Part 339		166, 168
3324	5 Part 300	136	40 Parts 22, 167
3392—3393	5 Part 317		

FIGURE 6–7   Example of parallel table of authorities from *LSA*

176

PARALLEL TABLE

7 U.S.C.—Con.	CFR
136w	40 Part 2
150bb	7 Part 301
161—162	7 Part 318
164a	7 Part 318
167	7 Part 318
394	9 Part 391
511b	7 Part 29
601—674	7 Parts 955, 998
612 note	7 Part 250
901 et seq	7 Parts 1709, 1754, 1762, 1763
901—950b	7 Part 1710
941 et seq	7 Part 1610
1308 et seq	7 Parts 1497, 1498
1308—1308a	7 Part 1413
1309	7 Part 1413
1360	19 Part 12
1413e	7 Part 726
1421	7 Parts 1413, 1425
1421 note	7 Part 1478
1423	7 Part 1413
1425	7 Part 1470
1431e	7 Part 250
1441-1	7 Parts 1413, 1421, 1470
1444	7 Part 1425
1444-1	7 Parts 1413, 1470
1444b	7 Parts 1413, 1421, 1470
1444b-2—1444b-4	7 Part 1470
1445b-2—1445b-4	7 Part 1413
1445b-2	7 Part 1421
1445c-2	7 Parts 729, 1421
1445d	7 Parts 1413, 1470
1445e	7 Part 1421
1445h	7 Part 1413
1461—1469	7 Parts 719, 1413
1471d note	7 Part 1479
1506	7 Parts 455, 456
1516	7 Parts 455, 456
1621 et seq	7 Part 68
1622	7 Part 27
	9 Part 391
1624	9 Part 391
1921 et seq	7 Parts 1762, 1763, 1754
1932 note	7 Part 1948
1989	7 Part 1946
2908	7 Part 1
3701 et seq	21 Part 5
4610	7 Part 1
4736	7 Part 27
4815	7 Part 1
4901—4916	7 Part 1210
4910	7 Part 1
8 U.S.C.:	
1101	8 Part 216
1101 note	8 Part 245a
	22 Part 44
1102	8 Part 212

8 U.S.C.—Con.	CFR
1103	8 Parts 210, 216, 217, 245a, 271, 286
	28 Part 44
1104	22 Part 44
1151	8 Part 245
1153	8 Part 245
	22 Part 44
1153 note	22 Part 44
1154	8 Part 216
1160—1161	29 Part 502
1160	8 Part 210
1161	29 Part 500
1182	8 Part 204
1184	8 Part 216
1186a	8 Parts 204, 205, 211, 214, 216, 223, 223a, 242, 245
1187	8 Parts 212, 214, 217, 236, 248
1251	8 Part 242
1255	8 Part 204
1255a	8 Part 245a
1255a note	8 Part 245a
1257	8 Part 245
1321	8 Part 271
1356	8 Part 286
1360	20 Part 422
10 U.S.C.:	
113	32 Parts 58, 95, 146, 191, 278, 356, 391
113 note	32 Part 105
131	32 Part 389
133	32 Parts 358, 374, 390, 390a
134	32 Part 385
135	32 Part 351
136	32 Parts 366, 383, 386, 387
137	32 Part 352
191—193	32 Parts 359, 360, 362
192	32 Part 388
814	32 Part 146
982	32 Part 144
1041	32 Part 887
1076a	32 Part 199
2131—2135	38 Part 21
2202	32 Part 173
	48 Parts 271, 5215
2301 et seq	48 Part 39
2304 note	48 Part 1246
2305	32 Part 838
2665	32 Part 265
2667	32 Parts 265, 863
2671	32 Part 265
3012	33 Part 245
7420	15 Part 777
7430	15 Part 777
8013	32 Parts 818, 855, 884
12 U.S.C.:	
1 et seq	12 Part 34
36	12 Part 208

FIGURE 6–7 *(continued)*

188   **PARALLEL TABLE OF AUTHORITIES AND RULES**

Removals from Table I, January through March 1989

This table lists the sections of the U.S. Code, U.S. Statutes at Large, Public Laws, and Presidential documents which are being removed from Table I as a result of documents published in the **Federal Register** during January through March 1989.

Table I is in the CFR Index and Finding Aids revised as of January 1, 1988. Removals during 1988 are in the December 1988 LSA (List of CFR Sections Affected).

In order to determine the **Federal Register** page number of a parallel CFR citation, consult this LSA and the appropriate Annual Issue of the LSA for that CFR title.

U.S. Code:	CFR	7 U.S.C.—Con.	CFR
2 U.S.C.:		1444-1	7 Parts 713, 770
441i	14 Part 1207	1444b	7 Parts 713, 770
5 U.S.C.:		1444b-2—1444b-4	7 Part 770
105	34 Part 31	1445b-2—1445b-4	7 Part 713
551	29 Part 101	1445d	7 Parts 713, 770
552	27 Parts 25, 250, 270, 275, 285, 290	1445h	7 Part 713
	30 Part 212	1446	7 Part 1425
	46 Part 162	1461—1469	7 Part 713
	49 Part 1004	1838	7 Part 719
552a	27 Part 70	2243	8 Part 103
552b	12 Part 790	2321 et seq	7 Part 180
553	20 Part 615	2372	7 Part 180
	47 Part 22	8 U.S.C.:	
	49 Part 1042, 1312	1101	8 Part 214
559	49 Part 1181		34 Part 603
1101 et seq	5 Part 1200	1101 note	8 Parts 210, 245a
1104	5 Part 300	1103	8 Part 233
1205	5 Part 1204	1159	8 Part 245
1211—1214	16 Part 1031	1181	8 Part 245
5405	5 Part 531	1184	8 Part 245
7151	5 Part 300	1186a	8 Parts 214, 235
7154	5 Part 300	1187	8 Part 214
7 U.S.C.:		1192	8 Part 204
136a	40 Part 162	1223	8 Parts 233, 235
136d	40 Part 162	1295	8 Part 204
136e	40 Part 167	1301—1302	8 Part 103
136q	40 Part 162	1321	8 Part 280
136s	40 Part 162	1351	8 Part 103
136v	40 Part 2	1362	8 Part 235
136w	40 Part 167	1434	8 Part 337
151—167	7 Part 318	1443	8 Part 103
428a	36 Part 251	1454	8 Part 103
450 et seq	9 Part 381	10 U.S.C.:	
601—674	7 Parts 1125, 1136	125	32 Part 366
931 et seq	7 Part 1610	131 et seq	32 Parts 359, 360, 362
1281 note	7 Part 719	133	32 Parts 191, 356
1305	7 Part 719	136	32 Parts 351b, 351c
1308—1308a	7 Part 713	2671	32 Part 232
1309	7 Parts 713, 719	7420	15 Part 377
1314c	7 Part 726	7430	15 Part 377
1421	7 Part 713	8012	32 Parts 818, 855, 884, 887
1423	7 Part 713	12 U.S.C.:	
1425	7 Part 770	1 et seq	12 Parts 1, 3, 18, 29, 30
1441 note	7 Part 719	93a	12 Parts 29, 30
1441-1	7 Parts 713, 770		

FIGURE 6–7 *(continued)*

AGENCY	OFFICIAL REPORTER OF ADMINISTRATIVE DECISION
Civil Aeronautics Board	Civil Aeronautics Board Reports
Consumer Product Safety Commission	Available on written request from Commission
Energy Department	Available for inspection and photocopying at DOE Public Docket Room, Washington, D.C.
Environmental Protection Agency	Formal adjudications in federal district
Federal Communications Commission	Federal Communications Commission Reports
Federal Energy Regulatory Commission	Federal Power Commission Reports (predecessor agency)
Federal Labor Relations Authority	Decisions of the Federal Labor Relations Authority
Federal Reserve System	Federal Reserve Bulletin; Federal Reserve Regulatory Service
Federal Service Impasses Panel (FLRA)	Federal Service Impasses Panel Releases
Federal Trade Commission	FTC Decisions
Immigration and Naturalization Service	Administrative Decisions under Immigration and Nationality Laws of the United States
Interstate Commerce Commission	ICC Reports
Mine Safety & Health Administration (Department of Labor)	Federal Mine Safety & Health Review Commission (an independent adjudicatory agency) Decisions 1979 to date.
National Labor Relations Board	Decisions and Orders of the NLRB
Nuclear Regulatory Commission	AEC Reports; Nuclear Regulatory Commission Issuances
Occupational Safety and Health Administration	Citations issued by OSHA. Appellate review by Occupational Safety and Health Review Commission. Administrative Law Judge and Comm. Decisions 1971 to date.
Securities and Exchange Commission	SEC Decisions and Reports
Social Security Administration (H.H.S.)	Social Security Rulings: On Federal Old-Age, Survivors Disability; Supplemental Security Income and Black Lung Benefits

FIGURE 6–8   Agencies that are official reporters of administrative decisions

of looseleaf services, including detailed information on how to use the services of the major publishers of these materials.

The commercial looseleaf publications of agency decisions are usually compiled by subjects, such as tax law, labor law, and insurance law. The looseleaf services, therefore, can provide quick access to decisions, particularly through their specialized and cumulative indexes. Figure 6–9 lists some looseleaf services that are unofficial reporters of administrative law decisions.

AGENCY	UNOFFICIAL REPORTER OF ADMINISTRATIVE DECISION
Civil Aeronautics Board	CCH Aviation Law Reporter (includes National Transportation Safety Board
Commodity Futures Trading Commission	CCH Commodity Futures Law Reporter
Consumer Product Safety Commission	CCH Consumer Product Safety Guide (digests)
Economic Regulatory Administration (DOE)	CCH Energy Management Vol. 6
Energy Department	Office of Hearings and Appeals Decisions and order (full texts and digest in Energy Management, Volume 7
Environmental Protection Agency	Chemical Regulation Reporter, Environment Reporter, ELI Environmental Law Reporter
Equal Employment Opportunity Commission	CCH Employment Practices Guide; CCH EEOC Decisions (1968-73); Fair Employment Practice Service of BNA Labor Relations Reporter (digests)
Federal Communications Commission	Pike & Fischer Radio Regulation; WESTLAW 1975 to date; LEXIS, 1965 to date.
Federal Energy Regulatory Commission	CCH Utilities Law Reports; LEXIS, 1977 to date.
Federal Reserve System	CCH Federal Banking Law Reporter
Federal Trade Commission	CCH Trade Regulation Reporter; LEXIS and WESTLAW
Food and Drug Administration	CCH Medical Services Reporter; Food, Drug, Cosmetic Reporter
Immigration and Naturalization Service	American Council for Nationalities Service Interpreter Releases (selected digests)
Interstate Commerce Commission (Department of Labor)	Federal Carriers Reporter, digests or full text (selected). Older cases cumulated in CCH Federal Carrier Cases.
National Labor Relations Board	CCH Labor Law Reporter, Vol. 5 (digests); Labor Management Relations binder (#2 of BNA Labor Relations Reporter); WESTLAW and LEXIS, 1972 to date. Older decisions cumulated in Labor Relations Reference Manual.
Nuclear Regulatory Commission	CCH Nuclear Regulation Reporter; LEXIS, beginning 1983.
Occupational Safety and Health Administration	CCH Employment Safety and Health Guide (selected full texts or digests, current) CCH Occupational Safety & Health Decisions, 1971 to date. WESTLAW 1971 to date.
Securities and Exchange Commission	CCH Federal Securities Law Reporter; P-H Securities Regulation Guide, digest or full text (selected), WESTLAW and LEXIS (selected) 1933 to date.

FIGURE 6–9   Looseleaf services that publish unofficial reports of administrative decisions

One unofficial publication of administrative decisions is Pike and Fischer's *Administrative Law Reporter Second,* published by Callaghan. This service indexes and reproduces decisions of most of the agencies. The decisions are arranged by subject. They are first published in a looseleaf format and later in bound volumes.

Judicial Review of Agency Decisions

Many agency decisions are subject to judicial review by a federal court. The specific court (federal district or federal court of appeals) with the power to review agency decisions is usually designated in the enabling act that established the agency. Since the designated court can vary and there is no pattern to the designations, you should review the statute if you are asked to address the issue of what court is the proper one with which to file an appeal of an agency decision.

Courts, however, have a relatively limited role in supervising agency conduct. Most courts take a "hands off" approach toward the agencies. When a court does review an agency decision, the court opinion may be important for the legal standards that are set. By using the appropriate finding tools discussed in later chapters, such as the digests, encyclopedias, treatises, and looseleaf services, judicial decisions on matters of administrative law may be located.

§ 6.3 Presidential Documents

The president has the power to issue **proclamations** and **executive orders**. A proclamation is a presidential action that generally has no legal effect. On the other hand, an executive order is used to direct officials or agencies to perform an act or refrain from an act. An executive order has legal effect. Presidential documents are published in a number of sources.

Since 1979, presidential documents have been compiled in a single publication known as the *Codification of Presidential Proclamations and Executive Orders*. This publication is arranged in fifty titles corresponding to the *Code of Federal Regulations*. Although first published in 1979, this

---

TERMS

proclamations†   Official announcements by the government.

executive orders†   Orders issued by the chief executive officer (e.g., the president of the United States; the governor of a state; the mayor of a city) of government, whether national, state, or local.

publication includes proclamations and executive orders dating back to 1961.

Title 3 of the *Code of Federal Regulations*, entitled "The President," issued annually since 1976 and dating back to 1936 with multi-year volumes, contains a full-text compilation of presidential documents and a codification of regulations issued by the Executive Office. (See Figure 6–10.) Presidential documents included are those that were required to be published in the *Federal Register*. Chapter 1, which contains regulations, is a true codification like other *C.F.R.* volumes in that its contents are organized by subject or regulatory area and are updated by individual issues of the *Federal Register*.

The Office of the Federal Register, which is a part of the National Archives and Records Administration, publishes White House materials weekly in the *Weekly Compilation of Presidential Documents*. This publication contains statements, messages, executive orders, proclamations, and other presidential materials released during the preceding week. Indexes provide subject access to these documents.

Another important source of presidential information is *Public Papers of the Presidents*. Published annually since Herbert Hoover was in office, many presidential speeches, public letters, and news conferences are accumulated in this publication. Access to those volumes is through indexes contained in each volume.

§ 6.4 State Agency Research

In General

State administrative practices and procedures vary. Many states have a statute similar to the federal Administrative Procedure Act and a publication similar to the *Federal Register*. In other states, agencies issue rules, regulations, and decisions directly, without publication in a specified general source. To determine a state's administrative laws and procedures, consult the state's administrative statute or contact the state administrative agency for access to its rules and procedures.

Texas Agencies

Texas has an extensive system of administrative agencies. See Appendix I for a directory of these agencies.

The Texas publication for all proposed and adopted rules and regulations of state administrative agencies is the *Texas Register* (cited as *Tex.*

Proclamation 6742 of October 14, 1994

Country Music Month, 1994

By the President of the United States of America
A Proclamation

Country music is a distinctly American treasure, drawing on the deepest cultural roots of our Nation's people. It reflects a storytelling impulse born of mountain balladry and cowboy songs. It combines an exciting instrumental texture of string bands and jazz orchestras, a heartfelt vocal style of religious and blues singing, and a contagious rhythm that inspires dancing in listeners of all ages.

The emotions of the myriad peaks and valleys of life find a vibrant voice in country music. Relating experiences all of us share, these songs boast a long and proud tradition in our national heritage. For the better part of our history, country music's many talented singers and songwriters from across the land have touched the hearts and minds of our citizens—rural and urban, rich and poor, young and old. Today, this wonderful art form is enjoyed and celebrated around the world as a uniquely American gift.

This month, we pause to commend and to appreciate the efforts of singers, songwriters, musicians, and all those in this thriving industry who work to maintain the vitality of the country music legacy.

The Congress, by Public Law 103-107, has designated October 1994 as "Country Music Month" and has authorized and requested the President to issue a proclamation in observance of this month. I urge all Americans to join me in recognizing the rich contributions that country music has made to our cultural heritage.

NOW, THEREFORE, I, WILLIAM J. CLINTON, President of the United States of America, do hereby proclaim October 1994 as Country Music Month.

IN WITNESS WHEREOF, I have hereunto set my hand this fourteenth day of October, in the year of our Lord nineteen hundred and ninety-four, and of the Independence of the United States of America the two hundred and nineteenth.

WILLIAM J. CLINTON

FIGURE 6–10   Sample page from Title 3 of the *C.F.R.*

Reg.). First published in 1975, the *Texas Register* is substantially similar to the *Federal Register*. See Figure 6–11 for a sample of pages from the *Texas Register*. The classification system of the rules and regulations in the *Texas Register* is a set of ten-digit numbers that identify the agency, individual rule, and the chapter and subchapter where the rule appears. Cumbersome and complicated to follow, this identification system is being phased out.

With the passage of the Administrative Procedure and Texas Register Act in 1975, the Texas Legislature determined that there should be public access to all proposed rules and regulations from Texas state agencies. The result was the passage in 1977 of the Texas Administrative Code, which requires the compilation, indexing, and publication of state administrative rules and regulations. The published verson of the code, entitled *Texas Administrative Code* (cited as *Tex. Admin. Code*) is published by West and is the state equivalent to the *Code of Federal Regulations*. (See Figure 6–12.)

All proposed administrative rules first appear in the *Texas Register* along with a proposed *Texas Administrative Code* citation. If adopted, the rule or regulation will appear in a later edition of the *Texas Register* in its full and final text.

In addition to administrative rules and regulations, the *Texas Register* also contains proclamations and executive orders and appointments of the governor, attorney general opinions, legislative actions, and status reports of proposed actions. Open meeting notices are also published in the *Texas Register*.

Often administrative research can be accomplished by directly corresponding with the appropriate state agency. Many Texas state administrative agencies, such as the Railroad Commission, the Texas Employment Commission, and the Insurance Board, publish their rules and regulations in pamphlet form. The complete updated text is provided either at no charge or for a nominal fee.

Other than those for statutes and case law, research sources focusing on Texas administrative law and agency information are limited. There are a few sources, however, that may provide a good starting point for legal research in certain administrative law areas. They are:

1. *Byram's Rules and Regulations of the Texas Railroad Commission* (Austin, Texas) (14 volumes)

2. Dorsaneo, William V., *Texas Litigation Guide: Administrative Proceedings* volume 17 (Matthew Bender)

3. *Guide to Texas State Agencies* (Austin: LBJ School of Public Affairs)

4. *Handbook of Government in Texas* (Austin: Texas Advisory Commission on Intergovernmental Relations)

5. *Opinions of the Texas Attorney General* (Austin: Attorney General's Office)

6. *Texas Legal Directory* (Dallas: Legal Directories) (4 volumes)

Texas Register

Volume 15, Number 75, October 2, 1990   Pages 5768–5830

In This Issue...

Governor

Appointments Made September 20, 1990

5779–Upper Colorado River Authority

5779–State Board of Barber Examiners

5779–Texas Children 2000 Organizational Committee

5779–Legal Committee of the Interstate Oil Compact Commission

5779–Texas Council on Alzheimer's Disease and Related Disorders

5779–Department of Information Resources

Appointments Made September 24, 1990

5779–Special Judge to Cause Number 2415

5779–Texas Health and Human Services Coordinating Council

5779–Texas Antiquities Committee

Appointments Made September 25, 1990

5779–Southern Regional Education Board

Proposed Sections

Banking Department of Texas

5781–Hearing

5781–Practice and Procedure

Railroad Commission of Texas

5789–Oil and Gas Division

5790–Transportation Division

Texas Workers'Compensation Commission

5790–Benefits-Calculation of Averaged Weekly Wage

Comptroller of Public Accounts

5793–Tax Administration

Texas Department of Public Safety

5794–Drivers License Rules

Texas Youth Commission

5798–Admission and Placement

Withdrawn Sections

Texas Water Well Drillers Board

5801–Substantive Rules

Adopted Sections

Office of the Secretary of State

5803–Health Spas

State Finance Commission

5804–Banking Sections

Railroad Commission of Texas

5804-Oil and Gas Division

Texas Department of Human Services

5805–Income Assistance Services

Texas Rehabilitaion Commission

5805–Memoranda of Understanding with Other State Agencies

5805–Special Rules and Policies

Open Meetings

5807–Texas Department of Agriculture

5808–Texas Employment Commission

5808–Texas Heroes Monument Commission

5808–State Department of Highways and Public Transportation

5809–Texas Historical Commission

5809–Texas Commission on Human Rights

CONTENTS CONTINUED INSIDE

FIGURE 6–11   Sample pages from the *Texas Register*

TAC Titles Affected

TAC Titles Affected–October

The following is a list of the administrative rules that have been published this month.

TITLE 1. ADMINISTRATION

Part IV. Office of the Secretarty of State

1 TAC §102.20—5803

1 TAC §102.40—5803

TITLE 7. BANKING AND SECURITIES

Part I. State Finance Commission

7 TAC §3.22—5804

7 TAC §§13.1-13.11, 13.21-13.37—5781

7 TAC §§13.1-13.12—5782

7 TAC §§13.21-13.26—5783

7 TAC §§13.31-13.35—5783

7 TAC §§13.41-13.44—5784

7 TAC §§13.51-13.55—5784

7 TAC §§13.61-13.70—5785

7 TAC §§13.81-13.89—5786

7 TAC §§13.101-13.106—5787

7 TAC §§13.121-13.131—5789

TITLE 16. ECONOMIC REGULATION

Part I. Railroad Commission of Texas

16 TAC §3.13—5789

16 TAC §3.32—5804

16 TAC §5.294—5790

TITLE 28. INSURANCE

Part II. Texas Workers' Compensation Commission

28 TAC §§28.1-28.6—5790

TITLE 31. NATURAL RESOURCES AND CONSERVATION

Part VII. Texas Water Well Drillers Board

31 TAC §§231.82, 231.84—5801

TITLE 34. PUBLIC FINANCE

Part I. Comptroller of Public Accounts

34 TAC §3.21—5793

TITLE 37. PUBLIC SAFETY AND CORRECTIONS

Part I. Texas Department of Public Safety

37 TAC §§15.1, 15.5-15.7—5794

37 TAC §§15.2-15.4—5796

37 TAC §15.9—5796

37 TAC §§15.91-15.93—5796

37 TAC §85.41—5798

TITLE 40. SOCIAL SERVICES AND ASSISTANCE

Part I. Texas Department of Human Services

40 TAC §3.1003—5805

Part II. Texas Rehabilitation Commission

40 TAC §115.8—5805

40 TAC §117.3—5805

♦ *TAC Titles Affected   October 2, 1990   15 TexReg   5673*

FIGURE 6–11   *(continued)*

Proposed Sections

Before an agency may permanently adopt a new or amended section, or repeal an existing section, a proposal detailing the action must be published in the *Texas Register* at least 30 days before any action may be taken. The 30-day time period gives interested persons an opportunity to review and make oral or written comments on the section. Also, in the case of substantive sections, a public hearing must be granted if requested by at least 25 persons, a governmental subdivision or agency, or an association having at least 25 members.

Symbology in proposed amendments. New language added to an existing section is indicated by the use of **bold text**. [Brackets] indicate deletion of existing material within a section.

TITLE 7. BANKING AND SECURITIES

Part II. Banking Department of Texas

Chapter 13. Hearing

- 7 TAC §§13.1-13.11, 13.21-13.37

(Editor's note: The text of the following sections proposed for repeal will not be published. The sections may be examined in the offices of the Banking Department of Texas or in the Texas Register office, Room 245, James Earl Rudder Building, 1019 Brazos Street, Austin.)

The Finance Commission of Texas proposed the repeal of §§13.1-13.11 and 13.21-13.37, concerning appeals to the banking section of the Finance Commission and hearings procedures of the Department of Banking. These sections are being repealed in order that a more comprehensive system of practice and procedure for hearings and appeals may be adopted.

Robert W. Potts, assistant general counsel, has determined that for the first five-year period the repeals are in effect there will be no fiscal implications for state or local government as a result of enforcing or administering the repeals. He has also determined that the repeals and new sections will not have an impact on local economies.

Mr. Potts, also has determined that for each year of the first five years the repeals are in effect the public benefit anticipated as a result of enforcing the repeals will be to provide for a more comprehensive system of practice and procedure before the department, commissioner, and commission to insure uniform standards of practice and a fair and expeditious determination of hearings. There will be no effect on small businesses. There is no anticipated economic cost to persons who are required to comply with the repeals as proposed.

Comments on the proposal may be submitted to Robert W. Potts, Assistant General Counsel, Texas Department of Banking, 2601 North Lamar Boulevard, Austin, Texas, 78705-4294, (512) 479-1200.

The repeals are proposed under Texas Civil Statutes, Article 342-113, which provide the Finance Commission of Texas with the authority to promulgate rules not inconsistent with the Constitution and statutes of this state; Texas Civil Statutes, Article 342-103, which provide the Finance Commission with the authority to adopt rules for the regulation of state banks; and Texas Civil Statutes, Articles 342-412 and 342-801a, which provide the Finance Commission with the authority to make rules regarding appeals to the commission.

§13.1　*Right to Review*

§13.2　*Contents of Review Application*

§13.3　*Filing*

§13.4　*Time of Filing*

§13.5　*Review of Public Hearing*

§13.6　*Precedence over Other Business*

§13.7　*Participation by Interested Persons*

§13.8　*Presiding Officer*

§13.9　*Transcripts*

§13.10　*Order of Participation*

§13.11　*Briefs*

§13.21　*Filing*

§13.22　*Form*

§13.23　*Depositions*

§13.24　*Subpoenas*

§13.25　*Adoption by Reference*

§13.26　*Motions*

§13.27　*Stipulations*

§13.28　*Service*

§13.29　*Attorneys*

§13.30　*Official Notice*

§13.31　*Evidence*

§13.32　*Cross-examination*

§13.33　*Oath*

§13.34　*Record*

§13.35　*Costs*

§13.36　*Hearing Officer*

§13.37　*Briefs*

This agency hereby certifies that the proposal has been reviewed by legal counsel and found to be within the agency's authority to adopt.

Issued in Austin, Texas, on September 24, 1990.

TRD-9010091　　　Ann Graham
　　　　　　　　　General Counsel
　　　　　　　　　Texas Department of
　　　　　　　　　Banking

Earliest possible date of adoption: November 2, 1990

For further information, please call: (512) 479-1200

♦　　　♦　　　♦

Chapter 13. Practice and Procedure

The Finance Commission of Texas proposes new §§13.1-13.12, concerning general provisions; §§13.21-13.26, concerning pleadings; §§13.31-13.35 concerning parties; §§13.41-13.44, concerning prehearing procedures; §§13.51-13.55, concerning discovery; §§13.61-13.70, concerning the hearing; §§13.81-13.89, concerning evidence; §§13.101-13.106, concerning the proposal for decision and orders and §§13.121-13.131, concerning appeals to the Finance Commission of actions of the banking commissioner which are appealable pursuant to the Banking Code. The new chapter was proposed before the Texas Department of Banking, the Banking Commissioner, and the Finance Commission of Texas. Subchapter A provides for hearing procedures in proceedings before the Banking Department and Banking Commissioner.

Robert W. Potts, assistant general counsel, has determined that for the first five-year period the sections are in effect there will be no fiscal implications for state or local government as a result of enforcing or administering the sections. He has also determined that the proposed sections will not have an impact on local economies.

FIGURE 6–11　*(continued)*

Adopted Sections

An agency may take final action on a section 30 days after a proposal has been published in the *Texas Register*. The section becomes effective 20 days after the agency files the correct document with the *Texas Register*, unless a later date is specified or unless a federal statute or regulation requires implementation of the action on shorter notice.

If an agency adopts the section without any changes to the proposed text, only the preamble of the notice and statement of legal authority will be published. If an agency adopts the section with changes to the proposed text, the proposal will be republished with the changes.

TITLE 1. ADMINISTRATION

Part IV. Office of the Secretary of State

Chapter 102. Health Spas

Subchapter B. Procedures For Registration

The Office of the Secretary of State adopts amendment to §102.20 and §102.40. Section 102.40 is adopted with changes to the proposed text as published in the August 17, 1990, issue of the *Texas Register* (15 TexReg 4575). Section 102.20 is adopted without changes and will not be republished.

The amendment to §102.2 clarifies the disclosure criteria to be included in the required registration statement. The amendment to §102.40 more clearly specifies the amount of security that is necessary for a health spa to file with the Office of the Secretary of State.

No comments were received regarding adoption of the amendments. However §102.40(a) was changed to indicate the correct section number for exemptions as §102.30 rather than §102.10.

• 1 TAC §102.20

The amendment is adopted under the Health Spa Act, Texas Civil Statutes, Article 5221L and Texas Civil Statutes, Article 6252-13a, which provide the secretary of state with the authority to adopt rules concerning procedures for registration.

This agency hereby certifies that the rule as adopted has been reviewed by legal counsel and found to be a valid exercise of the agency's legal authority.

Issued in Austin, Texas, on September 24, 1990.

TRD-9010115   Loma Wassdorf
                     Special Assistant
                     Office of the Secretary of
                     State

Effective date: October 16, 1990

Proposal publication date: August 17, 1990

For further information, please call: (512) 463-5701

◆   ◆   ◆

• 1 TAC §102.40

The amendment is adopted under the Health Spa Act, Texas Civil Statutes, Article 5221L and the Administrative Procedure and Texas Register Act, Texas Civil Statutes, Article 6252-13a, which provide the secretary of

state with the authority to adopts rules pertaining to health spa registration requirements to include the filing of security requirements established by 1989 amendments to the Health Spa Act.

§102.40. Security Requirements-General.

(a) The following is applicable to any health spa opened on or after September 1, 1989, other than those hereinafter described in subsection (b) of this section.

(1) When there is transfer of health spa ownership, the successor is subject to the security requirements that are in effect at the time of the transfer. The only exception is if the successor qualifies for an exemption under §102.30 of this title (relating to Exemptions).

(2) On or before the 30th day before the date a health spa opens a location for the use of its members, the health spa shall file with the secretary a surety instrument issued by a surety licensed to do business in this state. In lieu of, and in equal amount to the bond, the spa may submit a certificate of deposit, or a letter of credit issued by a financial institution in this state whose deposits are insured by the Federal Deposit Insurance Corporation or the Federal Savings and Loan Insurance Corporation. The bond, certificate of deposit, or letter of credit shall be payable in favor of the State of Texas and shall be held for the benefit of any members of the health spa who suffer financial losses due to the insolvency or cessation of operation of the health spa.

(3) The amount of the security required in subsection (b) of this section is $20,000.

(4) The health spa shall maintain in force and effect the security in the amount required by paragraph (3) of this subsection of this section for two years after the date on which the health spa ceases business or until the secretary determines that each claim to which the bond or other security deposit is subject has been satisfied or foreclosed by law.

(b) The following is applicable to the owner of any health spa in operation before September 1, 1989, and any additional locations opened by the owner of that health spa on or after September 1, 1989.

(1) Except as provided by paragraph (4) of this subsection, on or before the 30th day after the date a health spa

opens its facilities for the use of its members, the health spa shall file with the secretary of state a surety bond issued by a surety company licensed to do business in this state or, in lieu of and in equal amount to the bond, a certificate of deposit, letter of credit, or other negotiable instrument issued by a financial institution in this state whose deposits are insured by the Federal Deposit Insurance Corporation or the Federal Savings and Loan Insurance Association. The bond, certificate of deposit, letter of credit, or other instrument shall be payable in favor of the state and shall be held for the benefit of any members of the health spa who suffer financial losses due to the insolvency or cessation of operation of the health spa. The term "financial losses" shall mean and be limited to any unused or unearned portion of such member's dues or fees. Such a member may bring an action based on the bond and recover against the surety regardless of the number of claimants or claims filed against the bond but the liability of the surety may not exceed the aggregate amount of the bond. If the claims filed against the bond, exceed the amount of the bond, the surety shall pay the amount of the bond to the secretary of state.

(2) The amount of the security required under paragraph (1) of this subsection is 20% of the total value of the prepayments received by the health spa. However, the amount of the security may not be less than $20,000 or more than $50,000.

(3) The health spa shall maintain the security in the amount provided in paragraph (2) of this subsection in effect for two years after the date the security is filed with the secretary of state. Thereafter, the health spa shall continuously maintain security in the amount of $5,000.

(4) A health spa is exempt from the security requirements of this section if the "owner" of the health spa owned at least one other health spa in the state which had operations at one location for at least two years preceding September 1, 1985, and against which none of its members had initiated litigation or filed a complaint with any government authority in this state relating to the failure to open or the closing of said health spa.

(c) The following provisions shall apply to all security instruments referenced in this section.

(1) (4) (No change.)

FIGURE 6–11   *(continued)*

Texas Register

Volume 15, Annual Index, January 25, 1990

Pages 283–375

In This Issue...

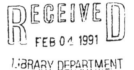
ANNUAL INDEX

VOLUME 15 NUMBERS 1-96

JANUARY 1990-DECEMBER 1990

Part I, January 25, 1991, Annual Index

FIGURE 6–11   *(continued)*

Agency Guide

FIGURE 6–11 *(continued)*

OFFICIAL

Texas Administrative Code

Title 16
Economic Regulation

1995

[Replaces 1994 Pamphlet]

Amendments effective through
January 1, 1995

Published by
West Publishing Co.
St. Paul, Minn.

FIGURE 6–12   Sample pages from the *Texas Administrative Code*

PART III. TEXAS ALCOHOLIC BEVERAGE COMMISSION

Authority: The provisions of this Part III issued under Acts 1977, 65th Legislature, ch. 194, effective September 1, 1977 (Alcoholic Beverage Code, §5.31), unless otherwise noted.

CHAPTER 31. ADMINISTRATION

§ 31.1. Powers Delegated to the Administrator

(a) The administrator is hereby given exclusive jurisdiction in the following matters:

(1) appointing, employing, and terminating all personnel and fixing their duties and salaries;

(2) commissioning inspectors, representatives, and employees;

(3) granting and refusing permits and licenses, and all other matters in connection with hearings thereon;

(4) cancellation and suspension of permits and licenses, and all matters in connection with hearings thereon;

(5) to designate representatives of the commission to hold hearings as provided by law;

(6) certifying to the authenticity of all records, notices, orders, publications, rules, and all other documents, records, and reports in possession of the commission;

(7) investigation of and all matters in connection with alleged violations of law by wholesalers, brewers, distillers, wineries, manufacturers and agents, servants, and employees of the same.

(b) The administrator is hereby given the power and it is hereby made his duty to make and execute the affidavits required by the provisions of an act of the legislature making appropriations for the support and maintenance of the administrative departments and agencies of the state government, which act requires that every month the head of each department shall attach to the pay roll of his department an affidavit to the pay roll of such department, stating that the persons listed on said payroll actually performed the duties for which they are being paid.

Source: The provisions of this §31.1 adopted to be effective January 1, 1976.

§ 31.2. Vehicle Inscription Exemption

State-owned vehicles utilized by the commission for the enforcement of the Alcoholic Beverage Code shall, in accordance with Texas Civil Statutes, Article 6701m-1, as amended, be exempt from the requirement that such vehicles bear inscriptions. The primary use of the exempt vehicles is by enforcement agents of the commission in the detection and investigation of criminal violations of the Code. The purpose served by not printing inscriptions on such vehicles is to increase the effectiveness of commission enforcement agents in detecting and investigating violations of the Code and to

FIGURE 6–12 *(continued)*

7. *Texas Natural Resources Reporter* (Austin: RPC Services) (2 volumes)

8. *Texas State Directory* (Austin: Texas State Directory)

At the city government level, a municipality is usually run pursuant to its city charter, which delegates authority to city administrative agencies. Much like state administrative agencies, city agencies have rules and regulations published in the city's code that identify the procedures of city agencies such as the Board of Adjusters, Urban Rehabilitation Board, and Tax Collector. These codes are often published and often can be found in local libraries. Administrative practices of local agencies also are often summarized and published and are available upon request at a city hall or in many local public libraries. If you cannot locate published materials readily, contact the agency directly to determine whether they can direct you to or supply you with the information you need.

§ 6.5 Checklist for Administrative Law Research

When beginning legal research on an administrative issue, use the following checklists. First determine whether your legal research problem involves a federal or state agency, then use the appropriate checklist for your research project.

Federal Research

1. Identify the possible agencies involved.

2. Go to the *Code of Federal Regulations* index to locate appropriate title, chapter, and sections.

3. Check cumulative *LSA: List of CFR Sections Affected.*

4. Check the monthly List of CFR Sections Affected in the *Federal Register* and *CIS: Federal Register Index.*

5. Go to the *Federal Register* index for the most recent update.

6. Consult official and unofficial publications for administrative decisions.

7. Check digests for possible federal or United States Supreme Court opinions.

State Research

1. Identify the possible agencies involved.

2. Go to the *Texas Administrative Code* to locate the appropriate chapter and section.

3. Check pocket parts of the *Texas Administrative Code* for any updates or changes.

4. Consult the *Texas Register* for recent agency developments.

5. Consult specific agency publications.

6. Check *Texas Digest* and appropriate case reporters for case law.

Summary

6.1   An Introduction to Administrative Law

Administrative law comprises that area of law that defines and regulates administrative agencies. Administrative law grew out of a congressional mandate establishing agencies to regulate certain aspects of American life. The main body of law comes from the Administrative Procedure Act, which sets forth procedures for administrative agencies. Agencies have the right to promulgate rules and regulations. The agencies also have the right to act like courts through their adjudication procedures.

6.2   Federal Agency Research

The two main sources for administrative rules and regulations are the *Federal Register* and the *Code of Federal Regulations*. The *Federal Register* is the first place administrative rules and regulations are published. General indexes provide access to the *Federal Register*, with the *CIS Federal Register Index* being more comprehensive. The final codification of administrative rules and regulations is found in the *Code of Federal Regulations,* published under fifty titles. The index to the *C.F.R.* is entitled *C.F.R. Index and Finding Aids*. Changes in *C.F.R.* titles can be found in *LSA: List of CFR Sections Affected* and the C.F.R. Parts Affected section of the *Federal Register*. In addition, agency adjudications are released in various forms, including official and unofficial publications

6.3   Presidential Documents

Presidential proclamations and executive orders are published in the *Codification of Presidential Proclamations and Executive Orders*. Title 3 of the *Code of Federal Regulations* cites all proclamations and orders as well. Another source of presidential documents is *Public Papers of the Presidents*.

6.4 State Agency Research

Texas has a number of administrative agencies, the proposed rules and regulations of which are published in the *Texas Register*. Texas also publishes an administrative code entitled the *Texas Administrative Code* that is similar to the *Code of Federal Regulations*. All rules and regulations are published in the *Texas Register*, as well as proclamations and executive orders of the governor.

Review Questions

1. Define administrative law.

2. What is the difference between informal and formal rule making?

3. What is the Administrative Procedure Act, and what acts have amended the APA?

4. What is the *Federal Register,* and what are some of its features?

5. How many titles are in the *Code of Federal Regulations?*

6. What two publications update *C.F.R.?*

7. Where can administrative agency decisions be found?

8. Where can presidential documents be found?

9. Identify the publications that publish Texas rules and regulations.

10. Where can the proclamations of the governor of the state of Texas be located?

Exercises

1. Using the Administrative Procedure Act (5 U.S.C. § 1 *et seq.*), answer the following:
   a. Under what section does the administration act begin?
   b. What section discusses rule making?
   c. Using section 553 of 5 U.S.C., what law commentary deals with wrap-around mortgages?
   d. What section of the APA deals with the scope of judicial review?

2. Locate the *Federal Register* dated Monday, May 8, 1995, and answer the following:
   a. What section deals with discrimination complaint procedures?
   b. Which section deals with the procedures for age discrimination complaints?

    c. Using the section dealing with procedures for age discrimination complaints, what is the proposed limitation for filing a lawsuit?

3. Using the *CIS Federal Register Index*, July–December 1994, on what page of the *Federal Register* can information on harassment in the workplace be found? On what page of the *Federal Register* can information on how to adopt an orphan alien (immigrant) child by a United States citizen be found?

4. Locate Title 27 of the *C.F.R.* and complete the following questions:

    a. What does this title deal with?

    b. On what page does the list of C.F.R. Sections Affected begin?

    c. How many volumes are in 27 C.F.R.?

    d. On what page does the alcohol beverage health warning statement begin?

    e. Under what section of the health warning is the mandatory label information set forth?

5. Using Title 3 of *C.F.R.*, 1994–1995, identify the following:

    a. On what page do the Executive Orders of the President begin?

    b. What proclamation by the president proclaims Cancer Control Month?

    c. What proclamation proclaims Safe Boating Week? What week was declared Safe Boating Week?

    d. What executive order implemented the National Voter Registration Act?

6. Locate 21 C.F.R. §§ 170–199 and answer the following:

    a. What is the subject of the title?

    b. On what page and in which section does "substances prohibited from use in human food" begin?

    c. What part of Title 21 deals with sea food inspection?

    d. Using the part dealing with sea food inspection, what section deals with the code-marking of oysters?

7. Locate volume 19 of the *Texas Register* and answer the following:

    a. On what page do the proposed standards of identity of wine begin?

    b. What section of the Alcohol Beverage Code will be affected by the change?

8. Using Title 43 of the *Texas Administrative Code*, answer the following:

    a. On what page does the section on aviation begin?

    b. In the section on aviation, under what conditions can case be dismissed without a hearing?

9. Use the general index of the *Texas Administrative Code* and answer the following:

    a. What title deals with hazardous substances and waste?

b. What title deals with the regulation of physicians and surgeons? What section of Title 22 deals with licensing and permits?

10. Using volume 19 of the *Texas Register*—the May 31, 1994, issue—which attorney general opinion concerns the term *child* and the extent of the definition on adult children?

CHAPTER 7

THE DIGEST SYSTEM

§ 7.1 Introduction to the Digest System

A legal **digest** is a collection of short **case annotations** (sometimes called **abstracts**) organized by legal issue. Digests are compiled on the basis of geography or jurisdiction, as are the reporters discussed in Chapter 4. Legal digests can greatly expedite the process of locating relevant case law on a particular topic or subject matter. In effect, digests serve as a summary index to case law, which can be of inestimable value when you consider that the number of reported decisions released by American courts annually is in excess of 65,000 and that these decisions are not published systematically by topic. Because the digests contain indexes and other finding aids, it is relatively easy to locate annotations that deal with the specific legal issues you are researching.

The annotation paragraphs that appear in digests have been prepared by editors at the publishing company who review and analyze reported decisions for the purpose of identifying and summarizing the courts' positions on every rule of law they address. These annotations appear as headnotes in case reporters, as discussed in Chapter 4. A concise statement of the facts of the case, the holding of the court based on a particular principle of law, and perhaps even the statement of law itself may be found in the annotation paragraph.

Numerous summary paragraphs are compiled into sections of books or complete volumes known as digests. These abstracts are organized by topics, such as mortgages, and subtopics, for example "assignability of mortgages." State, regional, court-specific, and specialty digest sets are available. The best known system of digests was developed by West Publishing Company and is discussed in detail in the following text.

A summary paragraph included in a digest is not legal authority. It has no precedential value and should *never* be cited as support for any proposition of the law. Although digests are excellent research tools, they serve only as case finders. You must read any case of interest in its entirety in the reporters, and you need to Shepardize (see Chapter 11) fully any cases you want to use as authority or identify as appropriate for further research.

TERMS

digest† A series of volumes containing summaries of cases organized by legal topics, subject areas, and so on; digests are essential for legal research.

case annotations Paragraphs that appear in digests, prepared by editors at publishing companies who review and analyze reported decisions to identify and summarize the courts' positions on every rule of law they address.

abstracts Another term for the case annotations found in digests.

§ 7.2 The West Digest System

Introduction

West Publishing Company offers the best known and most comprehensive sets of digests covering all units of the West reporter system. West digests are linked to West's key number system. Each abstract prepared as a headnote by West and intended for subsequent inclusion in a digest is assigned a topic and key number (or more than one topic and number if appropriate). Digests are assembled using these topic and key numbers so you can use them to find other cases that West's editors have identified as ones discussing the same issues.

All West's digests also include three valuable internal finding aids—a descriptive word index, a table of cases, and a defendant-plaintiff table.

Units

The following publications represent the five main divisions of West's digests.

American Digest System: The "Master Index"

The American Digest System consists of a massive collection of over five hundred volumes of material covering three hundred years of decisions handed down by courts in America, beginning with colonial courts and continuing to the present day. This collection contains digests for all reported state appellate court decisions and all reported federal trial and appellate court decisions.

The American Digest System encompasses three "series" of volumes: the *Century Digest,* the *Decennial Digest,* and the *General Digest.*

The *Century Digest* is a fifty-volume set of annotations of opinions issued between 1658 and 1896. Should you ever have occasion to refer to this digest, you will not be able to rely on the topic references you find as a means of locating key numbers in subsequent digest sets. The *Century Digest* does not use the same topic and key number system that West developed at the end of the nineteenth century. There is a conversion table, however, with corresponding key numbers for *Century Digest* topics at the front of volume 21 of the *First Decennial Digest* that can assist you in carrying a search forward from the *Century Digest* into the key number digests.

A *Decennial Digest* is a cumulative compilation of the annotations that appear in each volume of the *General Digest* that has been released after the publication of the last *Decennial Digest.* The *Decennial Digest* consists of nine numbered series, totaling over three hundred and fifty volumes, each covering a ten-year period between 1896 and 1986. Because the number of cases digested during a ten-year period has become quite large, West has begun (starting with the *Ninth Decennial Digest*) to publish each *Decennial* in two parts, each part covering a five-year period. *Decennial Digest* series are as follows:

Decennial Digest

Years	Digest
1658–1869	*Century Digest*
1896–1906	*First Decennial*
1906–1916	*Second Decennial*
1916–1926	*Third Decennial*
1926–1936	*Fourth Decennial*
1936–1946	*Fifth Decennial*
1946–1956	*Sixth Decennial*
1956–1966	*Seventh Decennial*
1966–1976	*Eighth Decennial*
1976–1981	*Ninth Decennial* (Part 1)
1981–1986	*Ninth Decennial* (Part 2)
1986–1991	*Tenth Decennial* (Part 1)
1991–Date	*General Digest* (8th series)

The *General Digest*, the third subdivision of the American Digest System, consists of a set of bound volumes (the set had fifty-five volumes as of mid-July 1991) that updates the most recent *Decennial Digest*. Once a new *Decennial Digest* is published, the obsolete *General Digest* set is removed from the shelves and a new series of *General Digest* begins, with each volume numbered sequentially as it is issued.

The first appearance of a case in the West Digest System is in the paperback advance sheet of a unit in the West National Reporter System. The advance sheets, including digests, are periodically cumulated into bound volumes, and the digests are added to the American Digest System as new *General Digest* volumes are released. Consult the copyright page of the most recent *General Digest* volume for a listing of the volume and advance sheet numbers of each reporter that is represented in the digest volume.

Federal Practice and Supreme Court Digests

A digest that covers ten years of case law in numerous courts can be unmanageable for research purposes. Smaller digests tied to regional and federal reporters, however, are available from West and other publishers. West has published five series of digests covering all three levels of federal courts (dates are not precise in terms of included decisions, since there are sometimes long delays in releasing decisions for publication):

Federal Digest, 1754–1938

Modern Federal Practice Digest, 1939–1961

West's Federal Practice Digest 2d, 1961–1975

West's Federal Practice Digest 3d, 1975–1983

West's Federal Practice Digest 4th, 1983–date

Cases within the *Federal Practice* series are arranged by court, circuit, and district. West also publishes separate digests for the Fifth and Eleventh circuits. In addition, West publishes the *United States Supreme Court Digest,* which contains digest annotations of only Supreme Court cases.

Regional Digests

Using the *Decennial Digest* or *General Digest* to locate all cases on a particular issue in all jurisdictions can be unwieldy and often unnecessary. If you are researching an issue that pertains to only federal law or to only one state's laws, time and effort are wasted in poring over these voluminous compendiums. In those instances, you should limit your search to federal, regional, or state digests.

A regional digest contains key number annotations of state court opinions that are printed in that particular regional reporter. Opinions of the California Supreme Court, for example, found in the *California Reporter* will be digested in the *Pacific Digest.*

West does not publish a regional digest for three of the seven regional reporters: *Southwestern, Northeastern,* and *Southern.* Regional digests that are currently available and their companion reporters are as follows:

Reporter	*States Covered*	*Digest*
Atlantic Reporter 2d	Conn., Del., Me., Md. N.H., N.J., Pa., R.I., Vt., D.C.	*Atlantic*
Northwestern Reporter 2d	Iowa, Mich., Minn., Nebr., N.D., S.D., Wis.	*Northwestern*
Pacific Reporter 2d	Alaska, Ariz., Cal., Colo., Hawaii, Idaho, Kan., Mont., Nev., N.M., Okla., Oreg., Utah, Wash., Wyo.	*Pacific*
Southeastern Reporter 2d	Ga., N.C., S.C., Va., W. Va.	*Southeastern*

To search for cases in the regional reporters for which there is no corresponding digest, you should use the appropriate state digest or the American Digest System. For example, Texas state court cases are in the *Texas Digest*. One additional, workable but less efficient, option is to consult the digest that appears in each volume of the regional reporter. If you have a specific and fairly limited time frame in mind, this can yield satisfactory results, but you must be sure to consult every volume that contains cases in the time frame in which you are interested. Remember, some courts release decisions for publication long after the date they are handed down, and there can be some lag time as well between the time the cases are released for publication and the time they actually appear in a reporter advance sheet.

State Digests

West publishes state-specific digests for all states except Nevada, Delaware, and Utah. The *Dakota Digest* covers North and South Dakota, and Virginia and West Virginia are combined into one digest. New York, California, Illinois, and Texas now have multiple series of digests.

A state digest consists of key number annotations of opinions from (1) the state courts of that state, (2) federal district courts sitting in that state, and (3) the United States Court of Appeals and the United States Supreme Court on cases that are appealed from that state's courts.

Although state digests cover a smaller geographical region, they are more comprehensive than regional digests. In addition to case annotations, state digests include summaries of legal periodical articles and opinions of that state's attorney general.

Figure 7–1 shows a typical page from the *Texas Digest*.

Specialty Digests

West also publishes the following specialty digests:

West's Bankruptcy Digest

West's Military Justice Digest

United States Court of Claims Digest

West's Education Law Digest

United States Merit Systems Protection Board Digest

The latter digest uses a key number system that is similar to but not the same as the standard key number system used in all other West digests (except the *Century Digest* edition of the American Digest System).

🔑380(5) WITNESSES

51 Tex D 2d—422

For later cases see same Topic and Key Number in Pocket Part

In prosecution for filing false income tax returns, wherein a witness was called by government in effort to prove purchases of cigarettes from defendant, and witness denied making such purchases, permitting the government, claiming surprise, to impeach witness by affidavit which he had given an internal revenue agent was reversible error, where 16 days before trial witness had told government attorney that witness had done no business with defendant during period involved, and that he had signed affidavit without reading it while confined with pneumonia, and the government did not show that witness' version of incident was incorrect. 26 U.S.C.A. (I.R.C.1954) § 7206(1).

Hooks v. U. S., 375 F.2d 212.

C.C.A.Tex. 1946. Where witness failed to testify as favorably for plaintiff as plaintiff had had reason to expect from an ex parte statement made by witness, but testimony did not tend to disprove any part of plaintiff's case, court properly excluded the ex parte statement and properly refused to permit plaintiff to cross-examine witness as a hostile witness for purpose of impeaching him.

Mitchell v. Swift & Co., 151 F.2d 770.

C.C.A.Tex. 1940. In prosecution for killing federal officer permitting district attorney to impeach witness, by showing inconsistent testimony in previous trial upon showing of surprise at testimony of witness was not error where district attorney showed that he did not know witness would change testimony and trial judge instructed jury that previous testimony was not usable as proof but only to destroy present testimony if jury thought it had that effect.

Young v. U. S., 107 F.2d 490.

C.C.A.Tex. 1938. Though trial courts, in the exercise of a sound discretion to prevent injury from the surprise testimony of a hostile or corrupt witness, should permit cross-examination and impeachment by contradictory statements, that rule should never be made an artifice to get before the jury favorable ex parte statements made by a witness whose testimony is known to be adverse.

Young v. U. S., 97 F.2d 200, 117 A.L.R. 316, rehearing denied 97 F.2d 1023.

Contradictory statements made by a party's own witness are not admissible unless there is surprise and damage, and damage claimed must not have been self-inflicted by continuing to put in damaging testimony after witness' hostility or change of front was discovered in order to let in his favorable ex parte statements.

Young v. U. S., 97 F.2d 200, 117 A.L.R. 316, rehearing denied 97 F.2d 1023.

A party should not be permitted to impeach his own witness by introducing his ex parte statement in contradiction of his testimony, unless party is really surprised at witness' testimony, and unless impeaching testimony is admitted not to supply what witness was expected to, but did not, say, as a basis for a verdict, but only to eliminate from jury's minds any positive adverse effect which might have been created by surprise testimony.

Young v. U. S., 97 F.2d 200, 117 A.L.R. 316, rehearing denied 97 F.2d 1023.

Tex.Cr.App. 1981. State's witness, by denying existence of relevant fact, had not, by denial, stated facts injurious to the State's case and since it could not be said that the witness' prior statement, admitted as impeachment rather than direct evidence, did not harm appellant, allowing the State to impeach its own witness resulted in prejudicial error requiring reversal.

Houston v. State, 626 S.W.2d 43.

Tex.Cr.App. 1980. Testimony by State's witness, that she saw two cars she recognized as belonging to deceased and defendant going down road at same time, was not injurious to State's case in murder prosecution, and thus it was error to allow the State to impeach the witness by introducing statement in which the witness purportedly said she saw, "[deceased] passing in his car, with [defendant] right behind him, driving real fast and real close behind him," even though record demonstrated that State made sufficient showing of surprise when witness testified inconsistently with previous written statement.

Lewis v. State, 593 S.W.2d 704.

Tex.Cr.App. 1975. State was entitled to rely upon its own witness' testimony at trial of defendant being consistent with witness's previous testimony at her own trial in which she admitted her guilt in robbery and stated under oath that defendant planned the robbery and participated in it as a principal.

Hunnicutt v. State, 523 S.W.2d 244.

Tex.Cr.App. 1974. Rule that the state may not impeach its own witness unless it shows the testimony to be harmful to its case and that such testimony was unexpected or a surprise did not apply to murder prosecution wherein state was allowed to show that accomplice witness gave prior inconsistent statements before his testimony at trial and that other witness gave prior inconsistent statements and had been convicted of a felony, since the state was not attacking the credibility of the two witnesses, as was shown by fact that its case depended on the truth of their trial testimony.

Jackson v. State, 516 S.W.2d 167.

For legislative history of cited statutes

FIGURE 7–1 A typical page from the *Texas Digest*

Digest Supplements

All West digests are kept current by frequent updates in several different formats. Cumulative annual pocket parts, supplement pamphlets, and the current volumes and advance sheets of West reporters are used to update digest coverage. You need to ascertain for each digest set you want to use how the set is kept current.

The American Digest System is supplemented by the bound volumes of the *General Digest* and by the current volumes and advance sheets of the various reporters.

The West Key Number System in Digests

In General

Locating all cases that have addressed a particular question or issue is often difficult because of the diversity and number of courts and the magnitude of opinions issued by those courts.

Digests enable you to find all cases isolated by West editors as dealing with a particular topic by simply identifying the appropriate topic and key number.

Each West digest annotation is assigned one or more topic and a key number within the topic. Each point of law under a topic is identified by a unique key number. All cases that apply to that particular point of law are classified by that same key number in every reporter or publication in which they subsequently appear.

If you are searching a particular state's digest and cannot locate any reference to the specific subject you are researching, you should expand your search to the digests of neighboring states, the series of federal digests, the *United States Supreme Court Digest*, the American Digest System, or *Corpus Juris Secundum*.

By using digests covering a designated period of time, you should be able to locate virtually all (remember, no single research method should be thought of as "foolproof") reported cases on a particular point that were decided during that time frame. Key number research can be facilitated by following the steps set out and discussed in the following text.

Locating the Key Number

One approach to finding a relevant West key number is to find a relevant decision published in a West reporter using some other research source. If you find, or already know of, such a case, you can consult its headnotes for the particular issue in which you are interested. Jot down the key number references that accompany the headnotes, and you can then access the digests.

Apart from this approach, there are three specific research methods that use the digests themselves to locate relevant key numbers. These methods should be used in the order listed as follows to facilitate fast and accurate research.

Descriptive Word Method The descriptive word method should be the first one you use to locate a needed key number. In preparing headnotes to accompany cases to be published in one of their reporters, West editors select words that are descriptive of the important facts or points of law in each such opinion. Those words are then arranged in alphabetical descriptive word indexes. These indexes can direct you to the topics and key numbers under which cases involving similar facts or legal issues have been previously classified. Every West key number digest contains a descriptive word index. There is also a cumulative descriptive word index in the tenth volume of the *General Digest*.

To begin the search for a key number using this method, you should first identify and list words that describe the pertinent facts or legal issues involved in the case. Developing skills in selecting the appropriate descriptive word requires practice. Keep in mind that many of the topics in the key number system are built around the basic matters that are a part of virtually every case:

1. parties,
2. type of action or issue,
3. defenses to the issues,
4. places and material items involved, and
5. relief sought by the parties

Figure 7–2 shows what is involved in a descriptive word search. Under the entry "abandonment" and the subentry "attachment" is a reference to "wrongful attachment, ground of action." The digest topic and key number for this entry are "Attach 360." This information will assist you in pursuing additional research in sources such as reporters or encyclopedias. Synonyms and antonyms are useful research tools for locating pertinent descriptive words.

Once you identify a topic and key number in the descriptive word index, you should continue your research using the digest volumes that contain that topic and key number. There you will find the case annotations dealing with the issue you are researching.

Topic Method A second digest research method for locating a topic and key number for the particular point of law being researched is to work

DESCRIPTIVE–WORD INDEX

References are to Digest Topics and Key Numbers

A

A MENSA ET THORO
DIVORCE. Divorce 155

A VINCULO MATRIMONII
DIVORCE. Divorce 157

AB INITIO
TRESPASS ab initio. Tresp 13

ABANDONED MOTOR VEHICLE
TOWING, detention and disposal of, due process, owner's entitlement to. Const Law 278(1.2)

ABANDONMENT
ACCIDENTAL loss, see this index Finding Lost Goods
ACTION. Action 70
    Costs as affected. Costs 46
ACTS constituting. Aband L P 3
ADMIRALTY proceeding. Adm 39
ADOPTION of children, forfeiting parent's rights. Adop 7.4
ADVERSE possession. Adv Poss 53
    Abandonment of title after acquisition. Adv Poss 109
AIRPORTS. Aviation 230
APPEAL or other proceedings for review—
        App & E 14(1), 805, 806
        Crim Law 1178
        Fed Cts 730
        J P 166
    Probate or contest of will. Wills 371½
    Workers' compensation, proceedings for review by court in proceedings to secure compensation. Work Comp 1908
ARBITRATION. Arbit 24
ASSAULT with intent to rape, abandonment of purpose, see this index Rape
ATTACHMENT—
    Dissolution of attachment. Attach 274
    Lien. Attach 184
    Wrongful attachment, ground of action. Attach 360
BROKER'S employment. Brok 45, 88(9)
BURDEN of proof—
    Homestead. Home 181(1)
CANALS. Canals 2, 22
CARRIERS, see this index Carriers
CEMETERY lands. Cem 14
CHILDREN, see this index Infants
CLAIMS—
    Against United States for proceeds of abandoned property. U S 103
COLLEGE or university. Colleges 12
COMMONS. Com Lands 13
CONTRACT. Contracts 256
    Contractor's right to mechanics' lien as affected by. Mech Liens 92
    Instructions in action for breach. Contracts 353(7)
    Land contracts, rights under. Ven & Pur 86

ABANDONMENT—Cont'd
CONTRACT—Cont'd
    Operation and effect. Contracts 274
    Sale contract. Sales 93
    Shipping contracts. Ship 108
    Subcontractors and materialmen, rights of. Mech Liens 111(2)
    Supply of water to municipality. Waters 200(2)
    Time for filing claim or statement. Mech Liens 132(9)
    To abandon action. Champ 4(3)
DEDICATION—
    By abandonment of property to public use. Dedi 20
    Dedicated property. Dedi 63
DEFENSE to criminal charge. Crim Law 31.10
DEMURRER, see this index Demurrer
DOMICILE. Domicile 4
DRAINS. Drains 65
EASEMENTS. Ease 30
EMPLOYMENT, see this index Labor and Employment
ESCHEAT, see this index Escheat
EVIDENCE. Aband L P 4
    Conclusions and opinions of witnesses in general. Evid 471(33)
FOREIGN land grants. Pub Lands 209
FRANCHISE, see this index Franchises
GARNISHMENT. Garn 198
HIGHWAYS. High 79
HOMESTEAD, see this index Homestead
HUSBAND or wife, see this index Abandonment of Husband or Wife
INDICTMENT of information for abandonment—
    Following language of statute. Ind & Inf 110(37)
INFANTS, see this index Infants
INSURANCE—
    Generally, see this index Insurance
    Marine insurance, see this index Marine Insurance
    Mutual benefit insurance, see this index Mutual Benefit Insurance
INTENT, see this index Intent
LABOR and employment, see this index Labor and Employment
LABOR Relations Board, proceedings. Labor 520
LEASED premises. Land & Ten 110
    Eviction, necessity to constitute. Land & Ten 171(3)
    Evidence, rent action. Land & Ten 231(5)
    Liability for rent. Land & Ten 195
    Termination of tenancy. Land & Ten 120(4)
LEGACY or devise. Wills 719
LICENSES or permits, see this index Licenses
LIMITATIONS, new action after abandonment of former action. Lim of Act 130(4)
LOGS and logging, matters concerning and relating to, see this index Logs and Logging
MINES and minerals—
    Lease. Mines 66, 77
    Location or claim. Mines 24

110 F P D 3d—1

FIGURE 7–2   A sample descriptive word index

through the lists of topics and key numbers that are provided within the digests. The alphabetic list of digest topics in the beginning of each digest volume can function as a quick reference tool. Because there are more than four hundred topics listed, however, you should not resort to this method unless you are thoroughly familiar with the key number classification system.

Once you have chosen a topic you think is relevant to your research, you should consult the analysis that appears at the beginning of the topic in every key number digest. This analysis, in effect a very detailed table of contents, lists topics that are covered and those that are excluded or covered by other topics. It also directs you to the ultimate topic and key number that will be used to locate cases in all key number digests. If the law under a particular topic has experienced significant growth or major redefinition in recent years, you may find a revised (usually more extensive) subdivision of individual key numbers in pocket part supplements or recent *Decennial Digests*.

Table of Cases Method

The Table of Cases If you know the name of a case that deals with a point of law you are researching, you can use the case name to locate other cases that deal with the same point. Through the name of a case, a key number from the table of cases in the state or regional digest or American Digest System can be located quickly and easily. The last volume of the state and regional digests normally contains a table of cases that is updated by pocket part supplements. Cases are listed in the table of cases alphabetically by plaintiff.

If you locate the case you are checking in the table of cases, you will find the following valuable research information:

1. the accurate title of the case;
2. parallel citations to both the national and state reporter systems;
3. the history of the case, including whether it has been affirmed, reversed, or modified on appeal or rehearing; and
4. topics and key numbers under which all points of law in that particular case have been classified in the West Digest System

Figure 7–3 is an example of a typical page from a West digest table of cases.

Defendant-Plaintiff Table of Cases In the event you do not know the plaintiff's name but you do know the defendant's, you can consult the special defendant-plaintiff table of cases that is included in several of West's digests. This table lists the defendant's name first, followed by the plaintiff's name and a citation to the location of the case in the National Reporter System. This enables you to either go directly to the case or

TABLE OF CASES DIGESTED

ABBREVIATIONS

aff	– affirmed	mand overr	– mandamus overruled
am	– amended	mod	– modified
cert	– certiorari	overr	– overruled
conf to	– conformed to	rearg	– reargument
den	– denied	ref w m	– refused for want of merit
dism	– dismissed	ref n r e	– refused no reversable error
foll	– followed	reh	– rehearing
gr	– granted	rev	– reversed
jur	– jurisdiction	transf	– transferred
mand gr	– mandamus granted	vac	– vacated

References are to Digest Topics and Key Numbers

P

Pabst v. Roxana Petroleum Co 30 F2d 953—Action 1; Courts 87; Rem of C 1, 48, 102.

Pabst v. Roxana Petroleum Corp, Tex CivApp, 51 SW2d 802, aff 125 Tex 52, 80 SW2d 956—Consp 18; Mines 78(1, 7); Plead 18, 34(4), 49

Pabst v. State 96 TexCrR 617, 259 SW 577—Crim Law 589(1), 627(2), 784(5), 814(17).

Pabst Brewing Co v. Emerson, Civ App, 36 SW 342—Corp 426(2), 432 (7).

Pace, Ex parte 16 TexApp 541—Bail 49.

Pace, Ex parte, CrApp, 20 SW 922—Bail 43.

Pace, In re FedCasNo10,640, 1 Tex LawJ 315—Bankr 484.

Pace v. American Freehold Land & Mortg Co 17 TexCivApp 506, 43 SW 36—Evid 596(3); Ref of Inst 36(1); Trial 255(1).

Pace v. Eoff, TexComApp, 48 SW2d 956—Ex & Ad 39, 176, 178, 180, 181, 182, 187, 195, 201; Hus & W 273(1); Statut 157, 223.2(12).

Pace v. Fishback 10 TexCivApp 450, 31 SW 424. See Page v. Fishback.

Pace v. Hollaman 31 Tex 158—App & E 338(2).

Pace v. J M Radford Grocery Co, CivApp, 152 SW 1130. See J H & J T Pace v. J M Radford Grocery Co.

Pace v. Moore, CivApp, 210 SW 238 —Autos 244(2).

Pace v. Munday, TexCivApp, 323 SW 2d 609—Mun Corp 741(1, 2); Neglig 54, 138(3).

Pace v. Olvey, TexCivApp, 282 SW 940, error dism—App & E 931(5), 1050(1); Damag 76, 157(3); Mines 74, 109; Trial 68(2).

Pace v. Ortiz 72 Tex 437, 10 SW 541 —Clerks of C 72.

Pace v. Pierson, TexCivApp, 145 SW 2d 929—Banks 241, 243, 278; Corp 123(5); Garn 105; Plead 430(1).

Pace v. Potter, CivApp, 20 SW 928, rev 22 SW 300—Anim 90; Appear 10; Tresp 10.

40B Tex.Dig.—1

Pace v. Price, CivApp, 45 SW 203—App & E 573.

Pace v. Shaw, TexCivApp, 13 SW2d 925, aff 29 SW2d 965—Banks 34, 40, 48, 48(1), 49(7).

Pace v. Smith 57 Tex 555—Garn 59.

Pace v. Sparks, Tex, 1 Posey Unrep Cas 402—Execution 24.

Pace v. State, CrApp, 20 SW 762—Crim Law 396(2), 419(10), 424(1), 781(8), 875(4), 1172(6).

Pace v. State, CrApp, 24 SW 297—Anim 13.

Pace v. State, CrApp, 31 SW 173—Crim Law 759(4), 780(2); Larc 77(3).

Pace v. State, CrApp, 32 SW 697—Bail 66.

Pace v. State, CrApp, 32 SW 700—Bail 66; Crim Law 1087(1).

Pace v. State 41 TexCrR 203, 51 SW 953, rev on rehearing 53 SW 689—Crim Law 594(1), 616, 784(1), 829 (1), 1172(6); Larc 75(2).

Pace v. State, CrApp, 79 SW 531—Assault 53, 56, 96(3); Crim Law 457, 763(8), 1038(3), 1056(1), 1092 (14), 1119(2), 1120(8); Witn 367 (2).

Pace v. State 58 TexCrR 90, 124 SW 949—Crim Law 369(3), 507(1), 719 (3), 742(2), 780(1, 3), 1099(6); Homic 169(2), 338(1).

Pace v. State 69 TexCrR 436, 135 SW 379—Crim Law 543(2), 737(1), 741 (1), 742(1), 790; Homic 178(1), 301; Witn 195.

Pace v. State 69 TexCrR 27, 153 SW 132—Crim Law 543(2), 547(4), 596 (1), 598(7), 603(10), 614(2), 778 (5), 1090(16), 1111(3); Homic 158 (3), 309(5).

Pace v. State 70 TexCrR 454, 156 SW 1192—Int Liq 50, 226.

Pace v. State 83 TexCrR 368, 203 SW 595—Crim Law 1090(16), 1144(13).

Pace v. State, CrApp, 31 SW2d 1081 —Crim Law 1090(1).

Pace v. State 132 TexCrR 647, 106 SW2d 323—Crim Law 479; Homic 338(3).

Pace v. State 171 TexCrR 219, 346 SW 2d 339—Crim Law 1171(5); Rob 24(1).

Pace v. State, TexCrApp, 398 SW2d 123—Crim Law 1170½(5); Witn 274(2).

Pace v. State, TexCrApp, 461 SW2d 409—Autos 349.

Pace v. U S, CCA, 94 F2d 591—Crim Law 730(1), 1141(2), 1163(2), 1173 (1); Licens 42(3, 5); Sec Reg 194, 195.

Pace v. Webb 79 Tex 314, 15 SW 269 —J P 159(8), 193.

Pace v. Wells, TexCivApp, 458 SW 2d 474, ref n r e—App & E 1151 (1); Bills & N 137(1); Costs 234.

Pace Corp v. Jackson 155 Tex 179, 284 SW2d 340—Contracts 10(1, 4); Corp 1.6(2), 306; Damag 40(2); Decl Judgm 142, 342; Salus 1(4), 19, 62, 64, 69, 71(4), 384(1), 418(1, 3, 15); Trial 25(4), 351(5).

Pace Corp v. Jackson, TexCivApp, 276 SW2d 849, aff 155 Tex 179, 284 SW2d 340—Contracts 9(1), 10(1), 143, 147(2), 175(2); Damag 40(1), 176; Decl Judgm 344, 347, 367; Evid 158(27), 461(1); Sales 81(2), 82(2), 411, 416(2), 421; Trial 25(4), 350(4).

Pace Grocery Co v. Guynes, CivApp, 204 SW 794. See S A Pace Grocery Co v. Guynes.

Pace Grocery Co v. Savage, CivApp, 114 SW 866. See S A Pace Grocery Co v. Savage.

Pace, State ex rel v. Logan, CivApp, 5 SW2d 247. See State ex rel Pace v. Logan.

Pacheco v. Allala, CivApp, 261 SW 168—Execution 171(4), 172(2); Inj 150.

Pacheco v. Fernandez, TexCivApp, 277 SW 197, error refused—Assign 73; Fraud Conv 240.

Pacheco v. State 128 TexCrR 473, 81 SW2d 690—Burg 41(4); Jury 131 (6).

Pacific Am Fire Underwriters of Liverpool & London & Globe Ins Co v. Atkinson, TexCivApp, 83 SW 2d 441—App & E 770(1); Insurance 574(5.1).

Pacific Am Gasoline Co of Tex v. Miller, CivApp, 61 SW2d 1024—Appear 19(1); Plead 236(1); Venue 77.

FIGURE 7–3   A typical page from a West digest table of cases

continue your key number research by going to the primary table of cases, since you now know the plaintiff's name. The defendant-plaintiff table of cases does not include key number classifications. An example of the defendant-plaintiff table of cases appears in Figure 7–4.

An additional value of the two tables of cases is that they give you the ability to locate all reported cases involving a particular plaintiff or defendant. Numerous lawsuits on the same issue may indicate problem areas in your firm's defense of a particular client. The fact that a particular plaintiff's name appears in the table six times may indicate that the party is extremely litigious.

Words and Phrases   A table of words and phrases lists alphabetically all words that have been judicially defined or defined by the court in the jurisdictions covered by that particular digest. A table of words and phrases volume is included with the *United States Supreme Court Digest*, the *Modern Federal Practice Digest, West's Federal Practice Digest 2d, West's Federal Practice Digest 3d,* and *West's Federal Practice Digest 4th.* Under each word or phrase are listed any cases, with their citations, in which the words have been defined. This table does not include the definitions themselves but allows you to go to the cases directly or move into the digests through the digests' tables of cases.

Supplements to these tables are found in the pamphlet and pocket part updates to each digest series. In addition, West publishes a set (more than ninety volumes) entitled *Words and Phrases* that consists of headnote annotations drawn from throughout the West reporter system.

See Figure 7–5 for an example of a table of words and phrases from the *Texas Digest,* a West publication.

§ 7.3   Non-West Digests

There are several digests available from publishers other than West. Another major digest publisher is Lawyers Cooperative Publishing Company (LCP). Its digest sets tend to be more specialized than West's. For example, the *United States Supreme Court Reports Digest, Lawyers' Edition*, published in approximately thirty volumes, covers some four hundred topics, with numerous subdivisions. It is not assembled with the West key number system. Because the publication is specifically created for Supreme Court decisions, many legal scholars consider it to be a more thorough reference source for Supreme Court cases than the West publications. The LCP digest is keyed to headnotes and annotations in the *United States Supreme Court Reports, Lawyers' Edition* and cross-references *A.L.R.* and *A.L.R. Federal.*

DEFENDANT-PLAINTIFF

TABLE OF CASES

Defendant Title appears in large type. Consult Plaintiff Table for
Key Number Digest Classification and Case History

A

A—State ex rel. Juvenile Dept. of Mult-
nomah County, OrApp, 660. P2d 707,
62 OrApp 293.
A-AAAABAAB'S ROOT RODDERS—
Blau Plumbing, Inc, CA7 (Wis), 781
F2d 604.
A-A-A ELEC. CO., INC.—U.S., CA4
(NC), 788 F2d 242.
A-A-A ELEC. CO., INC.—U.S., DCNC,
607 FSupp 266.
A-ABCO LAWN SPRINKLERS—Blaes-
er Development Corp. of Texas, Tex-
App 13 Dist, 664 SW2d 830.
A-COPY, INC.—Margaret Maunder As-
sociates, Inc, ConnSuper, 499 A2d
1172, 40 ConnSup 361.
A-COPY, INC.—Maunder Associates,
Inc, ConnSuper, 499 A2d 1172, 40
ConnSup 361.
A-OK ROOFING—Mohawk Green
Apartments, ColoApp, 709 P2d 955.
A-1 AUTO PARTS AND USED CARS—
Benham, WashApp, 683 P2d 1142.
A-1 AUTO SERVICE—King, LaApp 1
Cir, 450 So2d 1000.
A-1 BAIL BONDS—Ewing, FlaApp 3
Dist, 481 So2d 99.
A-1 BIT AND TOOL CO., INC.—Blanch-
ard, LaApp, 406 So2d 773.
A-1 BUS LINES, INC.—Kaufman, Fla-
App 3 Dist, 416 So2d 863.
A-1 CONTRACTING CO. OF LOUISI-
ANA, INC.—Commercial Union Ins.
Co., LaApp 1 Cir, 447 So2d 39.
A 1-800-A-M-E-R-I-C-A-N CORP.—
American Airlines, Inc, DCIll, 622
FSupp 673.
A-1, INC.—Matthews, CATex, 748 F2d
975.
A-1 INDUSTRIES, INC.—Richard, La-
App 5 Cir, 489 So2d 386.
A-1 INDUSTRIES, INC.—Wilson, La-
App 4 Cir, 451 So2d 1251.
A-1 KING SIZE SANDWICHES, INC.—
N.L.R.B., CA11, 782 F2d 872.
A-1 MAINTENANCE SERVICE—True
Vang, MinnApp, 376 NW2d 479.
A-1 MAINTENANCE SERVICE—
Vang, MinnApp, 376 NW2d 479.
A-1 MAINTENANCE SERVICE—Youa
True Vang, MinnApp, 376 NW2d
479.
A-1 MANAGEMENT, INC.—Ewing,
FlaApp 3 Dist, 481 So2d 99.

A-1 PETROLEUM, INC.—Johnson,
MinnApp, 352 NW2d 504.
A-1 PLUMBING AND HEATING CO.,
INC.—Thirteenth St. Corp., Colo,
640 P2d 1130.
A-1 SALES, INC.—Caldwell, Mass, 434
NE2d 174, 385 Mass 753.
A-1 SERVICES—Venus, IllApp 1 Dist,
82 IllDec 143, 468 NE2d 405, 127
IllApp3d 19.
A-1 24 HOUR TOWING, INC.—Long,
Nev, 707 P2d 1151, 101 Nev 682.
A-PAC LTD.—Anne Arundel County,
MdApp, 506 A2d 671, 67 MdApp 122.
A-PAC, LTD.—Shanor, Wyo, 711 P2d
420.
A-P-A SPORTS, INC.—Cherry, Colo-
App, 662 P2d 200.
A-Z ASSOCIATES—Lesser, DCNY, 48
BR 829.
A-Z ASSOCIATES—Lesser, BkrtcyNY,
46 BR 850.
A-Z ASSOCIATES—Lesser, BkrtcyNY,
44 BR 690.
AAA BEER STORE—Com., Pennsylva-
nia Liquor Control Bd, PaCmwlth,
456 A2d 1120, 72 PaCmwlth 305.
AAA BLDG. MAINTENANCE, INC.—
Service Emp. Health & Welfare
Trust Fund, WashApp, 704 P2d 644.
AAA CABINET CO.—Pierce, GaApp,
326 SE2d 575, 173 GaApp 463.
AAACON AUTO TRANSPORT, INC.—
Caspe, CAIowa, 658 F2d 613.
AAACON AUTO TRANSPORT, INC.—
Martin, NYCity CivCt, 495 NYS2d
602, 129 Misc2d 1012.
AAACON AUTO TRANSPORT, INC.—
Montagna, CAMass, 706 F2d 359.
AAACON AUTO TRANSPORT, INC.—
Porias, CAConn, 685 F2d 56.
AAA COOPER TRANSP.—Joyner, DC-
Ala, 597 FSupp 537.
AAA COOPER TRANSP.—Joyner, Ala,
477 So2d 364.
AAA EQUIPMENT SERVICE CO.—
Parks Corp., IllApp 4 Dist, 87 IllDec
467, 477 NE2d 68, 132 IllApp3d 417.
AAA HOMEBUILDERS, INC.—Collins,
WVa, 333 SE2d 792.
AAA INS. AGENCY, INC.—American
Auto. Ass'n (Inc.), DCTex, 618
FSupp 787.

AAA INS. CO.—Featherly, MichApp,
326 NW2d 390, 119 MichApp 182.
AAA MACH. CO., INC.—Equilease
Corp., BkrtcyFla, 30 BR 323.
AAA MACHINERY & EQUIPMENT
CO.—Fugate, DCTenn, 593 FSupp
392.
AAA PRO MOVING & STORAGE—Ver-
million, ArizApp, 704 P2d 1360, 146
Ariz 215.
AAA SERVICES, INC.—Holiday Inn,
IllApp 1 Dist, 88 IllDec 154, 478
NE2d 469, 182 IllApp3d 1061.
AAA SERVICES, INC.—Oak Lawn
Lodge, Inc, IllApp 1 Dist, 88 IllDec
154, 478 NE2d 469, 132 IllApp3d
1061.
AAA TRUCKING CORP.—Siravo, Pa-
Super, 452 A2d 521, 306 PaSuper
217.
A.A.A. UNIFORMS—Wunschel, NJ, 477
A2d 329, 96 NJ 651.
AA AUTO SALVAGE, INC.—South
Cent. Bell Telephone Co., LaApp 1
Cir, 481 So2d 641.
AAA WATERPROOFING CO., INC.—
Mancini, NYAD, 453 NYS2d 120, 89
AD2d 651.
A. A. BAXTER CORP.—Standard Pacif-
ic of San Diego, CalApp 4 Dist, 222
CalRptr 106, 176 CA2d 677.
AABBEY GALLERIES, INC.—Freehl-
ing, BkrtcyFla, 39 BR 196.
AABCO CONTRACTORS, INC.—Aleem,
LaApp 4 Cir, 422 So2d 1293.
A. A. BEIRO CONST. CO., INC.—Coun-
ty School Bd. of Fairfax County, Va,
286 SE2d 232, 223 Va 161.
A.A. BEIRO CONST. CO., INC.—Dono-
van, CADC, 746 F2d 894, 241 US-
AppDC 161.
A.A. BOCA, INC.—Pace, FlaApp 4 Dist,
429 So2d 415.
A.A. BOCA, INC.—Ponke, FlaApp 4
Dist, 429 So2d 415.
AAC SYDCO, INC.—Lansons, Inc, Fla-
App 3 Dist, 489 So2d 217.
A.A. ELEC.—Pacific Elec. Contractors
Ass'n, DCHawaii, 583 FSupp 472.
AA JOB PRINTING—New York Typo-
graphical Union No. 6, DCNY, 622
FSupp 566.
AAKER—Aaker, ND, 338 NW2d 645.

47–9th D Pt 2—1

FIGURE 7–4   An example of the defendant-plaintiff table of cases

Negligence Per Se WORDS AND PHRASES 42 Tex D—400

NEGLIGENCE PER SE,
St. Louis Southwestern R. Co. of Texas v. Hawkins, 108 S.W. 736, 740, 49 Tex.Civ.
App. 545.
J. M. Radford Grocery Co. v. Andrews, 5 S.W.(2d) 1010, 1013.
Ford Motor Co. v. Madden, 42 S.W.(2d) 165, 167.
Houston Oil Co. of Texas v. Wilson, 70 S.W.(2d) 285, 287.
Menefee v. State, 87 S.W.2d 478, 480, 129 Tex.Cr.R. 375.
Daugherty v. Chicago, R. I. & G. Ry. Co., 94 S.W.2d 587, 588.
Sage v. State, 124 S.W.2d 376, 377, 136 Tex.Cr.R. 252.
Hicks v. Brown, Tex.Civ.App., 128 S.W.2d 884, 888.
Wright v. McCoy, Tex.Civ.App., 131 S.W.2d 52, 53.
Gillette Motor Transport v. Fine, Tex.Civ.App., 131 S.W.2d 817, 823.
Womack v. Tripp, Tex.Civ.App., 137 S.W.2d 180, 182.
Bettis v. Watkins, Tex.Civ.App., 140 S.W.2d 280, 281.
Ruggles v. John Deere Plow Co., Tex.Civ.App., 146 S.W.2d 456, 460.
Russell v. Liggett Drug Co., Tex.Civ.App., 153 S.W.2d 231, 233.

NEGLIGENT,
Chicago, R. I. & P. Ry. Co. v. Gillett, 99 S.W. 712, 713.

NEGLIGENT CONDUCT,
Gulf, C. & S. F. Ry. Co. v. Bell, 101 S.W.2d 363, 364.

NEGLIGENT HOMICIDE.
Anderson v. State, 11 S.W. 33, 27 Tex.App. 177, 181, 3 L.R.A. 644, 11 Am.St.Rep. 189.
Clifton v. State, 84 S.W. 237, 239, 47 Tex.Cr.R. 472.
Gorden v. State, 90 S.W. 636, 637.
Saye v. State, 99 S.W. 551, 552, 554, 50 Tex.Cr.R. 569.
Joy v. State, 123 S.W. 584, 589, 57 Tex.Cr.R. 93.
Talbot v. State, 125 S.W. 906, 907, 58 Tex.Cr.R. 324.
Chant v. State, 166 S.W. 513, 515, 73 Tex.Cr.R. 345.
Egbert v. State, 176 S.W. 560, 562, 76 Tex.Cr.R. 663.
McPeak v. State, 187 S.W. 754, 756.
Simmons v. State, 3 S.W.(2d) 449, 451, 109 Tex.Cr.R. 157.
Abell v. State, 5 S.W.(2d) 139, 141, 109 Tex.Cr.R. 380, 61 A.L.R. 318.
Barfield v. State, 43 S.W.(2d) 106, 108, 118 Tex.Cr.R. 394.
Hillin v. State, 57 S.W.(2d) 843, 844, 123 Tex.Cr.R. 22.
Wilkerson v. State, 59 S.W.(2d) 392, 393, 123 Tex.Cr.R. 532.

NEGLIGENT HOMICIDE OF THE FIRST DEGREE,
Bowles v. State, 146 S.W.2d 183, 186, 140 Tex.Cr.R. 511.

NEGLIGENT HOMICIDE OF THE SECOND DEGREE,
Bowles v. State, 146 S.W.2d 183, 186, 140 Tex.Cr.R. 511.

NEGLIGENT PER SE,
Missouri Pac. Ry. Co. v. Lee, 7 S.W. 857, 70 Tex. 496.
Campbell v. Trimble, 12 S.W. 863, 75 Tex. 270.
Gulf, C. & S. F. Ry. Co. v. Anderson, 13 S.W. 196, 76 Tex. 244.
Calhoun v. Gulf, C. & S. F. Ry. Co., 19 S.W. 341, 84 Tex. 226.
Garteiser v. Galveston, H. & S. A. Ry. Co., 21 S.W. 631, 2 Tex.Civ.App. 230.
San Antonio & A. P. Ry. Co. v. Long, 23 S.W. 499, 4 Tex.Civ.App. 497.
San Antonio & A. P. Ry. Co. v. Connell, 66 S.W. 246, 248, 27 Tex.Civ.App. 533.
McAfee v. Travis Gas Corporation, 153 S.W.2d 442, 447, 137 Tex. 314.

NEGLIGENTLY,
Magnolia Petroleum Co. v. Dodd, 52 S.W.(2d) 670, 672.

NEGOTIABLE,
F. L. Shaw Co. v. Coleman, 236 S.W. 178, 180.
Hamilton Nat. Bank v. Pool, Tex.Civ.App., 144 S.W.2d 670, 671.
City of Ranger v. Wier, Tex.Civ.App., 148 S.W.2d 870, 873.

FIGURE 7–5 An example of a table of words and phrases

The LCP digest contains short paragraph summaries of all opinions from the United States Supreme Court from its inception to the present date. Figure 7–6 is an example of a page from the LCP digest.

Some state digests are available through publishers other than West, including the *California Digest of Official Reports, Third Series* (Bancroft-Whitney) and the *Illinois Digest, Third Edition* (Callaghan). The annotations in these digests are not assembled with the West key number system. The publishers, however, have developed their own unique classification schemes. For example, Bancroft-Whitney digests are linked to companion *A.L.R.* publications and its headnotes and indexing system.

§ 7.4 Using Digests in Legal Research

Learning how to use digests effectively and efficiently is essential to your being able to carry out legal research projects as thoroughly as you should. Do not, however, overestimate their value. For example, should an opinion have been wrongly digested by a digest editor, it is effectively lost to a researcher who is relying exclusively on digests to find relevant cases.

As a review of this chapter, and also to gain some additional specialized familiarity with the *Texas Digest*, consider the research process you should undertake to deal with a case involving the following facts:

> A three-year-old child accompanies his mother to work one day. The mother cleans apartments and commercial buildings. While cleaning an office, the mother hears a gunshot and runs to the next office. She sees an open desk drawer and her son lying on the floor with a gunshot wound to his head. She immediately calls for assistance. Within minutes her son is undergoing emergency surgery at the hospital for the removal of the bullet. The boy recovers. The mother believes that the office building was negligent in allowing tenants to have weapons hidden, especially since the building management knew the mother frequently brought her son to work.

Your assignment as a legal assistant in this case might be to research the following issues (among many that might ultimately play a role in an attorney's analysis of the strength of the mother's claim against the office building):

1. Is a child in Texas responsible for his or her own negligent actions? If so, what is the determinative age for such responsibility?

2. Is a parent in Texas responsible for a child's negligent actions? If so, what are the determining factors for that responsibility?

Evidence § 243

(K) AS TO JUDICIAL AND OTHER OFFICIAL ACTS; JURISDICTION; VENUE

1. IN GENERAL

§ 243 Generally.

(*In ALR Dig, see Evidence*, §§ 368–372.5; in *Am Jur, see Evidence*, §§ 167–177.)

Acts of corporate officers, see ante, § 205.
Chinese student's certificate issued by consul, see ante, § 115 c.
Compensation of officers, see post, § 388.
Correctness of decision of commissioner of patents, see post, § 336.
Issuance of municipal bonds, see post, § 305.
Issuing patent for invention, see post, §§ 333–336.
Judicial notice of official character and acts, see ante, §§ 19–30.
Presumed grant by, see post, § 355 c–g.
Presumption and burden of proof as to knowledge or notice of facts by public officers, see ante, § 160.
Presumption as to correctness of official action, see ante, § 180 p.
Presumption of intent to perform duty, see ante, § 166 i; post, §§ 257 a, 260 j, 261 a, b, 264 d, 271, 272 l, 299 a, 305 b, c, j, 449 b, 950 d, 1000 a.
Presumption of equality of right between states in boundary waters, see post, § 348 b.
Presumptions on appeal, see APPEAL AND ERROR, §§ 1278–1314.
Prima facie effect of discharge in bankruptcy, see post, § 951.
Sufficiency of evidence as to official acts and records, see post, § 943.

a. Every public officer is presumed to act in obedience to his duty until the contrary is shown.
Wilkes v. Dinsman, 7 How 89,
12 L ed 618
Ross v. Reed, 1 Wheat 482,
4 L ed 141
Martin v. Mott, 12 Wheat 19,
6 L ed 537
Pendleton County v. Amy, 13 Wall 297,
20 L ed 579

b. A presumption exists that every man in his private or official capacity does his duty, until the contrary is proved. Bank of United States v. Dandridge, 12 Wheat 64,
6 L ed 552

c. The law presumes that every man in his private and official character, does his duty until the contrary is proved, it will presume that all things are rightly done, unless the circumstances of the case overturn such presumption. Cincinnati, N. O.

& T. P. R. Co. v. Rankin, 241 US 319, LRA 1917A 265, 36 S Ct 555.
60 L ed 1022

d. Public policy forbids the imputation to authorized official action of any other than legitimate motives. Louisiana v. Texas, 176 US 1, 20 S Ct 251,
44 L ed 347

e. It is a presumption of law that all public officers perform their duties. Philadelphia & T. R. Co. v. Stimpson, 14 Pet 448,
10 L ed 535

f. Presumption is that all officers do their duty, until contrary is proved. Turner v. Yates, 16 How 14,
14 L ed 824

g. It is a general principle to presume that public officers act correctly until the contrary is shown. United States v. Weed, 5 Wall 62,
18 L ed 531

h. In the absence of clear evidence to the contrary, courts presume that public officers have properly discharged their official duties. United States v. Chemical Foundation, 272 US 1, 47 S Ct 1,
71 L ed 131

i. It will be presumed, unless the contrary be shown, that a public officer acted in accordance with the law and his instructions. Moral y Gonzales v. Ross (Gonzales v. Ross) 120 US 605, 7 S Ct 705,
30 L ed 801

j. The presumption always is, in the absence of anything to show the contrary, that a public officer while acting in his official capacity is performing his duty. Weyauwega v. Ayling, 99 US 112,
25 L ed 470

Distinguished in Coler v. Cleburne, 131 US 174, 175, 33 L ed 150, 9 S Ct 724, 725, and Anthony v. County of Jasper, 101 US 699, 25 L ed 1009.

k. Officers charged with the performance of a public duty are presumed to perform it correctly. Quinlan v. Greene County, 205 US 410, 27 S Ct 505.
51 L ed 860

l. Officers of the government are presumed, in the absence of anything to show the contrary, to have performed their duty when called upon to act in their official capacity. United States v. Pugh, 99 US 265,
25 L ed 322

m. No officer, without proof, will be presumed to have violated his duty. Bruce v. United States, 17 How 437,
15 L ed 129

n. The presumption is that a sworn officer, acting in the discharge of his duty, upon a subject over which jurisdiction is given him, has acted rightly. Muser v. Magone, 155 US 240, 15 S Ct 77,
39 L ed 135
439

FIGURE 7–6 A page from the LCP digest

After analyzing the facts in the case, you determine that there are several key words that should assist you in locating applicable case law. The first word that comes to mind is *children*. When you turn to the page from the *Texas Digest* descriptive word index that contains the word *children*, you find only a cross-reference, "see this index Infants." Turning to that section of the index, you discover that there are fourteen pages of subtopics under the word *infants*. The second page of Figure 7–7 shows, under the heading "negligence," the subtopic "Four-year-old child incapable of negligence as matter of law. Autos 223(2)." Using this topic and key number, you quickly locate several Texas cases that have held that a four-year-old is incapable of negligence.

Additional verification of the above finding might be pursued by researching the *Texas Digest* for the word *negligence* as it relates to children. The digest entries (Figure 7–8) reveal numberous Texas cases that have held that the test for negligence in a small child is the standard of conduct applicable to a child of the same age, and not the standard that is applicable to an adult. Notice there is one case that held that "a two-year-old is incapable of negligence."

Summarized in the following text are the steps you should follow with the previous fact scenario and in all research assignments relating to digests. If one step is unsuccessful, you should move on to the next step or try another digest.

Guidelines for Research in Digests

1. Select the digest that covers the jurisdiction of the research situation.
2. Write down words and phrases that may apply to your research situation.
3. Use the descriptive word index in the front of the digest selected to locate key numbers for the research situation.
4. If you are familiar with the topic to be researched, use the topic outline to locate pertinent key numbers.
5. Use the words and phrases outline to locate frequently used words and phrases that have been defined or construed by the courts in the jurisdiction of the research situation.
6. Once your topics and key numbers are located from the index, go to the main volume where the topics are located and identify the key numbers. Here you will find summaries of the cases. Begin reading the summaries.
7. *Make certain the research is as current as possible:* Use all the series of a digest. Check supplements.

CHICKENS

References are to Digest Topics and Key Numbers

CHICKENS

ATTORNEY fees, sufficiency of sworn account pleadings, quantum meruit. Costs 173(1)
HOMESTEAD, use of leased lots by chickens. Home 35
INJURING or killing, criminal liability. Anim 45
KEEPING or possessing within city—
 Const Law 278(4)
 Mun Corp 122(2, 4), 604
POISONING—
 Criminal responsibility. Anim 45
 Weight and sufficiency of evidence in prosecution for poisoning chickens. Anim 45
SALE of diseased chicks—
 Evidence in action for damages—
  Fraud 59(1)
  Neglig 134
 Fraud—
  Damages. Fraud 59(1)
  Reliance by buyer. Fraud 21
  Remedy for. Fraud 31
 Pleading in action for damages. Neglig 111(1)
THEFT of chickens as larceny. Crim Law 27
 Certainty of statute. Crim Law 13
 Different offenses in same transaction. Crim Law 29
 Statutory provisions. Larc 2
 Sufficiency of evidence. Larc 55

CHIEF

ARMY Corps of Engineers, refuse dumping standards, private parties' standing to compel setting. Nav Wat 35
FIRE department. Mun Corp 176(5), 196
 Disciplinary suspension, captain, three days. Const Law 277(2)
POLICE. Mun Corp 182
 Action against, to recover case of dice—
  App & E 931(1)
  Gaming 61
  Nuis 60
 Arrest, authority to arrest without warrant. Arrest 63.2
 Constitutional and statutory provisions. Mun Corp 176(5)
 Creation and abolition of office. Mun Corp 180(3)
 Evidence—
  Suspension of police inspector. Mun Corp 185(10)
 Hearing in jury's absence of evidence of probable cause for search. Crim Law 671
 In rem proceeding for destruction of pinball machine. Gaming 61
 Injunction, taking possession of automobile illegally parked—
  Const Law 235
  Inj 128
 Traffic regulations, delegation of municipal powers. Autos 8

CHIEF CLERKS

COMPTROLLER as public officer. States 44

CHIEF JUSTICE

ACTION by chief justice of county. Counties 217

CHILD CARE FACILITIES

INJURY to minor, liability. Asyl 8
RELIGIOUS organizations, licenses—
 Const Law 84
 Licens 7(1)

CHILD CARE LICENSING ACT

SAFETY, statewide minimum standards, religious belief—
 Asyl 3
 Const Law 84

CHILD LABOR

See this index—
 Infants
 Workers' Compensation

CHILD WELFARE

See this index Parental and Child Welfare

CHILDBEARING

PRESUMPTION of woman's capacity. Evid 58

CHILDBIRTH

ARMY officer's wife failing to receive medical service, liability of United States under Federal Tort Claims Act. U S 78

CHILD-PLACING AGENCY

CONSENT, placement of children for adoption. Adop 7

CHILDREN

See this index Infants

CHILDREN'S COURT

See this index Juvenile Courts

CHILDRENS' HOME

ALLOWANCE from minor wards' estate for maintenance and education. Guard & W 67, 121

CHILDREN'S NURSERY

VILLAGE restrictions as not prohibiting operation in private home. Mun Corp 631(2)

CHILI PARLORS

PROPRIETOR as merchant within statute of limitations. Lim of Act 29(2)

CHILLING BIDDING

AUCTION sale. Auctions 7
FORECLOSURE sale. Ven & Pur 287

CHILLING EFFECT

LOITERING, ordinance's alleged effect, sufficiency for Federal relief. Decl Judgm 128
REINDICTMENT, threat if appeal prosecuted. Const Law 271

CHILLING OF RIGHTS

LOYALTY oath, candidates, support of present representative form of government. Elections 21

CHINA

CONFLICT of laws relative to contract to sell goods to Republic of China. Sales 2

CHINCHILLAS

INFANTS—
 Disaffirmance of contract for purchase of chinchillas. Infants 58(1, 2)
 Individual liability of sellers to minor buyer though sellers were third party agent. Princ & A 136(3)
 Necessaries for minor. Infants 50
MONOPOLIES. Monop 17(2.5)

CHINESE

EXCLUSION or expulsion, see this index Exclusion or Expulsion of Aliens
LAW requiring citizenship qualification for wholesale license to sell fish as denying equal protection of law. Const Law 210

FIGURE 7–7   Pages from the *Texas Digest* descriptive word index

54 Tex D 2d—639

INFANTS

References are to Digest Topics and Key Numbers

INFANTS—Cont'd
NEGLECTED children, delinquent and dependent children, generally, see this index Delinquent and Dependent Children
NEGLIGENCE in general. Infants 61
Attractive nuisance, see this index Attractive Nuisances
Care as to children. Neglig 7
Licensees or invitees. Neglig 32(4)
Playground in drive-in-theater. Neglig 32(4)
Trespassers. Neglig 33(3)
Contributory negligence. Neglig 85
Failure to give warning to injured child. Neglig 52
Four-year-old child incapable of negligence as matter of law. Autos 223(2)
Landowners, failure to warn of dangers of playing upon scrap iron. Neglig 52
Motorboats, failure to seat infant and keep lookout for logs. Nav Wat 23
Notice to city of personal injury claim, minority excusing noncompliance with charter requirement. Mun Corp 741(1)
NEGOTIABLE instruments. Infants 52
NEW trial. Infants 103
Action for injuries to loss of services or society of child. New Tr 163(2)
Actions by or against—
Setting aside verdict in favor of father as affecting verdict in favor of minor in joint action. New Tr 163(2)
Evidence misinterpreted by jury. New Tr 52
NEXT friend, see this index Guardian Ad Litem or Next Friend
NOTICE, infancy as excuse for failure to give notice of tort claim. Mun Corp 741.1(8)
NURSERY, operation in church vicar's residence in violation of zoning code. Zoning 288
NUTRITION programs. Agric 2.7
OATH as witnesses. Witn 45(2)
OPINION evidence in action for injuries to, loss of services or society of child. Evid 506
ORPHAN societies. Infants 17
PARENT, definition. Parent & C 1
PARENT and child—
Abandonment or neglect to support. Parent & C 17
Actions between. Parent & C 11
Advances. Parent & C 10
Agency of child for parent. Parent & C 12
Immunity from liability, see this index Immunity
Notice of criminal proceedings. Infants 68.4
Services and earnings of child. Parent & C 5
Stepchildren. Parent & C 14
PARKS—
City's liability. Mun Corp 747(2)
Injuries in. Mun Corp 857
PARTIES. Infants 74, 75
Custody and control, ante
District Court of United States. Fed Civ Proc 113
Proceeding to determine right to custody and control of child. Parent & C 2(7)
PARTITION—
Appointment of guardian ad litem or next friend. Infants 78(4)
Avoidance by infant. Infants 58(1)
Estoppel against infant. Infants 29
Mother's estate, evidence warranting judgment for daughter for claims. Partit 89
Operation and effect of decree. Infants 113
Presumption as to incapacity of infants. Infants 98
Vacation of judgment by infant. Infants 111
PARTNERS, party to action. Partners 200
PARTNERSHIP—
Between father and son, extent. Partners 65
PASSENGERS, see this index Passengers

INFANTS—Cont'd
PATERNITY proceedings, see this index Illegitimate Children
PAVING lien against minor's property. Mun Corp 434(5)
PERJURY, statutory provisions. Perj 2
PERSONAL injuries—
Intentional infliction, vagueness of felony statute. Crim Law 13.1(8)
Railroad signaling device, negligence. Explos 10
PHYSICIANS and surgeons—
Liability for services performed at request of father. Phys 13
Plea of guilty in criminal prosecution. Crim Law 273
PINBALL machines, arrest and fine for playing. Action 18
PLEADING. Infants 91-95
Injuries or loss of services, control or society of child. Parent & C 7(11)
Proceeding to determine right to custody and control of child. Parent & C 2(7)
PLEADING in actions by or against in general. Infants 91-95
Law of foreign state. Statut 281
PLEAS in criminal prosecutions. Crim Law 273
POWER—
Guardian ad litem or next friend. Infants 84
PRENATAL injuries—
A live birth and survival, cause of action. Infants 72(2)
Right of action for. Infants 72(2)
PRESENTATION of claims, infancy as excuse for failure to present tort claim. Mun Corp 741.1(8)
PRESUMPTION that son's testimony would have been adverse to father who failed to call son as witness. Evid 77(4)
PRINCIPAL and agent, see this index Principal and Agent
PRIVILEGE, as to criminal prosecution. Infants 68
PROCESS, actions by or against. Infants 89
District Court of United States. Fed Civ Proc 424
Prerequisite to appointment of guardian ad litem or next friend. Infants 80(2)
PROCESS in proceedings to determine right to custody and control of child. Parent & C 2(6)
PROCHEIN AMI, see this index Guardian Ad Litem or Next Friend
PROOF of infancy. Infants 99
PROPERTY. Infants 21-45
Action for sale of property. Infants 39
Adverse possession. Infants 24
Cancellation. Infants 31
Capacity to—
Convey. Infants 23
Take and hold. Infants 22
Deeds and conveyances, generally, ante
Equity jurisdiction. Infants 33
Estoppel. Infants 29
Gifts. Infants 28
Judicial sales. Infants 36-45
Foreign and ancillary guardianship. Guard & W 169
Judgment. Infants 39
Jurisdiction of court. Infants 32-34
Lease of infant's property. Infants 44
Marriage, as ratification. Infants 30(3)
Mortgage of infant's property. Infants 43
Orders of court, mortgage or lease under. Infants 36-45
Proceeds of sale, mortgage or lease of property. Infants 45
Ratification of contracts. Infants 30
Rescission. Infants 31
Return of consideration on avoidance of transaction. Infants 31(2)
Sheriff's deed to property. Infants 42

FIGURE 7–7 *(continued)*

☞85(2) NEGLIGENCE

For later cases see same Topic and Key Number in Pocket Part

question of fact about which there might be reasonable difference of opinion.

> Rudes v. Gottschalk, 324 S.W.2d 201, 159 Tex. 552.

Tex. 1949. A child of tender years is not bound to exercise for its own safety the care required of an adult, but the standard by which to measure the child's conduct is that degree of care ordinarily exercised by children of the same age, intelligence, experience and capacity under the same or similar circumstances.

> Dallas Ry. & Terminal Co. v. Rogers, 218 S.W.2d 456, 147 Tex. 617.

Although a three year old child may be conclusively presumed to be incapable of contributory negligence and a sixteen year old may be presumed prima facie to have the capacity and discretion of an adult, the standard by which to measure conduct of an eleven year old child is the degree of care ordinarily exercised by children of the same age, intelligence, experience and capacity, and where his negligence is an issue, charge should set that standard and not standard applicable to an adult.

> Dallas Ry. & Terminal Co. v. Rogers, 218 S.W.2d 456, 147 Tex. 617.

Tex.App. 14 Dist. 1983. Where negligence of child above the age of five is at issue, child's negligence is to be judged by standard of conduct applicable to child of same age and not by that standard that is applicable to adult.

> Thompson v. Wooten, 650 S.W.2d 499.

Tex.Civ.App. 1964. The general rule is that a minor child is required to use only the care which a child of the same age, intelligence and experience would use.

> City of Austin v. Hoffman, 379 S.W.2d 103.

Tex.Civ.App. 1960. Standards of care for children less than 14 years of age are not as great as for adults.

> Kelly v. Hamm-Tex Distributing Co., 337 S.W.2d 608, ref. n.r.e.

Tex.Civ.App. 1959. The term "negligence" as applied to a minor plaintiff means the doing of that which an ordinarily prudent person of the age, intelligence, experience and capacity of the minor would not do or the failure to do that which an ordinarily prudent person of the age, intelligence, experience and capacity of the minor would do under similar circumstances. Rules of Civil Procedure, rule 434.

> Coates v. Moore, 325 S.W.2d 401, ref. n.r.e.

Tex.Civ.App. 1958. The standard of care for a child is not to be judged by that of the reasonably prudent man, but by that care which a child of the same age, intelligence, capacity and experience would ordinarily be expected to exercise under the same or similar circumstances.

> Gottschalk v. Rudes, 315 S.W.2d 361, affirmed 324 S.W.2d 201, 159 Tex. 552.

Tex.Civ.App. 1948. The standard to be applied in determining whether a child was contributorily negligent is that degree of care ordinarily exercised by children of like age, intelligence, capacity and experience under similar circumstances even though the particular child in question is intelligent or has had some experience in the matters involved.

> Rogers v. Dallas Ry. & Terminal Co., 214 S.W.2d 160, affirmed 218 S.W.2d 456, 147 Tex. 617.

Tex.Civ.App. 1943. The term "proper lookout", used in rule requiring an invitee to maintain a proper lookout as applied to eight-year-old child in a store, means such a lookout as a person of similar age, intelligence, and experience in exercise of ordinary care would have kept under similar circumstances.

> J. Weingarten, Inc. v. Carlisle, 172 S.W.2d 170, error refused.

In determining whether an invitee injured in a fall over a carton in the aisle of a store is guilty of contributory negligence, the law makes a reasonable distinction between degree of care required of adults and children based upon their comparable age, judgment and experience, exacting of child less than it does of an adult.

> J. Weingarten, Inc. v. Carlisle, 172 S.W.2d 170, error refused.

☞85(3). Age at which children are chargeable with contributory negligence.

C.A.Tex. 1983. Under Texas law, a two-year-old is incapable of negligence.

> Ellis v. K-Lan Co., Inc., 695 F.2d 157.

C.A.Tex. 1977. Both 13-year-old boy and 11-year-old defendant could be held responsible for their negligent acts under Texas law, and thus Texas doctrine of "unavoidable accident" did not apply in action brought for injuries sustained when 13-year-old boy was struck in head by golf club swung by 11-year-old defendant.

> Morrison v. Sudduth, 546 F.2d 1231.

D.C.Tex. 1975. If a child is under the common-law bracket of 14 years of age, Texas courts apply the standard of care applicable to children; if the child is above the age of 14, the adult standard of care is applied, unless it be shown that the child is wanting in discretion or laboring under the handicap of some mental disability.

> Starr v. U. S., 393 F.Supp. 1359.

For legislative history of cited statutes

FIGURE 7–8 Digest entries from the *Texas Digest*

8. If the name of one party in a case is known, use the table of cases index or the defendant-plaintiff table of cases index.

9. Once your topics and key numbers are identified, write down the applicable case citations.

10. Review the cases listed and determine applicability.

11. Copy any relevant cases for later use.

12. Shepardize all cases. (Refer to Chapter 11.)

Summary

7.1 Introduction to the Digest System

A legal digest, a collection of short case annotations (abstracts) organized by legal issue, expedites the process of locating relevant case law on a particular topic or subject matter. These case annotations are prepared by editors at the publishing company and first appear as headnotes in case reporters. Digests, like the reporters, are compiled by jurisdiction or geographical area. The best known system of digests was developed by West Publishing Company. A summary paragraph in a digest is not legal authority. It has no precedential value and should never be cited as support for any proposition of law. Digests are excellent research tools.

7.2 The West Digest System

West Publishing Company offers the best known and most comprehensive sets of digests, covering all units of the West reporter system. West digests are linked to West's key number system. Each abstract is assigned a topic and key number or numbers. All of West's digests include three valuable internal finding aids: a descriptive word index, a table of cases, and a defendant-plaintiff table. There are five main divisions of West's digests: (1) American Digest System; (2) federal practice and United States Supreme Court digests; (3) regional digests; (4) state digests; and (5) specialty digests.

7.3 Non-West Digests

There are several digests available from publishers other than West. Another major digest publisher is Lawyers Cooperative Publishing Company (LCP). Its digest sets tend to be more specialized than West's. The *United States Supreme Court Reports Digest, Lawyers' Edition* is keyed to headnotes and annotations in the *United States Supreme Court Reports*,

Lawyers' Edition and cross-references *A.L.R.* and *A.L.R. Federal*. Some state digests are available through publishers other than West, including the *California Digest of Official Reports, Third Series* (Bancroft-Whitney) and the *Illinois Digest, Third Edition* (Callaghan). These publishers have developed their own unique classification schemes.

7.4 Using Digests in Legal Research

Learning how to use digests effectively and efficiently is essential to being able to carry out legal research projects as thoroughly as you should. After analyzing a fact situation, determine the key words to locate applicable state law. Use the descriptive word index or its cross-reference. From the topic and key number, you can quickly locate cases on your research issue. Make certain that your research is as current as possible. Use all the series of a digest, and check supplements. Shepardize all cases located through the digest system.

Review Questions

1. Define digest.

2. What is the authority or precedential value of a digest?

3. List three finding aids contained in West's digests.

4. Identify the five main divisions of West's digests.

5. List the three regional reporters for which regional digests are not available.

6. Identify the states that do not have digests available.

7. List three research methods by which to locate relevant key numbers in a digest.

8. If you know only the name of a defendant in a case, which digest table should be used to locate the complete name of the case?

9. What information is available in a table of words and phrases?

10. Identify two non-West digests.

Exercises

1. Visit a law library and become familiar with the federal digests available.

2. Locate and review the state digests maintained by your firm or local law library.

3. Compare your state's digest with any federal digest and determine the similarities and differences.

4. Locate the key numbers applicable to the issue of whether a hotel in Texas is liable for the mugging of a guest in its parking lot.

5. List five descriptive words to assist in locating cases relevant to the facts in exercise 4.

6. Use the descriptive words listed in exercise 5 to begin a digest topic search for cases applicable to exercise 4. Modify the initial word list to the digest topics available.

7. Refer to the table of cases for the *Texas Digest* to locate three cases listed in the digest topics for your key number search in exercise 4.

8. Use the defendant-plaintiff table of cases to locate three cases from your digest topic/key word search.

9. Locate a non-West digest and determine the similarities and differences between that digest and the West digest used in the research topic for these exercises.

10. Review supplements to the *Texas Digest* and locate two cases relevant to the research issue in these exercises.

CHAPTER 8

LEGAL ENCYCLOPEDIAS AND AMERICAN LAW REPORTS

§ 8.1 Legal Encyclopedias

Their Purpose and Nature

Digests are only one of several valuable aids to use in finding the law. Another important set of research tools are legal encyclopedias. **Legal encyclopedias** are secondary sources that provide commentaries about, and case authority for, a myriad of legal subjects. Although most commentaries in legal encyclopedias are general in nature, they can provide important beginning points in legal research, particularly on topics with which the researcher is not already familiar.

Always use caution when researching with legal encyclopedias, for several reasons. First, legal encyclopedias most often present a broad, general overview of the law. Second, legal encyclopedias are secondary sources used as finding tools to lead to primary sources of the law (mainly cases). Never rely on statements of the law in an encyclopedia as authoritative. Encyclopedias may in some instances be used as persuasive authority, but they carry no weight as "law." Third, legal encyclopedias often cite representative cases in an area of law, but the general legal statements they support may not apply to your specific problem and may not at all reflect the case or statutory law in your jurisdiction. Fourth, despite claims of completeness and careful updating, legal encyclopedias do not present and analyze all new cases or changes in the law. Finally, take claims that a rule of law stated in an encyclopedia is the "majority rule" with a certain degree of skepticism. Make that conclusion one you draw yourself only after more comprehensive research in primary sources.

Do not rely on legal encyclopedias exclusively for your research. They are not intended to be, and indeed fall far short of being, exhaustive treatises on every aspect of American law. They are excellent, however, for the purposes for which they are intended.

There are two general legal encyclopedias known to everyone who practices law: *Corpus Juris Secundum* (*C.J.S.*), published by West Publishing Company, and *American Jurisprudence Second* (*Am. Jur. 2d*), published by Lawyers Cooperative Publishing Company, a division of Thomson Legal Publishing Inc.

TERMS

---

legal encyclopedias Secondary sources of law that provide commentaries about, and case authority for, a myriad of legal subjects; general in nature but important in legal research.

Corpus Juris Secundum

Overview

Corpus Juris Secundum (C.J.S.) is a dark blue, multivolume set of books that provides commentaries on the law and contains extensive footnotes to identify cases relating to the commentaries. *Corpus Juris Secundum* encompasses all jurisdictions and presents an overview of all American law. In the words of the publisher, in the preface to 53 *C.J.S.*:

> The basic objective of the C.J.S. set has been to reflect and present in concise and harmonious form the result of the steady stream of precedents which have replaced, modified, or supplemented older doctrines, while at the same time preserving those principles or statements of law which have withstood the test of time and are firmly embedded in our jurisprudence.

To obtain a quick overview of the range of main topics covered in *C.J.S.*, take a look at the list of titles that the publisher has inserted in the front matter section of each volume.

Note that *C.J.S.* was published between 1911 and 1936 in an earlier edition known as *Corpus Juris (C.J.)* The earlier edition has been totally superseded by *C.J.S.* but occasionally may be referenced in *C.J.S.*, citing older cases.

Since *C.J.S.* is a West publication, all West coordinate references are provided. At the beginning of the commentary, the related West topics and key numbers are identified under "Library References." The references permit quick access into the American Digest System, discussed in Chapter 7. (See Figure 8–1.)

As with most finding tools, *C.J.S.* has a pocket part supplement containing changes in the text of the main volume and new cases. This supplement must be consulted for complete and accurate research. In the pocket part, the page of the text in the main volume is referenced, as well as the specific footnote references for any additional cases. (See Figure 8–2.)

Indexes

Corpus Juris Secundum has two types of indexes: a multivolume, softbound general index at the end of the entire set and subject indexes at the end of most volumes in the set. The general index is new and supercedes and replaces the 1981 hardbound indexes. These indexes should be consulted when using *C.J.S.*

General Index   The general index provides access to the specific commentaries in *C.J.S.* To access a subject, look up general words and phrases to find the specific subject in which your area is listed. This process is

§§ 17–18 INNS, HOTELS, ETC. 43A C. J. S.

the innkeeper[1] or were the direct effects of the mental distress and anguish.[2] He may also recover for any unlawful restraint of his liberty.[3] Punitive damages which are not the direct consequence of the wrongful act are not recoverable.[4]

§ 18. Compensation

    a. In general
    b. Actions for compensation

a. In General

An innkeeper can charge only a reasonable compensation and he m' ! usually perform his whole obligation before being enti' d to it.

Research Note

Power to regulate and set rates is considered supra § 6 et seq.

Library References

Innkeepers ⊜12.

An innkeeper may charge for entertaining a guest at rates made by the innkeeper,[5] or by agreement of the parties.[6] Since a person who engages a room at a hotel impliedly promises to pay a reasonable compensation where there is no specific agreement as to payment of compensation,[7] the innkeeper may, in the absence of agreement, charge a reasonable compensation.[8] Under some statutory provisions, unless a person is an innkeeper, he cannot recover for entertainment furnished in the absence of an express agreement for compensation.[9] An undertaking to board and lodge a guest implies an engagement to pay the usual and reasonable attentions to his health and comfort without extra charge therefor, but not to provide the services of a nurse in a severe and protracted illness.[10]

Although it has been said to be a privilege of an inn to demand, in advance, compensation for the accommodation,[11] ordinarily, before being entitled to compensation the innkeeper or boardinghouse keeper must perform his whole obligation.[12] If the obligation is to furnish both room and board, the innkeeper cannot recover compensation, although he furnishes the room, if he has _failed to provide proper board,[13] but, although the innkeeper is forbidden by law to recover for liquor he has furnished to his guest, he may nevertheless recover the amount due for board.[14]

Under some circumstances, compensation may be recovered for a period of time when the guest was not present, as where the guest had made a contract for a definite time,[15] or where he was temporarily absent and a rule of the innkeeper provides for a reasonable charge in such cases.[16] However, recovery of compensation may be had only for the time of actual occupancy where a guest is removed from the premises by the innkeeper,[17] where the agreement is abrogated by mutual consent,[18] or where the guest or boarder, although under an agreement to remain, leaves the inn or motel because of its unsanitary condi-

---

1. N.Y.—Boyce v. Greeley Square Hotel Co., 126 N.E. 647, 228 N.Y. 106.
32 C.J. p 567 note 86.

2. N.Y.—Boyce v. Greeley Square Hotel Co., 126 N.E. 647, 228 N.Y. 106.

3. Mass.—Frewen v. Page, 131 N.E. 475, 238 Mass. 499.

4. **Assault by detective**
Punitive damages were held not recoverable for acts of hotel detective in pushing guest aside when opening door to her room.
Wis.—Meshane v. Second St. Co., 222 N.W. 320, 197 Wis. 382.

5. Pa.—Whalley v. Toddington, 13 Phila. 2.
32 C.J. p 568 note 99 [a].

6. Pa.—Shoemaker v. Beaver, 42 Leg.Int. 511.
32 C.J. p 568 note 1.

7. Ga.—Zappa v. Higgins, 156 S.E.2d 521, 116 Ga.App. 81.

8. Ga.—Baldwin v. Webb, 49 S.E. 265, 121 Ga. 416.

Ky.—Kemper v. Asher's Adm'x, 114 S.W. 2d 525, 272 Ky. 461.
Insurance claim
The fact that a motel operator was advised that the guest had a claim against his fire insurance company for additional living expenses which he incurred by being unable to use his premises does not amount to an agreement between the parties that the motel operator will look solely to the insurance company for compensation.
Ga.—Zappa v. Higgins, 156 S.E.2d 521, 116 Ga.App. 81.

9. Ky.—Rice v. Meade, 272 S.W. 415, 209 Ky. 173.
Snowden v. Snowden, 96 S.W. 922, 29 Ky.L. 1112—Ramsey v. Keith, 76 S.W. 142, 25 Ky.L. 582.

10. Del.—Kennard v. Hobson, 6 Del. 36.

11. Cal.—Orloff v. Hollywood Turf Club, 242 P.2d 660, 110 C.A.2d 340.

12. N.Y.—Wilson v. Martin, 1 Den. 602.

13. N.Y.—Wilson v. Martin, 1 Den. 602.

14. Pa.—Chase v. Burkholder, 18 Pa. 48—Scattergood v. Waterman, 2 Miles 323.

15. La.—Donlin v. Pierce, 133 So. 178, 16 La.App. 24.
32 C.J. p 568 note 11.

16. N.Y.—Smith v. Keyes, 2 Thomps. & C. 650.

17. Cal.—Roberts v. Casey, 93 P.2d 654, 36 C.A.2d Supp. 767.

18. **Airline personnel**
The operator of a motel is not entitled to recover compensation for a period of time after abrogation of an agreement with an airline to use premises for its personnel for a monthly payment where the relationship is not that of landlord and tenant, where the impetus of the abrogation of the agreement was the order of a public agency forbidding the use of particular food and drink from the motel on an interstate airline.
Tex.—Mallam v. Trans-Texas Airways, Civ.App., 227 S.W.2d 344.

FIGURE 8–1 West topic and key numbers are identified under "Library References" in *C.J.S.*

43A CJS 37

§ 333. Limitation by Scope and Penalties of Bond

page 744

83. U.S.—Buddy Systems, Inc. v. Exer-Genie, Inc., C.A.Cal., 545 So.2d 1164.

87. U.S.—National Maritime Union of America, AFL-CIO v. Commerce Tankers Corp., D.C.N.Y., 411 F.Supp. 1224, affd. in part, rev. in part on oth. gds., C.A., 553 F.2d 793, cert. den. 98 S.Ct. 400, 434 U.S. 923, 54 L.Ed.2d 280, two cases.
Fla.—City Nat. Bank of Miami v. Centrust Sav. Bank, App. 3 Dist., 530 So.2d 317.

Conduct in good faith
Fla.—Parker Tampa Two, Inc. v. Somerset Development Corp., App. 2 Dist., 522 So.2d 502, approved 544 So.2d 1018.

88. N.C.—Stevenson v. North Carolina Dept. of Ins., 262 S.E.2d 378, 45 N.C.App. 53.

91. Mass.—Financial Acceptance Corp. v. Garvey, 399 N.E.2d 506, 9 Mass.App. 94.

93. Utah—C.J.S. cited in Corporation of President, Etc. v. Wallace, 573 P.2d 1285, 1288.

§ 334. Particular Items

page 745

1. La.—Fontenot v. Petmecky, App., 386 So.2d 702, writ ref., Sup., 393 So.2d 747.

§ 335. —— Deprivation of Use or Occupation of Property

page 747

20. La.—Roy v. Union Bank, App., 347 So.2d 286, writ den., Sup., 350 So.2d 895, 902.

§ 338. —— Expenses and Costs in Procuring Dissolution

page 750

63. Wash.—Parsons Supply, Inc. v. Smith, 591 P.2d 821, 22 Wash.App. 520.

§ 339. —— Attorney Fees

page 753

88. Cal.—Melnyk v. Robledo, 134 Cal.Rptr. 602, 64 C.A.3d 618.
Wash.—Ritchie v. Markley, 597 P.2d 449, 23 Wash. App. 569.

89. Ala.—Luker v. Perry, Civ., 351 So.2d 591.
N.M.—Shultz v. Pascoe, 614 P.2d 1083, 94 N.M. 634.

page 755

15. La.—Lighthouse Life Ins. Co., Inc. v. Rich, App., 343 So.2d 444.

§ 340. —— —— For What Services Recoverable

page 757

38. Mass.—Financial Acceptance Corp. v. Garvey, 399 N.E.2d 506, 9 Mass.App. 94.
N.M.—Shultz v. Pascoe, 614 P.2d 1083, 94 N.M. 634.

39. Wash.—Cheney v. City of Mountlake Terrace, 583 P.2d 1242, 20 Wash.App. 854.

§ 341. —— —— Amount of Allowance

page 761

69. La.—Roy v. Union Bank, App., 347 So.2d 286, writ den., Sup., 350 So.2d 895, 902.

INNS, HOTELS, AND EATING PLACES

page 763

INJURE.

2. Mo.—C.J.S. cited in State ex rel. County of Shannon v. Chilton, App., 626 S.W.2d 426, 428.

INJURY.

page 770

15. Okl.—C.J.S. cited in Cartwright v. Atlas Chemical Industries, Inc., Okl., 593 P.2d 104, 122, 18 A.L.R.4th 180.

page 772

30. N.Y.—C.J.S. quoted at length in Lippes v. Atlantic Bank of New York, 419 N.Y.S.2d 505, 512, 69 A.D.2d 127.

INNS, HOTELS, AND EATING PLACES

§ 2. Definitions and General Considerations

page 786

42. N.C.—Williams v. Riley, 289 S.E.2d 102, 56 N.C. App. 427.

page 789

85. Or.—Babb v. Lewis, 419 P.2d 423, 244 Or. 537.

§ 3. —— Keeper of Inn, Hotel, Tavern, or Restaurant

page 790

11. Corporation which provides services
Mass.—Brandi v. National Bulk Carriers, Inc., 436 N.E.2d 444, 14 Mass.App. 916.

§ 5. —— Guests and Persons of Similar Status

page 793

66. N.J.—Blair Academy v. Sheehan, 373 A.2d 418, 149 N.J.Super. 113.

page 794

78. Conn.—C.J.S. cited in State v. Anonymous (1977-7), Super., 379 A.2d 1, 2, 34 Conn.Sup. 603.
80. Conn.—State v. Anonymous (1977-7), Super., 379 A.2d 1, 34 Conn.Sup. 603.

page 795

84. Conn.—State v. Anonymous (1977-7), Super., 379 A.2d 1, 34 Conn.Sup. 603.

page 798

16. N.C.—Rappaport v. Days Inn of America, Inc., 250 S.E.2d 245, 296 N.C. 382.
S.D.—Mortenson v. Braley, 349 N.W.2d 444.

§ 6. Power to Regulate in General

page 803

84. N.J.—Blair Academy v. Sheehan, 373 A.2d 418, 149 N.J.Super. 113.

§ 7. Particular Regulations

93. N.Y.—Wood v. Metropolitan Hotel Industry Stabilization Ass'n, 447 N.Y.S.2d 813, 112 Misc.2d 601.

INNS, HOTELS, AND EATING PLACES § 12

Requirement of night watchman
N.Y.—People v. Doria Hotels, Inc., 386 N.Y.S.2d 961, 88 Misc.2d 9.

Purpose of statute
Wash.—Herberg v. Swartz, 578 P.2d 17, 89 Wash.2d 916.

page 804

98. Posting of rates inadequate
Fla.—Motel 6, Operating L.P. v. Department of Business Regulation, Div. of Hotels and Restaurants, App. 1 Dist., 560 So.2d 1322.

2. N.Y.—First Colonie Co. v. Lyons, 425 N.Y.S.2d 667, 74 A.D.2d 696, affd. 426 N.E.2d 486, 54 N.Y.2d 719, 442 N.Y.S.2d 992.

5. Dormitories of private schools
N.J.—Blair Academy v. Sheehan, 373 A.2d 418, 149 N.J.Super. 113.

page 805

7. Ga.—Teachers Retirement System of Georgia v. City of Atlanta, 288 S.E.2d 200, 249 Ga. 196.

10. Privilege tax
Tenn.—Pete v. Cumberland County, 621 S.W.2d 731.

§ 8. —— Licenses

Owner lessor of hotel liable
8. Nev.—20th Century Hotel & Casino, Ltd. v. Clark County, 625 P.2d 576, 97 Nev. 155.

page 806

25. Boardinghouse not within hotel statute
Tex.—Bullock v. Ramada Texas, Inc., Civ.App., 586 S.W.2d 651, err. ref. no rev. err.

26. Operation and effect
Iowa—Fleur de Lis Motor Inns, Inc. v. Bair, 301 N.W.2d 685.

30. N.Y.—Turf House, Inc. v. Hammond, 445 N.Y. S.2d 296, 83 A.D.2d 367.

page 807

38. Tax based on gross receipts
Wis.—Blue Top Motel, Inc. v. City of Stevens Point, 320 N.W.2d 172, 107 Wis.2d 392.

page 808

60. College entitled to motel license
Fla.—City of Hallandale v. Prospect Hall College, Inc., App. 4 Dist., 414 So.2d 239.

§ 11. Offenses

page 811

1. Cal.—Archibald v. Cinerama Hotels, 140 Cal.Rptr. 599, 73 C.A.3d 152.

§ 12. —— By Guests, Boarders, or Lodgers

page 812

24. Ala.—C.J.S. quoted at length in Cottonreeder v. State, Cr.App., 389 So.2d 1169, 1173.

page 813

30. Ala.—C.J.S. quoted at length in Cottonreeder v. State, Cr.App., 389 So.2d 1169, 1174.

page 814

54. Intent to defraud
Okl.—Wagoner v. State, Cr., 617 P.2d 895.
55. La.—State v. Pope, 382 So.2d 912. **Page 814**

FIGURE 8–2 A pocket part supplement to *C.J.S.* contains changes in the text of the main volume and new cases

similar to using the descriptive word indexes of the West digests, which are discussed in Chapter 7. Once you have found your specific subject, next to the entry will be a boldfaced topic title and section number where the specific concept of law is addressed. Write the subject and section entry down and then retrieve the appropriate volume (clearly marked on the spine) from the library shelf and open to your subject and section. (See Figure 8–3.)

Avoid the seemingly sensible shortcut of directly retrieving a *C.J.S.* volume from the shelf. Often what you think should be a major subject in fact is not. Let the general index guide you to the appropriate subject and *C.J.S.* volume.

Subject Indexes At the end of most *C.J.S.* volumes is an index section containing separate indexes for each subject title covered in that volume. If you are already certain of the topic title you want to consult but need assistance in locating discussion of a specific subtopic within that title, you can go directly to the subject-specific index. (See Figure 8–4.)

In the subject-specific index, only section numbers within the title are given. The publisher assumes that you recognize that the index is a focused index and does not repeat the subject topic for each entry. Note that newer volumes of *C.J.S.* do not have a subject-specific index. Therefore, for those volumes, consulting the general index is appropriate.

Table of Contents

In addition to a subject-specific index, each *C.J.S.* main subject title begins with a detailed table of contents labeled "Analysis." The table of contents lists in an outline format the numbers and titles of all sections found in the title. This outline can give you a valuable "quick-glance" overview of a particular title. Although this overview represents the *C.J.S.* approach to classifying the law in the area, the likelihood is strong that most legal issues of interest in the topic area will be identified in the outline. (See Figure 8–5.)

American Jurisprudence

American Jurisprudence 2d: The Encyclopedia

American Jurisprudence 2d, cited as *Am. Jur. 2d*, is the title of the current edition of the multivolume, green legal encyclopedia published by Lawyers Cooperative Publishing Company (LCP). It consists of over eighty-two volumes containing coverage of various legal topics and six volumes of softbound indexes and tables. *American Jurisprudence 2d* has been published

INNOCENCE

INNOCENCE—Continued
Nuisances, innocent owners—Continued
    Destruction or forfeiture of innocent owner's property on abatement of nuisance, **Nuis** § 130
    Forfeiture as against, of personal property on abatement of public nuisance, **Nuis** § 129
Pardon and parole,
    Implication, operation and effect, **Pardon** § 18
    Presumptions, applications, **Pardon** § 13
Price control, violations, defenses, **War** § 109
Purchasers. Bona Fide Purchasers, generally, this index
Rape,
    Instruction that presumption of chastity will not control presumption of innocence, **Rape** § 82
    Instructions to jury, **Rape** § 82
    Presumption, **Rape** § 46
    Prosecutrix' failure to complain as evidence of accused's innocence, **Rape** § 54
Reformation of instruments, correction of misdescription without prejudice to rights of innocent third person, **Ref of Inst** § 42
Sales, innocent misrepresentation,
    Avoidance of contracts, **Sales** § 37
    Rescission, **Sales** § 95
Securities and securities regulation,
    Issuance in violation of statute, state regulation, **Sec Reg** § 232
    Protection, state regulation, **Sec Reg** § 192
Seduction, accused, presumption, **Seduct** § 45
Trespass, presumption, **Tresp** §§ 86, 163
Trover and conversion,
    Innocence of wrong, **Trover** § 7
    Innocent bailee, demand and refusal, **Trover** § 56
    Innocent transporter of stolen property, **Trover** § 36
Trusts and trustees, innocent third persons, estoppel and waiver, interest of beneficiary, **Trusts** § 191
Vendor and purchaser, innocent third person, election of remedies, **Ven & Pur** § 543

INNOCENT
Defined, Vol. 43A

INNOCENT PURCHASER
Bona Fide Purchasers, generally, this index
Defined, **Chat Mtg** § 263

INNOCENTLY
Defined, Vol. 43A

INNOCUOUS ACTS
Crimes and offenses, **Crim Law** § 37

INNOMINATE
Defined, Vol. 43A

INNOMINATE CONTRACT
Defined, **Contracts** § 10

INNOVATE
Defined, Vol. 43A

INNOVATION
Defined, Vol. 43A

INNS, HOTELS AND EATING PLACES
Generally, see Title Index to **Landlord and Tenant**
Abatement and revival, survival of action for injuries, **Abate & R** § 145
Abduction, liability, **Abduc** § 15
Actions,
    Generally, see Title Index to **Inns, Hotels and Eating Places**
    Contract or tort action for breach of duty toward guest, **Actions** § 49
Admissibility of Evidence, this index
Admission tax, **Theaters** § 20
Advertisements, this index
Agents and agency,
    Implied agency, **Agency** § 57
    Torts, warning tourists, duty of agent to principal, **Agency** § 272
Aliens, resident aliens, management, ordinances, **Aliens** § 8
Armed services, mortgage foreclosure, default judgment, opening judgment, **Armed S** § 146
Assault and battery, see Title Index to **Inns, Hotels and Eating Places**
Assumed or Fictitious Names, this index
Assumption of risk, see Title Index to **Inns, Hotels and Eating Places**
Baggage,
    Generally, see Title Index to **Inns, Hotels and Eating Places**
    Carriers, claim check including privilege of checking baggage, **Carr** § 866
    Transportation of baggage from station, **Commerce** § 24
Bailments, this index
Bathtubs, this index
Boarding and Lodging Houses, generally, this index
Buildings, this index
Burden of Proof, this index
Burglary, this index
Butcher, workmen's compensation, **Work C** § 36
Carpets, this index
Carriages of guests, right to keep in adjoining street, **Mun Corp** § 1709
Carriers,
    Claim check including privilege of checking baggage, **Carr** § 866
    Porter, acceptance of goods for as agent of carrier, liability for loss, **Carr** § 146
    Wrongful ejection of passengers, damages as recoverable for hotel expenses, **Carr** § 848
Chattel mortgages,
    Description of fixtures and furniture in mortgage, sufficiency, **Chat Mtg** § 57
    Furniture as subject to mortgage, **Chat Mtg** § 22
    Lien, priority over mortgage, **Chat Mtg** § 302
Checkrooms, see Title Index to **Inns, Hotels and Eating Places**
Children and minors, see Title Index to **Inns, Hotels and Eating Places**
Cigars, sale on Sunday, **Sunday** § 13
Civil rights, **Commerce** §§ 32, 63, 98
    See, also, Discrimination, generally, post
    Common law, **Civil R** § 11
    Improper seizure of property of guest, **Civil R** § 113

584

FIGURE 8–3 The general index provides access to the specific commentaries in *C.J.S.*

INDEX TO
INNS, HOTELS, AND EATING PLACES

Ab initio, custody of property, liability for loss, § 41

Abandoned or unclaimed property, sales, § 43

Abandonment, guest status, § 5, p. 801

Absconding debtors,
Entry without permission, § 17
Guests, § 12

Absence,
Mauager, protection of property, § 26
Rates and charges, payment, § 18

Act of God,
Loss of property, extent of liability, § 39
Property damage, § 37

Actions and proceedings,
Compensation, § 18
Guests, damages, § 15
Liens for charges, enforcement, § 19, p. 830
Personal injuries, §§ 29–35, pp. 859–879
Property damage, § 51
Evidence, § 52

Admissibility of evidence,
Eviction, § 15
Fire damage, § 13, n. 67
Personal injuries, § 31, p. 866
Property damage, § 52, p. 908

Advance payments, rates and charges, § 18
Regulations, § 14, n. 1

Advertisements,
Crimes and offenses, § 11
Occupation as innkeeper, § 3
Rates, rules and regulations, § 7

Affirmative defenses, personal injuries, § 30

Affray, officers and employees, injuries to guests, § 22

Agents,
Guests, property damage, § 37, n. 95
Licenses and permits, § 11

Alcoholic beverages. Intoxicating liquors, generally, post

Alcoholism. Drunkards and drunkenness, generally, post

American plan, license fees, § 8

Amusement area, safety of premises, § 24, p. 845, n. 9

Apartment hotel, distinguished, § 2, p. 786

Appliances, safety, § 24, n. 840

Apprehension, personal injuries, § 20

Arrest, guests, duties of innkeeper, § 14, n. 82

Arson, personal injuries, § 27, n. 15

Asphyxiation, heaters, safety of premises, § 25, p. 846, n. 34

Assault and battery,
Action for damages, § 29
Drunken guests, § 23, n. 33
Guests, § 14
Questions of law and fact, § 32
Third persons, § 23

Assault and battery—Continued
Officers and employees, § 22
Negligence, questions of law and fact, § 33
Off premises, evidence, § 31, p. 868, n. 6
Pleading, § 30, n. 3
Scope of employment, instructions to jury, § 35, n. 55
Weight and sufficiency of evidence, § 31, p. 868
Persons waiting for relatives in lobby, § 16, n. 54
Third persons, instructions to jury, § 35, n. 54

Assignments, guests, status, § 5, p. 801

Assumed or fictitious names,
Crimes and offenses, notice, § 11
Guests, § 5, p. 800, n. 49
Registration, § 12

Assumption of risk,
Instructions to jury, § 35
Personal injuries, § 28, p. 855
Burden of proof, § 31, p. 863
Evidence, § 31, p. 870
Third person, § 26, n. 87
Questions of law and fact, § 34

Auctions and auctioneers, abandoned property, disposition, § 43

Automobiles. Motor vehicles, generally, post

Baggage,
Accommodations, § 2, p. 785
Cab area, failure to watch, § 46, n. 86
Conditions precedent, § 14
Custody of property, liability for losses, § 41
Damage to property, § 40
Evidence of intent to refuse to pay rent, § 12
Liens and encumbrances, compensation, § 19, p. 825
Limitation of liability, § 44

Loss,
Amount of liability, § 48, n. 24
Limitation of liability, § 47
Personal property, generally, post
Protection of property, § 49
Surreptitious removal, fraud, § 12

Bailment,
See, also, C.J.S. Bailments
Liability of innkeeper, § 41
Loss of property, § 43
Evidence, § 52, p. 907
Limitation of liability, § 44
Property damage, actions and proceedings, § 51
Protection of property, § 49
Restaurants, § 50

Banquet room, fall over chairs, contributory negligence, § 34, n. 27

Banquets, guests, bailment, loss of property, § 43, n. 93

968

FIGURE 8–4 Subject-specific indexes are located at the end of most *C.J.S.* volumes

43A C. J. S.

INNS, HOTELS, AND EATING PLACES

Analysis

Sub-Analysis

See also descriptive word index in volume containing end of this Title

781

FIGURE 8–5   A detailed table of contents begins each *C.J.S.* main subject title

HOTELS, MOTELS, AND RESTAURANTS

Scope of Topic: This article covers the law relating to the operation of hotels, motels, restaurants, boarding or lodging houses, and other places furnishing shelter and accommodations for compensation. It discusses the regulation of such businesses and the status, rights, duties, and liabilities of the owners or operators thereof with respect to their guests, patrons, boarders, or lodgers.

Treated elsewhere are the sale of intoxicating liquor in such establishments (see INTOXICATING LIQUORS); liability with respect to the sale of unwholesome or unfit food (see 35 Am Jur 2d, FOOD §§ 94, 97); the applicability of zoning regulations (see ZONING AND PLANNING); restrictive covenants (see 20 Am Jur 2d, COVENANTS, CONDITIONS, AND RESTRICTIONS §§ 212, 215, 231); the use of a building, room, apartment, or premises as a place of abode or sojourn under a lease (see LANDLORD AND TENANT); offenses committed in the serving of fish and game in violation of the fish or game laws (see 35 Am Jur 2d, FISH AND GAME); and the keeping of disorderly houses (see 24 Am Jur 2d, DISORDERLY HOUSES).

✦ Table of Parallel References see p vii ✦

I. IN GENERAL; DEFINITIONS AND DISTINCTIONS (§§ 1–12)

II. GUEST OR OTHER RELATIONSHIP
   A. IN GENERAL (§§ 13–16)
   B. PARTICULAR MATTERS AFFECTING EXISTENCE OF STATUS (§§ 17–25)
   C. DURATION AND TERMINATION OF RELATIONSHIP (§§ 26, 27)

III. PUBLIC REGULATION
   A. IN GENERAL (§§ 28–32)
   B. PARTICULAR REGULATIONS (§§ 33–48)

IV. ESTABLISHMENTS AS NUISANCE; ABATEMENT (§§ 49–52)

V. RIGHTS, DUTIES, AND LIABILITIES, IN GENERAL (§§ 53–58)

VI. DUTIES AND LIABILITIES AS TO RECEPTION, ACCOMMODA-
   TION, AND SOJOURN
   A. IN GENERAL (§§ 59–61)
   B. DUTY TO RECEIVE AND ENTERTAIN (§§ 62–67)
   C. EJECTION OR REMOVAL; VOLUNTARY DEPARTURE (§§ 68–72)
   D. ACTIONS AND OFFENSES (§§ 73–80)

VII. LIABILITY FOR PERSONAL INJURIES OR INDIGNITIES
   A. IN GENERAL (§§ 81–86)
   B. DEFECTIVE OR DANGEROUS CONDITION OF PREMISES AND FURNISHINGS
      (§§ 87–106)
   C. OTHER CAUSES OR CIRCUMSTANCES OF INJURY OR DEATH (§§ 107–119)
   D. ACTIONS (§§ 120–125)

893

FIGURE 8–8   An illustrative outline from *Am. Jur. 2d* (compare with Figure 8–5)

since 1940. It replaced the original set that was entitled *American Jurisprudence (Am. Jur.)*.

Similar in format and design to *C.J.S.*, *Am. Jur. 2d* provides wide-ranging commentaries on diverse areas of the law, with cases, statutes, and administrative agency regulations cited in footnotes. Updating is through pocket part supplement pamphlets and periodically through revised volumes.

Citation of cases in *Am. Jur. 2d* is much more selective than in *C.J.S. Corpus Juris Secundum* purports to cite all relevant cases in its footnotes, while *Am. Jur. 2d* limits citations to only a sample of leading cases. This difference can be important if you are using an encyclopedia as a tool for finding cases in a particular jurisdiction rather than for learning general principles.

In terms of substantive coverage, the number of main topics in *Am. Jur. 2d* is virtually the same as in *C.J.S.*, although the topics may be named differently and the scope of coverage of each may differ between the two encyclopedias. For example, if you needed to research a question of agency, you would find in *Am. Jur. 2d* a subject title of "Agency," whereas in *C.J.S.* the corresponding title is "Principal and Agent." For a complete listing of titles in *Am. Jur. 2d*, you should refer to the listing in a separate volume entitled *American Jurisprudence 2d, Desk Book*.

American Jurisprudence 2d provides additional research references primarily to coordinate publications in LCP's Total Client Service Library (TCSL) system. These include *A.L.R.*, other *Am. Jur.* sets, and *U.S.C.S.* References to *C.F.R.* are also included. No West publications are referenced, nor are any topics and key numbers from the West Digest system given. For an example, review Figure 8–6.

Like *C.J.S.*, *Am. Jur. 2d* is designed so that users must rely heavily on indexes to access its subjects. There are both general and subject-specific indexes. The general index is a multivolume, softbound set at the end of the set of volumes. Subject-specific indexes, arranged in the order of the titles covered in the volume, appear at the end of each volume. The process of using these indexes is the same as that discussed earlier for the *C.J.S.* indexes. (See Figure 8–7.)

American Jurisprudence 2d also provides a detailed table of contents for each of its titles. This table of contents, or topic outline, is located at the beginning of each subject title. An illustrative outline is set out in Figure 8–8. Compare this outline with the *C.J.S.* outline for the same general topic area that is set out in Figure 8–5. You will notice that the editors and writers who compile each of these encyclopedias approach topics differently. As a result, you probably should review both *C.J.S.* and *Am. Jur. 2d* if you are going to use an encyclopedia for research. With either encyclopedia,

§ 33   HOTELS, MOTELS, ETC.   40 Am Jur 2d

compliance thereof a penal offense and prescribe penalties for their violation.[17] The imposition of penalties is a valid exercise of the police power, and they are upheld insofar as they are not unreasonable.[18] However, a penal clause which is highly unreasonable has been held to render the whole act void irrespective of whether its provisions would otherwise be valid;[19] but where a penal clause is not essential to the integrity of the act as a whole, it has been held not to invalidate the remainder of the act, being separable therefrom.[20] Statutes which have attempted to penalize by imprisonment the failure to pay required fees have, in some instances, been held unconstitutional as violative of the prohibition against imprisonment for debt.[1]

B. PARTICULAR REGULATIONS

1. IN GENERAL

§ 33. Generally.

Under the police power, reasonable regulations may be adopted and enforced governing the construction, operation, and use of buildings in which inns, hotels, motels, boardinghouses, restaurants, and similar places are conducted.[2] A municipal counsel has been held to have the power to require the keepers of boardinghouses, restaurants, and hotels to furnish the street commissioner with the names of persons liable to poll tax who are boarding or lodging in their houses, and to impose a fine for refusal to do so.[3] But an ordinance prohibiting the proprietor of a restaurant from permitting patrons to dance without extra charge while the place is open for the purchase of refreshments has been held invalid.[4]

A municipal ordinance requiring all lunch wagons to be closed from 1 a.m. to 7 a.m. on all days is unreasonable and unconstitutionally discriminatory in failing to include within its terms other establishments in the nature of restaurants since lunch wagons as purveyors of food do not differ essentially from restaurants in general.[5]

---

17. Adams v Miami Beach Hotel Asso. (Fla) 77 So 2d 465; State v Norval Hotel Co. 103 Ohio St 361, 133 NE 75, 19 ALR 637.
Annotation: 22 ALR2d 785, § 6 (motels, motor courts, and tourist camps).

18. Bonnett v Vallier, 136 Wis 193, 116 NW 885.

19. Bonnett v Vallier, supra, holding that where the penal feature of a police regulation is so severe, having regard to the nature of the regulation, as to efficiently intimidate property owners from using their property for tenements or lodginghouse purposes, and from resorting to the courts for redress or defense as to their honestly supposed rights, it is highly unreasonable.

20. Hubbell v Higgins, 148 Iowa 36, 126 NW 914.

1. Hubbell v Higgins, supra; State v McFarland, 60 Wash 98, 110 P 792.

2. The fact that the value of a hotelkeeper's investment will be lessened if he is required

to make improvements in lighting and ventilating rooms to conform with a municipal ordinance does not invalidate it. Daniels v Portland, 124 Or 677, 265 P 790, 59 ALR 512.

For a full discussion of building regulations generally, see 13 Am Jur 2d, BUILDINGS §§ 2 et seq.

3. Topeka v Boutwell, 53 Kan 20, 35 P 819.

4. Chicago v Drake Hotel Co. 274 Ill 408, 113 NE 718.
Annotation: 48 ALR 151, s. 60 ALR 173.

5. Hart v Teaneck Twp. 135 NJL 174, 50 A2d 856, 169 ALR 973, holding, however, that the fact that no restaurants except lunch wagons remain open all night was immaterial in determining the validity of the ordinance, since the validity thereof was to be tested not by what is actually done but by what it permits to be done, and voluntary compliance with a discriminatory ordinance contributes nothing to its validity.
Annotation: 169 ALR 979.

922

FIGURE 8–6   An example from *Am. Jur. 2d*

40 Am Jur 2d   HOTELS, MOTELS, ETC.   § 35

Regulations for the protection of civil rights with respect to the use of inns, hotels, motels, boardinghouses, and restaurants,[6] and those relating to the use and sale of intoxicating liquors in such places,[7] are treated in other articles.

§ 34. Inspection.

The police power justifies reasonable regulations providing for the official inspection of hotels, boardinghouses, restaurants, and similar places, to insure and check compliance with statutory requirements.[8] A statute providing for the inspection of hotels, and declaring that every structure kept, used, advertised, or held out to the public to be an inn, hotel, or public lodginghouse, or place where sleeping accommodations are furnished for hire to transient guests, in which 10 or more sleeping rooms are used for guests' accommodations, shall be deemed within the act, is not unconstitutional as arbitrary in its classification of hotels.[9] A statute may validly provide for the payment of an inspection fee and its collection in a civil action, but it may not make the mere failure to pay the inspection fee a misdemeanor, subjecting the hotelkeeper to a fine or imprisonment or both, for to do so would be unconstitutional as violative of the prohibition against imprisonment for debt.[10]

§ 35. Rates or charges.

The validity of regulations requiring innkeepers to file with the proper public authority schedules of the fixed prices for rooms and to give notice in advance of changes in such schedules has been sustained against various constitutional objections.[11] The purpose of such regulation is to prevent innkeepers from exacting exorbitant or unfair charges when there is an acute demand for facilities.[12] Under some early statutes, an innkeeper is expressly prohibited from charging higher prices than those fixed by statute or by the proper public authority,[13] and it is considered a penal offense to violate such a statute.[14] Some very early cases took the view that innkeepers were indictable for extortion for charging excessive prices for their accommodations.[15]

Although hotels are not public utilities subject to the regulatory powers of a public service or utilities commission,[16] such a commission has been held to have the authority to require the filing of tariff schedules fixing the rate that hotels may charge their guests for telephone services rendered.[17]

6. See 15 Am Jur 2d, Civil Rights §§ 28, 30.

7. See Intoxicating Liquors (Rev ed §§ 231, 232).

8. Chicago v R. & X. Restaurant, 369 Ill 65, 15 NE2d 725, 117 ALR 1313; Hubbell v Higgins, 148 Iowa 36, 126 NW 914; State v McFarland, 60 Wash 98, 110 P 792.

9. Hubbell v Higgins, 148 Iowa 36, 126 NW 914; State v McFarland, 60 Wash 98, 110 P 792.
Annotation: 172 ALR 203.

10. Hubbell v Higgins, 148 Iowa 36, 126 NW 914; State v McFarland, 60 Wash 98, 110 P 792.

11. State v Norval Hotel Co. 103 Ohio St 361, 133 NE 75, 19 ALR 637.

Annotation: 19 ALR 641.

12. State v Norval Hotel Co., supra.

13. Banks v Oden, 8 Ky (1 AK Marsh) 546; South v Grant, 7 NJL 26; Talbott v Southern Seminary, 131 Va 576, 109 SE 440, 19 ALR 534.
Annotation: 19 ALR 641.

14. State v Wynne, 8 NC 451.

15. Newton v Trigg, 1 Shower KB 268, 89 Eng Reprint 566; Luton v Bigg, Skinner 291, 90 Eng Reprint 131.

16. § 30, supra.

17. People ex rel. Public Service Com. v New York Tel. Co. 175 Misc 128, 22 NYS2d 837, affd 262 App Div 440, 29 NYS2d 513, affd 287 NY 803, 40 NE2d 1020.

923

FIGURE 8–6   *(continued)*

AMERICAN JURISPRUDENCE 2d

HOSTILITY—Cont'd
Jury, peremptory challenges in case of antagonistic interest, Jury §§ 261, 262, 264
Libel and Slander (this index)
Life tenants and remaindermen, hostility affecting virtual representation, Life Ten §§ 8-10
Limitation of actions, hostility of courts to, Lim Act § 5
Malicious prosecution, hostility as proof of malice, Mal Pros § 152
Monopolies, Restraints of Trade, and Unfair Trade Practices (this index)
Passports, hostile countries to U.S., Passp §§ 43, 44
Receivers, removal for hostility, Receiv § 197
Trusts, hostility between trustee and beneficiaries as ground for judicial removal or discharge, Trusts § 131
War, hostilities necessary for existence of, War § 3
Witnesses (this index)

HOTBOXES
Labor and labor relations, Labor § 2533

HOT CARGO CLAUSES
Labor and Labor Relations (this index)

HOTCHKISS PRINCIPLE
Patents, Pat § 147

HOTCHPOT
Advancements or Prepayment (this index)
Wills, bringing into "hotchpot," ademption, Wills §§ 1733, 1734

HOTDOGS
Products liability, Prod Liab §§ 498, 674

HOT DOG STANDS
Generally, Hotels §§ 10, 51

HOTELS AND MOTELS
Abatement of action for injuries resulting from failure to maintain safe premises, Hotels § 120
Abatement of nuisances, Hotels §§ 49-52
Absconding without payment for food or lodging, Hotels §§ 79, 80
Absence from premises, continuation of guest relationship during, Hotels § 26
Absolute liability of proprietor generally, Hotels § 82
– defective or dangerous condition of premises or furnishings, generally, Hotels § 87
– employees, servants, or agents, liability for injury or death caused by acts of, generally, Hotels §§ 107, 108
– fire, Hotels §§ 115, 167
– infant guest, Hotels § 85
– motor vehicle of guest, loss of or damage to, Hotels § 135
– property, liability for loss of, or damage to, generally, Hotels §§ 126, 127
– restaurants and other eating places, liability of proprietors of, for property of patrons, Hotels § 180
– statutory limitation of liability, generally, Hotels § 153
Abusive language by employee, servant, or agent, Hotels § 110
Accommodations, duties and liabilities as to. Reception, accommodations, and sojourn, infra
Actions and remedies
– damages, infra

HOTELS AND MOTELS—Cont'd
Actions and remedies—Cont'd
– evidence, infra
– failure to obtain license as barring civil action to recover for board and lodging, Hotels § 48
– personal injuries or indignities, liability for, infra
– pleading, infra
– property, liability for loss of or damage to, Hotels §§ 181-186
– reception, accommodations, and sojourn, duties and liabilities as to, infra
– reputation of establishment, action for wilful injury to, Hotels § 56
– trial, infra
– wrongful diversion of business from establishment, liability for, Hotels § 54
Act of God, loss of or damage to property caused by, Hotels §§ 126, 167
Actual notice. Notice or knowledge, infra
Additional license fee or tax, requirement of, Hotels § 46
Adequacy of lighting. Lighting, infra
Administrative bodies or agencies, regulation by, Hotels §§ 30, 43
Admissibility of evidence. Evidence, infra
Admissions against interest by employee or servant of proprietor, Hotels §§ 122, 184
Advance agreement as to length of stay, effect on status as guest, Hotels § 22,
Advance payment of rates and charges, requirement of, Hotels § 57
Advertising (this index)
Agents. Employees, servants, or agents, infra
Age of occupants, restrictions as to, Hotels § 41
Agreements. Contracts or agreements, infra
Alcoholic beverages. **Intoxicating Liquors** (this index)
Amount or quantity
– boardinghouse, number of guests as indicating status as, Hotels § 6
– license fee or tax based on number of rooms, Hotels § 47
– money lost by guest, amount of generally, Hotels § 134
– – statutory limitation of liability, Hotels § 156
– restriction as to number of occupants, Hotels § 41
– statutory limitation of amount of liability, Hotels §§ 156, 158
Animals (this index)
Animus revertendi on part of guest, Hotels § 26
Anticipation or contemplation
– defenses in pleading in action for personal injuries, anticipation of, Hotels § 121
– improper or tortious conduct by guest, patron, or third person, anticipation of, Hotels §§ 111, 112
– returning by guest, expectation of, effect of liability of proprietor for guest's property, Hotels § 146
Apartment house and apartment hotel, Hotels § 8
Apparent scope of employment, Hotels §§ 140, 164
Arbitrary refusal to receive and entertain patrons or guests, Hotels § 62
Arbitrary regulations, Hotels §§ 29, 31, 42
Arrest of guest, duty of innkeeper to prevent, Hotels § 56

HOTELS AND MOTELS—Cont'd
"Articles of gold or silver manufacture" within statute limiting liability of innkeeper, construction of phrase, Hotels § 157
Assault and Battery (this index)
Assets in receivership, hotel property as, Receiv § 155
Assignment of room or location, Hotels §§ 16, 20, 60
Associations and Clubs (this index)
Assumpsit action for loss of or damage to property of guest, Hotels § 181
Assumption of risk. Contributory negligence or assumption of risk, infra
Attachment and garnishment
– enforcement of proprietor's lien by garnishment of wages of guest or boarder, Hotels § 191
– loss of proprietor's lien by levy of, attachment on property, Hotels § 189
Attorneys' fees in action for loss of or damage to guest's property, Hotels § 186
Automobile insurance, hotel maintaining parking lot as engaging in "automobile business", Auto Ins § 94
Automobiles. Motor vehicles, infra
Aviation, federal regulation of hotel package tours, Avi § 46
Bad character or reputation. Character or reputation, infra
Baggage
– boarding, lodging, or rooming house proprietors, liability of, Hotels § 178
– defined or construed, Hotels §§ 133, 192, 193
– delivery of baggage check, effect of, Hotels § 144
– leaving baggage in custody of innkeeper, effect on status as guest, Hotels § 19
– lien of proprietor, property subject to, Hotels § 192
– ordinary bailee, liability as, Hotels § 129
– property for which proprietor liable, generally, Hotels § 131
– property subsequently brought into hotel by guest, liability for, Hotels § 132
– removal of baggage by use of fraud, Hotels § 79
– show or sale, goods of guest kept for, Hotels § 137
– sleeping car company's liability for baggage as that of innkeeper, Carriers §§ 1293, 1301
Bailments (this index)
Balcony railings, failure to provide, Hotels § 88
Ball or other special function, guest status of persons attending, Hotels § 15
Banisters for steps or stairs, Hotels § 97
Banquet or other special function, persons attending, as guests, Hotels § 15
Barber shop, right of innkeeper to conduct, Hotels § 54
Bar equipment as fixtures, Fixt § 94
Bar. Tavern or bar, infra
Basis of liability for loss of or damage to property, Hotels § 127
Bathhouse maintained or operated by innkeeper, Hotels §§ 18, 130
Bathroom
– defective or dangerous condition of bathroom fixtures in room, Hotels § 104
– leaving coat in powder room, Hotels § 176
– toilet facilities, Hotels §§ 18, 27, 91

FIGURE 8–7 A sample from an *Am. Jur. 2d* general index

HOTELS, MOTELS, AND RESTAURANTS

Scope of Topic: This article covers the law relating to the operation of hotels, motels, restaurants, boarding or lodging houses, and other places furnishing shelter and accommodations for compensation. It discusses the regulation of such businesses and the status, rights, duties, and liabilities of the owners or operators thereof with respect to their guests, patrons, boarders, or lodgers.

Treated elsewhere are the sale of intoxicating liquor in such establishments (see INTOXICATING LIQUORS); liability with respect to the sale of unwholesome or unfit food (see 35 Am Jur 2d, FOOD §§ 94, 97); the applicability of zoning regulations (see ZONING AND PLANNING); restrictive covenants (see 20 Am Jur 2d, COVENANTS, CONDITIONS, AND RESTRICTIONS §§ 212, 215, 231); the use of a building, room, apartment, or premises as a place of abode or sojourn under a lease (see LANDLORD AND TENANT); offenses committed in the serving of fish and game in violation of the fish or game laws (see 35 Am Jur 2d, FISH AND GAME); and the keeping of disorderly houses (see 24 Am Jur 2d, DISORDERLY HOUSES).

✦ **Table of Parallel References see p vii** ✦

I. IN GENERAL; DEFINITIONS AND DISTINCTIONS (§§ 1–12)

II. GUEST OR OTHER RELATIONSHIP
    A. IN GENERAL (§§ 13–16)
    B. PARTICULAR MATTERS AFFECTING EXISTENCE OF STATUS (§§ 17–25)
    C. DURATION AND TERMINATION OF RELATIONSHIP (§§ 26, 27)

III. PUBLIC REGULATION
    A. IN GENERAL (§§ 28–32)
    B. PARTICULAR REGULATIONS (§§ 33–48)

IV. ESTABLISHMENTS AS NUISANCE; ABATEMENT (§§ 49–52)

V. RIGHTS, DUTIES, AND LIABILITIES, IN GENERAL (§§ 53–58)

VI. DUTIES AND LIABILITIES AS TO RECEPTION, ACCOMMODA-TION, AND SOJOURN
    A. IN GENERAL (§§ 59–61)
    B. DUTY TO RECEIVE AND ENTERTAIN (§§ 62–67)
    C. EJECTION OR REMOVAL; VOLUNTARY DEPARTURE (§§ 68–72)
    D. ACTIONS AND OFFENSES (§§ 73–80)

VII. LIABILITY FOR PERSONAL INJURIES OR INDIGNITIES
    A. IN GENERAL (§§ 81–86)
    B. DEFECTIVE OR DANGEROUS CONDITION OF PREMISES AND FURNISHINGS (§§ 87–106)
    C. OTHER CAUSES OR CIRCUMSTANCES OF INJURY OR DEATH (§§ 107–119)
    D. ACTIONS (§§ 120–125)

893

FIGURE 8–8   An illustrative outline from *Am. Jur. 2d* (compare with Figure 8–5)

HOTELS, MOTELS, ETC.   40 Am Jur 2d

I. IN GENERAL; DEFINITIONS AND DISTINCTIONS

II. GUEST OR OTHER RELATIONSHIP

A. In General

B. Particular Matters Affecting Existence of Status

C. Duration and Termination of Relationship

III. PUBLIC REGULATION

A. In General

894

FIGURE 8–8   *(continued)*

however, remember to begin with the general index in order to locate the titles you should review more closely.

Distinguishing features of *Am. Jur. 2d* are its *New Topic Service* and *Desk Book*. The *New Topic Service* covers emerging legal topics. By placing in a separate binder releases in which titles not previously appearing in *Am. Jur. 2d* are covered, new topics can be introduced without reissuing an existing volume. It is always worth the two minutes it may take to pull the *New Topic Service* binder and open it to the gold Table of Contents card, which should be the first item filed in the binder. This card lists all new topics that are presently filed in the *New Topic Service*. Titles filed in the *New Topic Service* volume are updated through cumulative supplements, also filed in this binder.

The *Desk Book* contains a collection of legal and historical documents such as the Declaration of Independence, the United States Constitution, and the charter of the United Nations. It also contains charts, statistics, and tabulations. If you need statistics on population or the number of people who immigrated to the United States, the *Desk Book* can be consulted. If you need medical diagnosis of the human body, check the *Desk Book*. It has a myriad of general information, with a supplement updating the information previously published in the *Desk Book* hardbound volume.

American Jurisprudence: Coordinate Sources

As part of its TCSL system, Lawyers Cooperative Publishing Company (LCP) offers additional coordinate services under the generic *American Jurisprudence* title. These related services are heavily focused on practice matters, rather than on exposition of the law.

Chapter 12 of this book discusses many practice guides, including trial guides, and form books available from a number of commercial publishers. The LCP offerings are highlighted here only because of their position in the TCSL system. Being a part of that system in no way establishes these practice-oriented sets as "better" materials than those discussed in Chapter 12.

American Jurisprudence Proof of Facts   *American Jurisprudence Proof of Facts*, presently in its third series, is primarily a guide for lawyers preparing for trial. It is multivolume and provides point-by-point procedures for examining witnesses in both pretrial and trial proceedings, conducting discovery, and interviewing clients. It also sets out the necessary steps for proving a case at trial and presents other trial preparation techniques. The information in these volumes is kept current by annual pocket part supplements. The guide has a multivolume index, which assists in gaining access to the desired information. Use the same approach used for all other research, such as identifying general words and phrases.

***American Jurisprudence*: Trials**   This multivolume "trial guidelines" series is heavily practice-oriented. The first six volumes detail common types of trial practice problems, with the remaining volumes, referred to as *Modern Trials*, devoted to handling trials involving specific types of litigation—for example, malpractice, products liability, and security regulation. Use the general index to access the main volumes.

American Jurisprudence Legal Forms   This set of form books is designed to assist with the drafting of legal documents. With over thirty volumes, *American Jurisprudence Legal Forms 2d* offers an extensive guide for drafting such documents as powers of attorney, leases, contracts, and promissory notes. Never, however, overrely on the forms you find in this or any other set of form books, particularly where, as here, the sets purport to be "national" in scope. Forms must conform to the requirements of the jurisdiction in which you want to use them. Their appearance in a commercially published form book does not endorse them with any validity for a specific situation or jurisdiction. These volumes have a general index for access to the referenced legal forms.

American Jurisprudence Pleading and Practice Forms   A complement to *Am. Jur. Legal Forms* is *American Jurisprudence Pleading and Practice Forms, Revised,* which provides examples of court documents such as pleadings, motions, and discovery. Caution should be used when referring to this set. A form suggested here may not conform to the requirements of your jurisdiction. By using the general index, you will be directed to the general forms within the hardbound volumes. For an illustration of *Am. Jur. Pleading and Practice Forms*, review Figure 8–9.

State Encyclopedias

In General

A number of states have encyclopedias that focus on their respective laws and judicial decisions. The state encyclopedias have many of the same features as the general legal encyclopedias, such as commentaries, footnotes listing primary-source authority, and pocket part supplements. All are organized by subject and section numbers, and all have general and specific indexes. The state encyclopedias are a good beginning point for state-specific research. The following are the state-specific encyclopedias published by LCP and West:

Form 5   16 Am Jur Pl & Pr Forms (Rev)

Substantive issues relative to rent levels and termination of benefits under United States Housing Act of 1937 (42 USCS secs. 1437 et seq.). 77 ALR Fed 884.

A. In General

Governing Principles

A landlord and tenant relation is a prerequisite to liability for rent under an implied contract, but no particular words are needed to create either the relation or the obligation to pay rent. The relation is created by occupying premises with the owner's consent, or with the consent of one entitled to assert a right to possession; and the law will imply the tenant's agreement to pay the reasonable value of the use and occupancy in the absence of an agreement or of circumstances indicating a contrary intent. Owners have been permitted to recover the reasonable value for use and occupancy by wrongful possessors, but the general view is that an owner may not maintain an action for use and occupation against an adverse possessor. (49 Am Jur 2d *Landlord and Tenant* § 516.)

An action to recover rent should be brought after the rent has accrued and must be prosecuted within the time limited by the applicable statute of limitations. The court in which the action may or must be brought often depends on the amount involved, but title to land is not ordinarily an issue in such an action so as to oust a justice court or a court having similar jurisdiction. It is generally accepted that actions brought by a landlord to recover rent from the tenant are founded on privity of contract, are transitory, and may be brought outside the county or state in which the leased premises lie. (49 Am Jur 2d *Landlord and Tenant* §§ 626–628.)

In actions to recover rent, questions of trial practice, such as the right to open and close, are governed by the general rules of trial. And a tenant is entitled to the affirmative and to the right to open and close when the tenant alleges affirmative defenses after admitting the allegations of the complaint necessary for recovery. However, the tenant is not entitled to have a circumstance favorable to the tenant's defense singled out for jury instructions if the circumstance is only one of several facts in evidence bearing on the issues to be determined. (49 Am Jur 2d *Landlord and Tenant* § 640.)

ANNOTATIONS

What sort of claim, obligation, or liability is within contemplation of statute providing for attachment, or giving right of action for indemnity, before a debt or liability is due, 58 ALR2d 1451.

Construction and effect of lease provision relating to attorneys' fees. 77 ALR2d 735.

CHECK LIST

A complaint, petition, or declaration to recover rent for the use or occupation of real property or under a written lease or agreement, among other things, should allege:

◆ Jurisdictional facts, if required.

◆ Facts laying venue of action, if required.

◆ Plaintiff's status as landlord.

◆ Defendant's status as tenant.

◆ Location of premises for which rent is sought.

◆ Term of tenancy.

366

FIGURE 8–9   A sample from *Am. Jur. Pleading and Practice Forms*

LANDLORD AND TENANT   Form 11

- ◆ Plaintiff's consent to or permission for tenancy, if action is based on implied promise to pay rent.
- ◆ Defendant's actual occupation of premises, if action is based on implied promise to pay rent.
- ◆ Amount of agreed rent or reasonable value of defendant's use or occupation of premises, if amount of rent is not expressly agreed.
- ◆ Payment terms.
- ◆ When unpaid rent accrued.
- ◆ Amount of rent accrued and unpaid.
- ◆ Performance by plaintiff of conditions precedent to suit.
- ◆ Demand for payment.
- ◆ Request for relief.

Form 11   Complaint, petition, or declaration—To recover accrued rent
[Caption, Introduction, see CAPTIONS, PRAYERS. ETC.]

I

Plaintiff resides at .....1............. *[address].* ....2............. *[city],* ....3............. County, ...4............. *[state].*

II

Defendant resides at ....5............. *[address],* .....6............. *[city],* ....7............. County, ...8............. *[state].*

III

By instrument dated ....9............., plaintiff. as landlord, and defendant, as tenant, agreed for the lease of the premises at ....10............. *[address],* ....11............. *[city],* ....12............. County, ...13............. *[state],* for a term commencing ....14............. *[date]* and ending ....15............. *[date],* for a total rental payment of $....16...., payable as follows: ....17............. *[specify amount and intervals of rental payments].* A copy of the lease, marked Exhibit ....18...., is attached and made a part of this pleading.

IV

Plaintiff tendered possession of the leased premises to defendant on or about ....19............. *[date],* and defendant at that time took possession of the premises, pursuant to the lease terms.

V

....20............. *[Allege, in general terms, plaintiff's performance of conditions precedent to recovery of rent.]*

VI

Defendant failed to pay to plaintiff the rental installments due under the lease on ....21............. *[specify due dates],* and defendant now owes plaintiff $....22.... for accrued rents under the lease, no part of which has been paid.

VII

Plaintiff has demanded payment from defendant for the accrued rents, but

367

FIGURE 8–9   *(continued)*

Form 11   16 Am Jur Pl. & Pr Forms (Rev)

defendant has neglected and refused to pay the rents due and still refuses to do so.

Wherefore, plaintiff requests:

1. Judgment against defendant in the amount of $.....23...., as the rental payments due from defendant to plaintiff; and

2. Such other and further relief as the court deems just.

[Signature, Verification. see CAPTIONS. PRAYERS, ETC.]

Notes

Liability under express agreement to pay rent. 49 Am Jur 2d LANDLORD AND TENANT § 440.

**Form 12   Complaint, petition, or declaration—To recover accrued rent—
              Against tenant failing to take possession**

[Caption, Introduction, see CAPTIONS, PRAYERS, ETC.]

I

Plaintiff resides at ___1_____ *[address]*, ___2_____ *[city]*, ___3_____ County, ___4_____ *[state]*.

II

Defendant resides at ___5_____ *[address]*, ___6_____ *[city]*, ___7_____ County, ___8_____ *[state]*.

III

At the times mentioned, plaintiff was and now is the owner of the building located at ___9_____ *[address]*, ___10_____ *[city]*, ___11_____ County, ___12_____ *[state]*.

IV

By instrument dated and executed ___13_____ *[date]*, plaintiff agreed to erect a second story to the building, to vacate the first story then occupied by plaintiff, to occupy the second story on its completion, and to lease to defendant the first story for a term of ___14_____ *[number]* ___15_____ [months or years], commencing ___16_____ *[date]*, for a total rental payment of $___17__, with the last month's rent of $___18___ payable concurrently with the execution of the agreement, and the remainder payable in advance in equal installments of $___19___ on the ___20____ day of each month of the lease term. By the same instrument, defendant agreed to lease the first story of the building for such term at the agreed rental payment and subject to the terms and conditions set forth. A copy of such lease agreement, marked Exhibit ___21___, is attached and made a part of this pleading.

V

Concurrently with the execution by the parties of the lease agreement, defendant paid to plaintiff $___22___ as the last month's rental installment.

VI

Within the time and in the manner required by the parties' lease agreement, plaintiff completed construction of the second story of the building, vacated the first story, delivered to defendant written notice that the first story of the building was ready for use and occupancy pursuant to the terms of the parties' lease agreement, and tendered possession of the first story of the building to

368

FIGURE 8–9   *(continued)*

LCP

California Jurisprudence 3d

Florida Jurisprudence 2d

Kentucky Jurisprudence

New York Jurisprudence 3d

Ohio Jurisprudence 3d

Texas Jurisprudence 3d

West

Illinois Law and Practice

Maryland Law and Practice

Michigan Law and Practice

Pennsylvania Law Encyclopedia

The state encyclopedias follow the formats used by West and LCP with their general encyclopedias, discussed earlier in this chapter. Consequently, the West publications reference the West Digest System and West coordinates, and the LCP publications cross-reference the units in the TCSL system.

Texas Jurisprudence

Texas has its own legal encyclopedia, *Texas Jurisprudence* (*Tex. Jur.*), which is published by Lawyers Cooperative Publishing Company. Presently in its third series (*Tex. Jur. 3d*) this encyclopedia's focus is exclusively on Texas law.

Texas Jurisprudence 3d is a very useful research tool. Following the format of *Am. Jur. 2d, Tex. Jur. 3d* includes both general indexes and subject-specific indexes. Using research methods previously discussed, you should begin research in *Tex. Jur. 3d* by writing down relevant words and phrases. Look up the words and phrases and find the subject and sections for your topic in the general index. (See Figure 8–10.)

Next, locate the subject in one of the main volumes and open to the specific section of the subject. Begin reading the commentary and refer to footnotes for specific cases in Texas on that point of law. (See Figure 8–11.)

Be sure to consult the pocket part supplement at the end of the volume for changes in the text and for new cases and statutory changes.

Refer to Figure 8–12 for examples of a subject-specific index and a table of contents found in *Tex. Jur. 3d.*

Hostile Possession	**72 Tex Jur 2d**

Tort liability—Cont'd
  physician of patient, liability for torts of. Hospit § 6
  private institutions. Hospit § 7
  railroad employee hospitals. Hospit § 8
  state asylum, liability of superintendent of. Hospit § 6
Workmen's Compensation (this index)
Zoning. Zon § 43

HOSTILE POSSESSION

Adverse Possession (this index)

HOSTILITY

Juror's hostility toward participant. Jury §§ 204, 211
Threat, hostility as evidence of. Threat. § 5

HOT CHECK LAW

Swindling and Cheating (this index)

HOTCHPOTCH

Community property as subject to. Advance § 19
Interest on advancements. Advance § 22
Order of. Dec Est § 905
Property subject to. Advance §§ 17–19; Dec Est § 888
Time element in valuation of advancements. Advance § 21
Valuation of advancement. Advance §§ 20–22

HOTELS

Innkeepers (this index)

HOURS OF WORK

Policeman. Pol § 20
Prisoners. Pris & P § 23

HOUSES OF CORRECTION, REFORMATION, AND REFUGE

Assistance of inmate to escape, offense of. House of Corr § 3
Coercion of child to leave institution as offense. House of Corr § 3

Commitment to. Del Child § 42; House of Corr §§ 1, 2
Concealment of escaped inmate as offense. House of Corr § 3
Corsicana State Home for Orphans. House of Corr § 1
Court order, visitation of institution receiving child under. House of Corr § 2
Crippled and deformed children, institutions for treatment of. House of Corr § 2
Discharge of children from state institutions. House of Corr § 2
Education of inmates of institutions, regulation of. House of Corr § 2
Escape of children from state institution, offenses in connection with. House of Corr § 3
Foreign corporation empowered to establish home for fallen women. House of Corr § 3
Gatesville State School For Boys. House of Corr § 1
  escape of inmate from, offenses in connection with. House of Corr § 3
Gainesville State School for Girls. House of Corr § 1
Governmental institutions for care of delinquent children. House of Corr § 1
Guardianship of institution. House of Corr § 2
Home for fallen women, foreign corporation empowered to establish. House of Corr § 3
Inducing child to leave institution as offense. House of Corr § 3
Offenses in connection with escape from institution. House of Corr § 3
Ordinance prohibiting home for fallen women, invalidity. House of Corr § 9
Orphan asylum. House of Corr § 1
  Corsicana State Home. House of Corr § 1
  establishment. House of Corr § 2
Regulation of institutions for children. House of Corr § 2

[80]

FIGURE 8–10   A sample from a *Tex. Jur. 3d* general index

HOTELS, Etc.   § 11

those facts that will exonerate him.[70] However, under the statute limiting an innkeeper's liability for loss of valuables,[71] where the innkeeper has met the conditions prescribed by the statute, the guest, in order to make out a case for full damages, may not rely on the presumption arising from the loss but must affirmatively show negligence. On the other hand, to recover the sum fixed by the statute he may rely on the presumed negligence, that is, the failure of the innkeeper to show freedom from negligence in all degrees.[72]

Ordinarily, the question of negligence must be resolved by the jury and not by the court.[73]

IV. COMPENSATION [§§ 11, 12]

Research References

ALR Second Series Quick Index (1980 ed.), Innkeepers § 1; Motor Courts and Motels; Restaurants § 1
ALR3d-4th Quick Index (1980 ed.), Innkeepers; Motor Courts and Motels; Restaurants § 1
Texas Forms—Legal and Business—Liens § 18:71 et seq.
13 Am Jur Pl & Pr Forms (Rev), Hotels, Motels, and Restaurants, Form 2 et seq.

§ 11. In general

An innkeeper is entitled to be paid for the accommodations he has furnished, either in accordance with the terms of his agree-

70. Southwestern Hotel Co. v Rogers (1945) 143 Tex 343, 184 SW2d 835.

71. RS art 4592.

72. Southwestern Hotel Co. v Rogers (1944, CA) 183 SW2d 751, affd 143 Tex 343, 184 SW2d 835.

For discussion of statute and its conditions, see § 8.

73. Hadley v Upshaw (1864) 27 Tex 547 (contributory negligence); Dallas

Hotel Co. v Davison (1930, Com) 23 SW2d 708; Kieffer v Keough (1916, CA) 188 SW 44, writ ref; Dallas Hotel Co. v Richardson (1925, CA) 276 SW 765 (gross negligence); Smith v Robinson (1927, CA) 300 SW 651, writ dism w o j; Driskill Hotel Co. v Anderson (1929, CA) 19 SW2d 216 (contributory negligence.).

As to role of jury in resolving questions of negligence, see NEGLIGENCE (2d ed., rev., § 153).

43 Tex Jur 3d   657

FIGURE 8–11   Commentary and footnotes from *Tex. Jur. 3d*

§ 11   HOTELS, Etc.

ment or according to their reasonable worth.[74] If payment is refused, he may recover the price in an ordinary suit on the contract.[75] The innkeeper has, however, the duty to minimize his damages.[76]

The legislature has not attempted to prescribe the rates that may be charged by innkeepers, but it has provided against fraud and imposition by requiring the owner or keeper of a hotel to post the prices of his rooms, and, in some cases, to furnish his guests with rate cards, and by limiting the time within which prices may be advanced.[77] Also by statute, all persons who obtain board or lodging by means of trick, deception, or false misrepresentations, and who fail to pay will be deemed to have obtained them with intent to defraud and are subject to fine or imprisonment or both.[78]

§ 12. Lien for sums due

By statute the proprietors of hotels, boarding houses, rooming houses, inns, tourist courts, and motels have a lien on baggage and other property of guests for all sums due, and may retain the property until the amount is paid.[79]

---

74. McDaniel v Turner (1924, CA) 269 SW 496.

Forms: Petition to recover for board and lodging, 13 Am Jur Pl & Pr Forms (Rev), Hotels, Motels, and Restaurants, Forms 2, 3.

75. McDaniel v Turner (1924, CA) 269 SW 496.

For general discussion of contract actions, see CONTRACTS § 308 et seq.

76. Mallam v Trans-Texas Airways (1949, CA) 227 SW2d 344.

As to duty to minimize damages, see DAMAGES § 29 et seq.

77. RS arts 4596b, 4596c.

Annotations: Validity and construction of statute or ordinance restricting outdoor rate advertising by motels, motor courts, and the like, 80 ALR3d

740; Maintenance or regulation by public authorities of tourist or trailer camps, motor courts, or motels, 22 ALR2d 774; Validity and construction of statute or ordinance requiring or prohibiting posting or other publication of price of commodity or services, 89 ALR2d 901.

Forms: Notice of rules, 9 Am Jur Legal Forms 2d, Hotels, Motels, and Restaurants, Form 137:15.

78. See CRIMINAL LAW § 534.

79. RS art 4594 (While in possession of innkeeper, baggage and other property are exempt from attachment or execution).

Innkeeper's lien did not attach to sample merchandise put in guest's possession by non-guest owner, for pur-

FIGURE 8–11   *(continued)*

HOTELS, Etc. § 12

When an innkeeper seizes or detains the belongings of his guest under an unauthorized claim of lien he is guilty of a wrongful conversion.[80] On the other hand, if a valid lien has arisen in favor of an innkeeper he may sell at public auction the property covered by the lien in satisfaction of his claim, on giving due notice and otherwise complying with the requirements of the statute.[81]

pose of exhibiting it for sale, where hotel manager knew nature and ownership of property involved and where guest gave no indication that property was owned by him. Torrey v McClellan (1897) 17 CA 371, 43 SW 64 (construing predecessor to RS art 4594).

It may be stated that lien given to proprietors of hotels may attach to property in possession of his guests though it belongs to third person, provided proprietor of hotel had no notice of that fact. Kieffer v Keough (1916, CA) 188 SW 44, writ ref (construing predecessor to RS art 4594).

As to creation, effect, and enforcement of liens generally, see LIENS (2d ed., § 4 et seq.).

Annotations: Modern views as to validity, under Federal Constitution, of state prejudgment attachment, garnishment, and replevin procedures, distraint procedures under landlords' or innkeepers' lien statutes, and like pro-

cedures authorizing summary seizure of property, 18 ALR Fed 223.

Law Reviews: Summary of rights and liabilities of innkeepers regarding property of guests, 1 So Tex LJ 63.

80. Torrey v McClellan (1897) 17 CA 371, 43 SW 64.

As to conversion generally, see CONVERSION.

81. RS art 4595.

As to conduct of auctions generally, see AUCTIONS AND AUCTIONEERS.

Law Reviews: Innkeeper's lien, 23 Tex LR 289.

Forms: Notice of sale of personal property to satisfy lien, Texas Forms —Legal and Business, Liens § 18:71 et seq.; Forms relating to enforcement of innkeeper's lien, 13 Am Jur Pl & Pr Forms (Rev), Hotels, Motels, and Restaurants, Form 4 et seq.; Notice of lien and sale, 9 Am Jur Legal Forms 2d, Hotels, Motels, and Restaurants § 137:17.

HOURS OF LABOR

See EMPLOYER AND EMPLOYEE

HOUSEBREAKING

See CRIMINAL LAW

FIGURE 8–11 *(continued)*

INDEX

FIGURE 8–12 Examples of a subject-specific index and a table of contents in *Tex. Jur. 3d*

INDEX

FIGURE 8–12   *(continued)*

HOTELS, MOTELS, AND RESTAURANTS

by

Michael P. Walsh, J.D., editor

Scope of topic:

This title discusses the duties and responsibilities of owners and operators of inns, hotels, motels, and restaurants.

Treated elsewhere:

Admissibility in evidence of hotel records, see EVIDENCE.

Bailees' rights and liabilities, see BAILMENTS.

Business districts and building restrictions, see ZONING.

Constitutionality of regulations, see CONSTITUTIONAL LAW.

Construction and operation of buildings, see BUILDING AND CONSTRUCTION CONTRACTS; BUILDING REGULATIONS.

Employee compensation and benefits, see EMPLOYER AND EMPLOYEE.

Exemption of furniture from levy and execution, see CREDITORS' RIGHTS AND REMEDIES.

Fire regulations, see FIRES AND FIRE DISTRICTS; HEALTH AND SANITATION.

Health and medical regulations, see HEALTH AND SANITATION.

Homestead of business, see HOMESTEADS.

Labelling regulations, see AGRICULTURE; CONSUMER AND BORROWER PROTECTION LAWS.

Landlords' and tenants' rights and responsibilities, see LANDLORD AND TENANT.

Liability for injury on premises, see PREMISES LIABILITY (2d ed., rev., NEGLIGENCE). Pending publication of Tex Jur 3d, PREMISES LIABILITY, see reprint of Tex Jur 2d, NEGLIGENCE in the Unreplaced Topics division of the Topic Service binders.

Liability of processors, handlers, and distributors of food, see PRODUCTS LIABILITY (2d ed., FOOD; SALES).

Licenses, see BUSINESS AND OCCUPATION LICENSES.

Liens, see LIENS.

Liquor, see INTOXICATING LIQUORS.

43 Tex Jur 3d **641**

FIGURE 8–12 *(continued)*

HOTELS, Etc.

Negligence, see NEGLIGENCE.
Nuisances, see NUISANCES.
Poisoning, see CRIMINAL LAW.
Pullman cars, see RAILROADS (2d ed., SLEEPING CAR COMPANIES).
Regulations governing handling and processing of food, see FOOD.
Sales, see MARKETING ASSOCIATIONS AND COOPERATIVES (2d ed., MARKETS AND MARKETING); SALES.
Sleeping cars, see RAILROADS (2d ed., SLEEPING CAR COMPANIES).
Taxes, see TAXATION.
Theft of services, see CRIMINAL LAW.
Workers' compensation, see WORK INJURY COMPENSATION (2d ed., WORKMEN'S COMPENSATION).

Research References

Text References:
40 Am Jur 2d, Hotels, Motels, and Restaurants

Annotation References:
ALR Second Series Quick Index (1980 ed.), Drive-in Restaurants; Innkeepers; Motor Courts and Motels; Restaurants
ALR3d-4th Quick Index (1980 ed.), Drive-in Restaurants; Innkeepers; Motor Courts and Motels; Restaurants
Federal Quick Index 3d (1980 ed.), Hotels, Motels, and Innkeepers; Restaurants
L Ed Index to Annotations, Hotels; Innkeepers; Motels; Restaurants
U.S. Supreme Court Reports (L Ed 2d) Desk Book, Index to Cases and Annotations, Hotels, Motels, and Innkeepers; Restaurants

Practice References:
6 Tex Jur Pl & Pr Forms 2d, Food
7 Tex Jur Pl & Pr Forms 2d, Hotels, Motels, and Restaurants
Texas Forms—Legal and Business—Bailments and Deposits; Liens
13 Am Jur Pl & Pr Forms (Rev), Hotels, Motels, and Restaurants
9 Am Jur Legal Forms 2d, Hotels, Motels, and Restaurants
6 POF p. 353, Innkeepers
11 POF p. 379, Negligence of Restauranteur in Causing Trichinosis
23 POF p. 194, Intentionally Caused Emotional Distress by Innkeeper
11 POF 2d p. 499, Failure to Use Due Care in Employment of Security Guard
14 POF 2d p. 657, Failure to Protect Guests From Fire

FIGURE 8–12 *(continued)*

HOTELS, Etc.

24 POF 2d p. 385, Inadequate or Defective Interior Illumination of Change in Floor Level

Tax References:

Am Jur 2d (1985), Federal Taxation ¶ 5961 (investment tax credit; lodging facility use rule)

RIA Federal Tax Coordinator 2d ¶ L-9852 et seq. (investment tax credit; lodging facility use rule)

Federal Legislation:

12 United States Code Service § 1731b (prohibition against use of insured multi-family housing for transient or hotel purposes)

18 United States Code Service § 245 (prohibition against discrimination and enumeration of certain protected activities)

42 United States Code Service § 2000a et seq. (Civil Rights Act of 1964)

Auto-Cite®:

Any case citation herein can be checked for form, parallel references, later history, and annotation references through the Auto-Cite computer research system.

_____

I. GENERALLY [§§ 1, 2]

II. GUEST-INNKEEPER RELATIONSHIP [§§ 3-5]

III. CARE OF PERSONAL PROPERTY [§§ 6-10]

IV. COMPENSATION [§§ 11, 12]

_____

I. GENERALLY
§ 1.   In general
§ 2.   Definitions and distinctions

II. GUEST-INNKEEPER RELATIONSHIP
§ 3.   In general; establishment and existence
§ 4.   Termination
§ 5.   Comparison with landlord-tenant relationship

43 Tex Jur 3d   **643**

FIGURE 8–12   (continued)

A Checklist for the Encyclopedias

When using a legal encyclopedia:

1. Begin with a general index and look up words and phrases related to the research problem.
2. Under the words and phrases chosen, locate applicable areas of interest.
3. Identify the general encyclopedia subject or topic and the section number.
4. Write down the subject and section number.
5. Retrieve the appropriate volume based upon the subject identified.
6. Open to the specific section number under the subject.
7. Begin reading commentary.
8. Refer to footnotes for specific case, constitution, and statutory references.
9. Write down applicable case, statutory, and constitutional references.
10. Check pocket part supplements for text changes, law updates, and new cases.
11. Be sure to reference correct subject and section for coordinate pocket part references.
12. Retrieve any cases or statutes in the references written down from the footnotes.
13. Read the cases retrieved and determine applicability.
14. Copy cases intended for use or reference.
15. Check for any publisher coordinate publications: West's Digest System and West publications or LCP's Total Client Service Library.

§ 8.2 *American Law Reports*

Introduction

American Law Reports (*A.L.R.*), published by Lawyers Cooperative Publishing Company, is well known for its extensive annotations on a wide rage of American legal subjects. Each annotation is preceded by the text of a carefully selected case that focuses on, or raises, important issues that define current legal trends. The annotations are comprehensive and are based on case law and statutes from all jurisdictions. Each annotation provides seemingly exhaustive coverage of its subject.

As with the encyclopedias (*C.J.S.* and *Am. Jur. 2d*) discussed earlier in this chapter, use of *A.L.R.* annotations requires a degree of caution and skepticism. The annotations are secondary sources and, therefore, are only as good as the research, analysis, and writing that have gone into them. Conclusions offered in these annotations and the rules identified as "majority" and "minority" rules need to be verified through other research. That said, *A.L.R.* annotations can be extremely useful in legal research. They are comprehensive in scope, based on comprehensive research, and, importantly, make an effort to present all perspectives in areas where there is disagreement among courts about what the legal rules should be.

A.L.R. Series

First published in 1919, *A.L.R.* has grown to massive size. It now consists of over six hundred volumes of material collected in five numbered series and a federal-specific series, as follows:

A.L.R.: 1919–1948

A.L.R.2d: 1948–1965

A.L.R.3d: 1965–1980

A.L.R.4th: 1980–1992

A.L.R.5th: 1992–present

A.L.R. Fed.: 1969–present

A.L.R. Indexes and Finding Aids

Indexes provide the best means of access to cases and annotations in *A.L.R.*Until recently, all *A.L.R.* series had an alphabetical *Quick Index*. Currently, only *A.L.R.* (the first series) has an index referred to as a *Quick Index*. All the other series' annotations are referenced in the cumulative multivolume *A.L.R. Index*. Annotations found in LCP's *United States Supreme Court Reports, Lawyers' Edition 2d* are also referenced in the cumulative index.

The *A.L.R.* and *A.L.R.2d* have case locators in their respective tables of cases. By looking up a case in these tables, you can find the citation and the annotation reference. Note that the tables of cases include only cases set forth in their entirety in *A.L.R.* and *A.L.R.2d*. They do not include cases that have been merely cited in the annotations.

There is an additional finding aid of value located in the final volume of the *A.L.R. Index.* This is a table of laws, rules, and regulations that, as explained by the publisher, "shows where federal statutes, regulations, and court rules, uniform and model acts, restatements of law, and professional codes of ethics are cited" in annotations in *A.L.R.3d, A.L.R.4th, A.L.R. Fed.,* and *L. Ed. 2d.*

The *A.L.R.* and *A.L.R.2d* each have a set of digests. The *A.L.R.3d, A.L.R.4th, A.L.R.5th,* and *A.L.R. Fed.* share a separate digest. By using the headnote references in cases reported in *A.L.R.* and *L. Ed. 2d* (also units in LCP's Total Client Service Library system), you can locate other cases, as well as annotations, that deal with the topic you are researching.

Updating *A.L.R.* Annotations

Making sure that you have consulted the most recent updates to *A.L.R.* annotations is crucial for thorough research in this source. Annotations are supplemented in various ways, as described below. Whether an annotation was first published in 1919 in the first *A.L.R.* series or in a recent volume in *A.L.R.5th,* any changes to the original text will be found in one of the updating series.

A.L.R.

Early *A.L.R.* annotations are kept current through the *A.L.R. Blue Book of Supplemental Decisions.* Entries in the *Blue Book* are arranged in sequential order by volume and page reference. For example, you will find in permanent volume 6 of the *Blue Book,* on page 567, a reference to "134 ALR 927–941." If that is the citation to the annotation you are researching, you will find additional cases and other updating information located under this reference in the *Blue Book.* So access is through the annotation citation alone, and the updating information pertains to the subject of the annotation—it is not identified in regard to its relevance to any specific point within the annotation. (See Figure 8–13.)

A.L.R.2d

The *A.L.R.2d* began publication in 1948. The updating service for this series is called *A.L.R.2d Later Case Service.* This service provides (1) updates of case and other authority for the original annotations, and (2) expanded coverage where needed to bring the annotations up to date. The references in the *Later Case Service* entries are far more precise than those in the *Blue Book,* as they identify the sections, by number and title, in the original annotations to which they pertain.

162 ALR   SUPPLEMENTAL DECISIONS   724

Va.—Virginia & M. R. Co. v W.,
319 SE2d 755

162 ALR 180-197
Superseded 3 ALR2d 466♦

162 ALR 202-204
N.Y.—P. v Castro, 68 NY2d 850,
508 NYS2d 407, 501 NE2d 15

162 ALR 220-223
Superseded 72 ALR2d 1156♦

162 ALR 237-240
U.S.—Donovan v M & M W. Service, Inc. (CA10 Okla) 733 F2d
83
Brock v G. S. C. (CA11 Ga) 765
F2d 1026, 37 CCH EPD ¶ 35470
Halferty v P. D. Co. (CA5 Tex)
826 F2d 2, 28 BNA WH Cas 495
Brock v S. (CA9 Or) 833 F2d
1326, 28 BNA WH Cas 625
Blackmon v B. G. Co. (CA5 Tex)
835 F2d 1135, 28 BNA WH Cas
718
Cook v U. S. (CA FC) 855 F2d
848, 28 BNA WH Cas 1363, 110
CCH LC ¶ 35113
Hudson v M. B. F., Inc. (ND Cal)
609 F Supp 467, 37 BNA FEP
Cas 1672, 37 CCH EPD ¶ 35285
Carpenters Local Union No. 1846
etc. v P.-F., Inc. (ED La) 609 F
Supp 1302, 119 BNA LRRM
3525
U.S. EEOC v Green County (WD
Wis) 618 F Supp 91, 37 CCH
EPD ¶ 35390
Brock v E. P. N. G. Co. (WD Tex)
644 F Supp 1202
Shelton v E. (MD Ga) 646 F Supp
1011
Donovan v M.-C. Co. (SD Ohio)
653 F Supp 1159
Hartt v U. C. Co. (WD Mo) 655 F
Supp 937, 28 BNA WH Cas 31
Brock v C. H. & C. (DC NJ) 664 F
Supp 899, 28 BNA WH Cas 577
Donovan v U. R. & H. C., Inc.
(ED NY) 674 F Supp 77, 28
BNA WH Cas 913
Veitz v U. Corp. (ED Va) 676 F
Supp 99
Brown v K. C. I., Inc. (ND Ill) 680
F Supp 1212, 46 BNA FEP Cas
98, 3 BNA IER Cas 26, 127 BNA
LRRM 2934
Amos v U. S., 13 Cl Ct 442, 28
BNA WH Cas 569
Blair v U. S., 15 Cl Ct 763, 29
BNA WH Cas 147, 110 CCH LC
¶ 35136
Nerseth v U. S., 17 Cl Ct 660, 29
BNA WH Cas 639, 112 CCH LC
¶ 35243
Ill.—Cuevas v B. T., Inc. (2d Dist)
149 Ill App 3d 977, 102 Ill Dec
946, 500 NE2d 1047, 27 BNA
WH Cas 1713
La.—Johnson v C. S. F. B., Inc.
(App) 449 So 2d 56, 101 CCH LC
¶ 55476

Cedotal v F. (App 1st Cir) 516 So
2d 405, 28 BNA WH Cas 989
N.C.—Jones v J., 91 NC App 289,
372 SE2d 80, 28 BNA WH Cas
1483, 110 CCH LC ¶ 35143
W.Va.—Ingram v C., 376 SE2d
327, 29 BNA WH Cas 226
McCarty v H., 384 SE2d 164, 29
BNA WH Cas 753

162 ALR 244-249
U.S.—Nationwide Mut. Ins. Co. v
B. (CA4 SC) 779 F2d 984
State Farm Fire & Casualty Co. v
B. (CA9 Cal) 849 F2d 1218
Terra Nova Ins. Co. v T. K. S.,
Inc. (ED Pa) 679 F Supp 476
Iowa—Altena v U. F. & C. Co.,
422 NW2d 485
La.—Paul v M., (App 4th Cir) 535
So 2d 6
Md.—Harpy v N. M. F. I. Co., 76
Md App 474, 545 A2d 718
Minn.—Economy Fire & Casualty
Ins. Co. v M. (App) 427 NW2d
742
N.Y.—Pawelek v S. M., I. Co. (4th
Dept) 143 App Div 2d 514, 533
NYS2d 161
Pa.—Gene's Restaurant, Inc. v N.
I. Co., 548 A2d 246
Ohio Casualty Group of Ins. Cos.
v B. (Super) 355 Pa Super 345,
513 A2d 462
Tex.—Garrison v F. R., Inc. (App
Dallas) 765 SW2d 536
Wash.—Farmers Ins. Co. v E., 52
Wash App 411, 763 P2d 454

162 ALR 261-263
U.S.—County of Johnson by Board
of Education v U. S. G. Co. (ED
Tenn) 580 F Supp 284
N.J.—Port Authority of New
York & New Jersey v B., 193
NJ Super 696, 475 A2d 676
N.C.—Rowan County Bd. of Education v U. S. G. Co., 87 NC App
106, 359 SE2d 814

162 ALR 288-292
F.—Re R & J Constr. Co. (BC ED
Mo) 43 BR 29

162 ALR 305-312
U.S.—D'Camera v D. of C. (DC
Dist Col) 693 F Supp 1208, 28
BNA WH Cas 1476, 109 CCH
LC ¶ 35102
Kan.—Dollison v O. Co., 243 Kan
763, 763 P2d 1101, 29 BNA WH
Cas 55

162 ALR 323-327
Superseded 52 ALR2d 1016♦

162 ALR 373-390
Supplemented 172 ALR 231♦

162 ALR 420-422
U.S.—Federal Land Bank v B. of
C. C. (CA10 Colo) 788 F2d 1440

Federal Land Bank v B. of C. C.
(DC Colo) 607 F Supp 1137, 84
OGR 616

162 ALR 446-477
Superseded 90 ALR 3d 1173 and
92 ALR3d 1164♦

162 ALR 495-535
U.S.—McCandless v B. (CA3 NJ)
835 F2d 58
Lancaster v N. (CA11 Ga) 880
F2d 362
American Library Asso. v T. (DC
Dist Col) 713 F Supp 469
Ala.—Watts v S. (App) 435 So 2d
129
Cal.—P. v Shelton (4th Dist) 150
Cal App 3d 946, 198 Cal Rptr
589
P. v Anderson (4th Dist) 210 Cal
App 3d 414, 258 Cal Rptr 482
D.C.—Re L.E.J. (App) 465 A2d 374
Reid v U. S. (App) 466 A2d 433
Fla.—Yost v S. (App D4) 542 So
2d 419, 14 FLW 989
Ill.—P. v Embry (4th Dist) 177 Ill
App 3d 96, 126 Ill Dec 503, 531
NE2d 1130
P. v Hester (1st Dist) 178 Ill App
3d 360, 127 Ill Dec 335, 532
NE2d 1344
P. v Garofalo (2nd Dist) 181 Ill
App 3d 972, 130 Ill Dec 837, 537
NE2d 1166
La.—S. v Densereaux (App 4th
Cir) 496 So 2d 423
N.J.—S. v Latimore, 197 NJ Super 197, 484 A2d 702
State v O., 220 NJ Super 104, 531
A2d 741
Ohio—S. v Snowden, 7 Ohio App
3d 358, 7 Ohio BR 458, 455
NE2d 1058
W.Va.—S. v Curry, 374 SE2d 526

162 ALR 556-570
U.S.—Marker v U.S. (DC Del) 646
F Supp 433
Ala.—Blair v K.-C. Corp., 474 So
2d 661
Ariz.—Lake Havasu Community
Hospital, Inc. v A. T. L & T. Co.
(App) 141 Ariz 363, 687 P2d 371
Ark.—Opaline King Hill v G., 284
Ark 383, 682 SW2d 737
Ill.—Hawkeye-Security Ins. Co. v
R., 128 Ill App 3d 352, 83 Ill Dec
683, 470 NE2d 1103
La.—Kalmn, Inc. v W. L. P. (App
3d Cir) 488 So 2d 340
Witter v B. R. (App 1st Cir) 546
So 2d 848
Mont.—Erickson v F. N. B., 697
P2d 1332
N.Y.—P. v Stack (App Div, 2d
Dept) 527 NYS2d 569
Ohio—Finomore v E. (C. C.) 18
Ohio App 3d 88, 18 Ohio BR
403, 481 NE2d 1193
Tex.—Equitable Trust Co. v R.
(App Corpus Christi) 721 SW2d
530
Jordan v B. (App Beaumont) 739
SW2d 629

♦When Supplemented see later Note and Blue Book under caption of later Note

FIGURE 8–13   The *A.L.R. Blue Book of Supplemental Decisions* keeps early *A.L.R.* annotations current

A.L.R.3d, A.L.R.4th, and *A.L.R.5th*

These series each have a simplified updating system in the form of a cumulative pocket part supplement inserted inside the back cover of each volume. When reading an annotation, refer to the pocket part for changes in the commentary as well as for new cases. With pocket parts, which are usually issued annually, make sure that the one you are consulting is the most current. If you are suspicious about the recentness of a supplement, then check with a librarian to determine whether the supplement is the most recent one that has been published.

In 1969, *A.L.R.* began publishing a series exclusively for federal case annotations. Therefore, some of *A.L.R.3d* and all of *A.L.R.4th* and *A.L.R.5th* are dedicated exclusively to state case annotations.

The update service for *A.L.R. Fed.* consists of cumulative pocket part supplements, which are inserted at the back of each volume. They should never be overlooked.

Finding the Most Current Annotation: The History Table

The *A.L.R.* annotations report the law as it exists at the time the annotations are written. The law, however, is dynamic. Some areas change rapidly. The result is that annotations do become dated, and even with the upkeep service, they may not capture the state of the law as it has evolved. Consequently, *A.L.R.* annotations are often revised, or new annotations are written that combine topics that may have been covered earlier in two or more annotations, or a topic initially covered in a single annotation may be subsequently broken down and covered in multiple annotations. It is therefore crucial to the use of the *A.L.R.* sets that you not assume that an annotation you have found is still offered by the publisher as a usable statement of the law. You must find out whether your annotation has been superseded or supplemented by another annotation (or even a string of subsequent annotations).

To determine if an *A.L.R.* annotation is "current," you must consult the annotation history table that is found in the last volume of the *A.L.R. Index.* This table tells whether an annotation has been superseded or supplemented and, if so, where those updates can be found. Remember to check the pocket part supplement to that volume to locate the most recent superseding changes in the annotations. The annotation history table includes references to all the *A.L.R.* series, including *A.L.R.* (the first series).

Using *A.L.R.*

Each *A.L.R.* annotation is, more or less, based on the text of a selected court opinion. The earlier series have the cases immediately preceding the annotation, whereas the latest series reports the cases at the end of the volume. The annotation covers a legal subject addressed by, or related to, the preceding case.

At this point, refer to Figure 8–14, which consists of the first seven pages of the annotation appearing at 30 A.L.R.4th 742, entitled Advertising as Ground for Disciplining Attorney. The first page states the title, followed by references to directly related materials in other units of the TCSL. Next, an extensive table of contents outlines the topic breakdown with section designators and topics. Then an index offers a different means of accessing a specific topic within the annotation. Following the index is a table of jurisdictions represented by cases cited in the annotation, which provides a quick means of locating cases from a specific jurisdiction, the references being to those sections of the annotation in which the cases are cited. Then, the annotation itself comes next.

Most annotations begin with an introduction (usually section 1) that should be read to facilitate more in-depth use of the annotation. The introduction includes subsections detailing the scope of the annotation, references to other annotations dealing with matters related to those covered in the annotation, and, if appropriate, practice pointers. Also useful as a preliminary matter is the summary (usually section 2), which is a treatise-like overview of the subject matter covered in the annotation, with references to specific sections of the annotation interspersed throughout the text of the summary. This section can give you a good idea of what to expect should you go further into the annotation. The remaining sections provide the in-depth treatment of the subject of the annotation.

A Checklist for *A.L.R.* Research

1. Begin by writing down words and phrases that apply to the problem.
2. Check the *A.L.R. Index* to see if the subject is covered.
3. Locate an *A.L.R.* annotation that may apply and write down the reference.
4. Check the annotation history table to determine if the annotation has been superseded or supplemented.
5. Retrieve the appropriate *A.L.R.* volume and open to the designated page. Be sure the correct *A.L.R.* series is used.
6. Begin reading the annotation.
7. Check pocket part supplements.

ANNOTATION

ADVERTISING AS GROUND FOR DISCIPLINING ATTORNEY

by

Gregory G. Sarno, J.D.

TOTAL CLIENT-SERVICE LIBRARY® REFERENCES

3 Am Jur 2d, Advertising §§ 8 et seq.; 7 Am Jur 2d, Attorneys at Law § 66

Annotations: See the related matters listed in the annotation, infra.

1 Am Jur Pl & Pr Forms (Rev), Advertising, Forms 31, 32; 2 Am Jur Pl & Pr Forms (Rev), Attorneys at Law, Forms 281 et seq.

1 Am Jur Proof of Facts 297, Advertisements

14 Am Jur Trials 265, Actions Against Attorneys for Professional Negligence

USCS Constitution, Amendment 1; Court Rules, Supreme Court Rule 8; Federal Rules of Appellate Procedure, Rule 46(b)

US L Ed Digest, Attorneys § 8; Constitutional Law §§ 953, 954

L Ed Index to Annos, Advertising; Attorney and Client; Disciplinary Measures; Fraud and Deceit; Freedom of Speech, Press, Religion, and Assembly

ALR Quick Index, Advertising; Attorneys; Disciplinary Action; Ethics and Ethical Matters; Fraud and Deceit; Freedom of Speech and Press

Federal Quick Index, Advertising; Attorneys; Canons of Ethics; Disciplinary Action; Fraud and Deceit; Freedom of Speech and Press

Auto-Cite®: Any case citation herein can be checked for form, parallel references, later history, and annotation references through the Auto-Cite computer research system.

Consult POCKET PART in this volume for later cases

742

FIGURE 8–14   A sample of material from *A.L.R.*

30 ALR4th   DISCIPLINE OF ATTORNEY FOR ADVERTISING
30 ALR4th 742

Advertising as ground for disciplining attorney

I. PRELIMINARY MATTERS

§ 1. Introduction:
 [a] Scope
 [b] Related matters
§ 2. Summary
§ 3. First Amendment guidelines

II. PROPRIETY OF PARTICULAR ADVERTISEMENTS

§ 4. Magazine or newspaper ads—fields or specialties:
 [a] Unconstitutional rule
 [b] Violation
§ 5. —Fees; free consultations:
 [a] Unconstitutional rule
 [b] No violation
 [c] Violation
§ 6. —Divorce information or instigation
§ 7. —Bar memberships
§ 8. —Anonymity; pseudonymity
§ 9. —Other or unspecified facets:
 [a] Unconstitutional rule
 [b] No violation
 [c] Violation
§ 10. Radio or television ads:
 [a] Unconstitutional rule
 [b] No violation
 [c] Violation
§ 11. Telephone directory listings:
 [a] Unconstitutional rule
 [b] No violation
 [c] Violation
§ 12. Mailings—technical announcements; letterheads:
 [a] Unconstitutional rule
 [b] No violation
 [c] Violation
§ 13. —Greeting cards
§ 14. —Other or unspecified facets:
 [a] Unconstitutional rule
 [b] No violation
 [c] Violation
§ 15. Business cards; flyers; inserts:
 [a] No violation
 [b] Violation
§ 16. Signs; posters:
 [a] Unconstitutional rule
 [b] No violation
 [c] Violation

FIGURE 8–14   (continued)

DISCIPLINE OF ATTORNEY FOR ADVERTISING   **30 ALR4th**
30 ALR4th 742

§ 17. Other or unspecified media:
  [a] Unconstitutional rule
  [b] No violation
  [c] Violation

III. SANCTIONS FOR UNETHICAL ADVERTISING

§ 18. Advertising improprieties alone:
  [a] Disbarment
  [b] Suspension
  [c] Censure or reprimand
  [d] Other disciplinary action
  [e] No disciplinary action
§ 19. Advertising and other improprieties:
  [a] Disbarment
  [b] Suspension
  [c] Censure or reprimand
  [d] Other disciplinary action
  [e] No disciplinary action

INDEX

FIGURE 8–14   *(continued)*

30 ALR4th   DISCIPLINE OF ATTORNEY FOR ADVERTISING
30 ALR4th 742

Detective services, § 8

Diary, advertisement in, §§ 17[b, c], 18[c]

Direct mail advertising, §§ 14, 18[e], 19[a]

Directory listings, § 11

Disbarment, §§ 18[a], 19[a]

Disclaimer of expertise, § 4

Discount coupons, §§ 14[c], 18[c]

Discount price or free services, §§ 5, 10[b], 11[a], 14[c], 16[c], 18[c]

Divorce services, §§ 4[b], 5[a, c], 6, 8, 11[c], 14[b, c], 15[b], 17[c], 19

"Do it yourself" divorce business, § 6

Dramatics in advertising, §§ 4[b], 10[a], 16[c]

Drug cases, § 10[b]

Endorsement of products, §§ 9[c], 18[b]

Envelope indicating nature of advertisement, § 12[a]

Explosion victims, transportation offered to families, § 10[b]

Extortion, § 19[a]

Fees, §§ 5, 10[a, b], 11[a], 14[c], 15[b], 16[c], 17[c], 18[b, c]

Fictitious name, § 16[c]

Fields or specialties, generally, §§ 4, 11

First Amendment guidelines, § 3

Flamboyant advertising, §§ 4[b], 10[a], 16[c]

Flyers, § 15

Foreign divorce, §§ 6, 14[b, c]

Foreign languages, ability to speak, § 9[c]

Free services or discount prices, §§ 5, 10[b], 11[a], 14[c], 16[c], 18[c]

Full-page newspaper advertisement, § 5[b]

Garish format, §§ 4[b], 10[a], 16[c]

Genealogical research services, § 8

Governor's use of attorney, § 17[c]

Greeting cards, §§ 13, 18[c]

Group divorce, § 19[b]

Group legal services plan, §§ 15[b], 17[c]

Home-office advertisement, §§ 16[c], 18[b]

Hotel lobby, business cards placed in, § 15[a]

Hourly fees, § 5[b]

Immigration services, §§ 9[c], 10[c], 11[c], 14[b]

Income tax service, §§ 14[c], 16[c]

Independent directories for attorney advertising, § 11[a]

Indigents, advertising directed at, § 17[b]

Inserts, § 15

Insurance business solicitation, § 15[b]

International trade bureau, letter to, § 14[c]

Interstate practice, §§ 7, 9[c], 10[c], 11[a, c], 12[b, c], 15[b], 16[a], 17[c], 18[c], 19[b, c]

Intoxicating liquor, attorneys linked with brand of, §§ 9[c], 18[b]

Investigatory services, § 8

Judge, libelous statement against judiciary, § 6

Judge, reference to attorney as, § 14[c]

Jurisdictions of practice, §§ 7, 9[c], 10[c], 11[a, c], 12[b, c], 15[b], 16[a], 17[c], 18[c], 19[b, c]

Kickback of fee to union, § 17[c]

"King of Torts", reference to attorney as, § 14[c]

Labor unions, advertising directed at, § 17[c]

Laudatory statements, §§ 9[c], 11[b], 14[c], 18[b]

"Laundry list" type of ad, § 11[a]

Lecture bureau services, §§ 9[c], 10[b], 14[c], 15[a], 16[b], 17[b]

Legal clinic, §§ 5[a], 9[a], 18[c], 19[c]

Legal services plan, §§ 15[b], 17[c]

Letterhead, §§ 12, 18[e], 19[b, c]

Libelous statements against judiciary, § 6

Loan scheme, § 17[b]

Magazine ads, §§ 4-9, 19[b]

Mailings, §§ 12-14

Martindale-Hubbell Law Directory, § 17[c]

Matchbook advertising, §§ 17[c], 19[c]

Matrimonial services, §§ 4[b], 5[a, c], 6, 8, 11[c], 14[b, c], 15[b], 17[c], 19

Mental incapacity of attorney, § 9[c]

Mexican divorces, § 6

Mortgage services, §§ 9[c], 14[b, c]

Multistate practice, §§ 7, 9[c], 10[c], 11[a, c], 12[b, c], 15[b], 16[a], 17[c], 18[e], 19[b, c]

Name change, §§ 5[a, c], 9[a], 11[c]

Naturalization services, §§ 9[c], 10[c], 11[c]

Negro population, advertisement directed at, §§ 17[a], 18[b]

Neighborhood newspaper, §§ 4, 11[a], 18[c]

Neon sign, §§ 16[c], 19[c]

Nevada divorces, § 6

Newspaper ads, §§ 4-9, 18[c], 19[b]

Nonprofit legal service, misrepresentations as, §§ 17[c], 19[c]

Office signs, § 16

Opening of offices, announcements of, § 12[a]

745

FIGURE 8–14   (continued)

DISCIPLINE OF ATTORNEY FOR ADVERTISING   **30 ALR4th**
30 ALR4th 742

TABLE OF JURISDICTIONS REPRESENTED
Consult POCKET PART in this volume for later cases

FIGURE 8–14   *(continued)*

30 ALR4th   Discipline of Attorney for Advertising   § 1[a]
30 ALR4th 742

Ill: §§ 6, 8, 14[b, c], 15[a, b], 17[b, c], 18[a, c]

Iowa: §§ 11[c]

Kan: §§ 9[c], 11[b], 12[b, c], 14[c], 15[b], 16[b], 17[b], 18[c], 19[a, b]

Ky: §§ 7, 8, 12[c], 14[b, c], 16[c], 17[c], 18[c], 19[c]

La: §§ 18[e]

Mass: §§ 5[c], 6, 8, 17[b], 18[b]

Minn: §§ 6, 12[c], 14[a], 17[a], 18[d], 19[b, c]

Miss: §§ 11[a, b]

Mo: §§ 4[b], 6-8, 10[b], 11[c], 12[b, c], 14[c], 17[c], 18[c, e], 19[b, e]

Mont: §§ 11[c], 17[b]

Neb: §§ 6, 16[c], 18[b]

Nev: §§ 6, 8, 11[c], 15[a], 16[c], 17[c], 18[b], 19[b]

NJ: §§ 9[c], 10[b, c], 12[a-c], 15[a], 16[a], 18[b, c]

NM: §§ 17[c], 19[c]

NY: §§ 6, 9[b, c], 11[c], 12[c], 14[a-c], 15[b], 16[c], 17[c], 18[a-e], 19[a-c]

Okla: §§ 5[a], 9[a], 14[c], 19[a]

Pa: §§ 6, 8, 19[a]

RI: §§ 11[b, c], 18[e]

SC: §§ 4[b], 11[c], 18[c], 19[a]

SD: §§ 8, 17[c], 18[b], 19[b]

Tenn: §§ 10[a]

Utah: §§ 16[c], 17[c]

Va: §§ 11[c], 18[d, e]

Wis: §§ 5[b], 9[b], 16[c], 19[c]

I. Preliminary matters

§ 1. Introduction

[a] Scope

This annotation[1] collects and analyzes the state and federal decisions which decide or discuss whether non-political[2] advertising[3] by a lawyer may or does constitute a ground for disciplinary action, and, if so, what is the appropriate sanction for an unethical advertisement. The annotation focuses on those decisions which remain, or evidently remain, viable after the United States Supreme Court's seminal ruling in Bates v State Bar of Arizona (1977) 433 US 350, 53 L Ed 2d 810, 97 S Ct 2691, 51 Ohio Misc 1, 5 Ohio Ops 3d 60, 1977-2 CCH Trade Cases ¶ 61573, reh den 434 US 881, 54 L Ed 2d 164, 98 S Ct 242 (hereinafter occasionally referred to as the "Bates Case"), infra §§ 3, 5[a], and hence it does not cover those decisions, antedating the Bates Case, which upheld or imposed discipline for presently protected conduct then considered to be unethical under the theretofore common type of blanket prohibition against attorney advertising no longer constitutionally permissible.[4]

Since relevant legislation and judicial or bar association rules of ethics are considered herein only to the extent that they are reflected in the

---

1. The present annotation supersedes the one at 39 ALR2d 1055.

2. The propriety of political activities by attorneys is considered generally in 7 Am Jur 2d, Attorneys at Law § 70.

3. Cases involving pure publicity or solicitation, in contrast to pure advertising or mixed advertising-publicity or -solicitation, are excluded from the present treatment; for their coverage, see the annotations at 4 ALR4th 306, "Lawyer publicity as breach of legal ethics," and 5 ALR4th 866, "Modern status of law regarding

solicitation of business by or for attorney," as well as § 18 of 56 L Ed 2d 841, "Licensing and regulation of attorneys as restricted by rights of free speech, expression, and association under First Amendment."

4. For pre-Bates cases involving merely the application of a blanket lawyer-advertising proscription, and apparently no longer constituting viable legal precedent, see the annotation at 39 ALR2d 1055, supra.

747

FIGURE 8–14   *(continued)*

§ 1[a]   DISCIPLINE OF ATTORNEY FOR ADVERTISING   30 ALR4th
                         30 ALR4th 742

reported cases within the scope of this annotation, the reader is advised to consult the latest statutes and rules of pertinent jurisdictions.

[b] Related matters

Use of assumed or trade name as ground for disciplining attorney. 26 ALR4th 1083.

Mental or emotional disturbance as defense to or mitigation of charges against attorney in disciplinary proceeding. 26 ALR4th 995.

Validity and construction of statutes or ordinances prohibiting or restricting distribution of commercial advertising to private residences—modern cases. 12 ALR4th 851.

Modern status of law regarding solicitation of business by or for attorney. 5 ALR4th 866.

Lawyer publicity as breach of legal ethics. 4 ALR4th 306.

Practices forbidden by state deceptive trade practice and consumer protection acts. 89 ALR3d 449.

Unsolicited mailing, distribution, house call, or telephone call as invasion of privacy. 56 ALR3d 457.

Attorney at law: publication and distribution of announcement of new or changed associations or addresses, change of firm name, or the like as ground for disciplinary action. 53 ALR3d 1261.

Validity and construction of state court's pretrial order precluding pub-

licity or comment about pending case by counsel, parties, or witnesses. 33 ALR3d 1041.

Maintenance of lawyer reference system by organization having no legal interest in proceedings. 11 ALR3d 1206.

Commercial tax preparer's advertising as unfair or deceptive act or practice under § 5 of Federal Trade Commission Act (15 USCS § 45(a)). 37 ALR Fed 81.

Actionability under Federal Civil Rights Acts with respect to proceedings to discipline attorney, to regulate admission to practice of law, or to restrain unauthorized practice of law. 9 ALR Fed 422.

Licensing and regulation of attorneys as restricted by rights of free speech, expression, and association under First Amendment. 56 L Ed 2d 841.

Applicability to advertisements of First Amendment's guaranty of free speech and press—Federal cases. 37 L Ed 2d 1124.

Misconduct other than criminal as ground for disbarment or suspension of attorney from practicing in federal court or before federal administrative agencies. 3 L Ed 2d 1960.

§ 2. Summary

The question of the permissible extent of attorney advertising has been highly volatile in recent years,[5]

---

5. See, for instance, the following articles: Muris & McChesney, "Advertising and the price and quality of legal services: The case for legal clinics," 1979 American Bar Foundation Res J 179 (Winter 1979); Andersen, "How lawyers are playing the advertising game," 1 Calif Lawyer 34 (September 1981); Beck, "Advertising, specialization and warranty liability," 16 Forum 248 (1980–1981); Murdock & Linenberger, "Legal Advertising and Solicitation," 16 Land & Water L Rev 627

(1981); Khactu, "Advertising, market power and the public interest: The lawyers' case," 55 ND L Rev 525 (1979); Mitchell, "The impact, regulation and efficacy of lawyer advertising," 20 Osgoode Hall L J 119 (March 1982); Devine, "Lawyer advertising and the Kutak Commission: a refreshing return to the past," 18 Wake Forest L Rev 503 (June 1982); and Hudec & Trebilcock, "Lawyer advertising and the supply of information in

748

FIGURE 8–14   *(continued)*

8. Review Total Client Service Library references in the box on the first page of the annotation for additional legal research sources that you may find useful to consult.

A word of caution here: Do not rely exclusively on these references for your research beyond *A.L.R.* This is a "closed-system" approach to research, limited to the resources provided by a single commercial publisher. As a general rule, you should be more expansive in your approach.

You should also be aware that *A.L.R.* is contained in the LEXIS database, which is discussed in detail in Chapter 13. The on-line access through LEXIS is handy, as it eliminates the necessity of updating annotations and conducting multiple lookups in the various series of bound volumes. The AUTO-CITE system on LEXIS also provides references to *A.L.R.* annotations.

Summary

8.1 Legal Encyclopedias

Legal encyclopedias are secondary sources that provide commentaries on the law and cases. The two main legal encyclopedias are *Corpus Juris Secundum* (*C.J.S.*) and *American Jurisprudence 2d* (*Am. Jur. 2d*). Both legal encyclopedias have general indexes and subject-specific indexes. *Corpus Juris Secundum* is a West publication and references the West key system and other West legal research sources. *American Jurisprudence 2d* is a Lawyers Cooperative Publishing (LCP) publication and references only LCP's coordinate publications. Some coordinate LCP offerings are *American Jurisprudence Proof of Facts, American Jurisprudence Trials, American Jurisprudence Legal Forms 2d,* and *American Jurisprudence Pleadings and Practice Forms, Revised.* Some states, including Texas, have state-specific legal encyclopedias. The Texas legal encyclopedia is entitled *Texas Jurisprudence 3d* (*Tex. Jur. 3d*), which is published by LCP.

8.2 *American Law Reports*

American Law Reports (*A.L.R.*) is now published in five numbered series and a federal-specific series. The *A.L.R.* primarily contains annotations that are extensive articles on a variety of legal subjects. The *A.L.R.* is published by Lawyers Cooperative Publishing (LCP). To use *A.L.R.*, the indexes and annotation history tables should be consulted. Most *A.L.R.* annotations have the same basic structure and normally include a table of jurisdictions represented, general reference material and introduction, and a summary followed by an in-depth treatment of the subject of the annotation.

Review Questions

1. Define legal encyclopedia.

2. Why should caution be used when using a legal encyclopedia?

3. Identify the two general legal encyclopedias.

4. What is the best method to use when beginning legal research in a legal encyclopedia?

5. What special features does *American Jurisprudence 2d* have?

6. Name the four coordinate *American Jurisprudence* resource materials.

7. How many series does *A.L.R.* now have?

8. What are some of the features of *A.L.R.* annotations?

9. How does a researcher find the most current *A.L.R.* annotation?

10. What is the name of the index used in the *A.L.R.* annotations?

Exercises

1. Using 77 *C.J.S.*, answer the following:
   a. On what page does the topic dealing with the Right of Privacy and Publicity begin?
   b. What section of Right of Privacy discusses false light?
   c. What are the library references under section 20?
   d. What is the black letter law in 77 C.J.S. § 20?
   e. In footnote 6 of 77 C.J.S. § 20, what case deals with a beautician?

2. Using the general indexes of *C.J.S.*, answer the following questions:
   a. Under what topic and section can the adulteration of canned spaghetti and cheese be found?
   b. Where are the words "sail close to the wind" defined?
   c. What topic deals with custom duties for lipstick?

3. Locate 22A *American Jurisprudence 2d* and answer the following questions:
   a. What topics are located in 22A *Am. Jur.*?
   b. Look up the topic "death penalty." Where is information found on this topic?

    c. Use the subject-specific index to determine what topic and section discusses damages for the wrongful death of a musician?

    d. What footnote and Texas case is referenced in section 328?

4. Your attorney has asked you to draft a promissory note.

    a. Which book from the *American Jurisprudence* coordinate sources would you use?

    b. In what section are promissory notes found?

    c. What section has an example of a promissory note with installments?

5. Your attorney has asked you to identify the categories for nongenuine signatures to prove a handwriting forgery case.

    a. Which legal sources could assist you?

    b. What article generally deals with identification?

    c. In the article, which section deals with types of forgeries?

    d. What are four categories for nongenuine signatures?

6. Locate 51 *Texas Jurisprudence 3d*, Mental Anguish, and answer the following:

    a. What sections deal with what constitutes mental anguish?

    b. Have any of sections 24 through 28 been supplemented?

    c. Is there a case in the supplement under sections 24 through 28 that sets forth what must be proven to recover for mental anguish?

    d. Using the subject-specific index, under what section would you find grief for loss of a spouse?

7. Your attorney has stated to you that an emergency has occurred in a case and asks you to do some research. The case involves the need for an injunction. Use *Texas Jurisprudence 3d* to answer the following:

    a. What volume deals with injunctions?

    b. What sections deal with the difference between a temporary restraining order and a temporary injunction?

    c. What is a temporary restraining order?

    d. What is a temporary injunction?

    e. Are there any law review articles surveying temporary restraining orders and injunctions in Texas?

8. Identify the section of *Texas Jurisprudence 3d* that sets forth the elements of negligence.

9. Using the *A.L.R. Index:*

    a. Find an article that discusses a physician's liability to third parties contracting the AIDS virus or other contagious disease from a doctor's patient.

    b. What section of *American Jurisprudence 2d* covers this topic?

    c. What federal statute relates to this topic?

    d. How many jurisdictions are cited in this article?

    e. Are there any new cases cited in the supplement?

10. Find 122 A.L.R. Fed. 375 and answer the following:
  a. What is the title of the article?
  b. What case is the basis of the annotation?
  c. On what page of the *A.L.R. Fed.* is the *Urbina* case reported?
  d. What is the citation for the case?
  e. What sections of *American Jurisprudence 2d* relate to this topic?

CHAPTER 9

TEXAS WRIT AND PETITION HISTORIES

§ 9.1 Introduction

In general terms, a **writ or petition history** is simply the information about how a higher court has responded to an application for a review of the final judgment of a lower court. In Texas, the term *writ history* refers to a notation included in all citations to court of appeals cases that either (1) notes "no writ history" if the case was not appealed, or (2) includes one of several notations available to indicate the action taken by the Texas Supreme Court upon an application for a writ of error filed by the party seeking review of the court of appeal's decision. In addition, the term *writ history* as used in Texas includes United States Supreme Court action on appeals from decisions of the Texas Supreme Court where an appeal has actually been filed. A petition history is different. Although it provides important information, the significance is less than with a writ history, as a petition history does not indicate a court's approval or disapproval.

All Texas cases must have their writ or petition histories checked. There are two important reasons for this. First, the writ or petition history must be included in the citation. The general rule for writ or petition histories is that every Texas Court of Appeals case has a writ or petition history notation in its citation, even if it is "no writ history" or "no petition history." Second, the writ or petition history provides a quick means of ascertaining whether there is a higher court decision in the same case that you need to consult before concluding research.

§ 9.2 Appeals to the Texas Supreme Court and the Texas Court of Criminal Appeals

Texas Supreme Court

When parties are dissatisfied with a trial court decision, an appeal may be filed with the Texas Court of Appeals. An appeal to a higher court in a civil case is not mandatory. The parties, along with their attorneys, normally make the decision whether to appeal a trial court decision. If an appeal is requested, the Texas Court of Appeals will hear the case and render a decision.

TERMS

writ or petition history The information about how a higher court has responded to an application for a review of the final judgment of a lower court.

A party who is dissatisfied with a final decision by the Texas Court of Appeals may request review by the Texas Supreme Court by filing a petition called an application for a *writ of error*. The granting of a writ of error by the Texas Supreme Court is within the court's discretionary powers. The court does not have to grant the request. The possible responses by the Texas Supreme Court to a request for a writ of error are:

1. *Granted:* The Texas Supreme Court agrees to hear the appeal.

2. *Refused:* The Texas Supreme Court will not hear the appeal, as the court of appeals decision in all respects is correct.

3. *Denied:* Although the Texas Supreme Court is not agreeing with the reasoning of the court of appeals, the Texas Supreme Court is refusing to hear the case because the decision of the court of appeals presents no error that requires reversal. The Texas Supreme Court may also deny a writ of error because the opinion is not significant to the jurisprudence of the state.

4. *Dismissed:* Normally a case is dismissed because the Texas Supreme Court does not have jurisdiction. This often is due to a procedural error of the appealing party.

Texas Court of Criminal Appeals

On the criminal side, a dissatisfied party may appeal a case to the Texas Court of Criminal Appeals by filing a *petition for discretionary review*. As with the Texas Supreme Court, the justices of the Texas Court of Criminal Appeals can grant, refuse, deny, or dismiss the request for a petition for discretionary review.

§ 9.3   Writ History Notations

Texas Supreme Court

In Texas, the *Texas Subsequent History Table,* or what most legal professionals call the *"Writ History Book,"* is the book that tells whether a case has been appealed to the Texas Supreme Court. The *Texas Subsequent History Table* is published by West Publishing Company. The *Writ History Book* gives the history of all Texas cases on appeal beginning with volume 20 of the *Southwestern Reporter*. Writ histories are supplemented daily by INSTA-CITE on WESTLAW, a computerized legal research tool that is discussed in Chapter 13, and weekly by the Cumulative Table of the advance sheets of the *Southwestern Reporter Texas Cases* and *Texas Supreme Court Journal*.

The writ history notation will appear at the end of the citation. Over the years, the writ history notations have changed. Many previously used notations are no longer used, and most of the current writ history notations were not used in older cases. The writ history notations in effect at the time the case was decided apply and are included in the citation. The following is a list of all writ history notations for Texas civil appeals cases with an explanation of the notation and its proper form for citations.

1. writ requested	A party has requested the Supreme Court to review a lower court decision.
2. writ granted	The Texas Supreme Court has agreed to review the case.
3. writ refused (writ ref'd)	The Texas Supreme Court has rejected review of a case because the court of appeals correctly stated the law.
4. writ dismissed (writ dism'd)	At the direction of the Texas Supreme Court, the request for appeal has been dismissed.
5. writ dismissed for want of jurisdiction (writ dism'd w.o.j.)	The Texas Supreme Court has dismissed the request for review for lack of jurisdiction.
6. writ dismissed, judgment corrected (writ dism'd judgmt cor.)	This is an older notation used from 1939 to 1941. The Texas Supreme Court has dismissed the request as the judgment was correct and the court of appeals properly declared the law.
7. writ refused for want of merit (writ ref'd w.o.m.)	This notation was used from 1941 to 1946. The Texas Supreme Court has rejected the request for review because the judgment was correct, but the court of appeals did not correctly state the law.
8. writ refused, no reversible error (writ ref'd n.r.e.)	This notation was used from 1946 to January 1, 1988. The Texas Supreme Court has rejected the request for review as the case presented no error that required reversal, but the court does not agree with the court of appeals' declaration of the law.
9. writ denied	This notation became effective on January 1, 1988. The Texas Supreme Court has rejected review of the case as the judgment of the court of appeals does not require reversal, but the law was not correctly stated in all respects or is not of such importance to the body of law in Texas

	to require correction. (The latter situation must be agreed to by at least four justices for review.)
10. writ dismissed by the agreement (writ dism'd by agr.)	The request has been dismissed by agreement of the parties to the case.
11. no writ	No appeal has been taken by the parties at the appeals level.
12. no writ history (n.w.h.)	Although a request for review has not been filed, the time for filing has not expired. This designation means a request for review could still be filed by the dissatisfied party in a case. If the time for review has completely expired, the designation in number 11 is used.

The *Texas Rules of Form,* published by the Texas Law Review Association and known as the *"Greenbook,"* discusses how to properly cite a Texas writ history and should always be consulted for proper citation form. The *Greenbook* should be used in conjunction with the *Texas Subsequent History Table,* as each supplies different information.

Texas Court of Criminal Appeals

The petition history for criminal cases is also found in the *Texas Subsequent History Table* and is supplemented in the *Southwestern Reporter Texas Cases* advance sheets. For the petition history of recent cases, check the *Slip Opinions of the Court of Criminal Appeals of Texas* or the advance sheets of West's *Southwestern Reporter* "Orders List." INSTA-CITE on WEST-LAW provides computer databases for recent petition histories as well.

Like civil writ histories, criminal petition histories have specific designation that are used in citations. The designations signal whether the Texas Court of Criminal Appeals granted or denied a request for a petition for discretionary review. The notation designations for criminal cases are as follows:

| 1. no petition (no pet.) | No petition has been filed for a request for discretionary review. |
| 2. no petition history (no pet. h.) | Although a petition has not been filed, the time for filing has not expired. This designation means that a petition for review could |

still be filed by the dissatisfied party in a case. If the time for review has completely expired, the designation in number 1 is used.

3. petition dismissed (pet. dism'd)	This designation is used when the parties dismiss the petition by agreement or when the Court has dismissed a previously granted petition because it was improvidently granted.
4. petition filed (pet. filed)	This notation signifies a petition has been filed but the court has made no decision about whether it will be granted or denied.
5. petition granted (pet. granted)	The petition for review has been granted by the court but no final decision has been rendered.
6. petition refused (pet. ref'd)	The court has refused to grant the petition for review. Note: Only capital cases must be heard for review by the court. All other cases are discretionary with the court.
7. petition refused untimely filed (pet. ref'd untimely filed)	The petition for review was filed out of time and has not been granted due to a procedural technicality.
8. review granted without petition (rev. granted, without pet.)	The court has filed an order for review of a case on its own motion.

Unlike civil writs for review, petition histories do not indicate a court's approval or disapproval of a lower court's decision. Consequently, do not read anything into a case's petition history.

§ 9.4 Using the *Texas Subsequent History Table*

In addition to checking writ and petition histories, the subsequent history of a case must be checked. The subsequent history tells what happened to a case after the Texas Supreme Court granted a writ, after the Texas Court of Criminal Appeals granted a petition or reviewed the case on its own motion, or after the United States Supreme Court accepted or rejected review.

The *Texas Rules of Form* (the *Greenbook*) states that a disposition by the Texas Supreme Court or the Texas Court of Criminal Appeals is to be given in lieu of writ or petition history, but a disposition by the United States Supreme Court is to be given *in addition* to writ or petition history.

Examples of possible subsequent history designations are:

Abbreviation	*Explanation*
aff'd	affirmed
aff'd on other grounds	affirmed on other grounds
aff'd per curiam	affirmed per curiam
cert. denied	certiori denied
cert. dismissed	certiori dismissed
rev'd	reversed
rev'd on other grounds	reversed on other grounds
rev'd per curiam	reversed per curiam
vacated	vacated; voided by court

The *Writ History Book* is easy to use. Look up the citation by identifying the volume, series of the reporter, and the page where the case begins. The volume and reporter will be isolated in a column. Under the volume and reporter, a list of page numbers appears. Find the page number on which the case in the reporter begins. Once you have located the page number, you may see various entries at that point.

First, a new citation may be given next to the page reference. (See Figure 9–1.) This indicates that the case was appealed to the Texas Supreme Court or Texas Court of Criminal Appeals and accepted for review by the court. The case from either high court is given a new citation. At this point, it is wise to retrieve the case cited. Read the case to learn what happened. More likely than not, the case that should be relied upon is the higher court case.

The second possible writ history entry is a reference appearing in the writ history book such as "n.r.e.," "ref'd," or "denied." These notations indicate that the higher court viewed the case and why it was rejected. Certain notations have more precedential value than others. For example, if a notation is "writ ref'd," this indicates that the Texas Supreme Court completely agrees with the Texas Court of Appeals decision and acknowledges that the court properly stated the law. Most view a writ refused case as having the same effect as though the Texas Supreme Court actually heard the case. However, the notation "n.r.e.," no reversible error, has a less positive effect on the Texas Court of Appeals decision. By refusing to hear a case based upon an "n.r.e." notation, the Texas Supreme Court is the stating that the decision of the Court of Appeals has not correctly stated the law in all respects, but the error in the decision presented does not require reversal by the court. In other words, although agreeing with the lower court's result, the Texas Supreme Court did not like how the court arrived at the result.

The last possibility is that when looking up the case, no page reference will appear. This simply means the case was not appealed, and the history reference will be "no writ" or "no pet.," meaning no writ or petition

165   **TEXAS SUBSEQUENT HISTORY TABLE**   650 S.W.2d

18—Refused
26—Refused
31—Refused
44—Ref. N.R.E.
46—721 SW2d 530
61—Ref. N.R.E.
64—697 SW2d 387
69—Ref. N.R.E.
71—Ref. N.R.E.
90—Ref. N.R.E.
92—Refused
116—Refused
123—Ref. N.R.E.
135—692 SW2d 712;
   701 SW2d 696
144—Ref. N.R.E.
154—647 SW2d 660
166—656 SW2d 421
170—668 SW2d 319
177—Ref. N.R.E.
185—Ref. N.R.E.
194—Refused
209—653 SW2d 799
446—704 SW2d 403
492—Ref. N.R.E.
494—Refused
500—Refused
503—Refused
506—Refused
510—Dismissed
512—Ref. N.R.E.
540—689 SW2d 450
546—646 SW2d 449
554—Refused
558—Ref. N.R.E.
560—Ref. N.R.E.
566—Ref. N.R.E.
574—Ref. N.R.E.
758—652 SW2d 923;
   661 SW2d 159
764—758 SW2d 255
774—Ref. N.R.E.
786—Ref. N.R.E.
791—Ref. N.R.E.
795—Ref. N.R.E.
797—Ref. N.R.E.
804—Ref. N.R.E.
808—Ref. N.R.E.
813—Refused
815—Ref. N.R.E.
823—Ref. N.R.E.
828—650 SW2d 61
831—Dismissed
833—674 SW2d 751
835—Ref. N.R.E.
856—Ref. N.R.E.
879—665 SW2d 124;
   737 SW2d 315
900—657 SW2d 782
903—658 SW2d 561
905—Ref. N.R.E.
911—Refused
915—Ref. N.R.E.
950—Refused

645 S.W.2d
279—104 SCt 1318
284—677 SW2d 562
340—Ref. N.R.E.
427—711 SW2d 628
477—659 SW2d 820
482—Refused
486—Ref. N.R.E.
493—Ref. N.R.E.
496—Ref. N.R.E.
498—770 SW2d 778
506—661 SW2d 911;
   914, 917;
   104 SCt 1911,
   2691
534—Ref. N.R.E.

542—Ref. N.R.E.
550—Ref. N.R.E.
555—Refused
562—Ref. N.R.E.
573—Ref. N.R.E.
575—Dismissed
579—691 SW2d 586
589—652 SW2d 368
591—660 SW2d 807
596—670 SW2d 250
625—Ref. N.R.E.
629—Ref. N.R.E.
645—Ref. N.R.E.
652—Refused
772—104 SCt 422
798—651 SW2d 409
824—Refused
827—647 SW2d 253
836—Ref. N.R.E.
845—Dismissed
855—Refused
861—Ref. N.R.E.
866—Refused
874—Ref. N.R.E.
885—Refused;
   686 SW2d 157;
   696 SW2d 282
888—660 SW2d 825
906—Refused
915—Refused
925—Ref. N.R.E.
928—659 SW2d 638

646 S.W.2d
246—673 SW2d 558;
   676 SW2d 183
255—Ref. N.R.E.
263—Ref. N.R.E.
270—Ref. N.R.E.
288—Ref. N.R.E.
292—Ref. N.R.E.
298—Ref. N.R.E.
302—Ref. N.R.E.
309—Dismissed;
   730 SW2d 857
320—Refused
330—657 SW2d 432
463[11]—658 SW2d 169
466—699 SW2d 334
469—Refused
474—649 SW2d 297
485—662 SW2d 357
474—Refused
489—661 SW2d 101
491—Ref. N.R.E.
497—652 SW2d 410
506—662. SW2d 362
514—Refused
516—Ref. N.R.E.
520—Refused
528—Refused
536—Refused
543—Ref. N.R.E.
   691 SW2d 747
554—683 SW2d 379
561—Ref. N.R.E.
573—657 SW2d 813;
   Ref. N.R.E.
576—683 SW2d 729
581—649 SW2d 296
594—670 SW2d 255
595—654 SW2d 701;
   104 SCt 497, 749
599—704 SW2d 21
602—Refused
606—Dismissed
610—Ref. N.R.E.
612—Refused
615—Refused
630—688 SW2d 486
633—Refused

641—Refused
648—Refused—
   untimely filed
655—Ref. N.R.E.
662—Refused
663—661 SW2d 957
673—Dismissed
676—650 SW2d 839;
   657 SW2d 166
953—Refused

647 S.W.2d
1[2]—641 SW2d 532
3—103 SCt 2086
5—Dismissed
18—Refused
22—Refused
27—Refused
44—Ref. N.R.E.
51—650 SW2d 67;
   659 SW2d 30
55—682 SW2d 550;
   719 SW2d 205
59—Ref. N.R.E.
62—Ref. N.R.E.
70—Dismissed
82—Dism. Agr.
102—Ref. N.R.E.
110—Ref. N.R.E.
249—652 SW2d 563
268—655 SW2d 284
304—Refused
306—Refused
310—Refused
319—Ref. N.R.E.
338—Dismissed
350—Refused
353—Refused
369—656 SW2d 518
384—Ref. N.R.E.
393—Ref. N.R.E.
400—650 SW2d 431
413—650 SW2d 813
675—Refused
686—652 SW2d 773
692—Ref. N.R.E.
708—Refused—
   untimely filed
726—Ref. N.R.E.
742—719 SW2d 320
749—Ref. N.R.E.
751—Refused
773—Ref. N.R.E.
786—Refused

648 S.W.2d
25—Ref. N.R.E.
30—Refused—
   untimely filed
31—677 SW2d 507;
   687 SW2d 65
312—103 SCt 3113
324—Ref. N.R.E.
335—Ref. N.R.E.
344—658 SW2d 148
351—Ref. N.R.E.
358—Ref. N.R.E.
363—Ref. N.R.E.
368—Ref. N.R.E.
380—Refused
387—Ref. N.R.E.
398—Dismissed
410—Ref. N.R.E.
418—Ref. N.R.E.
430—Ref. N.R.E.
667—104 SCt 136
712—646 SW2d 448
715—Refused
743—Ref. N.R.E.

746—654 SW2d 442;
   709 SW2d 225
768—Refused
773—Ref. N.R.E.
782—717 SW2d 1
783—Refused
790—726 SW2d 107

649 S.W.2d
30—104 SCt 122
46—104 SCt 496
59—770 SW2d 778
73—Ref. N.R.E.
81—652 SW2d 939
83—660 SW2d 521
96—661 SW2d 933
111—662 SW2d 368
121—Ref. N.R.E.
128—Ref. N.R.E.
139—Refused
142—Refused
303[7]—105 SCt 1876
314—Refused
342—Ref. N.R.E.
347—Ref. N.R.E.
361—Refused
363—Refused
368—Ref. N.R.E.
380—Refused
384—Refused
610—104 SCt 242
613—104 SCt 156
643—Ref. N.R.E.
647—Refused
649—Ref. N.R.E.
652—Ref. N.R.E.
658—Ref. N.R.E.
677—737 SW2d 805;
   750 SW2d 17
679—Ref. N.R.E.
700—Ref. N.R.E.
724—Ref. N.R.E.
728—Refused
731—Ref. N.R.E.
740—Ref. N.R.E.
749—Ref. N.R.E.
752—Refused
780—Ref. N.R.E.
786—Refused
791—Ref. N.R.E.
794—Dismissed
798—Ref. N.R.E.
801—681 SW2d 602;
   685 SW2d 131
809—Ref. N.R.E.
814—658 SW2d 760;
   678 SW2d 75
826—Ref. N.R.E.

650 S.W.2d
89—662 SW2d 595
97—672 SW2d 233
104—Ref. N.R.E.
123—Ref. N.R.E.
131—696 SW2d 178
135—Ref. N.R.E.
145—Dismissed
158—Ref. N.R.E.
177—Dismissed
181—Ref. N.R.E.
185—Ref. N.R.E.
189—Ref. N.R.E.
193—Ref. N.R.E.
198—Refused
203—Refused
213—Ref. N.R.E.
432—683 SW2d 702
436—702 SW2d 597
441—660 SW2d 822
445—Refused

Supplemented by **Texas Cases Advance Sheet Table** and **INSTA-CITE** on **WESTLAW.**

FIGURE 9–1   A sample from the *Texas Subsequent History Table*

history. Do not read anything into a "no writ" or "no pet." case. Often a case is not appealed simply because of lack of finances.

For recently appealed cases, the writ history notations may be "writ requested" or "writ granted." These notations mean that an appeal is pending before the Texas Supreme Court. This must be included in the citation as well.

§ 9.5   A Checklist

1. Locate a copy of the *Texas Subsequent History Table*.

2. If the case is recent, also check advance sheets for *Southwestern Reporter* or INSTA-CITE on WESTLAW.

3. Look up the citation by finding the volume and reporter.

4. After locating the appropriate volume, identify the page number of the citation.

5. If a page number appears, write down the writ or petition history.

6. If no page number appears, the history is a no writ or no petition history.

7. If a new citation appears for either the *Southwestern Reporter* or a United States Supreme Court reporter, or both, retrieve the book and review the case.

8. Add all subsequent writ or petition histories to the final citation.

Summary

9.1 Introduction

A writ or petition history shows how a higher court has responded to an application for a writ of error or a petition for discretionary review. All intermediate appealed cases have a writ or petition history in Texas that must always be checked in legal research. The writ or petition history is the part of the citation and tells how a higher court has viewed a lower court's decision.

9.2 Appeals to the Texas Supreme Court and the Texas Court of Criminal Appeals

A party dissatisfied with a civil decision by the Texas Court of Appeals can apply for a writ of error. The granting of a writ is discretionary with the Texas Supreme Court. Criminal cases are appealed through a petition for discretionary review to the Texas Court of Criminal Appeals. Granting or denying a petition is also discretionary.

9.3 Writ History Notations

The *Texas Subsequent History Table*, commonly known as the "*Writ History Book*," is used to locate writ and petition histories. All writ and petition history notations are designated at the end of the citation and have various explanations. Each writ or petition history, whether civil or criminal, has a specific meaning. To properly cite writ or petition history notations, consult the Texas *Greenbook*.

9.4 Using the *Texas Subsequent History Table*

Using the *Writ History Book* is easy. Look up each citation by first identifying the volume and locating the page of the case. If no page number is located, the notation is "no writ." If the page number appears, there will be corresponding notation to review.

Review Questions

1. What is a writ history?

2. What is the request for review to the Texas Supreme Court called? What is the request for review to the Texas Court of Criminal Appeals called?

3. What are the possible responses of the Texas Supreme Court to a writ of review?

4. What is the proper name of the *Writ History Book*?

5. Where can recent writ histories be located?

6. In what year was the notation "n.r.e." eliminated?

7. What replaced the notation "n.r.e."?

8. What does the notation "writ denied" signify?

9. What is the procedure for looking up a writ history? A petition history?

10. What notation appears when your citation does not appear in the *Writ History Book*?

Exercises

1. Identify the writ or petition histories for the following cases:

   a. 94 S.W.2d 514

   b. 435 S.W.2d 569

   c. 832 S.W.2d 147

   d. 234 S.W. 684

   e. 537 S.W.2d 304

   f. 853 S.W.2d 70

2. What is the writ history for 667 S.W.2d 887?

3. What is the writ history for 494 S.W.2d 865?

4. The following cases were appealed to the Texas Supreme Court. Did the court grant or deny the petition for writ of error?

   a. 869 S.W.2d 478

   b. 757 S.W.2d 103

   c. 609 S.W.2d 590

   d. 458 S.W.2d 696

   e. 241 S.W.2d 616

   f. 158 S.W.2d 569

5. Find *Savin Corp. v. Copy Distributing Co.*

   a. What is the citation?

   b. What is the writ history?

6. Find *Tuloma Gas Products Co. v. Lehmbers.*

   a. What is the citation?

   b. What is the writ history?

7. Identify the writ histories for the following cases:

   a. 91 S.W. 640

   b. 344 S.W.2d 426

   c. 585 S.W.2d 796

   d. 707 S.W.2d 930

   e. 878 S.W.2d 248

8. Using the most recent *Texas Subsequent History Table* book, what cases are covered in that volume?

9. Find *Haverfield Co. v. Siegel.*

   a. What is the citation?

   b. What is the writ history?

10. What is the writ history for *Kasmir v. Suburban Homes Realty,* 824 S.W.2d 239?

CHAPTER 10

PROPER
CITATION FORM

§ 10.1 Citation Form in General

Use of Legal Authorities

In legal memoranda and briefs, legal authorities must be used to support the propositions asserted. As discussed in earlier chapters, a legal authority is referenced by its "citation" or "cite," as it is commonly called. From cases to legal encyclopedias, all legal authorities have a specific citation form. The rules of form for citations are necessary for completeness, accuracy, and uniformity of presentation. The proper citation form allows easy access to legal material. You should think of proper citation form as a substantive, as well as "style," issue. If your citation form is inaccurate, whoever reads your research may tend to question its substantive accuracy.

The widely accepted authority for proper citation form is *The Bluebook—A Uniform System of Citation* (15th ed. 1991). In Texas, a separate citation book was created, *Texas Rules of Form* (8th ed. 1992), known as the *"Greenbook."* Each citation book is discussed in detail below.

The Bluebook

Jointly produced by the Harvard, Columbia, Yale, and Pennsylvania law review staffs, published by Harvard University, and presently in its fifteenth edition, *The Bluebook* is the most widely used and accepted book on citation form. *Bluebook* rules, however, can be complex and, at points, confusing. There has been a movement in recent years toward a simpler system set forth in the *University of Chicago Manual of Legal Citation*, known as the *"Maroon Book."* The Chicago manual, however, has not been adopted as authoritative. Therefore, continue to follow *The Bluebook* form unless you are asked to do otherwise.

The best way to become familiar with *The Bluebook* is simply to scan its contents. A lengthy index at the back of the book details the contents. Within its pages are examples of how to cite legal authorities ranging from primary sources such as cases, statutes, administrative regulations, and constitutions to secondary authorities such as treatises, legal periodicals, and law reviews. Perhaps some of the most important pages in *The Bluebook* are the inside front and back covers and the first page, which give examples of basic citation forms. For state-specific citation forms, *The Bluebook* contains a state-specific section, with the states arranged alphabetically. This section is located within the blue-colored pages.

The Bluebook is divided into a number of sections: (1) an introduction, (2) practitioners' notes, (3) structure and use of citations, (4) tables and abbreviations, and (5) an Index. Each section contains important information on proper citation form.

The Introduction   The introduction in *The Bluebook* presents an overview of the general principles of legal citation. It gives a number of examples of general citation form, mainly those that are more commonly used. The introduction also sets forth the basic structure of *The Bluebook*, highlighting its three major parts.

Practitioners' Notes   Since *The Bluebook*'s citations illustrate the form used for law review articles, the section referred to as "practitioners' notes" (printed on light blue paper) identifies how to adapt law review citation form to a simpler style used in court documents. This section gives numerous examples of the typeface conventions used in court documents and legal memoranda, citing the rules the legal practitioner should use.

Structure and Use of Citations   This section is the heart of *The Bluebook*, detailing the rules for proper citation. It sets forth the rules for all types of legal authorities, both primary and secondary. Specifically, this section identifies such important rules as the order of legal authorities, law review citation form, short forms of citations, use of quotations, abbreviations, and basic citation form.

Tables and Abbreviations   All jurisdictions, both federal and state, are listed in this section, giving the proper citation form for each. Printed on light blue paper, seventeen tables are identified for quick and easy reference to any jurisdiction's citation form, including cases and statutes.

Index   At the end of *The Bluebook* is an alphabetically arranged index, covering over thirty pages of information. This index provides an access guide to *The Bluebook*'s parts and information.

The fifteenth edition of *The Bluebook* contains a number of revisions and changes to previous editions. These changes are clearly noted in the "Preface to the Fifteenth Edition." There are over twenty changes in the fifteenth edition. For those who were familiar with the fourteenth edition of *The Bluebook*, perhaps the most notable change deals with the use of parallel citations in state court decisions. The previous rule required that all parallel citations be given in state court decisions. This was sometimes a difficult task when books were unavailable to lawyers and paralegals. The new rule provides that parallel citations are to be used only in documents submitted to a court that decided the case. All other state cases can be cited to the West regional reporter only.

A *Bluebook* user should always study the preface to the edition carefully whenever a new edition is published as a quick and efficient means to becoming familiar with important changes that occur from one edition to the next.

The Bluebook adds uniformity to citation form. It sets standards that are generally followed in all jurisdictions. Some states, such as Texas, have published their own rules of form books, and these should be consulted along with *The Bluebook*.

The *Greenbook*

As a general rule, *The Bluebook* is *the* authority on proper citation form, and its rules must be followed. *The Bluebook*, however, does not adequately address Texas citation form, particularly writ and petition histories that are crucial to Texas Court of Appeals and Texas Court of Criminal Appeals citations. In response to these inadequacies, the University of Texas Law Review Association created a Texas-specific citation book—the *Texas Rules of Form,* or the *Greenbook*. First published in 1966, the *Greenbook* is now in its eighth edition and has become the "Bible" for citing Texas legal authorities. Although *The Bluebook* is still the primary citation authority, the *Greenbook* should be followed when conflicts arise in citing Texas authorities.

The *Texas Rules of Form* is easy to use and organized in a logical and manageable fashion. The pages at the front of the book give a quick reference to basic Texas citation forms. Following these general rules is a detailed table of contents that breaks down Texas legal authorities into the following general categories:

1. Typeface conventions
2. Texas cases
3. Texas constitutions and prestatehood documents
4. Texas statutes
5. Quasi-statutory material
6. Secondary material
7. Order of citation

The general categories are then subdivided into specific areas. For example, the section on Texas cases is divided into the Texas Supreme Court, the Texas Court of Criminal Appeals, Commission of Appeals, Courts of Appeals, District Courts, and Miscellaneous Cases. Under each subtopic, the dates of citation modification are given. To identify the citation form desired, review the table of contents. The *Greenbook* also has an extensive index.

The *Greenbook* gives examples of proper citation form and often an explanation of changes that have occurred and why. When using the *Texas*

Rules of Form, pay close attention to dates of cases, as they will dictate the proper citation form.

The last pages list the writ history notations, discussed in Chapter 9. This section is expanded further in the section on Texas cases, which explains Texas writ and petition histories and proper citation forms.

If your specific question is not addressed in the *Greenbook*, you might consult the Texas Tech Law Review's *"Redbook"* which emphasizes citation forms for Texas administrative materials. In addition, there are some useful compilations of legal citations and abbreviations that are much more exhaustive than either *The Bluebook* or the *Greenbook* in terms of examples of specific publications that are listed, for example, Bieber's *Dictionary of Legal Citations, 3d ed.,* published in 1988 by Hein.

§ 10.2 The Cases

Legal professionals must often rely upon cases as their primary source of legal authority. When citing a case in legal memoranda and court documents, always include:

1. the name of the case underlined [Note: underlining signifies that the word(s) underlined should be italicized. If you have access to a word processing system that allows you to print with an italics font, then these word(s) should in fact be italicized, as they are in this set of materials.];

2. the reporter or source where the case can be found, including volume and page number on which the case begins;

3. the court that decided the case; and

4. the date of the decision.

The information included in a citation varies from state to state, jurisdiction to jurisdiction, and court to court. For example, in Texas, writ or petition history notations are included in a citation for a Texas Court of Appeals decision, whereas in New York, they are not. Pay close attention to state citation form.

United States Supreme Court

The United States Supreme Court should be cited only by using its official reporter, *United States Reports*, when this citation is available:

World-Wide Volkswagen Corp. v. Woodson, 444 U.S. 286 (1980).

Many attorneys believe that the parallel citations to the United States Supreme Court cases should be used in the citation. This is neither correct nor necessary, at least for formal legal writing in the form of briefs and memoranda to be filed with a court. Parallel citations, however, may be very useful for internal communications within a law office, particularly if the office has only one of the series of reporters. So you should clarify what is expected in this regard as you discuss the assignment with the person making it.

If parallel citations are required, shepardizing (discussed in detail in Chapter 11) will quickly provide you with the needed citation. The following is the acceptable order of presentation:

> *World-Wide Volkswagen Corp. v. Woodson,* 444 U.S. 286, 100 S. Ct. 559, 62 L. Ed. 2d 490 (1980).

Recent United States Supreme Court Cases

There is an exception to the above rule. When a case is cited prior to its publication in *United States Reports,* cite to *United States Law Week* or the *Supreme Court Reporter.* Both are published far in advance of *United States Reports* and give the complete texts of United States Supreme Court decisions. The following is an example of a citation for which a *United States Reports* reference is not yet available:

> *Harris v. Forklift Sys., Inc.,* ____ U.S. ____, 114 S. Ct. 367, 126 L. Ed. 2d 295 (1993).

Federal Courts of Appeals

Federal Reporter

Decisions of the United States Courts of Appeals are published in West's *Federal Reporter.* When citing a *Federal Reporter* case, always identify the name of the case, the volume of the reporter, and the page on which the case begins. In addition, the appeals circuit must be identified in the parenthetical along with the date of the decision. The circuit is identified with its arabic number and abbreviation of the word "circuit." All federal courts of appeals cases are cited with the name of the case underlined (or italicized):

> *Neifeld v. Steinberg,* 438 F.2d 423 (3d Cir. 1971).

Texas Cases in the *Federal Reporter*

When citing a federal court of appeals case from Texas, use the same form as that used for other *Federal Reporter* cases. The circuit will always be the fifth:

> *Marsh v. United States,* 334 F.2d 317 (5th Cir. 1965).

Federal District Courts

Federal Supplement

Federal Supplement citations differ slightly from *Federal Reporter* citations. The most notable difference is in the parenthetical. When citing a case from the *Federal Supplement*, the district where the case originates must be identified along with the state in which the district is located and the year of the decision. Although the citation form remains consistent for all fifty states, attention must be paid to the variation in districts. The possible districts at the federal trial level are listed below:

N.D.   Northern District

S.D.   Southern District

E.D.   Eastern District

W.D.   Western District

D.   District (referring to a state that has only one federal district court)

C.D.   Central District

M.D.   Middle District

You will not find all of these in every state. Some states have multiple districts, while others have but one. Do not include the division in the citation. A *Federal Supplement* case is cited as follows:

Reyno v. Piper Aircraft Co., 479 F. Supp. 727 (M.D. Pa. 1979).

Texas Cases in the *Federal Supplement*

Follow *The Bluebook* form when citing Texas federal district court cases appearing in the *Federal Supplement.* Note that Texas has four districts: Northern (N.D.), Southern (S.D.), Eastern (E.D.), and Western (W.D.). See Chapter 2 for a listing of which counties are located in each district. A Texas *Federal Supplement* citation is as follows:

Port Neches Indep. School Dist. v. R.F.C., 121 F. Supp. 561 (S.D. Tex. 1954).

Federal Rules Decisions

Federal Rules Decisions (*F.R.D.*) contains district court decisions on issues involving the federal rules of civil procedure, rules of criminal procedure, and rules of evidence. When citing a case from *F.R.D.*, always include in the parenthetical the district of origination, the state, and the year of the decision. The format is similar to that used in citing cases in the *Federal Supplement*:

> *Marks v. Spitz*, 4 F.R.D. 348 (D. Mass. 1945).

State Cases

When submitting legal documents to courts of a deciding state, cite all parallel citations. Otherwise, cite only to the regional reporter:
In California:

> *Bryant v. Blevin*, 9 Cal. 4th 47, 884 P.2d 1034, 36 Cal. Rptr. 2d 86 (1994).

Outside California:

> *Bryant v. Blevin*, 884 P.2d 1034 (Cal. 1994).

Texas State Courts

As discussed earlier in this chapter, *Texas Rules of Form* provides proper citation forms for Texas state cases. One of the inadequacies of *The Bluebook* is the failure to give full treatment of Texas writ and petition histories. Although the *Greenbook* is more helpful in citing Texas writ and petition histories, do not use it to the exclusion of *The Bluebook* on other matters of style.

Texas Supreme Court

Prior to July 1962, Texas had two reporters for Texas Supreme Court cases: *Texas Reports* and *Southwestern Reporter*. *Texas Reports* was the official reporter, and its citation must be included with the unofficial citation for any Texas Supreme Court case prior to 1962:

> *Gouldy v. Metcalf*, 75 Tex. 455, 12 S.W. 830 (1889).

Since July 1962, Texas Supreme Court cases have not been published in an official reporter, but they continue to be published in the *Southwestern Reporter*. The citation for cases after July 1962 is as follows:

> *Wal-Mart Stores, Inc. v. Street*, 754 S.W.2d 153 (Tex. 1988).

Note that the *Texas Reports* reference has been dropped from the citation, and Texas (Tex.) is added to the parenthetical information along with the year of the decision.

For Texas Supreme Court cases reported between 1846 and 1886, reference only *Texas Reports*, as the *Southwestern Reporter* does not contain Texas decisions prior to 1886:

Reese v. Medlock, 27 Tex. 120 (1886).

Cases decided recently may first appear in the *Texas Supreme Court Journal*. Until published in the *Southwestern Reporter*, your only reference may be to the *Texas Supreme Court Journal*. Cite these cases as follows:

Payne & Keller, Inc. v. P.P.G. Indus., Inc., 33 Tex. Sup. Ct. J. 603 (June 23, 1990).

Note that the date in the parenthetical is the date of publication of the *Texas Supreme Court Journal*, and not the date the case was decided.

Texas Commission of Appeals During the years 1918 to 1945, Texas had a Commission of Appeals of the Texas Supreme Court. Although the court no longer exists, its cases remain. To cite a Commission of Appeals case, use the following form:

Republic Ins. Co. v. Highland Park Indep. School Dist., 141 Tex. 224, 171 S.W.2d 342 (Tex. Comm'n App. 1943, opinion adopted).

In the parenthetical, the words "opinion adopted" or "holding approved" refer to the situation in which the Commission of Appeal's opinion was subsequently adopted or approved by the Texas Supreme Court. The notation is located at the end of the case in the *Southwestern Reporter*.

Texas Courts of Appeals

When the Texas Court of Civil Appeals was eliminated in 1980, changes in citation form occurred. Texas Court of Appeals cases decided prior to September 10, 1981, are cited:

Lubbock Radio Paging Serv., Inc. v. Southwestern Bell Tel. Co., 607 S.W.2d 29 (Tex. Civ. App.—Beaumont 1980, writ ref'd n.r.e.).

Within the parenthetical, the court, city of the court of appeals district, the date, and the writ history of the case must be included. There are fourteen court of appeals districts, called supreme judicial districts, in Texas:

Supreme Judicial District	*City*
First	Houston [1st Dist.] (formerly Galveston)
Second	Fort Worth
Third	Austin
Fourth	San Antonio
Fifth	Dallas
Sixth	Texarkana

Seventh	Amarillo
Eighth	El Paso
Ninth	Beaumont
Tenth	Waco
Eleventh	Eastland
Twelfth	Tyler
Thirteenth	Corpus Christi
Fourteenth	Houston [14th Dist.] (formerly Houston)

Because Houston has two districts, the citation to a Houston court of appeals case must include the numerical district designation:

> *Bottinelli v. Robinson,* 594 S.W.2d 112 (Tex. Civ. App.—Houston [1st Dist.] 1979, no writ).

After 1981, the Texas Court of Civil Appeals and the Texas Court of Criminal Appeals were replaced by one intermediate level of appellate courts for both civil and criminal decisions: the Texas Courts of Appeals, with the fourteen districts listed above. A change has occurred in the citation form. The word "Civ." has been removed from the parenthetical.

> *Jarett v. Warhola,* 695 S.W.2d 8 (Tex. App.—Houston [14th Dist.] 1985, writ ref'd).

Texas Court of Criminal Appeals

Prior to 1962, two reporters published Texas Court of Criminal Appeals cases: *Texas Criminal Reports* and the *Southwestern Reporter*. The official reporter was *Texas Criminal Reports*. Both reporters must be cited. Texas Court of Criminal Appeals decisions prior to 1962 should be cited as follows:

> *Hale v. State,* 164 Tex. Crim. 482, 300 S.W.2d 75 (1957).

Since 1962, the *Southwestern Reporter* has served as the only reporter for the Texas Court of Criminal Appeals. Cases from this court decided after 1962 are cited only to the *Southwestern Reporter:*

> *Roach v. State,* 586 S.W.2d 866 (Tex. Crim. App. 1979).

Local Rules

The local rules in Texas are numerous, and the *Greenbook* offers some guidance in citing them. The *Greenbook* suggests that a local rule citation should identify the court location and rule number:

> Dallas (Tex.) Civ. Dist. Ct. Loc. R. 1.3.

§ 10.3 Statutes and Administrative Rules and Regulations

Federal Statutes

Important legal authority is often found in statutes. When citing a statute, always refer to its official version. The official compilation of federal statutes is the *United States Code.* Always include:

1. the title number,
2. the statutory code,
3. the section number of the code, and
4. the year the code was published.

For example:

> 25 U.S.C. § 409a (1983) or 25 U.S.C. section 409(a) (1983).

Unless the *United States Code* does not in any of its volumes yet contain the statute you want to cite, it is incorrect to cite to an unofficial source such as the *United States Code Annotated* or the *United States Code Service.* However, you may see them cited as follows:

> 25 U.S.C.A. § 409a (West 1983) or 25 U.S.C.S. section 409(a) (Law. Coop. 1983).

To properly cite to the above sources, simply eliminate the "A" from the U.S.C.A. and the "S" from the U.S.C.S.

Texas Statutes

The Texas statutes are being reorganized from articles to subject-specific codes. Consequently, there are two basic variations of citations to Texas statutes. Citations to Texas statutes should include the following elements:

1. reference to the official statutory name,
2. the abbreviated code or noncode name,
3. the section or article number of the statute, and
4. the year the code or noncode was published.

The two methods of citing Texas statutes are:

- Uncodified statutes with articles:

    Tex Rev. Civ. Stat. Ann. art. 6132b, § 6 (Vernon 1970) or Tex. Ins. Code Ann. art 21.24 (Vernon 1981).

- Codified statutes (codes):

    Tex. Civ. Prac. & Rem. Code Ann. § 15.001 (Vernon 1986).

Administrative Rules and Regulations

The two main sources for administrative rules and regulations are the *Code of Federal Regulations* (*C.F.R.*) and the *Federal Register* (*Fed. Reg.*). When citing *C.F.R.*, include:

1. the title number,
2. the code (C.F.R.),
3. the section and chapter of the regulation, and
4. the most recent edition of *C.F.R.*

An example of a citation to the *Code of Federal Regulations* is:

    25 C.F.R. § 151.1 (1990).

An example of a citation to the *Federal Register* is:

    45 Fed. Reg. 58,837 (1980) (to be codified at 21 C.F.R. pt. 182).

Texas Administrative Rules and Regulations

The two places to locate general information on Texas administrative rules and regulations are the *Texas Administrative Code* and the *Texas Register*. When available, cite to the *Texas Administrative Code*. The citation should include the following information:

1. the agency issuing the rule,
2. the title of the code,
3. the code,
4. the section reference,
5. the date (including month, day, and year), and
6. the publisher.

The *Texas Administrative Code* is cited as follows:

    Tex. R.R. Comm'n, 16 Tex. Admin. Code § 4.1 (Hart, Jan. 15, 1981).

The *Texas Register* publishes proposed rules or rules that have not yet appeared in the *Texas Administrative Code*. The citation should include:

1. the agency;
2. the volume, page, and year of the *Texas Register*; and
3. the proposed *Texas Administrative Code* citation.

Cite the *Texas Register* as follows:

> State Sec. Bd., 9 Tex. Reg. 5807 (1984) (prop. amend. do be codified at 7 Tex. Admin. Code § 109.4).

Federal Rules of Procedure and Evidence

There are federal civil and criminal rules of procedure and evidence that have a specific citation form. They should be cited in all capital letters:

> FED. R. CIV. P. 11.

> FED. R. CRIM. P. 8.

> FED. R. EVID. 403.

Do not cite these rules as F.R.C.P. or F.R.E., as is often seen, and do not cite a date.

Texas Rules of Procedure and Evidence

The Texas rules of procedure are promulgated by the state's highest courts. As with the federal rules, do not cite a date of publication:

> TEX. R. CIV. P. 166a.

> TEX. R. CRIM. P. 11.

The Texas rules of evidence went into effect September 1, 1983, and generally parallel the federal rules of evidence. The Texas rules of criminal evidence went into effect two years later and also parallel the federal rules of evidence. These rules are cited as follows:

> TEX. R. CIV. EVID. 601.

> TEX. R. CRIM. EVID. 801.

§ 10.4   Constitutions and Court Rules

Constitutions

The format for citing the United States Constitution and the Texas Constitution is the same. Both include the following:

1. name of country or state,
2. abbreviation of the word "Constitution" (Const.)
3. the name of the constitutional provision (art. or amend.) and the number (shown in Roman numerals), and
4. the section or paragraph reference.

The methods of citing the constitutions are:

- The United States Constitution:

    U.S. CONST. art. III, § 2 or U.S. CONST. amend. XIV, § 1.

- The Texas Constitution:

    TEX. CONST. art. I, § 3 or TEX. CONST. art. V, § 6 (1891, amended 1978).

§ 10.5   Secondary Sources

Often it is necessary to cite secondary sources in legal research. The main secondary sources are books, including encyclopedias and treatises, and law review journals.

Books

Citations to books are the same for all jurisdictions. Include in your citation:

1. the author's name, beginning with the author's first initial and then the last name;
2. the title of the book, italicized (or underlined);
3. the section or paragraph of the book, if needed;

4. the edition number; and

5. the year of publication.

For example:

> W. Prosser & K. P. Keeton, *Handbook on the Law of Torts* § 119 (1984).

Law Reviews

When citing a law review article, include the following information:

1. the author's name, first and last;

2. the title of the article, italicized (or underlined);

3. the volume, law review name, and page where the article begins; and

4. the year of publication, in parentheses.

For example:

> Allan E. Parker, Jr., *Public Free Schools: A Constitutional Right to Educational Choices in Texas*, 45 Sw. L.J. (1991).

Restatements

Citations to the restatements should identify the title of the restatement referenced, the edition, the section cited, and the date of adoption:

> *Restatement (Second) of Contracts* § 90 (1981).

Dictionaries

The two main legal dictionaries are *Black's* and *Ballentine's*. When citing either dictionary, identify its name, the page on which the definition appears, and, in parentheses, the edition and year of the publication:

> *Black's Law Dictionary* 1085 (6th ed. 1990).

> *Ballentine's Law Dictionary* 178 (3d ed. 1969).

Often people disagree about the definition of a word in the law. Attorneys can resort to a law dictionary, but that may not be sufficient. Courts are asked to define words, terms, and legal phrases when a dispute arises about their meaning. For example, suppose the parties in a lawsuit are in disagreement about the meaning of the word *nightclub*. Does it necessarily include the serving of food or liquor? A secondary source that provides case law definitions of legal terms is *Words and Phrases*. A West publication, *Words and Phrases* provides thousands of "judicial definitions" that have come from judicial decisions defining words and phrases over the years. The words and phrases are arranged alphabetically and contain the verbatim definition supplied by the court.

If the definition of a term is in dispute, try using *Words and Phrases* for a guide in locating a case law definition. But remember, the words and phrases defined are from courts all around the country, not just your jurisdiction, and the definitions may not be those your judge would give for the words and phrases. If the word or phrase is not from your jurisdiction, it is only persuasive authority for your jurisdiction.

Attorney General Opinions

For attorney general opinions, cite the volume number, the page on which the opinion appears, the state of the opinion, and the year:

19 Op. Att'y Gen. 20 (1995).

American Law Reports

American Law Reports (*A.L.R.*) annotations should include basic information such as the author's complete name, the title of the annotation (underlined or italicized), the volume, the page number, and the year the annotation was written:

Debra T. Landis Annotation, *What Corporate Documents Are Subject to Shareholder's Right to Inspection*, 88 A.L.R.3d 693 (1978).

Encyclopedias

There are two general encyclopedias to cite: *Corpus Juris Secundum* (*C.J.S.*) and *American Jurisprudence 2d* (*Am. Jur. 2d*). Include the name of the encyclopedia, the topic title you are referencing, the volume and section, and the year:

52 C.J.S. Landlord & Tenant § 427 (1968).

49 Am. Jur. 2d Landlord & Tenant § 223 (1970).

§ 10.6 General Citation Issues

Many questions can arise in citing legal authorities. This section addresses some of the common questions asked. For example, can *id.* or *supra* be used for previously cited material? How do you refer to material quoted from a case? What is the difference between emphasis added and emphasis supplied? Can words be omitted from a quote?

Underlining (Italicizing) Sources of the Law

Case names, titles of books, and titles of articles need to be underlined (or italicized) and unbroken in legal briefs and memoranda according to *The Bluebook*. The name is always followed by a comma:

> *Smith v. Johnson,* 112 S.W.2d 401 (Tex. 1978).

Constitutions, statutes, restatements, and procedural rules are not underlined (italicized).

Names in a Case

In the citation of cases in legal documents and memoranda, do not use the full name of the parties to a case. Use the last names of the two main parties, which usually appear in all caps in the actual case in the reporter. For example:

> *Michelson v. Hamada*

In the actual case, the parties are listed as *G. Karlin Michelson, M.D. v. James S. Hamada, M.D., et al.* Note that in the citation example, not only were the complete names shortened, but also the initials *M.D.* and the *et al.,* which indicates there were multiple parties in the case, were omitted.

Do not abbreviate the United States government when it is a party. Write out the full name, without including "of America":

> *United States v. Smith*

When citing a criminal case, a Texas state case may be cited as:

> *Bedford v. State*

But when citing the case in another jurisdiction, cite the name as:

> *Bedford v. Texas*

A case that was decided by another court is also identified by the name of the state:

> *California v. Rodrigues*

Using *Id.* and *Supra* in Citing Legal Material

It is generally inappropriate to use *id.* or *supra* in substitution for a case reference. The main reason *id.* and *supra* are not used is because of the confusion created. Using *id.* is considered acceptable if the case you are citing is the immediately preceding authority cited. If another case or other authority is cited in between citations, do not use *id.*

The Bluebook says not to use *supra* to refer to cases. *Supra* refers to previously cited material. Do not use *supra* in legal research or writing.

The following example shows the proper use of *id:*

> When a party's address is known to the city, notice by publication does not constitute adequate notice. *Jones v. City of Odessa*, 574 S.W.2d 850 (Tex. Civ. App.—El Paso 1978, writ ref'd n.r.e.). Notice by publication in a newspaper is appropriate only when addresses are unobtainable. *Id.* at 852.

Omitting Language in a Quote

When using quoted material, it is acceptable to use ellipsis points (. . .) to show where material has been omitted. This is a clear signal to the reader that material has been omitted from the quote. The ellipsis points can be used at the beginning, middle, or end of a quotation, or whenever necessary. For example:

> As early as 1856, the state of Texas defined a nuisance as: "Anything that works hurt, inconvenience, or damage, or which is done to hurt the lands . . . and which renders the enjoyment of life and property uncomfortable." *Burditt v. Swenson*, 17 Tex. 489, 491 (1856)

When omitting language at the end of a quote, use three periods followed by the punctuation of the quote (usually a period):

> "Which renders the enjoyment of life. . . ."

Using Brackets in Quoted Material

When a quote is used and a capital letter is changed to lowercase, or vice versa, a bracket is appropriate:

> Original material: "The definition of assault is . . ."

> Changed material: In *White v. Black*, "[t]he definition of assault is . . ."

Differentiating Between Emphasis Supplied and Emphasis Added

The words "emphasis added" are used when the author wants to bring attention to a passage and underscores the important language. "Emphasis added" must appear in parentheses at the end of the quote. However, when the text being quoted includes the emphasis, the term "emphasis supplied" is added in parentheses at the end of the quote.

Citing Information Directly from a Case

When quoting a case, the exact page reference must appear in the citation. The specific page reference appears *after* the page on which the case begins, separated by a comma:

723 S.W.2d 521, 522 (Tex. 1986).

Using Introductory Signals

A signal before a citation indicates that additional reference material may be reviewed that supports the general statement of law preceding the citation. A signal such as *See* or *e.g.,* must be italicized (or underlined) when it is used. Common introductory signals are:

eg.,	This signal is used when several authorities can be given for the proposition of laws cited.
See	This signal is commonly used for points of law that indirectly support the proposition cited.
See also	Distinguished from *See*, this signal is used when additional material is referenced that supports the general proposition cited.
See generally	This signal is used to refer the reader to general background information on the point cited.

The following shows how these signals are used in text:

Texas case law places a strict burden of proof on a city to establish as a matter of law that repairs could not be made to a dwelling without substantial reconstruction. *Crossman v. City of Galveston*, 112 Tex. 303, 247 S.W. 810 (1923). *See also Gonzales v. City of Lancaster*, 675 S.W.2d 293 (Tex. App.—Dallas 1984, no writ); *Hart v. City of Dallas*, 565 S.W.2d 373 (Tex. Civ. App.—Tyler 1978, no writ).

When a citation is not preceded by a signal, the citation reference applies directly to the preceding sentence or sentences. No other legal authorities are being referenced for additional review.

Using "Hereafter"

Many legal authorities become cumbersome to use every time the authorities are referenced. It is appropriate to shorten the name of the authority by using the reference "hereafter" or "hereinafter referred to as . . ." For example:

> The government of the United States (hereinafter "Government") is planning to review welfare reform.

Using the Short Form of a Case Name in a Citation or Reference

Once a case has been completely cited, a shortened case name form may be used when it is repeated. The general rule is to refer to the first party in the case name:

> In *Gouldy,* the court established the rules of construction.

Using the Short Forms for Citations

After a complete citation has been used, a shortened form may be used for later reference. Shortened citations normally appear when later quoted material is used. Always reference the exact page of the quoted material. The following are acceptable variations of *Price v. Price,* 732 S.W.2d 316 (Tex. 1987):

1. *Price v. Price,* 732 S.W.2d at 318.
2. *Price,* 732 S.W.2d at 318.
3. 732 S.W.2d at 318.

The last choice should be used only if the case has been recently presented or if the case name appears in the text to which the footnote relates.

Order of Presentation of Cited Cases

When listing more than one citation for a proposition of law, known as string citing, the following is a guide for the order of presentation:

1. United States Supreme Court cases are cited first in reverse chronological order (newest to oldest).

2. Federal circuit court of appeals cases are cited next, also in reverse chronological order.

3. Federal district court cases are cited after federal circuit court of appeals cases in reverse chronological order.

4. State cases are cited next, beginning with a state's highest court, in reverse chronological order.

When citations are included at the end of a sentence, they stand alone as a separate sentence. If more than one citation is referenced, each should be separated by a semicolon with a period following the last citation. For example, if one citation were referenced:

> A party must supplement discovery thirty days prior to trial or the offered information will not be allowed at trial. *Ramons v. Champlin Petroleum Co.*, 750 S.W.2d 873 (Tex. App.—Corpus Christi 1983, writ denied).

If more than one citation were referenced:

> A party must supplement discovery thirty days prior to trial or the offered information will not be allowed at trial. *Ramons v. Champlin Petroleum Co.*, 750 S.W.2d 873 (Tex. App.—Corpus Christi 1983, writ denied); *Morrow v. H.E.B.*, 714 S.W.2d 297 (Tex. 1986); *Yeldell v. Holiday Hills Retirement Nursing Center, Inc.*, 701 S.W.2d 243 (Tex. 1985).

However, try to stay away from using string cites, no matter how tempted. Courts prefer you cite the strongest authority for the proposition stated. Unless you are trying to change the law and want to show the numbers of jurisdictions following a particular path, avoid string citing.

§ 10.7   A Quick Checklist for Citations

Federal Cases

United States Supreme Court

> *World-Wide Volkswagen Corp. v. Woodson,* 444 U.S. 286 (1980).

Federal Reporter

> *Marsh v. United States,* 334 F.2d 317 (5th Cir. 1965).

Federal Supplement

> *Port Neches Indep. School Dist. v. R.F.C.,* 121 F. Supp. 561 (S.D. Tex. 1954).

Federal Statutes

25 U.S.C. § 409a (1932).

Federal Constitution

U.S. CONST. art III, § 2.

Texas Cases

Texas Supreme Court prior to 1962

Gouldy v. Metcalf, 75 Tex. 155, 12 S.W. 455 (1889).

Texas Supreme Court after 1962

Wal-Mart Stores, Inc. v. Street, 754 S.W.2d 153 (Tex. 1988).

Texas Court of Criminal Appeals prior to 1962

Hale v. State, 164 Tex. Crim. 482, 300 S.W.2d 75 (1957).

Texas Court of Criminal Appeals after 1962

Roach v. State, 586 S.W.2d 866 (Tex. Crim. App. 1979).

Texas Court of Appeals prior to 1981

Lubbock Radio Paging Serv., Inc. v. Southwestern Bell Tel. Co., 607 S.W.2d 29 (Tex. Civ. App.—Beaumont 1980, writ ref'd n.r.e.).

Texas Court of Appeals after 1981

Jarrett v. Warhola, 695 S.W.2d 8 (Tex. App—Houston [14th Dist.] 1985, writ ref'd).

Texas Statutes

TEX. REV. CIV. STAT. ANN. art. 6132b, § 6 (Vernon 1970).

TEX. CIV. PRAC. & REM. CODE ANN. § 15.001 (Vernon 1986).

Texas Constitution

TEX. CONST. art. I, § 3.

Summary

10.1 Citation Form in General

The most widely accepted authority for proper citation form is *The Bluebook—A Uniform System of Citation*. To get familiar with *The Bluebook*, scan its contents. *The Bluebook* gives uniformity to all legal citation forms. The so-called *Greenbook*, the *Texas Rules of Form*, complements *The Bluebook* but gives only Texas forms of citations. The *Greenbook* focuses on such areas of citation form as writ and petition histories and Texas statutes. Both books should always be consulted.

10.2 The Cases

Properly citing cases is important. Always include the name of the case, volume, page, reporter, the court that decided the case, and the date of the decision. Check *The Bluebook* and the *Greenbook* for proper citation form, including changes such as the proper method of citing state cases.

10.3 Statutes and Administrative Rules and Regulations

When citing a federal statute, reference the title, statutory code, section number, and year published. However, when citing a Texas statute, identify the abbreviated code name of the Texas statutes, the section, and the year the code was published. For the *Code of Federal Regulations*, use the same guide as with statutes, but be sure you are citing to the most recent *C.F.R.* edition.

10.4 Constitutions and Court Rules

When citing to the constitution, the word Constitution should be abbreviated as Const. in capital letters. If referencing a section of an article or an amendment, that information should be included in the citation. Follow the same rules for the Texas Constitution. In citing court rules, abbreviate the name of the rules followed by the court rule referenced.

10.5 Secondary Sources

There are a number of secondary sources that must have proper citation form. General books should always have the author's name, book title, referenced section, edition, and year of publication. With law review articles, the citation must include the author's name, title of article, volume and page of article, law review journal name, and year of publication. Other general research sources also can be cited as authority, including *A.L.R.*, legal encyclopedias, and dictionaries.

10.6 General Citation Issues

There are always issues that arise regarding proper citation form. One typical citation issue is case names, which are always underlined or italicized. Learning when to use *id.* or *supra*, and how to use "emphasis added" or "emphasis supplied," is also important. When citing information directly from a case, always cite the page from which the reference is taken. When citing more than one authority, all citations should be in the proper order of presentation.

Review Questions

1. What is the most widely accepted book for proper citations?

2. What citation book is used in Texas for guidance on Texas citations?

3. What should be included when citing a case?

4. What change occurred in 1981 in citing a Texas Court of Civil Appeals case?

5. How many judicial districts are in Texas?

6. What information should be included when citing a federal statute? A Texas statute?

7. Distinguish between using *id.* and *supra*.

8. Distinguish between "emphasis supplied" and "emphasis added."

9. What are introductory signals and how should they be used?

10. What is the proper order of presentation for cited cases?

Exercises

1. Correct the following citations:
    a. 109 S.Ct. 1591 490 U.S. 19, 104 L.Ed. 2d 18 (1989)
    b. 51 F.3rd 780 (CA. Eighth, 1995)
    c. 760 Fed.Supp. 1486 (M.D. Florida, 1991)
    d. 690 S.W.2d 546 (Tex.Sup.Ct. 1985)
    e. 856 So.W.2d 230 (Civ.Ct. Tex. Dallas 1993)

2. Using *The Bluebook*, properly cite the following law review articles:

   a. *Freedom of Speech and Work Place Harassment*, Vol. 39 of the University of California at Los Angeles Law Review page 17910, 1992 by Eugene Volokh

   b. *Title VII as Censorship: Hostile Environment Harassment and the First Amendment*, Vol. 52 of the Ohio State Law Journal at page 481 (1991) by Kingsley R. Browne

3. Properly cite the following:

   a. Section 90 of the Restatement of Contracts, Second Series

   b. Article Four of the United States Constitution

   c. Title 42 of the United States Code Section in 2000e

   d. Black's Law Dictionary 6th edition 1990 page 1080

4. Create the proper citation from the following information:

   a. Name: Keith J. Hudson versus Jack McMillian
      Court: U.S. Supreme Court
      Year: 1991
      Volume and page: volume 499 and page 958

   b. Name: Herbert Whitlock versus Salvador Godinez
      Court: Federal Court of Appeals, Seventh Circuit
      Year: March 9, 1995
      Volume and page: volume 51 and page 59 in the third series

   c. Name: OKC Corporation versus UPG, Inc.
      Court: Texas Court of Appeals, Civil, Dallas Division
      Year: 1990
      Volume and page: volume 798 and page 300
      Writ history: no writ

5. Prepare the proper citations for the following statutes:

   a. Title 34 of the United States Code Section 505

   b. Title 42 of the United States Code Annotated Section 2000e(d) (e) a West Publication 1991

   c. Texas Government Code in Vernon's Annotated Texas Statutes (1988) section 73.001

   d. Vernon's Annotated Texas Code, Family Code, Section 54.03 published 1986 and supplemented in 1994

6. Properly cite the case of Arnold versus the City of Siminole, in the Federal Supplement at volume 614 and page 853. The district is the eastern district of Oklahoma decided in 1985.

7. Properly cite Jones versus Flagship International. The case was appealed from the fifth circuit but denied certiori by the United States Supreme Court in 479 U.S. 1065, 107 S.Ct. 952 93 L.Ed. 2d 1001 in 1987. The original federal appeals case was decided in 1986 in volume 793 at page 714.

8. Properly cite *The Law of Trusts* by Austin W. Scott and William F. Fratcher section 156, in the 4th edition published in 1989 in volume 2A.

9. Prepare the citation for The Code of Federal Regulations located in Chapter 20, Section 404.1545.

10. Correct the following citations:

   a. 46 Federal 3rd 37 (8th Circuit 1995)
   b. V.I.C.A. Family Code (1986) in Section 54.03
   c. 651 S.W.2d 364 (Tex. Civ.App.— Tyler [1st Dist.] 1983, no writ history)
   d. 690 So.W.2d 546, Tex Supreme Court 1985
   e. 635 S.W.2d 780 (Court of Appeals Texas ——Corpus Christ 1982 petition refused)

CHAPTER 11

SHEPARD'S CITATORS

§ 11.1   Introduction to Shepard's Citators

In General

Law is dynamic, not static. Court decisions may be reversed, overruled, criticized, questioned, distinguished, followed, or simply cited by subsequent courts. Statutes may be amended, superseded, repealed, and declared unconstitutional. In order for an attorney to rely on a case as legal authority, there must be precidential value, which means that the prior cases cited in support of the researcher's argument are similar in facts or legal principles to the case presently under consideration.

Attorneys and paralegals have a professional responsibility to determine the current status and validity of a case or statute. Assume that Attorney Jones relies on the case of *Smith v. Acme Corp.* in a brief filed with the court. Subsequently, he discovers not only that the case has been reversed but, even worse, that the reversal had been reported before he submitted his brief. Not only should Attorney Jones be disconcerted at the discovery, but he also may have exposed himself to a malpractice suit should an adverse outcome to his client occur in part because of his failure to uncover the reversal of the case in question.

To determine the legal status of a case or statute, researchers rely on **citators**, sets of books that provide (1) the subsequent judicial histories of reported decisions, and (2) lists of cases and legislative enactments construing, applying, or interpreting the cited cases and statutes. In addition to ascertaining the status of a case or statute, the citator is an outstanding research tool in that it lists cases citing the cases being checked, which often involve similar facts and legal issues, and sometimes includes references to legal periodicals and *A.L.R.* annotations.

Shepard's Citations, published by Shepard's/McGraw-Hill, Inc., is the most widely used citator series. This citator's popularity is evident by the fact that for years the term **Shepardizing** has been a synonym for **"cite checking."**

Until recently, Shepardizing has required the researcher to systematically review printed volumes of material, as discussed in detail in the rest of this chapter. Recent applications of computer technology to the legal profession, however, have revolutionized the process of Shepardizing.

─────────────── **TERMS** ───────────────

citators†   Systems of books, the use of which allows a person doing legal research to locate every court opinion in which a particular case is cited, and to determine the context in which it is cited as well as whether it has been affirmed, distinguished, followed, overruled, or simply mentioned.

Shepardizing   Using a citator to determine the legal status of a case or statue.

cite checking   Using a citator to determine the legal status of a case or statute.

Today, cite checking can be performed on-line in a much more time-efficient manner than is possible by using the printed volumes. (See Chapter 13 for discussion of these on-line systems.)

You cannot, however, access all *Shepard's* volumes through an on-line service. For example, no statutory *Shepard's* are included in LEXIS or WESTLAW, nor do some of the specialized *Shepard's* appear in the databases. Cost, too, may be a factor. On-line services tend to be expensive, and in some instances, cost considerations may outweigh the time savings that might be realized.

Whether cite checking on-line or through the traditional processes, the underlying premises and goals are the same. The purpose of Shepardizing is not dependent on method, so you need to understand the material in this chapter even if you have access to an on-line cite checking system.

Shepard's citators offer a composite verification of the validity of a case and its prior and subsequent histories. Specialty citators serve as excellent indexes for locating the names of a party, the particular court in which a decision was rendered, and the volume and page of the reporter in which the case or statute may be located. Another important use of *Shepard's* is as a locator for additional research. The citator series will direct you to a variety of authorities that discuss your particular case, statute, or constitutional provision.

The first appearance of a *Shepard's* citator is in the form of an advance sheet, usually issued monthly. These advance sheets are subsequently cumulated into a red paperback pamphlet that is published quarterly. Some of the citator series also have yellow annual cumulative supplements. The so-called "main volumes" of a *Shepard's* citator set consist of one or more bound volumes with deep maroon–colored covers.

Because of the large number of bound volumes, pamphlets, and advance sheets of a citator series, *Shepard's* includes a clearly marked listing on the front cover of the most recent paper supplement (advance sheet) of the casebound volumes and softcover pamphlets that constitute a complete up-to-date set of *Shepard's* in a particular area. It is absolutely essential that you gather together every volume and pamphlet that could conceivably have a reference to the case you are interested in from the very first time it appears in *Shepard's* to the present. You *cannot* Shepardize accurately unless you consult each relevant volume and pamphlet.

To use a citator, one must begin with a citation. A citation is the volume number, source, and page number where a case or statute is reported. For example:

645	F.2d	555
(volume)	(source)	(page number)

Later opinions, referred to as the citing cases, are the cases that affect, mention, or discuss the earlier case, referred to as the cited case. For example, assume that in 645 F.2d 555, the citing case, there is a reference to 444 F.2d 333. This second reference is a cited case.

Shepard's references are not in *Bluebook* format. For example, 342 S.W.2d 184 would appear as 342SW184 (with the "2" written over the "W"), and 93 L. Ed. 2d 598 would appear as 93LE598 (with the "2" written over the "E"). To assist in the interpretation of these unique abbreviations, the front of each volume of *Shepard's* contains a table of abbreviations.

A standard case citation is always to the page on which a case begins. However, a *Shepard's* reference is to the exact page on which your case is discussed. If your case is mentioned on several pages, *Shepard's* will list each page. You can determine the more recent references by the volume number, as the latest volume number represents the most recent reference.

The appearance of a lowercase "n" at the end of a reference indicates that the reference to your case appears in an *A.L.R.* annotation. A small "s" at the end of a reference indicates that the reference to your case is in a supplement (pocket part or softcover supplement) to an *A.L.R.* annotation.

Initial Shepardizing Decisions

When to Shepardize

The determination of when to Shepardize is at the discretion of the individual researcher. If you are asked to cite check a brief or legal memorandum written by an attorney in your firm, that attorney will determine when he or she is ready for the Shepardizing process. Often you will be given a Shepardizing assignment when a final draft of the brief is completed. That may afford you only a short time to accomplish a lengthy process. One danger of this last-minute Shepardizing effort is the possibility that you will discover that an important case or cases have been overruled or reversed.

If you are the author of the brief or legal memorandum, you should consider Shepardizing early in the research process. Not only will you avoid last minute surprises, but you will locate other authorities. A positive aspect of Shepardizing on an ongoing basis throughout the writing process is the ability to rule out cases immediately that are not favorable to your argument, without wasting precious time and effort.

Which Citator to Use

The determination of which citator should be used is an important beginning step in the Shepardizing process. Is the case being Shepardized a state or federal court case? Should the state or regional reporter citator be checked first? If a state reporter citator is to be checked, is the official or unofficial state reporter citator the appropriate choice? Not all *Shepard's* volumes contain the same citations. For example, state attorney general opinions and selected law review articles appear only in the state *Shepard's* edition. Citations from other states appear only in the regional *Shepard's* edition.

Shepard's Regional Reporter Citations parallels the regional reporter series. All state and federal citations to cases in a particular regional reporter are compiled in the regional citator. Citations to law review articles and attorney general opinions contained in the state citators are not repeated in the regional citators.

Listed below are all the *Shepard's* citators. You should have no problem finding the ones you are most likely to need. Some, however, are very specialized and may not be available in all law libraries. If not readily available in print form, you can access most of these volumes through an on-line service (see Chapter 13).

List of Shepard's Citators

Acts and Cases by Popular Names

Banking Law Citations

Bankruptcy Case Names Citator

Bankruptcy Citations

Code of Federal Regulations Citations

Corporation Law Citations

Criminal Justice Citations

Federal Case Names Citators

Federal Circuit Table

Federal Citations

Federal Energy Law Citations

Federal Labor Law Case Names Citator

Federal Labor Law Citations

Federal Law Citations in Selected Law Reviews

Federal Occupational Safety and Health Citations

Federal Rules Citations

Federal Tax Citations

Federal Tax Locator

Immigration and Naturalization Citations

Insurance Law Citations

Law Review Citations

Medical Malpractice Citations

Military Justice Citations

Ordinance Law Annotations

Partnership Law Citations

Products Liability Citations

Professional and Judicial Conduct Citations

Regional Reporter Citations

Restatement of the Law Citations

State Case Names Citator

State Citations

Texas Law Locator

Uniform Commercial Code Case Citations

United States Administrative Citations

United States Citations

United States Patents and Trademarks Citations

United States Supreme Court Case Names Citator

This chapter provides a general set of rules for and approaches to Shepardizing, but all cases, unless you are already familiar with the *Shepard's* set you are consulting, you should also review two items that are included in the front of each *Shepard's* hardbound volume and each softbound annual and cumulative supplement pamphlet: (1) the list of citations included in the volume or pamphlet, and (2) the preface, which offers the publisher's guidelines for using the volume or pamphlet.

§ 11.2   Sheparding Federal Cases

Federal Case Citators

Lower Federal Courts

Shepard's Federal Citations consists mainly of two separate multivolume sets. One set covers decisions of federal courts of appeals that are published in the *Federal Reporter*, and the other set covers decisions of federal district courts that are reported in the *Federal Supplement*. Although the title *Shepard's Federal Citations* is prominently displayed on each volume in both sets, the volumes are clearly marked on their spines and covers as to whether they belong to the *Federal Reporter* or *Federal Supplement* set. In addition, there is a one-volume set covering decisions of various courts that are published in *Federal Rules Decisions*, also clearly marked.

Once you locate the case you are researching in the citator, you will find citing cases (if any) listed at that point by the judicial circuit or federal court from which the citation originated. This is a helpful feature when you have been asked to limit your research to the decisions of a particular court, for example, the Fifth Circuit, particularly where the cases you are researching have achieved a lot of recognition and have been often cited in later decisions from numerous courts.

Shepard's Federal Citations also includes citations to *A.L.R.* annotations, articles from the *American Bar Association Journal* and other legal periodicals, and opinions from the United States Attorney General.

United States Supreme Court Cases

Another federal case law citator with which you must become familiar is *Shepard's United States Citations, Case Edition*. This comprehensive multivolume set lists citations by both federal and state courts to decisions of the United States Supreme Court that have been reported in the official and unofficial reporters. Supreme Court cases in each volume are clearly arranged in separate sections (note the running head at the top of each page) for each of the three reporters in which Supreme Court cases appear—*United States Reports* (the official reporter), *Supreme Court Reporter* (West's unofficial reporter), and *Supreme Court Reports, Lawyers' Edition* (LCP's unofficial reporter).

To ensure completeness, you must Shepardize your case through each of the reporters. They do not contain the same information. For example, if you Shepardize through the *United States Supreme Court Reports* section, you will locate where your case has been cited not only by any federal court but also by any state court whose opinions appear in a unit of the National Reporter System. If, however, you Shepardize through one of the unofficial reporters, you will not find the citing state court references. If you are unsure about what is included in each section, consult the page *Shepard's* has inserted at the beginning of each section for a listing of the citing sources included in that particular division.

Regional *Shepard's* Citators

Many cases are published in both an official reporter and a West regional reporter. You may Shepardize such cases by using either the state's citator or the relevant regional citator. One advantage of Shepardizing with the regional citator rather than the state citator is that you will find references to cases from other states in the regional reporter. A disadvantage is that you will not locate law review articles or attorney general opinions through the use of a regional reporter. To obtain the most complete results, you should Shepardize in both the state and regional reporter.

What Shepardizing Cases Reveals

Shepardizing reveals six types of information about a case:

1. parallel citations,
2. history of cited case—subsequent and prior,
3. citing cases,
4. citing legal periodicals,
5. citing annotations, and
6. citing opinions of the attorney general.

Parallel Citations

A *parallel citation*, referring to another reporter location where you can find a case that is published in more than one reporter. parentheses directly below the *Shepard's* page entry c However, the parallel citation appears *only* in the first cit the case was published. As shown in Figure 11–1, the citatic 404 indicates a parallel citation to 153 Tex. 449. General the parallel citations must be Shepardized to obtain the subs of the case. It may be advisable, however, to Shepardize bo unofficial reporter citations (assuming you have access to th *Shepard's* sets) because each may include citing sources that the not.

Citing Cases

A **citing case** is a later case that mentions or discusses the cited case. The citators include cases that establish the subsequent history of the case you are researching. Citing cases may reverse, affirm, overrule, follow, distinguish, or simply mention the cited case.

────────────────── TERMS ──────────────────

citing case A later case that mentions or discusses a cited case.

SOUTHWESTERN REPORTER, 2d SERIES (Texas Cases)   **Vol. 271**

439SW[5]365	d319SW[2]435	401SW[1]794	544SW[3]199	352SW[3]785	349SW[1]621	527SW[3]794	407SW[10]330
527SW[5]254	d320SW[7]205	403SW[2]892	544SW[3]635	352SW[5]786	358SW[1]887	549SW[3]433	407SW[4]330
322SW[2]390	322SW[2]390	404SW[7]292	545SW[3]277	374SW[1]283	372SW[1]564	565SW[3]918	407SW[6]330
—347—	323SW[4]145	q404SW294	565SW[2]513	385SW[1]280	382SW[1]343	602SW[6]523	407SW[5]331
RNRE	326SW[2]590	d404SW[1]844	e565SW[3]516	403SW[4]523	384SW[1]735	609SW[3]659	407SW[8]333
393SW[4]657	327SW[3]452	d404SW[6]845	q565SW518	410SW[1]62	385SW[1]715	668SW[8]324	409SW[3]933
660SW[1]159	328SW[3]470	410SW[3]220	570SW[2]549	417SW[4]435	397SW[1]551	692SW[3]115	410SW[3]815
45Æ109n	335SW[2]668	410SW[2]676	572SW[2]44	f462SW[1]562	405SW454	157Tex[6]481	410SW[4]815
45Æ125n	337SW[3]201	411SW[3]413	j573SW847	f462SW[2]563	405SW642	d162Tex[7]86	410SW[7]815
45Æ151n	337SW[4]202	412SW[3]355	618SW[7]419	f469SW[1]487	407SW[1]9	j162Tex[6]98	410SW[9]815
45Æ276n	340SW[7]504	413SW[7]813	f655SW[2]243	474SW[1]31	425SW7	e162Tex[6]106	410SW[10]816
46Æ196n	345SW[4]774	414SW[1]146	683SW[4]194	j474SW[1]32	432SW[1]167	e162Tex[7]107	418SW[6]896
46Æ224n	346SW[1]647	414SW[7]146	f154Tex[1]338	476SW[1]665	436SW[1]587	Cir. 5	419SW[8]900
46Æ321n	346SW[3]648	415SW291	160Tex[3]174	616SW[1]325	456SW[1]475	220F2d[6]705	424SW[8]498
—350—	348SW[3]96	416SW[2]392	Cir. 5	j679SW97	483SW[1]503	257F2d[7]159	431SW[3]386
RNRE	f348SW[4]200	419SW[2]684	224F2d[1]585	679SW[1]101	510SW[1]374	340FS1234	436SW[4]591
358SW[1]248	f348SW[4]200	419SW[4]685	f228F2d[2]511	e679SW[4]102	f545SW[1]21	13BLR204	438SW[4]157
d358SW[2]720	f348SW[5]200	427SW[3]329	232F2d[2]18	701SW[5]70	559SW[1]684	10HUL267	438SW[8]595
29SLJ185	f348SW[3]201	428SW[1]361	236F2d[1]52	Cir. 5	f638SW913	17SLJ25	438SW[6]597
30SLJ234	349SW[5]761	428SW[7]362	236F2d[2]52	d229F2d[2]892	710SW87	30SLJ108	438SW[10]903
32SLJ348	350SW[1]869	j428SW364	236F2d[2]53	21SLJ79	j156Tex[1]536	17TTR1364	438SW[11]903
—388—	350SW[2]869	f428SW[3]484	236F2d[7]57	30SLJ217	f158Tex[1]487	35TxL2	438SW[7]903
(153Tex460)	353SW[2]330	430SW[2]583	j236F2d[4]60	31SLJ314	159Tex[1]589	19Æ1025s	438SW[8]903
s280SW636	354SW[3]651	430SW[1]910	244F2d[3]130	—400—	12BLR362	51Æ322n	438SW[9]903
294SW[4]915	355SW[7]825	j430SW[6]939	251F2d[1]834	(153Tex474)	—410—	51Æ338n	439SW[11]119
301SW[2]75	f356SW[2]816	432SW[3]744	276F2d[2]755	s268SW767	(153Tex465)	51Æ401n	439SW[3]897
312SW[1]720	f356SW[3]816	433SW695	j276F2d[2]762	f280SW[2]318	s265SW199	53Æ335n	443SW[3]779
316SW[1]313	f357SW[3]411	434SW[2]404	290F2d[1]194	317SW[1]522	f274SW[1]161	53Æ369n	443SW[8]979
381SW[1]932	f358SW[1]204	434SW[4]404	294F2d[2]582	j317SW[2]524	280SW[5]302	53Æ394n	451SW[3]771
398SW[4]600	f358SW[2]205	434SW[3]907	d311F2d[2]389	354SW[3]925	d290SW[5]698	—414—	453SW[4]195
398SW[2]601	f358SW[4]205	436SW[7]414	319F2d[3]116	356SW[1]327	292SW[6]375	(153Tex566)	453SW[9]195
400SW[2]385	f358SW[4]206	436SW[3]573	354F2d[7]968	f391SW165	295SW[1]478	s263SW299	453SW[9]197
406SW[1]777	f358SW[2]765	437SW[1]388	362F2d[4]688	453SW[1]238	295SW[4]696	278SW[8]871	463SW[3]267
418SW[1]285	d360SW[2]168	441SW[4]834	427F2d[3]250	461SW680	295SW[5]697	282SW[9]85	464SW[4]952
435SW[1]900	d361SW[7]584	442SW[7]801	455F2d[1]635	d469SW[1]21	e303SW[7]809	282SW[8]380	468SW[8]189
514SW[1]334	d362SW[2]313	444SW[1]957	460F2d[6]489	496SW747	[1]304SW[6]363	294SW[14]157	d473SW[11]494
f517SW[1]892	f362SW[2]371	j450SW[2]751	477F2d127	561SW873	314SW[7]156	295SW[6]676	478SW[7]850
526SW714	363SW[3]165	451SW[2]754	d488F2d[1]260	704SW[1]89	323SW[2]67	307SW[1]648	478SW[8]850
584SW[2]946	e364SW[7]710	451SW[4]754	d488F2d[2]260	159Tex[1]212	f326SW[4]583	307SW[6]649	481SW[7]482
596SW[1]601	366SW[3]95	j451SW[2]756	580F2d[5]795	j159Tex[2]215	334SW[7]619	312SW[4]898	481SW[8]483
157Tex[2]135	366SW634	452SW[3]945	580F2d[7]797	163Tex[2]359	335SW[6]231	314SW[7]625	489SW[8]642
1986TxAG	367SW[4]371	455SW[7]702	607FS[1]555	61Æ1035n	[1]340SW[6]880	314SW[6]625	490SW[3]204
[JM-467	367SW[7]400	d456SW[2]199	Cir. 9	—404—	e344SW[6]669	314SW[7]626	501SW[5]694
—391—	d367SW[2]915	461SW[2]443	174FS[1]766	(153Tex449)	e344SW[7]670	314SW[5]626	509SW[3]678
(153Tex517)	d367SW[3]928	461SW[4]443	174FS[3]766	s263SW313	ld344SW[7]865	314SW[4]627	510SW[10]383
s263SW326	j367SW[3]932	461SW[7]443	Cir. 10	274SW[1]880	j344SW[6]873	319SW[9]158	510SW[11]383
f279SW[7]930	d369SW[3]79	463SW[2]241	d239F2d[3]552	281SW[1]107	363SW[7]494	324SW[7]167	510SW[8]383
f280SW[1]239	f369SW[3]302	464SW[2]158	13BLR216	286SW[1]957	d363SW[5]830	329SW[3]850	514SW[6]784
283SW[2]112	q370SW920	f465SW[2]441	16BLR112	287SW[1]273	f371SW[7]585	j329SW[3]852	514SW[11]787
284SW[2]414	371SW[7]377	466SW[4]838	11HUL1070	289SW[1]812	e380SW[2]574	331SW[10]340	521SW[3]658
287SW[3]278	h371SW[2]381	d468SW[7]168	20SLJ11	290SW[1]398	384SW[6]759	336SW[14]295	521SW[4]659
287SW[5]287	q371SW[3]84	q469SW[3]387	26SLJ850	292SW[1]810	384SW[5]787	339SW[6]267	521SW[7]659
293SW[3]838	371SW[3]753	470SW[2]638	29SLJ3	293SW[1]504	389SW[1]738	346SW[6]192	521SW[8]659
293SW[7]860	q371SW753	471SW[4]88	9SMJ269	j297SW[1]128	413SW[6]415	f359SW[4]957	521SW[12]660
294SW[3]894	373SW342	473SW[5]74	33TxL1	f297SW[1]354	417SW[1]490	f359SW[5]957	523SW[8]420
f297SW[2]730	q373SW360	476SW[7]352	35TxL768	301SW[1]227	420SW[6]134	f359SW[6]957	525SW[8]37
297SW[3]732	373SW[3]736	476SW[2]892	40TxL196	d309SW[1]947	422SW[6]593	367SW[6]957	f528SW[1]346
d299SW[7]160	375SW[2]762	476SW[4]897	TCLM§11.02	310SW[1]397	435SW[6]553	371SW[8]589	f528SW[2]347
301SW[7]214	378SW[7]421	d476SW[6]948	20Æ868s	310SW[1]587	d443SW[6]137	381SW[9]99	f528SW[8]348
f305SW[2]625	d378SW[6]99	f480SW[7]291	35Æ238n	310SW[1]623	453SW[6]137	386SW[2]576	533SW[13]889
306SW[8]940	382SW[2]923	f480SW[3]791	35Æ241n	311SW[1]94	453SW[6]855	386SW[8]576	535SW[8]729
307SW[2]133	382SW[3]925	483SW[3]454	—397—	311SW[1]447	458SW695	386SW[5]577	544SW[1]485
d308SW[2]937	d384SW[2]400	483SW[4]454	(153Tex470)	f314SW[1]282	j458SW[7]98	386SW[12]637	e544SW[14]487
308SW[7]940	f385SW[3]742	e484SW[7]557	s267SW191	321SW[1]596	j470SW[2]624	389SW[10]170	549SW37
311SW[4]514	f385SW[1]742	487SW[3]447	d279SW[1]400	324SW[1]265	[1]473SW[1]673	389SW[12]609	552SW[3]585
312SW[2]308	386SW[2]561	493SW534	281SW499	324SW[1]550	473SW[4]673	390SW[14]366	552SW[8]586
313SW[4]913	387SW[7]84	493SW[4]747	d290SW[2]364	329SW[1]346	473SW[7]673	392SW[7]896	552SW[8]586
d314SW[3]357	f392SW[2]596	493SW[5]747	d291SW[1]375	329SW909	483SW[8]811	398SW[3]439	552SW[10]592
d315SW[7]613	f392SW[3]596	499SW[9]30	d308SW[1]551	337SW403	f495SW[7]62	401SW[3]706	f552SW[4]935
315SW[4]614	393SW[9]632	512SW[3]41	d313SW[2]629	337SW[1]703	495SW[5]63	402SW[6]529	f552SW[6]935
315SW[6]614	396SW[1]480	515SW[4]325	320SW[4]59	341SW[1]950	f495SW[4]64	402SW[8]556	558SW[7]527
316SW[2]951	396SW[4]480	518SW[2]538	326SW[1]728	342SW184	497SW[1]75	402SW[11]557	558SW[8]527
f319SW[2]381	396SW[4]542	518SW[3]538	338SW[1]417	343SW[1]776	508SW[3]155	403SW[8]518	563SW[11]342
	d399SW[7]185	518SW[5]538	341SW[2]494	346SW[1]508	508SW815	406SW[11]84	567SW[8]854
	399SW[3]186	522SW[1]540	344SW[1]939		512SW[3]784	406SW[3]86	Continued
	401SW[4]793	529SW[3]758					

FIGURE 11-1   Reproduced with permission of Shepard's/McGraw-Hill, Inc. Any further reproduction is strictly prohibited.

Your decision about whether to rely on the cited case may hinge on how a later court treated the cited case or the amount of credence given the cited case. For example, if there were seven citing cases in a *Shepard's* citation, and two contained the note "f" for "followed," but five contained the note "c" for criticized, the case might have little persuasive precedential value. This decision, of course, cannot be made until you determine in each instance whether the courts were addressing the same issues, whether their analyses were based on the same premises, and whether their reasoning was similar. This assessment cannot be made until you "pull" these cases and read them.

The difference between the *history* of a case and the *treatment* of a case is whether the reference is to the same case (*history*) or the position that a court takes several months or several years later about the earlier case (*treatment*). For example, a later court may decide that the reasoning in an earlier case was erroneous and subsequently *overrule* the earlier court's decision. The absence of any letter in the *Shepard's* citation indicates that later cases have mentioned your case, but the editors at *Shepard's* have not determined the impact of that later case on your case. A quick review of the *Shepard's* illustrations in this chapter will reveal that most references have no letters preceding them.

The following is a list of the history and treatment case notations used in *Shepard's*. You should become generally familiar with them. If needed, you can refresh your memory by consulting the table of abbreviations page that appears in the front of each *Shepard's* volume.

History and Treatment Citing References

History of a Case

a	(affirmed)	Same case affirmed on rehearing.
cc	(connected case)	Different case from cited case but arising out of same subject matter or connected subject matter.
d	(dismissed)	Appeal of cited cases dismissed.
m	(modified)	Same case modified on appeal.
r	(reversed)	Same case reversed on appeal.
s	(superseded)	Substitution of cited case.
U.S.	app pndg	Appeal pending before U.S. Supreme Court.
U.S.	cert den	Certiorari denied by U.S. Supreme Court.
U.S.	cert dis	Certiorari dismissed by U.S. Supreme Court.
U.S.	reh. den	Rehearing denied by U.S. Supreme Court.
U.S.	reh. dis	Rehearing dismissed by U.S. Supreme Court.

Treatment of a Cited Case

c	(criticized)	Reasoning or soundness of decision in cited case criticized for reasons given.

d	(distinguished)	Case different either in law or fact from case cited for reasons given.
e	(explained)	Statement of impact of decision.
f	(followed)	Cited as controlling.
h	(harmonized)	Apparent inconsistency explained and shown not to exist.
j	(dissenting opinion)	Citation in dissenting opinion.
L	(limited)	Refusal to extend decision of cited case beyond precise issues.
o	(overruled)	Ruling in cited case expressly overruled.
p	(parallel)	Citing case substantially like or on all fours with cited case in its law or facts.
q	(questioned)	Soundness of decision or reasoning in cited case questioned.

References to cases are arranged in chronological order, beginning with the earliest cases.

History of the Case—Subsequent and Prior

The *history of a case* includes all cases that are part of the same litigation. That history has two components: subsequent history and prior history.

An example of subsequent history is a cited case that has been appealed to a higher court. For example, in Figure 11–2, the citator reports a case at 698 F. Supp. 1258, which was affirmed in a decision located at 878 F.2d 570.

Some cases have rather complicated histories. For example, a federal appeals court can reverse a district court decision and remand for further proceedings. The subsequent district court decision can again be reversed by the court of appeals, with an appeal then taken to the United States Supreme Court. The Supreme Court can reverse the appeals court decision, effectively reinstating the district court decision. A sense of the innumerable combinations that are possible can be gleaned from paying close attention to the *Shepard's* entries. What has really happened, though, can be learned only by reading the cases themselves. Begin by reading the latest decision in the subsequent history series first, and work your way back to the original district court decision.

The prior history of a case may be particularly important if less than a full written opinion in the subsequent appeal is issued by the appellate court. Assume that a case has been appealed to the Supreme Court. The Supreme Court affirms, but issues only a memorandum decision, which is simply a summary statement of a court's decision that gives no explanation, ruling, or rationale for the decision. *Shepard's*, however, does not

FEDERAL SUPPLEMENT   **Vol. 698**

720FS293 Cir. 8 e871F2d¹¹721 e871F2d¹²721 N Y 146NYA⚫ [216	723FS¹1093 —867— cc697FS859 Cir. 2 d707FS²91 714FS683 Cir. 3 699FS1090 cc699FS1091 722FS159 723FS¹1093	—1031— (9PQ2d1226) Cir. 7 727FS²1239 —1036— s896F2d255	—1218— a877F2d889 NOCA§ 24. [65 —1222— s687FS614	—1339— Cir. 7 717FS1369 —1344— m881F2d1236	719FS⁹1060 —1500— a870F2d1250 s697FS1489 —1505— Cir. 8 697FS¹1507	—111— Cir. 5 709FS²719 —139— Cir. 7 723FS³98 AGSS§ 7.06	—254— s873F2d1450 CIT 709FS¹1166 719FS1095 —266— CIT 706FS51
—748— (9PQ2d1155) Cir. 9 881F2d⁶776	—883— Cir. 3 715FS¹717 e725FS¹270	—1040— a896F2d255 —1048— Wis 194Wis 216NW	—1229— s690FS1133 —1231— s690FS1133	—1360— (9PQ2d1985) s711FS759 cc109FRD673 Cir. 7 716FS¹329	—1506— Cir. 2 715FS¹609 —1508— cc854F2d1127	—141— s703FS742 —149— s695FS410	—268— CIT 727FS1469 —275— s698FS285 CIT 701FS238 707FS¹557 AABA§ 3.11
—752— (9PQ2d1181) Cir. 2 882F2d¹⁶639 725FS1293 NOCA§ 19. [05	—896— (9PQ2d1523)	—1063— m884F2d381 —1058— a886F2d986 10CoLR72 10CoLR73	—1234— Cir. 2 126FRD¹439 f126FRD¹453 NOCA§ 7.06	—1366— s723FS234 Vt 569A2d470	—1538— Nev 781P2d764 13PST113§ [144	—150— s717FS1330 Cir. 1 716FS¹54	—285— s698FS275 CIT 714FS¹1222
—765— a878F2d638	—908— r883F2d1251	—1088— s691FS1243	—1248— cc697FS1254 Cir. 2 e728FS161	—1377— a835F2d479 s122FRD175	—1570— MMBL§ 4.40	—178— Cir. 6 f718FS¹663 Cir. 7 f719FS¹750 Cir. 9 e884F2d²1308	—290— a862F2d323 s795F2d139 s611FS823 cc788F2d728 cc802F2d697 cc821F2d750
—777— Cir. 2 895F2d²891	—921— a889F2d633	—1094— Cir. 8 721FS¹208	—1254— cc697FS1248 Cir. 2 d718FS²1218	—1394— Cir. 3 711FS203	—1577— a880F2d419 **Vol. 698**	—187— Cir. 11 710FS1335	—300— s859F2d216 s708FS389 cc881F2d1088 Cir. DC 713FS¹1447 f726FS⁵932 f726FS⁴937 Cir. 4 715FS³147
—779— s689FS339	—946— s816F2d264	—1102— DRE§ 3.18	—1258— a878F2d570 Conn 214Ct205	—1417— Cir. 5 728FS¹1304	—1— (7PQ2d1904)	—190— (7PQ2d1811)	
—784— Cir. 2 722FS986	—968— Cir. 2 875F2d¹362	—1108— (7PQ2d1409)	—1274— Cir. 6 728FS467	—1423— (7PQ2d1850) a888F2d1392	—4— Cir. DC 884F2d¹1452 d716FS¹665 FID§ 5.04	—195— Cir. 9 d726FS⁴782 11InL49 11InL159 11InL412	—316— s708FS389
—794— a888F2d1376 Cir. 2 884F2d³73	—962— s697FS965	—1113— (7PQ2d1789)	—1280— s117FRD359	—1431— a888F2d127	—10— (9PQ2d1234)	—196— r887F2d949	—322— s708FS389
—808— Cir. 3 722FS⁴200 e722FS¹1186 Cir. 10 730FS1050	—965— s697FS962 —974— Cir. 7 701FS673	—1125— m872F2d837 —1136— (7PQ2d1295)	—1282— (9PQ2d1201) Cir. 2 725FS⁶1299 726FS⁶973	—1437— r892F2d79 Cir. 4 q712FS507 f712FS¹⁰507 717FS¹⁰394 Cir. 9 714FS¹284	—47— s722FS68	—199— (7PQ2d1885) s713FS1329	—332— Cir. DC 695FS1229 DRE§ 2.08
—817— 11InL123 14PcL32 1PPR(2)9	—983— Cir. 2 701FS36 Cir. 3 711FS¹1252 711FS²1254 727FS871	—1161— Cir. 2 d97BRW²775 —1165— Cir. 7 887F2d⁹756	—1314— Cir. 8 886F2d³995	—1457— (9PQ2d1799) Cir. 2 705FS¹975 Cir. 3 709FS⁴536 d709FS³540 716FS146 716FS⁴147 e716FS³148 Cir. 7 705FS¹1347 Calif 211CA3d [1381	—52— a877F2d1154 Cir. 2 705FS¹975 FID§ 17.09	—204— s669FS317 FID§ 17.09	—348— cc460US1001 cc464US1013 cc75LE472 cc78LE719 cc103SC1240 cc104SC542 cc797F2d1082 cc552FS131 cc569FS1057 cc578FS668 cc627FS1090
—821— a860F2d1074 Pa cc481Pa62 cc391A2d [1316	—988— (9PQ2d1138) s726FS1525 —1007— Ill cc154Ill2l1161 cc519NE729 Cir. 7 723FS³36	—1183— a859F2d840 —1190— Cir. 2 c696FS³880 715FS⁴35 Cir. 7 703FS³1338	—1314— s887F2d1200 s123FRD80 Cir. 2 713FS698 Cir. 3 727FS²173 Cir. 4 718FS³1253 Cir. 6 730FS776 Md 81MdA525 568A2d1133 11InL60 LPIB§ 3.04	—1474— a876F2d563	—74— a872F2d413 —80— a875F2d309	—209— s677FS1491 s708FS1561	
—845— s676FS597 cc833F2d1113 DRE§ 8.13	—1016— s684FS973 —1025— s719FS707 Cir. 10 706FS²775		—1324— Fla s886F2d1339 s704FS1247 Cir. 2 726FS949	—1489— s697FS1500 cc479US995 cc479US1047 cc93LE598 cc93LE862 Ill cc109Il2d484 cc488NE529 Cir. 11	—85— a872F2d414 —89— a875F2d309 a875F2d312	—217— s879F2d789 —232— s893F2d301 cc681FS1562	—369— Cir. 4 f709FS²116
—859— cc697FS867 Cir. 2 d707FS¹91 714FS683 Cir. 3 699FS1090 cc699FS¹1091 710FS138 713FS745 722FS¹159 722FS²160					—99— m872F2d1144 s736F2d96 s564FS375 s637FS930 s640FS1329	—234— s655FS487 s682FS60 AABA§ 3.11 —240— s678FS285 s706FS908 cc718FS63	

FIGURE 11–2 Reproduced with permission of Shepard's/McGraw-Hill, Inc. Any further reproduction is strictly prohibited.

indicate that the opinion is a memorandum decision. You must go to the appropriate reporter to discover this information. If the Supreme Court relied on (in effect adopted) the lower court's earlier decision in affirming, you should cite the lower court's decision in addition to the Supreme Court decision.

Citing Secondary Sources

In *Shepard's*, inclusion of a citing secondary source is usually limited to citations to the *American Bar Association Journal*, legal treatises published by Shepard's/McGraw-Hill, Inc., and annotations appearing in *United States Supreme Court Reports, Lawyers' Edition* and the various *American Law Reports (A.L.R.)* units.

Citing Opinions of Attorney General

A citing opinion of an attorney general is a written opinion or legal advice given by an attorney general to government officials on critical legal issues in which the cited case is either analyzed or mentioned.

Steps for Shepardizing a Federal Case

Once you are familiar with the citator system, Shepardizing a federal case involves the following six steps:

1. Start with the appropriate *Shepard's Federal Citations* or *United States Citations* set that covers the reporter in which the cited case appears. Check the cover page of the advance sheet or pamphlet for the current or previous month to determine that all required volumes are available. The information on the front cover of this advance sheet or pamphlet enumerates the *Shepard's* volumes and supplements that constitute a complete set.

2. Become familiar with abbreviations used in Shepardizing. Check the abbreviations tables, the preface, and the illustration or explanation pages that are at the beginning of most *Shepard's* volumes. The preface often contains abbreviations for sources you may not encounter in the tables.

3. The volume of the cited material is in black bold print at the top of each page, and the page numbers on which each case in a volume begins appear in black bold print in the columns on the page, as shown in Figure 11–2. Remember that the page number of the citing case is the page on which the cited case is mentioned, *not* the page on which the cited case begins.

4. Review *Shepard's* for parallel citations.

5. Work back from the most recent supplement to the hardbound volume in which the citation being researched first appears.

6. Review the subsequent history entries in *Shepard's* to determine (a) whether the cited case has been appealed to a higher court, and (b) whether that court has acted on the case. Use the table of *Shepard's* abbreviations for subsequent case history provided in this chapter.

7. It is necessary to determine how the citing cases listed have treated the cited case. Have they followed the case? Have they criticized it? Notice the small letters that precede the citing citations. One abbreviation that should be noted carefully in any citation is the "o," indicating that a holding in the cited case has been expressly overruled. When a case has been overruled, its precedential value may be reduced or destroyed. In many instances, only a part of a decision is overruled. You may then cite the case as authority, with the caveat that the case was "overruled in part" or "overruled on another issue."

Not all citations are preceded by an abbreviation. The absence of an abbreviation does not mean that the citing case is unimportant. You must read *all* cases listed in *Shepard's* to ensure that the research is complete and accurate. If time constraints preclude this, however, you should first read the cases with notations suggesting possibly important reactions to the case you are researching.

Sheparardizing Headnotes

Cases often involve multiple legal issues, with any number of them capable of generating enough attention from the legal community and courts to be referred to in subsequent cases. Where citing cases are numerous (they can run into the dozens, if not hundreds), you are confronted with the somewhat difficult task of trying to limit your research to only the citing cases that are relevant to the specific issues you are researching in the cited case.

Sheparardizing a case using West headnotes or the syllabus paragraph number in an official reporter eliminates the need to read cases that do not relate to the issue in the cited case. In Figure 11–2, for example, note the small raised number within the citing case, 715 F. Supp. 609, for the cited case, 698 F. Supp. 1506. This figure shows that the citing case concerns the issue summarized in that numbered headnote in the cited case.

Frequently the issues you are researching involve only one or two headnote numbers. If you make a careful note of these numbers initially, you can save a great deal of time during subsequent research by focusing your research on only those issues of interest to you. Also important, of course, is that you pay careful attention to which headnotes you are using.

The headnotes in a West reporter will differ from those in the official reporter or in another publisher's version of the same case. The absence of any headnote number reflects that a later case discusses your case only generally, rather than focusing on a specific legal issue covered by a headnote.

Shepard's Federal Case Names Citator

Decisions of federal courts of appeals since 1940 are listed alphabetically by circuit in a *Shepard's Federal Case Names Citator* for each circuit. (See Chapter 2 for a listing of states in each federal circuit.) Each citation incorporates the following research information:

1. primary source (*F.2d, F. Supp., F.R.D.,* or *Bankr.*),
2. federal circuit court,
3. year of decision, and
4. proper spelling of plaintiff/defendant names.

Updates of this citator consist of four cumulative supplements each year.

§ 11.3 Sheparding Federal Statutes and Regulations

Introduction

The process for Sheparding cases is repeated in researching federal law, including statutes, agency regulations, and the United States Constitution. *Shepard's United States Citations, Statute Edition,* is a multivolume set that shows, in the words of the publisher, "all citations to the United States Constitution, United States Code, United States Code Annotated, Federal Code Annotated, United States Code Service, Tariff Schedules of the United States, United States Statutes at Large (not in the United States Code), United States Treaties and Other International Agreements, General Orders in Bankruptcy, and United States Court Rules." It is important, therefore, that you pull the appropriate volumes containing the item you want to research. This should be relatively easy if you pay attention to the information on the front cover of each volume. For example, if you have a reference to a Statute at Large, you should first determine whether it is in the *United States Code* (use the tables discussed in Chapter 5). If it is in the *U.S.C.*, you will not find it in the *Statutes at Large* volumes of *Shepard's United States Citations: Statute Edition.* You will, however, find it in the

United States Code volumes. (Note: some Statutes at Large will never be codified due to the lack of any public interest value.)

After each boldfaced cited source in *Shepard's*, citing sources are listed. Citing sources include legislative enactments, cases, attorney general opinions, and legal periodicals.

What Shepardizing Statutes Reveals

Shepardizing statutes can reveal seven basic types of information:

1. parallel citation in parentheses after section number of statute to session law edition of statute;

2. history of statute in the legislature, including amendments, sections repealed, new sections added, or renumbering of statutes (see Figure 11–3 for abbreviations). A statute citation may appear to contain a discrepancy. For example, a session law may cite "1987," the year in which the legislature enacted the statute, while the code cites "1990," the year of codification;

3. history of statute in courts—citing cases that have analyzed, mentioned, or declared statute unconstitutional (see Figure 11–4 for abbreviations);

4. citing administrative decisions, for example, where an agency such as the EPA or the Social Security Administration has analyzed or mentioned the statute in its administrative proceedings;

5. citing legal periodicals—a law review or law journal article that has analyzed or mentioned the statute;

6. citing annotations in *A.L.R.*; and

7. citing opinions of the attorney general.

Steps for Shepardizing Federal Statutes

The steps for Shepardizing statutes are similar to those followed in Shepardizing a case.

1. Start with *Shepard's United States Citations, Statute Edition*. Determine by following step one for Shepardizing a case whether all of the required *Shepard's* volumes are available. Check the appropriate *Shepard's* volume.

2. If the statute has been codified, Shepardize it through its latest code citation. Use the tables in the current code to translate a session law citation into a codified citation. In the case of a statute that has not been codified, Shepardize the citation only through the session law citation.

3. Shepardize the citation in every volume of *Shepard's* by working backward from the most recent pamphlet to the bound volume containing the initial citation being researched or working from the initial citation forward to the current pamphlet. Exercise caution if the statute you are researching appears in a blocking, which is a group of statutes cited by a court. That blocking must be Shepardized in addition to the individual section of the statute. For Shepardizing material appearing in blocking, return to step 1 and proceed through the process.

The pages from *Shepard's* in Figure 11–3 show what you will encounter in Shepardizing a statute that has been codified through the *Shepard's United States Code* volumes, here sections of Title 20 of the *United States Code*, 1982 edition and 1986 supplement.

Six groups of citations appear on the page in Figure 11–3:

1. sections of the code that have been amended, repealed, and so on by congressional action;

2. citations by the United States Supreme Court and lower federal courts, analyzed as to constitutionality or validity of the statute;

3. citations to articles in the *American Bar Association Journal*;

4. citations to annotations in *United States Supreme Court Reports, Lawyers' Edition* and *American Law Reports*;

5. citations to legal texts and treatises; and

6. citations to specific subdivisions of the code.

Note that section 921, subsection c, was added by an act of Congress and was printed in 99 *United States Statutes at Large* (St) on page 720.

There are numerous citations to decisions of the United States Supreme Court and lower federal courts, as shown in Figure 11–3. Under section 1001 *et seq.*, there is a citation to a case reported in 15 *American Law Reports, Second Series* (AL2) at page 500. Citations by all federal courts except the United States Supreme Court appear under headings that indicate the federal court or judicial circuit from which the citation originated. For example, under section 902, subsection a, there is a citation to a case from the Fourth Circuit: 879 F.2d 1229.

Shepardizing the United States Constitution

Citations to the United States Constitution, including the Preamble, articles, and amendments, are found in *Shepard's United States Citations, Statute Edition*. The process involved with Shepardizing the federal Constitution mirrors the steps used to Shepardize a statute.

UNITED STATES CODE '82 Ed. & '86 Supp.   T. 20 § 1002

Subsec. a Cir. 2 690FS1353 Cir. 9 812F2d1153 Cir. 10 632FS1572 Subsec. b Cir. DC 795F2d93 Cir. 2 690FS1347 Cir. 8 862F2d685 Cir. Fed. 796F2d428 Subd. 1 Cir. 2 690FS1348 Cir. Fed. 796F2d421 Subd. 2 Cir. DC 795F2d93 Cir. 2 690FS1348 Cir. 5 826F2d327 Cir. 10 632FS1570 Subsec. c Cir. DC 795F2d93 Cir. 2 690FS1348 Cir. 5 826F2d327 Subsec. d Subd. 1 Cir. DC 795F2d94 § 107b Cir. DC 695FS1236 Subsec. 6 Cir. DC 695FS1239 Cir. 6 700FS23 Cir. 8 862F2d686 Cir. 10 632FS1572 § 107b-1 Cir. DC 695FS1238 Subsec. 1 Cir. DC 695FS1241 Subsec. 3 Cir. DC 695FS1241	§ 107b-3 Cir. 9 812F2d1154 § 107d-1 Cir. DC 695FS1236 Cir. 5 826F2d327 Cir. 6 700FS23 Cir. 10 632FS1572 796F2d428 Subsec. a 795F2d94 Subsec. g 795F2d94 Cir. 2 695FS1239 Cir. 5 690FS1348 Cir. 5 826F2d328 Cir. 6 700FS22 Cir. 8 862F2d682 Cir. 10 632FS1572 Cir. Fed. 796F2d403 Subsec. b Cir. DC 795F2d94 Cir. 2 690FS1348 Cir. 5 826F2d328 § 107d-2 Cir. DC 795F2d109 695FS1236 Cir. 2 690FS1349 Cir. 5 826F2d327 Cir. 6 700FS22 Cir. Fed. 796F2d428 Subsec. a Cir. DC 795F2d94 Cir. 2 690FS1348 Cir. 6 700FS22 Cir. 8 862F2d682 Subsec. d Cir. 8 862F2d687 § 107d-3 Cir. DC 795F2d94 Cir. 6 700FS22 Cir. 9 812F2d1152 624FS521 Cir. Fed. 796F2d421	Subsec. a Cir. 2 690FS1348 Subsec. b Cir. Fed. 796F2d427 Subd. 1 Cir. Fed. 796F2d403 Subsec. d Cir. Fed. 796F2d403 Subsec. e Cir. DC 795F2d94 Subsec. g Cir. Fed. 796F2d416 § 107e Subsec. 3 Cir. Fed. 796F2d421 Subsec. 7 Cir. DC 795F2d94 Cir. 10 632FS1570 § 236 et seq. 469US267 470US646 §§ 236 to 244 Cir. Fed. 824F2d1576 § 236 A102St294 § 237 et seq. Cir. DC 640FS471 § 237 Subsec. a A102St294 Subd. 1 ¶ c Cir. DC 640FS471 § 238 Cir. Fed. 824F2d1577 Subsec. a Subd. 4 56USLW [4833 Subsec. d A100St739 ¶ D A102St300 Subd. 3 Cir. Fed. 824F2d1576 ¶ C RnSubd d [100St740 ¶ C (100St740) Ad100St740 Subsec. b A102St295	§ 239 Subsec. a A102St294 § 240 A102St296 Subsec. f A102St296 § 241 Cir. DC 870F2d699 Cir. 2 855F2d938 Cir. 4 838F2d130 Cir. 6 875F2d1180 Cir. 11 860F2d397 Subsec. a Cir. DC 870F2d700 Cir. 2 855F2d942 Cir. 4 838F2d130 Cir. 6 875F2d1185 Cir. 11 860F2d403 ClCt 15ClC284 Subsec. c Cir. 6 875F2d1185 Subsec. e Cir. 2 855F2d943 Subsec. 15 838F2d130 Cir. 11 860F2d403 Subsec. i Ad102St294 § 241-1 Subsec. a A102St299 Subd. 1 A102St294 ¶ A A102St4709 Subd. 3 A102St300 Subd. 4 56USLW [4833 Subsec. d A102St294 Subsec. f Ad102St300 § 241a et seq. 470US634 Cir. 9 831F2d876 Cir. 11 853F2d867 § 241a 470US634 § 241c 470US634 § 241e 470US635 470US660 Cir. 8 848F2d885	§ 241f 470US636 470US663 § 241g 470US635 470US671 § 241aa Rs102St414 § 241bb Rs102St414 § 241cc Rs102St414 Subsec. 3 Ad100St [3207-133 § 241dd Rs102St414 § 241ee Rs102St414 § 241ff Rs102St414 § 242 Subsec. b Cir. 9 833F2d831 § 244 Subsec. 5 A102St300 Subsec. 6 Cir. 9 833F2d828 Subsec. 7 833F2d829 § 351a Subsec. 12 Subsec. 15 A99St902 § 351b Subsec. a Subd. 4 A102St2862 Subd. 5 A102St2862 § 351c Subsec. d Subd. 2 A99St902 § 351d Subsec. b Subd. 4 A99St903 § 353 Subsec. b Subd. 1 A99St903 § 401 et seq. Cir. 11 700FS27 §§ 421 to 429 Cir. 9 829F2d740 § 425 Cir. 9 788F2d619 829F2d742 § 631 A102St301 A102St302	§ 633 A102St301 § 644 Subsec. d Rs102St301 § 645 Subsec. 14 A102St301 Subsec. 15 A102St301 § 646 Subsec. a A102St301 Subd. 1 ¶ A A102St4709 Subsec. c A102St301 §§ 681 to 685 Rs100St794 §§ 691 to 691g Rs100St794 §§ 693 to 693h Rs100St794 §§ 695 to 695c Rs100St794 § 701 et seq. 56USLW [4823 § 811 Cir. DC 870F2d664 § 821 et seq. Cir. DC 657FS1555 § 871 et seq. 56USLW [4093 § 901 et seq. Cir. DC 863F2d989 Cir. Fed. 786F2d1127 § 901 Cir. Fed. 786F2d1127 § 902 Subsec. a Cir. 4 879F2d1229 Subd. 4 Cir. DC 863F2d991 Subd. 6 Cir. DC 863F2d991 § 905 Cir. Fed. 786F2d1127 § 921 et seq. Cir. Fed. 786F2d1127 §§ 921 to 923 Cir. Fed. 801F2d1304	§ 921 Subsec. c Ad99St720 § 923 Subsec. d Ad99St721 § 928 Subsec. a Subd. 1 A99St720 Subsec. b A99St720 § 929 Subsec. a A99St720 ¶ A A99St720 Subsec. b Subd. 1 A99St721 § 951 et seq. ClCt 15ClC449 § 951 A99St1332 Subsec. 1 Cir. 10 622FS695 § 952 A99St1332 § 953 Subsec. a A99St1333 § 954 Cir. 10 622FS695 Subsec. b Subd. 1 A99St1333 Subsec. b Subd. 4 A99St1333 Subd. 4 (99St1333) Ad99St1333 Subd. 5 RnSubd 7 [99St1333 Subd. 5 (99St1333) Ad99St1333 RnSubd 8 [99St1333 Subsec. g Subd. 2 A99St1333 ¶ D Ad99St1334 ¶ E Ad99St1334 Subsec. i Subd. 1 A99St1334 ¶ D A99St1334 Subsec. m Ad99St1334 § 955 A99St1335 § 956 A99St1335	§ 956a A100St [1783-281 A101St [1329-250 § 957 A99St1338 § 958 A99St1339 § 959 A99St1339 § 960 Subsec. a A99St1342 Subd. 2 A100St769 Subsec. c A99St1343 Subsec. d RnSubsec e [99St1343 Subsec. d (99St1343) Ad99St1343 § 963 A99St1344 § 964 Subsec. a Subd. 2 A99St1344 § 967 Subsec. a A99St1344 A99St1334 § 971 Subsec. b Subsec. b A99St1345 § 972 Subsec. b Subd. 1 A99St1345 § 974 Subsec. b A99St1345 A101St [1329-249 Subsec. c A99St1345 A101St [1329-249 § 1001 et seq. Cir. DC 624FS917 Cir. 7 698FS1466 125FRD692 Cir. 9 656FS571 95BRW166 Cir. 11 700FS363 Cir. Fed. 787F2d1568 15Æ500s §§ 1001 to 1145e A102St837 § 1001 A100St1278 § 1002 A100St1278

439

FIGURE 11–3 Reproduced with permission of Shepard's/McGraw-Hill, Inc. Any further reproduction is strictly prohibited.

Sheshardizing Administrative Regulations

In General

Shepard's Code of Federal Regulations Citations includes citations to regulations, executive orders, and reorganization plans. The *C.F.R.* citator currently consists of two bound volumes, an annual supplement pamphlet, and advance sheets. Included in this citator are federal and state court decisions citing the *C.F.R.*, presidential proclamations, executive orders and reorganization plans, and citations found in annotations in *A.L.R.* and *L. Ed. 2d,* selected law reviews, the *ABA Journal*, and several legal texts. Research in the *Shepard's* for *C.F.R.* follows the same steps as statute research. The lists of citations are arranged by title and then *C.F.R.* section.

Shepard's contains only citations of court actions relating to the cited regulation. To determine whether an administrative agency has taken any action, it is necessary to search the List of CFR Parts Affected tables of the *Federal Register* and the List of Sections Affected at the end of the *C.F.R.* volumes.

Note that *Shepard's* incorporates some citing sources by year of *C.F.R.* edition and some without the year notation. An elevated asterisk before the year indicates the year of the cited regulation, not the year of the citing case.

In Shepardizing a regulation, you may discover an elevated triangle prior to the year of the citing source. It indicates that the citing case discussed the section but did not refer to either the year or edition of the regulation. In that instance, the year reflected is the year of the citing case, and not the year of the cited regulation.

Tips for Shepardizing a Federal Regulation

1. Determine whether you have a complete set of *Shepard's Code of Federal Regulations Citations*.
2. Shepardize the regulation through each one of the volumes in the set.
3. To find out what has happened to the regulation in an agency, check the List of CFR Parts Affected table in the *Federal Register*.

§ 11.4 Shepardizing Federal Court Rules

Procedural court rules, like other legal authority, should be Shepardized for accuracy and to locate additional sources that cite, construe, or mention a particular rule. *Shepard's United States Citations, Statute Edition* offers a comprehensive compilation of citations to federal court rules, as listed below:

Rules of the Supreme Court of the United States

Rules of Bankruptcy Procedure

Rules of Practice in Admirality and Maritime Cases

Federal Rules of Appellate Procedure

Rules of the United States Courts of Appeals

Revised General Rules of the Temporary Emergency Court of Appeals

Rules of the Judicial Panel on Multi-District Litigation

Rules of Procedure for the Trial of Minor Offenses before United States Magistrates

Rules of the Special Court, Regional Rail Reorganization Act

Rules Governing Section 2254 Cases

Rules Governing Section 2255 Proceedings

Rules of Civil Procedure for the United States District Courts

Rules of Criminal Procedure for the United States District Courts

Federal Rules of Evidence

Rules of the United States District Courts

Rules of the United States Claims Court

Rules of the United States Court of Customs and Patent Appeals

Rules of the United States Court of International Trade

Rules of Practice before the United States Tax Court

Code of Judicial Conduct of United States Judges

Code of Professional Responsibility

Citations by Texas state courts to federal court rules may be found in *Shepard's Texas Citations. Shepard's Federal Law Citations in Selected Law Reviews* and *Shepard's Federal Rules Citations* contain additional citations to a federal court rule in law reviews and legal periodicals. The cited source or rule number is printed in boldface at the top of the listing of these citing sources. A letter abbreviation may precede the citations for some citing sources. This abbreviation indicates the history and treatment of a case or statute.

Once the citing cases have been located, you must Shepardize and read those cases to determine their impact.

§ 11.5 Sheparding Law Review Articles

As will be discussed in Chapter 12, law review articles are an important secondary research tool. Often law review articles either influence the reasoning of a court or are thought of highly enough by the writer of an opinion to be included in textual or footnote references. *Shepard's Law Review Citations* provides an excellent means of accessing decisions that have cited an article you are either researching or suspect may have drawn judicial attention. This set, as described in its preface, "is a comprehensive system showing citations since 1957 to articles in law reviews and legal periodicals" by virtually all federal and state courts.

§ 11.6 Sheparding Texas Cases and Statutes

Cases

In General

Shepard's publishes individual state citators as a complement to the individual state reporter system. These citators consist of parallel citations, history citations, citing references by state and federal courts, attorney general opinions that cite the case, and law review citations. In *Shepard's Texas Citations*, the references are to cases decided by Texas and federal courts, as well as to law review articles from Texas and numerous national periodicals such as the *Yale Law Review*.

Shepard's has introduced a publication called *Shepard's Express Citations* that is described as an "advance supplement to your regular state citator subscription." This publication is available for Texas under the name *Shepard's Texas Express Citations*. Issued twice a month, this *Shepard's* offers a much faster updating of the *Shepard's* state citator than was previously available in printed form.

You may easily ascertain from the abbreviation preceding the citation if a case has been affirmed, dismissed, reversed, overruled, criticized, distinguished, or followed. For example, in Figure 11–4, the case at 773 S.W.2d 665 was reversed at 788 S.W.2d 569.

Researching by reference to a particular West headnote will permit you to narrow the search to one or more particular issues of a case. The process for Shepardizing state cases is the same as that followed in Shepardizing federal cases, discussed previously in this chapter.

Shepard's Texas Case Names Citator

This specialized *Shepard's* is a fast and accurate index of Texas cases. It is not itself really a citator; it is to be used only for finding cases, not for ascertaining the full history as in the state and regional citators. However, *Shepard's Texas Case Names Citator*, combined with the state and regional *Shepard's*, provides a comprehensive research tool for state citations for each case decided by the Texas Supreme Court, the Texas Court of Appeals, the Texas Court of Civil Appeals, the Texas Court of Criminal Appeals, and the Texas Commission of Appeals from 1940 to the present, including annotations, legal periodicals, and legal texts that subsequently referred to a case.

Features of this citator include:

1. case names, alphabetically by plaintiff-defendant;

2. court;

3. date of the decision;

4. reverse defendant-plaintiff listing; and

5. official state and regional reporter citations, if available.

For example, this specialized citator can be used to obtain the correct spelling of a party's name or the official state and regional citation for that case.

State Statutes

Shepard's Texas Citations includes citing references to state statutes by both federal and Texas appellate courts, action by the state legislators in the form of amendment or repeal of statutes, attorney general opinions, and citations in annotations, law reviews, law journals, and other legal texts. It also includes a section of judicial decisions involving local ordinances and municipal charters, by city and county.

State Court Rules

The statute section of *Shepard's Texas Citations* includes citations to state court rules, as shown in Figure 11–5.

SOUTHWESTERN REPORTER, 2d SERIES (Texas Cases)　　Vol. 774

—545— 44SLJ213	**—283—** 44SLJ602 44SLJ640	**—543—** 786SW562	**—674—** f792SW¹578 f797SW¹273 j797SW275	**—808—** 43SLJ1066 44SLJ257	486US1004 44SLJ3	**—368—** 44SLJ11	**—656—** f786SW³264 798SW⁵²07
—556— s788SW18	**—296—** 788SW591 31SoT639	**—553—** 787SW¹393 787SW³394 j790SW627	o797SW¹683	**—948—** 44SLJ369	**—229—** US cert den in110SC1535 787SW¹⁸120 787SW¹¹153	**—371—** US cert den in110SC3248	44SLJ522
—559— 44SLJ291	**—302—** 787SW67 794SW¹397 j794SW401	**—568—** 44SLJ599	**—676—** Cir. 5 f732FS⁴720	**Vol. 774**	787SW¹²153 787SW¹⁵153 44SLJ595	**—379—** 786SW²481 786SW¹482	**—659—** 44SLJ384
—563— j792SW245			**—681—** 794SW³448	**—22—** 44SLJ539	44SLJ619		**—661—** 44SLJ691
—571— 786SW³482	44SLJ602 44SLJ649	**—595—** 795SW²321 21SMJ890	44SLJ294 PLU§ 10.02	**—31—** 788SW⁵668	**—247—** US cert den in110SC519	**—380—** 44SLJ12	**—662—** 791SW531 Cir. 5
—580— 44SLJ35	**—322—** 44SLJ641	**—599—** cc99LE483 cc108SC1272	**—687—** 44SLJ288 44SLJ474	**—45—** 44SLJ528	790SW²⁶362 791SW²⁷344	**—384—** 21SMJ885	f903F2d¹376 42BLR601 21SMJ693
—946— 790SW705 794SW³808 794SW⁶812	**—332—** 787SW197 790SW614 44SLJ610	f787SW¹562 Cir. 5 113BRW³328	**—693—** 44SLJ563	44SLJ575 44SLJ583 21SMJ936	792SW²83 797SW331	**—387—** US cert den in111SC51 790SW⁴721	21SMJ753 31SoT121
Vol. 773	**—338—** 44SLJ213	**—601—** d791SW³541	**—698—** 798SW⁹299 44SLJ49	**—56—** 44SLJ625	**—270—** a790SW299 44SLJ683	44SLJ4 44SLJ50	**—666—** s790SW738 21SMJ907
—13— Case I 44SLJ156 44SLJ389	**—346—** 44SLJ196	**—607—** 44SLJ311	44SLJ519	**—63—** 44SLJ547	**—276—** s797SW658 786SW¹312	**—391—** 44SLJ288 11CoLR27	**—668—** s789SW656 44SLJ581
—28— 44SLJ50 21TTR1338	**—352—** 44SLJ124	**—616—** 791SW318 791SW³319 44SLJ143 44SLJ174	**—707—** 21SMJ893	**—73—** WD 788SW²154 44SLJ344	44SLJ625	**—411—** 789SW²425 21SMJ908	**—673—** 787SW955 797SW⁵398 44SLJ512
—34— e795SW¹778	**—354—** 44SLJ161 44SLJ195 44SLJ534	44SLJ536 21SMJ921	**—711—** DAP	**—75—** 786SW¹386	**—284—** WD 788SW³429	**—415—** WD 44SLJ303	68TxLL947
		—626— 21SMJ883	**—718—** 44SLJ561 31SoT535	**—86—** r786SW263	**—299—** 788SW⁵207	**—638—** 21SMJ753	**—679—** 44SLJ145 44SLJ184 44SLJ508
—44— 792SW190 792SW194 794SW111 795SW³303 798SW321	**—369—** 794SW¹65 Cir. 5 911F2d1154 44SLJ520	80AL521n	**—721—** 787SW442 792SW497 794SW111 795SW²305	s790SW403 s795SW741	44SLJ46	31SoT121	21SMJ694
		—631— 787SW115		**—88—** c786SW¹6	**—307—** 44SLJ50	**—639—** 797SW252	**—693—** 44SLJ531
—60— 788SW¹921	**—384—** 44SLJ244	**—637—** 44SLJ514	**—735—** 21SMJ906	786SW735 q786SW¹736	**—308—** 21SMJ921	21SMJ907	**—697—** 788SW⁵665
—63— 44SLJ53	**—391—** 44SLJ363	**—642—** d790SW³756 794SW608 21SMJ919	**—749—** 44SLJ612	**—107—** r787SW948 794SW⁴956	**—316—** 786SW²773 789SW¹687	**—644—** US cert den in110SC1122 s794SW479	791SW302
—68— r788SW566 44SLJ368	**—393—** 44SLJ220	**—645—** 44SLJ46	**—759—** 44SLJ298	44SLJ157 44SLJ337	21SMJ934 31SoT512 31SoT521	787SW42 787SW¹126 787SW²126	**—706—** 44SLJ59
—75— 44SLJ71	**—396—** r786SW259 d791SW⁵256 797SW285	**—649—** 21SMJ886	**—771—** s796SW190	**—111—** d785SW²950 785SW³950	**—319—** 786SW¹¹311 44SLJ626	787SW⁴126 788SW²703 788SW²708 793SW²730 795SW235	**—707—** 44SLJ304
		—652— 794SW68 795SW¹¹260	**—785—** 44SLJ76 44SLJ536	**—195—** f740SW²869 f740SW⁸869	**—344—** 794SW²410	**—719—** j797SW63 42BLR406	**—717—** 44SLJ305
—263— 790SW⁴82 795SW²273 44SLJ668	**—398—** 44SLJ269 **—401—** 44SLJ57	44SLJ550 1AtSN10	**—792—** 787SW⁶197	787SW¹71 788SW625 788SW³855	**—352—** 44SLJ370 44SLJ530	44SLJ567	**—719—** 42BLR483 44SLJ455
		—662— 790SW57 44SLJ553	**—797—** 44SLJ407 44SLJ554 44SLJ950	788SW²902 788SW⁴904 790SW²354 790SW⁴356	1ExER98	**—650—** 786SW28 44SLJ385	**—730—** 794SW¹440 794SW¹490 794SW³490
—271— US cert den in110SC209 s111SC1 cc741FS126 785SW⁵390 792SW¹100	**—408—** 44SLJ303 **—525—** US cert den in110SC257 788SW⁴666 44SLJ619 44SLJ642	**—665—** r788SW569 44SLJ14 44SLJ276 21SMJ920	**—800—** 44SLJ61 **—802—** 21SMJ879 31SoT66 1AtSN15	791SW307 793SW293 793SW⁴294 795SW²33 e795SW²193 796SW¹542 796SW³720 796SW²729 796SW⁴741 796SW⁴819	**—359—** 787SW427 795SW³2 44SLJ159 44SLJ199 44SLJ529 21SMJ894	**—653—** 789SW⁵691 791SW⁵581 1990TxAG [JM-1230 44SLJ479	**—741—** r796SW700 44SLJ584 **—743—** s787SW953 q795SW218 44SLJ528

FIGURE 11–4　Reproduced with permission of Shepard's/McGraw-Hill, Inc. Any further reproduction is strictly prohibited.

Ordinances and Municipal Charters

Shepard's Texas Citations includes citations to ordinances and charters of a city or other municipality, subdivided into topics, or by alphabetical topics, subdivided by city or other municipality.

State Constitution

Shepard's state edition for Texas also contains citations to the Texas Constitution. A list of citing sources reported in this citator can be found on the table page at the front of the book.

When Shepardizing a state constitution, follow the same steps used in Shepardizing the federal Constitution. The same information can be obtained. In Figure 11–6, note that Art. 7, Subd. 4, Sec. 3 of the Texas Constitution was upheld at 421 U.S. 291.

Summary

11.1   Introduction to Shepard's Citators

Law is dynamic, not static. Thus, attorneys and paralegals have a professional responsibility to determine the current status and validity of a case or statute. To make that determination, researchers rely on citators, sets of books that provide: (1) the subsequent judicial histories of judicial decisions, and (2) lists of cases and legislative enactments construing, applying, or interpreting the cited cases and statutes. *Shepard's Citations* is the most widely used citator service.

11.2   Sheppardizing Federal Cases

Shepard's Federal Citations consists mainly of two separate multivolume sets. One set covers decisions of federal courts of appeals that are published in the *Federal Reporter*, and the other set covers decisions of federal district courts. Another federal case law citator is *Shepard's United States Citations, Case Edition*. This comprehensive multivolume set lists citations by both federal and state courts to the decisions of the United States Supreme Court that have been reported in the official and unofficial reporters. Shepardizing reveals six types of information about a case: parallel cites, history of cited cases—subsequent and prior, citing cases, citing legal periodicals, citing annotations, and citing opinions of the attorney general.

TEXAS CONSTITUTION, 1876 AS AMENDED 1984							Art. 7
689SW897	181SW712	479SW33	184SW644	499FS1334	195SW423	208SW412	§1
692SW481	183SW175	500SW103	191SW762	648FS613	196SW546	212SW625	160SW1178
707SW262	191SW115	525SW518	196SW60	25SLJ416	198SW262	271SW834	166SW377
717SW51	194SW263	579SW463	208SW415	17TTR1502	209SW364	291SW406	170SW840
717SW612	218SW207	584SW948	212SW625	11TxL382	212SW630	299SW934	185SW591
719SW655	227SW227	108Tex578	213SW469	35TxL1032	212SW968	361SW225	195SW1132
724SW83	227SW228	110Tex374	252SW720	35TxL1041	214SW847	412SW954	201SW413
725SW727	279SW362	111Tex538	264SW135	37TxL683	240SW329	Va414SW685	202SW966
726SW127	297SW732	114Tex176	271SW391	54CaL610	243SW832	110Tex395	272SW559
64TxCr43	301SW71	133Tex493	280SW638	29StnL683	260SW227	114Tex205	278SW516
131TxCr310	342SW622	147Tex74	291SW723	31LE888n	270SW235	115Tex205	280SW1070
148TxCr651	396SW895	90TxCr254	294SW160	§2a	273SW96	117Tex165	300SW211
162TxCr161	401SW854	380US94	295SW409	25SLJ416	281SW356	133Tex114	3SW420
346US181	410SW63	400US228	302SW627	§3	281SW746	147Tex74	14SW1052
97LE1540	416SW907	13LE679	312SW721	195SW643	295SW408	157Tex5	17SW36
73SC1091	448SW198	27LE340	337SW134	228SW1112	299SW933	61TxCr368	22SW476
29SLJ490	583SW665	85SC779	342SW1	243SW287	304SW543	64TxCr262	23SW431
32SLJ508	108Tex476	91SC316	359SW910	261SW430	337SW134	64TxCr315	34SW656
36SLJ561	157Tex130	C575F2d1111	361SW225	261SW434	342SW1	75TxCr436	35SW123
39SLJ525	79TxCr437	726F2d198	378SW41	266SW782	372SW752	124TxCr182	35SW781
13SMJ233	108TxCr653	252FS239	C378SW304	299SW221	373SW844	6F827	37SW829
16SMJ150	139TxCr142	25SLJ416	389SW946	52SW757	378SW41	482F2d1230	40SW31
17TTR79	146TxCr380	34SLJ460	Va414SW685	71SW233	387SW697	25FS285	41SW513
11TxL19	147TxCr177	5SMJ227	415SW701	82SW680	397SW944	224FS518	93SW180
35TxL958	147TxCr586	35TxL1032	435SW896	105SW659	411SW566	351FS883	95SW1032
59TxL216	149TxCr326	35TxL1041	479SW32	111SW1225	C464SW638	35TxL1031	106SW288
§28	153TxCr100	44TxL469	575SW84	116SW823	466SW75	35TxL1041	108SW257
150SW312	154TxCr322	54CaL435	579SW463	127SW208	C518SW923	§5	114SW947
157SW1169	154TxCr339	20AE732s	110Tex369	128SW786	544SW957	144SW1167	190SW406
198SW1006	161TxCr564	Subd. 4	110Tex375	136SW808	123Tex365	228SW1116	195SW436
201SW986	37TxL851	220SW99	111Tex538	196SW546	129Tex627	281SW837	205SW97
247SW263	§30	87TxCr163	114Tex176	304SW543	134Tex442	115Tex205	292SW886
2SW270	332SW553	380F2d450	115Tex205	321SW322	145Tex320	380US94	317SW99
177SW975	534SW887	341FS180	133Tex492	337SW134	147Tex79	13LE679	330SW710
181SW75	160Tex384	C341FS183	147Tex74	342SW1	150Tex591	85SC779	334SW574
215SW325		§§2 to 3a	153Tex464	373SW844	156Tex365	23BLR50	348SW18
291SW349	Art. 6	415SW701	156Tex21	378SW42	157Tex91	35TxL1041	348SW245
294SW202	227SW181	§2	156Tex366	480SW273	161Tex327	399US213	363SW747
332SW553	228SW1115	135SW587	157Tex316	C518SW923	399US213		366SW850
460SW401	93SW746	146SW633	161Tex327	114Tex241	Up421US291	Art. 7	376SW331
525SW716	252SW726	149SW803	61TxCr369	117Tex159	439US69	211SW327	429SW918
651SW373	264SW135	161SW412	90TxCr254	123Tex365	26LE530	251SW210	450SW719
106Tex138	291SW409	189SW960	120TxCr562	129Tex635	58LE301	278SW183	488SW521
112Tex198	324SW542	206SW958	123TxCr270	133Tex493	90SC1996	24SW449	502SW671
147Tex248	378SW305	208SW574	126TxCr119	134Tex444	Up95SC1638	35SW780	683SW839
160Tex321	575SW83	208SW963	321US653	161Tex327	99SC389	40SW20	695SW559
83TxCr135	718SW428	217SW431	339US285	Up421US291	142F2d794	40SW35	704SW916
108TxCr653	111Tex38	218SW479	U380US89	Up44LE175	352FS489	47SW268	711SW425
147TxCr18	159Tex581	221SW880	383US666	Up95SC1638	Up377FS1017	97SW1054	106Tex270
147TxCr399	130TxCr264	225SW266	400US228	6F827	28BLR31	101SW360	109Tex51
325US399	25SLJ417	228SW1112	412US447	456F2d572	25SLJ417	120SW945	120Tex383
420US87	5TTR345	234SW910	88LE991	Up252FS255	30SLJ379	280SW583	162Tex392
89LE1694	21TxL485	242SW749	94LE846	352FS489	35TxL1036	363SW747	132TxCr540
43LE41	28TxL40	243SW277	U13LE677	Up377FS1016	35TxL1041	435SW896	C411US7
65SC1276	35TxL1041	251SW277	16LE172	399FS783	§4	590SW554	C36LE27
95SC877	§§1 to 5	251SW302	27LE340	28BLR31	135SW585	653SW560	C93SC1279
16SLJ216	351FS883	265SW1019	37LE69	25SLJ376	144SW544	695SW559	392F2d697
21SLJ478	§1	277SW218	64SC757	27SLJ199	144SW570	120Tex360	648F2d436
16TxL501	1967p1861	278SW919	70SC629	30SLJ379	144SW1167	120Tex395	261FS545
44TxL1098	189SW961	281SW837	U85SC776	35TxL915	171SW716	121Tex148	308FS571
§29	196SW511	24SW767	86SC1081	35TxL1041	187SW1115	154Tex555	320FS729
165SW139	217SW434	29SW451	91SC316	§3a	221SW881	29SLJ478	321FS1044
176SW818	218SW479	47SW613	93SC2234	71SW233	228SW1114	21TxL48	325FS1021
185SW580	228SW1112	52SW757	6F824	82SW679	243SW287	35TxL916	393FS1150
196SW1166	234SW910	52SW801	131F2d593	95SW150	265SW1023	35TxL1004	501FS562
273SW318	242SW749	58SW519	496F2d113	100SW1067	281SW837	§§1 to 8	11HUL890
284SW991	265SW1023	70SW431	U498F2d244	105SW655	299SW222	363SW774	16HUL329
2SW270	277SW218	93SW747	526F2d290	111SW1188	61SW1005	§§1 to 7	23SLJ203
65SW817	95SW151	95SW151	224FS518	116SW823	75SW150	223SW281	29SLJ491
91SW841	96SW994	411SW1225	U232FS930	123SW1029	111SW1225	363SW780	27TxL345
113SW644	127SW207	123SW794	Up252FS234	127SW212	112SW782	§§1 to 4	51TxL900
115SW1183	128SW786	127SW208	259FS122	130SW925	120SW956	16TTR677	63TxL815
136SW615	212SW625	128SW786	320FS134	136SW808	126SW4		59Cor209
139SW275	359SW910	133SW177	U321FS1101	138SW896	155SW618		38LCP384
175SW420	361SW225	146SW455	346FS529	139SW307	203SW320		
179SW574	478SW78	155SW618	422FS920	191SW757			

FIGURE 11–5 Reproduced with permission of Shepard's/McGraw-Hill, Inc. Any further reproduction is strictly prohibited.

TEXAS COURT RULES

Rules of Civil Procedure							
Rules	347SW917	336SW434	636SW212	250SW253	Rule 3a	463SW261	724SW415
of Civil	543SW400	341SW887	644SW910	253SW315	291SW887	464SW209	144Tex11
Procedure	605SW301	343SW553	648SW765	256SW202	23SW812	467SW618	146Tex396
	619SW611	345SW797	649SW680	267SW439	24SW346	469SW323	148Tex443
as amended	636SW445	346SW911	651SW353	279SW589	188SW678	472SW211	152Tex23
	651SW845	348SW71	657SW497	302SW697	462SW317	472SW296	160Tex292
	689SW463	356SW354	662SW706	321SW321	492SW348	475SW403	162Tex331
1986	140Tex40	356SW460	664SW418	336SW229	512SW777	477SW693	163Tex450
248SW1013	154Tex151	366SW648	667SW343	341SW918	519SW633	484SW587	155TxCr99
249SW588	156Tex158	393SW819	671SW618	342SW371	530SW930	487SW436	425FS689
250SW310	156Tex613	393SW827	682SW431	352SW358	539SW203	490SW236	531FS191
272SW948	157Tex464	397SW217	683SW184	356SW354	550SW268	500SW212	25BLR206
273SW63	162Tex378	407SW277	684SW750	373SW527	554SW835	501SW729	32BLR493
292SW845	147TxCr106	408SW543	685SW379	508SW455	573SW182	514SW812	33BLR585
319SW137	276FS392	416SW529	691SW715	520SW820	609SW258	516SW696	38BLR558
322SW501	6TTR915	424SW898	692SW561	548SW13	144Tex45	517SW838	19SLJ745
324SW163	37TxL857	430SW254	696SW153	596SW178	10BLR132	518SW578	39SLJ71
328SW295	43ABA217	446SW733	696SW158	613SW761	33BLR591	531SW373	17SMJ363
328SW324	8At739n	450SW389	711SW236	653SW336	15SLJ371	534SW891	17SMJ371
333SW636		457SW123	713SW153	660SW812	21SLJ462	535SW681	4TTR3
344SW938	Rule 1	459SW190	720SW599	667SW587	4TTR16	538SW490	14TTR14
344SW959	161SW358	461SW116	143Tex612	675SW810	20TxL632	540SW733	
346SW827	165SW935	462SW126	144Tex44	677SW228	21TxL793	542SW883	Rule 5
346SW890	172SW395	465SW820	145Tex290	690SW299	26TxL814	545SW19	159SW574
351SW254	173SW549	467SW618	149Tex223	714SW387	35TxL386	552SW183	163SW886
351SW659	174SW101	468SW121	151Tex238	719SW242		554SW795	166SW383
352SW489	177SW301	471SW888	151Tex313	148Tex447	Rule 4	561SW798	169SW501
360SW176	187SW363	472SW540	153Tex41	149Tex44	167SW808	561SW800	170SW629
360SW521	188SW676	477SW681	153Tex250	154Tex466	168SW891	569SW877	179SW959
361SW477	196SW950	484SW127	153Tex279	147TxCr108	188SW144	571SW860	189SW633
361SW925	198SW256	484SW139	154Tex23	170TxCr451	208SW363	572SW811	194SW583
365SW843	200SW844	486SW179	154Tex124	28SLJ191	214SW480	574SW192	200SW844
368SW600	201SW115	489SW458	154Tex335	36SLJ26	219SW1014	577SW559	203SW796
370SW419	203SW800	496SW957	156Tex235	25TxL182	222SW262	579SW545	207SW362
372SW352	203SW955	497SW109	159Tex275		226SW116	580SW127	214SW331
373SW535	216SW848	501SW868	161Tex337	Rule 3	228SW580	581SW774	228SW548
373SW570	222SW262	502SW922	491FS1316	140SW1145	230SW812	582SW616	228SW580
380SW753	228SW542	507SW818	32BLR493	158SW298	233SW188	583SW645	234SW901
380SW892	229SW1012	507SW859	33BLR583	165SW533	235SW927	584SW705	241SW196
385SW443	234SW898	514SW141	38BLR261	175SW1129	254SW104	586SW137	241SW311
391SW504	235SW238	515SW930	22SLJ182	206SW703	254SW405	596SW571	243SW196
151Tex308	236SW642	517SW331	23SLJ190	211SW535	254SW548	598SW659	244SW989
154Tex27	248SW472	517SW627	37SLJ433	223SW231	267SW479	601SW60	246SW493
159Tex455	249SW590	519SW640	3SMJ214	265SW1012	286SW669	602SW130	246SW854
159Tex560	254SW548	521SW930	15SMJ770	265SW1021	298SW279	608SW239	249SW590
162Tex355	260SW625	522SW695	17SMJ779	273SW1109	305SW377	608SW263	252SW604
168TxCr398	261SW465	525SW313	2SoT2	281SW1084	306SW383	614SW177	256SW162
171TxCr425	263SW770	527SW263	4TTR3	296SW1070	312SW408	615SW268	257SW456
337F2d618	267SW137	529SW850	20TxL27	58SW74	321SW161	618SW136	260SW620
15BLR381	267SW541	534SW878	20TxL46	78SW209	322SW661	628SW176	263SW621
4TxL475	273SW59	541SW474	20TxL634	78SW1081	324SW431	629SW838	263SW631
5TxL52	274SW432	542SW884	21TxL317	123SW794	326SW564	643SW200	264SW209
28TxL435	274SW538	545SW765	21TxL337	125SW1063	329SW845	650SW949	266SW241
30TxL512	275SW213	545SW904	22TxL503	180SW466	336SW224	656SW510	269SW415
31TxL843	277SW92	546SW126	23TxL398	298SW845	336SW452	658SW282	272SW938
35TxL954	279SW175	547SW56	24TxL221	404SW631	342SW371	671SW128	274SW538
38TxL824	280SW616	548SW418	25TxL397	620SW899	347SW250	671SW616	274SW761
38TxL880	284SW939	548SW452	25TxL432	114Tex177	352SW358	672SW44	276SW414
Rule 1	287SW314	552SW183	29TxL372	116Tex329	354SW645	673SW392	277SW159
et seq.	288SW900	555SW556	30TxL122	116Tex580	354SW683	674SW762	279SW171
166SW103	294SW375	562SW924	31TxL8	70TxCr546	356SW774	675SW810	280SW788
178SW688	294SW412	564SW178	38TxL361	132US508	356SW804	676SW442	281SW230
183SW183	297SW367	564SW457	42TxL340	33LE399	374SW418	680SW73	281SW377
190SW426	300SW219	564SW474		10SC147	375SW518	682SW368	283SW817
198SW117	302SW214	579SW459	Rule 2	28SLJ248	375SW557	686SW350	286SW698
203SW811	303SW840	589SW493	170SW238		381SW140	691SW772	290SW576
205SW796	304SW246	589SW860	170SW789	Rule 3A	400SW863	698SW369	290SW922
206SW629	308SW557	590SW605	178SW689	671SW508	414SW537	699SW282	291SW425
275SW463	311SW438	592SW58	203SW548	679SW580	415SW717	699SW620	296SW238
293SW495	313SW131	596SW178	222SW262	39SLJ460	418SW861	699SW705	297SW255
297SW867	317SW917	600SW402	225SW651	17SMJ776	421SW682	702SW671	301SW700
299SW275	324SW433	602SW349	226SW116		422SW15	704SW938	303SW466
302SW767	328SW231	616SW646	228SW130		422SW240	711SW725	306SW385
304SW111	329SW137	616SW687	234SW118		432SW79	712SW541	308SW592
328SW475	331SW250	620SW615	235SW946		450SW773	716SW731	*Continued*
	336SW229	635SW207	244SW358		457SW123	721SW489	

FIGURE 11–6 Reproduced with permission of Shepard's/McGraw-Hill, Inc. Any further reproduction is strictly prohibited.

11.3 Sheperdizing Federal Statutes and Regulations

The process for Sheperdizing cases is repeated in researching federal law, including statutes, agency regulations, and the United States Constitution. *Shepard's United States Citations, Statute Edition* is a multivolume set that shows all citations to the United States Constitution, *United States Code, United States Code Annotated, United States Code Service*, and United States court rules. Sheperdizing furnishes parallel cites, history of a statute, treatment of a statute by court, citing administrative decisions, citing legal periodicals, citing annotations, and citing opinions. The process involved with Sheperdizing the United States Constitution mirrors the steps used to Sheperdize a statute. *Shepard's Code of Federal Regulations Citations* includes federal and state court decisions citing the *C.F.R.*, presidential proclamations, executive orders and reorganization plans, and citations found in annotations in *A.L.R.* and *L. Ed. 2d*, selected law reviews, the *ABA Journal*, and several legal texts.

11.4 Sheperdizing Federal Court Rules

Shepard's United States Citations, Statute Edition offers a comprehensive compilation of citations to federal court rules. Citations by Texas state courts to federal court rules may be found in *Shepard's Texas Citations, Shepard's Federal Law Citations in Selected Law Reviews* and in *Shepard's Federal Rules*, which contains additional citations to federal court rules in law reviews and legal periodicals.

11.5 Sheperdizing Law Review Articles

Law review articles are an important secondary research tool. Often law review articles either influence the reasoning of a court or are thought of highly enough by the writer of an opinion to be included in textual or footnote references. *Shepard's Law Review Citations* contains citations since 1957 to articles in law reviews and legal periodicals by virtually all federal and state courts.

11.6 Sheperdizing Texas Cases and Statutes

Shepard's publishes individual state citators as a complement to the individual state reporter system. These citators consist of parallel citations, history citations, citing references by state and federal courts, attorney general opinions that cite the case, and law review citations. In *Shepard's Texas Citations*, those references would be to cases decided by Texas and federal courts, or to law review articles from Texas, as well as numerous national periodicals, such as *Yale Law Review*, which have cited your case. *Shepard's Texas Case Names Citator* may be used to find a case and, combined with the state and regional *Shepard's*, provides a comprehensive research tool for state citations for each case decided by the Texas Supreme Court, the Texas Court of Appeals, the Texas Court of Civil Appeals, the Texas Court of Criminal Appeals, and the Texas Commission of Appeals from 1940 to the present, including annotations, legal periodicals, and legal texts that subsequently referred to a case. *Shepard's Texas Citations* also includes citing references to state statutes by both federal and Texas appellate courts, action by the state legislators in the form of amendments or repeal of statutes, attorney general opinions, and citations in annotations, law reviews, law journals, and other legal texts. This publication also includes citations to state court rules, ordinances and charters of a city, and the Texas Constitution.

Review Questions

1. Define *citator*.

2. List three types of information about a case or statute that is available in a citator.

3. What is the first form in which a *Shepard's* citator appears?

4. What determines when a researcher begins to Shepardize a case or statute?

5. Identify the courts whose decisions are published in the two sets of *Shepard's Federal Citations*.

6. Which courts' decisions are contained in *Shepard's United States Citations, Case Edition*?

7. List one advantage and one disadvantage of using the regional citator rather than a state citator for Shepardizing.

8. What is a parallel citation and where does it appear in *Shepard's*?

9. Explain the differences between history and treatment of a case.

10. List the four types of information obtained from Shepardizing a statute.

Exercises

Use the appropriate citator to answer the following questions:

1. List the parallel citations for 471 U.S. 462 (1985).

2. Has the case in number 1 above been followed by the Fifth Circuit Court of Appeals? If yes, list the citations from the entry.

3. Has the Fifth Circuit distinguished 471 U.S. 462? If yes, write down the entry.

4. Has the State of Texas cited 471 U.S. 462 (1985)? If yes, list the entries from *Shepard's*.

5. Has the case in number 4 above been cited in Texas law reviews? If yes, list the law reviews.

6. Has headnote number 3 in the case in number 4 above been cited by a Texas state court? If yes, state the entry.

7. Has headnote number 7 in the case in number 4 above been cited by a Fifth Circuit court? If yes, state the entry.

8. Using the *Supreme Court Reporter* section of *Shepard's United States Citations: Cases,* identify the lower court decision from 105 S. Ct. 2174, and identify the parallel citations to 105 S. Ct. 2174.

CHAPTER 12

ADDITIONAL LEGAL RESEARCH MATERIALS

§ 12.1 Introduction

In addition to the primary sources of law and the finding tools discussed in previous chapters, there are other important sources of materials that can assist in conducting comprehensive legal research. This chapter discusses various looseleaf services, periodicals, and other legal research materials such as restatements, treatises, dictionaries, directories, form books, and continuing legal education handbooks.

§ 12.2 Looseleaf Reporter Services

Generally

Many of the traditional methods of legal research are insufficient for the timely needs of the paralegal and the attorney. Statutes are passed, cases are decided, and agencies act on a daily basis. The need for immediate or quick access to the most recent materials is evident. In response to this need, looseleaf reporter services were created.

Looseleaf reporters are published in a notebook-style format with separate hole-punched pages for easy insertion, removal, and substitution of pages or updated pamphlets. They should not be confused with looseleaf treatises that are similar in that they allow for substitution of specific pages. The looseleaf treatises are different in that they contain primarily textual analysis of the law in a specific area, rather than primary sources such as court opinions and statutes, and are updated much less frequently than looseleaf reporter services. The treatises are discussed in more detail later in this chapter.

Looseleaf reporters are essentially a hybrid publication, containing primary and secondary sources as well as finding tools. Although the looseleaf reporters vary in content and coverage, most consolidate into a single source materials focused on a specific legal subject, including current statutes, court decisions, and analyses and commentaries. Their main value is the "one-stop shopping" they make possible for all relevant primary sources: cases, statutes, and administrative regulations and decisions. They also contain valuable indexes that allow the researcher to access the primary source materials.

As laws change or decisions are rendered, the publisher may create a single page or a number of pages that address that topic for inclusion into the looseleaf binder. The process of updating is continual, with releases published monthly, weekly, or in some cases daily.

To locate material in a looseleaf reporter service, use the indexes. Most looseleaf services contain cumulative subject or topical indexes as well as indexes to current releases.

Looseleaf services can be cumbersome to use due to the comprehensive materials included and their frequent updating. When first using a specific reporter service, it is advisable to read the introductory section that discusses the organization and format of the service before turning to the index.

Specific Publications

There are three main publishers that specialize in looseleaf services. They are Commerce Clearing House (CCH), Prentice Hall (PH) (part of which was purchased by Maxwell Macmillan), and the Bureau of National Affairs (BNA).

Commerce Clearing House Looseleaf Services

Commerce Clearing House provides a myriad of looseleaf services, as listed in Figure 12–1. These services have comprehensive indexes referred to as "topical" indexes. The index is found in the last binder in the set. It will assist in locating special topics of interest and the specific volume that contains the legal material. Since the pages of the looseleaf service are constantly changing, topics are assigned numbered paragraph designators to allow for flexibility in changing or supplementing the material in the looseleaf series. Consequently, standard page references are unimportant. Your focus should be on the numbered paragraph assigned to each topic area for quick access to a desired topic. (See Figure 12-2.)

Included in the CCH looseleaf services are full texts of court decisions, statutory changes, and administrative agency rulings. In CCH, the court decisions or agency rulings are often placed in a separate volume or a separate section. By using an appropriate table found in the indexes, cases and agency decisions may be cross-referenced and located under the particular paragraph numbers assigned from the indexes.

Often current developments in a particular area are reported in the form of weekly bulletins that are retained as part of the looseleaf service. The publisher will include text-type comments prepared by its staff of authors. These analytical paragraphs are an important feature of many looseleaf services and enhance their value as comprehensive research tools.

Using CCH Looseleaf Services   When beginning your research in CCH, you should:

ILLUSTRATION 12B
COMMERCE CLEARING HOUSE SERVICES

ACCOUNTING AND AUDITING
    Accountancy Law Reports
    Accounting Articles
    Cost Accounting Standards Guide
    Federal Audit Guides
    SEC Accounting Rules

AVIATION
    Aviation Law Reporter

BANKING
    Federal Banking Law Reports

CARRIERS
    Federal Carrier Reports
    Federal and State Carrier Reports (combines
       Federal Carrier Reports and State Motor
       Carrier Guide)
    State Motor Carrier Guide

COMMERCIAL LAW AND CONSUMERISM
    Consumer Credit Guide
    Secured Transactions Guide

CORPORATIONS
    Business Franchise Guide
    Capital Changes Reporter
    Professional Corporation Handbook

EDUCATION, FOUNDATIONS AND CHARITIES
    College and University Reporter
    Exempt Organizations

ELECTIONS
    Federal Election Campaign Financing Guide

ENERGY
    Economic Regulation Administration
       Enforcement Manual
    Energy Management and Federal Energy Guidelines
    Federal Energy Regulatory Commission Reports
    Nuclear Regulation Reporter

ENVIRONMENT
    Pollution Control Guide

ESTATES, WILLS, TRUSTS
    Estate Planning Review
    Financial and Estate Planning

FAIR EMPLOYMENT
    EEOC Compliance Manual
    Employment Practices Guide

FOOD, DRUG, AND MEDICAL
    Food, Drug, Cosmetic Law Reporter
    Medical Devices Reporter

FRANCHISES
    Business Franchise Guide

GOVERNMENT CONTRACTS
    Contract Appeals Decision
    Government Contracts Reporter
    OFCCP Federal Contract Compliance Manual

INSURANCE
    Automobile Law Reports
    Fire & Casualty Insurance Law Reports
    Insurance Law Reporter (combines Automobile
       Law Reports, Fire & Casualty Insurance Law
       Reports and Life, Health & Accident Law Reports)
    Life, Health, & Accident Law Reports
    Workmen's Compensation Law Reporter

LABOR AND EMPLOYMENT RELATIONS
    Employment Practices Guide
    Human Resources Management
    Labor Arbitration Awards
    Labor Law Reporter-Labor Relations-Wages-Hours
    NLRB Case Handling Manual
    Public Employee Bargaining

LEGISLATION
    Advance Session Law Reporter
    Congressional Index
    Congressional Legislative Reporting
    State Legislative Reporting Service (guide to
       each state is published individually)

LIQUOR CONTROL
    Liquor Control Law Reporter

MEDICARE AND MEDICAID
    Medicare and Medicaid Guide

OCCUPATIONAL SAFETY AND HEALTH
    Employment Safety and Health Guide
    OSHA Compliance Guide

PATENT AND COPYRIGHT
    Copyright Law Reporter

PENSIONS AND COMPENSATION
    Compliance Guide for Plan Administrators
    Individual Retirement Plans Guide
    Payroll Management Guide
    Pension Plan Guide

PRODUCTS LIABILITY
    Consumer Produt Safety Guide
    Products Liability Reporter

FIGURE 12–1   Looseleaf services provided by the Commerce Clearing House (CCH)

PUBLIC UTILITIES
Utilities Law Reporter

SECURITIES
American Stock Exchange Guide
Blue Sky Law Reporter
Commodity Futures Law Reports
Chicago Board Options Exchange Guide
New York Futures Exchange Guide
Coffee, Sugar and Coca Exchange, Inc. Guide
Executive Disclosure Guide
Federal Securities Law Reporter
MSRB Manual
Mutual Funds Guide
NASD Manual
New York Exchange Guide
Boston, Philadelphia, Midwest and Pacific
Stock Exchange Guides
California Eligible Securities List
Stock Transfer Guide

SOCIAL SECURITY
Unemployment Insurance-Social Security Reporter

SUPREME COURT
U.S. Supreme Court Bulletin

TAXATION
Code and Regulations
Executive Tax Review
Farmers Tax Watch
Federal Income Tax Regulations
Federal Tax Articles
Federal Tax Compliance Reporter
Federal Tax Guide
Federal Tax Guide Reports-Control Ed.
Federal Texas-IRS Letter Rulings
Interest Dividend-Withholding
-Information Returns
IRS Positions Reports
IRS Publications
Internal Revenue Manual
Standard Federal Tax Reports
Tax Court Decisions Reports
Tax Court Reports
Tax Planning Review

TAXATION, ESTATE AND GIFT
Estate Planning Review
Financial and Estate Planning
Inheritance Estate and Gift Tax Reports

TAXATION, EXCISE
Federal Excise Tax Reports

TAXATION, INTERNATIONAL AND FOREIGN
Tax Treaties

TAXATION, STATE
All-State Sales Tax Reports
State Tax Cases Reports
State Tax Guide
State Tax Reports

TRADE, INTERNATIONAL
Common Market Reporter

TRADE REGULATION
Trade Regulation Reporter

URBAN PROBLEMS
Urban Affairs Reporter

FIGURE 12–1   *(continued)*

Topical Index

How to Use the Topical Index

The Topical Index, printed on white paper beginning at page 10,201, is to be used for approach to the basic Compilations by subject or key word. The Topical Index covers the Compilations devoted to the income tax published in the Index Volume and Volumes 1 through 12, inclusive. Each topic in the index is followed by one or more paragraph numbers covering a specific provision of the Code or Regulations, CCH Explanations or digests of decisions or rulings. After checking the direct paragraph references provided by the Topical Index, you should also examine related information appearing in the same area of a Compilation.

Arrangement of the index is strictly alphabetical. An abbreviation such as "A.R.M." will be found after "Arkansas" and before "Armed Forces"; hyphenated words are treated as two words; in headings of more than one word, the first word of the heading governs the alphabetical order so that "Gift tax" precedes "Gifts."

Rapid Finder Index

Use the Rapid Finder Index, printed on green paper and beginning at page 10,111, for quick reference to broad subjects.

For New Developments

The Cumulative Index, beginning at page 75,201, Volume 13, should always be checked after you have consulted the Compilations. The arrangement of the Cumulative Index is exactly the same as that of the Compilations. Refer to the same paragraph number used for the Compilations in the Cumulative Index and you obtain the new matters. Noting a decision in an annotation in the Compilations, take its paragraph number to the Cumulative Index and you learn of affirmance or reversal, if any, as well as of any related new matters. Generally, the latest decision is that of the highest authority—the controlling decision. Therefore, make it a rule to complete each inspection of the Reporter by consulting the Cumulative Index.

New developments can also be located through the Topical Index for the current year. The Cumulative Index is usually the main direct approach to new matters. But the Current Topical Index is helpful where the subject matter is newly conceived and not previously mentioned in the Compilations. The Topical Index to 1991 Developments begins at page 75,101 in Volume 13.

'91 CCH Index—Standard Federal Tax Reports

FIGURE 12–2 A sample of material from the *CCH Standard Federal Tax Reports*

24   5-29-91   **Topical Index**
                     References are to paragraph (¶) numbers.

RETURNS—continued
. failure to report income—continued
. . negligence v. fraud penalties 40,445.356
. . no attempt to conceal transactions . . .
. . . . 40,445.345
. . nontaxability claimed 40,445.358
. . overpaid income 40,445.346
. . partnerships 40,445.3585
. . recklessness 40,445.344
. . stock received for services 40,445.359
. failure to sign 40,375.635
. failure to verify 40,375.635
. false
. . conviction for preparation 42,033.02
. . erroneous work sheets of Internal Rev-
. . . enue Service 42,033.15
. . prosecutor's comment. effect on con-
. . . viction 42,033.156
. . suit by United States 41,520.484
. . venue 42,033.172
. . willfulness, defined 42,033.175
. false v. fraudulent 40,445.352
. . assistance in preparing 42,033.169
. family member filing. timeliness . . . . . .
. . . . 39,913.459
. farmers and fishermen 656.01; 1386.007
. farmers' cooperatives
. . time for filing 37,720; 37,724
. fictitious, penalties 40,445.3596
. fiduciaries—see Fiduciaries: returns by
. filing 37,723.01
. . before due date, refunds and credits
. . . . 40,030.011
. . by mail 37,723.016
. . copies of federal returns required to be
. . . filed with local returns 37,894.593
. . extension granted 40,375.492
. . late, delay due to mails 37,723.016
. . late, reasonable cause 40,375.361
. . necessary to allegation of fraud . . . .
. . . . 40,445.363
. . personal holding companies 3325C.012
. . postponed due to war . . . . 43,586—43,587.22
. . Sunday as last day 43,535.40
. . willful failure 42,015
. . wrong form 40,375.63
. . wrong period, deficiencies 38,539.51
. final returns
. . decedents 37,723.01
. . liquidating corporation 36,450.209
. fiscal year, deficiency determined . . . . .
. . . . 38,539.32
. fiscal years
. . tax rate change 36,450.03
. foreign corporations 28,200; 36,445;
. . . . 36,450.11
. . exempt income 36,445; 36,450.834
. . failure to file necessary information . . .
. . . . 28,209.05
. . form used 36,445
. . formation of . . . . 37,040—37,045.50
. . late filing 28,209.06
. . reorganization of . . . . 37,040—37,045.50
. . statute of limitations 39,913.431;
. . . . 39,913.511
. . time for filing 37,720; 37,724
. foreign personal holding companies . . . 3376
. . officers, directors, and shareholders
. . . . 36,680—36,685.10
. foreign trusts 37,721
. forms reproduced . . . . 43,600—43,602.50
. fractional part of dollar disregarded . . . .
. . . . 37,860—37,863.01
. fractional part of year . . . . 2731—2751
. fraudulent 42,034; 42,038.01
. . acquittal as to indictment, bar to fur-
. . . ther penalties 40,445.204; 40,445.206
. . ad valorem penalty paid. bar to crimi-
. . . nal prosecution 42,018.07
. . admission of taxpayer 40,445.208
. . aliases 40,445.218

RETURNS—continued
. fraudulent—continued
. . amended returns later filed 40,445.219
. . assistance in preparation 42,018.1467
. . attorney not having complete data . . .
. . . . 40,445.38
. . attorney's advice 40,445.21
. . bank deposits as basis 40,445.242
. . basis used, erroneous 40,445.32
. . bookkeeper's errors 40,445.243;
. . . . 40,445.375; 40,445.39
. . books changed to cover up understate-
. . . ment 40,445.245
. . burden of proof 39,917.28
. . circumstantial evidence 42,018.116
. . conviction, imposition of penalty . . . .
. . . . 42,018.068
. . corporation 39,917.284
. . corporation officer making returns,
. . . deceased 40,445.305
. . correction after allegation of fraud . . .
. . . . 40,445.487
. . decedents 39,917.286
. . deductions established 39,917.287
. . defenses 42,018.07; 42,018.0997
. . deficiencies partially due to fraud . . . .
. . . . 40,445.4565
. . directed verdict of acquittal 42,018.35
. . disclosures made prior to investigation.
. . . effect on prosecution 42,018.37
. . double jeopardy . . . . . 42,018.08—42,018.0844
. . erroneous deductions claimed . . . .
. . . . 40,445.321
. . facts falsified 40,445.27
. . failure to report constructively
. . . received income 40,445.286
. . false returns distinguished 40,445.352
. . fraud asserted at court hearing . . . .
. . . . 40,445.23
. . husband and wife, incomplete report-
. . . ing of income 40,445.364
. . income reported in wrong year . . . .
. . . . 40,445.374
. . intent to punish for illicit liquor dealing
. . . . 42,018.096
. . mental illness 39,917.319
. . motion to sever offense 42,033.117
. . offsetting items in returns 40,445.455
. . partnerships 40,445.315; 40,445.457;
. . . . 42,018.1298
. . penalties 40,445.19; 42,030; 42,033.01;
. . . . 42,034; 42,038.01
. . predecessor trustees filing 40,030.249
. . preparation by District Directors . . . 36,540
. . presumption as to fraud 40,445.46
. . proof lacking 42,018.116
. . request for prompt assessment . . . .
. . . . 39,919.15
. . res judicata 39,917.322
. . schedules omitted 40,445.485
. . statute of limitations 39,916; 39,917.045;
. . . 39,917.279—39,917.32; 39,970.12; 42,033.169
. . suspicion of fraud 40,445.42
. . transferee liability 41,520.4842
. . unintentional errors 39,917.29
. . venue 42,033.172
. . willfulness 42,018.41
. frivolous, penalty for 40,840; 40,843.01
. . omissions 40,843.60; 40,843.70
. full and honest, penalties 40,445.33
. general stock ownership corporations
. . . (repealed) 36,821.01
. group-term life insurance 899D.06
. guardian for missing spouse 36,450.7305
. guardian or committee filing
. . date of filing returns 36,450.731
. husband and wife—see also Joint returns
. . . . 36,460
. . income and deductions to wife . . . .
. . . . 40,445.364
. . interlocutory divorce 36,471.6363

1991 CCH Index—Standard Federal Tax Reports   **RET**

FIGURE 12–2   (continued)

1. Write down words and phrases that may apply to the topic you are researching.
2. Locate the words and phrases in the topical index at the end of the series.
3. Locate and note the pertinent paragraph reference numbers found in the index.
4. Go to the specific paragraph number in one of the main volumes of the looseleaf series.
5. Locate any case citations that have been referenced and identified in the text.
6. Review any current weekly bulletins that may provide additional material.

Prentice Hall Looseleaf Services

Prentice Hall Law and Business (PH), a division of the Simon and Schuster Professional Information Group, is another major publisher of looseleaf services. Some of its product line has been sold to Maxwell Macmillan, and some of its publications have undergone title changes. The PH reporter services are listed in Figure 12–3.

The PH looseleaf services are similar in format to those of CCH. Access to a number of topics is provided through the indexes, the most important being the "Master Index." To begin research in a PH looseleaf service, begin with this index.

First, identify the topic of interest. Once you locate the topic of interest in the Master Index, you will find a paragraph number assigned to it. This system is almost exactly the same as the CCH system. Again, specific page references are irrelevant. Use the paragraph number assigned to locate in various segments of the service the specific types of materials you need (cases, statutes, agency rulings).

There are weekly bulletins that report any current developments or changes of interest. These bulletins should be consulted in addition to the indexes.

When beginning your research, follow the procedure for beginning research in the CCH looseleaf services.

Bureau of National Affairs Looseleaf Services

The last major publisher of looseleaf services is the Bureau of National Affairs (BNA). The major BNA publications are listed in Figure 12–4.

The BNA looseleaf services differ significantly from those of CCH and Prentice Hall. Periodic pamphlet inserts are published to be filed in chronological order, rather than single-page inserts. As a subject changes,

PRENTICE HALL LOOSELEAF SERVICES

ADMINISTRATIVE LAW
  Federal Regulatory Week

ATTORNEYS
  Manual for Managing the Law Office

BANKING
  Banking (Control of Banking;
    Federal Aids to Financing)

COMMERCIAL LAW AND CONSUMERISM
  Consumer and Commercial Credit
    -Credit Union Guide
  Consumer and Commercial Credit
    -Installment Sales Service

CORPORATIONS
  Corporation Management Edition
  Professional Corporation Guide

EDUCATION, FOUNDATIONS AND CHARITIES
  Charitable Giving and Solicitation

ENERGY
  Energy Controls

ESTATES, WILLS, TRUSTS
  Successful Estate Planning Ideas and Methods
  Wills, Estates and Trusts

EXECUTIVES
  Executive Action Report

FAIR EMPLOYMENT
  EEOC Compliance Manual

GOVERNMENT INFORMATION
  Government Disclosure

INSURANCE
  Insurance Guide

LABOR AND EMPLOYMENT RELATIONS
  Compensation
  Industrial Relations Guide
  Labor Relations Guide
  Personnel Policies and Practices
  Public Personnel Administration
    -Labor Management Relations
  Wage-Hour Guide

OCCUPATIONAL SAFETY AND HEALTH
  Labor Relations Guide: Occupational
    Safety and Health

PENSIONS AND COMPENSATION
  Plan Administrator's Compliance Manual

REAL PROPERTY
  Real Estate Guide

SECURITIES
  SEC Compliance-Financial Reporting and Forms
  Securities Regulation Service and Guide

TAXATION
  American Federal Tax Reports
  Capital Adjustments
  Cumulative Changes
  Divorce Taxation
  Federal Tax Guide
  Federal Taxes-Private Letter Rulings
  Federal Taxes Service
  Oil and Gas-Natural Resources Taxes
  Publications of the IRS
  Tax Court Service
  Tax Exempt Organizations
  Tax Ideas

TAXATION, ESTATE AND GIFT
  Inheritance Taxes
  Successful Estate Planning Ideas and Methods
  Wills, Estates and Trusts

TAXATION, EXCISE
  Excise Taxes

TAXATION, INTERNATIONAL AND FOREIGN
  Tax Treaties
  U.S. Taxation of International Operations

TAXATION, PROPERTY
  Property Tax Service
  Real Estate Federal Tax Guide

TAXATION, STATE
  All-States Tax Guide
  Sales Taxes Service
  State and Local Taxes
  State Income Taxes

URBAN PROBLEMS
  Equal Opportunity in Housing

FIGURE 12–3   Reporter services from Prentice Hall

BUREAU OF NATIONAL AFFAIRS LOOSELEAF SERVICES

BANKING
  Washington Financial Reports

COMMUNICATIONS
  Media Law Reporter

CORPORATIONS
  Corporate Practice Series

CRIMINAL LAW
  Criminal Law Reporter

ENVIRONMENT
  Chemical Regulation Reporter
  Environment Reporter
  Noise Regulation Reporter
  Water Pollution Control

ENVIRONMENT, INTERNATIONAL
  International Environment Reporter

FAIR EMPLOYMENT
  Affirmative Action Compliance Manual for
    Federal Contractors
  Fair Employment Practice Series

FAMILY LAW
  Family Law Reporter

GOVERNMENT CONTRACTS
  Federal Contracts Reports

HUMAN REPRODUCTION
  Family Law Reporter

INSURANCE
  Loss, Prevention and Control

LABOR AND EMPLOYMENT RELATIONS
  Collective Bargaining Negotiations and Contracts
  Construction Labor Report
  Daily Labor Report
  Employment and Training Reporter
  Government Employee Relations Report
  Labor Arbitrations Reports
  Labor Relations Reporter
    Labor-Management Relations
    State Laws
    Fair Employment Practice
    Wages and Hours
    Labor Arbitration
  Retail/Services Labor Report
  Union Labor Report

OCCUPATIONAL SAFETY AND HEALTH
  Job Safety and Health
  Mine Safety and Health Reporter
  Occupational Safety and Health Reporter

PATENT AND COPYRIGHT
  Patent, Trademark & Copyright Journal
  United States Patent Quarterly

PENSIONS AND COMPENSATION
  Payroll Guides
  Pension Reporter

PRODUCTS LIABILITY
  Product Safety and Liability Reporter

SECURITIES
  Securities Regulation and Law Report

SUPREME COURT
  United States Law Week

TAXATION
  Tax Management Financial Planning Journal
  U.S. Income
  Primary Sources

TAXATION, INTERNATIONAL AND FOREIGN
  Tax Management-Foreign Income

TRADE REGULATION
  Antitrust and Trade Regulation Reporter

URBAN PROBLEMS
  Housing and Development Reporter

FIGURE 12–4   Major publications from the Bureau of National Affairs (BNA)

it is updated in the most recent pamphlet. Earlier issues are not revised. Unlike CCH and PH, BNA does not use a paragraph numbering system.

The BNA reports relevant information regarding new developments in a particular area of legal interest, including changes in legislation, court decisions, and administrative agency action rulings. The two pages shown in Figure 12–5 illustrate typical BNA approaches.

The primary means of accessing information in BNA reporters is the same as for the other looseleaf services. A topical index is provided at the end of each volume in a set (a new volume number is usually assigned annually). Begin your research by using this and any other specialized finding aids, such as a table of cases, that you find at the back of each volume in which you are interested. These finding aids, which are volume-specific, will direct you to the pages in the volume that contain the material that is listed. Finding aids, including indexes, are updated cumulatively with each release of the reporter, so they are always current.

Additional Looseleaf Services

A number of other publishers also publish looseleaf services. These publishers generally employ formats similar to those used by CCH, PH, and BNA. Consequently, you should be able to use these services by following the same steps that are appropriate for using one of the major services.

§ 12.3 Legal Periodicals

Legal periodicals are important sources of secondary materials used in legal research. Many legal periodicals provide scholarly analyses, and many offer excellent coverage of current trends in the law. The major types of legal periodicals are law reviews, magazines and journals, and legal newspapers.

Law Reviews

Generally

Law reviews are the most significant periodical sources of secondary legal research materials. A law review is a softbound pamphlet, usually issued quarterly, published by a law school. Virtually every law school in the country publishes its own law review, with its students acting as editors

The United States
LAW WEEK

**Court Decisions
Agency Rulings**

June 26, 1990 • THE BUREAU OF NATIONAL AFFAIRS, INC., WASHINGTON, D.C. • Volume 58, No.50

NEW COURT DECISIONS
Digests of Significant Opinions Not Yet Generally Reported

Antitrust

TYING ARRANGEMENTS—
Advertising agency's allegations that auto manufacturer's institution of national advertising campaign, in which it raised prices of its cars to fund national advertising efforts and stopped paying for advertising by individual dealerships, caused dealerships to cease doing business with local advertising agencies in independent advertising market are sufficient to state claim of illegal tying in violation of Sherman Act.

(Faulkner Advertising Association Inc. v. Nissan Motor Corp., CA 4, No. 89-1548, 6/12/90)

An advertising agency brought this action against Nissan Motor Corp., alleging that it was engaged in an illegal "tying" arrangement in violation of the Sherman Act. The district court granted Nissan's motion to dismiss under Fed.R.Civ.P. 12(b)(6). In particular, the court held that the agency had failed to allege in its complaint all the essential elements of a tying violation, especially Nissan's sale of a "tied" product.

Until 1988 the agency was engaged exclusively in the business of creating and placing advertising for local Nissan dealer associations. That year, however, Nissan increased the price of its automobiles to finance a new "local market advertising" plan, under which it increased advertising at the national level. Its new national advertising firm was to develop advertising for the regional and local levels. In addition, while it did not preclude local dealers from developing and placing their own advertising, Nissan ceased making monetary contributions to the advertising efforts of the local dealer associations. As a consequence, the local dealer associations terminated their business relationships with the agency.

A tying arrangement is an agreement whereby a seller conditions the sale of one product or service (the tying product) upon the buyer's purchase of a second product or service (the tied product). A tying arrangement that poses an unacceptable risk of stifling competition in the sale and purchase of a tied product or service constitutes a violation of the antitrust laws. The essential characteristic of an invalid tying arrangement lies in the seller's exploitation of its control over the tying product to force the

buyer into the purchase of a tied product that the buyer either did not want at all, or might have preferred to purchase elsewhere on different terms. When such forcing is present, competition on the merits in the market for the tied item is restrained and the Sherman Act is violated. See *Jefferson Parish Hospital District No. 2 v. Hyde,* 466 U.S. 2 (1984).

In this case, the sole issue is whether the agency properly alleged in its complaint that Nissan had linked together two distinct product or service markets in order to sell a tied product or service. Nissan argues that it is engaged exclusively in selling cars and trucks, while the advertising agency insists that Nissan is selling two linked products, vehicles and advertising.

In *Jefferson Parish,* the court made the following observations comparing the sale of a single product to the linked sale of two distinct products or services: "Thus, the law draws a distinction between the exploitation of market power by merely enhancing the price of the tying product, on the one hand, and by attempting to impose restraints on competition in the market for a tied product, on the other. When the seller's power is just used to maximize its return in a tying product market, where presumably its product enjoys some justifiable advantage over its competitor, the competitive ideal of the Sherman Act is not necessarily comprised. But if the power is used to impair competition on the merits in another market, a potentially inferior product may be insulated from competitive pressures. This impairment could either harm existing competitors or create barriers to entry of new competitors in the market for the tied product . . . ." The court went on to emphasize that the answer to the question whether one or two products are involved turns not on the functional relation between them, but rather on the character of the demand for the two items. Thus, if a sales arrangement in one product market impinges upon competition in another market, a tying arrangement will be recognized.

In *Jefferson Parish,* the court suggested that the market interference test for determining product linkage should be applied from the viewpoint of the purchaser and not the seller. From the perspective of Nissan's independent dealers and their local dealer associations, Nissan's new advertising plan

does integrate what many of them consider to be two distinct markets, one for Nissan's vehicles and the other for advertising. Indeed, there is little doubt that the sale of Nissan automobiles under the company's new local market advertising program has caused an adverse competitive impact in what previously was an independent market for advertising services. Thus, it is apparent that Nissan is engaged in selling a tied product, that the agency's complaint was sufficient to withstand a motion to dismiss, and that this case should have been permitted to go to trial to resolve the question of whether the tying arrangement was illegal.—Ervin, C.J.

Dissent. The majority holds that a manufacturer may not increase its advertising budget, expend that budget as it sees fit, and include the increased cost in the price of its only product, without the risk of running afoul of the Sherman Act. Because the antitrust laws do not prohibit such conduct, I would affirm the Rule 12(b)(6) dismissal.—Hall, J.

Armed Forces

MILITARY BASES—
1988 Base Closure and Realignment Act's grant of authority to secretary of defense regarding base closures does not amount to unconstitutional delegation of legislative power or violate separation of powers principle.

(Federal Employees, NFFE v. U.S., CA DC, No. 90-5004, 6/5/90, aff'g 58 LW 2377)

A union appeals the dismissal of a suit to enjoin the closure or realignment of any of 145 domestic military bases under the 1988 Base Closure and Realignment Act. It challenges the constitutionality of the act under the non-delegation and separation of powers doctrines. Alternatively, it seeks Administrative Procedure Act review of the decisions by the secretary of defense to close and realign bases under the act.

In May 1988, the secretary of defense chartered the Commission on Base Realignment and Closure to study the issues surrounding military base realignment and clo-

FIGURE 12–5 A sample of material from BNA's *U.S. Law Week* and *Environment Reporter*

ENVIRONMENT REPORTER Current Developments

A weekly review of pollution control and related environmental management problems

Volume 22, Number 5   THE BUREAU OF NATIONAL AFFAIRS, INC.   May 31, 1991

HIGHLIGHTS

EXXON WITHDRAWS GUILTY PLEAS in litigation over the 1989 oil spill in Prince William Sound. A Justice Department official urges the company to return to the bargaining table (p. 251) ... Attorney General Richard L. Thornburgh oversaw the Exxon case for a year before seeking a waiver concerning his oil company investments (p. 253) ... Exxon sues more than 5,000 fishermen and other parties to stave off multiple claims (p. 254).

CABINET STATUS for the Environmental Protection Agency moves one step closer to reality as the Senate Governmental Affairs Committee approves legislation to elevate the agency. Sen. John Glenn (D-Ohio) says problems that held up previous bills have been worked out (p. 251).

A FLEXIBLE DEFINITION of sources under the Clean Air Act's new early reduction program is expected to induce more companies to participate in a drive to reduce toxic emissions (p. 252).

BOILERS AND FURNACES that burn hazardous waste as fuel are inadequately regulated, environmentalists and a waste treatment industry group charge in a lawsuit (p. 252).

A MAN WHO EXPORTED WASTE to Mexico pleads guilty in federal court, marking the first such conviction under the Resource Conservation and Recovery Act. A Mexican national pleads guilty to similar charges under California law in a separate case (p. 253).

SIX WICHITA BANKS PLEDGE to make loans on contaminated property that city officials seek to clean up. Landowners can obtain certificates releasing them from liability (p. 255).

EARLY AUCTIONS OF ALLOWANCES under EPA's acid rain control program are expected to allow more companies to take part in the trading scheme (p. 256) ... Full Text (p. 272).

FUEL AND BUS STANDARDS would be rolled back under an EPA proposal required by the 1990

Clean Air Act amendments (p. 257) ... Full Text (p. 287).

A CONSENT DECREE PRECLUDES an environmental group from pressing a citizen suit even if the suit preceded the decree, a federal appeals court rules (p. 257) ... Arkansas residents urge the Supreme Court to allow their Clean Water Act suit to continue despite a consent decree between the defendant and the United States. Their suit also came first (p. 260).

RISK ASSESSMENT GUIDANCE issued by EPA provides less protection for human health by changing the worst-case exposure scenario, an environmental scientist says. Industry and government officials say the scenario is more realistic (p. 258).

ACCESS TO YUCCA MOUNTAIN should be granted to the Energy Department by law; otherwise the department must halt work at the proposed radioactive waste disposal site in Nevada, a DOE official tells a Senate panel (p. 258).

DOE IS ADDRESSING PROBLEMS in its environmental programs, cited in an Office of Technology Assessment report, and deserves the full $4.2 billion requested for 1992 for environmental restoration, the department's top cleanup official testifies (p. 259).

STATE CLEAN AIR PLANS would receive a separate, preliminary completeness review that would take no more than six months under an EPA proposal (p. 261) ... Full Text (p. 269).

This week's supplement to Environment Reporter reference file binders includes amendments to the National Environmental Policy Act on environmental review procedures for public and other federal agencies, changes to CERCLA's reportable quantities and notification requirements list of hazardous substances, amended motor vehicle fuel and fuel additives rules, changes to the state hazardous waste program regulations and various state Clean Air Act implementation plans.

FIGURE 12–5 *(continued)*

and writers. In most cases, these law reviews are general in scope, covering a tremendous range of legal topics within one issue and from issue to issue.

Many law schools also publish subject-specific law reviews, such as *The Harvard Civil Rights–Civil Liberties Law Review, American Journal of Criminal Law* (University of Texas), *New York University Journal of International Law and Politics,* and *The Columbia Human Rights Law Review.*

Most law reviews contain lead articles written by legal scholars, most often professors and accomplished practicing attorneys, and secondary articles, often referred to as "Notes" or "Comments," written by law students who have been selected for membership on the editorial board of the law review in which their work appears.

Law reviews are excellent tools for legal research. Most articles are extensively researched and footnoted, so focus on both the text and the footnotes. The students who participate on the law review staffs devote substantial time and effort to making sure that the sources cited in the footnotes are completely accurate. Consequently, law review articles can be a valuable source for legal research material and can add a new perspective to an area you are researching.

Texas

Texas has nine law schools that publish law reviews. All are recognized in Texas as scholarly journals and are important sources for the analysis of Texas law. The Texas law review journals are:

1. Baylor University School of Law

    Baylor Law Review (published quarterly)
    Journal of Church and State (published quarterly)

2. St. Mary's University School of Law

    St. Mary's Law Journal (published quarterly)

3. Southern Methodist University School of Law

    Journal of Air Law and Commerce (published quarterly)
    S.M.U. Law Review (published quarterly) (formerly *Southwestern Law Journal*) (one issue is entitled *Annual Survey of Texas Laws*)

4. South Texas College of Law

    South Texas Law Review (published three times a year) (formerly known as *South Texas Law Journal*)

5. Texas Southern University (Thurgood Marshall School of Law)

    Texas Southern University Law Review (published three times a year)
    Thurgood Marshall Law Review (published three times a year)

6. Texas Tech University School of Law

    Texas Tech Law Review (published quarterly)

7. University of Houston School of Law

   Houston Journal of International Law (published three times a year)
   Houston Law Review (published five times a year)

8. University of Texas School of Law

   American Journal of Criminal Law (published three times a year)
   Review of Litigation (published three times a year)
   Texas International Law Journal (published three times a year)
   Texas Law Review (published seven times a year)
   Urban Law Review (published three times a year)

9. Texas Wesleyan University School of Law

   Texas Wesleyan Law Review (published three times a year)

Magazines and Journals

Bar Associations' General Interest Publications

The most widely circulated legal periodicals are magazines and journals published by various national, state, and local bar associations. The best known of these publications is *The American Bar Association Journal*, published monthly by the ABA. Although bar journals focus on issues that should be of interest to attorneys throughout the country, many magazines are more limited in scope, reflecting the geographic or practice interests of their specialized memberships.

The primary value of these periodicals is their coverage of current developments and trends in the law—including articles, commentaries, and reviews of recent case decisions and legislation. They do not purport to be law reviews, although they do contain articles (usually only a few pages in length) with commentary and footnote citations on selected topics. Law review articles in general are more theoretical and comprehensive, while bar association publications tend to be more practical and focused on issues of concern to their specific memberships.

The State of Texas Bar Association publishes its own periodical, the *Texas Bar Journal,* which contains articles on state and national topics of interest to Texas practitioners. Each issue usually contains a number of articles, which are useful not only for the discussions they offer but for the significant bibliographies that are included.

Special Interest Group Publications

In addition to general bar association periodicals, including those that are limited by the geographic range of the association's membership, there are a number of subject-specific journals published by a variety of organizations and associations. These journals explore current topics in the law and usually are limited to the subject of the periodical. Representative special interest periodicals include: *The Judges' Journal, The Women's Lawyers' Journal, The Litigation Lawyer,* and *The Business Lawyer.* Many attorneys who are interested in a specific area of the law subscribe to the special interest periodicals.

In Texas, there are specific interest groups, referred to as bar sections, within the Texas Bar Association that are concerned with single areas of practice. Among the more active sections of the Texas Bar Association are those that focus on family law, litigation, and probate law. Most of these sections publish periodicals in which coverage is limited to cases and current trends within their areas of focus. These periodicals often provide excellent analysis of recent case decisions, including their legal effect.

There are a number of periodicals that are geared for paralegals only. The most widely circulated publication is *Legal Assistant Today.* This publication focuses on current paralegal issues and concerns. Most of the articles are written by paralegals. The National Association of Legal Assistants (NALA) also publishes a paralegal newsletter, known as Facts and Findings, that provides information on current paralegal issues, and the National Federation of Paralegal Assistants (NFPA) publishes *Reporter.*

Many local paralegal associations publish newsletters citing current trends and topics in a particular state. Texas has a number of paralegal associations, such as the Dallas Association of Legal Assistants (DALA), which provides a newsletter for its members. All these paralegal legal publications assist paralegals in staying current on the issues that affect their profession.

Legal Newspapers

There are several national legal newspapers and others that are state-specific. The two leading national weeklies are *The Legal Times,* which has several regional editions, and *The National Law Journal.* The *American Lawyer* is a monthly legal newspaper that also publishes information of national interest to lawyers.

Among the states that have a state-specific legal newspaper are New York, California, and Texas. The *Texas Lawyer* is a monthly publication devoted to matters of importance to Texas lawyers and legal assistants.

In addition, there are weekly newspapers that update the current status of the law in Texas. For those who must keep abreast of developments in civil law, *The Texas Lawyers' Civil Digest* is an important resource. It contains a summary of recent civil court decisions from the Texas Supreme Court and Texas Courts of Appeals. The counterpart to that publication is *The Texas Lawyers' Criminal Digest,* which focuses on criminal practice. This digest summarizes recent criminal court decisions from both the Texas Court of Criminal Appeals and the Texas Court of Appeals.

Both digests include a summary of each case cited and list the court, the city of origination, and the date of the decision. Although not yet published in a reporter, new decisions may be reviewed by ordering a **fastback decision** of the case through one of the *Texas Lawyers' Digests*. This is a copy of the decision directly from the court. The fastback decision does not have headnotes, summaries, or specific reporter volume and page. Ordering information for fastback decisions is found in every issue and specifies the necessary information for quick return. This service is provided by the State Bar of Texas.

A separate journal, *The Texas Supreme Court Journal*, provides full-text coverage of Texas Supreme Court cases. Often, this source provides the first opportunity to review a recent decision. In addition to reproducing the court decisions, the *Texas Supreme Court Journal* also lists cases that the court intends to hear at a later date, as well as cases the court has declined to review.

Finding Legal Periodicals

To find articles and information that have been published in legal periodicals, including law reviews, magazines, journals, and newspapers, you *must* consult the guides to legal periodicals. The quantity of published materials in the periodicals is so great that use of the guides offers virtually the only systematic and sensible method of finding information published in the periodicals.

Prior to 1908, the only guide to legal periodicals was known as the *Jones-Chipman Index*. This six-volume index to periodicals tracked articles from 1888 to 1937. Since 1908, most articles have been indexed in what has become the standard guide, the *Index to Legal Periodicals*. This is a comprehensive index of over five hundred legal periodicals published in the United States, Canada, Great Britain, Ireland, Australia, and New Zealand.

The *Index to Legal Periodicals* contains both author and subject entries and is extensively cross-referenced. In addition to multiyear indexes covering specific years of issues, an index pamphlet is published monthly, and an annual cumulative index is published each September.

Other law indexes that can be used in locating periodicals are the *Current Law Index* and the *Legal Resource Index*. These indexes were intro-

━━━━━━━━━━━━━━━━━━━━ **TERMS** ━━━━━━━━━━━━━━━━━━━━

fastback decision   A copy of a decision ordered directly from the court.

duced in 1980 and are computer-produced. They contain separate author-title and book review listings, and both encompass all Texas periodicals.

Sponsored by the American Association of Law Librarians, the *Legal Resource Index* is published monthly as a totally new cumulated index. It indexes over a thousand legal periodicals, including law reviews, magazines, journals, newspapers, and selected legal articles from academic periodicals, general newspapers, and government publications.

The *Legal Resource Index* is issued in various formats. The microfilm format it used when it initially began publication is now obsolete and is rarely found in libraries. There is a CD-ROM version, LegalTrac, that is available in most academic law libraries. It offers Boolean (word) searching and easy printing. Those advantages are also available in the computerized versions of this index on LEXIS and WESTLAW.

The *Current Law Index* and *Legal Resource Index* are the preferred tools for locating articles published since 1980. Both the coverage and the indexing in these sources is superior to that in the *Index to Legal Periodicals*. Use the latter only for pre-1980 research or in the absence of access to the other two indexes.

§ 12.4 Legal Treatises

In General

In general terms, legal treatises are books, or sets of books, written for practicing attorneys that explain in detail the law relating to a particular subject matter. They tend to be scholarly, with ample use of footnote authority to back up textual analysis, and they usually offer far more in-depth coverage of a specific area than do encyclopedias, which, as we saw in Chapter 8, try to cover all areas of American law. Consequently, treatises can be particularly valuable in obtaining a good overview of the legal rules and concepts that may be applicable to your research problem.

Treatises vary enormously in the depth and quality of their coverage. Some treatises, usually multivolume, purport to cover all concepts and provide analyses of significant cases relating to the entire subject field. Others are far more limited and function primarily as a beginning point for attorneys who may not be particularly well informed about a subject area. Some publishers, in fact, offer different versions of the same treatise to satisfy the differing needs of attorneys. For example, Larson's *Workmen's Compensation Law*, first published in 1952, is acknowledged by all as the leading treatise in this field. For the specialist, an eleven-volume version is available. For the attorney who is not a specialist but occasionally handles a workers' compensation case, a three-volume **Desk Edition** is available. The latter is an abridgement of the larger set but does not include as in-depth coverage or as many case citations as are found in the eleven-volume set.

As a general rule, publishers supplement their treatises with what is called "upkeep," or "releases." Upkeep consists of issuing, at least annually, but more often if necessary, revision pages that can be inserted where they belong in the text portion of the treatise and supplement pamphlets that contain additional recent case authority for text materials not yet revised. The integration of revision pages is possible because of the looseleaf binders used for many treatises. Other publishers rely exclusively on pocket part pamphlets to upkeep their hardcover treatises. Whatever the method of upkeep used by the publisher, you need to be sure to consult any upkeep materials in your treatise research.

Most publishers provide, inside the first volume of a treatise, some guidelines for conducting research. And, of course, do not overlook the other research sources that can give you more current coverage than is available through any treatise upkeep program.

Student Texts (Hornbooks)

In addition to practitioner-oriented treatises, you should be aware of a category of single-volume treatises that are more instructional in intent. They present a general overview of the law and focus on the major court decisions in that area. These treatises are often described as "hornbooks." Treatises of this type are in most instances single-volume works that have been written, at least in theory, for law students. West Publishing Company also issues practitioner editions of some of their texts, which they update through pocket part supplements.

Probably the best known student texts are those in the West Hornbook series, such as Prosser and Keeton, *Law of Torts (Fifth Edition)*; Tribe, *Constitutional Law*; and Weihofen, *Legal Writing*. Foundation Press, Little Brown, and Michie are other law school publishers who offer single-volume texts.

Practice Guides

Several major law book publishers have developed highly practice-oriented books that in effect lead attorneys step-by-step through the processes they need to use to deal with pretrial and trial matters. These

---

TERMS

Desk Edition   An abridgement of a large set of reference books.

guides are a hybrid type of treatise. They usually have minimal treatise-type commentary, but they may heavily cross-reference standard treatises (particularly those of the same publisher).

Trial guides are specialized practice guides that focus on helping attorneys prepare for a specific trial. See Figure 12–6 for a complete description of the *Texas Civil Trial Guide*.

Form Books

Form books assist lawyers and legal assistants in drafting legal documents. The term "form books" can be misleading. As used here, it includes treatises and practice guides that have a heavy form-preparation component, usually accompanied by sample documents. In a strict sense, however, form books differ from treatises in that treatises focus on analysis of the law, whereas form books are intended to assist an attorney in generating finished forms appropriate for use in an actual business, litigation, or other law-related setting. In form books, legal analysis is secondary to form preparation. The confusion results from the development by legal publishers in recent years of fairly comprehensive all-purpose "treatises" that not only provide legal analysis but offer all varieties of practical guidance, including form generation. Accordingly, what is said about the use of form books here applies equally to the use of sample forms wherever found.

Form books are a guide and should be used with caution. Form books are often general in nature and do not contain model forms or document segments that address all the specific situations in which clients may be involved. Reliance on form books to the exclusion of everything else could lead to unfortunate results. For example, a form you find in *American Jurisprudence, Legal Forms 2d* may not conform to Texas rules. Preparing a Texas pleading from such a form without modifying it could result in a form that would be insufficient under Texas law and, therefore, wholly incorrect or not acceptable to the court or agency to which it is submitted.

There are several multivolume national form sets that are familiar to most legal professionals. The three that are probably best known and most widely used are *American Jurisprudence, Legal Forms 2d*, published by Lawyers Cooperative Publishing Company; *West's Legal Forms*, published by West Publishing Company; and Rabkin and Johnson, *Current Legal Forms with Tax Analysis*, published by Matthew Bender. There are also a number of subject-specific (but non–state-specific) form books such as *Collier Forms Manual*, a two-volume unit of Matthew Bender's fifteen-volume treatise, *Collier on Bankruptcy*; Melville, *Forms and Agreements on Intellectual Property*; and *Arnold's Modern Real Estate and Mortgage Forms*.

HOW TO USE THE TEXAS CIVIL TRIAL GUIDE

Description of the Trial Guide

The Texas Civil Trial Guide differs from traditional publications in its organization and features. The set contains materials for trial preparation and presentation in four Office Books (Volumes 1–4) and one Trial Book (Volume 5). These materials may be used to plan for trial and may be taken into court for direct use in conducting the voir dire examination of the jury panel, making motions, arguing points, and examining witnesses.

The four Office Books contain comprehensive coverage of issues pertinent to pretrial and trial motions, evidentiary trial objections, foundations for the introduction of evidence, and the jury selection process. It is intended that you copy the Office Book pages you will need, take notes in the convenient wide margins, and place the copied pages behind the appropriate tabs in the Trial Book, the working record of your case.

Volume 1 also contains a three-part Master Checklist that provides information relating to the timeliness of motions, potential problems with the admissibility of particular pieces of evidence, and the requirements for laying a legally sufficient foundation for specific kinds of evidence. The Master Checklist cross-refers to pertinent sections of all four Office Book volumes.

The Trial Book is used to organize your case. It is equipped with tabs behind which you can place material copied from the Office Books or other items essential to the presentation of your case. The Trial Book also has a number of worksheets and checklists useful for trial preparation. These forms should be duplicated and used as needed for each case.

When to Use the Trial Guide

You will generally use the Guide after the pleadings have been filed and discovery has been performed. However, many of the materials can be used in discovery preparation as well.

To begin trial preparation, all case materials should be assembled and placed behind the proper tabs in the Trial Book. The first three features to consult in the Trial Guide are: in the Office Book, the three-part Master Checklist; and, in the Trial Book, the Case Analysis Sheet and the Trial Planning Checklist. The following discussion fo-

FIGURE 12–6   Material from the *Texas Civil Trial Guide*

cuses on how you should use the Office Books and the Trial Book together and describes the features of both.

How to Use the Office Books

The Master Checklist

The first Office Book of the Trial Guide contains a three-part Master Checklist, a quick reference that allows you speedy access to material in the Office Books. The first checklist, Master Checklist A, provides a list of motions that are appropriate to specific stages of trial
proceedings, with cross-references to Trial Guide materials for each
motion.

You should go through Checklist A to find the motions that you
believe you will want to make. You should then turn to the referenced
section in the proper Office Books for a discussion of the law governing the motion and the form in which it should be made. For example, suppose a motion in limine would be appropriate to obtain a preliminary ruling on the admissibility of certain evidence. Checklist A
will identify where in the Office Books you can find this motion covered. You may want to see if there is a sound legal basis for the motion or whether it is an appropriate trial tactic. Alternatively, you
may want to copy the section covering motions in limine, make notes
on the copied pages, and place them in your Trial Book.

Master Checklist B provides a listing of potential problems related
to the introduction of specific kinds of evidence, with cross-references
to related Trial Guide materials. For instance, if you plan to introduce a deed into evidence, you can look down the checklist under the
heading, "DEED" to determine potential objections to the deed. If
one or more objections appear likely, you may then consult the referenced section or sections for the legal and evidentiary issues involved.
If, for example, Best Evidence Rule and hearsay objections seem
likely, go to the appropriate Trial Guide sections, copy any helpful
arguments and examinations, and place them behind the proper tab in
the Trial Book.

Master Checklist C is a list of the foundational requirements for
common kinds of evidence, with cross-references to Trial Guide materials. If, for instance, as in the deed example, above, Best Evidence
Rule and hearsay objections seem likely, you can consult this checklist to quickly ascertain the legally sufficient foundation required for
its admission. You may also take Checklist C along with you to court
to ascertain if your opponent has laid a proper foundation for evidence.

FIGURE 12–6   *(continued)*

Contents of the Office Books

All parts of the Master Checklist cross-refer to sections in the Office Books that give you information for a particular issue. Once you have located the appropriate section in the Office Book, you can expect that Unit to contain one or more of the following features:

1. Legal Background, presenting a brief, concise overview of the issue that gives you a quick understanding of legal requirements.

2. Trialforms and Trialexams, offering invaluable guidance on legally sufficient wording of motions, objections, responses, arguments, and juror and witness examinations. These scripts offer you a quick reference to (a) proper wording of motions, objections, and responses, (b) correct construction and wording of arguments, (c) legally sufficient examinations of witnesses, and (d) questions to elicit desired information from potential jurors.

3. Authority, containing direct quotes of relevant statutes and rules and eliminating the need to carry along the primary source.

4. Case summaries and editorial commentary for the scripted arguments, placing at your fingertips the authority to support the in-court arguments.

5. Practice Points, advising of potential pitfalls, providing tactical suggestions, or advising how to use a particular form. The practice points allow you to be aware of potential problem areas with positions being taken in court. They can also give you information on how to best approach a particular issue. This practice point always starts and stops with a filled in black square, like this ■.

How To Use the Trial Book

The Trial Book contains worksheets and checklists to help you prepare for trial and to conveniently organize trial materials for in-court presentation.

Tabs divide the Trial Book into several useful sections with some special features that you can photocopy and use for all your cases, as follows:

(1) Trial Plan, with a detailed listing of trial preparation steps and a Case Analysis Sheet to outline the proof required;

(2) Legal Research, with a form to record case authorities for key propositions of law;

FIGURE 12–6   *(continued)*

(3) Jury Plan, including a checklist of things to do before the panel appears in the courtroom, a short summary of claims and defenses, and a juror profile form to list desirable and undesirable characteristics of prospective jurors;

(4) Voir Dire Questions, providing a place to file copies of pertinent examinations from the Office Book, a checklist for conducting the voir dire, a checklist for areas of inquiry that should be covered, and a form for recording information about each prospective juror;

(5) Opening Statement (Optional), with a form to outline your opening remarks;

(6) Plaintiff's and Defendant's Exhibits, containing forms to plan the introduction of each exhibit;

(7) Plaintiff's and Defendant's Witnesses, with a general information sheet for each witness, forms to list all witnesses and related exhibits, forms to plan or note both the direct and cross examinations, and additional tabs for individual witnesses behind which you can file specific Trialexams, objections and responses, arguments, deposition summaries, and copies of statements;

(8) Trial Notes, with forms to record information about a witness's testimony, each exhibit offered, and all motions filed, plus a form to plan necessary rebuttal testimony;

(9) Closing Argument, with a form to place notes on critical points;

(10) Jury Instructions, providing a form to list requested questions, definitions, and instructions and record the court's action on each;

PLUS tabs for sections in which to file live pleadings, motions, orders, and trial briefs and to note challenges to prospective jurors.

FIGURE 12–6   *(continued)*

In addition to the national form books, there are many state-specific form books available from a variety of sources. Texas has a number of these, including treatises with a strong forms component, as listed below:

1. Dorsaneo, *Texas Litigation Guide* (Matthew Bender) (nineteen volumes with updates.)

2. Johnson and Dorsaneo, *Texas Civil Trial Guide* (Matthew Bender) (five volumes)

3. Kazen, *Family Law: Texas Practice and Procedure* (Matthew Bender) (six volumes with updates)

4. Kendrick and Kendrick, *Texas Transaction Guide—Legal Forms* (Matthew Bender) (sixteen volumes with updates)

5. *Legal Forms Manual for Real Estate Transactions* (State Bar of Texas) (three volumes)

6. *Legal Forms Manual for Family Law* (State Bar of Texas) (four volumes)

7. *Legal Forms Manual for Collections* (State Bar of Texas) (three volumes)

8. Robertson, *Family Law Trial Guide* (Matthew Bender) (one volume)

9. Robins, *Texas Special Issues Forms* (Butterworth) (one volume)

10. Simkins, *Texas Family Law with Forms* (Lawyers Cooperative) (five volumes)

11. Stayton, *Stayton Texas Forms with Practice Commentaries* (Vernon) (five volumes)

12. Stevenson and Taylor, *Texas Legal Practice Forms* (Callaghan) (four volumes)

13. Teague, *Texas Criminal Practice Guide* (Matthew Bender) (six volumes)

14. *Texas Forms: Legal and Business* (Lawyers Cooperative) (twelve volumes with updates)

15. *Texas Corporations—Law and Practice* (Matthew Bender) (five volumes)

16. *Texas Jurisprudence Pleading and Practice Forms 2d* (Lawyers Cooperative) (thirteen volumes)

17. *Texas Pattern Jury Instructions* (State Bar of Texas) (five volumes)

18. *West's Texas Forms* (West) (nineteen volumes projected)

Although there is an abundance of published form books and other materials with sample or representative forms, the most productive form-finding exercise may be conducted in the files of the firm where you are working. Ask your supervisor or the attorney who assigns a form-drafting project whether the firm has handled similar matters, then find and pull those files and review the forms they contain for guidance. It is possible that your firm may have automated certain types of forms for production. You also can go to a court clerk's office and review forms filed in similar cases, since these are public records. But regardless of your source, never assume that a sample form is particularly good or appropriate for your assignment. Such forms can be helpful and instructive but must be used with caution.

Finding the Right Treatise

Although you should be willing to consult a treatise whenever appropriate, you should do so carefully to ensure that the set or title you use is the best available for your purposes. There are a lot of legal publishers, and the 1980s saw a rapid expansion in the number of legal treatises being published. Some are considered to be standard references that should not be ignored. Some, however, are not highly regarded. All treatises, even if addressing the same topic area, will not offer the same materials. The place to begin is to ask the attorney who has initiated the research project you have been assigned whether he or she can recommend the best treatises, should you need to consult one. The firm librarian or any other legal librarian should be in a good position to steer you to appropriate treatises. You can ask specific questions if you have already identified the major works available by consulting a card catalog or reviewing catalogs of the major legal publishers, which should be available in your firm's offices or in a nearby law library.

§ 12.5   Miscellaneous Legal Research Sources

There are several additional secondary sources that can be of great assistance to legal research. The major ones are restatements of the law, uniform laws, attorney general opinions, legal dictionaries, legal directories, and continuing legal education materials. Each is discussed separately in the following text.

Restatements of the Law

Restatements of the law are scholarly compilations of the common law (the body of law that is made up of court decisions rather than being based on statutes) produced by the American Law Institute (ALI). The *Restatements* give a general overview of generally accepted rules of law. Restatement rules may be adopted independently of one another, with or without modification, by courts on a state-by-state basis. Unless adopted by a state's high court, a Restatement rule is not considered the law of that state. Courts, however, are free to base their decisions on Restatement positions unless to do so would be contrary to an existing state statute.

The *Restatements* have played a major role in the development of the common law in the United States over the past several decades, particularly in such important areas as the imposition of liability in defective products and other personal injury cases. Should a state's high court adopt a Restatement position, that position is thereafter the law of the state until reversed by a subsequent court decision or legislation.

There are various series of the *Restatements*. The first series was prepared and adopted by the ALI between 1923 and 1944 and included the areas of agency, conflicts of laws, contracts, judgments, property, restitution, security, torts, and trusts. With the second series of the *Restatements*, some of the initial volumes were revised (*e.g.,* the torts volume, now *Restatement Torts 2d*), and the scope of the set was expanded to include new subjects such as foreign relations law and landlord-tenant law. The ALI is now releasing a *Restatement 3d* series, beginning with the *Law of Foreign Relations.*

The *Restatements* are organized by chapters and divided into sections. Each chapter represents a major topic withing the field of that Restatement. The sections of each Restatement define a generally accepted proposition of law, referred to as the black letter law. This statement of the law is followed by a commentary concerning the legal principle and its application. A valuable research aid included with each subject area is an index of cases in which pertinent Restatement sections have been cited or discussed. These references to the use of the *Restatements* in court are periodically updated through supplement pamphlets or pocket parts.

Uniform Laws

Because of the disparity among the various jurisdictions on general laws, a commission was formed to provide a guide to basic laws that affect everyone in the United States. This commission is known as the National Conference of Commissioners on Uniform State Laws. Those who participate in the commission develop laws that are presented to the individual state legislators and territories for adoption and approval. The hope of the commission is that a proposed uniform law will be adopted verbatim and in its entirety, but that does not always happen. States are free to adopt all or part of a uniform law and even add their own twist to a law.

The most popular uniform law that has been adopted in whole or in part by every state is the Uniform Commercial Code (U.C.C.), which governs commercial transactions. This code provides for continuity in transactions from sales to secured transactions. Since every state has adopted the U.C.C. in some form, the continuity of commercial law is a plausible goal.

Over 160 uniform laws have been proposed, but not all have been adopted by the states. Uniform laws relating to children have gained wide acceptance, such as the Child Custody Jurisdiction Act and the Regional Enforcement of Child Support Act. Others, such as the Brain Death Act, have not received wide acceptance.

The commission also drafts model acts, such as the Model Penal Code. But the model acts have been received with less enthusiasm, since they are, by their very nature, more state-specific.

The best source for locating the uniform laws and model acts is West's *Uniform Laws Annotated, Master Edition*. This set provides both text and comments of the uniform laws as well as a listing of vehicle states that have adopted the various uniform laws or model acts.

Attorney General Opinions

Legal questions arise about a variety of matters, such as the interpretation of statutes, political occurrences, and how to legally hire and fire state employees. These questions are often posed by the heads of executive departments, agencies, or commissions within state, United States territory or federal governments. The chief legal officer who responds to these questions is the attorney general.

There are two types of attorneys general. The most visible and important legal officer in the United States is the United States Attorney General, appointed by the president and confirmed by the Senate. This Attorney General is the highest law enforcement officer, whose opinion has great weight in rendering answers to questions posed by government officials. Although the Attorney General's legal opinion is not a primary source of authority, it is persuasive when seeking information on sources. All United States Attorney General opinions are compiled in a multivolume set entitled *Opinions of the United States Attorney General*. Most large law libraries have the United States Attorney General's opinions in their collections.

The second type of attorney general is the state attorney general. The fifty states and United States territories have either an elected or appointed attorney general who renders opinions based on questions posed by officials within their respective jurisdictions. Most states collect their attorney general opinions in bound volumes that can be referenced in your research. Remember that attorney general opinions are clearly a secondary source and, more importantly, are only persuasive in the jurisdiction for which they are being used. If you are researching a Texas issue and you locate an attorney general opinion on the issue in a California attorney general opinion, stay away from it. California attorney general opinions have very little weight, if any, in Texas.

Attorney general opinions are not always updated and, worse, are difficult to locate. Although most volumes of attorney general opinions have a general index, the index often is not current. Consequently, the way a paralegal finds an attorney general opinion is often through other sources and, unfortunately, happenstance. If you believe an attorney general opinion may have been rendered by your state attorney general, a simple method of locating such a current interpretation of your issue is to directly contact your attorney general's office by telephone or mail and simply ask whether any opinions have been rendered by the attorney general on that issue. Usually, the staff of the attorney general's office will be happy to send you a copy of the opinions. If this is the route you take, contact the attorney general in your state's capital or one of the satellite offices.

Legal Dictionaries

Legal dictionaries can be valuable resources. Legal terminology can be very precise and, at the same time, very confusing, particularly when different courts use the same words to mean different things. If you are confronted with a word or term that is unfamiliar, you might first consult a legal dictionary in an effort to unravel the mystery. All law dictionaries present a short definition of the word and, in many instances, give variations of how the word is used and treated in a legal context.

The best known and most widely respected (and probably most widely used) legal dictionary is *Black's Law Dictionary* published by West Publishing Company. *Black's Law Dictionary* provides extensive definition and pronunciation guides for the legal professional. There are several other legal dictionaries that you may find useful, including *Ballentine's Law Dictionary* (3d ed. 1969); *Bouvier's Law Dictionary & Concise Encyclopedia* (8th ed. 1984); Gilmer, *Law Dictionary* (6th ed. 1986); and Garner, *Dictionary of Modern Legal Usage* (1987).

A legal dictionary can only facilitate your understanding of words and terms. It does not offer legal analyses, and its definitions are not binding. Courts, however, often cite dictionaries such as *Black's* because many definitions presented are definitions that over time have become established through common usage.

Legal Directories

Law directories are invaluable guides to locating lawyers, courts, and legal support services in various states. The most comprehensive and widely used national directory is the multivolume *Martindale-Hubbell Law Directory*. It is also available as a single CD-ROM disc. This directory lists all lawyers admitted to the bar in all the jurisdictions in the United States. It is updated and republished in its entirety each year. For firms purchasing a full biographical entry, it includes a biographical entry for each lawyer in the firm and lists the specialties and representative clients of the firm.

One of the most important features of *Martindale-Hubbell* is found in the final volume of each annual set—a digest of the statutory laws for all fifty states, Canada, and some foreign countries. This volume gives a general overview of the law from the various jurisdictions and serves as a quick introductory reference guide for any legal professional.

Most states have their own independent law directory. In Texas, this directory is the four-volume *Texas Legal Directory*, more commonly known as the *Texas Blue Book*. This directory is invaluable. It includes a listing of all lawyers in Texas, as well as a listing of all state and federal courts, with their addresses and telephone numbers. In addition, this directory lists all state agencies in Austin and their branches throughout the state.

Another directory that identifies all Texas state agencies is the *Handbook of Government in Texas*. This directory contains extensive discussion of the agencies and their organizations and functions. A similar directory of state agencies is the *Texas State Directory*, which also lists county and city government officials. Also of interest to legal professionals is a directory of Texas banks, the *Texas Banking Redbook*. This directory contains useful information about Texas banks, ranging from assets and liabilities to names of officers and directors.

Continuing Legal Education Handbooks

The law is dynamic, not only in terms of the sheer volume of case law and statutory developments but also in terms of new technologies and other societal reorderings that require a legal framework. As a matter of professionalism, lawyers and legal assistants should keep up-to-date on new developments in the law. Many state bar licensing agencies have institutionalized this need through mandatory continuing legal education (CLE) programs that require licensed professionals to attend a certain number of hours of seminars or other approved program instruction annually or over a specified number of years.

Continuing legal education seminars and symposiums are offered by a variety of providers, including established organizations such as the American Bar Association, state bar associations, the American Law Institute, the Practicing Law Institute, and law schools. Each program or provider must be approved for CLE credit in advance by the agency that oversees the state's CLE system. Apart from possibly attending one of these programs, a legal researcher might benefit from reviewing the materials that are prepared and distributed at a program of interest. Often, these handbooks or other compilations are extensive and contain well-researched and well-written overviews, analyses, and practice materials prepared by the lawyers and legal professionals who make up the faculty for the program.

Texas offers a variety of CLE seminar and symposium handbooks that contain a wealth of information for the legal practitioner. These handbooks often prove to be a practical starting point for research. Since Texas lawyers now are required to attend annually a minimum of fifteen hours of continuing legal education, the legal subjects addressed each year are extensive. When attendance at a continuing legal education seminar or symposium is impossible, you can order most handbooks through the Texas Bar Association. Some of the titles currently available are listed below.

Advanced Administrative Law (October 1990) (one volume)

Advanced Civil Trial (September 1990) (four volumes)

Advanced Family Law (August 1990) (four volumes) ·

Alternative Dispute Resolution (September 1990) (one volume)

Discovery (January 1991) (one volume)

Family Law: The Team Approach for the Legal Assistant and the Lawyer (May 1990) (one volume)

Legal Aspects of the Music Industry (March 1991) (one volume)

Marriage Dissolution (May 1990) (two volumes)

Practicing Sports Law in Texas (October 1990) (one volume)

Trial and Tactics (April 1991) (one volume)

In addition, law schools have active CLE programs that publish their course materials. Audio-and videotapes of many CLE programs in Texas are available. You should check with various program sponsors for lists of materials available for distribution.

§ 12.6 Checklists

A hard-and-fast guide for the general sources would be difficult to compile. But the following checklist provides some general reminders when using some of the miscellaneous sources cited in this chapter.

Often in the law, persons disagree about the definition of a word. Attorneys can resort to a law dictionary, but that may not be sufficient. Courts are asked to define words, terms, and legal phrases when a dispute arises about their meanings. A secondary source that provides case law for defining legal terms is *Words and Phrases*. A West publication, *Words and Phrases* provides thousands of "judicial definitions" from judicial decisions that have defined words and phrases over the years. The words and phrases are arranged alphabetically and contain the verbatim definition supplied by a court. For example, suppose that the parties in a lawsuit disagree about the meaning of the word *nightclub*. "Does it necessarily include the serving of food or liquor?" If the definition is in dispute, try using *Words and Phrases* for a guide in locating a definition.

Remember, however, the words defined are from courts all around the country. Be careful because the words and phrases defined may not be from your jurisdiction and may not be how your judge will define the word. If the word or phrase is not from your jurisdiction, it is only persuasive authority for your jurisdiction.

Looseleaf Series

1. Always consult the "How to Use This Book" at the beginning of each set.
2. Locate the index for the volume of the set you intend to use.
3. Determine whether the series you are using has page inserts or pamphlet updates.
4. Find the most current update for your series.

Legal Periodicals

1. Write down words and phrases that pertain to your topic.
2. Locate a copy of a legal periodical index that is organized by subject matter and author.
3. Look up your words and phrases in the index.
4. Write down the referenced law review, magazine, journal, or legal newspaper citation.
5. Retrieve the cited sources from the stacks in the law library.

Legal Treatises

1. Go to a card or computer catalog in the law library to locate specific legal treatises.
2. Write down the call number and locate the book or volume set on the library shelves.
3. Use the general index to locate the topic.

4. Review the section in the main volume.

5. Write down any noteworthy cases cited in the text or footnotes.

6. Shepardize all the cases for current status and cases from your jurisdiction.

7. If using a West or LCP publication, look for coordinate reference systems.

8. If using a form book, copy the desired form. Remember, if it is a general form, check any local laws for variations in the form.

Restatements

1. Locate a copy of the *Restatements of the Law* through the card or computer catalog.

2. Write down the call number.

3. Check the general index for the specific topic.

4. Write down the sections of the Restatement.

5. Review the Restatement section and the corresponding comments.

6. Determine whether your jurisdiction has adopted the Restatement by case law or statute by consulting the Restatement in the courts.

Attorney General Opinions

1. Determine whether your topic is federal or state.

2. Locate the collection of attorney general opinions in your library.

3. Review the attorney general opinions to determine if any are relevant.

4. Contact the state attorney general's office for advice on whether an attorney general opinion exists on your issue.

Uniform Laws and Model Acts

1. Consult West's *Uniform Laws Annotated, Master Edition*.

2. Review the text and comments of the section consulted.

3. Determine whether your state has adopted, in whole or in part, the uniform law or model act.

Summary

12.1 Introduction

In addition to primary sources and finding materials, there are other sources of research material, including looseleaf services, periodicals, treatises, and dictionaries, to name a few.

12.2 Looseleaf Reporter Services

Looseleaf services are generally published in a notebook-style format by Commerce Clearing House, the Bureau of National Affairs, and Prentice Hall, the leading publishers. Looseleaf services provide the most current law and court opinions. Each looseleaf service has its own format, and therefore, the "How to Use This Book" section should be consulted before using any series.

12.3 Legal Periodicals

Legal periodicals include law reviews, journals, magazines, and legal newspapers. There are also special interest group publications such as the *Women's Lawyers' Journal*. Consult a guide to legal periodicals to locate general journals or publications.

12.4 Legal Treatises

Legal treatises are books that detail the law relating to a specific subject. Treatises vary in depth and quality. Treatises are updated by either supplements or releases. Student treatises, usually used in law school, are called "hornbooks" and are usually one comprehensive volume. Other legal-type treatises are practice guides and form books. Form books offer guides to drafting legal documents and are often state-specific.

12.5 Miscellaneous Legal Research Sources

There are a number of additional sources, such as the *Restatements* and uniform laws. Both these sources set forth general principles of the law. Legal dictionaries help define legal terminology, with *Black's* and *Ballentine's* as the most notable legal dictionaries. Attorney general opinions also can be an invaluable source of law for guidance of legal issues and questions in individual states and the federal government. Other legal sources are directories and continuing legal education handbooks.

12.6   Checklists

Words and Phrases is another secondary source. This source provides reference to thousands of judicial definitions from judicial opinions that have defined words and phrases. The volumes are arranged alphabetically for easy access and are updated by annual pocket parts.

Review Questions

1. What are the three main looseleaf service publishers? Identify some of the features found in their books.

2. What is a law review?

3. What is the best known bar journal?

4. In what source can all legal periodicals be found?

5. Define a legal treatise.

6. What are hornbooks?

7. What are form books?

8. Distinguish between the *Restatements of the Law* and the uniform laws.

9. Identify the two most widely used law dictionaries.

10. What is the purpose of *Words and Phrases*?

Exercises

1. Using a guide to legal periodicals, answer the following:
    a. You are researching an article on termination of parental rights, and you want to read an article from the child's perspective. What recent article from the *Cornell Law Review* addresses this?
    b. Is there a Minnesota article on this same topic?

2. Using a guide to legal periodicals, answer the following:
    a. You are researching the consequences of same sex marriages, and you have heard about an article but know only the author's name, James Trosino. Find the article.
    b. What law journal contains this article?

3. You have found an article listed in an index to legal periodicals but do not understand the abbreviations. Using the abbreviations table, identify the following:
    a. Arb. J.
    b. Loy. L.A. Ent. L.J.

   c. Tex. B.J.
   d. SW. L. J.

4. Locate *The Law of Torts*, by Prosser and Keeton, and answer the following:

    a. What section defines negligence? Gross negligence?
    b. What sections discuss strict liability in torts?

5. Using *Corbin on Contracts*, answer the following:

    a. What section defines an offer?
    b. What are the library references for section 1.11?

6. Find the *Texas Litigation Guide*, and answer the following:

    a. In what chapter can a suit on a sworn account be found?
    b. What Texas Rule of Civil Procedure deals with sworn accounts?
    c. Under what section can an example of an original petition for a sworn account be found?

7. Find the *Texas Transaction Guide*, and answer the following:

    a. In what chapter can mechanics' liens be found?
    b. What section deals with perfecting a lien for the original contractor?
    c. In which section do the forms for mechanics' liens begin?

8. Find the *Restatement (Second) of Contracts*, and answer the following:

    a. What section of the Restatement deals with supplying an omitted essential term?
    b. On what page does the comment of this section begin?
    c. Under the "Reporter's Note" of this section, what law review article is cited?

9. Find copies of *Black's Law Dictionary* (6th ed. 1990) and *Ballentine's Law Dictionary*.

    a. What is the definition of *defamation*?
    b. Is it exactly the same in both dictionaries?

10. Locate a copy of *Martindale-Hubbell's Law Directory*.

    a. What law firm in Kilgore, Texas, does work in the area of oil and gas?
    b. Locate the law firm of Jackson and Walker, LLP, in Houston. How many other offices does it have?
    c. Does the Jackson and Walker firm practice in tax law?

CHAPTER 13

LEGAL RESEARCH BY COMPUTER

§ 13.1 Introduction to Computer-Assisted Legal Research

Overview

The cost and space requirements for maintaining a complete law library are enormous. Few law firms today can afford the luxury of maintaining a comprehensive collection of reporters, statutes, encyclopedias, periodicals, looseleaf services, treatises, and law reviews. The computer addresses the concerns of both cost and space. It stores a massive quantity of material without tying up expensive office space. The task of rapidly sorting and retrieving a large amount of research can normally be accomplished using a computer at less cost than the investment in a complete law library, when one includes, in addition to the staffing requirements, billing time for attorneys and legal assistants to perform manual research through several hundred volumes.

Assume that a computer search may be executed in a matter of minutes for approximately $80. Assume also that the same search performed by a legal assistant requires two hours in the typical law books. The legal assistant's billing rate is $75 an hour. The savings to the client from the use of the computer for research is $70.

In earlier chapters, the manual research process was examined. This "yellow pad" method consists of identifying a research issue, determining sources that may contain the answer, and locating the pertinent cases or statutes. The computer performs the same function through a process known as **CALR**, computer-assisted legal research, which uses special software programs to search the full text of cases, statutes, and other legal sources.

The purpose of this chapter is not to make you proficient in CALR. The range of services that are available and the involved technical search details that are needed to access and manipulate the various databases as thoroughly as possible would require volumes of materials to present. In fact, should you decide to explore CALR, you will find that each major service has available extensive reference manuals; in addition, most periodically issue newsletter-type updates that detail new services (which are frequently added to the major databases) and address specific search issues that have been raised by users as ones needing more clarification than already appears in the manuals. In addition, the major services provide

---

■■■■■■■■■■■■■ **TERMS** ■■■■■■■■■■■■■

CALR Computer-assisted legal research in which special software programs are used to search the full text of cases, statutes, and other legal sources.

excellent toll-free telephone assistance to users, including help in formulating specific search inquiries.

The intent of this chapter is simply to introduce you to the major legal databases that are available and give you a basic idea of how they are structured and used. CALR is becoming an increasingly important tool for the researcher. You need to understand in broad terms what it is and how it works.

The two major computer-assisted legal research services are LEXIS and WESTLAW. These services are **on-line**, meaning the information in each service is stored in a database at a remote location. The database is accessed by a telecommunications system consisting of a telephone line, special telecommunications software, and a **modem**, which is a device used to convert digital impulses from the computer to analog impulses for transmission by the telephone line. Information from the database is viewed on a **terminal** or computer screen at the law firm, law library, or any other location that has computer availability.

Advantages of Computer-Assisted Legal Research

Computer-assisted legal research offers five major advantages over using traditional bound volumes:

1. *Timeliness.* Computer-assisted legal research services generally place information on-line before it appears in printed format because the information can be instantly transmitted by the computer while the printed format requires additional preparation and mailing time by a publisher.

2. *Speed.* A search on CALR is much faster than manual research. Because of the speed, CALR research may be more cost-effective than standard research. It is also time-effective because you always have access to everything in the database. There is no waiting for another user to return the volume you need to the library or waiting for a volume through inter-library loan.

3. *Completeness.* Computer-assisted legal research permits virtually instant access to a multitude of legal research source materials. Most law

---

TERMS

on-line The accessing of information stored in a computerized legal research database at a remote location by use of a telecommunications system.

modem A device used to convert digital impulses from a computer to analog impulses for transmission by telephone line.

terminal A computer with a screen on which information retrieved from a computerized legal research database can be viewed.

libraries, particularly those in law firms or those maintained by local bar associations, do not have comparably extensive collections of printed volumes.

4. *Flexibility.* Computer-assisted legal research permits searches of entire libraries of materials (for example, all volumes of West regional reporters) simultaneously or searches of limited segments of a library, depending on your research needs. Similarly, as described later in this chapter, CALR allows either the broadest of searches in terms of topic (for example, all state cases dealing with the responsibility of social hosts for injuries caused by drunken guests at the party or later) or the narrowest of searches (for example, Nevada Supreme Court cases since January 1991 discussing the same issue in terms of the host's knowledge that the guest was drunk).

5. *Convenience.* Only CALR offers the convenience of performing thorough research at home, the client's office, or other locations away from the law library.

6. *Full-text searching.* Computer-assisted legal research allows you to make full-text searches of all cases or other sources contained in the files you want to review. This means that each word or item in the selected files is reviewed electronically to identify every appearance of the search request you have entered. This allows you to structure requests that need not correspond, for example, to the words and phrases used by a publishing company in labeling annotations prepared for digests. Full-text search capability is a tremendous advantage of CALR.

Disadvantages of Computer-Assisted Legal Research

Computer-assisted legal research is not without its problems. The major flaw is that the computer is literal. A computer recognizes only words, not ideas or concepts. Synonyms create a difficulty for the computer. You realize that house, home, and apartment have the same or similar meanings in a legal sense, but the computer does not.

Also, the English language is imprecise. A computer does not recognize the differences between different meanings of the same word. For example, the computer does not understand that *duck* may be either a bird or the act of bending to avoid hitting an object.

Computer-assisted legal research offers no "prompt" such as cross-references or possible synonyms and antonyms to suggest alternative words or terms as do traditional research sources.

Cost may be another disadvantage of CALR. Not all research applications lend themselves to the computer. Researching a very broad legal concept, for example, may be both difficult and costly. The costs associated with CALR vary, depending on the type and length of the search and the databases searched. Both of the major CALR services, LEXIS and WEST-LAW, publish price lists that should be consulted prior to beginning a complicated search on the computer.

§ 13.2 WESTLAW

Introduction

WESTLAW was developed and marketed by West Publishing Company in the late 1970s. This service is patterned after the West manual research system. The West topic and key number system on WESTLAW permits the research to be focused and facilitates the retrieval of relevant cases that do not comply exactly with the original search terms.

When WESTLAW was first introduced, it contained only headnotes and case synopses. Within a short time, the full text of cases was included.

All information available in WESTLAW is divided into five "databases":

General Materials

Topical Materials

Texts and Periodicals

Citators

Specialized Materials

These databases are further subdivided into "files."

WESTLAW may be combined with the West **CD-ROM** Libraries, which are specialized libraries on compact discs, and standard West legal publications for complete, coordinated research.

Slip opinions, discussed later in this chapter, are placed on-line immediately upon their receipt by West. Since slip opinions are added before they go through the West editorial process, they do not have the West synopsis, key number, or headnote features. These features are added

---

TERMS

WESTLAW   A computerized legal research system, developed and marketed by West Publishing Company, that is patterned after the West manual research system.

CD-ROM   A system in which a read only memory compact disc, which stores large amounts of information, can provide access through a computer modem and terminal to mini-libraries for purposes of legal research.

several weeks later as West editors complete their reviews and preparation of each opinion for inclusion in the National Reporter System.

The Search Process

Formulating the Query

Assume that you have been asked to research case law in a case in which an infant in a car seat became entangled in the belt restraints and was killed. The plaintiff alleges that the firm's client, the manufacturer of the car seat, is liable for the death because of a defect in the car seat construction.

A basic understanding of computer research concepts and terminology is necessary before beginning the research process. An initial decision is how to structure the search to retrieve the right response from the computer. Once the search has been defined, you must then address where the cases or statutes on point for the research are most likely to be found.

A **search query** is a search for a particular word, series of words, or concept that appears in the question you are researching. The first step in developing a search query is to write out the question being researched or to identify the key words in the question and prompt the computer to search for these key phrases by using custom software designed to retrieve pertinent cases or statutes. This search query should be carefully drafted *before* accessing the computer to reduce the cost of the search.

Once the question to be researched has been phrased, target the important terms in the question. For example, in the case involving the infant car seat death, you might ask this question: Was the manufacturer liable for the death of the infant in the defective infant car seat? Determine which terms within the question are important. Remember that the critical part of the question may be a "concept" or "theory" instead of an actual word. In this example, the important words, terms, phrases, or concepts would be "manufacturer," "liability," "death," "infant," "defective," and "car seat."

TERMS

---

search query   A particular word or series of words that represent a concept being researched on a computerized database.

Search Words or Terms

A **word** is either a single character or a group of characters with a space on both sides. For example:

7:00   A   search   C.F.R.   F.B.I.

Certain types of words, such as plurals/singulars, possessives, and possessive plurals, call for special search techniques. When a singular form of a word is entered, WESTLAW automatically retrieves the plural of words that are pluralized by adding "s" or "es" or by changing "y" to "ies." WESTLAW also automatically retrieves irregular plural forms. When the regular plural form of a word is entered, however, WESTLAW does not automatically locate the singular. WESTLAW retrieves singular and plural possessive forms with the entry of a singular form, but only the plural possessive form when a plural form is entered.

Root Expansion   **Root expansion** is a method used to search for different words that share the same root without having to type each of those words again. WESTLAW utilizes two root expansion symbols, an exclamation mark (!) and an asterisk (*). The root expansion symbol lessens the variations of word searches entered separately, reduces the cost of the search, and increases the likelihood that all possible forms of a word will be retrieved.

An exclamation mark at the end of a root word instructs the computer to search for all words that begin with that root. For example: "instruc!" retrieves "instruction," "instructed," "instructor," "instructing," "instructional," and "instructive." The asterisk substitutes for a character within a word or at the end of a root word. Placing two asterisks in a word indicates two missing characters. In such a case, the search request will not find a word with three character variations. For example, "instruct**" retrieves "instructed" but not "instruction."

Neither the asterisk nor the exclamation mark may be used at the beginning of a word.

Remember that searching on WESTLAW is literal. The use of synonyms, antonyms, and other alternative terms increases the success ratio in searches.

TERMS

word   As used in reference to a computerized database, a single character or group of characters with a space on both sides.

root expansion   A method used in computer-assisted legal research to search for different words that share the same root without having to type each of those words again.

WESTLAW publishes a table called "Automatic Equivalencies." Entry of a word with an equivalent automatically retrieves the equivalent.

Alternatives WESTLAW has developed a system to retrieve other forms of initials automatically when a series of initials with periods but no spaces is entered. For example, [f.t.c.] would retrieve "F.T.C.," "F. T. C.," "FTC," and "F T C." WESTLAW will not retrieve documents containing the full form of the abbreviation, "Federal Trade Commission."

In some cases, a term may be written as one word, a hyphenated word, or multiple words. WESTLAW retrieves all three forms only when the hyphenated form is entered. For example, the entry of "first-born" retrieves "firstborn" and "first born."

A phrase sometimes represents a single concept, for example, "agent orange." WESTLAW requires the use of quotation marks around such a phrase before the system will look for the words as a single phrase and not retrieve documents that contain either word only in separate form.

Connectors Assume that you have selected the important words in the search query for the car seat case to locate pertinent state court cases. Before beginning the actual search, several words should be connected to avoid numerous time-consuming, expensive searches. **Connectors**, words that connect words and phrases for search purposes, include such words as "or," "and," "but not," and "w/n."

The connector "or" locates documents in which either one or both linked words or phrases appear, such as "death or casualty." This search tool is valuable for synonyms, antonyms, and alternative spellings of a word, for example, "house or home or residence or apartment." A space between words may be used instead of the word "or" on WESTLAW.

The "and" connector instructs the computer to retrieve a document only if it contains all words joined by "and." Plurals and possessives will automatically be retrieved. WESTLAW permits the substitution of the "&" symbol in lieu of writing out the word.

The "but not" connector may be used to exclude a document if it contains a designated term. WESTLAW uses either "but not" or the "%" symbol, for example, "belt but not seat belt" or "belt % seat belt."

WESTLAW permits the user to stipulate that search terms appear within a specified number of terms of each other (1 to 255 words) by using "w/n." The "n" represents the desired number which you insert in the "n"

TERMS

connectors Words used in computer-assisted legal research that will connect words and phrases for search purposes; for example, "or," "and," "but not," and "w/n."

position, for example, "infant w/10 car seat." WESTLAW offers the option of typing only "/" followed by the desired number, for example, "infant/10 car seat." If you want the term on the left of the connector to precede the term on the right, the "+n" connector must be used. The "+s" connector may be used to further require that the term to the left of the connector precede the term to the right with a sentence. This is particularly useful in names and volume/page number searches. For example: "John +s Anding" requires that the name "John Anding" must appear in that order within the same sentence.

Often it is difficult to determine how close to one another the designated search words will appear. Selecting the appropriate number designator, therefore, is difficult. If the number is too restrictive, important documents may be missed. An overly broad number may retrieve several hundred irrelevant documents.

Because the connectors do not differentiate sentences and paragraphs, the connectors may retrieve documents in which the terms are several sentences or paragraphs apart and have no relationship. WESTLAW permits you to require that the terms appear in the same sentence by using "/s," for example, "infant /s death," or in the same paragraph by using "/p," for example, "infant /p death."

Sequence of Connectors The table in Figure 13–1 is a summary of connectors for WESTLAW searches. The order in which the computer searches the connectors has an impact on the search results. WESTLAW searches should be conducted in this manner:

1. Phrases
2. "or"
3. "pre/n"
4. "w/n"
5. "+s"
6. "/s"
7. "/p"
8. "and"
9. "but not"

Accessing WESTLAW

WESTLAW may be accessed by using a WALT II custom terminal or a personal computer or terminal, using West's telecommunications software and network. EZ ACCESS, a new menu-driven option from West, enables researchers with no computer experience to research quickly and accurately by simply typing "ez" and the citation to be researched.

FIGURE 13–1
WESTLAW
connectors

Description	Connector
Search terms—alternatives	or *or* space
Within the same sentence	/s
Within the same paragraph	/p
Within the same document	and *or* &
Within the same sentence—term on left must precede term on right	+s
Terms must appear within a specified number of each other	wn/ *or* /n
Terms must appear within a specified number of each other and the term on left must precede the term on right	pre/n *or* +n
Exclude terms following the connector	but not *or* %
Phrase search	"agent orange"

Signing onto WESTLAW

The initial procedures for signing onto WESTLAW may vary, depending on the type of computer. However, the steps are generally as follows:

1. Select the WESTLAW option from the general menu.
2. Type your assigned password and press Enter. For security purposes, your password will not be displayed on the computer screen. If you accidentally enter your password incorrectly, you will receive a message to re-enter the correct password.
3. Read the "Welcome to WESTLAW" screen for information about recent changes in WESTLAW.
4. Transmit your client identification number.
5. Begin the research process.

Selecting the Database

An important decision early in your computer research is which database you should search. The research strategy is the same as that utilized in traditional research. For example, is the issue a federal or state issue? Does the research question involve judicial decisions or statute interpretation? WESTLAW's database directory is user-friendly. However, if you encounter problems with determining the appropriate database in which to begin your search, WESTLAW technical assistance is available at 1-800-WESTLAW.

Entering a Query

WESTLAW offers two options when entering a query: (1) "AGE"—documents retrieved by your search are arranged in a rank format by "age" with the most recent documents first, or (2) by the documents containing the largest number of search terms. You have the option to receive prompts relating to the ranking of documents as you enter a query and perform research. If you do not make such a determination, the standard option (NOPROMPTS) will apply. Documents will be ranked by age, and no extra prompts will appear.

Once you have typed your search query and verified that it is typed correctly, press Enter. A prompt will appear, stating that the search is proceeding.

Modifying the Search

The results of your search query will be displayed on the screen. The search will yield no documents or a certain number of documents. A "no documents" response may be more beneficial than a search that results in 1,112 documents.

If your search query retrieves a large number of cases, you might limit your search through the selection of a different database, by narrowing your search terms, or by using restrictive connectors. In the event that your search produces a small number of documents, you might reverse this strategy and search a broader database or more databases, add other search terms, or increase your use of connectors.

You might determine that your search query is poorly constructed and decide to modify the query itself. A query edit is simple. To edit your query, type "q" and press Enter to display your new search results.

If you decide that editing a query is not enough, you can choose to enter a new search by typing "s" and hitting Enter. Although you have structured a new search, you have not changed databases.

Field Searches

Another means of modifying a search is the use of a "field search." WESTLAW fields include:

1. *Title*. If you already know the title (or style) of a case, search only the title field:

   a.   Enter the name of at least one of the parties. It is not necessary to enter all of the parties' names.

   b.   Use a portion of a name, rather than the entire name.

c. Avoid retrieving the wrong case in the event the party's name is a common name by combining the title and subject fields in the search.

2. *Citation.* Use the citation of a case, if known.

3. *Court.* This field is used to restrict a search to a particular court or courts within a database. Assume that your query relates to an interpretation of a Texas statute by Texas state courts. Begin your search by entering the word "court" followed, without a space, by parentheses containing the postal abbreviation for Texas. Select the district court database (db dct).

4. *Date.* Use of this field generally limits the search results. You might restrict the query to a year (1996), a month and year (February 1996), or a certain day (February 14, 1996). In addition, you have the option of limiting a search to cases decided before, after, or between a certain time period. WESTLAW accepts the entry of a date in virtually any format. For example:

date (1996) & search terms

date (February 1996) & search terms

date (February 14, 1996) & search terms

date (after 2/14/96) & search terms

date (>2/14/96) & search terms

date (<2-14-96) & search terms

5. *Judge.* The judge field is the appropriate field to use when you want to know if a particular judge has written a majority opinion on your research topic. Suppose your query relates to prison reform in Texas. Use this field to find out whether federal Judge William Wayne Justice has written a majority opinion on this topic.

6. *Synopsis.* The results of your search for cases relating to prison reform in Texas will likely be voluminous. The synopsis field can limit your results to only the cases with search terms related to certain issues.

7. *Topic.* You can use a WESTLAW topic number or name in a search. Information to formulate a topic record is available on the directory screen or in the WESTLAW reference manual.

8. *Headnote/Digest.* The WESTLAW digest field contains the title, citation, court, topic, and text of headnotes. This field prevents the retrieval of an otherwise unmanageable number of cases.

9. *Opinion.* The value of this field is its ability to determine cases where a certain attorney has appeared as counsel. If your employer, a Texas computer manufacturing company, has asked that you investigate a

list of attorneys who have experience in trademark litigation, you could use the opinion field to determine if the attorneys' names have previously appeared in a number of opinions relating to trademark litigation.

Displaying the Search Results

At the top of each retrieval, a line containing the citation to your document, the page of the document that you are reviewing, the total number of pages in the document, the database accessed, and the search mode you are currently using will appear. There are two search modes: term mode and page mode. In term mode, you will browse only those pages containing your search terms. Page mode permits browsing your entire document, one page at a time. A page mode display, however, will include pages that do not contain your search terms.

Next Document

When you have completed your review of a document, you can move to another document on the search results screen by entering "r" and the rank number of the document or by simply typing that rank number.

Locate

This feature of WESTLAW enables a researcher to quickly review documents for a specific word or terms, including words and terms not found in the initial query. Type "locate," "loc," or "l," followed by a space and the search term. In the locate mode, the term to be located is highlighted, but the original query terms are not. Remember that your request to locate must occur at the beginning of the documents to be searched. If you are reviewing a document ranked tenth, return to the first ranked document before entering the locate command.

Shepard's

Shepard's citations on WESTLAW consist of the full range of case citators for federal and state court cases. Shepard's statutory citators are not available on-line.

You may access Shepard's at any time from any database by typing "SH" and pressing Enter, then entering the citation of the case to be Shepardized in the following order: volume, reporter series, and page. Remember to use the appropriate Shepard's abbreviations for the reporter or other publications. If you are uncertain about the abbreviation, type "pubs" and press Enter for a directory of publication abbreviations.

To limit the number of cases retrieved, use "loc" in combination with a restricting word, such as "hist" (history) or "tr" (treatment). Use a state's postal abbreviation to restrict your results to a particular state.

Shepard's on-line version on WESTLAW is easier to read and understand than the manual citators because it combines the information from the hardbound volumes and the supplements. Not as many Shepard's volumes need to be searched on-line as must be researched manually. Also, with Shepard's on-line, the search can be limited to citing cases that discuss a particular headnote issue. This feature reduces irrelevant case retrieval and requires less search time.

West Publishing Company and Shepard's/McGraw-Hill, Inc., have recently developed an important enhancement to the Shepard's on-line service. Known as Shepard's PreView, this enhancement gives citing information much earlier than was previously possible with Shepard's citations on WESTLAW, which had been timed closely to the release of the advance sheets to Shepard's in printed form. This enhancement is unique to WESTLAW.

INSTA-CITE

INSTA-CITE serves a different purpose from Shepard's on-line. It is limited to the case cited and the verification that the case is still good law. INSTA-CITE does not cite every case that refers to the case, as Shepard's does. In addition to its primary purpose of providing prior and subsequent case history, however, INSTA-CITE also offers an easy means for finding parallel citations, which are added as they become available.

Information available on INSTA-CITE includes:

1. Case name
2. Official and parallel citations
3. Court issuing decision
4. Filing date
5. Docket number
6. Format (memorandum or table)
7. History of a case

Federal and state court case histories are available from 1938 to the present, and the overruling history of a case is available from 1972 to the present. WESTLAW's electronic citator normally contains direct case history for a case within five days of receipt of the case.

West has also added references to *Corpus Juris Secundum*, the West legal encyclopedia discussed in Chapter 8, to the INSTA-CITE service.

INSTA-CITE may be accessed in one of the following methods:

1. Type "ic" and press Enter when viewing or Shepardizing a case.
2. Type "ic," followed by a space and the case citation.
3. Access the INSTA-CITE database and type the case citation.

Star Paging

An opinion in an official reporter (for example, the *United States Reports*, or *U.S.*) will be repeated verbatim in an unofficial reporter but not necessarily on the same page. To ensure that accurate official reporter page references can be obtained when using an unofficial reporter, the unofficial reporters make use of star paging. This is a notation system using an asterisk or a star along with a page number, usually in bold print, that refers to the page number of the same case in an official reporter. (See Chapter 4 for a more detailed discussion of star paging.) Using this feature on WESTLAW, you may go directly to a particular page of text without additional charge. Figure 13–2 is an example of a star-paging screen.

WIN

Comptuer expertise is not a prerequisite for using WESTLAW. WIN (WESTLAW Is Natural) permits a user to enter a search query in plain English and does not require the use of root expanders or connectors. For example, if you were researching the issue relating to negligence and the three-year-old child discussed in Chapter 6, your query would be: "Is a three-year-old liable for his or her negligence?" Follow these steps to research this negligence issue:

1. Access the appropriate database for Texas cases.
2. Type the query as drafted above and press Enter.
3. Review WESTLAW's display of the twenty documents most responsive to the query.
4. Browse the twenty documents by selecting a command from the following choices:
   a.   Best (highest rated portion of each of the twenty documents)
   b.   Nxt (next document in the search)
   c.   T (five highest rated portions of each document)
   d.   p (next page)
   e.   p- (previous page)
   f.   r (next ranked document)
   g.   L (list of all documents)

```
┌─────────────────────────────────────────────────────────────┐
│  ╭──────────────────────────────────────────────────────────╮ │
│  │          COPR. (C) WEST 1989 NO CLAIM TO ORIG. U.S. GOVT. WORKS │
│  │ 633 F.Supp. 257                    P 16 OF 28    DCT      P │
│  │ (Cite as: 633 F.Supp. 257, *259)                           │
│  │   On January 13, 1986, Wanner filed his Petition for Writ of habeas corpus in │
│  │ the above-entitled action in Federal District Court alleging seven │
│  │ grounds.  ...                                              │
│  │   Respondent's Brief in Support of Return to Petition for Writ of Habeas Corpus │
│  │ 2-4.  This statement represents a fair rendering of the procedural background │
│  │ of this case.                                              │
│  │                         Decision                           │
│  │   Exhaustion of State Remedies                             │
│  │   The State argues that Mr. Wanner's petition should be dismissed because he has │
│  │ not exhausted his available state remedies.  Specifically, the State asserts │
│  │ that Mr. Wanner, to the best of anyone's knowledge, has never appealed his │
│  │ conviction under the Post-Conviction Relief Act, N.D.C.C. ch. 29-32.1.  Section │
│  │ 29-32.1-01 provides, in pertinent part:                    │
│  │   1. A person who has been convicted of and sentenced for a crime may institute │
│  │ a proceeding applying for relief under this chapter under the ground that: │
│  │   *260 a. The conviction was obtained or the sentence was imposed in │
│  │ violation of the laws or the Constitution of the United States or of the laws │
│  │ or Constitution of North Dakota.                           │
│  │   ....                                                     │
│  │   e. Evidence, not previously presented and heard, exists requiring vacation of │
│  │ the conviction or sentence in the interest of justice;     │
│  ╰──────────────────────────────────────────────────────────╯ │
└─────────────────────────────────────────────────────────────┘
```

FIGURE 13–2   Example of a star-paging screen

5. Modify your search, if necessary, by typing "q" and pressing Enter.

It is possible to select WIN as your default search method through the WESTLAW Options Directory ("OPT") in the event you would like to primarily search in WIN. You can also change the number of documents to be retrieved from the initial setting of twenty documents, up to a maximum of one hundred documents, through the "OPT" directory.

Find

WESTLAW offers a fast, easy retrieval method through its "Find" feature. Enter "fi" and a citation from any point in any database to quickly locate a case.

WESTLAW Assistance

Technical assistance is available by calling WESTLAW at 1-800-937-8529, Monday through Friday from 7:00 A.M. to midnight, Saturday from

8:00 A.M. to 6:00 P.M., and Sunday from 10:00 A.M. to 6:00 P.M. (Central time). For assistance in formulating or executing search queries, call 1-800-REF-ATTY.

§ 13.3   LEXIS

Introduction

LEXIS, the first CALR service, was introduced by the Ohio State Bar in 1967. Mead Data Central marketed this "experiment" in 1973. Effective in 1995, LEXIS became a division of Reed Elsevier, Inc. According to LEXIS, its service is the "world's largest full-text database." One factor that may contribute to the size of LEXIS is the decision to report all available cases without any editorial determination of whether a case merits publication. Annotations in *A.L.R.* are also available on LEXIS, with some 13,000 *A.L.R.* topics indexed and analyzed on-line. Through designating the files you want to search, you can include or exclude the *A.L.R.* materials, as appropriate.

The Search Process

Formatting the Query

The process for formulating a query on LEXIS is identical to that described earlier for WESTLAW. However, database construction differences require some modification in the query.

Plurals and possessives are handled differently on LEXIS in some instances than on WESTLAW. LEXIS retrieves words that are pluralized by adding "s" or by changing a "y" to "ies." However, to retrieve the irregular plural of a singular word, it is necessary to enter both the singular and plural terms or use universal characters to retrieve both forms. When the regular plural form of a word is entered, LEXIS automatically locates the singular. LEXIS also automatically retrieves the singular and plural possessive forms when either the singular or plural form of a word with a regular plural is entered.

───────────■ **TERMS** ■───────────

LEXIS   The first computer-assisted legal research service, introduced by the Ohio State Bar and marketed by Mead Data Central; it contains all available cases, *A.L.R.* annotations, and other features.

Connectors

The theory of connections in a search query is quite similar to that described in the discussion of WESTLAW techniques.

Root Expansion

LEXIS utilizes the same two root expansion symbols as WESTLAW: the exclamation mark and the asterisk.

Alternatives

Because LEXIS, like WESTLAW, performs literal searches, it is necessary to consider word or term variations. The LEXIS reference manual lists equivalent terms for such terms as "F.C.C.," days of the week, months, and states. Thus, LEXIS will retrieve a document containing "FCC," even though you enter "F.C.C." A hyphen is treated as a space. For example, "post-trial" retrieves "posttrial" or "Post trial." Formulate your query to search for the term as one word or two. Otherwise, you will miss many pertinent documents.

Segment Searches

One extremely important feature of LEXIS is the ability it gives you to search selected files by "segments." Segment searches permit you to limit your search, for example, to locating decisions by specific judges, courts, or time periods.

LEXIS segments include the following:

1. *Name.* Only one party's name is required to retrieve the correct case.
2. *Citation.* The citation will retrieve a case when the correct citation is known.
3. *Court.* This retrieves a case from a particular court or courts.
4. *Written by.* A case with a decision written by a particular judge is retrieved.
5. *Date.* Documents retrieved are restricted to a particular time period.

Accessing LEXIS

A computer novice should have no difficulty accessing and searching on LEXIS. No special search language or complicated computer commands are required. An on-screen menu provides clear guidance through the simple research process.

Initial access to LEXIS on a dedicated system (a system on which only LEXIS can be used) consists of these steps:

1. Press the On/Off key on the computer terminal. Wait 30 seconds for the message that LEXIS is available until 2:00 a.m.
2. Type the personal 7-character LEXIS number that you are assigned through the firm and press TRANSMIT or ENTER.
3. Transmit research or client identifier.
4. Transmit your library (e.g., GENFED) and appropriate file (e.g., U.S.) requests.
5. Transmit search request.
6. Display search results using LEXIS' five specially programmed keys:

    a. FULL – retrieves the full text of the search results in reverse chronological order, with the higher court listed before the lower court cases. Use of the NEXT PAGE key in conjunction with a number permits the researcher to move to other pages in the case

    b. KWIC – or key word in context key displays 25 words on either side of the highlighted search word or terms

    c. VAR KWIC – or variable key word in context displays 50 words on either side of the highlighted search word or terms

    d. CITE – displays only the citation for the search results

    e. SEGMTS – restricts the search results displayed to a particular section of the decision, such as a particular court or judge

The dedicated LEXIS terminal contains programmed function keys. Using the personal computer, a series of **dot commands**, a dot or period followed by initials are used to indicate the action which the computer should perform. For example, ".np" accesses the next page of a document. Figure 13–3 is a chart of dot commands for use with LEXIS.

Changing Libraries

Assume that you are in the middle of researching the issue of whether your client's former employees may sue for overtime once they have signed a settlement with the Department of Labor that includes a waiver of all right to pursue litigation in the future. Your attorney calls and asks that you research whether there are federal cases involving this issue. To

---

TERMS

---

dot commands A dot, or period, followed by initials; used in LEXIS research to indicate the action the computer should perform.

FIGURE 13–3
LEXIS dot
commands

LEXIS DOT COMMANDS

Command	Results
.np	Next page
.pp	Previous page
.fp	First page
.nd	Next document
.pd	Previous document
.fd	First document
.ns	New search
.cf	Change file
.cl	Change library
.ss	Select service
.es	Exit service
.kw	KWIC
.vk	Variable KWIC
.fu	Full
.se	Segment
.dl	Display different level
.so	Sign off
.ke	Keep search in log
.log	Display search log
.sp	Print screen
.pr	Print document
.pa	Print all documents
.ci	CITE list
.fo	FOCUS
.ef	Exit FOCUS
.fr	FREESTYLE
.bool	Standard boolean search

access federal cases, you must leave the states library, where you have been researching Texas case law, and go to the library for federal cases. To begin this new assignment, access the federal library (gen fed) by hitting the Transmit key.

Changing Files

Your attorney has added a second step to your assignment relating to the issue of whether an employee can sue for overtime after a settlement has been entered into with the Department of Labor. He has asked that you determine how other states have treated the issue. Using the same query, press the CHG File key. Although you remain in the states library, you can access other state files. Type "la, ark" and press the Transmit key to begin your research for Texas's neighboring states.

Modifying the Search

An innovation found only on LEXIS is the ability to modify a search by adding up to 255 levels of research while saving the results of earlier searches. To modify a search to search level 2, type "m" and press Transmit. Your first query remains in search level 1. Type your modification and press Transmit. A connector word such as "and" is necessary to link the two levels. Place the cursor at the end of your modification before pressing the Transmit key.

Printing

Figure 13–4 describes the printing process and options for LEXIS.

Storing Results

Imagine that you have spent an hour on LEXIS, researching an extremely complicated issue. Your attorney telephones you in the law library to ask for your assistance in obtaining records on another case from the courthouse. You do not want to lose your research. How can you save the previous results? Simply type ".ke" to keep the search in a log. Later that afternoon when you access the LEXIS terminal again, you can display the stored search log by typing ".log." Once you are certain that you have completed a research assignment, type ".delall" to delete the contents of your log.

Shepard's

Approximately eight hundred divisions of Shepard's citations service, discussed in Chapter 11, are available on-line with LEXIS.

Once the relevant cases have been located, you may wish to Shepardize them on LEXIS. After exiting the library in which the cases are located, SHEPARD'S may be accessed by transmitting "sh" followed by the citation, or by typing the citation and then pressing the SHEP key on the computer.

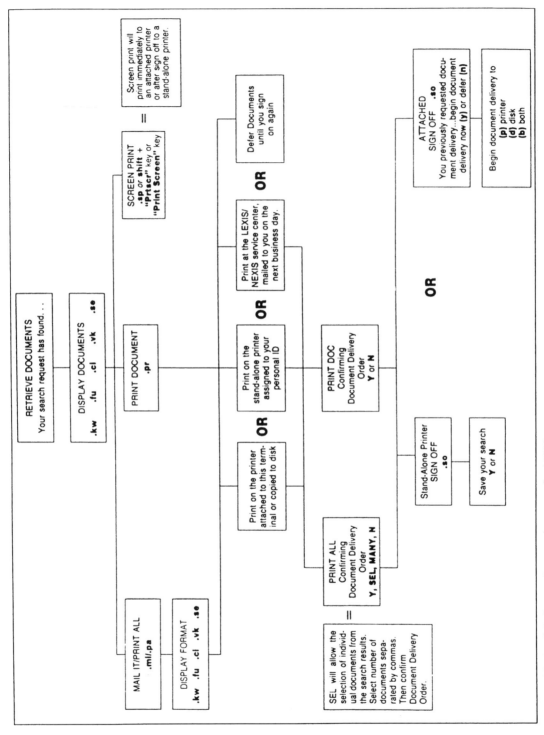

FIGURE 13–4 Printing options and process for LEXIS

Figure 13–5 reflects the Shepard's information available on LEXIS, including parallel citations, references to citing cases, and an "editorial analysis."

AUTO-CITE

A second cite checking feature of LEXIS is AUTO-CITE, which contains in excess of four and one-half million federal and state case law citations from over three hundred reporters. AUTO-CITE retrieves the following information:

1. Parties' names
2. Official or parallel citations
3. Validity of the case
4. Prior history
5. Subsequent history
6. ALR annotations discussing the case

The abbreviations in AUTO-CITE are similar to those in the bound volumes of Shepard's citators.

AUTO-CITE can be accessed at any point in the research by either transmitting "ac" followed by the citation or by typing the citation and then pressing the AUTO-CITE key.

Figure 13–6 is an example of the first screen of a citation on AUTO-CITE.

Special Features of LEXIS

In addition to the basic research and cite checking functions of LEXIS, several special features are available, including the following.

LEXSEE

Once you determine the citation of a case, administrative decision, law review article, *A.L.R.* annotation, or other document in the LEXIS database, you may transmit "LEXSEE" followed by the citation or type the citation and press the LEXSEE key to immediately view the full text of that particular item.

Shepard's citation format
The format for requesting Shepard's is:

volume	*reporter*	*page number*
738	f2d	1249

Note that it is not necessary to include spaces or punctuation in the reporter abbreviation, but there must be a space between the volume number and the reporter and the reporter and the page number. "Page number" refers to the page upon which the case begins. Do not include paragraph numbers or editorial designations in your search. (After you have completed your search, you can limit the display of citing references to those with a particular paragraph, history or treatment).

(c) 1987 McGraw-Hill, Inc.—DOCUMENT 1 (OF 3)

CITATIONS TO: 738 F.2d 1249
SERIES: SHEPARD'S FEDERAL CITATIONS
DIVISION: FEDERAL REPORTER, 2d SERIES
COVERAGE: Shepard's 1969-1985 Supplements Through 01/87 Supplement.

NUMBER	ANALYSIS	CITING REFERENCE	PARA	NOTES
1	parallel citation	(238 App.D.C. 103)		
2	US cert den	105 S.Ct. 2357		
3	same case	508 F.Supp. 690		
4		92 L.Ed.2d 372	64	
5		106 S.Ct. 3037	64	
6		54 U.S.L.W 4992		
7		U.S. Dkt.No. 84-1656 Cir. D.C.		
8	distinguished	747 F.2d 1473		
9	dissenting opinion	747 F.2d 1487		
10		748 F.2d 706		

to see the text of a citing case, press the citing reference NUMBER and then the TRANSMIT key.
for further explanation, press the H key (for HELP) and then the TRANSMIT key.

FIGURE 13–5   Shepard's information available on LEXIS

Auto-Cite Service, Copyright (c) 1987, VERACORP:

66 LED2D 621:

United States v Cortez*1 (1981) 449 US 411, 66 L Ed 2d 621, 101 S Ct 690, on remand United States v Cortez (1981, CA9 Ariz) 653 F2d 1253, cert den Cortez v United States (1982) 455 US 923, 71 L Ed 2d 464, 102 S Ct 1281, reh den Cortez v United States (1982) 455 US 1008, 71 L Ed 2d 877, 102 S Ct 1648 and (disagreed with by multiple cases as stated in United States v Magana (1986, CA9 Or) 797 F2d 777)

PRIOR HISTORY:

United States v Cortez (1979, CA9 Ariz) 595 F2d 505, revd (BY CITATION YOU ENTERED)

CITATION YOU ENTERED MAKES NEGATIVE REFERENCE TO

Gray v United States (1972, Dist Col App) 292 A2d 153
State v Ochoa (1976) 112 Ariz 582, 544 P2d 1097

AUTO-CITE information continues, press the NEXT PAGE key.
To return to LEXIS, press the EXIT SERV key.

FIGURE 13–6 The first screen of a citation in AUTO-CITE

LEXSTAT

A similar feature is LEXSTAT, which allows you to go directly to the text of a statutory section by transmitting "LEXSTAT" followed by the citation.

ECLIPSE

Research results are not static. New court decisions constantly alter case law. A case may be modified or overruled. ECLIPSE, an Electronic Clipping Service, allows the computer to monitor LEXIS for new information related to the search. LEXIS automatically forwards the reports to the law firm daily, weekly, or monthly, as requested. For example, in the car seat case, the legal assistant might request that ECLIPSE monitor all Texas cases involving a child's death in a car seat. LEXIS would automatically send updates.

LEXIS recently added valuable Texas-specific material to its services, including:

Texas Administrative Code

The Texas Register

Texas regulation tracking

Texas statutes and codes

Texas bill tracking

Texas Advance Legislative Service

Texas Constitution and court rules

FREESTYLE

LEXIS offers a computer novice the option of searching in plain English through the use of FREESTYLE. Follow these steps to utilize FREESTYLE:

1. Select a library.
2. Select a file.
3. Type ".fr" after a message appears to type your request.
4. Enter your search description in plain English.
5. Use the Search Options screen to confirm your search and make adjustments to your original search. You will be directed on how to make revisions.
6. Once your revisions to the request are complete, move your cursor to the end of the search description and press Enter.
7. Select an option from the search results screen to view your results.

FREESTYLE recognizes common phrases automatically. You should place a phrase within quotation marks to make certain that two or more words are retrieved only if they are linked together as a phrase.

Another feature of FREESTYLE is the mandatory terms option. Use this option only when you want a word or term to appear in every document retrieved.

Hot Topics Library

The Hot Topics (HOTTOP) Library includes topic summaries in such practice areas as international law, taxation, utilities, and medical and health law. Use this library to research major trends in pending federal or state legislation.

The Easy Search Library

Easy Search (EASY) uses information you supply in response to preset questions to select the appropriate library and file, and then constructs and runs your search.

The LEXIS-NEXIS Legal Toolbox

LEXIS has developed specialized software to permit the litigation paralegal and attorney to work faster and with greater accuracy. Software currently available includes:

1. CheckCite: This software locates and verifies the accuracy and standing of all citations and quotations in a document. Through a useful report feature, errors and negative treatment of a case are highlighted.

2. CiteRite II: Every citation in a document is automatically located and checked against *The Bluebook* or the *California Style Manual*. You are notified of errors through a simple error message.

3. CompareRite: Through the use of this software package, you can produce a document with additions and deletions appearing side by side. Another useful feature is the list of revisions created.

4. FullAuthority: FullAuthority automatically locates all citations in a brief or legal memorandum, alphabetizes the citations, and sorts the citations by source (cases, statutes, books, and law review articles) to create a complete table of authorities. With FullAuthority, you can be confident that minor errors, such as abbreviations, punctuation, and underlining, will be corrected.

5. Case Pull: Assume that your update of research on the infant car seat case has yielded four recent cases on the issue of negligence by a manufacturer. With Case Pull, you have immediate access to a printed copy of those cases without leaving the LEXIS terminal.

6. LEXIS Counsel Connect: An electronic mail and conferencing network enables law firms, government agencies, and corporate legal departments to combine their expertise to resolve a myriad of legal issues. In addition, this feature acts as a gateway for accessing LEXIS-NEXIS services.

Shepard's Overnight Citations

This new product, offered only by LEXIS, is initially available only for California and Texas. Each night, Shepard's is updated to include all new history information and treatment analysis.

Search Costs

LEXIS and WESTLAW rates are structured quite differently and are difficult to compare. LEXIS charges for each search or citation entered, with no additional charge for level searches. WESTLAW charges strictly by the time used. Thus, the research project may dictate which service is more economical.

While cost is obviously a factor in selecting the computer research service, it should not be the controlling factor. Timeliness, accuracy, and completeness of the particular database to be searched also must be factored into the selection process.

LEXIS Assistance

Technical assistance is available from LEXIS by calling 1-800-433-8416 at any time except between the hours of 2:00 A.M. and 10:00 A.M. (EST) on Sunday.

§ 13.4 Computer-Assisted Legal Research Database Structure

Information in the CALR database is organized into federal and state **libraries**, which are all materials on a particular subject area, and **files**, which are separate groups of related documents that are searchable as a group on LEXIS and as a database on WESTLAW. There is no difference in the database and library/file organization except for the titles. Knowledge of the CALR organization is necessary for successful computer research.

LEXIS and WESTLAW are full-text retrieval systems. Every word of cases, statutes, administrative decisions, rules, and other legal documents is assigned an "address" or location in the database and subsequently forms a concordance, which is an index of every word, number, or symbol in a document.

Libraries are made up of files, which are documents that are searchable as a group. Figure 13–7 shows a library-selection screen.

TERMS

libraries As used in reference to computerized legal research databases, groupings of all materials into particular subject areas; both federal and state libraries are available.

files As used in reference to computerized legal research databases, separate groups of related documents that can be searched as groups on LEXIS or as databases on WESTLAW.

```
                        LIBRARIES -- PAGE 1 of 3
Please ENTER the NAME (only one) of the library you want to search.
- For more information about a library, ENTER its page (PG) number.
- To see a list of additional libraries, press the NEXT PAGE key.
 NAME    PG NAME    PG NAME    PG NAME    PG NAME    PG NAME    PG NAME    PG

   -------General Legal-------- --Public Records--- --Helps-- Financial --Nexis-
 MEGA     1 2NDARY   6 LAWREV   6 ALLREC   5 INCORP   6 EASY     1 COMPNY 17 NEWS   14
 GENFED   1 ALR      6 MARHUB   6 ASSETS   6 LEXDOC   9 GUIDE   13 NAARS  12 REGNWS 14
 STATES   1 BNA      6 LEXREF   6 DOCKET   6 LIENS    6 PRACT   13 QUOTE  17 TOPNWS 14
 CODES    1 ABA      6 HOTTOP   1 FINDER   9 VERDCT   9 TERMS   13            LEGNEW 15
 CITES    6 CAREER   6 CLE      5 INSOLV   5            CATLOG  13            CMPGN  15
 LEGIS    1 CUSTOM   9 MODEL    5                                            WORLD  18


   ------------------------------Area of Law---------------------------- Medical
 ACCTG   12 EMPLOY   2 FEDCOM   3 INSURE   3 MEDMAL   3 PRLIAB   4 TAXANA   6 GENMED 16
 ADMRTY   2 ENERGY   2 FEDSEC   3 INTLAW   3 MILTRY   4 PUBCON   4 TAXRIA   6 EMBASE 16
 BANKNG   2 ENVIRN   2 FEDSEN   3 ITRADE   3 MSTORT   5 PUBHW    4 TRADE    5 MEDLNE 16
 BKRTCY   2 ESTATE   2 FEDTAX   3 LABOR    3 PATENT   4 REALTY   4 TRANS    5
 COPYRT   2 ETHICS   2 HEALTH   3 LEXPAT   3 PENBEN   4 STSEC    4 TRDMRK   5
 CORP     2 FAMILY   2 IMMIG    3 M&A      4            STTAX    4 UCC      5

Enter .NP for Individual States, International Law and more News information
```

```
                        LIBRARIES -- PAGE 2 of 3
Please ENTER the NAME (only one) of the library you want to search.
- For more information about a library, ENTER its page (PG) number.
- To see a list of additional libraries, press the NEXT PAGE or PREV PAGE key.
 NAME    PG NAME    PG NAME    PG NAME    PG NAME    PG NAME    PG NAME    PG

   ---------Individual States-----------   -----Int'l Law----- ------News--------

 ALA      7 IND      7 NEV      8 SD       8 AUST    10 MEXICO 18 APOLIT 12 EXEC   15
 ALAS     7 IOWA     7 NH       8 TENN     8 CANADA  18 NILAW  10 BUSFIN 14 INVEST 17
 ARIZ     7 KAN      7 NJ       8 TEX      8 COMCAS  10 NZ     10 BUSREF 14 MARKET 15
 ARK      7 KY       7 NM       8 UTAH     8 ENGGEN  10 SAFRCA 12 CMPCOM 14 PEOPLE 15
 CAL      7 LA       7 NY       8 VT       9 EURCOM  10 SCOT   10 ENTERT 14 SPORTS 14
 COLO     7 MAINE    7 NC       8 VA       9 HKCHNA  12 SING   12
 CONN     7 MD       7 ND       8 VI       9 IRELND  10 UKJNL  10
 DEL      7 MASS     7 OHIO     8 WASH     9 MALAY   12 UKTAX  10   ----Int'l News---
 DC       7 MICH     7 OKLA     8 WVA      9            UK     10 ASIAPC 18 MDEAFR 18
 FLA      7 MINN     7 ORE      8 WISC     9                      DUTCH  18 NSAMER 18
 GA       7 MISS     8 PA       8 WYO      9  -French Language- EUROPE 18 TXTLNE 18
 HAW      7 MO       8 PR       8                INTNAT  11 PRIVE  11 GERMAN 10
 IDA      7 MONT     8 RI       8              LOIREG  11 PUBLIC 11
 ILL      7 NEB      8 SC       8              PRESSE  11 REVUES 11            PROFIL 18
```

FIGURE 13–7 Sample library-selection screen

§ 13.5   Governmental Databases

Three databases have been developed for use by the federal government.

JURIS is a Department of Justice database for the exclusive use of federal attorneys. The following partial list of the database contents is indicative of the specialized needs of that agency: recent lower federal court cases; United States Supreme Court cases from 1900; United States Codes; current uncodified public law; West's *Federal Digest*; and decisions from the Court of Military Review.

Searches on JURIS can be performed by an index search that is restricted to a search of West's headnotes or full-text searching. This database bears many similarities to WESTLAW and LEXIS, including a concordance method of indexing each word and the method of formulating a search query.

FLITE is a system that permits departments and agencies of the federal government to mail a search request to the database computer. Attorneys perform the requested search and mail the results. This system lacks the interactive ability of databases such as WESTLAW and LEXIS. It is not possible to change the search query based on initial results. Additional research time is also required by the use of the mail for sending a request and receiving the research results.

In addition to accessing the federal cases and codes on the JURIS database, FLITE accesses Lockheed's DIALOG databases, which are discussed in Chapter 14. This service also contains the following specialty research sources:

1. *Military Justice Reporter*
2. *Court Martial Reports*
3. Labor law database
4. Tax library
5. Federal administrative, management, and procurement information

The RIRA database is utilized exclusively by the IRS. Its contents incorporate both federal and tax court cases, regulations, and rulings of the IRS.

§ 13.6   Tracking Legislation by Computer

The computer facilitates the difficult and often lengthy process of tracking a particular bill through the state or federal legislative systems.

Many corporate clients are impacted by major legislation, such as the Clean Water Act, and must be aware of any legislative changes. With a computerized tracking system, an attorney or paralegal can remain current at all times on a bill of interest to the firm's clients.

The major national database system covering all state legislatures and Congress is the Electronic Legislative Search System (ELSS) produced by Commerce Clearing House. The ELSS services are aimed primarily at the legal profession. The charge is on the basis of use after the payment of an initial registration fee based on the number of subjects and jurisdictions to be utilized. The services are available by telecommunication and are compatible with most word processors and microcomputers.

The most important database service focused exclusively on federal law is LEGI-SLATE, which is a product of Legi-Slate, Inc. It offers on-line, the afternoon of each day they are released, the full texts of the *Congressional Record* and the *Federal Register*. Full texts of bills are available the day they are received from the Government Printing Office, as are congressional committee reports. LEGI-SLATE also provides the full text of each day's articles in *The Electronic Washington Post*, indexing and text of articles in the *National Journal*, indexing of articles in the *Congressional Quarterly Weekly Report*, schedules of congressional committee meetings, and transcripts of press briefings and congressional hearings.

LEGI-SLATE has recently added two new services to facilitate federal statutory research. The Daily CFR service updates the *C.F.R.* each day, incorporating final rules and regulations announced in the previous day's *Federal Register*. The Current USC service updates the *United States Code* every time a new law is enacted and assigned a specific location in *U.S.C.* by the Congressional Law Revision Counsel.

Numerous state governments and the federal government maintain legislative databases for legislative tracking and statutory searches. LEGIS is the federal government's comprehensive legislative database. An example of a comparable state database is the LRS (Legislative Retrieval System) maintained by the State of New York Legislative Bill Drafting Commission. This database contains complete texts of all codes, rules, and regulations of the state of New York, which includes all state agencies.

Another important statutory database is the State Net Legislative and Regulatory Service (State Net), a service of Information for Public Affairs, Inc. This service is accessed through a WESTLAW gateway (a means of using WESTLAW to connect into third-party on-line services). It is a comprehensive service that provides state and federal legislative and administrative information. It is the only on-line service that covers proposed regulations for all fifty states.

13.7 Research by CD-ROM

The introduction of the CD-ROM, a read only memory compact disc, revolutionized legal research. With a CD-ROM drive, a computer modem, and a terminal with 640K storage capacity, the researcher can access mini-libraries on a particular subject through a single compact disc. Each compact disc can contain between 150,000 and 300,000 pages of printed text. Companies that offer CD-ROM libraries or services provide updates every few weeks or months, at which time the obsolete CD-ROM is discarded.

The CD-ROM became a viable option for legal research in the late 1980s. Publications available on CD-ROM are quickly being added by traditional law book publishers. For a complete listing of publications available on CD-ROM, contact your area representative for that publisher. The following is a partial listing of CD-ROMs available at the end of 1995 from West Publishing Company:

1. Bankruptcy Library
2. Federal Civil Practice Library
3. Federal Tax Library
4. *United States Code Annotated*
5. West's *Code of Federal Regulations*

West's Texas-specific CD-ROMs include:

1. Texas Cases
2. *Vernon's Texas Statutes and Codes Annotated*
3. West's *Texas Digest* CD-ROM Edition
4. *Texas Administrative Code*
5. Texas Practice Guides on CD-ROM
6. West's Fifth Circuit Reporter
7. West's Federal District Court Reporter—Fifth Circuit

Figure 13–8 shows guides for using West's CD-ROM libraries for research in Texas statutes, codes, and cases.

Lawyers Cooperative Publishing Company had the following CD-ROM available at the end of 1995: Law Desk, Federal Court Rules.

Matthew Bender & Company's "Search Master" CD-ROM series includes the following:

1. Collier Bankruptcy
2. Intellectual Property
3. Business Law

TEXAS ADMINISTRATIVE CODE™

When You Know the Citation [1]

1. From the Library, select the **Texas Administrative Code** book and choose **Search Book**.
2. At the Search Book - Fields Template dialog box, press **Tab** to reach the *Citation* text box and type the title number and section number.[2]

   For example, to retrieve Tex. Admin. Code title 4, § 3.5, type
   4 3.5
3. Choose **OK**.

When You Know the Name [1]

1. From the Library, select the **Texas Administrative Code** book and choose **Search Book**.
2. At the Search Book - Fields Template dialog box, press **Tab** to reach the *Headings* text box and type significant terms from the code's name.

   For example, to retrieve sections dealing with election procedures under the Boll Weevil Eradication Program, type
   election & boll weevil
3. Choose **OK**.

When You Know the Title and Part [1]

1. From the Library, select the **Texas Administrative Code** book and choose **Search Book**.
2. At the Search Book - Fields Template dialog box, press **Tab** to reach the *Prelim* text box and type the title and part numbers.[2]

   For example, to retrieve Title 4, Part I, type
   "title 4" "part I"
3. Choose **OK**.

When You Have an Issue [1]

1. From the Library, select the **Texas Administrative Code** book and choose **Search Book**.
2. At the Search Book - Fields Template dialog box, type a query in the *All Fields* text box using key terms, root expanders, universal characters and connectors.

   For example, to retrieve administrative code sections that deal with the tabulation of votes in an election, under the Boll Weevil Eradication Program, type
   tabulat! vot! or ballot & boll weevil
3. Choose **OK**.

[1] These queries use the default /p connector between terms unless you specify another connector.

[2] This search can also be restricted to the headings field.

Using Field Restrictions

The following fields are available in the Texas Administrative Code book. By restricting your search to the appropriate field, you limit your search to the portion of an administrative code with the most pertinent information; the entire document, however, is retrieved for viewing.

Field	Abbrev.	Description
Headings	he	Citation, prelim and caption fields
Citation	ci	Unique references for citing specific documents
Prelim	pr	Headings preceding caption
Caption	ca	Section name and number
Text	te	Text of document
Credit	cr	Authority and source of the section
References	re	Cross-references and miscellaneous references

Citation — 4 TAC Sec. 3.5 AGRICULTURE

Headings
Prelim —
OFFICIAL TEXAS ADMINISTRATIVE CODE
TITLE 4. AGRICULTURE
PART I. TEXAS DEPARTMENT OF AGRICULTURE
CHAPTER 3. BOLL WEEVIL ERADICATION PROGRAM
SUBCHAPTER A. ELECTION PROCEDURES

Caption — Sec. 3.5. Canvassing of Ballots

Text —
(a) Ballots in all board elections and referenda will be counted at the headquarters of the foundation by a canvassing committee consisting of a representative of the county judge's office from the county in which the ballots are counted by the committee, a representative of the Texas Agricultural Extension Service, a representative of the foundation, and a representative of the Texas Department of Agriculture.

(b) In all elections, results will be certified by the canvassing committee and submitted to the commissioner of agriculture for verification.

(c) Votes will be tabulated and recorded by zone, with the following tabulations recorded for each zone:
(1) total number of valid votes;
(2) total voting for proposition;
(3) total voting against proposition;
(4) percentage voting for proposition;
(5) total cotton acreage in the zone;
(6) total cotton acreage voting for proposition;
(7) total cotton acreage voting against the proposition;
(8) percentage of cotton acreage voting for the proposition; and
(9) if applicable, total votes for each board candidate.

(d) Upon completion of canvassing of the ballots, the ballots shall be stored at the department's offices located in Austin for a period of 30 days. Thereafter, the ballots shall be destroyed.

Credit —
Authority: The provisions of this Subchapter A issued under the Texas Agriculture Code, Sec. 74.114.

Source: The provisions of this Sec. 3.5 adopted to be effective August 9, 1993, 18 TexReg 4949; amended to be effective December 31, 1993, 18 TexReg 9754.

References —
Cross References: This Section cited in 4 TAC Sec. 3.3, (relating to Conduct of Elections; Notice).

West Documentation. Printed in September 1994. For additional copies, ask for Pub. # 13669. This replaces the version of # 13669 printed in August 1994.

© 1994 WEST PUBLISHING CORPORATION 4-9331-7/9-94

For assistance with research questions, call the West Reference Attorneys at 1-800-62-CDROM (1-800-622-3766).

FIGURE 13–8 Guides for using West's CD-ROM libraries

For technical assistance, call West Customer Service at 1-800-888-9907.
For research assistance, call the West Reference Attorneys at 1-800-62CDROM (1-800-622-3766).

QuickScan
ON
Vernon's®
TEXAS STATUTES AND CODES UNANNOTATED™

RETRIEVING A STATUTE OR RULE

When You Know the CITATION*
1. From the Library, select the **Texas Statutes and Codes Unannotated** or **Texas Court Rules** book and choose **Search Book**.
2. At the Search Book - Fields Template dialog box, enter a query restricted to the citation field.†

   Press **Tab** to reach the *Citation* text box and type the citation, e.g.,

   To retrieve Article 1.07 of the Insurance Code in the Texas Statutes and Codes Unannotated book, type

   ins 1.07

   To retrieve Rule 10 of the Texas Rules of Civil Procedure in the Texas Court Rules book, type

   rcp 10

   Do not include a subsection with a section or rule number.
3. Choose **OK**.

   The first page of the statute or rule is displayed.

   Note: See the Code and Rule Abbreviation card for additional abbreviations.

* These queries use the default. /p connector between terms unless you specify another connector.

When You Know the NAME*
1. From the Library, select the **Texas Statutes and Codes Unannotated** or **Texas Court Rules** book and choose **Search Book**.
2. At the Search Book - Fields Template dialog box, enter a query restricted to the headings field.

   Press **Tab** to reach the *Headings* text box and type significant terms from the name, e.g.,

   To retrieve the article of the Insurance Code regarding the Workers' Compensation Commission, type

   Insurance & worker compensation commission
3. Choose **OK**.

   The first page of the statute or rule is displayed, and your search terms are highlighted.

When You Know the TITLE, CHAPTER or SUBCHAPTER*
1. From the Library, select the **Texas Statutes and Codes Unannotated** or **Texas Court Rules** book and choose **Search Book**.
2. At the Search Book - Fields Template dialog box, enter a query restricted to the prelim field.†

   Press **Tab** to reach the *Prelim* text box and type the code name and title or chapter number, e.g.,

   To retrieve Chapter One of the Insurance Code in the Texas Statutes and Codes book, type

   "insurance code" "chapter 1"
3. Choose **OK**.

   The first page in that chapter is displayed, and your search terms are highlighted.

   Note: This type of search may retrieve several documents. See the PREMISE® QuickScan mat for more information about browsing search results.

When You Know the SESSION LAW That Created, Amended or Revised the Statute*
1. From the Library, select the **Texas Statutes and Codes Unannotated** or **Texas Court Rules** book and choose **Search Book**.
2. At the Search Book - Fields Template dialog box, enter a query restricted to the credit field.

   Press **Tab** to reach the *Credit* text box and type the session law numbers, e.g.,

   To retrieve statutes in the Texas Statutes and Codes book amended by chapter 499, section 2 of the Acts of 1957, type

   499 2 1957
3. Choose **OK**.

   The first page of the first document that satisfies your query is displayed. Your search terms are highlighted in each document.

When You Have an ISSUE
1. From the Library, select the **Texas Statutes and Codes Unannotated** or **Texas Court Rules** book and choose **Search Book**.
2. At the Search Book - Fields Template dialog box, enter a query using key terms, root expanders, universal characters and connectors.

   For example, in the Texas Statutes and Codes book, press **Tab** to reach the *All Fields* text box and type a query, e.g.,

   insur! /p unfair or deceptive /s trade /s practice

   or

   unemploy! /s compensat! or benefit /p base-period
3. Choose **OK**.

   The first page of the first document that satisfies your query is displayed. Your search terms are highlighted in each document.

Using the INDEX*
1. From the Library, select the **Index** book and choose **Search Book**.
2. At the Search Book - Fields Template dialog box, enter a query restricted to the citation field.

   Press **Tab** to reach the *Citation* text box and type significant terms from the subject name, e.g.,

   To retrieve the index entry for Limitation of Actions, type

   limitation action
3. Choose **OK**.

   The first page of the index for that subject is displayed.

Updating Your Research
Use session laws to update your statutes research.

NOTE

To display the Search Book - Fields Template dialog box, choose **Fields Template** in the Search Book - Terms and Connectors dialog box.

To display the Search Book - Terms and Connectors dialog box, choose **Term Search** in the Search Book - Fields Template dialog box.

Some of the features described in this QuickScan mat may be set differently in your software. Refer to the "Changing Workstation Preferences" section in your user manual for information about changing your settings.

† This search also can be restricted to the headings field (he).

FIGURE 13-8 (continued)

For technical assistance, call West Customer Service at 1-800-888-9907.
For research assistance, call the West Reference Attorneys at 1-800-62-CDROM (1-800-622-3766).

QuickScan
ON TEXAS CASES™

RETRIEVING CASE LAW

When You Know the South Western Reporter®, 2d CITATION

1. From the Library, select the appropriate book and choose **Retrieve Document**.
2. Type the citation, e.g.,
172 texcrim 303

   Note: Using spaces and periods when typing the citation is optional.
3. Choose **OK**.
4. Move to the next search term to see your citation. You can now jump directly to the case.

   Note: Refer to your user manual or your PREMISE QuickScan mat for more information about moving to the next search term and jumping to the case's full text.

When You Know the Parallel CITATION

1. From the Library, highlight the **Texas Table of Cases** book and choose **Retrieve Document**.
2. Type the citation, e.g.,
772 sw2d 470

   Note: Using spaces and periods when typing the citation is optional.
3. Choose **OK**. The first page of the case is displayed.

When You Know the Party NAMES*

1. From the Library, select the **Texas Table of Cases** book and choose **Search Book**.
2. At the Search Book-Fields Template dialog box, you can enter a query that searches for a title. Press **Tab** to reach the *Title* text box and type significant terms from the party names, e.g.,

   To retrieve *Byler v. Garcia*, type
byler garcia
3. Choose **OK**.
4. Move to the next search term to see your case. You can now jump directly to the case.

   Note: Refer to your user manual or your PREMISE QuickScan mat for more information about moving to the next search term and jumping to the case's full text.

NOTE

To display the Search Book-Fields Template dialog box, choose **Fields Template** in the Search Book-Terms and Connectors dialog box.

To display the Search Book-Terms and Connectors dialog box, choose **Term Search** in the Search Book-Fields Template dialog box.

Some of the features described in this QuickScan mat may be set differently in your software. Refer to the "Changing Workstation Preferences" section in your user manual for information about changing your settings.

When You Know the TOPIC and KEY Numbers

1. From the Library, select the appropriate book and choose **Search Book**.
2. At the Search Book-Fields Template dialog box, you can retrieve all cases containing headnotes classified under a specific topic and key number. Type the topic and key number in the *All Fields* text box, e.g.,

   343k426
   Topic Number 343 – Sales,
   Key Number 426 – Provisions of contract as to remedy
   (Use the letter *k* between the topic and key numbers.)

   110k1120!
   Topic Number 110 – Criminal Law,
   Key Number 1120 – Admissibility of Evidence
   (Use the exclamation point (!) to retrieve all subsections of the key number.)

   You can also retrieve all cases classified under a particular topic only by pressing **Tab** to reach the *Topic* text box and typing the topic name, e.g., **contracts**
3. Choose **OK**.

When You Have an ISSUE

1. From the Library, select the appropriate book and choose **Search Book**.
2. At the Search Book-Fields Template dialog box, you can enter a query using field restrictions, key terms, universal characters and connectors. Type a query in the *All Fields* text box, e.g.,

   direct! /5 verdict /p slip! /s fail! or fell
   or
   discover! /s sanction /p expert /s test! or witness
3. Choose **OK**.

RETRIEVING ATTORNEY GENERAL OPINIONS

When You Know the CITATION, NAME or AUTHOR*

1. From the Library, select the **Texas Attorney General Opinions** book and choose **Search Book**.
2. At the Search Book-Fields Template dialog box, enter a citation, name or author, e.g.,

   To retrieve Tex. Atty. Gen. Op. DM-125, press **Tab** to reach the *Citation* text box and type
dm-125

   To retrieve an opinion letter addressed to Georgia Flint, press **Tab** to reach the *Name* text box and type
georgia flint

   To retrieve opinion letters prepared by Kymberly Oltrogge, press **Tab** to reach the *Author* text box and type
kymberly oltrogge
3. Choose **OK**.

When You Know the DATE

1. From the Library, select the **Texas Attorney General Opinions** book and choose **Search Book**.
2. At the Search Book-Fields Template dialog box, you can enter a date restriction. Press **Tab** to reach the *Date* text box and type the date using the appropriate format, e.g.,
6/9/92
3. Choose **OK**.

*These queries use the default /p connector.

FIGURE 13–8 *(continued)*

4. Federal Practice

5. Tax

6. Banking/Commercial Law

7. Personal Injury

8. California Practice

9. Texas Practice

The *Martindale-Hubbell Law Directory* is also available on CD-ROM.

The cost of CD-ROM libraries varies from company to company and is subject to constant reevaluation and changes in pricing structure. For example, West does not sell CD-ROM libraries. The services are available for a monthly service fee based on the number of discs each library service contains.

A major drawback to the CD-ROM service is the time required for update and the possibility that information accessed may be obsolete. However, the negative aspects may be outweighed by the ability to access veritable libraries on a single compact disc, immediately search the full text of the actual reporter or statute by using compatible software specially developed for the CD-ROM, and transfer sections of the legal decision or statute to a floppy disk for use with the firm's word processing software.

The CD-ROM concept is particularly attractive for the law firm that specializes in a particular area such as bankruptcy or tax. An attorney or paralegal may well be in a position to walk into the courtroom with a laptop computer, disc player, and a box of CD-ROM discs and instantly access volumes of legal material on a specialty area. This convenience and speed cannot be realized in the courtroom with only the traditional law library.

This area of legal research is undergoing constant change. Additional legal publishers are in the process of introducing products and services on CD-ROM. Within the next several years, virtually all legal libraries and periodicals may be available on the tiny discs. Paralegal and other legal trade publications often contain sections on computerized legal research and are excellent sources of information about new CD-ROM products.

§ 13.8 Effective Computer Research Guidelines

Computer research is effective only when carefully planned and executed. The researcher must be proficient in the use of the computer and knowledgeable about the database contents. The following guidelines increase the effectiveness of CALR research:

1. Understand the assignment. Request clarification if necessary.
2. Learn the basic information about the case: the parties, the date the lawsuit was filed, the docket number, the court, the judge, and the type of litigation.
3. Use the LEXIS or WESTLAW query planner to develop a concise query.
4. *Do not* "sign on" the computer until a query has been developed and you understand the libraries and files in which the search should be conducted.
5. Once the search query is entered, check it for accuracy before transmitting.
6. *Do not read while on-line—merely scan.* Print citations and read from the bound-volume reporters, encyclopedias, and so on, when available.
7. If the initial search query is not successful, immediately sign off and restructure the query.
8. Use the toll-free attorney reference number provided by both CALR services to answer nontechnical questions.

Just as the law is not static, neither is the CALR process. Once you become proficient with the basic concepts of computer research, you should set specific goals for increasing your computer research skills. Both LEXIS and WESTLAW provide excellent training materials and updates on their services. Seminars and one-on-one training sessions in specialized areas of the law are generally available. Use any "free" time by these CALR services to become more adept in executing computer research. The secret to fast and accurate computer research is *practice.*

Summary

13.1   Introduction to Computer-Assisted Legal Research

The cost and space requirements for maintaining a complete law library are enormous. Few law firms today can afford a comprehensive library. Computer-assisted legal research (CALR) has reduced the need for a large library. The two major CALR services are WESTLAW and LEXIS. Advantages of CALR include timeliness, speed, completeness, flexibility, convenience, and full-text searching. However, CALR is not without its problems. The major flaw is that the computer is literal. A second major disadvantage of CALR is cost.

13.2 WESTLAW

WESTLAW, developed and marketed by West Publishing Company in the late 1970s, was patterned after the West manual research system. All information available on WESTLAW is divided into five "databases," which are further subdivided into "files." INSTA-CITE offers a variety of information on a case, including the case name, official and parallel citations, the court issuing the decision, filing date, docket number, format, and history. Shepard's citations are available by computer in lieu of Shepardizing manually. Computer expertise is not a prerequisite for using WESTLAW. WIN (WESTLAW Is Natural) permits a computer novice to structure research queries using only plain English.

13.3 LEXIS

LEXIS, the first CALR service, was introduced by the Ohio State Bar in 1967. Research on LEXIS utilizes a "library" instead of a "database." The "files" configuration used by WESTLAW is also found in LEXIS. The process for formulating a query for LEXIS is the same as for WESTLAW, although the difference in database construction requires some modification in the query. An innovation found only on LEXIS is the ability to modify a search by adding up to 255 levels of research while saving the results of earlier searches. Special features available on LEXIS include LEXSEE, the ability to immediately view the full text of a retrieved document; LEXSTAT, which allows you to go directly to the text of a statutory section; and ECLIPSE, an Electronic Clipping Service, which monitors LEXIS for new information relating to a search and automatically forwards the reports to the law firm daily, weekly, or monthly, as requested. LEXIS offers a computer novice the option of searching in plain English through the use of FREESTYLE.

13.4 Computer-Assisted Legal Research Database Structure

LEXIS and WESTLAW are full-text retrieval systems. Every word of cases, statutes, administrative decisions, rules, and other legal documents is assigned an "address" or location in the database. These subsequently form a concordance, which is an index of every word, number, and symbol in a document.

13.5   Governmental Databases

Three databases have been developed for use by the federal government. JURIS is a Department of Justice database for the exclusive use of federal attorneys. FLITE is a system that permits departments and agencies of the federal government to mail a search request to the database computer. FLITE also accesses Lockheed's DIALOG database. The RIRA database, which includes federal and tax court cases, regulations, and rulings of the IRS, is utilized exclusively by the IRS.

13.6   Tracking Legislation by Computer

With a computerized legislative tracking system, a law firm can remain current at all times on the status of a bill that is of interest to a firm client. LEGI-SLATE is a database service focused exclusively on federal law.

13.7   Research by CD-ROM

The introduction of the CD-ROM, a read only memory compact disc, revolutionized legal research. With a CD-ROM drive, a computer modem, and a terminal with at least 640K storage capacity, the legal researcher can access mini-libraries on a particular subject through a single compact disc. Each disc contains between 150,000 and 300,000 pages of printed text. West Publishing offers a wide variety of subjects in its CD-ROM libraries, including bankruptcy, federal civil practice, and federal tax. Texas-specific CD-ROMs are also available: *Texas Digest, Texas Cases,* and *Texas Statutes and Codes Annotated. Shepard's Citations—Texas* is another library available on CD-ROM.

A recent addition to the CD-ROM library is the *Martindale-Hubbell Law Directory.*

Matthew Bender became a minor player in the CD-ROM legal market with its introduction of the Search Master CD libraries, including *Collier Bankruptcy, Intellectual Property, Business Law, Federal Practice, Tax, Banking/Commercial Law, Personal Injury, California Practice,* and *Texas Practice.*

The cost for the CD-ROM libraries varies from company to company and is subject to constant reevaluation and changes in pricing structure. A major drawback to the CD-ROM is the update time required and the possibility that information accessed may be obsolete. However, the negative aspects are outweighed by the ability to access veritable libraries on a single compact disc, immediately search the full text of the actual reporter or statute by using compatible software specifically developed for the CD-ROM, and copy sections of the legal decision or statute to a floppy disk for use with the firm's word processing software.

The CD-ROM concept is particularly attractive for the law firm that specializes in a particular area such as bankruptcy or tax.

13.8 Effective Computer Research Guidelines

Computer research is effective only when carefully planned and executed. The researcher must be proficient in the use of the computer and knowledgeable about the database contents. Guidelines to increase the effectiveness of CALR research include understanding the assignment, learning the basic information about the case, using a LEXIS or WESTLAW query planner to develop a concise query, planning the query completely before signing on the computer, and checking the query for accuracy before transmitting. You should not read on-line. Sign off and restructure the query if the initial search query is not successful. Use the toll-free attorney reference number provided by both CALR services to answer nontechnical questions.

The CALR process is not static. Once you are proficient with the basic concepts of computer research, set specific goals for increasing your computer research skills. Remember that the secret to fast and accurate computer research is *practice*.

Review Questions

1. Define CALR.

2. List five advantages of CALR.

3. Identify three disadvantages of CALR.

4. What are the five West databases?

5. List five categories of information available on INSTA-CITE.

6. Define star paging.

7. Explain WIN.

8. What information is available an AUTO-CITE?

9. Explain the purpose of LEXSEE.

10. What is FREESTYLE?

Exercises

1. Contact your law firm's librarian and determine whether your firm subscribes to WESTLAW and/or LEXIS. Arrange for any free training sessions available.

2. Obtain copies of WESTLAW and LEXIS training materials and review them.

3. Locate a query form planner for WESTLAW or LEXIS. Use that form to construct a query for the infant car seat case discussed in this chapter.

4. Schedule time with your firm's WESTLAW or LEXIS representative to research the infant car seat case, using your previously constructed query.

5. Review your law firm's facilities and determine whether your firm is a subscriber to CD-ROM services. Schedule any free training available on the use of CD-ROMs.

6. Contact your local and state bar associations to find out if a computerized litigation section exists and determine the membership requirements. Arrange to attend a meeting of the section, if possible.

7. Ask your law firm's librarian to order any videos or films available on the subject of computer-assisted legal research.

8. Contact your state legislative office and determine what information relating to current or prior legislation is available on computer.

9. Locate information relating to the cost of computer-assisted legal research. Estimate the cost of conducting the research project relating to the infant car seat case on WESTLAW and LEXIS.

10. Determine the length of time that is normally required for a Texas state court decision to be available on WESTLAW and LEXIS.

CHAPTER 14

RESEARCH IN THE NONLEGAL DATABASES

§ 14.1   An Overview of the Nonlegal Databases

As explained in Chapter 13, LEXIS and WESTLAW have revolutionized the legal research process through the development of computer-assisted legal research (CALR) systems. Not all research in the legal profession, however, is directed toward finding case law, statutes, or administrative agency rules or decisions. Typical of the research questions that may be directed to a legal assistant are: How many stockholders does Corporation *X* have? Which pharmaceutical company manufactures a new antibiotic? What was the closing price of *ABC* stock for the previous sixty days? Who are potential expert witnesses in a major airline crash?

Several databases contain the answers to general reference questions. Major nonlegal computer-assisted research services include LEXIS and its counterpoint, NEXIS, DIALOG (developed by Lockheed Corporation), Information America, and Prentice Hall Online.

The materials that follow are intended only to *introduce* you to the major nonlegal databases and to give you an *overview* of how research can be conducted in each. Using computer-assisted research methods efficiently and thoroughly requires the development of working familiarity and good skills with each database. If you want to learn, for example, how to use DIALOG in all of its nuances, you should ask a librarian or other researcher familiar with it to instruct you and assist you with some "practice assignments." You should also obtain any available instructional manuals. They often offer excellent step-by-step tutorials. Such instruction also may be available on-line through the database service itself.

It is extremely important that you keep current as to the libraries and files of information available from the various services to which you have access. The databases are constantly being expanded and restructured. You cannot rely on "old" guidebooks. You need to confirm with the librarian in charge of the database terminals that you have the most current compiled listing of libraries and files available, and you also need to review any informational releases and user updates for the services you want to use.

§ 14.2   LEXIS

LEXIS offers excellent research tools for nonlegal searches in specialty areas such as business, finance, accounting, news, wire services, politics, and medicine.

LEXIS Financial Information Service

The COMPNY library of the LEXIS Financial Information Service contains more than seventy-five files of business and financial information. It includes such basic information on a company as its state of incorporation, the filing date for proxy statements, and a list of subsidiaries. Much more sophisticated materials are also available. These include research reports from leading investment banks and brokerage houses; Securities and Exchange Commission filings in full text, including 10-Ks, 10-Qs, proxy statements, and annual reports; extracts of reports from more than 11,000 public companies listed on major and over-the-counter exchanges; and abstracts of registration statements, 13-Ds, 14-Ds, and Form 4s.

Information contained in the COMPNY database may be critical in assessing the merits of bringing a lawsuit and in evaluating various business strategies. For example, from the myriad financial and corporate information available on COMPNY, an attorney may be able to arrive at a realistic recovery potential in the infant car seat death case discussed in Chapter 13. If the company's annual report, for example, indicates a minimal net worth, the projected recovery may not merit lengthy and expensive litigation.

Information in the COMPNY files is organized in the following five major categories.

Company Identifiers

Information concerning companies listed in the COMPNY database is broken down into segments for search purposes, similar to the LEXIS research process outlined in Chapter 13. Figure 14–1 demonstrates search applications for these various identifier segments.

Share Information

Another category of information on COMPNY is share information. This segment reports the distribution of a company's shares, including the number of outstanding shares and the number of shares held by the company's officers and directors. A summary of ownership of the company is also available. It contains the names of stockholders who own at least five percent of the company's stock, the names of insiders (corporate officers or directors), and investment companies or institutional holders of the company's stock. Figure 14–2 is an example of a screen printout of share information. The source of each item of information, such as filed corporate reports (10-K, proxy, and 10-Q) is indicated.

COMPANY IDENTIFIERS

Segment name	Application	Example
Address Includes street address, city, two-letter state abbreviation, ZIP code and country[1]	Find annual corporate reports, filed with the SEC, summarizing the management and financial position of Ohio's forest product companies	FILE TRANSMIT	10-K *address (oh)* AND *forest products*
Company-name Complete or partial name of a company (NAME is an equivalent segment name)	Find annual reports to stockholders on a corporation	FILE TRANSMIT	ARS *name (mead)*
Document-date Ending date of the period that document was filed	Find proxy statements filed in 1989 that mention forest products	FILE TRANSMIT	PROXY *document-date (is 1989)* AND *forest w/3 products*
Exchange The exchange on which the company is traded, e.g. American Stock Exchange, New York Stock Exchange, etc.	Look at the recent financial condition of companies, traded on the New York Stock Exchange, associated with paper mills	FILE TRANSMIT	10-Q *exchange (nys)* AND *paper w/3 mills*
Filing-date The date a report was filed with the SEC	View important corporate financial information of a company, for example, Form 8Ks filed in a specific time frame	FILE TRANSMIT	EVENTS *filing-date (=12/1989)* AND *mead*
Incorporation State or country in which company is incorporated	Locate reports on companies incorporated in Michigan that mention paper or forest products	FILE TRANSMIT	DISCLO *incorporation (oh)* AND *paper* OR *forest w/3 product*
Subsidiaries List of subsidiaries of a company	Locate a parent company by conducting a search mentioning a subsidiary or subsidiaries	FILE TRANSMIT	DISCLO *subsidiaries (mead data central)*
Telephone Phone number of a company	Identify companies through their telephone numbers	FILE TRANSMIT	10-K *telephone (513 222 6323)*
Ticker symbol Abbreviated symbol for a company on the stock exchange	Retrieve documents that relay transaction information, such as buying and selling specific securities, by searching by ticker symbols	FILE TRANSMIT	MG *ticker (mea)*

---

[1] When choosing search words in the ADDRESS segment, use the AND connector. To search foreign companies spell out full name of the country.

[Reproduced with permission of Mead Data Central, Inc.]

FIGURE 14–1   LEXIS search applications for identifier segments

Corporate Financial Record in the DISCLO file (DISCLOSURE Database)

```
                    LEVEL 1 — 1 OF 1 REPORT

           Copyright (c) 1989 Disclosure Online Database

                         MEAD CORP
           DISCLO COMPANY NUMBER: M339900000
           TICKER SYMBOL: MEA EXCHANGE: NYS

                COURTHOUSE PLAZA NORTHEAST
                     DAYTON, OH 45463
                       513-222-6323

     *******************OWNERSHIP*******************
     THE EQUITABLE LIFE ASSURANCE SOCIETY OF U.S., 5.1% (PRX 03-14-88)
```

Corporate Financial Record in the DISCLO file (DISCLOSURE Database)

```
                    LEVEL 1 — 1 OF 1 REPORT

           Copyright (c) 1989 Disclosure Online Database

                         MEAD CORP
           DISCLO COMPANY NUMBER: M339900000
           TICKER SYMBOL: MEA EXCHANGE: NYS

                COURTHOUSE PLAZA NORTHEAST
                     DAYTON, OH 45463
                       513-222-6323

     SHARE INFORMATION:
     63,218,405 CURRENT OUTSTANDING SHARES (SOURCE: 10-Q 08/04/89)

     1,736,250 SHARES HELD BY OFFICERS AND DIRECTORS (SOURCE: PROXY)

     23,294 SHAREHOLDERS (SOURCE: 10-K)
```

[Reproduced with permission of Mead Data Central, Inc.]

FIGURE 14–2   An example of a screen printout of share information on Mead Corporation

SIC Codes

The Standard Industrial Classification (SIC) code is a descriptive code developed by the Office of Budget and Management. Each industry is assigned a unique identifier code. Major codes are then subdivided to reflect variations of the particular industry. Federal and state agencies employ the SIC codes for consistency in such areas as developing federal unemployment insurance rates.

If the researcher is asked to locate all companies that manufacture infant car seats, the SIC code may be a quick and accurate source for that information. Figure 14–3 is an example of a screen displaying SIC codes. These codes indicate that the corporate entities include several paper and computer companies.

Company Characteristics

A company has many unique characteristics that may be important in a lawsuit. For example, the "filing-person" segment tracks the purchases and sales of a company's stock. This information might indicate substantial stock purchases by a competitor in anticipation of a corporate takeover. The "auditor" segment indicates the auditing firm employed by a company. Current financial information on the company can be obtained quickly from the company's auditors and used in a lawsuit.

Company characteristics also may be used to research a statement by management in the report to the shareholders relating to the financial position of the company, as shown in Figure 14–4. Such a discussion often summarizes a company's financial position and projected growth. In the car seat case, the statement by management may confirm that the plaintiffs should be able to collect on any substantial judgment rendered in their favor.

Corporate Executives

Figure 14–5 shows the results from searching the "officers" segment and includes the names, ages, salaries, and titles of the top corporate officers of a company.

Assume that the attorney in the car seat litigation is preparing to take the deposition of the defendant's key employees. The "officers" segment may be used to determine the name and location of the car seat manufacturer's chief financial officer and the department head who was responsible for quality control.

Corporate Statement from the PROXY file
(Proxy Statements)

LEVEL 1 — 1 OF 2 REPORTS

[*Summary]   COPYRIGHT (c) 1989 SEC ONLINE, INC.

Proxy Statement

FILING-DATE: 03/15/89   DOCUMENT-DATE: 03/13/89

MEAD CORP

SIC-CODE:

SIC-CODES: 2621, 2651, 2631, 2649, 5111, 7374
PRIMARY SIC: 2621

Corporate Financial Record in the DISCLO file
(DISCLOSURE Database)

LEVEL 1 — 1 OF 1 REPORT
Copyright (c) 1989 Disclosure Online Database

MEAD CORP
DISCLO COMPANY NUMBER: M339900000
TICKER SYMBOL: MEA EXCHANGE: NYS

COURTHOUSE PLAZA NORTHEAST
DAYTON, OH 45463
513-222-6323

SIC CODES: 2649;
SIC CODES: 5111;
SIC CODES: 5113;
SIC CODES: 2621;
SIC CODES: 2651;
SIC CODES: 2631

[Reproduced with permission of Mead Data Central, Inc.]

FIGURE 14-3   An example of a screen printout of share information on Mead Corporation

Corporate Statement from the PROXY file (Proxy Statements)

LEVEL 1 — 1 OF 1 REPORT
Copyright (c) 1989 Disclosure Online Database
MEAD CORP
DISCLO COMPANY NUMBER: M339900000
TICKER SYMBOL: MEA EXCHANGE: NYS

COURTHOUSE PLAZA NORTHEAST
DAYTON, OH 45463
513-222-6323

MANAGEMENT DISCUSSION: Operating Results—Management Analysis and Discussion Mead set new records in both sales and earnings in 1988. Sales grew by 6%, despite the sizeable divestitures of 1987 and 1988. (The company estimates sales growth would have been 13%, excluding the sales of divested units.) Operating earnings before non-recurring gains increased 33% to $3.70 per share, or $240.8 million, which compares to $2.79 per share, or $175.5 million. That made 1988 Mead's second consecutive record earnings year. Mead's manufacturing operations benefitted from strong demand and high operating rates throughout 1988. In pulp, paper, paperboard and school and office products businesses, these conditions permitted both efficient operations and improved prices. Earnings per share from continuing operations rose to $5.54 (including non-recurring gains of $1.84), or $364.1 million. That compares with $3.47 a . . .

[Reproduced with permission of Mead Data Central, Inc.]

FIGURE 14–4   Company characteristics may be used to research a statement by management in the report to the shareholders relating to the financial position of the company

The LEXIS Public Records Online Service

LEXIS has recently introduced a number of new subjects of interest to the legal profession through its Public Records Online Service.

LEXDOC

Once the researcher has located the pertinent public record, the LEXDOC feature permits the researcher to order certified or uncertified copies of the record or order a manual search of filings from any state, the District of Columbia, the Virgin Islands, or Canada while on-line. Public documents available include certificates of good standing, articles of incorporation, Uniform Commercial Code information, tax liens, judgments, patents, and pending lawsuits. LEXDOC also allows a user to check name availability and obtain assistance in filing a corporate name reservation. Document orders or requests go directly to LEXIS Document Services for processing.

DISCLO File
(DISCLOSURE Database)

LEVEL 1 — 1 OF 1 REPORT

Copyright (c) 1989 Disclosure Online Database

MEAD CORP
DISCLO COMPANY NUMBER: M339900000
TICKER SYMBOL: MEA EXCHANGE: NYS

COURTHOUSE PLAZA NORTHEAST
DAYTON, OH 45463
513-222-6323

OFFICERS (NAME/AGE/TITLE/REMUNERATION):
(SOURCE: 10K)
ENOUEN, WILLIAN A./ 60/ SENIOR VICE PRESIDENT, CHIEF FINANCIAL OFFICER /
$479,997
HERBERT, JOHN W./ 64/ SENIOR VICE PRESIDENT / $487,176
KARTER, ELIAS M./48/VICE PRESIDENT/NA
MASON, STEVEN C./ 53/ PRESIDENT, CHIEF OPERATING OFFICER / $826,502
MAZZA, CHARLES J./ 46/ VICE PRESIDENT / NA
NUGENT, WALLACE O./ 50/ VICE PRESIDENT / NA
RAPP, GERALD D./ 55/ SENIOR VICE PRESIDENT, LEGAL COUNSEL / NA

LEVEL 1 — 1 OF 1 REPORT

Copyright (c) 1989 Disclosure Online Database

MEAD CORP
DISCLO COMPANY NUMBER: M339900000
TICKER SYMBOL: MEA EXCHANGE: NYS

COURTHOUSE PLAZA NORTHEAST
DAYTON, OH 45463
513-222-6323

DIRECTORS/NOMINEES (NAME/AGE/TITLE/REMUNERATION):
(SOURCE: PROXY 03/13/89)
BREEN, JOHN G./ 54/ NOMINEE / NA
MECHEM, CHARLES S., JR./ 58/ NOMINEE / NA
SPENCER, WILLIAM M. III/ 68/ NOMINEE / NA
STANLEY, THOMAS B./ 62/ NOMINEE / NA
GREGORY, VINCENT L., JR./ 65/ NA/ NA
MASON, STEVEN C./ 53/ PRESIDENT, CHIEF OPERATING OFFICER / $826,502
MILLER, PAUL F., JR./ 61/ NA/ NA
SPICOLA, JAMES R./ 58/NA/ NA
BOGIE, JOHN C./ 59/ NA/ NA

[Reproduced with permission of Mead Data Central, Inc.]

FIGURE 14–5   An example of a screen printout of share information on Mead Corporation

INCORP Library

The INCORP library available through LEXIS offers the legal professional direct access to current records for limited partnerships and corporations. Information found in this library includes:

1. articles of incorporation
2. amendments to articles of incorporation
3. annual reports
4. various public filings

The paralegal should consider this service for tasks such as checking corporate name availability, determining the registered agent and office for service of process, identifying corporate officers, and reviewing stock and capitalization information.

ASSETS Library

LEXIS offers a separate library of information concerning asset ownership and location. If you need to locate a mailing address for an asset's owner, the assessed value of a property, or land use restrictions in a particular area, check this library.

A recent addition to the ASSETS library is the Texas Motor Vehicle Registration (TXMVR) file. This file offers access to current Texas registration information, including owner name and address, license plate number, VIN, purchase price, lien holder, and previous owner and license plate number.

LIENS Library

Records of Uniform Commercial Code (UCC) lien filings on personal property are maintained by LEXIS in its LIENS library. Information for this library is compiled from financing statements, terminations, continuations, and so on, filed under the UCC. An outstanding feature of LIENS is the ability to search full text. You might use LIENS to obtain a list of secured creditors for bankruptcy filings, to determine the indebtedness of an individual or company, or to perform due diligence.

Miscellaneous Libraries

Other information available in the LEXIS Public Records Online Service includes:

1. Bankruptcy filings (INSOLV)
2. Docket (DOCKET)

3. Civil and criminal filings (see Docket)
4. Verdicts (VERDCT)

Quote Library

The quote library of the LEXIS Financial Information Service permits immediate access to equity quotes from the North American stock exchanges and NASDAQ, in addition to quotes for bonds traded on the United States Exchanges. Information available includes price quotes; open, high, and low prices; changes; and volume. The quote can be requested by either the company name or ticker symbol, the official symbol utilized by stock exchanges to identify a particular stock. For example, "MEAD" is the ticker symbol for the Mead Corporation.

Individual quotes may be checked quickly by using the QUOTE FINDER (QF). QUOTE SAVER (QS) saves up to fifty quotes and organizes and values the stock.

Other market indicators are also available through the Quote Library, as indicated in Figure 14–6.

Associated Press Political Service

Current and historical political information is featured in the Associated Press Political Service. The subject matter of this library includes

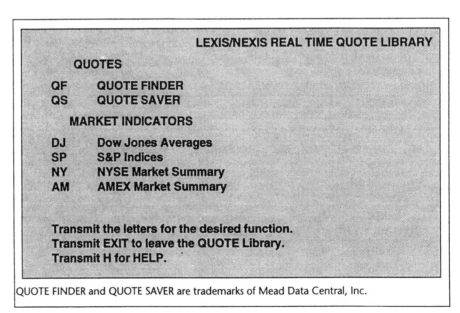

QUOTE FINDER and QUOTE SAVER are trademarks of Mead Data Central, Inc.

FIGURE 14–6 Market indicators that are available through the Quote Library.

national polls, candidates' positions on political issues, congressional ratings, a historical calendar, and information on statewide referenda and propositions.

MEDIS Service

LEXIS has created specialized medical libraries in areas such as medical journals and textbooks, both current and archived; drug information; pharmacy journals; cancer information; physician data query (PDQ); and specialty journals and articles.

The researcher, for example, may access MEDIS to locate an article from the *Journal of the American Medical Association* and may find other information on the same topic by accessing the PDQ Reference File, PDQ Physician Directory, PDQ Cancer Information for Patients, *Journal of the National Cancer Institute* (from January 1983) and pediatrics journals (from 1980).

§ 14.3   The NEXIS Service

Since NEXIS is part of the LEXIS system and is searched by the same protocol, it is the nonlegal database most heavily used in law offices. One of its strengths is its access to information on pending litigation before the Supreme Court (*United States Law Week Daily*). Another is the information it may supply, through a wide array of financial and business publications in its library, on the activities of companies that may be actual or potential clients or adversaries.

The NEXIS library consists of a wide variety of general and specialized business, finance, news, and technical publications in full text. NEXIS contains a section of Legal News files, which, in addition to *United States Law Week*, includes *Legal Times, The American Lawyer, The National Law Journal,* and the *Texas Law Journal* (from January 1990). All files on NEXIS may be searched separately or collectively by using the OMNI file listed on the NEXIS menu.

The CURRNT file contains all full-text documents in the NEXIS library from 1988 to the current date. Full-text documents before that time are in the group file labeled ARCHIV.

Full-text files are organized into groups by the type of publication—MAGS, PAPERS, WIRES, and NWLTRS—and by subject matter—BUS, FIN, INTL, NEWS, PERSON, LGLNEW, and TRDTEC (trade/technology). For example, the MAGS group includes such magazines as *Fortune* and *Newsweek.* Papers on-line include *The New York Times* and *The Wall Street Journal.*

Another valuable group classification on NEXIS is the regional group file: NEAST, MWEST, SEAST, and WEST. The regional group file consists of selected regional sources of full-text information, including newspapers and periodicals such as the *Nashville Business Journal*, the *Alaska Journal of Commerce*, the *Cincinnati Business Courier*, and *The Boston Globe*.

Two abstract files complement the full-text files: CURABS includes all current abstract documents from 1988 to date, and ARCABS consists of all archived abstract documents prior to that time.

Libraries available through the NEXIS service include the following:

Business & Finance (BUSFIN)

Business Reference (BUSREF)

Campaign News (CMPGN)

Computers and Communications (CMPCOM)

Entertainment (ENTERT)

Executive Branch (EXEC)

Legal News (LEGNEW)

Legislation (LEGIS)

Markets and Industry (MARKET)

News and Business (NEWS)

People (PEOPLE)

Sports (SPORTS)

Top News (TOPNWS)

Figure 14–7 depicts the first page of the NEXIS library's massive twenty-one page menu (as of April 1990).

§ 14.4 DIALOG

Lockheed has developed and marketed DIALOG, which offers approximately two hundred and fifty databases consisting of more than fifty million records. The subject areas covered range from agriculture and art to business economics, expert witnesses, literature, mathematics, medicine, products, social sciences, and travel. Information found in these databases is made available to DIALOG by government agencies, corporations, associations, and major publishers. These database sources are responsible for the accuracy and completeness of the information supplied to DIALOG.

SAMPLE PAGES OF THE MENU OF FILES AVAILABLE IN THE NEXIS LIBRARY
AS OF APRIL 1990

Please TRANSMIT, separated by commas, the NAMES of the files you want to search. You may select as many files as you want, including files that do not appear below, but you must transmit them all at one time. To see a description of a file, TRANSMIT its page (PG) number.

FILES — PAGE 1 of 21 (NEXT PAGE for additional files)

NAME	PG	DESCRIP	NAME	PG	DESCRIP	NAME	PG	DESCRIP
— FULL-TEXT FILES —			— SOURCE FILES —			— SUBJECT FILES —		
CURRNT	1	NEXIS 1988-Current	PAPERS	2	Newspapers	BUS	3	Business
ARCHIV	1	NEXIS Prior to 1988	MAGS	2	Magazines	FIN	3	Finance
OMNI	1	All NEXIS Files	NWLTRS	2	Newsletters	LGLNEW	3	Legal News
			WIRES	2	Wires	INTL	3	International
— ABSTRACT FILES —			— REGION FILES —			NEWS	3	News
CURABS	1	ABSTRACTS 1988-1989	NWEST	3	Midwest	PERSON	3	People Info
ARCABS	1	ABSTRACTS Pre-1988	NEAST	3	Northeast	GUIDE	3	Descriptions
ALLABS	1	All Abstracts	SEAST	3	Southeast	TRDTEC	3	Trade/Tech
INFOBK	1	Combined ABS & AMI	WEST	3	West	GUIDE	3	Descriptions

WHAT'S NEW IN NEXIS? PRESS NEXT PAGE TO SEE THE NEW FILE ADDITIONS

[Reproduced with permission of Mead Data Central, Inc.]

FIGURE 14–7   The first page of NEXIS library's menu

The DIALOG database is located in Menlo Park, California, and may be accessed directly, using a personal computer equipped with a modem and communications software, or through WESTLAW. Many DIALOG databases are available as WESTLAW files and can be searched using standard WESTLAW protocols.

DIALOG is relatively inexpensive and easy to use. The charge for searches varies according to the database, but information on the cost of the search is available at the time the database is accessed.

Two major categories of DIALOG information that are often research subjects in the legal profession are the business and medical databases.

Business

DIALOG's Business Connection offers outstanding sources of information in the corporate and financial areas, including Dun & Bradstreet, Inc.; Moody's Investors Service, Inc.; and Standard & Poor's Corporation. Dun & Bradstreet, Inc., can be used to obtain, for example, complete information on the car seat manufacturer involved in the infant death case discussed in Chapter 13, including assets, debts, net worth, and corporate structure. The Business Connection may also be used to analyze business and marketing trends to determine the future growth potential of the car seat manufacturer.

More than two million commercial and industrial companies with five or more employees are listed on DIALOG. Information available on these companies includes officers, parent company, subsidiaries, related companies, sales volumes, banks, and accounting firms engaged by the company.

Another valuable feature of DIALOG's business information databases is the Electronic Yellow Pages. By using this feature, you can, for example, locate the address of the car seat manufacturer's satellite plants by entering the state or city where the plant is located.

Dow Jones Disclosure II on DIALOG includes Securities and Exchange Commission filings for approximately eighty-five hundred publicly held corporations.

Medical

Personal injury and medical malpractice litigation often require information about a particular medication, doctor, hospital, treatment, or medical research. DIALOG's Medical Connection answers questions on a variety of subjects, including:

- Who manufactures a particular medicine?

- Has the medicine been recalled, and if so, when and why?

- Have any doctors testified before Congress about the side effects of the medicine, and if so, who are those doctors?

- How many times has a doctor been sued for malpractice?

- How often has a particular doctor testified as an expert witness?

- Has a medical expert witness always testified for the plaintiff?

- How many lawsuits have been filed against a particular hospital?

MEDLINE

MEDLINE, a comprehensive database on DIALOG, indexes over three thousand medical journals from the United States and seventy foreign countries, published from 1970 to the present. This database can be an excellent tool for locating helpful articles on medical topics; for example, those which address the issue of infant strangulation in car seats. MEDLINE is also available on LEXIS.

Product Standards

DIALOG may be used to research information in products liability cases where product standards are at issue. Over two hundred thousand domestic, international, and military standards are maintained on the International Standards & Specifications database.

Once the standards by which an infant car seat should be measured have been determined, the performance of the product in question can be compared with that of similar products through the Thomas Register Online, another DIALOG specialty database.

Patents and Trademarks

In many products liability cases, the manufacturer of a product may not be known. TRADEMARKSCAN is an excellent source of information about the manufacturer because it lists the trademark owners of particular products. The Claims/United States Patent Abstracts database contains data on all patents issued since 1978.

News

Several DIALOG databases contain regional, national, and international news. For example, NEWSEARCH indexes on a daily basis over two thousand news stories, articles, and book reviews from some fourteen hundred major newspapers, magazines, and periodicals. Another news database, The National Newspaper Index, is updated monthly. This index includes data from such publications as *The New York Times* and *The Wall Street Journal*.

Congressional Activities

The Congressional Information Service (CIS) database on DIALOG contains information on the activities of approximately three hundred house, senate, joint committee, and subcommittee activities from 1970 to the present. Information on the status of bills and all roll-call votes from 1976 to the present can be located through the Congressional Records Abstracts database on DIALOG.

§ 14.5 Information America

Overview

A legal assistant who specializes in corporate matters may expend much time and effort attempting to access secretaries of state offices. A typical scenario would be: the telephone line is busy. Once the telephone is answered, a recording suggests multiple answers for the caller's question. None of the answers, however, really respond to the precise problem faced by the caller.

Information America (acquired by WESTLAW in 1994) offers a fast and inexpensive alternative—on-line access to many state and municipal records databases. The Texas databases that are currently available include:

- Lawsuits filed in Dallas County, Texas

- County and court records for the Dallas–Fort Worth metroplex area and Harris County, Texas

- Bankruptcy court records for all Texas districts

- Uniform Commercial Code and lien records for all areas of Texas

Information America may be accessed through WESTLAW, dedicated Information America terminals, or personal computers equipped with a modem to communicate with the Information America database in Atlanta, Georgia.

Services

Corporate and Limited Partnership Records

Services available on Information America include Texas corporate and limited partnership records, as well as such records for more than twenty other states. This database provides important corporate information such as an officer's name, registered agent, state corporate identification number, good standing status, and the company's principal address. With the Corporate Global feature, all states may be searched on-line simultaneously. This speeds up the search process and reduces the cost of the search.

Dun's Business Records Plus

This specialized database contains information on three million public and private companies nationwide. Included is information on the company's financial affairs, executive personnel, operations, and intracompany relationships.

The Family Scan service of this database reveals intracompany relationships and nonmortgaged asset information. This database would indicate, for example, whether the infant car seat manufacturer has any assets that have not already been pledged to secure indebtedness. If the search reveals only a few assets, it may indicate a limited potential for recovery of a judgment in the infant death case.

People Finder

Personal information on more than one hundred million individuals and eighty million households and some sixty million telephone numbers are captured in the People Finder feature. This database can reveal an individual's:

- Current address

- Telephone number

- Birth date

- Type of residence

- Length of time at residence

- Family members

- Birth dates of family members

In addition to information on a particular individual or family, the Neighbor Listing function reveals information on ten neighbors, identified by name, address, telephone number, and type of residence.

Information for the People Finder database is obtained by Information America from databases of sources such as the United States Census Bureau and major national businesses.

If, for example, you were searching in the infant car seat case for a witness who has moved to another state, Person Locator could be used to find the witness simply by entering the name of the state. If the forwarding address is unknown, however, Skip Tracer would supply the individual's new address. Both of these features are helpful in the specialty of collection law.

State UCC and Lien Filings

Much information about an individual or company may be ascertained from state Uniform Commercial Code (UCC) and lien filings, including assets that have been pledged, the institution or individual to whom they have been pledged, and the amount of the lien. Information America currently contains state UCC filings for California, Colorado, Florida, Illinois, Iowa, Maryland, Massachusetts, Missouri, Nebraska, North Carolina, Pennsylvania, and Texas. All states that are on-line can be searched simultaneously.

The UCC information available on-line includes the following:

- Debtor

- Secured party

- Assignee name and address

- Collateral

- Type of instrument

- Filing date and time

- Instrument number

Information America offers a unique service, DOX (document ordering express), through which state corporate and UCC documents can be ordered electronically or through Information America's corporate offices in Atlanta, Georgia.

Bankruptcy Records

Company and individual bankruptcy filings for all district courts in California and Texas, the Eastern District of Pennsylvania, and the Northern District of Georgia are on-line with Information America. Data available includes the debtor's name, case number, bankruptcy filing location, date of the filing, and bankruptcy chapter number.

Local Court Records

Information America offered the local county and court records for ten counties (including two locales in Texas—Dallas/Fort Worth metropolitan area and Harris County) on-line in 1995 and is in the process of adding additional counties. Court records available generally include abstracts of judgment, assumed name, civil lawsuits, county UCC records, lis pendens, real property filings, tax appraisal records, and tax liens.

Venue/County Determination

Entering a zip code, city, or state discloses the proper venue for legal actions. If the paralegal is asked to file a subpoena in another state, this function of Information America supplies fast and accurate venue information.

§ 14.6   Prentice Hall Online

Another comprehensive source for information on tax liens and bankruptcy information is available through Prentice Hall Online. Small claims and civil judgments can also be accessed through this service. For additional information on services and costs, check with Prentice Hall's technical assistance representatives at 1-800-333-8356. Refer to Figure 14–8 for a list of Prentice Hall Online services offered nationwide and to Figure 14–9 for a detailed listing of services available in Texas.

§ 14.7   Recent Developments in Nonlegal Databases

The initial developers of nonlegal databases are expanding their computer services and products. Many new nonlegal publishers have entered the rapidly developing computer market. Conservative estimates indicate that over fifteen hundred nonlegal databases were available in mid-1990. Much of this nonlegal information can be accessed through the law firm's

ACTIVE COLLECTION AREAS
FOR CLIENT SUPPORT CALL 800-333-8356

	Bankruptcy	Tax Lien – County State & Federal	Judgments	Notice of Default	Uniform Commercial Code Lien Information SOS & County*	Corporation – Incorporation/Qualification	Limited Partnership Information	Board of Equalization Sales Tax	Franchise Tax	General Index	Real Estate	Fictitious Owner/Assumed Name	Environmental	Superior Court/County Court Civil Index	Federal Aviation
ALASKA					●	●							●		●
ARIZONA	●					●							●		●
ARKANSAS						●							●		●
CALIFORNIA	●	●	●	●	●	●	●	●		●***	●		●	●**	●
COLORADO					●	●	●						●		●
CONNECTICUT						●						●	●		●
DELAWARE						●	●						●		●
FLORIDA					●	●							●		●
GEORGIA	●					●	●						●		●
HAWAII	●	●	●										●		●
IDAHO						●							●		●
ILLINOIS					●	●							●		●
IOWA						●	●						●		●
MARYLAND					●	●	●						●		●
MASSACHUSETTS					●	●	●					●	●		●
MISSISSIPPI						●	●						●		●
MISSOURI					●	●	●					●	●		●
NEBRASKA					●	●							●		●
NEW HAMPSHIRE						●	●						●		●
NEW YORK					●	●						●	●		●
NEVADA	●	●	●			●	●						●		●
OREGON	●	●	●		●	●	●						●		●
PENNSYLVANIA	●				●	●						●	●		●
RHODE ISLAND						●	●					●	●		●
TENNESSEE						●	●						●		●
TEXAS	●	●	●		●*	●	●	●	●			●*	●	●**	●
UTAH	●				●	●	●						●		●
VERMONT						●	●						●		●
WASHINGTON	●	●	●			●	●						●		●
WISCONSIN						●	●						●		●
WYOMING						●							●		●

  * Texas: Dallas and Harris Counties
 ** California: Los Angeles, Orange, Riverside, San Diego, San Bernardino, Santa Barbara, Santa Clara, San Francisco, San Joaquin, San Luis Obispo, and Ventura Counties

 ** Texas: Harris County
*** California: L.A. County and San Francisco County

NOTE: ENVIRONMENTAL DATA and FEDERAL AVIATION DATA is available in all 50 states.

FIGURE 14–8 Prentice Hall's online public information services

Active Collection Areas
Texas Local Records

TAX LIENS and JUDGMENTS

County	Tax Liens (Earliest Date)	Judgments (Earliest Date)
Atascosa	06/84	08/84
Bastrop	01/86	01/86
Bexar	06/84	06/84
Brazoria	01/86	01/86
Burnet	01/86	01/86
Chambers	01/86	01/86
Collin	01/85	01/85
Comal	06/84	06/84
Dallas	01/85	01/85
Denton	01/85	01/85
Ellis	01/85	01/85
Fannin	01/91	01/91
Fort Bend	01/86	01/86
Grayson	01/91	01/91
Guadalupe	06/84	07/84
Harris	01/86	01/86
Hays	01/86	01/86
Hood	01/86	01/86
Hopkins	01/91	01/91
Hunt	01/91	01/91
Johnson	01/86	01/86
Kaufman	01/86	01/86
Liberty	01/86	01/86
Medina	06/84	01/85
Montgomery	01/86	01/86
Parker	01/86	01/86
Rockwall	08/85	08/85
Tarrant	01/85	01/85
Travis	01/86	01/86
Wharton	01/86	01/86
Williamson	01/86	01/86
Wise	01/86	01/86

BANKRUPTCY

Court	District	Bankruptcy (Earliest Date)
Plano	Eastern	05/92
Tyler	Eastern	01/86
Dallas	Northern	01/85
Fort Worth	Northern	01/85
Lubbock	Northern	11/82
Corpus Christi	Southern	01/86
Houston	Southern	01/86
Austin	Western	01/86
Del Rio	Western	01/86
El Paso	Western	11/82
Midland	Western	11/82
San Antonio	Western	01/86
Waco	Western	01/86

* 1) Dates reflect earliest collection dates in database.
2) PHO collects State and Federal Tax Liens.
3) PHO collects Small Claims Judgments and Civil Judgments.
4) Please refer to the coverage appendix of the Prentice Hall Online manual for exact county coverage within other states.

FIGURE 14–9   Prentice Hall's online services available in Texas

existing computer equipment and services, such as LEXIS/NEXIS, WEST-LAW, DIALOG, Information America, and Prentice Hall Online.

Information brokers, companies that specialize in locating and furnishing information in such areas as business, finance, legislation, and patents, are available to assist law firms that lack the capacity to access the massive number of nonlegal databases. Libraries in major cities and law schools provide computer search services for nominal fees.

The ability to quickly access information on a virtually unlimited number of nonlegal topics was previously lacking in many law firms. Advanced technology and the reduced cost of computer services ensure that nonlegal databases will be as accessible as the major legal databases, WESTLAW and LEXIS.

Summary

14.1 An Overview of the Nonlegal Databases

Not all legal research is directed toward finding case law, statutes, and administrative agency rules or decisions. Several databases contain the answers to general fact questions. Major nonlegal computer-assisted research services include LEXIS/NEXIS, DIALOG, Information America, and Prentice Hall Online. All research on nonlegal databases should utilize the most current reference material and user information.

14.2 LEXIS

LEXIS offers excellent research tools for nonlegal searches in specialty areas such as business, finance, news, wire services, politics, and medicine within the following libraries: COMPNY, INCORP, ASSETS, LIENS, Quote, AP Political, and MEDIS service.

14.3 The NEXIS Service

NEXIS, which is part of the LEXIS system and searched by the same protocol, offers access to information on pending litigation before the Supreme Court with its coverage of *United States Law Week Daily*. The NEXIS library consists of a wide variety of general and specialized business, finance, news, and technical publications in full text, including *Legal Times, The American Lawyer, The National Law Journal,* and *The Texas Law Journal*.

14.4 DIALOG

Lockheed has developed and marketed DIALOG, which contains information on diverse subjects within two major categories: business and medical. Many DIALOG databases are also available on WESTLAW. DIALOG's Business Connection offers outstanding sources of information in the corporate and financial areas, for example, Dun & Bradstreet, Inc.; Moody's Investors Service, Inc.; and Standard & Poor's Corporation. Dow Jones Disclosure II includes Securities and Exchange Commission filings for approximately eighty-five hundred publicly held corporations. Medical databases available on DIALOG are Medical Connection and MEDLINE. For research on products, DIALOG offers the Product Standards database, the Thomas Register Online, and TRADEMARKSCAN. News databases that can be accessed through DIALOG include NEWSEARCH and the National Newspaper Index.

For information on congressional activities, refer to either the Congressional Information Service (CIS) or the Congressional Records Abstract database.

14.5 Information America

Information America, which was acquired by WESTLAW in 1994, offers a fast and inexpensive alternative on-line access to many state and municipal records databases. Services offered include corporate and limited partnership records, Dun's Business Records Plus, People Finder, state UCC and lien filings, bankruptcy records, and local court records.

14.6 Prentice Hall Online

Prentice Hall Online offers comprehensive information on tax liens, bankruptcies, small claims, and civil judgments.

14.7 Recent Developments in Nonlegal Databases

The initial developers of nonlegal databases are expanding their computer services and products. In addition, many new nonlegal publishers have entered the rapidly developing computer market.

Information brokers, companies that specialize in locating and furnishing information in such areas as business, finance, legislation, and patents, are available to assist law firms that lack the capacity to access the massive number of nonlegal databases. Libraries in major cities and law schools provide computer search services for nominal fees.

Advanced technology and the reduced cost of computer services ensure that nonlegal databases will soon be as accessible as the major legal databases, LEXIS and WESTLAW.

Review Questions

1. Identify three nonlegal computer-assisted research services.

2. Discuss the information contained in the LEXIS COMPNY library.

3. List the five major categories of information in the LEXIS COMPNY library.

4. What is an SIC code and what is its purpose?

5. What information is contained in the LEXIS Quotes library?

6. Name three legal publications found in the NEXIS library.

7. What are the two major categories of DIALOG information?

8. List three types of information available on Information America for Texas subscribers.

9. How are actual documents obtained after a search on Information America?

10. Identify two sources for information from nonlegal databases for law firms that are not subscribers to such databases.

Exercises

1. Check with your law firm's librarian or a local law school, if any, to determine the nonlegal databases available. Obtain copies of any available brochures on those services.

2. Contact LEXIS/NEXIS and request a copy of all publications relating to its nonlegal database services.

3. If available, schedule training on your law firm's nonlegal databases.

4. Contact a medical school library in your area, if any, and obtain information on medical databases utilized by that institution. Obtain a copy of any brochures that are available.

5. Telephone your state senator or representative's office to determine what databases that office uses to track legislation.

6. Contact your local office of the Department of Labor and obtain a copy of SIC codes. Review the codes and determine the appropriate listing for the manufacturer in the child's car seat litigation.

7. Research the databases used by a local brokerage house for tracking securities transactions—stock prices, stock ownership, and volume of shares sold.

8. Telephone your local newspaper office and inquire about the news and political databases it utilizes.

9. Contact Information America and request information on services available to an individual who is not a subscriber to Information America.

10. Review recent editions of legal computer publications and become familiar with recent or planned databases similar to those discussed in this chapter.

APPENDIX

TEXAS STATE AGENCIES

A

A & M UNIVERSITY SYSTEM,
THE TEXAS BOARD OF
College Station, TX 77483-1123   409/845-9600

ACCOUNTANCY, TEXAS STATE
BOARD OF PUBLIC
1033 La Posada, Suite 340
Austin, TX 78752-3892   512/450-7075

AGING, TEXAS DEPARTMENT ON
1949 IH35 South 3rd Floor
P.O. Box 12786
Austin, TX 78711   512/444-2727

AGRICULTURE, TEXAS DEPARTMENT OF
Stephen F. Austin Bldg.
P.O. Box 12847
Austin, TX 78711   512/463-7476

AGRICULTURAL DIVERSIFICATION
BOARD, TEXAS
c/o Texas Department of Agriculture
P.O. Box 12847
Austin, TX 78711   512/463-7624

AGRICULTURE FINANCE AUTHORITY, TEXAS
c/o Texas Department of Agriculture
P.O. Box 12847
Austin, TX 78711   512/463-7624

AIR CONTROL BOARD, TEXAS
6330 Highway 290 West
Austin, TX 78723   512/451-5711

AIRCRAFT POOLING BOARD, STATE
4900 Old Manor Road
Austin, TX 78723   512/477-8900

ALCOHOL AND DRUG ABUSE,
TEXAS COMMISSION ON
720 Brazos, Suite 403
Austin, TX 78701   512/867-8700

ALCOHOLIC BEVERAGE COMMISSION,
TEXAS
5806 Mesa Drive
P.O. Box 13127
Austin, TX 78711   512/458-2500

ANGELINA AND NECHES RIVER AUTHORITY,
Board of Directors
210 Lufkin Avenue
P.O. Box 387
Lufkin, TX 75902-0387   409/632-7795

ANIMAL HEALTH COMMISSION, TEXAS
210 Barton Springs Road
P.O. Box 12966
Austin, TX 78711-2966   512/479-0697

ANTIQUITIES COMMITTEE
105 W. 16th St.
P.O. Box 12276
Austin, TX 78711   512/463-6098

ARCHITECTURAL EXAMINERS,
TEXAS BOARD OF
8213 Shoal Creek Boulevard, Suite 107
Austin, TX 78758   512/458-1363

ARTS, TEXAS COMMISSION ON THE
920 Colorado
P.O. Box 13406
Austin, TX 78756   512/459-2952

ATHLETIC TRAINERS, ADVISORY BOARD OF
c/o Texas Department of Health
1100 W. 49th
Austin, TX 78756   512/459-2952

ATTORNEY GENERAL'S OFFICE
Supreme Court Building
P.O. Box 12548
Austin, TX 78711-2548   512/463-2063

AUDITOR'S OFFICE, STATE
206 E. 9th
P.O. Box 12067
Austin, TX 78711-2067   512/479-4700

AUSTIN STATE HOSPITAL
4110 Guadalupe St.
Austin, TX 78751   512/452-0381

AVIATION, TEXAS DEPARTMENT OF
410 E. 5th Street
Box 12607
Austin, TX 78711   512/476-9262

B

BANKING BOARD, STATE
2601 North Lamar
Austin, TX 78705   512/479-1200

BANKING DEPARTMENT OF TEXAS
2601 North Lamar
Austin, TX 78705   512/479-1200

BARBER EXAMINERS, STATE BOARD OF
9101 Burnet Road, Suite 103
Austin, TX 78758   512/835-2040

BATTLESHIP TEXAS ADVISORY BOARD
3527 Battleground Road
LaPorte, TX 77571   713/471-3200

BLIND, TEXAS COMMISSION FOR THE
4800 N. Lamar
P.O. Box 12866
Austin, TX 78711   512/459-2500

BRAZORIA COUNTY CONSERVATION
AND RECLAMATION DIST. #3
P.O. Box 789
1318 Rosharon Road
Alvin, TX 77512   713/331-3433

BRAZOS RIVER AUTHORITY
P.O. Box 7555
Waco, TX 76714-7555   817/776-1441

BRAZOS RIVER HARBOR NAVIGATION
DISTRICT—PORT OF FREEPORT
P.O. Box 615
1001 Pine Street
Freeport, TX 77541   409/233-2667

C

CANADIAN RIVER MUNICIPAL
WATER AUTHORITY
P.O. Box 99
Sanford, TX 79078   806/865-3325

CHIROPRACTIC EXAMINERS,
TEXAS STATE BOARD OF
8716 MoPac Expressway North, Suite 301
Austin, TX 77002   713/658-9020

COASTAL WATER AUTHORITY
1299 Smith Street
Citicorp Center, Suite 2260
Houston, TX 77002   713/658-9020

COLORADO RIVER AUTHORITY, CENTRAL
P.O. Box 964
Coleman, TX 76834   915/636-4373

COLORADO RIVER AUTHORITY, LOWER
3700 Lake Austin Boulevard
P.O. Box 220
Austin, TX 78767   512/473-3200

COMMERCE, TEXAS DEPARTMENT OF
First City Centre
816 Congress, 12th Floor
P.O. Box 12728
Austin, TX 78711   512/472-5059

COMMUNITY JUSTICE ASSISTANCE DIVISION,
TEXAS DEPARTMENT OF CRIMINAL JUSTICE
8100 Cameron Road
Suite 600 Building B
Austin, TX 78753   512/834-8188

COMPTROLLER OF PUBLIC ACCOUNTS
Lyndon B. Johnson Building
111 E. 17th Street
Austin, TX 78774   512/463-4000

CONCHO RIVER WATER AND SOIL
CONSERVATION AUTHORITY
Paint Rock, TX 76866

CONSUMER CREDIT COMMISSIONER
2601 N. Lamar
Austin, TX 78705-4207   512/479-1280

CONSUMER PROTECTION, OFFICE OF
333 Guadalupe, Suite 800
One Republic Plaza, Box 44
Austin, TX 78701-3938   512/322-4143

COORDINATING BOARD, TEXAS
HIGHER EDUCATION
7745 Chevy Chase Drive
P.O. Box 12788
Austin, TX 78711   512/483-6100

COSMETOLOGY COMMISSION, TEXAS
1111 Rio Grande
Austin, TX 78701   512/463-5540

COUNCILS OF GOVERNMENTS

Alamo Area Council of Government (AACOG)
118 Broadway, Suite 400
San Antonio, TX 78205   512/225-5201

Ark-Tex Council of Government (Ark-Tex COG)
P.O. Box 5307
Texarkana, TX 75505   214/832-8636

Brazos Valley Development Council (BVDC)
P.O. Drawer 4128
Bryan, TX 77805-4128   409/776-2277

Capital Area Planning Council (CAPCO)
2520 IH-35, S. Suite 100
Austin, TX 78704   512/443-7653

Central Texas Council of Government (CTCOG)
P.O. Box 729
Belton, TX 76513   817/939-1801

Coastal Bend Council of Government (CBCOG)
P.O. Box 9099
Corpus Christi, TX 78469   512/883-5743

Concho Valley Council of Governments (CVCOG)
P.O. Box 60050
San Angelo, TX 76906   915/944-9666

Deep East Texas Council of Government
(DETCOG)
274 E. Lamar
Jasper, TX 75951   409/384-5704

East Texas Council of Governments (ETCOG)
3800 Stone Road
Kilgore, TX 75662   214/984-8641

Golden Crescent Regional Planning
Commission (GCRPC)
P.O. Box 2028
Victoria, TX 77902   512/578-1587

Heart of Texas Council of Government
(HOTCOG)
320 Franklin
Waco, TX 76701-2297   817/756-7822

Houston-Galveston Area Council of Government
(H-GCOG)
P.O. Box 22777
3555 Timmons #500
Houston, TX 77227   713/627-3200

Lower Rio Grande Development Council
(LRGVDC)
4900 North 23rd St.
McAllen, TX 78504   512/682-3481

Middle Rio Grande Development Council
(MRGDC)
P.O. Box 1199
Carrizzo Springs, TX 78834   512/876-3533

Nortex Regional Planning Commission (NRPC)
P.O. Box 5144
Wichita Falls, TX 76307   817/322-5281

North Central Texas Council of Government
(NCTOCOG)
P.O. Box COG
Arlington, TX 76005-5888   817/640-3300

Panhandle Regional Planning Commission
(PRPC)
P.O. Box 9257
Amarillo, TX 79105-9257   806/372-3381

Permian Basin Regional Planning Commission
(PBRPC)
P.O. Box 60660
Midland, TX 78711-0660   915/563-1061

Rio Grande Council of Governments (RGCOG)
1014 N. Station, Suite 100
El Paso, TX 79902   915/553-0998

South East Texas Regional Planning
Commission (SETRPC)
P.O. Drawer 1387
Nederland, TX 77627   409/727-2384

South Plains Association of Governments (SPAG)
P.O. Box 3730
Lubbock, TX 79452   806/762-8721

South Texas Development Council (STDC)
P.O. Box 2187
Laredo, TX 78044-2187   512/722-3995

Texoma Council of Governments (TCOG)
1000 Grayson Drive
Dennison, TX 75020   214/786-2955

West Central Texas Council of Governments
(WCTCOG)
P.O. Box 3195
Abilene, TX 79604   915/672-8544

COUNSELORS, TEXAS STATE BOARD OF
EXAMINERS OF PROFESSIONAL
1100 West 49th
Austin, TX 78756-3183   512/459-2900

CREDIT UNION DEPARTMENT
914 East Anderson Lane
Austin, TX 78752-1699   512/837-9236

CRIMINAL JUSTICE, TEXAS DEPARTMENT OF
816 Congress, Suite 400
P.O. Box 13084
Austin, TX 78711   512/463-9988

CRIMINAL JUSTICE, TEXAS DEPARTMENT
OF—INSTITUTIONAL DIVISION
P.O. Box 99
Huntsville, TX 77342   409/295-6371

CRIMINAL JUSTICE POLICY COUNCIL
Sam Houston State Office Building
P.O. Box 13332
Austin, TX 78711   512/463-1810

D

DEAF, TEXAS COMMISSION FOR THE
1524 So. IH 35 #200
P.O. Box 12904
Austin, TX 78711   512/444-3323

DENTAL EXAMINERS, TEXAS STATE BOARD OF
327 Congress, Suite 500
Austin, TX 78701-4037   512/834-6021

DEPOSITORY BOARD, STATE
Lyndon B. Johnson State Office Building
P.O. Box 12608
Austin, TX 78711   512/463-6000

DEVELOPMENTAL DISABILITIES, TEXAS
PLANNING COUNCIL
4900 N. Lamar
Austin, TX 78751   512/483-4800

DIABETES COUNCIL, TEXAS
c/o Texas Department of Health
1100 W. 49th
Austin, TX 78756   512/458-7534

DIETITIANS, STATE BOARD OF EXAMINERS OF
c/o Texas Department of Health
1100 W. 49th
Austin, TX 78756   512/459-2945

DISABLED PERSONS, GOVERNOR'S
COMMITTEE FOR
4900 N. Lamar
Austin, TX 78751-2316   512/483-4300

E

EAST TEXAS STATE UNIVERSITY, BOARD OF
REGENTS
East Texas Station
Commerce, TX 75429   903/886-5014

EDUCATION, STATE BOARD OF
c/o Texas Education Agency
1701 N. Congress Avenue
Austin, TX 78701-1494   512/463-9007

EDUCATION AGENCY, TEXAS
1701 N. Congress Avenue
Austin, TX 78701   512/463-9734

EDUCATION BOARD, SOUTHERN REGIONAL
592 Tenth Street, N.W.
Atlanta, GA 30318-5790   404/875-9211

EDWARDS UNDERGROUND WATER DISTRICT
P.O. Box 15830
San Antonio, TX 78212   512/222-2204

EGG MARKETING ADVISORY BOARD
c/o Department of Agriculture
P.O. Box 12847
Austin, TX 78711   512/463-7624

EMERGENCY COMMUNICATIONS, ADVISORY
COMMISSION ON STATE
1101 Capital of Texas Hwy., S, Suite B-100
Austin, TX 78746   512/327-1911

EMERGENCY MANAGEMENT, DIVISION OF
5805 N. Lamar Blvd.
P.O. Box 4087
Austin, TX 78773   512/465-2138

EMPLOYERS RETIREMENT SYSTEM OF TEXAS
18th & Brazos
P.O. Box 13207
Austin, TX 78711-3207   512/476-6431

EMPLOYMENT COMMISSION, TEXAS
TEC Bldg.
Congress Avenue & 15th Street
Austin, TX 78778   512/463-2222

ENGINEERS, STATE BOARD OF
REGISTRATION FOR PROFESSIONAL
1917 IH 35 South
P.O. Drawer 18329
Austin, TX 78760   512/440-7723

F

FAMILY FARM AND RANCH ADVISORY
COUNCIL
SFA Bldg., Dept. of Agriculture
P.O. Box 12847
Austin, TX 78711   512/463-7569

FEED AND FERTILIZER CONTROL SERVICE,
TEXAS/OFFICE OF THE TEXAS STATE CHEMIST
Texas Agricultural Experiment Station
Texas A & M University System
P.O. Box 3160
College Station, TX 77841   409/845-1121

FILM COMMISSION, TEXAS
c/o Texas Dept. of Commerce
P.O. Box 12728
Austin, TX 78711   512/469-9111

FINANCE COMMISSION, STATE
2601 North Lamar
Austin, TX 78705   512/479-1200

FIRE DEPARTMENT EMERGENCY BOARD
c/o State Fire Marshall, State Board of Insurance
1110 San Jacinto Blvd.
Austin, TX 78701-1998   512/322-3550

FIRE FIGHTER'S RELIEF AND RETIREMENT
FUND, BOARD OF TRUSTEES
c/o Fire Fighter's Pension Commissioner
3910 S. I-35, Suite 235
Austin, TX 78704   512/462-0222

FIRE FIGHTER'S PENSION COMMISSIONER
3910 S. I-35, Suite 235
Austin, TX 78704   512/463-0222

FIRE MARSHALL, STATE
c/o State Board of Insurance
1110 San Jacinto Blvd.
Austin, TX 78701-1998   512/322-3550

FIRE PROTECTION PERSONNEL STANDARDS
AND EDUCATION, COMMISSION ON
9800 N. Lamar, Suite 160
Austin, TX 78753   512/837-9851

FOOD AND FIBER COMMISSION, TEXAS
17360 Coit Road
Dallas, TX 75252   214/231-0852

FOREST SERVICE, TEXAS
Texas A & M University Research Park
College Station, TX 77843-2136   409/845-2641

FUNERAL SERVICE COMMISSION, TEXAS
8100 Cameron Rd. Bldg. B, Suite 550
Austin, TX 78753   512/834-9992

G

GUADALUPE-BLANCO RIVER AUTHORITY
P.O. Box 271
Seguin, TX 78156-0271   512/379-5822

GUADALUPE RIVER AUTHORITY, UPPER
P.O. Box 1278
Kerrville, TX 78029   512/896-5445

GULF COAST WASTE DISPOSAL AUTHORITY
910 Bay Area Blvd.
P.O. Box 58150
Houston, TX 77258-8150   713/488-4115

GULF STATES MARINE FISHERIES COMMISSION
Box 726
Ocean Springs, MS 30564   601/875-5912

H

HEALTH, TEXAS DEPARTMENT OF
1100 West 49th Street
Austin, TX 78756   512/458-7111

HEALTH AND HUMAN SERVICES
COORDINATING COUNCIL, TEXAS
9101 Burnet Road, Suite 216
Austin, TX 78758   512/873-2400

HEALTH COORDINATING COUNCIL, TEXAS
STATEWIDE
c/o Texas Dept. of Health
1100 West 49th Street
Austin, TX 78756   512/458-7261

HEARING AIDS, TEXAS BOARD OF EXAMINERS
IN THE FITTING AND DISPENSING OF
4800 N. Lamar, Suite 150
Austin, TX 78756   512/459-1488

HIGH SPEED RAIL AUTHORITY, TEXAS
823 Congress, Suite 1502
Austin, TX 78701   512/478-5484

HIGHWAY AND PUBLIC TRANSPORTATION
COMMISSION, TEXAS
Dewitt C. Greer State Highway Building
11th & Brazos Streets
Austin, TX 78701-2483   512/463-8576

HIGHWAYS AND PUBLIC TRANSPORTATION,
TEXAS STATE DEPARTMENT OF
Dewitt C. Greer State Highway Building
11th & Brazos Streets
Austin, TX 78701-2483   512/463-8585

HISTORICAL COMMISSION, TEXAS
1511 Colorado Street
P.O. Box 12276
Austin, TX 78711   512/463-6100

HISTORICAL RECORDS ADVISORY BOARD,
TEXAS
State Library and Archives Bldg.
P.O. Box 12927 Capitol Station
Austin, TX 78711   512/463-5480

HOME HEALTH SERVICES ADVISORY COUNCIL
c/o Texas Department of Health
1100 W. 49th Street
Austin, TX 78756   512/458-7240

HOSPITAL LICENSING ADVISORY COUNCIL
c/o Texas Department of Health
1100 West 49th Street
Austin, TX 78756   512/458-7531

HOUSING AGENCY, TEXAS BOARD
OF DIRECTORS
811 Barton Springs, Suite 300
Austin, TX 78704   512/474-2974

HUMAN RIGHTS, STATE COMMISSION ON
8100 Cameron Rd. #525
P.O. Box 13493
Austin, TX 78711   512/837-8534

HUMAN SERVICES, TEXAS DEPARTMENT OF
701 West 51st Street
P.O. Box 149030
Austin, TX 78714-9030   512/450-3011

I

INCENTIVE AND PRODUCTIVITY
COMMISSION, TEXAS
E.O. Thompson Bldg. Room 103
P.O. Box 12482
Austin, TX 78711   512/475-3293

INDUSTRIALIZED BUILDING CODE
COUNCIL
c/o Dept. of Licensing & Regulation
920 Colorado St.
P.O. Box 12157
Austin, TX 78711   512/463-7348

INFORMATION RESOURCES, TEXAS
DEPARTMENT OF
3307 Northland Drive, Suite 300
Box 13564
Austin, TX 78711   512/371-1120

INSURANCE, STATE BOARD OF
1110 San Jacinto
Austin, TX 78701-1998   512/463-6464

INTERSTATE MINING COMPACT
COMMISSION (IMCC)
459B Carlisle Drive
Herndon, VA 22070   703/709-8654

INTERSTATE OIL COMPACT COMMISSION
900 N.E. 23rd St.
P.O. Box 53127
Oklahoma City, OK 73152   405/525-3556

IRRIGATORS, TEXAS BOARD OF
1700 N. Congress Avenue Room 647
P.O. Box 12337
Austin, TX 78711   512/463-7990

J

JAIL STANDARDS, TEXAS COMMISSION ON
611 South Congress, Suite 200
P.O. Box 12985
Austin, TX 78711   512/463-5505

JUVENILE PROBATION COMMISSION, TEXAS
2015 S. IH-35
P.O. Box 13547
Austin, TX 78711   512/443-2001

L

LAMAR UNIVERSITY SYSTEM, BOARD OF
REGENTS
P.O. Box 11900
Beaumont, TX 77710   409/880-2304

LAND OFFICE, GENERAL
1700 N. Congress Avenue
Austin, TX 78701-1945   512/463-5001

LAVANCA-NAVIDAD RIVER AUTHORITY
P.O. Box 429
Edna, TX 77957   512/782-5229

LAW ENFORCEMENT OFFICER STANDARDS-
EDUCATION, TEXAS COMMISSION OF
1033 LaPosada, Suite 175
Austin, TX 78752   512/450-0188

LEGISLATIVE BUDGET BOARD
State Capitol
P.O. Box 12666
Austin, TX 78711   512/463-1166

LEGISLATIVE COUNCIL, TEXAS
Capitol, 1st Floor, Room 155
P.O. Box 12128
Austin, TX 78711   512/463-1151

LEGISLATIVE REFERENCE LIBRARY
Capitol Building, 2nd Floor
P.O. Box 12488
Austin, TX 78711   512/463-1252

M

MEDICAL EXAMINERS, TEXAS STATE BOARD OF
1101 Camino La Costa #201
P.O. Box 13562, Capitol Station
Austin, TX 78711   512/452-1078

MEDICAL EXAMINERS, BOARD OF DISTRICT
REVIEW COMMITTEES
1101 Camino La Costa #201
P.O. Box 13562, Capitol Station
Austin, TX 78711   512/452-1078

MENTAL HEALTH AND MENTAL
RETARDATION, TEXAS DEPARTMENT OF
909 West 45th Street
P.O. Box 12668
Austin, TX 78711-2668   512/454-3761

MIDWESTERN STATE UNIVERSITY,
BOARD OF REGENTS
3400 Taft Boulevard
Wichita Falls, TX 76308   817/692-6611

MOTOR VEHICLE COMMISSION, TEXAS
300 Brazos Building
815 Brazos
Austin, TX 78701   512/476-3587

MUNICIPAL RETIREMENT SYSTEM, TEXAS
1200 N. Interstate 35
Austin, TX 78701   512/476-7577

MUSIC OFFICE, TEXAS
c/o Texas Dept. of Commerce
P.O. Box 12728
Austin, TX 78711   512/320-9474

N

NATIONAL GUARD ARMORY BOARD, TEXAS
Camp Mabry
P.O. Box 5426
Austin, TX 78763   512/451-6394

NATIONAL RESEARCH LABORATORY
COMMISSION, TEXAS
1801 North Hampton, Suite 400
DeSoto, TX 75115   214/709-3800

NECHES RIVER, UPPER, MUNICIPAL
WATER AUTHORITY
P.O. Drawer 1965
Palestine, TX 75802   214/876-2237

NECHES VALLEY AUTHORITY, LOWER
7850 Eastex Freeway
P.O. Box 3464
Beaumont, TX 77704

NORTH TEXAS, UNIVERSITY OF,
BOARD OF REGENTS
P.O. Box 13737
Denton, TX 76203   817/565-2904

NUECES RIVER AUTHORITY
First State Bank Building, Suite 206
P.O. Box 349
Uvalde, TX 78802-0349

NURSE EXAMINERS FOR THE STATE OF
TEXAS, BOARD OF
9101 Burnet Road, Suite 104
Austin, TX 78758   512/835-4880

NURSE EXAMINERS, BOARD OF VOCATIONAL
9101 Burnet Road, Suite 105
Austin, TX 78758   512/835-2071

NURSING HOME ADMINISTRATORS,
TEXAS BOARD OF LICENSURE FOR
4800 North Lamar, Suite 310
Austin, TX 78756   512/458-1955

O

OCCUPATIONAL THERAPY,
ADVISORY BOARD OF
4900 N. Lamar
Austin, TX 78751-2316   512/483-4072

OPTOMETRY BOARD, TEXAS
9101 Burnet Road, Suite 214
Austin, TX 78758   512/835-1938

P

PARDONS AND PAROLES DIVISION, TEXAS
DEPARTMENT OF CRIMINAL JUSTICE
8610 Shoal Creek Blvd.
P.O. Box 13401
Austin, TX 78711   512/459-2700

PARKS AND WILDLIFE DEPARTMENT, TEXAS
4200 Smith School Road
Austin, TX 78744   512/389-4800

PECOS RIVER COMPACT COMMISSIONER
401 North Main Office
Fort Stockton, TX 79735   915/336-3989

PENSION REVIEW BOARD
Employee Retirement System Bldg.
18th & Brazos
P.O. Box 13498
Austin, TX 78711   512/463-1736

PEST CONTROL BOARD, TEXAS STRUCTURAL
9101 Burnet Road, Suite 201
Austin, TX 78758   512/835-4066

PHARMACY, TEXAS STATE BOARD OF
8505 Cross Park Drive, Suite 110
Austin, TX 78754-4594   512/832-0661

PHYSICAL THERAPY EXAMINERS, TEXAS
STATE BOARD OF
313 Rundberg, Suite 113
Austin, TX 78753   512/835-1846

PLUMBING EXAMINERS, STATE BOARD OF
929 East 41st Street
Austin, TX 78751   512/458-2145

PODIATRY EXAMINERS, TEXAS
STATE BOARD OF
3420 Executive Center Drive, Suite 305
Austin, TX 78731   512/794-0145

POLYGRAPH EXAMINERS BOARD
5805 N. Lamar
P.O. Box 4087
Austin, TX 78773   512/465-2058

PRESERVATION BOARD, STATE
P.O. Box 13286
Austin, TX 78711   512/463-5495

PRIVATE INVESTIGATORS AND PRIVATE
SECURITY AGENCIES, TEXAS BOARD OF
313 E. Anderson Lane, Suite 200
P.O. Box 13509
Austin, TX 78711   512/463-5545

PRODUCE RECOVERY FUND BOARD
c/o State Dept. of Agriculture
Stephen F. Austin Bldg.
P.O. Box 12847
Austin, TX 78711   512/463-7604

PROPERTY TAX BOARD, STATE
4301 Westbank Drive
Bldg. B, Suite 100
Austin, TX 78746   512/329-7901

PSYCHOLOGISTS, TEXAS BOARD OF
EXAMINERS OF
9101 Burnet Road, Suite 212
Austin, TX 78758   512/835-2036

PURCHASING AND GENERAL SERVICES
COMMISSION, STATE
Central Services Bldg.
1711 San Jacinto
P.O. Box 13047
Austin, TX 78711   512/463-3446

R

RACING COMMISSION, TEXAS
9420 Research, Suite 200
P.O. Box 12080
Austin, TX 78711   512/794-8461

RADIOACTIVE WASTE DISPOSAL AUTHORITY,
TEXAS LOW-LEVEL
7701 N. Lamar Blvd., Suite 300
Austin, TX 78752   512/451-5292

RAILROAD COMMISSION OF TEXAS
William B. Travis Bldg.
P.O. Box 12967
Austin, TX 78711   512/463-7288

REAL ESTATE COMMISSION OF TEXAS
1101 Camino La Costa
P.O. Box 12188
Austin, TX 78711   512/459-6544

REAL ESTATE RESEARCH CENTER
Texas A & M University
College Station, TX 77843-2115   409/845-2031

RED RIVER AUTHORITY OF TEXAS
520 Hamilton Bldg.
Wichita Falls, TX 76301   817/723-8697

RED RIVER COMPACT COMMISSIONER
P.O. Box 6660
Texarkana, TX 75505   214/792-1988

REHABILITATION COMMISSION, TEXAS
4900 N. Lamar Blvd.
Austin, TX 78751-2316   512/483-4000

RETIREMENT SYSTEM OF TEXAS, TEACHER
1000 Red River
Austin, TX 78701   412/397-6400

RETIREMENT SYSTEM, TEXAS COUNTY AND
DISTRICT
400 West 14th Street
Austin, TX 78701   512/476-6651

RIO GRANDE COMPACT COMMISSIONER
FOR TEXAS
5812 Cromo Drive, Suite 105
P.O. Box 12785
El Paso, TX 79913   915/581-1161

RIO GRANDE VALLEY MUNICIPAL WATER
AUTHORITY
3505 Boca Chica, Suite 303
Brownsville, TX 78521   512/541-1660

S

SABINE RIVER AUTHORITY OF TEXAS
P.O. Box 579
Orange, TX 77630   409/746-2192

SABINE RIVER COMPACT COMMISSION,
TEXAS
Box 579
Orange, TX 77630   409/746-2192

SAN ANTONIO RIVER AUTHORITY
100 East Guenther Street
P.O. Box 830027
San Antonio, TX 78283-0027   512/227-1373

SAN JACINTO HISTORICAL ADVISORY BOARD
c/o Parks Section
Parks & Wildlife Dept.
4200 Smith School Road
Austin, TX 78744   512/389-4889

SAN JACINTO RIVER AUTHORITY
P.O. Box 329
Conroe, TX 77305   409/588-1111

SAVINGS AND LOAN DEPARTMENT OF TEXAS
2601 North Lamar, Suite 201
Austin, TX 78705   512/479-1250

SCHOOL LAND BOARD
c/o General Land Office
Stephen F. Austin State Office Building
Austin, TX 78701   512/463-5016

SECRETARY OF STATE
State Capitol Building
Austin, TX 78711   512/463-5701

SECURITIES BOARD, STATE
1800 San Jacinto Street
P.O. Box 13167
Capitol Station
Austin, TX 78711-3167   512/474-2233

SEED AND PLANT BOARD, STATE
c/o Texas Department of Agriculture
Stephen F. Austin Building
P.O. Box 12847
Austin, TX 78711   512/463-7614

SOIL AND WATER CONSERVATION BOARD,
TEXAS STATE
311 North 5th Street
P.O. Box 658
Temple, TX 76503   817/773-2250

SPEECH-LANGUAGE PATHOLOGY AND
AUDIOLOGY, STATE COMMITTEE OF
EXAMINERS FOR
c/o Texas Department of Health
1100 W. 49th
Austin, TX 78756   512/459-2935

STEPHEN F. AUSTIN STATE UNIVERSITY,
BOARD OF REGENTS
Box 6078 SFA Station
Nacogdoches, TX 75962   409/568-2201

STUDENT LOAN CORPORATION, TEXAS
GUARANTEED
1609 Centre Creek Drive
P.O. Box 15996
Austin, TX 78761   512/835-1900

SUNSET ADVISORY COMMISSION
Reagan Building, Room 305
P.O. Box 13066
Austin, TX 78711   512/463-1300

SURPLUS PROPERTY AGENCY, TEXAS
2103 Ackerman Road
P.O. Box 8120
San Antonio, TX 78208-0120   512/661-2381

SURVEYING, TEXAS BOARD OF
PROFESSIONAL LAND
7701 N. Lamar, Suite 400
Austin, TX 78752   512/452-9427

T

TAX PROFESSIONAL EXAMINERS BOARD
4301 Westbank Drive
Building B, Suite 140
Austin, TX 78746-6565   512/329-7982

TEACHERS PROFESSIONAL PRACTICES
COMMISSION
1701 N. Congress Avenue
William B. Travis Building
Austin, TX 78701   512/463-9337

TEXAS SOUTHERN UNIVERSITY, BOARD OF
REGENTS
3100 Cleburne Avenue
Houston, TX 77004   713/527-7900

TEXAS STATE TECHNICAL INSTITUTE,
BOARD OF REGENTS
Waco, TX 76705   817/799-3611

TEXAS STATE UNIVERSITY SYSTEM, BOARD
OF REGENTS
505 Sam Houston Building
Austin, TX 78701   512/463-1808

TEXAS TECH UNIVERSITY, BOARD OF REGENTS
TEXAS TECH UNIVERSITY HEALTH SCIENCES
CENTER, BOARD OF REGENTS
P.O. Box 4039
Lubbock, TX 79409   806/742-2161

TEXAS WING, CIVIL AIR PATROL
Building 4212
Bergstrom AFB, TX 78743   512/389-3000

TEXAS WOMAN'S UNIVERSITY, BOARD OF
REGENTS
P.O. Box 23025 TWU Station
Denton, TX 76204   817/898-3250

TREASURY DEPARTMENT, STATE
LBJ Building
P.O. Box 12608
Austin, TX 78711   512/463-6000

TRINITY RIVER AUTHORITY OF TEXAS
P.O. Box 60
Arlington, TX 76004-0060   817/467-4343

TURNPIKE AUTHORITY, TEXAS
3015 Raleigh St.
P.O. Box 190369
Dallas, TX 75219   214/522-6200

U

UNIVERSITY OF TEXAS SYSTEM
BOARD OF REGENTS
Sam Houston Building, 5th Floor
Austin, TX 78711   512/463-1808

V

VETERANS COMMISSION, TEXAS
E.O. Thompson Building
10th & Colorado, 6th Floor
P.O. Box 12277
Austin, TX 78701   512/463-5538

VETERANS LAND BOARD
Stephen F. Austin Building
Austin, TX 78701   512/463-5350

VETERINARY MEDICAL EXAMINERS,
TEXAS BOARD OF
1946 South IH 35, Suite 306
Austin, TX 78704   512/447-1183

VOCATIONAL EDUCATION,
TEXAS COUNCIL ON
1717 West 6th Street, Suite 360
P.O. Box 1886
Austin, TX 78767   512/463-5490

W

WATER COMMISSION, TEXAS
1700 North Congress
P.O. Box 13087
Austin, TX 78711   512/463-7830

WATER DEVELOPMENT BOARD, TEXAS
1700 North Congress
P.O. Box 13231
Austin, TX 78711   512/463-7847

WATER WELL DRILLERS BOARD, TEXAS
1700 N. Congress
P.O. Box 13087
Austin, TX 78711   512/371-6299

WEATHERIZATION POLICY ADVISORY
COUNCIL
c/o Texas Dept. of Community Affairs
P.O. Box 13166, Capitol Station
Austin, TX 78711   512/834-6050

WORKERS COMPENSATION
COMMISSION, TEXAS
4000 S. IH-35
Austin, TX 78704-1287   512/448-7900

Y

YOUTH COMMISSION, TEXAS
4900 N. Lamar
P.O. Box 4260
Austin, TX 78765   512/483-5000

GLOSSARY

abstracts Another term for the case annotations found in digests.

adjudication procedures Proceedings similar to those of a court that take place before, and under the guidance of, an agency administrative law judge who makes a final decision on the issue in question.

administrative agency† A board, commission, bureau, office, or department, of the executive branch of government, that implements the law that originates with the legislative branch.

administrative law† The body of law that controls the way in which administrative agencies operate; regulations issued by administrative agencies.

administrative procedure act† A statute enacted by Congress and statutes enacted by state legislatures that regulate the way in which administrative agencies conduct their affairs and that establish procedures for judicial review of the actions of agencies.

advance sheet† A printed copy of a judicial opinion published in looseleaf form shortly after the opinion is issued.

advisory opinions† Judicial interpretations of legal questions requested by the legislative or executive branch of government.

affirmed† The upholding of a lower court's decision or judgment by an appellate court.

answer† A pleading in response to a complaint. An answer may deny the allegations of the complaint, demur to them, agree with them, or introduce affirmative defenses intended to defeat the plaintiff's lawsuit or delay it.

appeal† The process by which a higher court is requested by a party to a lawsuit to review the decision of a lower court.

appeals court† A court in which appeals from a lower court are heard and decided.

appellant† A party who appeals from a lower court to a higher court.

appellee† A party against whom a case is appealed from a lower court to a higher court.

bench trial† A trial before a judge without a jury.

Bill of Rights† The first ten amendments to the United States Constitution; the portion of the Constitution that sets forth the rights that are the fundamental principles of the United States and the foundation of American citizenship.

binding precedent† Previous decisions of a higher court that a judge must follow in reaching a decision in a case.

branches of government† Three divisions into which the Constitution separates the government of the United States, specifically, the executive branch, the legislative branch, and the judicial branch.

CALR Computer-assisted legal research in which special software programs are used to search the full text of cases, statutes, and other legal sources.

caption† A heading; in legal practice, it generally refers to the heading of a court paper.

case annotations Paragraphs that appear in digests, prepared by editors at publishing companies who review and analyze reported decisions to identify and summarize the courts' positions on every rule of law they address.

case brief† An outline of the published opinion in a case, made by an attorney or a paralegal for the purpose of understanding the case.

case law† The law as laid down in the decisions of the courts in similar cases that have previously been decided.

case reporter† Official, published reports of cases decided by courts, giving the opinions rendered in the cases, with headnotes prepared by the publisher.

CD-ROM A system in which a read only memory compact disc, which stores large amounts of information, can provide access through a computer modem and terminal to mini-libraries for purposes of legal research.

challenge for cause† An objection, for a stated reason, to a juror being allowed to hear a case.

citation† A writ issued by a judge, ordering a person to appear in court for a specified purpose.

citators† Systems of books, the use of which allows a person doing legal research to locate every court opinion in which a particular case is cited, and to determine the context in which it is cited as well as whether it has been affirmed, distinguished, followed, overruled, or simply mentioned.

cite checking Using a citator to determine the legal status of a case or statute.

citing case A later case that mentions or discusses a cited case.

civil law† Law based upon a published code of statutes, as opposed to law found in the decisions of courts.

closing statement† Making the closing argument (also referred to as a final argument) in a case; summing up.

codification† The process of arranging laws in a systematic form covering the entire law of a jurisdiction or a particular area of the law; the process of creating a code.

common law† Law found in the decisions of the courts rather than in statutes; judge-made law; English law adopted by the early American colonists, which is part of the United States' judicial heritage and forms the basis of much of its law today.

compensatory damages† Damages recoverable in a lawsuit for loss or injury suffered by the plaintiff as a result of the defendant's conduct.

complaint† The initial pleading in a civil action, in which the plaintiff alleges a cause of action and asks that the wrong done him or her be remedied by the court.

concurrent jurisdiction† Two or more courts having the power to adjudicate the same class of cases or the same matter.

concurring in part and dissenting in part opinion An opinion of the court in which the judges agree with a part of a decision and disagree with another part of the decision.

concurring opinion† An opinion issued by one or more judges that agrees with the result reached by the majority opinion rendered by the court, but reaches that result for different reasons.

connectors Words used in computer-assisted legal research that will connect words and phrases for search purposes; for example, "or," "and," "but not," and "w/n."

constitution† The system of fundamental principles by which a nation, state, or corporation is governed.

counterclaim† A cause of action on which a defendant in a lawsuit might have sued the plaintiff in a separate action, which is stated in a separate division of a defendant's answer.

court† A part of government, consisting of a judge or judges and, usually, administrative support personnel, whose duty it is to administer justice; the judicial branch of government.

court of general jurisdiction† Generally, another term for trial court; that is, a court having jurisdiction to try all classes of civil and criminal cases except those which can be heard only by a court of limited jurisdiction.

court of limited jurisdiction†   A court whose jurisdiction is limited to civil cases of a certain type or which involve a limited amount of money, or whose jurisdiction in criminal cases is confined to petty offenses and preliminary hearings.

courts of original jurisdiction   Trial courts, where cases are filed and initially tried, as distinguished from appellate courts.

courts of record†   Generally, another term for trial courts.

crime†   An offense against the authority of the state; a public wrong, as distinguished from a private wrong; an act in violation of the penal code; a felony or a misdemeanor.

criminal law†   Branch of the law that specifies what conduct constitutes crime and establishes appropriate punishments for such conduct.

cross-claim†   A counterclaim against a coplaintiff or a codefendant.

cross-examination†. The interrogation of a witness for the opposing party by questions designed to test the accuracy and truthfulness of the testimony the witness gave on direct examination.

defendant†   The person against whom an action is brought.

deponent†   A person who gives a deposition.

depositions†   Transcripts of witnesses' testimonies given under oath outside of the courtroom, usually in advance of the trial or hearing, upon oral examination or in response to written interrogatories.

Desk Edition   An abridgement of a large set of reference books.

dicta (obiter dictum)†   Expressions or comments in a court opinion that are not necessary to support the decision made by the court; they are not binding authority and have no value as precedent.

digest†   A series of volumes containing summaries of cases organized by legal topics, subject areas, and so on; digests are essential for legal research.

direct examination†   The first or initial questioning of a witness by the party who called the witness to the stand.

discovery†   A means for providing a party, in advance of trial, with access to facts that are within the knowledge of the other side, to enable the party to better try his or her case.

disposition†   A court's ruling, decision, or judgment in a case.

dissenting opinion†   A written opinion filed by a judge of an appellate court who disagrees with the decision of the majority of judges in a case, giving the reasons for his or her differing view.

distinguishing a case†   To explain why a particular case is not precedent or authority with respect to the matter in controversy; to point out significant differences.

diversity jurisdiction†   The jurisdiction of a federal court arising from diversity of citizenship, i.e., the existence of a controversy between citizens of different states, when the jurisdictional amount has been met.

docket†   A list of cases for trial or other disposition; a court calendar.

docket number†   The number given to a case when it is on a list of cases for trial or other disposition.

dominant jurisdiction   The power of one court over another to adjudicate the issues where two suits involving the same parties and issues are filed in courts of concurrent jurisdiction.

dot commands   A dot, or period, followed by initials; used in LEXIS research to indicate the action the computer should perform.

enabling act†   A statute that grants new powers or authority to persons or corporations.

equitable relief† A remedy available in equity rather than at law; generally relief other than money damages.

exclusive jurisdiction† Jurisdiction when only one court has the power to adjudicate the same class of cases or the same matter.

executive branch† With the legislative branch and the judicial branch, one of the three divisions into which the Constitution separates the government of the United States; the executive branch is primarily responsible for enforcing the laws.

executive orders† Orders issued by the chief executive officer (e.g., the president of the United States; the governor of a state; the mayor of a city) of government, whether national, state, or local.

exemplary damages† Damages that are awarded over and above compensatory or actual damages for the purpose of making an example of the plaintiff to discourage others from engaging in the same kind of conduct in the future.

fact† An actual occurrence, as distinguished from the legal consequences of the occurrence.

fastback decision A copy of a decision ordered directly from the court.

federal question jurisdiction† The power of federal courts to adjudicate a question created by any case arising under the Constitution or any treaty or statute of the United States; it also exists in any case based upon diversity of citizenship.

felony† A general term for more serious crimes, as distinguished from lesser offenses, which are known as misdemeanors; in many jurisdictions, felonies are crimes for which the punishment is death or more than one year of imprisonment.

files As used in reference to computerized legal research databases, separate groups of related documents that can be searched as groups on LEXIS or as databases on WESTLAW.

final judgment† A judgment that determines the merits of the case by declaring that the plaintiff is or is not entitled to recovery.

forcible entry and detainer action† An action to obtain a summary remedy for obtaining possession of real property by a person who has been wrongfully put out or kept out of possession.

formal rule making The procedure by which a proposed rule is published in a manner provided by law and a trial-type proceeding is held to which all interested parties are invited to appear before the agency and present testimony, documentation, or any information relevant to final agency action on the proposed rule.

front matter Materials at the beginning of a book that can provide valuable research guidance, *e.g.,* tables of contents, cases, statutes, rules, and cross-references.

general damages† Damages that are the natural and probable result of the wrongful acts complained of.

headnote† A summary statement that appears at the beginning of a reported case to indicate the points decided by the case.

holding† The proposition of law for which a case stands; the "bottom line" of a judicial decision.

impeach† To charge a public officer with defective performance in office.

informal rule making The procedure by which a proposed rule is published in a manner provided by law, the public is given an opportunity to submit comments about it to the agency sponsoring the rule, and the agency reviews all information and makes a final determination whether to pass the proposed rule.

injunction† A court order that commands or prohibits some act or course of conduct.

interlocutory order† An order that is not final, but only intermediate, and does not determine or complete the action.

interrogatories† Written questions put by one party to another, or, in limited situations, to a witness in advance of trial.

issue† A material point or question arising out of the pleadings in a case, which is disputed by the parties and which they wish the court to decide.

judgment† In a civil action, the final determination by a court of the rights of the parties, based upon the pleadings and the evidence; in a criminal prosecution, a determination of guilt.

judicial branch† With the legislative branch and the executive branch, one of the three divisions into which the constitution separates the government of the United States; the judicial branch is primarily responsible for interpreting the laws.

jurisdiction† In a general sense, the right of a court to adjudicate lawsuits of a certain kind; in a specific sense, the right of a court to determine a particular case.

jury instructions† Directions given to the jury by the judge, just before the jurors are sent out to deliberate and return a verdict, explaining the law that applies in the case and spelling out what must be proven and by whom.

jury trial† A trial in which the jurors are the judges of the facts and the court is the judge of the law.

law† The entire body of rules of conduct created by government and enforced by the authority of government.

lawsuit† An informal term for an action or proceeding in a civil court, but not for a criminal prosecution.

legal encyclopedias Secondary sources of law that provide commentaries about, and case authority for, a myriad of legal subjects; general in nature but important in legal research.

legal research† A study of precedents and other authority for the purpose of developing or supporting a legal theory or position.

legislative branch† With the judicial branch and the executive branch, one of the three divisions into which the Constitution separates the government of the United States; the legislative branch is primarily responsible for enacting the laws.

legislative history† Recorded events that provide a basis for determining the legislative intent underlying a statute enacted by a legislature.

LEXIS The first computer-assisted legal research service, introduced by the Ohio State Bar and marketed by Mead Data Central; it contains all available cases, *A.L.R.* annotations, and other features.

liability† A legal responsibility such as a debt one is required to pay, an obligation one must discharge, the circumstance one is in when he or she has breached a contract, or a person's responsibility after he or she has committed a tort that causes injury.

libraries As used in reference to computerized legal research databases, groupings of all materials into particular subject areas; both federal and state libraries are available.

litigation† A legal action; the area of the law concerning trial work.

looseleaf reporter services Official reports of cases decided by courts that are published in a notebook-style format that can be easily updated by substituting more recent pages for the original ones.

majority opinion† An opinion issued by an appellate court that represents the view of a majority of the members of the court.

mandatory authority Binding legal authority that a court must follow in making a decision in a case.

masters† Persons appointed by the court to assist with certain judicial functions in specific cases.

memorandum opinion† A court decision, usually consisting of a brief paragraph announcing the court's judgment, without an in-depth opinion.

misdemeanor†   A crime not amounting to a felony; in many jurisdictions, misdemeanors are offenses for which the punishment is incarceration for less than a year or the payment of a fine.

modem   A device used to convert digital impulses from a computer to analog impulses for transmission by telephone line.

monetary damages†   The sum of money that may be recovered in the courts as financial reparation for an injury or wrong suffered as a result of breach of contract or a tortious act.

mootness†   Of no actual significance; a case is moot when it involves only abstract questions, without any actual controversy between the parties.

motion†   An application made to a court for the purpose of obtaining an order or rule directing something to be done in favor of the applicant.

motion in limine†   A motion made before the commencement of a trial that requests the court to prohibit the adverse party from introducing prejudicial evidence at trial.

motion for summary judgment   An application made to the court requesting that the action be disposed of without further proceedings.

nominal or token damages†   Damages awarded to a plaintiff in a very small or merely symbolic amount where no actual damages have been incurred, but the law recognizes the need to vindicate the plaintiff, or some compensable injury has been shown, but the amount of that injury has not been proven.

nominative reporters   Early reports of United States Supreme Court cases that were compiled by individuals and identified by the individuals' names.

nonbinding precedent   Previous decisions of a higher court that a judge may, but does not have to, follow in reaching a decision in a case.

notice and comment rule making   Another term for informal rule making.

official reporter   The publication containing reports of cases that has been designated by or on behalf of a court as the one that is to be accepted as a matter of law as containing the final valid versions of the opinions issued by that court.

on-line   The accessing of information stored in a computerized legal research database at a remote location by use of a telecommunications system.

opening statement†   A statement made by the attorney for each party at the beginning of a trial, outlining to the judge and jury the issues in the case and the facts that each side intends to prove.

opinion†   A written statement by a court that accompanies its decision in a case and gives the court's reasons for its decision. Although "decision" and "opinion" are often used interchangeably, the terms are not synonymous: a decision is the judgment in the case; an opinion gives the reasoning on which judgment is based.

oral argument†   A party, through his or her attorney, usually presents the party's case to an appellate court on appeal by arguing the case verbally to the court, in addition to submitting a brief.

original jurisdiction†   The jurisdiction of a trial court, as distinguished from the jurisdiction of an appellate court.

parallel citation†   A citation to a court opinion or decision that is printed in two or more reporters.

peace bonds†   Bonds that a court requires be posted by a person who has threatened to commit a breach of the peace.

peremptory challenge†   A challenge to a juror that a party may exercise without having to give a reason.

per curiam opinion†   An opinion, usually of an appellate court, in which the judges are all of one view and the legal question is sufficiently clear that a full written opinion is not required and a one- or two-paragraph opinion suffices.

persuasive authority† Authority that is neither binding authority nor precedent, but which a court may use to support its decision if it chooses.

petition† The name given in some jurisdictions to a complaint or other pleading that alleges a cause of action.

petitioner† A person seeking relief by a petition.

petition for discretionary review† A request that the appellate court review a case even though review is not required by law but takes place solely at the discretion of the court.

plaintiff† A person who brings a lawsuit.

plurality opinion† An appellate court opinion joined in by less than a majority of the justices, but by more justices than the number joining any other concurring opinion.

precedent† Prior decisions of the same court or a higher court that a judge must follow in deciding a subsequent case presenting similar facts and the same legal problem, even though different parties are involved and many years have elapsed.

pretrial conference† A conference held between the judge and counsel for all parties prior to trial, for the purpose of facilitating disposition of the case by, among other actions, simplifying the pleadings, narrowing the issues, obtaining stipulations to avoid unnecessary proof and limiting the number of witnesses.

primary sources The collective term for the main sources of the law: constitutions, judicial opinions, statutes and treaties, and administrative law.

private laws† The rules of conduct that govern activities occurring among or between persons, as opposed to the rules of conduct governing the relationship between persons and their government.

procedural law† The law governing the manner in which rights are enforced; the law prescribing the procedure to be followed in a case.

proclamations† Official announcements by the government.

public law number The number of a statute in the slip laws that is assigned once the statute has completed the legislative process.

public laws† Laws dealing with the relationships between the people and their government, between agencies and branches of government, and between governments themselves.

punitive damages† Damages that are awarded over and above compensatory damages or actual damages because of the wanton, reckless, or malicious nature of the wrong done by the plaintiff.

reasoning The legal basis upon which the court relies to reach its result in a case.

regulation† A rule having the force of law, promulgated by an administrative agency.

relief† A person's object in bringing a lawsuit; the function or purpose of a remedy.

remanded† A case that is returned by an appellate court to the trial court for further proceedings, for a new trial, or for entry of judgment in accordance with an order of the appellate court.

remedy† The means by which a right is enforced, an injury is redressed, and relief is obtained.

reporter† Court reports, as well as official, published reports of cases decided by administrative agencies.

request for admission† Written statements concerning a case, directed to an adverse party, that he or she is required to admit or deny. Such admissions or denials will be treated by the court as having been established, and need not be proven at trial.

request for production of documents A request to a party to produce documents and other tangible evidence that is relevant to the case.

respondent† The party against whom an appeal is taken to a higher court, *i.e.*, the successful party in the lower court; the appellee.

reversed†   The overthrow or annulment of a prior decision.

root expansion   A method used in computer-assisted legal research to search for different words that share the same root without having to type each of those words again.

rule†   An order of a court or an administrative agency made in a particular proceeding with respect to the disposition of the case or some aspect of the case; a regulation issued by an administrative agency.

search query   A particular word or series of words that represent a concept being researched on a computerized database.

secondary authority†   Nonbinding or persuasive authority that is not the law itself but simply commentary upon or a summary of the law.

service of process†   Delivery of a summons, writ, complaint, or other process to the opposite party, or other person entitled to receive it, in such manner as the law prescribes, whether by leaving a copy at the party's residence, by mailing a copy to the party or the party's attorney, or by publication.

session laws†   The collected statutes enacted during a session of a legislature.

Shepardizing   Using a citator to determine the legal status of a case or statue.

slip law†   A single judicial decision published shortly after it has been issued by the court and well before it is incorporated into a reporter.

slip opinion†   A single judicial decision published shortly after it has been issued by the court and well before it is incorporated into a reporter.

small claims jurisdiction†   The power of a court of limited jurisdiction to adjudicate the litigation of small claims, that is, claims not exceeding a specified limited amount, which varies according to state statute.

special damages†   Damages that may be added to the general damages in a case, and arise from the particular or special circumstances of the case; the natural but not necessary result of a tort; damages arising naturally but not necessarily from a breach of contract.

specific performance†   The equitable remedy of compelling performance of a contract, as distinguished from an action at law for damages for breach of contract due to nonperformance.

standing†   The position of a person with respect to his or her capacity to act in particular circumstances.

stare decisis†   The doctrine that judicial decisions stand as precedents for cases arising in the future.

star paging   A pagination system used in unofficial reporters to reference the official reporter pages that correspond to the pages in the unofficial reporters.

statutory codes†   The published statutes of a jurisdiction, arranged in systematic form.

statutory law†   Law that is promulgated by statute, as opposed to law that is promulgated by the judiciary.

subpoena duces tecum†   A written command requiring a witness to come to court to testify and at that time to produce for use as evidence the papers, documents, books, or records listed in the subpoena.

substantive law†   Area of the law that defines right conduct, as opposed to procedural law, which governs the process by which rights are adjudicated.

summons†   The process by which an action is commenced and the defendant is brought within the jurisdiction of the court.

syllabus†   The headnote of a reported case.

terminal   A computer with a screen on which information retrieved from a computerized legal research database can be viewed.

third-party complaint†   A complaint filed by the defendant in a lawsuit against a third person whom he or she seeks to bring into the action because of that person's alleged liability to the defendant.

trial† A hearing or determination by a court of the issues existing between the parties to an action.

trial courts† Courts that hear and determine cases initially, as opposed to appellate courts; courts of general jurisdiction.

trial de novo† A new trial, a retrial, or a trial on appeal from a justice's court or a magistrate's court to a court of general jurisdiction.

unofficial reporter A publication containing reports of cases that has not been endorsed by the court as containing the official versions of the cases heard by the court.

vacated† A judgment, decree, or other order of a court that is annulled, set aside, made void, or canceled.

verdict† The final decision of a jury concerning questions of fact submitted to it by the court for determination in the trial of a case.

voir dire A process by which the lawyers for both parties examine potential jurors to determine whether they are qualified and acceptable to act as jurors in the case.

WESTLAW A computerized legal research system, developed and marketed by West Publishing Company, that is patterned after the West manual research system.

word As used in reference to a computerized database, a single character or group of characters with a space on both sides.

writ of certiorari† A writ issued by a higher court to a lower court requiring the certification of the record in a particular case so that the higher court can review the record and correct any actions taken in the case which are not in accordance with the law; the Supreme Court of the United States uses the writ of certiorari to select the state court cases it is willing to review.

writ of error† A formal order issued by an appellate court, directed to the lower court, ordering it to transfer the record for review and for the correction of errors of law that the appellant alleges were committed by the lower court.

writ or petition history The information about how a higher court has responded to an application for a review of the final judgment of a lower court.

INDEX

17585403R00274

Printed in Great Britain
by Amazon